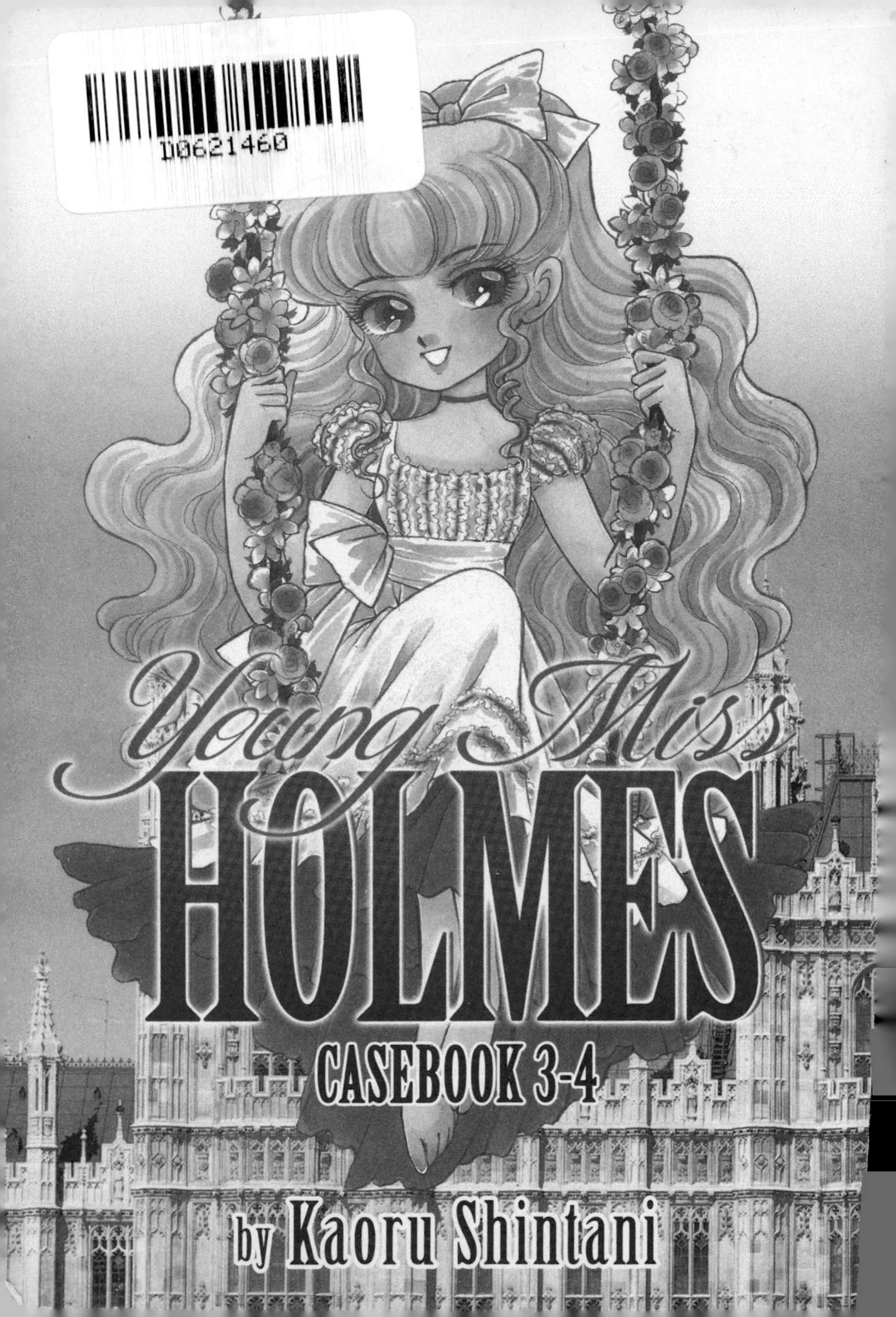
Young Miss
HOLMES
CASEBOOK 3-4
by Kaoru Shintani

Young Miss
HOLMES
CASEBOOK 3-4

story & art by Kaoru Shintani

STAFF CREDITS

translation	**Adrienne Beck**
adaptation	**Shanti Whitesides**
lettering/layout	**Mia Chiresa**
cover design	**Nicky Lim**
assistant editor	**Janet Houck**
editor	**Adam Arnold**
publisher	**Jason DeAngelis**
	Seven Seas Entertainment

YOUNG MISS HOLMES CASEBOOK 3-4
Originally published in Japan as CHRISTIE: HIGH TENSION Vol. 3 & 4
Copyright © 2008-2009 Kaoru Shintani
First published in 2008-2009 by MEDIA FACTORY, Inc., Tokyo, Japan.
English translation rights reserved by Seven Seas Entertainment, LLC.
under the license from MEDIA FACTORY, Inc., Tokyo, Japan.

Seven Seas and the Seven Seas logo are trademarks of
Seven Seas Entertainment, LLC. All rights reserved.

ISBN: 978-1-935934-94-3

Printed in the USA

First Printing: November 2012

10 9 8 7 6 5 4 3 2 1

FOLLOW US ONLINE: www.gomanga.com

READING DIRECTIONS

This book reads from *right to left*, Japanese style.
If this is your first time reading manga, you start
reading from the top right panel on each page and
take it from there. If you get lost, just follow the
numbered diagram here. It may seem backwards
at first, but you'll get the hang of it! Have fun!!

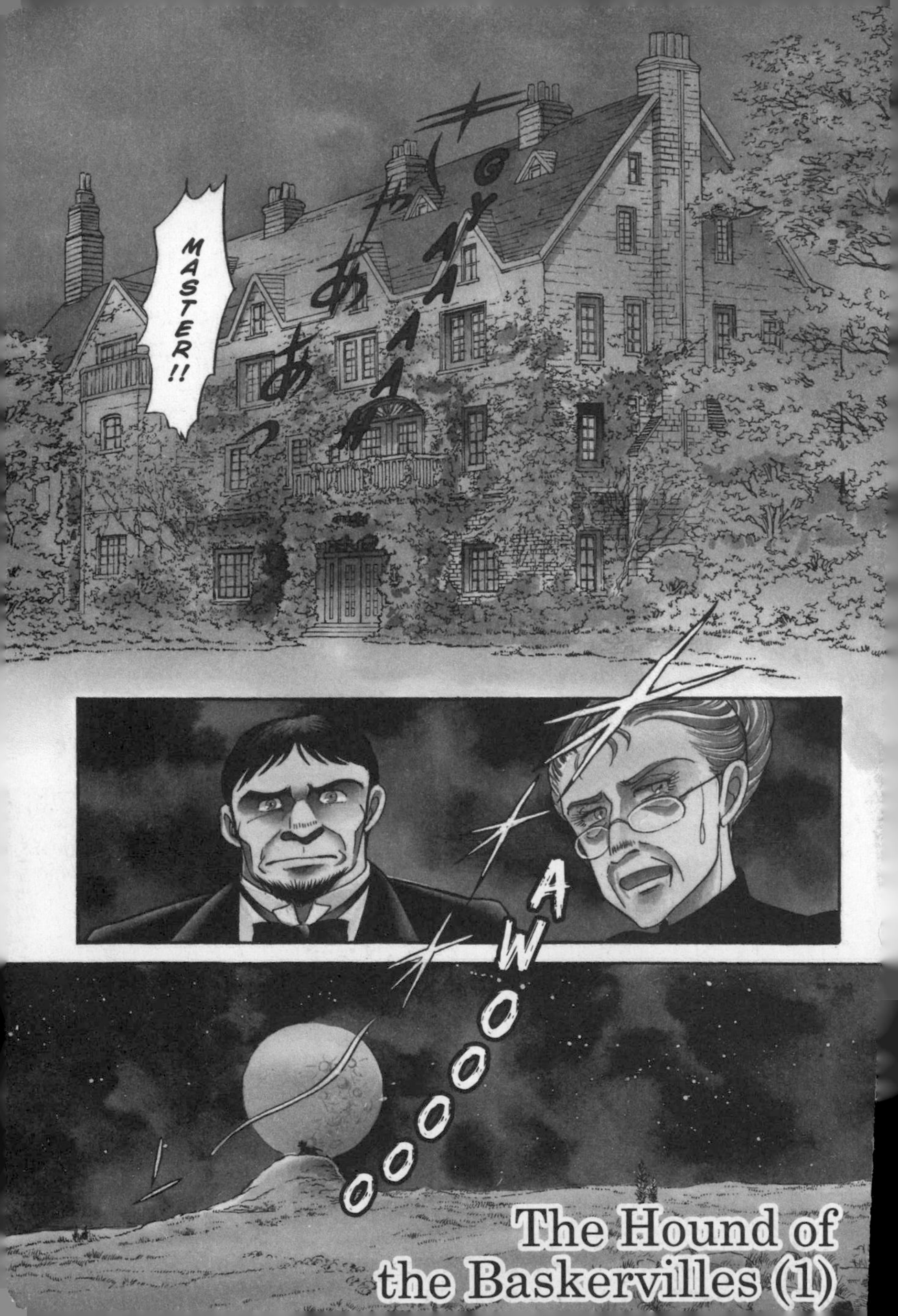
MASTER!!
GYAAAAH
きゃああっ
AWOOOOO
The Hound of the Baskervilles (1)

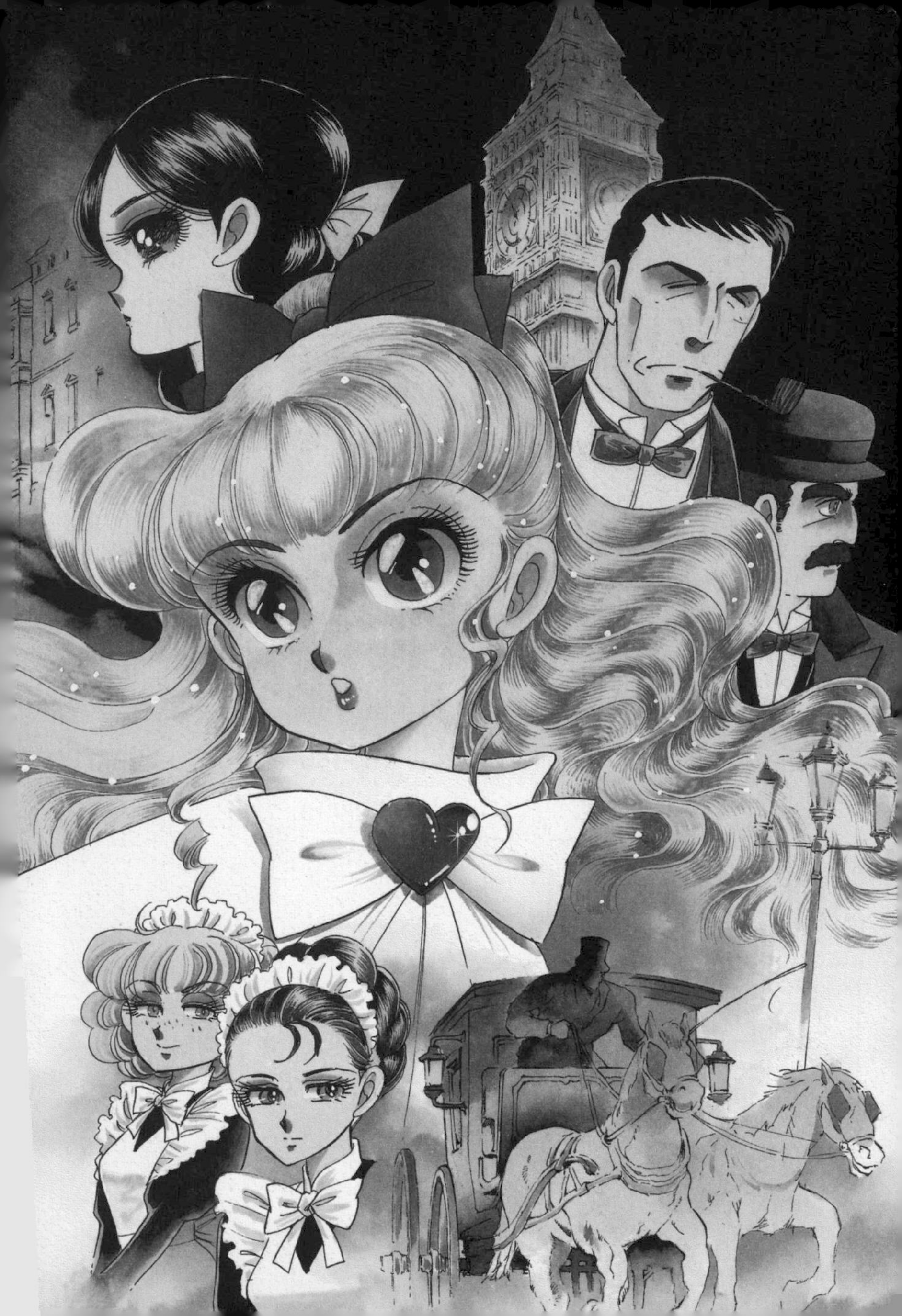

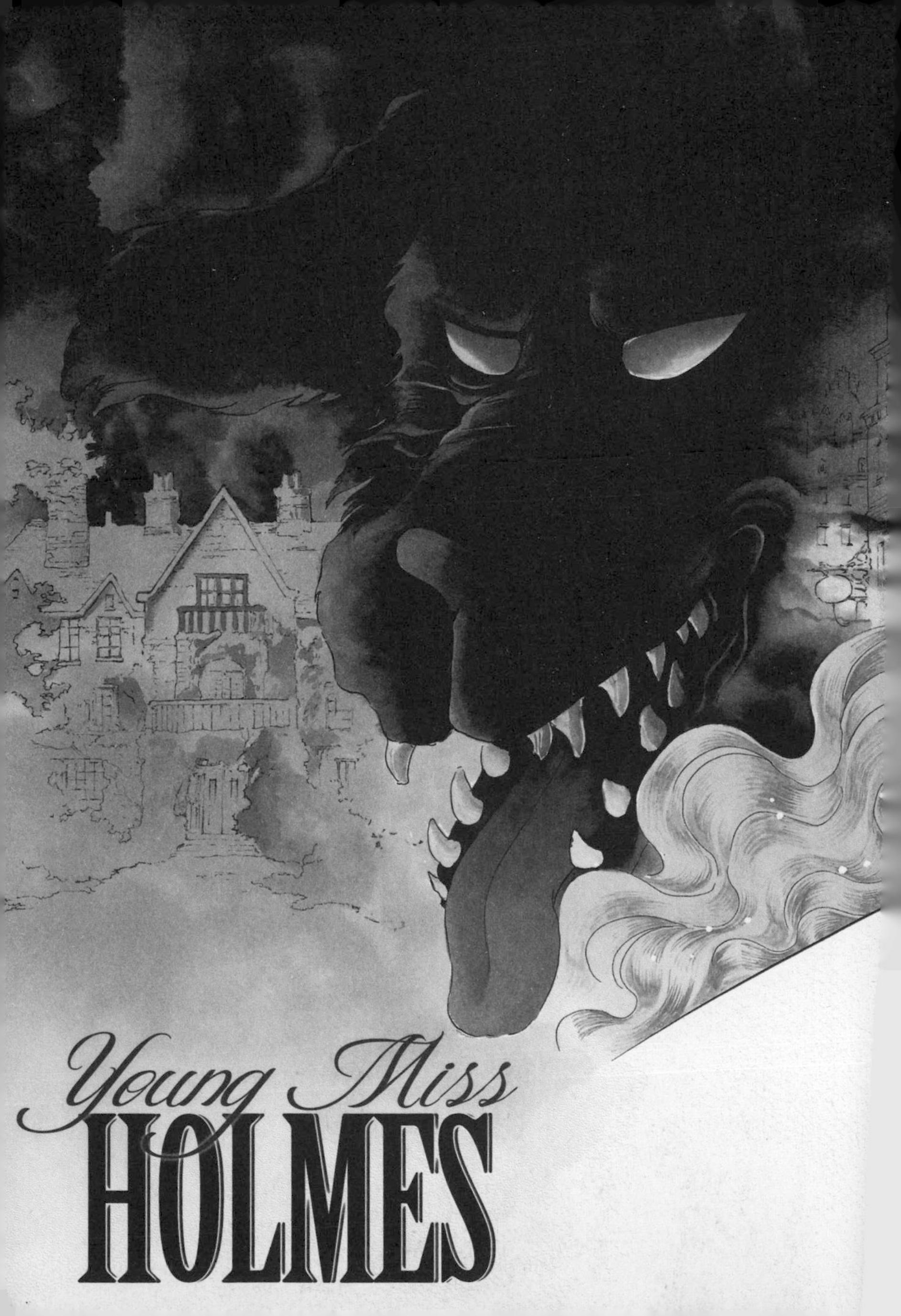
Young Miss
HOLMES

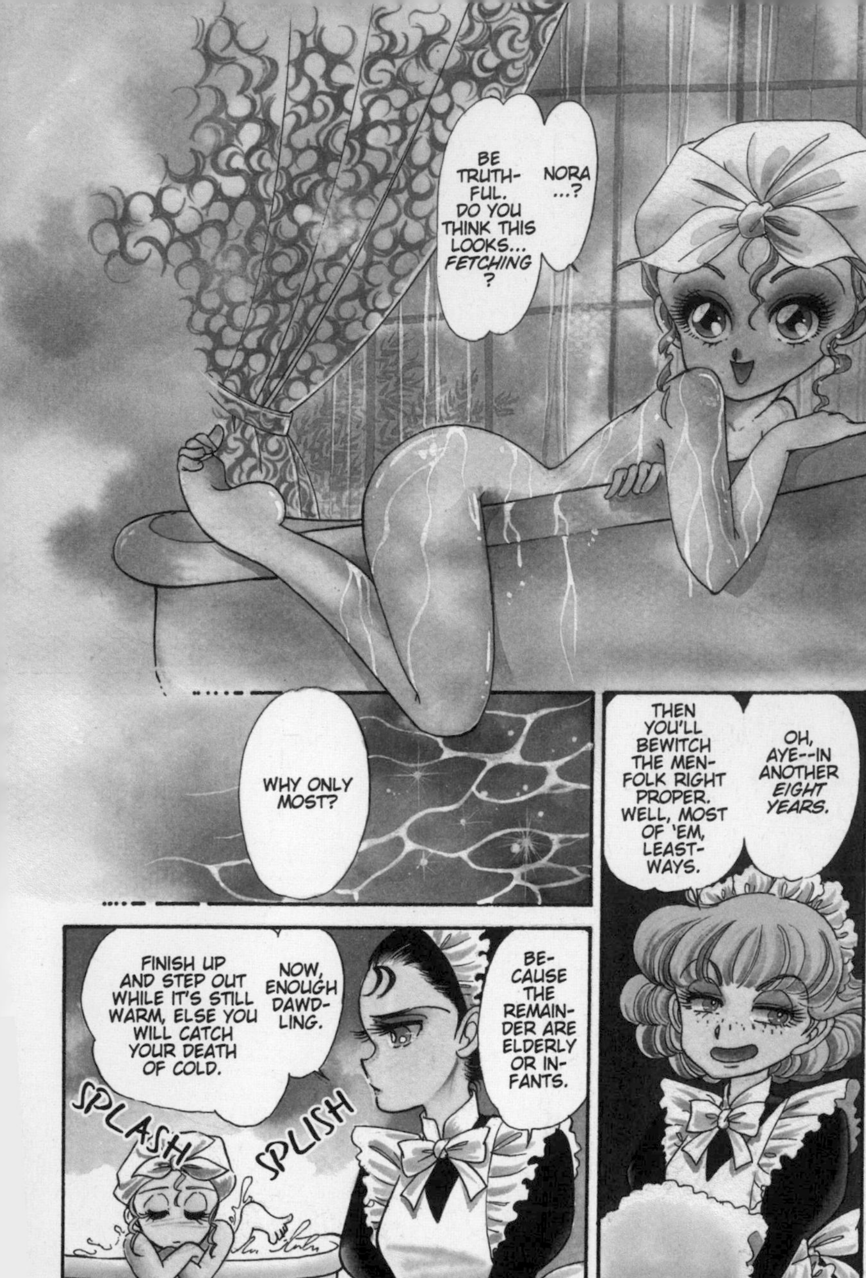
NORA ...?
BE TRUTH-FUL. DO YOU THINK THIS LOOKS... FETCHING?
OH, AYE--IN ANOTHER EIGHT YEARS.
THEN YOU'LL BEWITCH THE MEN-FOLK RIGHT PROPER. WELL, MOST OF 'EM, LEAST-WAYS.
WHY ONLY MOST?
BE-CAUSE THE REMAIN-DER ARE ELDERLY OR IN-FANTS.
NOW, ENOUGH DAWD-LING.
FINISH UP AND STEP OUT WHILE IT'S STILL WARM, ELSE YOU WILL CATCH YOUR DEATH OF COLD.
SPLISH
SPLASH

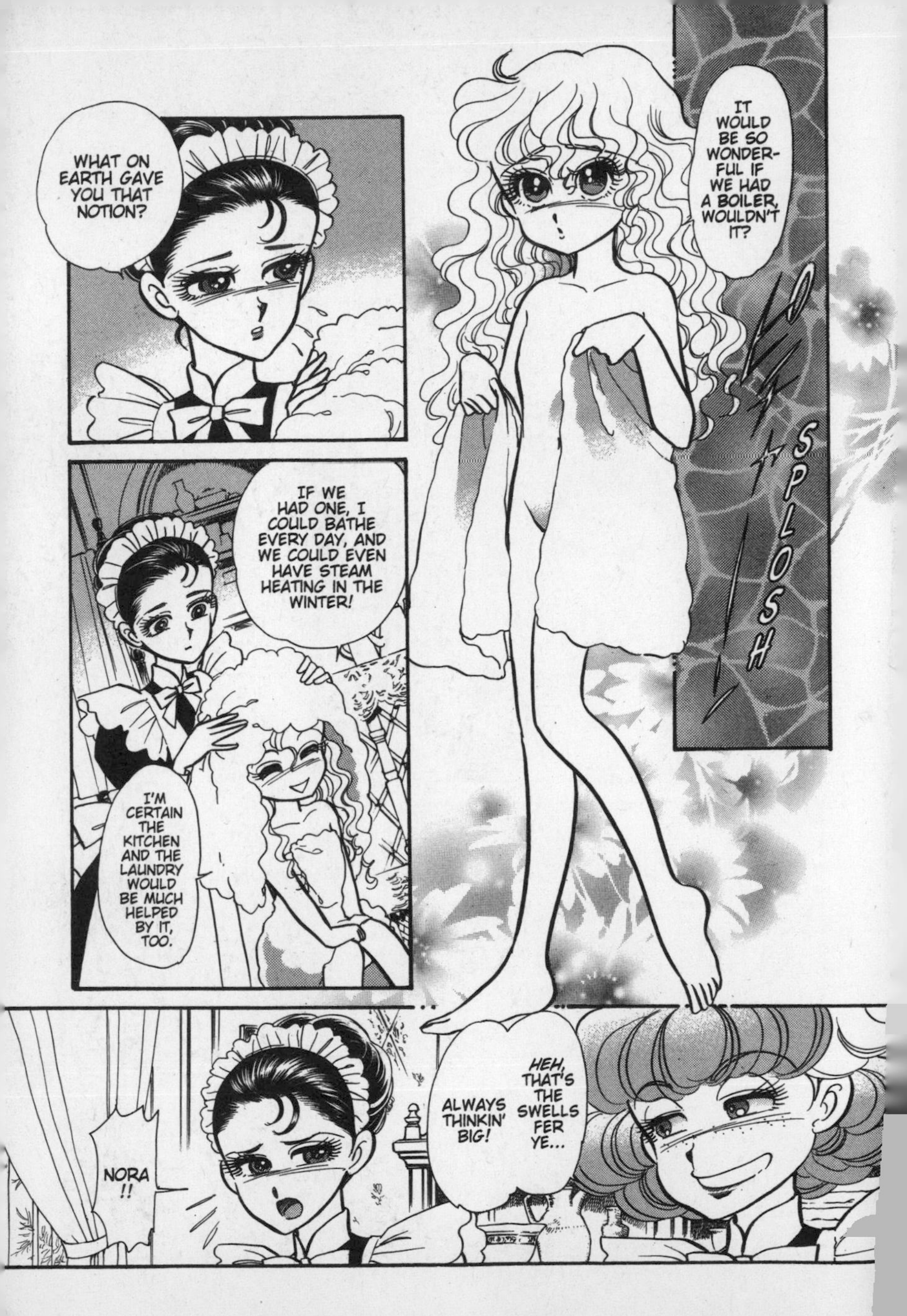
IT WOULD BE SO WONDER-FUL IF WE HAD A BOILER, WOULDN'T IT?
SPLOSH
WHAT ON EARTH GAVE YOU THAT NOTION?
IF WE HAD ONE, I COULD BATHE EVERY DAY, AND WE COULD EVEN HAVE STEAM HEATING IN THE WINTER!
I'M CERTAIN THE KITCHEN AND THE LAUNDRY WOULD BE MUCH HELPED BY IT, TOO.
HEH, THAT'S THE SWELLS FER YE...
ALWAYS THINKIN' BIG!
NORA !!

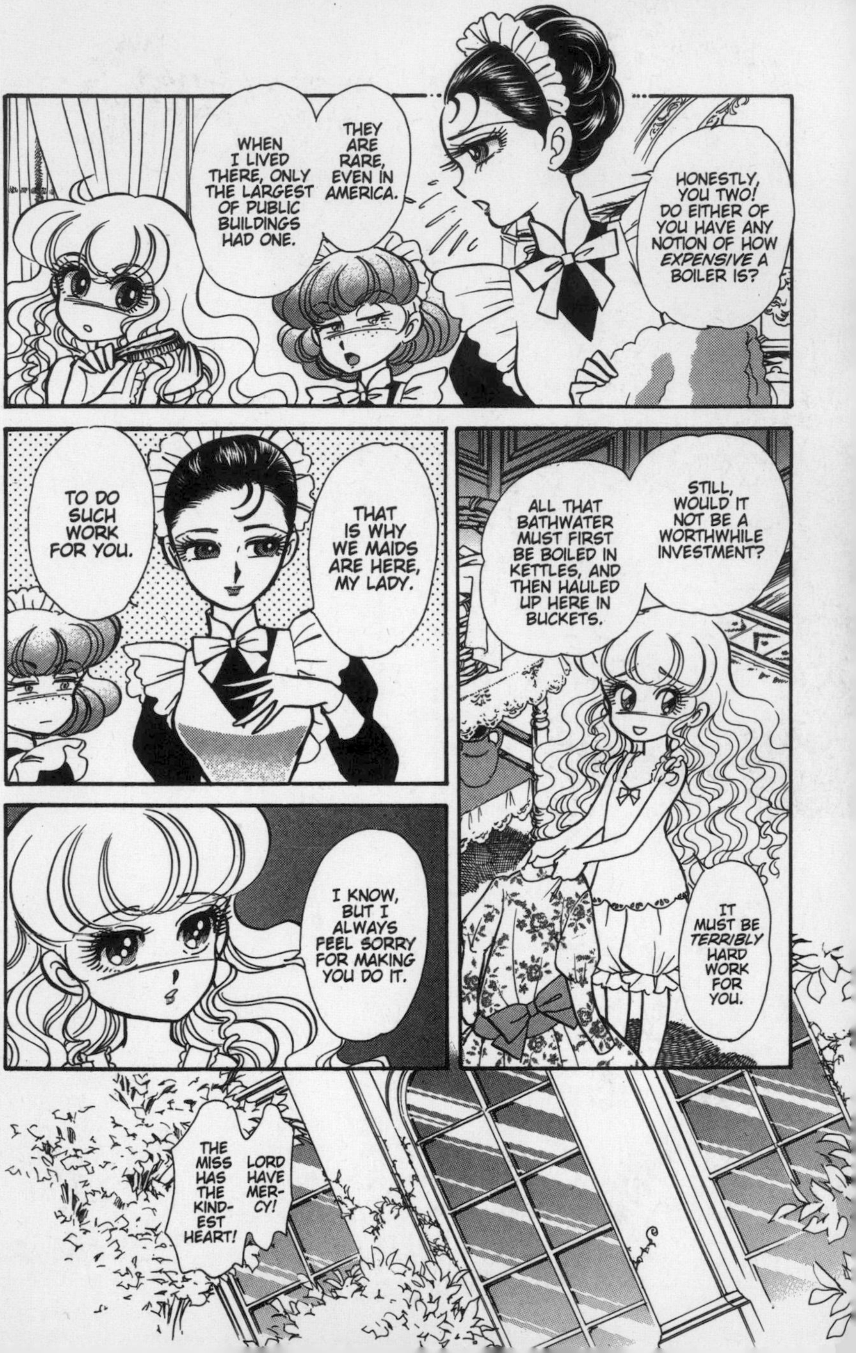
HONESTLY, YOU TWO! DO EITHER OF YOU HAVE ANY NOTION OF HOW *EXPENSIVE* A BOILER IS?
THEY ARE RARE, EVEN IN AMERICA.
WHEN I LIVED THERE, ONLY THE LARGEST OF PUBLIC BUILDINGS HAD ONE.
STILL, WOULD IT NOT BE A WORTHWHILE INVESTMENT?
ALL THAT BATHWATER MUST FIRST BE BOILED IN KETTLES, AND THEN HAULED UP HERE IN BUCKETS.
IT MUST BE *TERRIBLY* HARD WORK FOR YOU.
THAT IS WHY WE MAIDS ARE HERE, MY LADY.
TO DO SUCH WORK FOR YOU.
I KNOW, BUT I ALWAYS FEEL SORRY FOR MAKING YOU DO IT.
LORD HAVE MERCY!
THE MISS HAS THE KINDEST HEART!

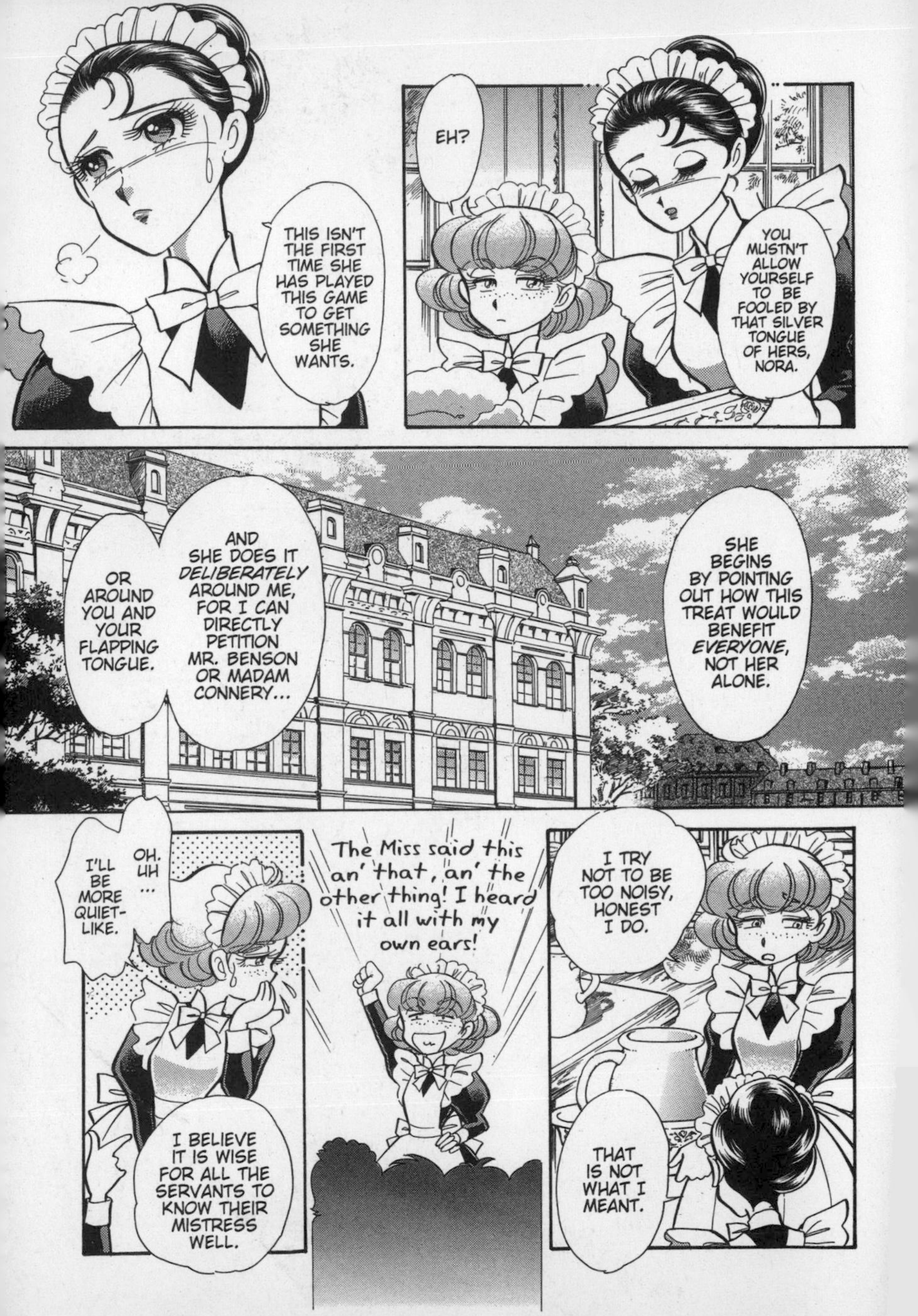
YOU MUSTN'T ALLOW YOURSELF TO BE FOOLED BY THAT SILVER TONGUE OF HERS, NORA.
EH?
THIS ISN'T THE FIRST TIME SHE HAS PLAYED THIS GAME TO GET SOMETHING SHE WANTS.
SHE BEGINS BY POINTING OUT HOW THIS TREAT WOULD BENEFIT *EVERYONE*, NOT HER ALONE.
AND SHE DOES IT *DELIBERATELY* AROUND ME, FOR I CAN DIRECTLY PETITION MR. BENSON OR MADAM CONNERY...
OR AROUND YOU AND YOUR FLAPPING TONGUE.
I TRY NOT TO BE TOO NOISY, HONEST I DO.
THAT IS NOT WHAT I MEANT.
The Miss said this an' that, an' the other thing! I heard it all with my own ears!
OH. UH ...
I'LL BE MORE QUIET-LIKE.
I BELIEVE IT IS WISE FOR ALL THE SERVANTS TO KNOW THEIR MISTRESS WELL.

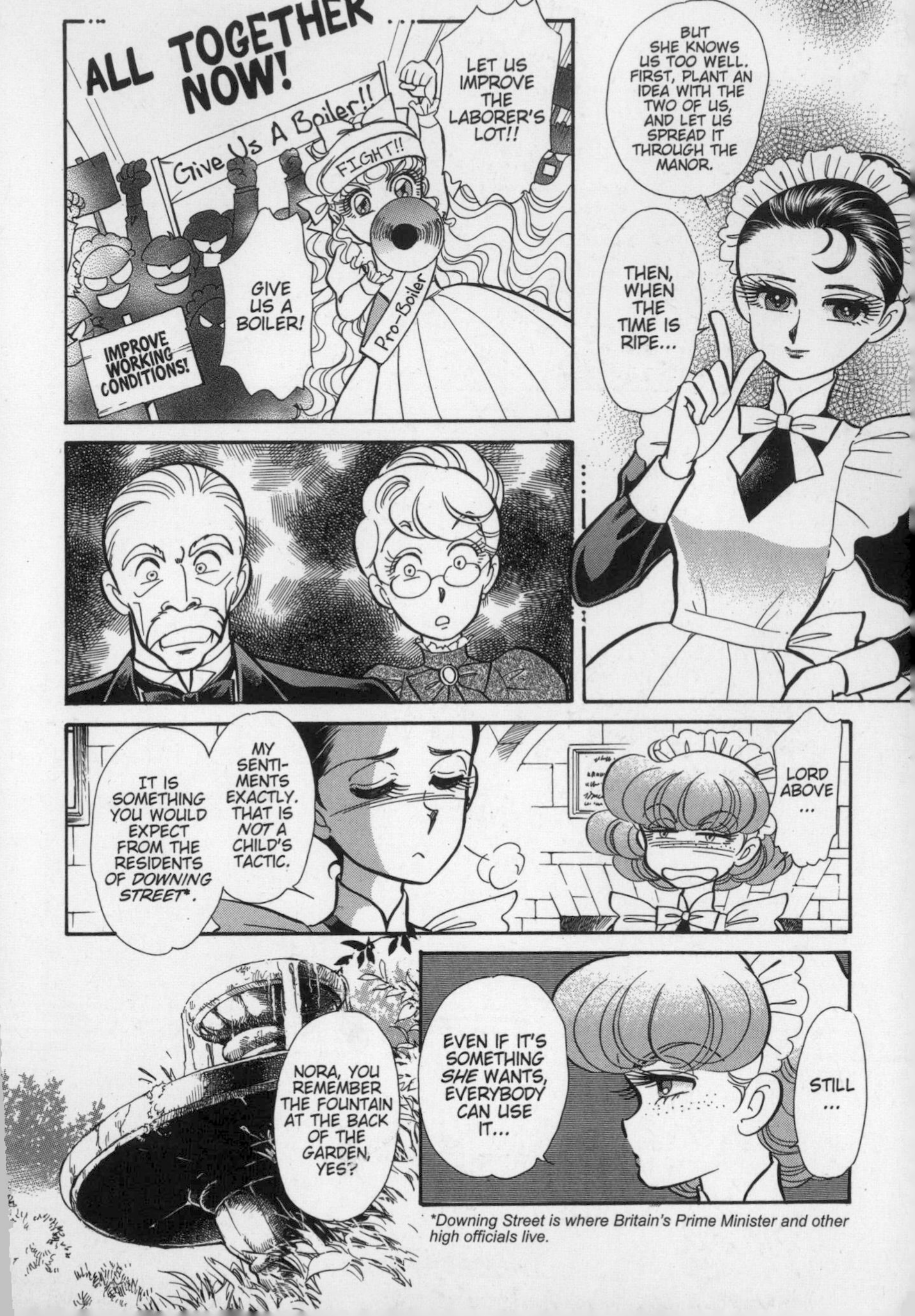
BUT SHE KNOWS US TOO WELL. FIRST, PLANT AN IDEA WITH THE TWO OF US, AND LET US SPREAD IT THROUGH THE MANOR.
THEN, WHEN THE TIME IS RIPE...
LET US IMPROVE THE LABORER'S LOT!!
ALL TOGETHER NOW!
Give Us A Boiler!!
FIGHT!!
GIVE US A BOILER!
Pro-Boiler
IMPROVE WORKING CONDITIONS!
LORD ABOVE...
MY SENTIMENTS EXACTLY. THAT IS *NOT* A CHILD'S TACTIC.
IT IS SOMETHING YOU WOULD EXPECT FROM THE RESIDENTS OF *DOWNING STREET**.
STILL...
EVEN IF IT'S SOMETHING *SHE* WANTS, EVERYBODY CAN USE IT...
NORA, YOU REMEMBER THE FOUNTAIN AT THE BACK OF THE GARDEN, YES?

**Downing Street is where Britain's Prime Minister and other high officials live.*

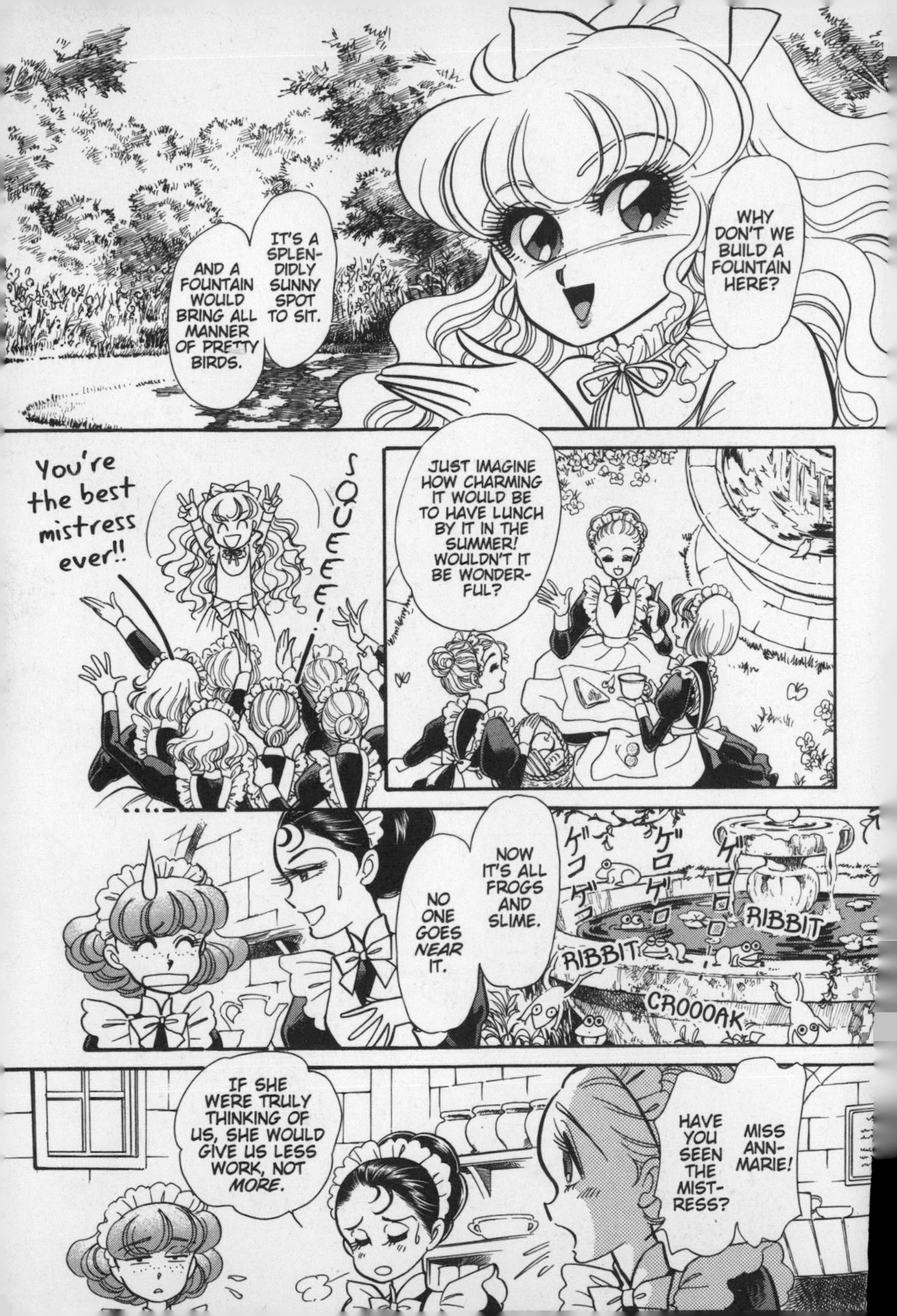
WHY DON'T WE BUILD A FOUNTAIN HERE?
IT'S A SPLEN-DIDLY SUNNY SPOT TO SIT.
AND A FOUNTAIN WOULD BRING ALL MANNER OF PRETTY BIRDS.
JUST IMAGINE HOW CHARMING IT WOULD BE TO HAVE LUNCH BY IT IN THE SUMMER! WOULDN'T IT BE WONDER-FUL?
SQUEEEE...!
You're the best mistress ever!!
ゲロゲロ
ゲコゲコ
RIBBIT
RIBBIT
CROOOAK
NOW IT'S ALL FROGS AND SLIME.
NO ONE GOES *NEAR* IT.
MISS ANN-MARIE!
HAVE YOU SEEN THE MIST-RESS?
IF SHE WERE TRULY THINKING OF US, SHE WOULD GIVE US LESS WORK, NOT *MORE*.

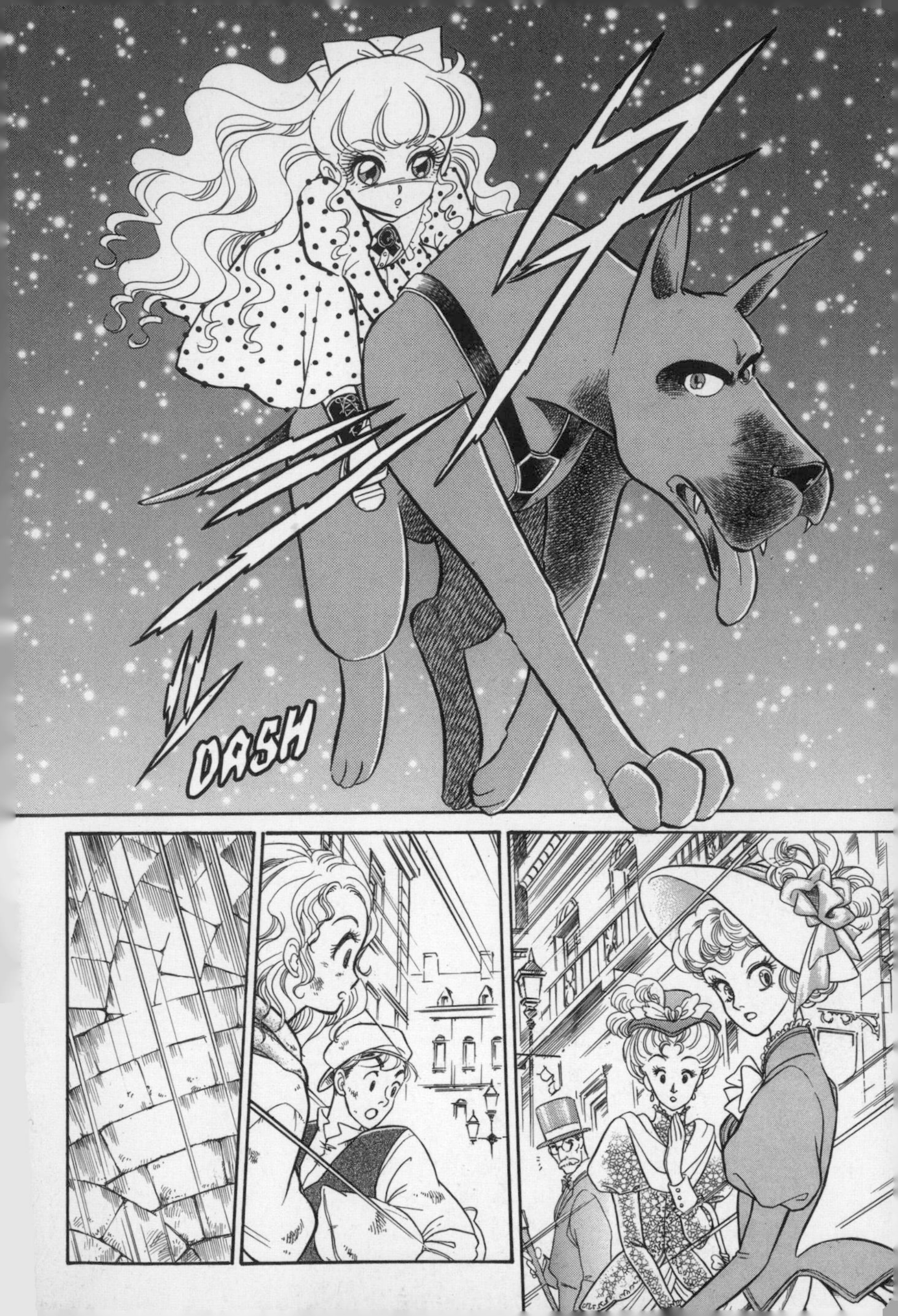
DASH

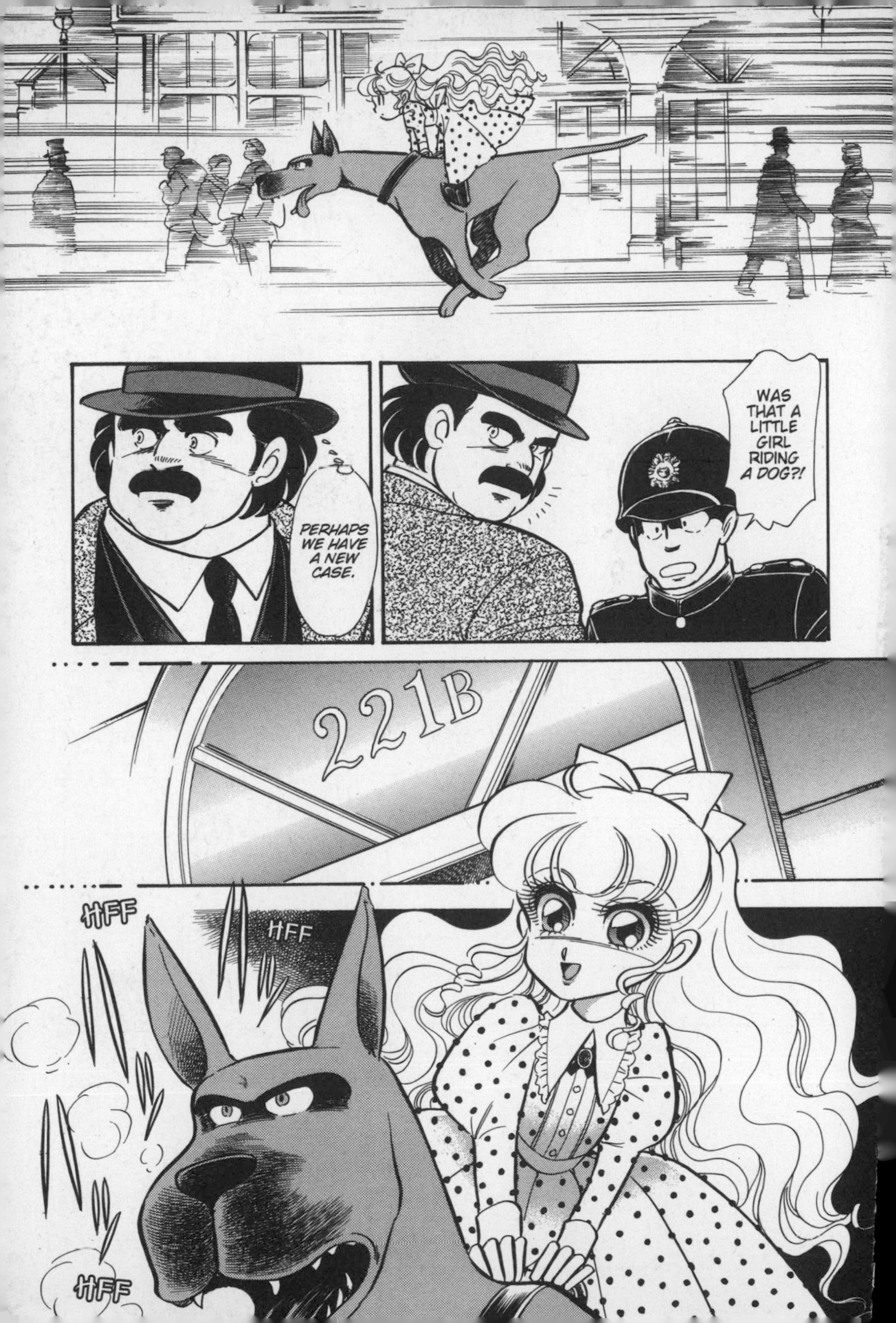
WAS THAT A LITTLE GIRL RIDING A DOG?!
PERHAPS WE HAVE A NEW CASE.
221B
HFF
HFF
HFF

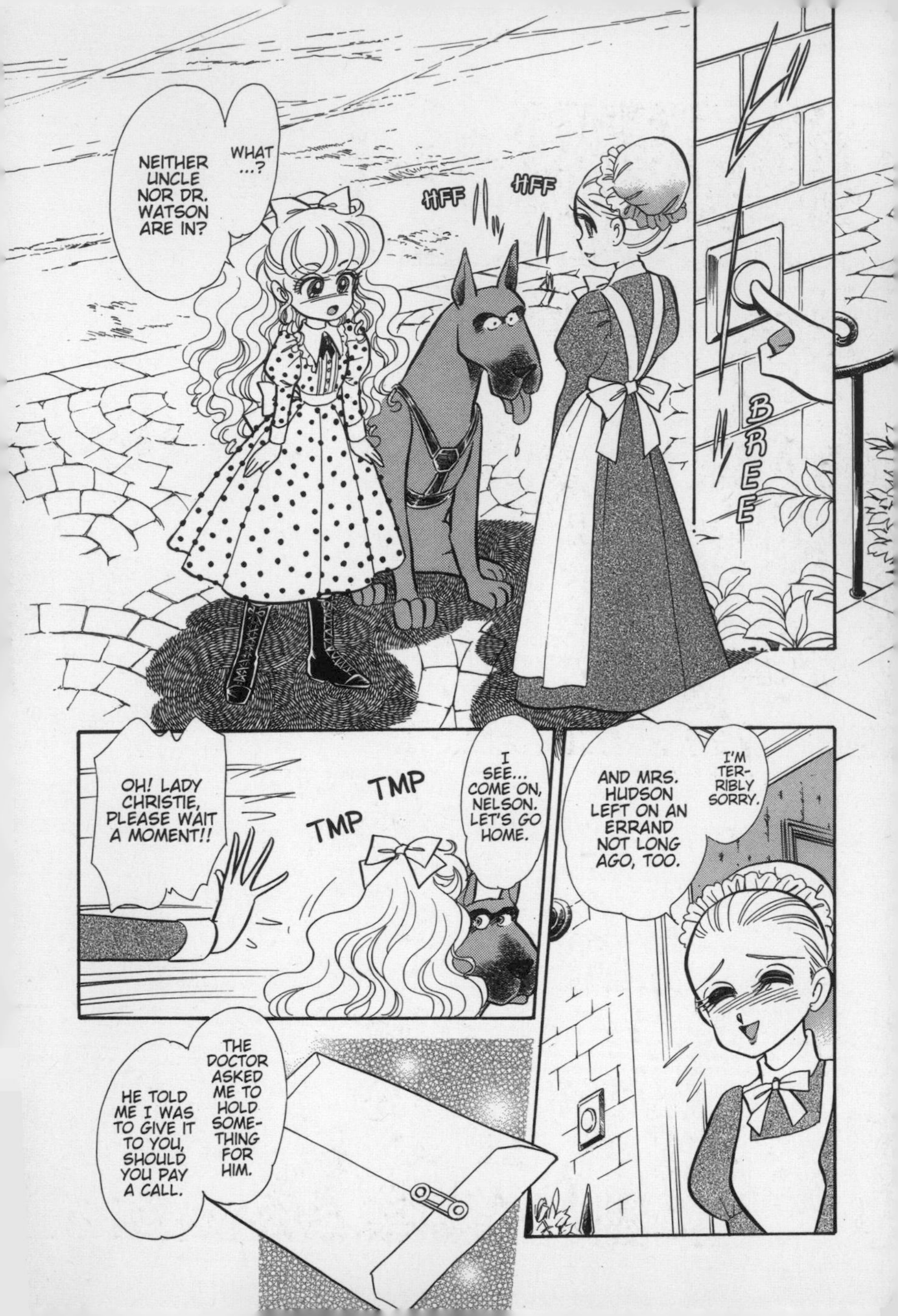
BREE
HFF HFF
WHAT ...?
NEITHER UNCLE NOR DR. WATSON ARE IN?
I'M TER-RIBLY SORRY.
AND MRS. HUDSON LEFT ON AN ERRAND NOT LONG AGO, TOO.
I SEE... COME ON, NELSON. LET'S GO HOME.
TMP TMP
OH! LADY CHRISTIE, PLEASE WAIT A MOMENT!!
THE DOCTOR ASKED ME TO HOLD SOME-THING FOR HIM.
HE TOLD ME I WAS TO GIVE IT TO YOU, SHOULD YOU PAY A CALL.

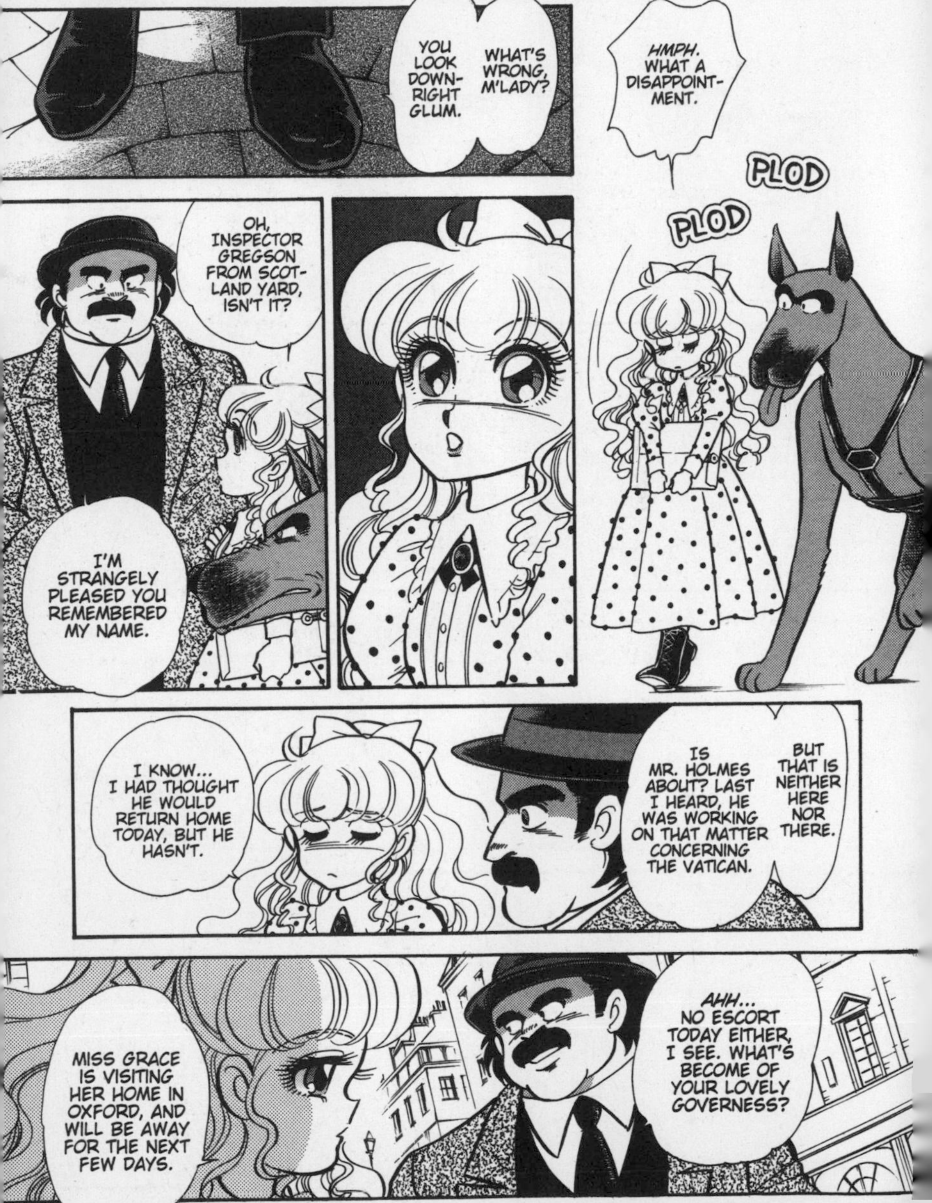
HMPH. WHAT A DISAPPOINTMENT.
PLOD
PLOD
WHAT'S WRONG, M'LADY?
YOU LOOK DOWNRIGHT GLUM.
OH, INSPECTOR GREGSON FROM SCOTLAND YARD, ISN'T IT?
I'M STRANGELY PLEASED YOU REMEMBERED MY NAME.
BUT THAT IS NEITHER HERE NOR THERE.
IS MR. HOLMES ABOUT? LAST I HEARD, HE WAS WORKING ON THAT MATTER CONCERNING THE VATICAN.
I KNOW... I HAD THOUGHT HE WOULD RETURN HOME TODAY, BUT HE HASN'T.
AHH... NO ESCORT TODAY EITHER, I SEE. WHAT'S BECOME OF YOUR LOVELY GOVERNESS?
MISS GRACE IS VISITING HER HOME IN OXFORD, AND WILL BE AWAY FOR THE NEXT FEW DAYS.

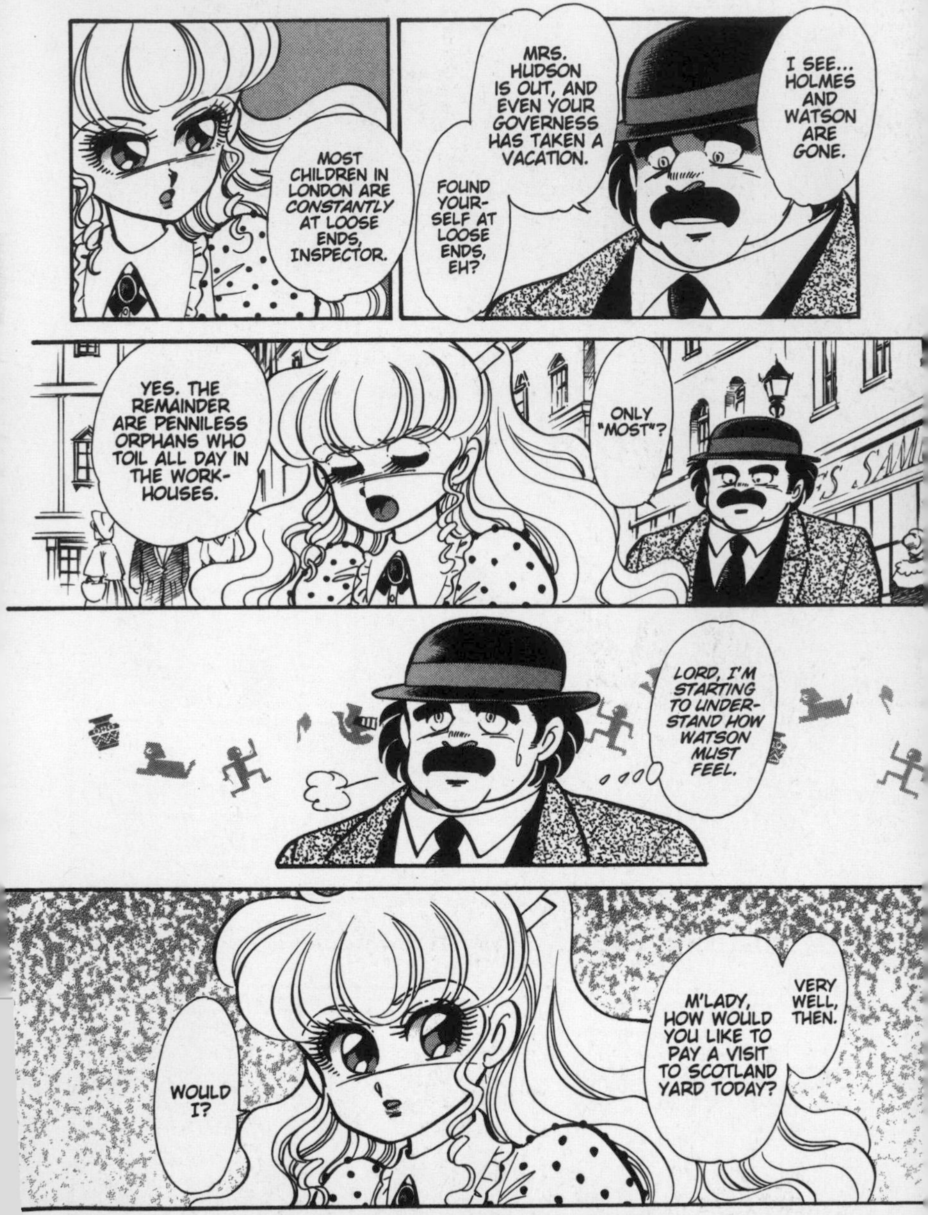
I SEE... HOLMES AND WATSON ARE GONE.
MRS. HUDSON IS OUT, AND EVEN YOUR GOVERNESS HAS TAKEN A VACATION.
FOUND YOURSELF AT LOOSE ENDS, EH?
MOST CHILDREN IN LONDON ARE *CONSTANTLY* AT LOOSE ENDS, INSPECTOR.
ONLY "MOST"?
YES. THE REMAINDER ARE PENNILESS ORPHANS WHO TOIL ALL DAY IN THE WORKHOUSES.
LORD, I'M STARTING TO UNDERSTAND HOW WATSON MUST FEEL.
VERY WELL, THEN.
M'LADY, HOW WOULD YOU LIKE TO PAY A VISIT TO SCOTLAND YARD TODAY?
WOULD I?

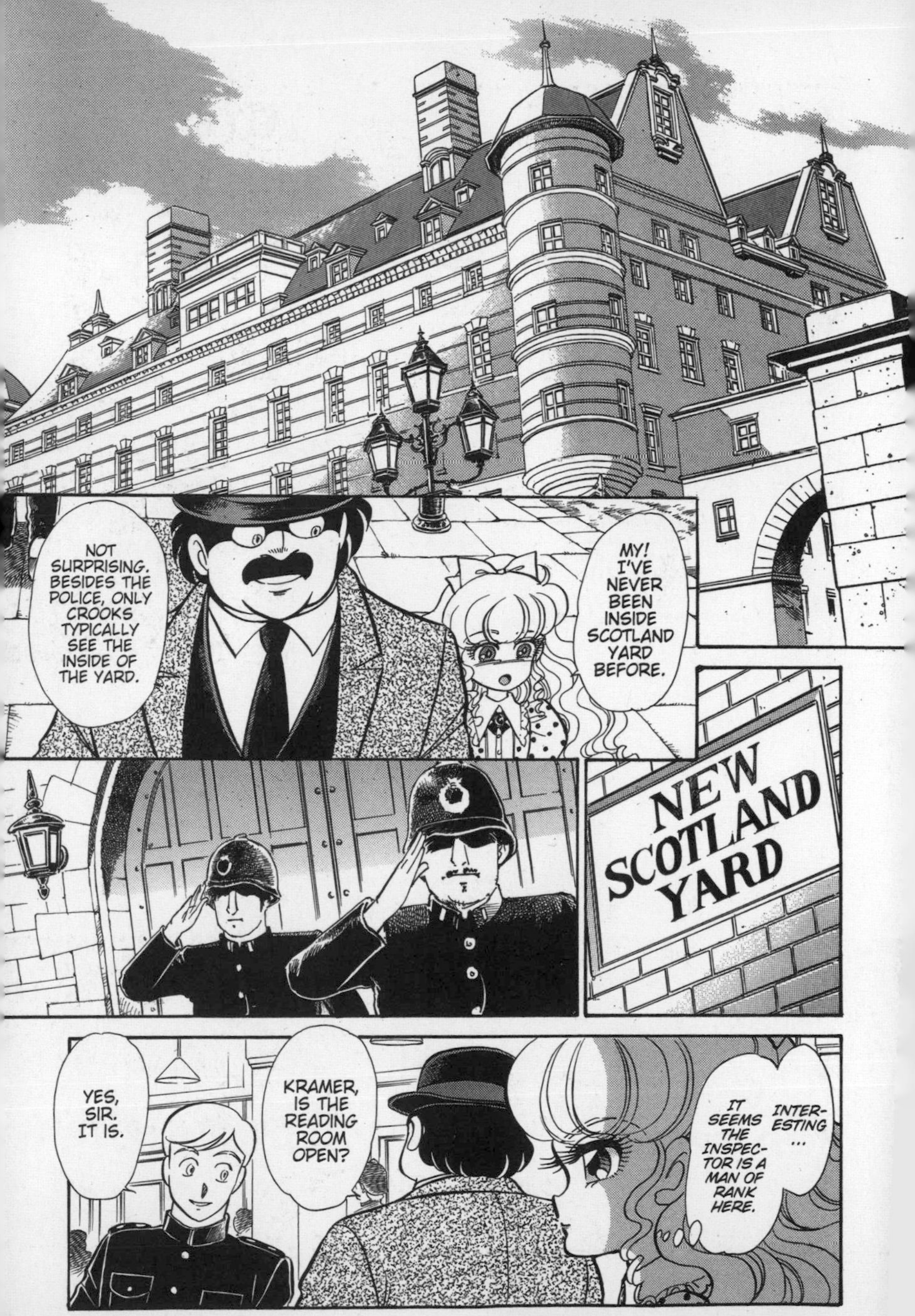
MY! I'VE NEVER BEEN INSIDE SCOTLAND YARD BEFORE.
NOT SURPRISING. BESIDES THE POLICE, ONLY CROOKS TYPICALLY SEE THE INSIDE OF THE YARD.
NEW SCOTLAND YARD
INTER-ESTING ...
IT SEEMS THE INSPEC-TOR IS A MAN OF RANK HERE.
KRAMER, IS THE READING ROOM OPEN?
YES, SIR. IT IS.

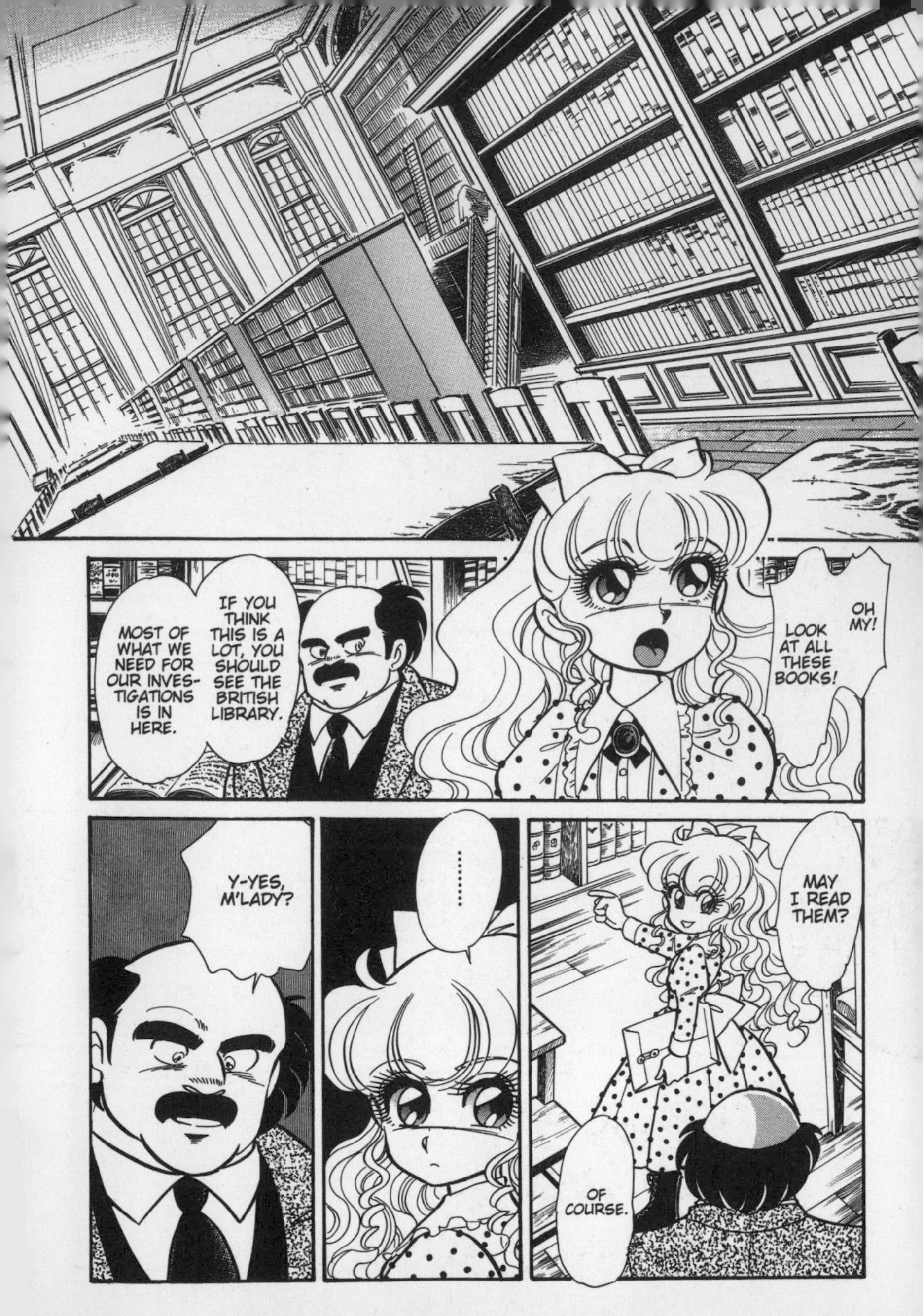
OH MY! LOOK AT ALL THESE BOOKS!
IF YOU THINK THIS IS A LOT, YOU SHOULD SEE THE BRITISH LIBRARY.
MOST OF WHAT WE NEED FOR OUR INVES-TIGATIONS IS IN HERE.
MAY I READ THEM?
OF COURSE.
....
Y-YES, M'LADY?

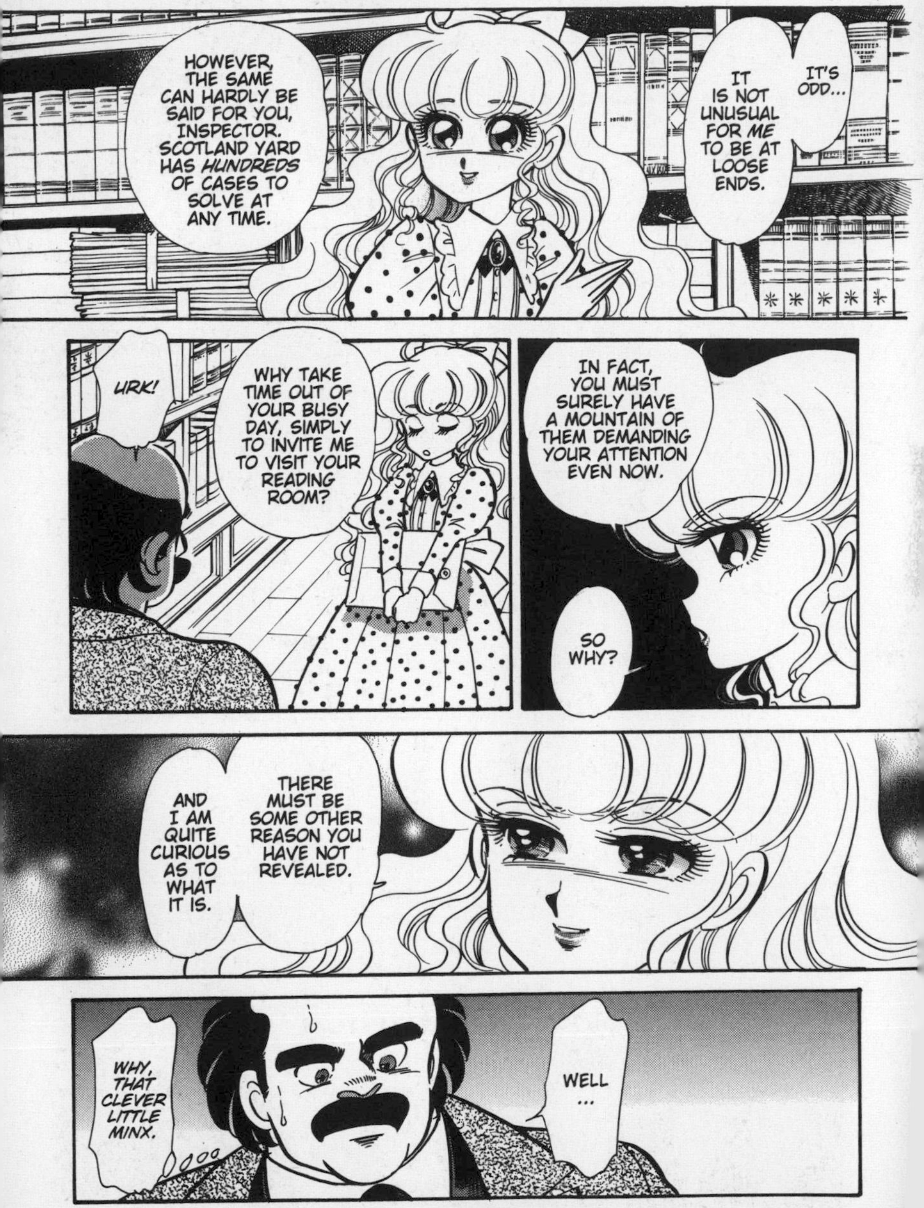
IT'S ODD...
IT IS NOT UNUSUAL FOR *ME* TO BE AT LOOSE ENDS.
HOWEVER, THE SAME CAN HARDLY BE SAID FOR YOU, INSPECTOR. SCOTLAND YARD HAS *HUNDREDS* OF CASES TO SOLVE AT ANY TIME.
IN FACT, YOU MUST SURELY HAVE A MOUNTAIN OF THEM DEMANDING YOUR ATTENTION EVEN NOW.
SO WHY?
WHY TAKE TIME OUT OF YOUR BUSY DAY, SIMPLY TO INVITE ME TO VISIT YOUR READING ROOM?
URK!
THERE MUST BE SOME OTHER REASON YOU HAVE NOT REVEALED.
AND I AM QUITE CURIOUS AS TO WHAT IT IS.
WELL ...
WHY, THAT CLEVER LITTLE MINX.

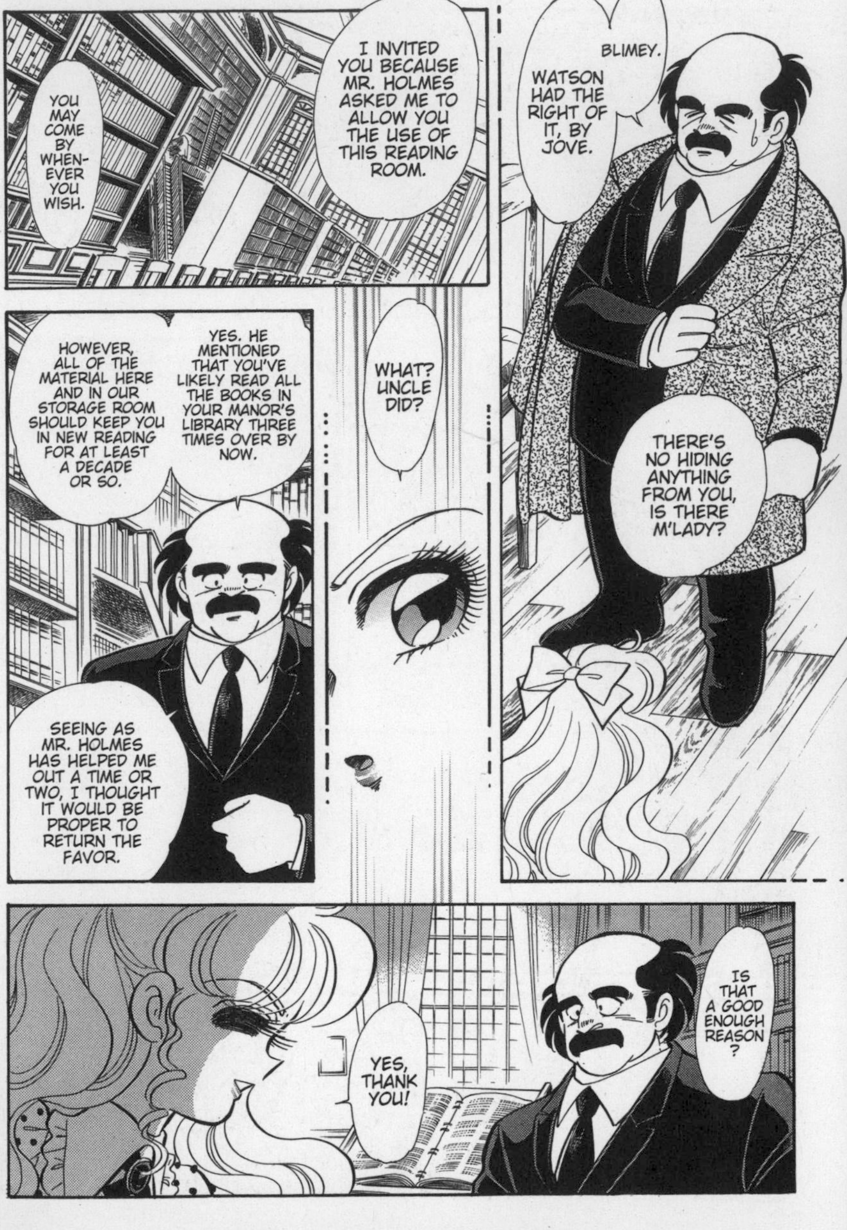
BLIMEY.
WATSON HAD THE RIGHT OF IT, BY JOVE.
THERE'S NO HIDING ANYTHING FROM YOU, IS THERE M'LADY?
I INVITED YOU BECAUSE MR. HOLMES ASKED ME TO ALLOW YOU THE USE OF THIS READING ROOM.
YOU MAY COME BY WHEN-EVER YOU WISH.
WHAT? UNCLE DID?
YES. HE MENTIONED THAT YOU'VE LIKELY READ ALL THE BOOKS IN YOUR MANOR'S LIBRARY THREE TIMES OVER BY NOW.
HOWEVER, ALL OF THE MATERIAL HERE AND IN OUR STORAGE ROOM SHOULD KEEP YOU IN NEW READING FOR AT LEAST A DECADE OR SO.
SEEING AS MR. HOLMES HAS HELPED ME OUT A TIME OR TWO, I THOUGHT IT WOULD BE PROPER TO RETURN THE FAVOR.
IS THAT A GOOD ENOUGH REASON?
YES, THANK YOU!

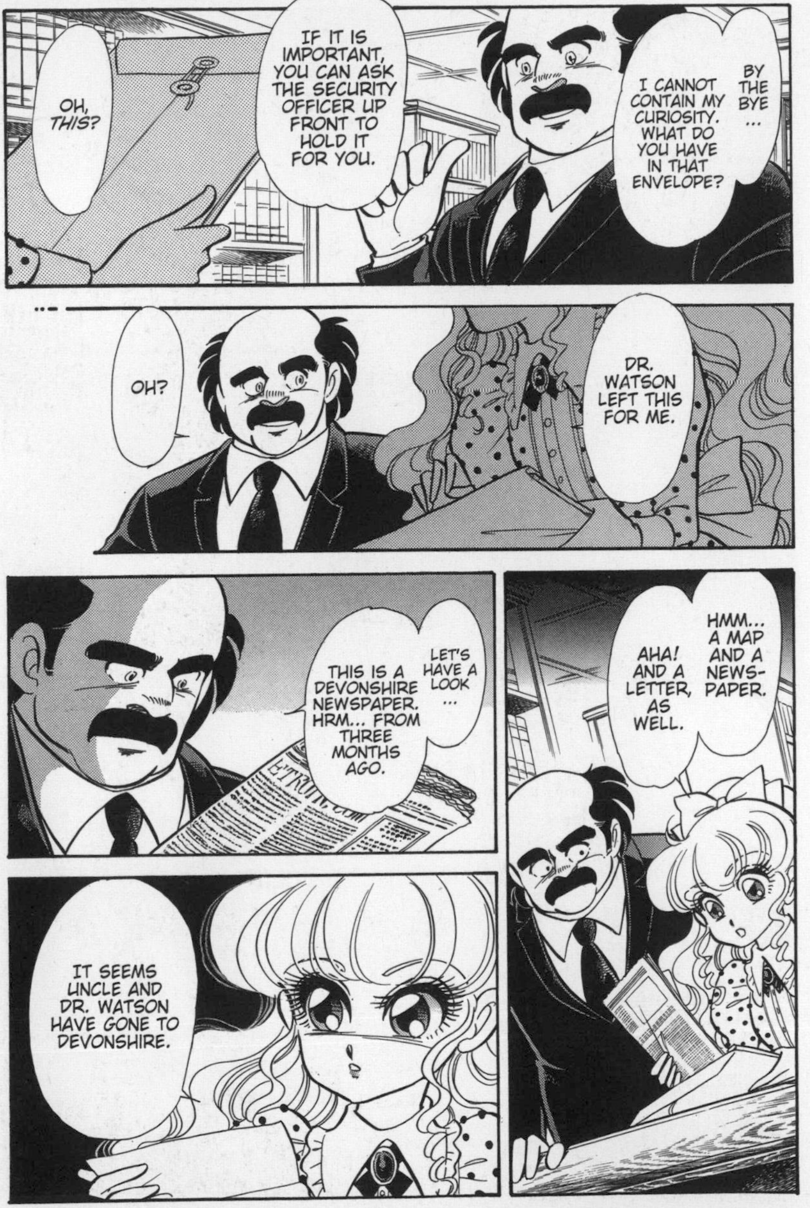
BY THE BYE ...
I CANNOT CONTAIN MY CURIOSITY. WHAT DO YOU HAVE IN THAT ENVELOPE?
IF IT IS IMPORTANT, YOU CAN ASK THE SECURITY OFFICER UP FRONT TO HOLD IT FOR YOU.
OH, THIS?
DR. WATSON LEFT THIS FOR ME.
OH?
HMM... A MAP AND A NEWS-PAPER.
AHA! AND A LETTER, AS WELL.
LET'S HAVE A LOOK ...
THIS IS A DEVONSHIRE NEWSPAPER. HRM... FROM THREE MONTHS AGO.
IT SEEMS UNCLE AND DR. WATSON HAVE GONE TO DEVONSHIRE.

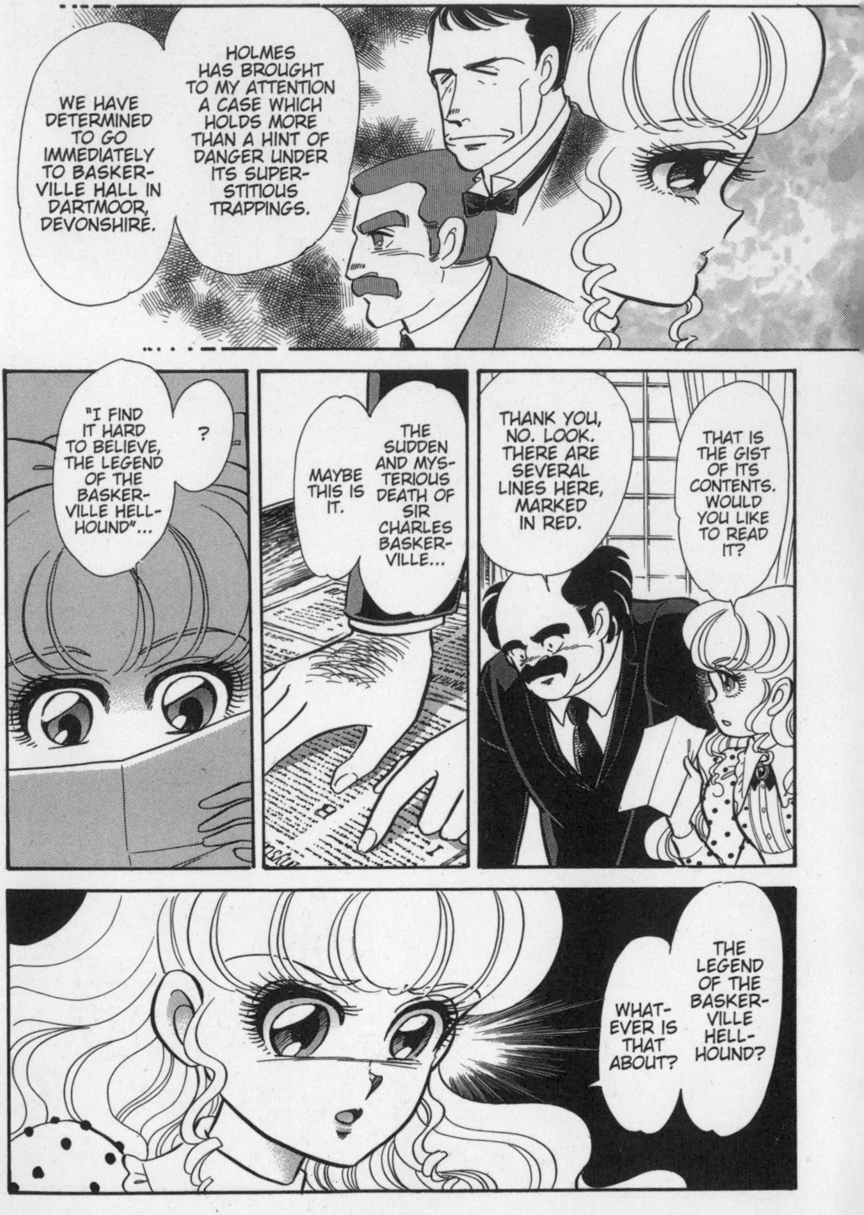
HOLMES HAS BROUGHT TO MY ATTENTION A CASE WHICH HOLDS MORE THAN A HINT OF DANGER UNDER ITS SUPER-STITIOUS TRAPPINGS.
WE HAVE DETERMINED TO GO IMMEDIATELY TO BASKER-VILLE HALL IN DARTMOOR, DEVONSHIRE.
THAT IS THE GIST OF ITS CONTENTS. WOULD YOU LIKE TO READ IT?
THANK YOU, NO. LOOK. THERE ARE SEVERAL LINES HERE, MARKED IN RED.
THE SUDDEN AND MYS-TERIOUS DEATH OF SIR CHARLES BASKER-VILLE...
MAYBE THIS IS IT.
?
"I FIND IT HARD TO BELIEVE, THE LEGEND OF THE BASKER-VILLE HELL-HOUND"...
THE LEGEND OF THE BASKER-VILLE HELL-HOUND?
WHAT-EVER IS THAT ABOUT?

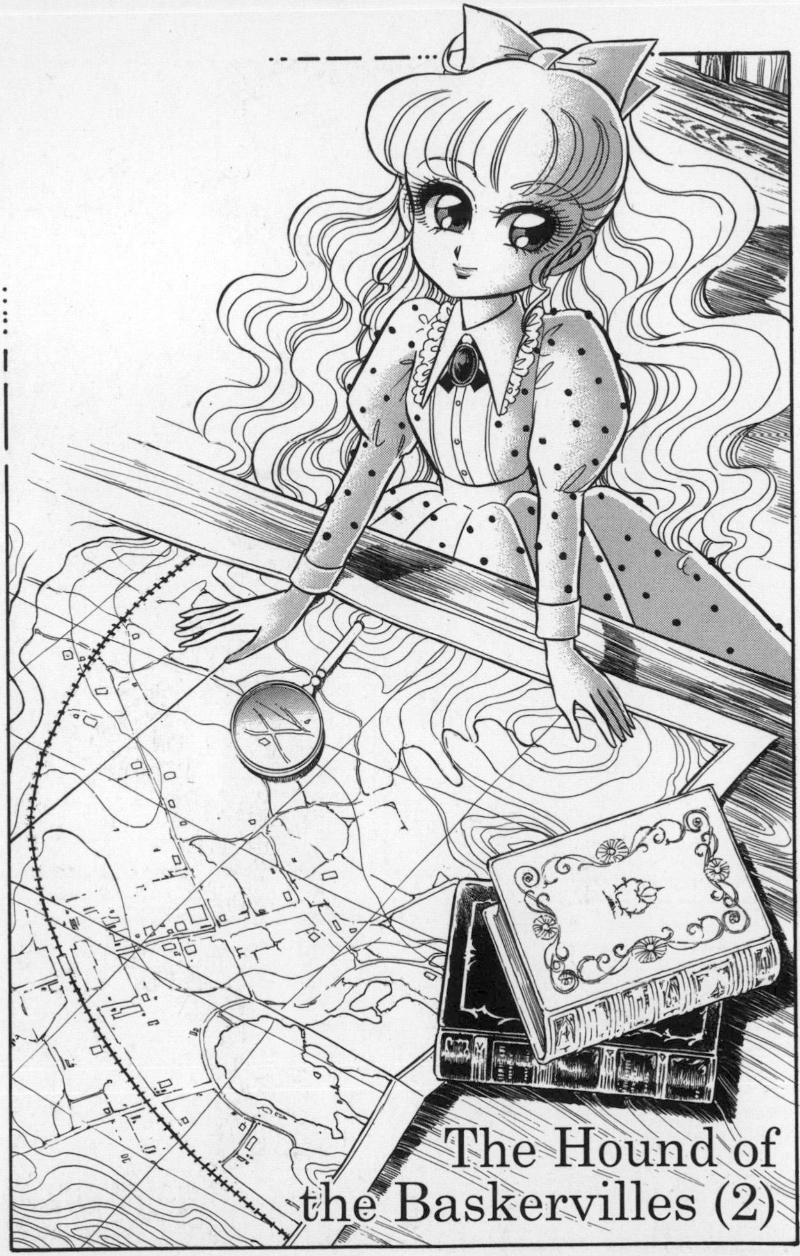

The Hound of the Baskervilles (2)

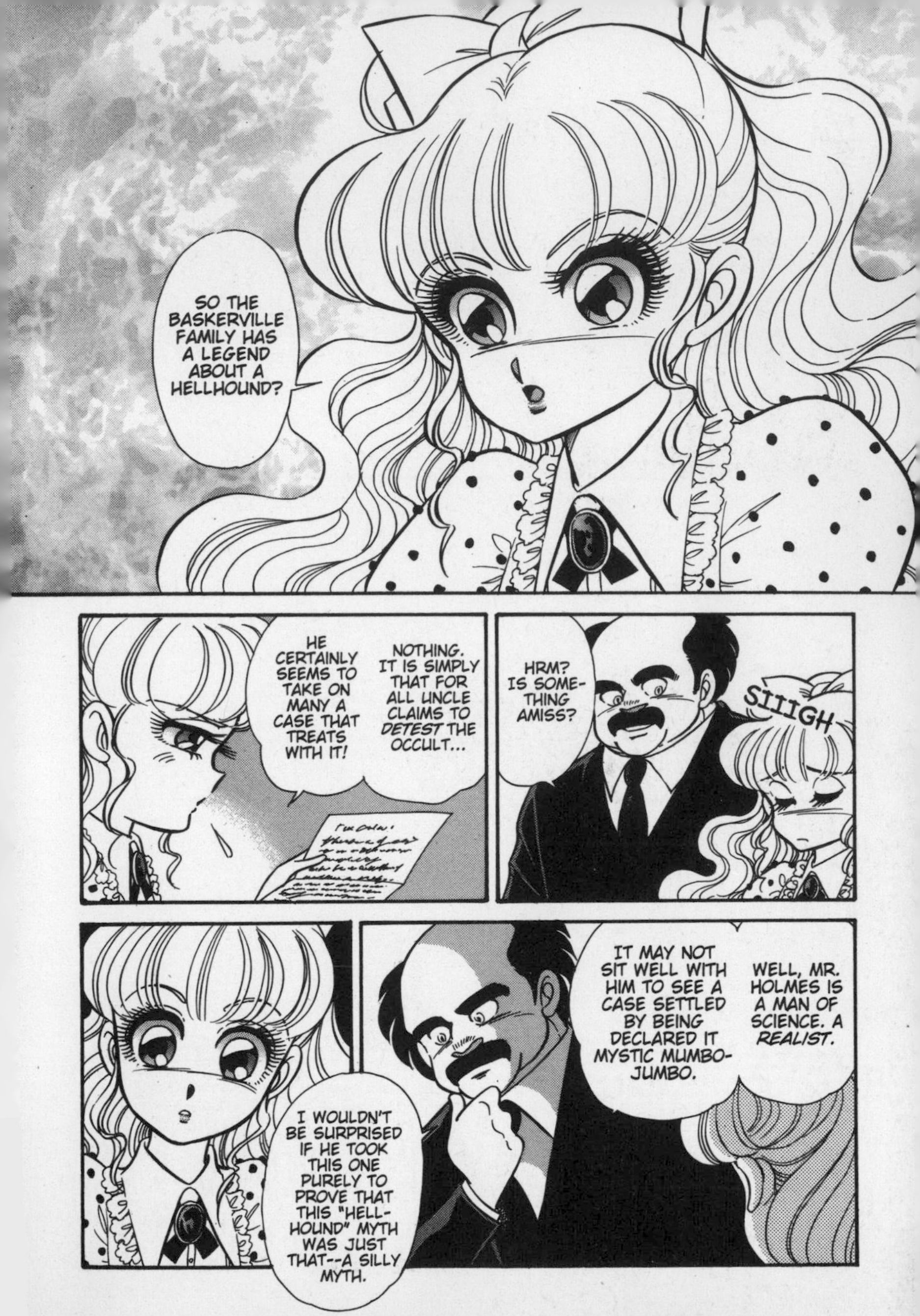
SO THE BASKERVILLE FAMILY HAS A LEGEND ABOUT A HELLHOUND?
HRM? IS SOMETHING AMISS?
SIIIGH
NOTHING. IT IS SIMPLY THAT FOR ALL UNCLE CLAIMS TO *DETEST* THE OCCULT...
HE CERTAINLY SEEMS TO TAKE ON MANY A CASE THAT TREATS WITH IT!
WELL, MR. HOLMES IS A MAN OF SCIENCE. A *REALIST*.
IT MAY NOT SIT WELL WITH HIM TO SEE A CASE SETTLED BY BEING DECLARED IT MYSTIC MUMBO-JUMBO.
I WOULDN'T BE SURPRISED IF HE TOOK THIS ONE PURELY TO PROVE THAT THIS "HELL-HOUND" MYTH WAS JUST THAT--A SILLY MYTH.

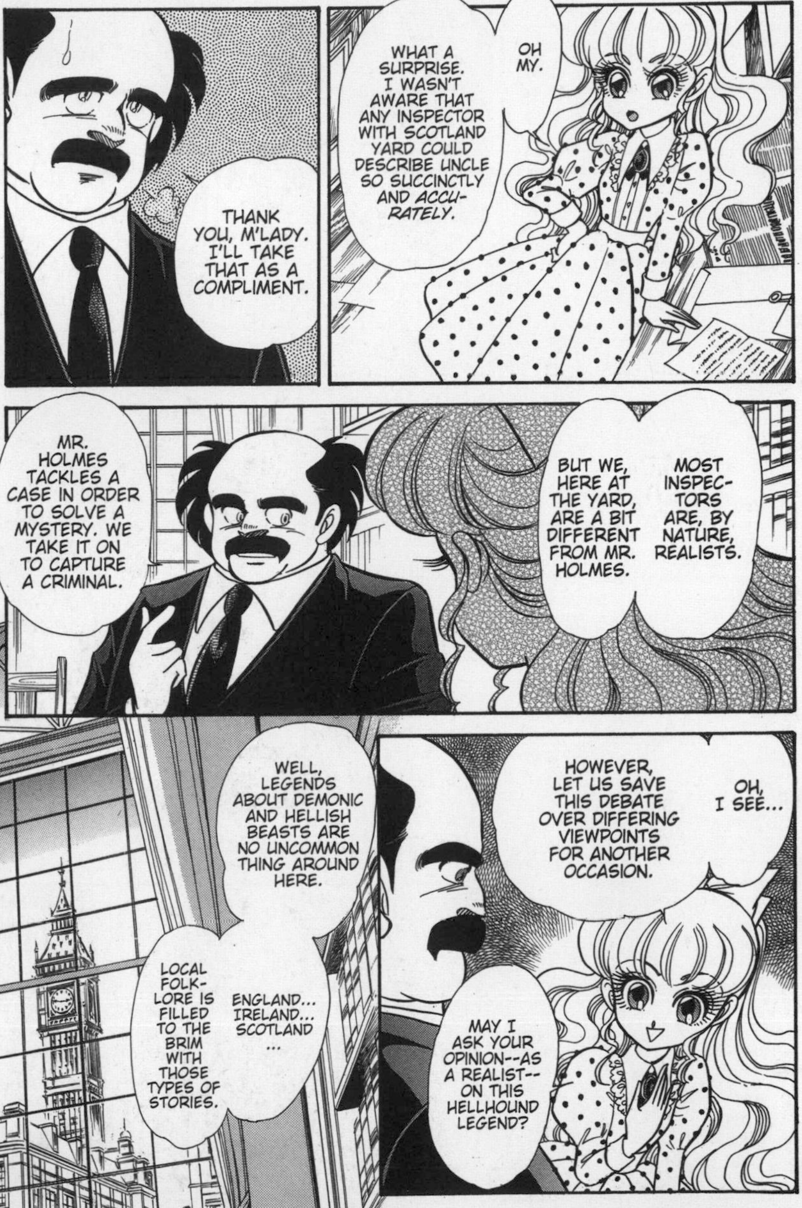
OH MY.
WHAT A SURPRISE. I WASN'T AWARE THAT ANY INSPECTOR WITH SCOTLAND YARD COULD DESCRIBE UNCLE SO SUCCINCTLY AND *ACCURATELY*.
THANK YOU, M'LADY. I'LL TAKE THAT AS A COMPLIMENT.
MOST INSPECTORS ARE, BY NATURE, REALISTS.
BUT WE, HERE AT THE YARD, ARE A BIT DIFFERENT FROM MR. HOLMES.
MR. HOLMES TACKLES A CASE IN ORDER TO SOLVE A MYSTERY. WE TAKE IT ON TO CAPTURE A CRIMINAL.
OH, I SEE...
HOWEVER, LET US SAVE THIS DEBATE OVER DIFFERING VIEWPOINTS FOR ANOTHER OCCASION.
MAY I ASK YOUR OPINION--AS A REALIST--ON THIS HELLHOUND LEGEND?
WELL, LEGENDS ABOUT DEMONIC AND HELLISH BEASTS ARE NO UNCOMMON THING AROUND HERE.
ENGLAND... IRELAND... SCOTLAND...
LOCAL FOLKLORE IS FILLED TO THE BRIM WITH THOSE TYPES OF STORIES.

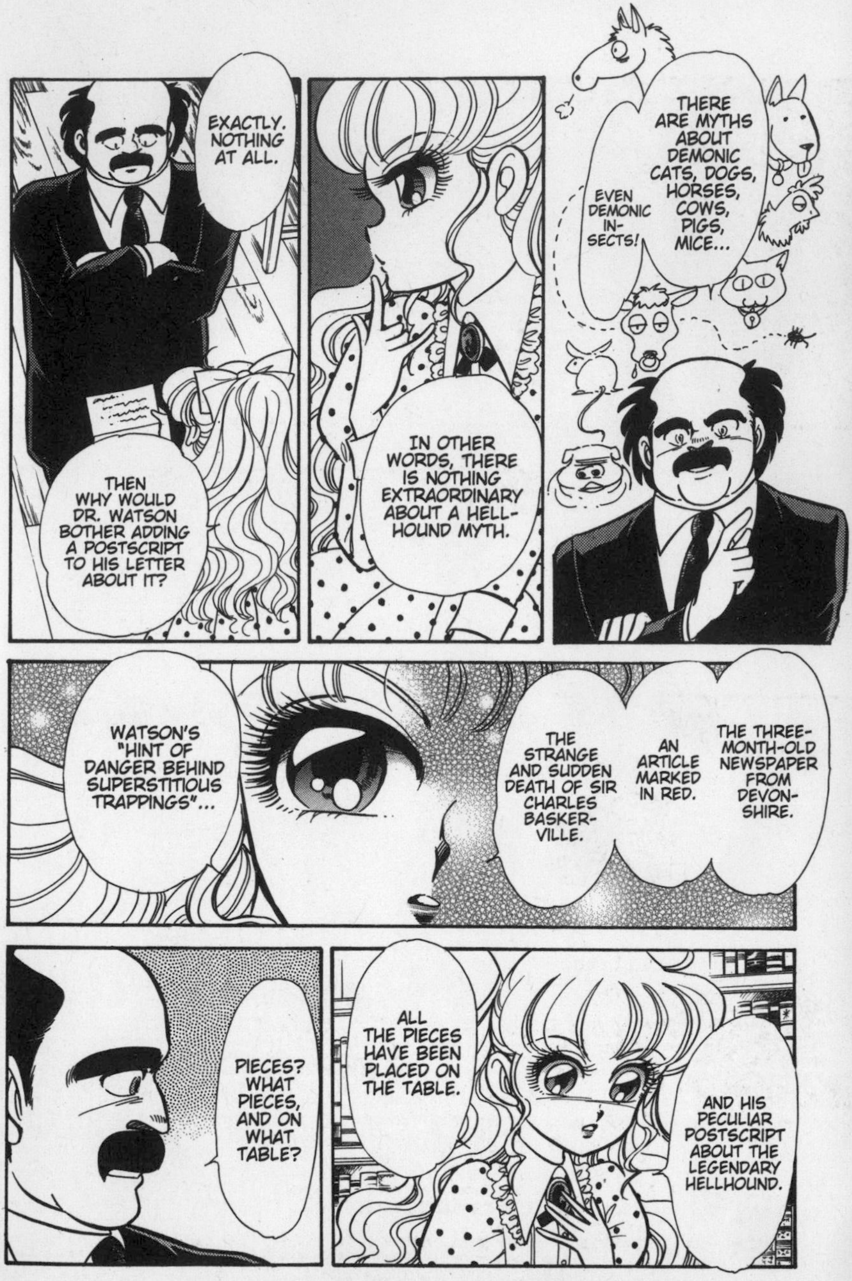
THERE ARE MYTHS ABOUT DEMONIC CATS, DOGS, HORSES, COWS, PIGS, MICE...
EVEN DEMONIC IN-SECTS!
IN OTHER WORDS, THERE IS NOTHING EXTRAORDINARY ABOUT A HELL-HOUND MYTH.
EXACTLY. NOTHING AT ALL.
THEN WHY WOULD DR. WATSON BOTHER ADDING A POSTSCRIPT TO HIS LETTER ABOUT IT?
THE THREE-MONTH-OLD NEWSPAPER FROM DEVON-SHIRE.
AN ARTICLE MARKED IN RED.
THE STRANGE AND SUDDEN DEATH OF SIR CHARLES BASKER-VILLE.
WATSON'S "HINT OF DANGER BEHIND SUPERSTITIOUS TRAPPINGS"...
AND HIS PECULIAR POSTSCRIPT ABOUT THE LEGENDARY HELLHOUND.
ALL THE PIECES HAVE BEEN PLACED ON THE TABLE.
PIECES? WHAT PIECES, AND ON WHAT TABLE?

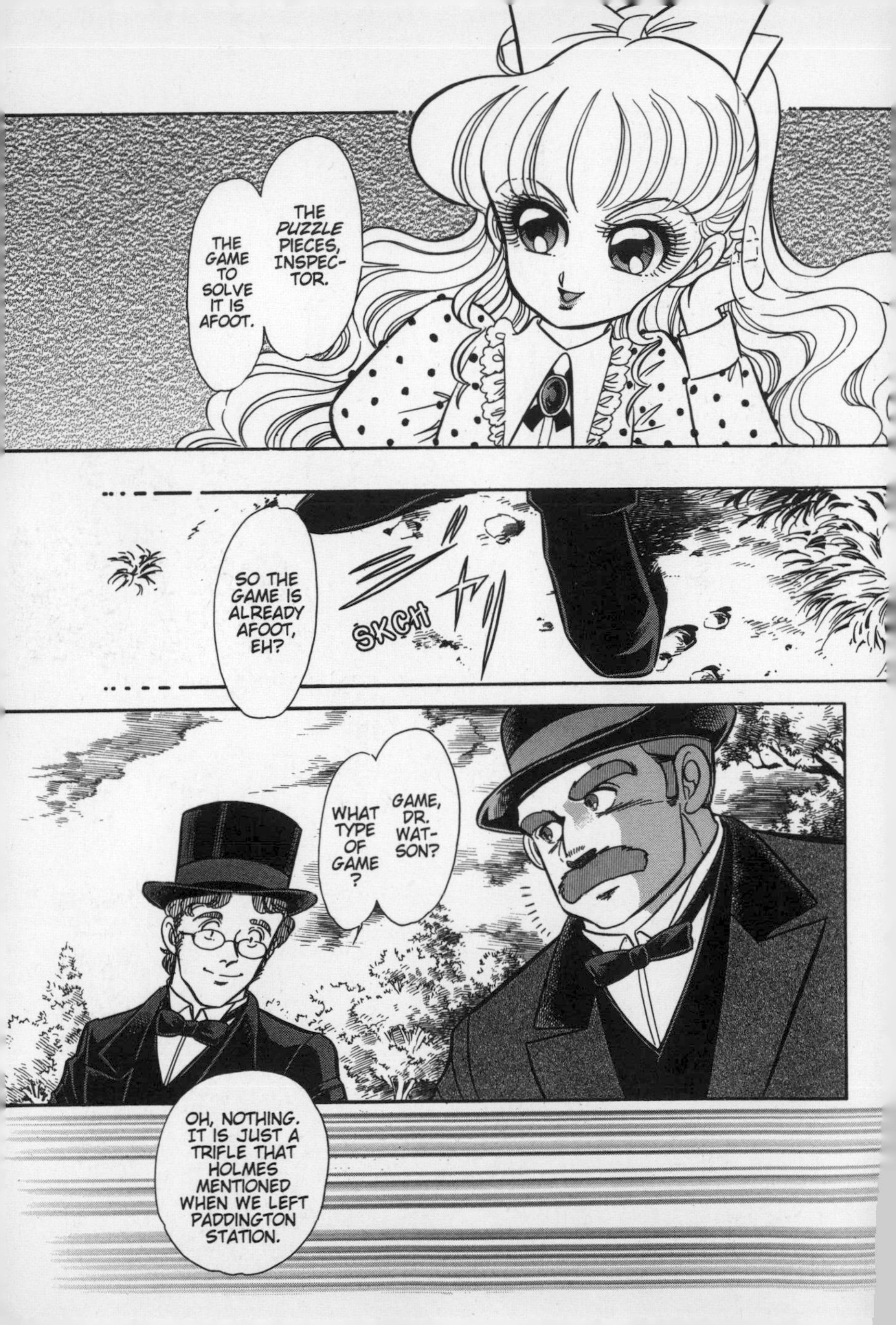
THE *PUZZLE* PIECES, INSPECTOR.
THE GAME TO SOLVE IT IS AFOOT.
SO THE GAME IS ALREADY AFOOT, EH?
SKCH
GAME, DR. WATSON?
WHAT TYPE OF GAME?
OH, NOTHING. IT IS JUST A TRIFLE THAT HOLMES MENTIONED WHEN WE LEFT PADDINGTON STATION.

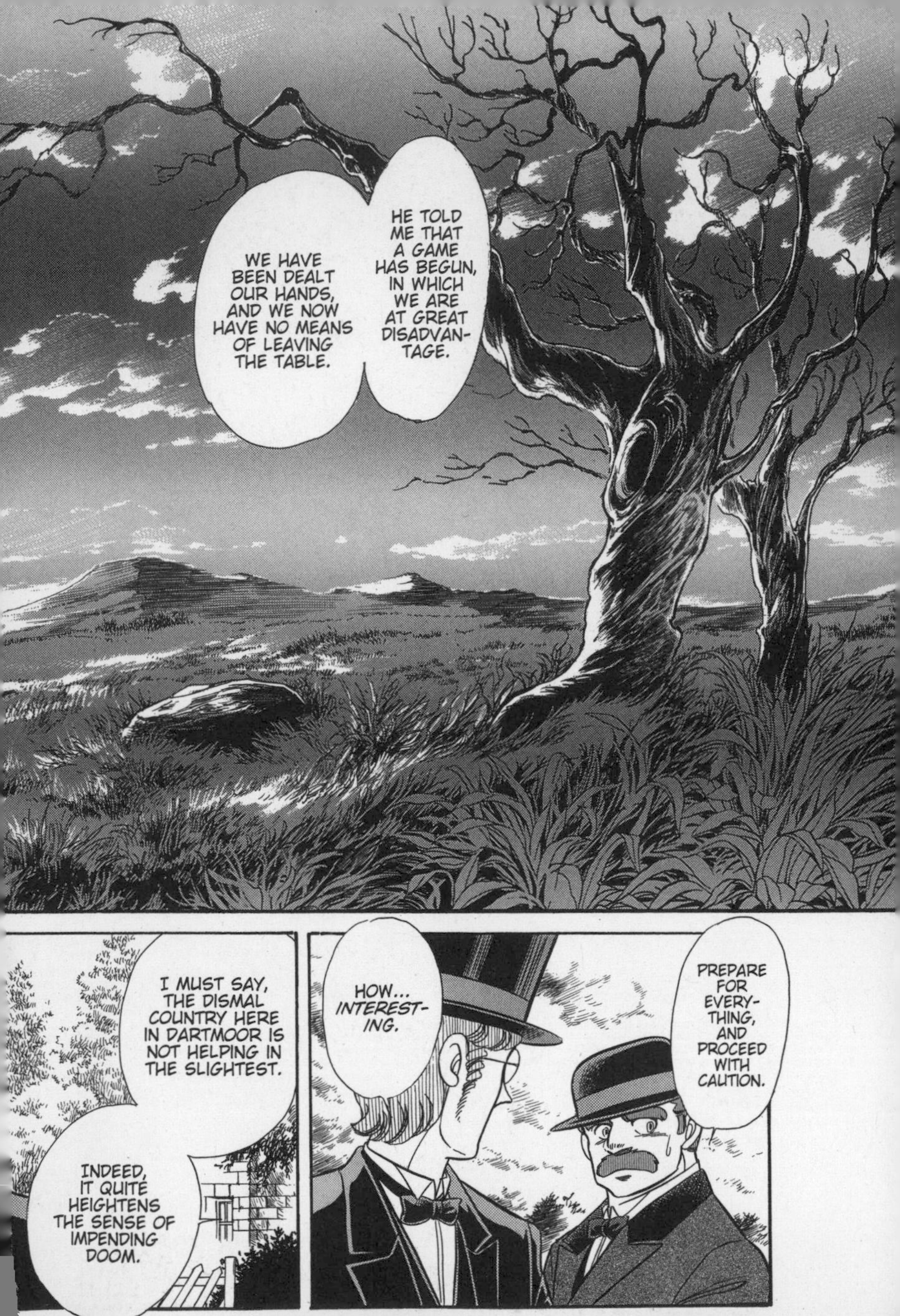
HE TOLD ME THAT A GAME HAS BEGUN, IN WHICH WE ARE AT GREAT DISADVAN-TAGE.
WE HAVE BEEN DEALT OUR HANDS, AND WE NOW HAVE NO MEANS OF LEAVING THE TABLE.
PREPARE FOR EVERY-THING, AND PROCEED WITH CAUTION.
HOW... *INTEREST-ING.*
I MUST SAY, THE DISMAL COUNTRY HERE IN DARTMOOR IS NOT HELPING IN THE SLIGHTEST.
INDEED, IT QUITE HEIGHTENS THE SENSE OF IMPENDING DOOM.

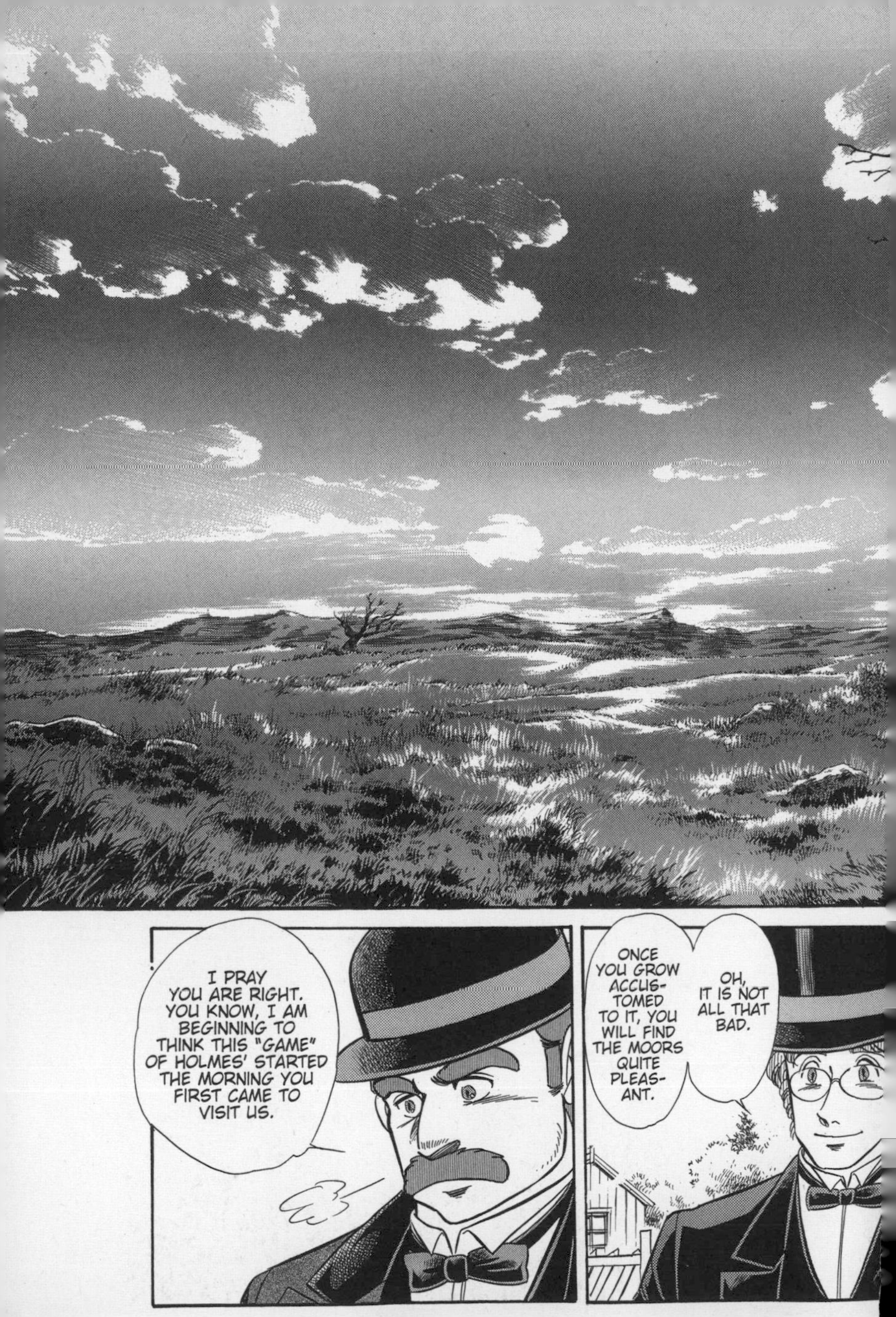
OH, IT IS NOT ALL THAT BAD.
ONCE YOU GROW ACCUSTOMED TO IT, YOU WILL FIND THE MOORS QUITE PLEASANT.
I PRAY YOU ARE RIGHT. YOU KNOW, I AM BEGINNING TO THINK THIS "GAME" OF HOLMES' STARTED THE MORNING YOU FIRST CAME TO VISIT US.

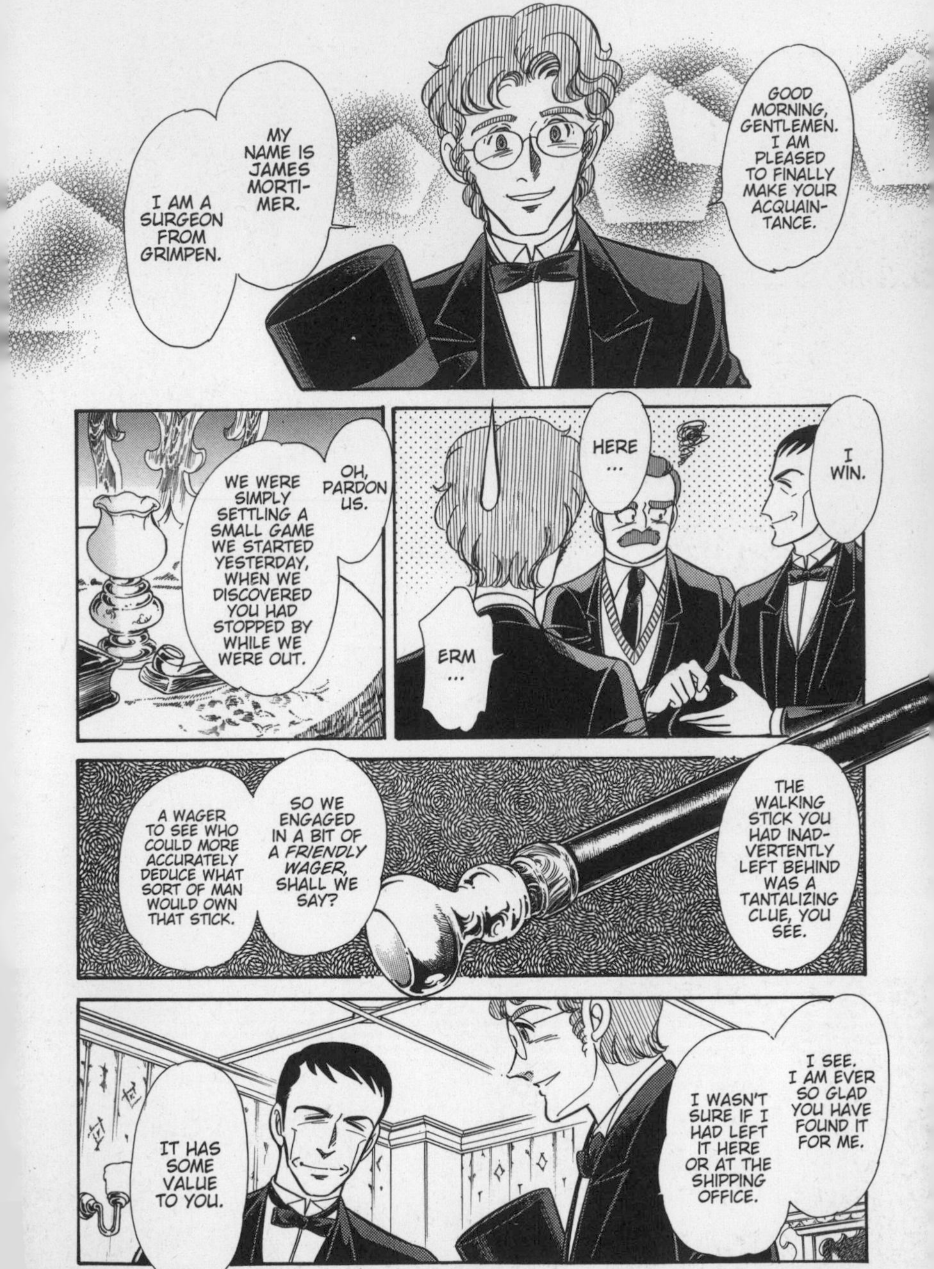
GOOD MORNING, GENTLEMEN. I AM PLEASED TO FINALLY MAKE YOUR ACQUAINTANCE.
MY NAME IS JAMES MORTIMER.
I AM A SURGEON FROM GRIMPEN.
I WIN.
HERE ...
ERM ...
OH, PARDON US.
WE WERE SIMPLY SETTLING A SMALL GAME WE STARTED YESTERDAY, WHEN WE DISCOVERED YOU HAD STOPPED BY WHILE WE WERE OUT.
THE WALKING STICK YOU HAD INADVERTENTLY LEFT BEHIND WAS A TANTALIZING CLUE, YOU SEE.
SO WE ENGAGED IN A BIT OF A *FRIENDLY WAGER*, SHALL WE SAY?
A WAGER TO SEE WHO COULD MORE ACCURATELY DEDUCE WHAT SORT OF MAN WOULD OWN THAT STICK.
I SEE. I AM EVER SO GLAD YOU HAVE FOUND IT FOR ME.
I WASN'T SURE IF I HAD LEFT IT HERE OR AT THE SHIPPING OFFICE.
IT HAS SOME VALUE TO YOU.

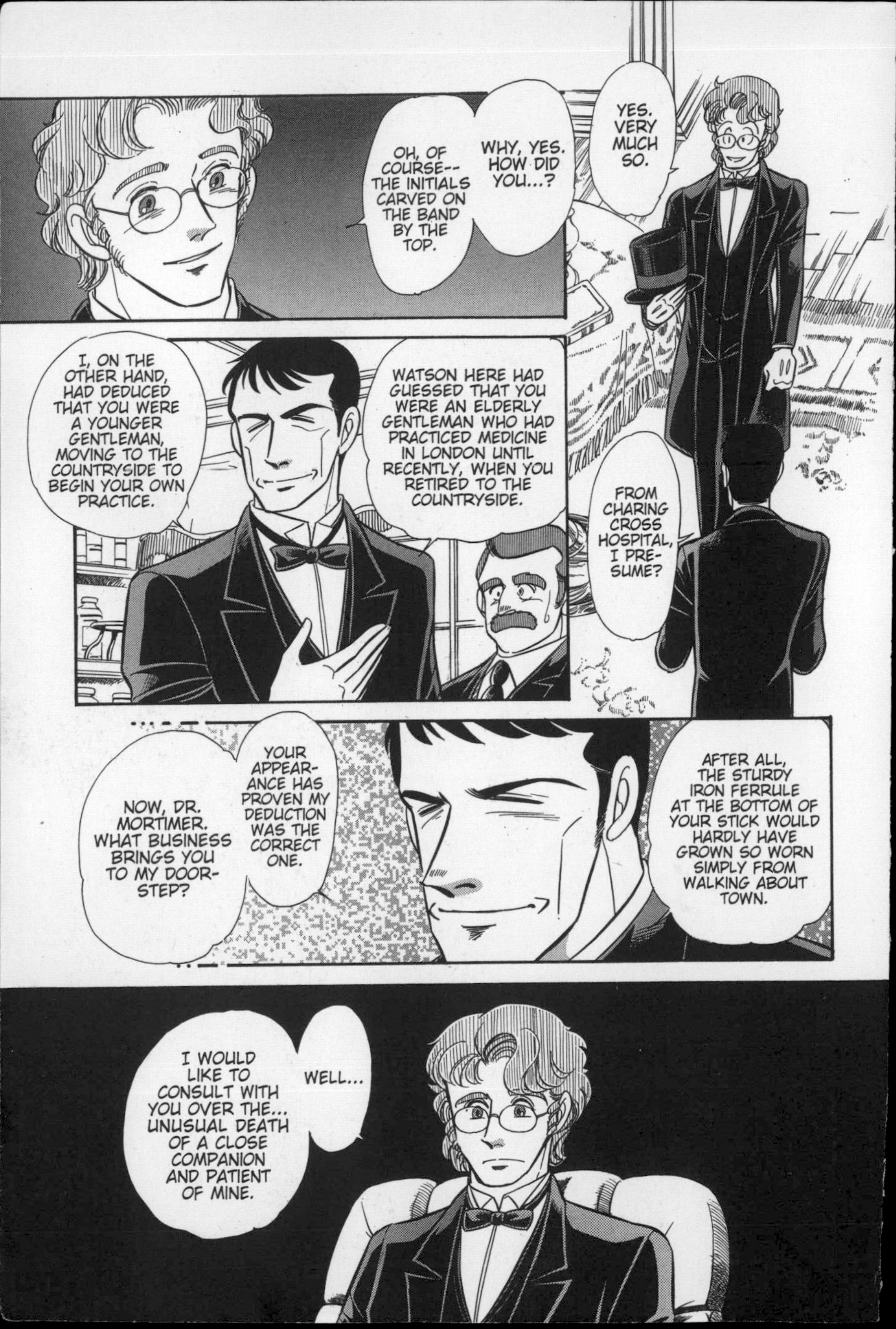
YES. VERY MUCH SO.
FROM CHARING CROSS HOSPITAL, I PRE-SUME?
WHY, YES. HOW DID YOU...?
OH, OF COURSE-- THE INITIALS CARVED ON THE BAND BY THE TOP.
WATSON HERE HAD GUESSED THAT YOU WERE AN ELDERLY GENTLEMAN WHO HAD PRACTICED MEDICINE IN LONDON UNTIL RECENTLY, WHEN YOU RETIRED TO THE COUNTRYSIDE.
I, ON THE OTHER HAND, HAD DEDUCED THAT YOU WERE A YOUNGER GENTLEMAN, MOVING TO THE COUNTRYSIDE TO BEGIN YOUR OWN PRACTICE.
AFTER ALL, THE STURDY IRON FERRULE AT THE BOTTOM OF YOUR STICK WOULD HARDLY HAVE GROWN SO WORN SIMPLY FROM WALKING ABOUT TOWN.
YOUR APPEAR-ANCE HAS PROVEN MY DEDUCTION WAS THE CORRECT ONE.
NOW, DR. MORTIMER. WHAT BUSINESS BRINGS YOU TO MY DOOR-STEP?
WELL...
I WOULD LIKE TO CONSULT WITH YOU OVER THE... UNUSUAL DEATH OF A CLOSE COMPANION AND PATIENT OF MINE.

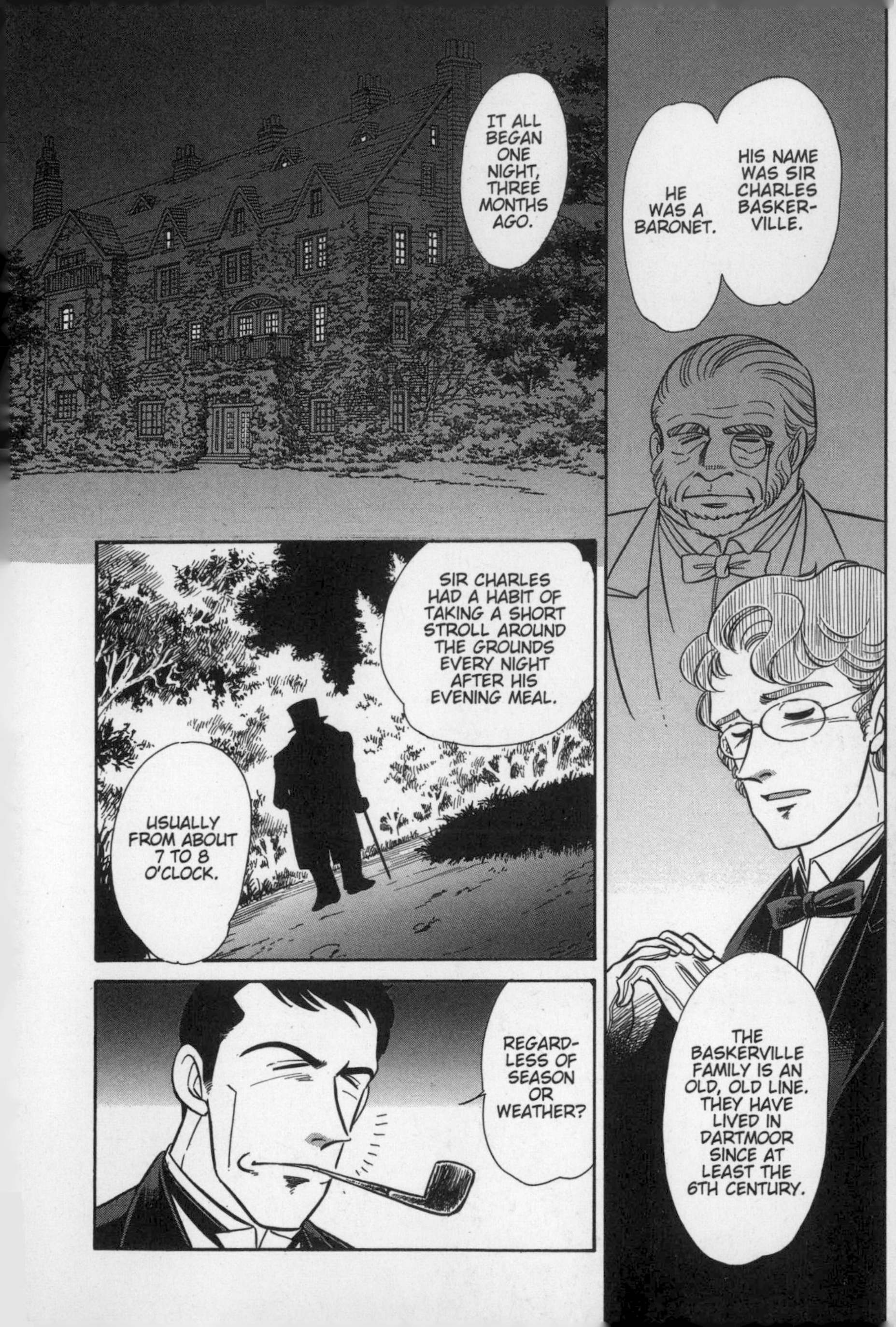
HIS NAME WAS SIR CHARLES BASKER-VILLE.
HE WAS A BARONET.
THE BASKERVILLE FAMILY IS AN OLD, OLD LINE. THEY HAVE LIVED IN DARTMOOR SINCE AT LEAST THE 6TH CENTURY.
IT ALL BEGAN ONE NIGHT, THREE MONTHS AGO.
SIR CHARLES HAD A HABIT OF TAKING A SHORT STROLL AROUND THE GROUNDS EVERY NIGHT AFTER HIS EVENING MEAL.
USUALLY FROM ABOUT 7 TO 8 O'CLOCK.
REGARD-LESS OF SEASON OR WEATHER?

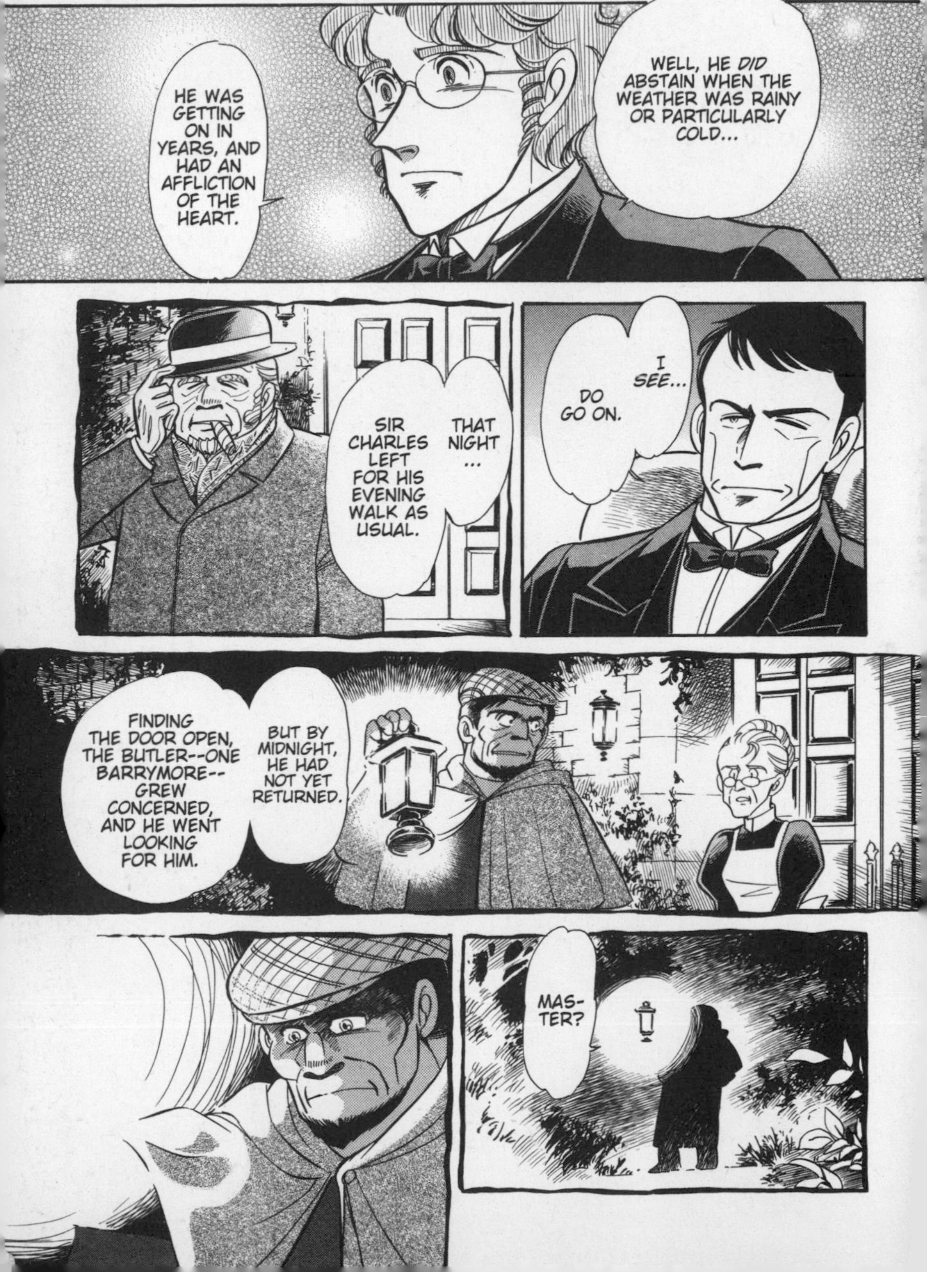
WELL, HE *DID* ABSTAIN WHEN THE WEATHER WAS RAINY OR PARTICULARLY COLD...
HE WAS GETTING ON IN YEARS, AND HAD AN AFFLICTION OF THE HEART.
I SEE...
DO GO ON.
THAT NIGHT...
SIR CHARLES LEFT FOR HIS EVENING WALK AS USUAL.
BUT BY MIDNIGHT, HE HAD NOT YET RETURNED.
FINDING THE DOOR OPEN, THE BUTLER--ONE BARRYMORE--GREW CONCERNED, AND HE WENT LOOKING FOR HIM.
MAS-TER?

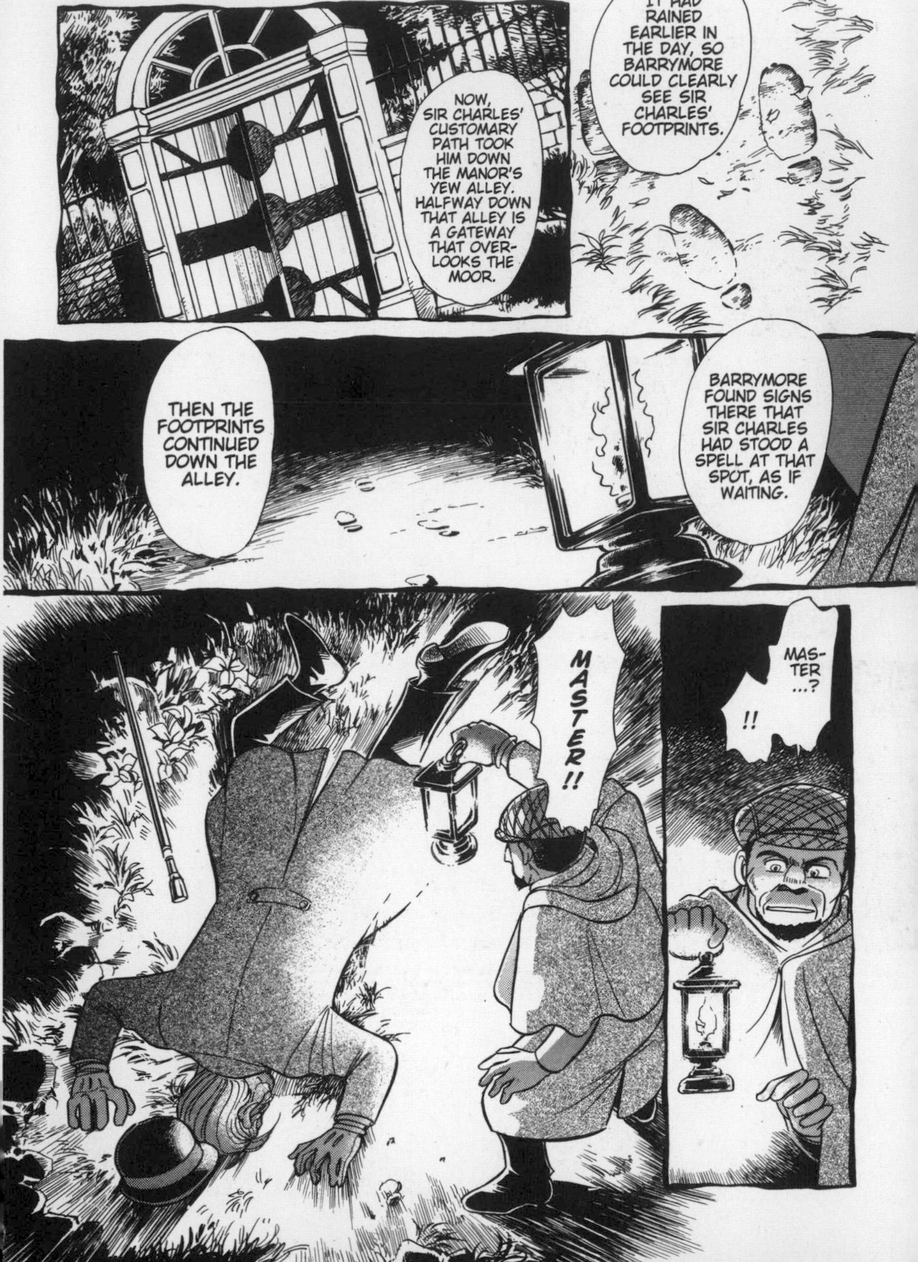
IT HAD RAINED EARLIER IN THE DAY, SO BARRYMORE COULD CLEARLY SEE SIR CHARLES' FOOTPRINTS.
NOW, SIR CHARLES' CUSTOMARY PATH TOOK HIM DOWN THE MANOR'S YEW ALLEY. HALFWAY DOWN THAT ALLEY IS A GATEWAY THAT OVER-LOOKS THE MOOR.
BARRYMORE FOUND SIGNS THERE THAT SIR CHARLES HAD STOOD A SPELL AT THAT SPOT, AS IF WAITING.
THEN THE FOOTPRINTS CONTINUED DOWN THE ALLEY.
MAS-TER ...?
!!
MASTER!!

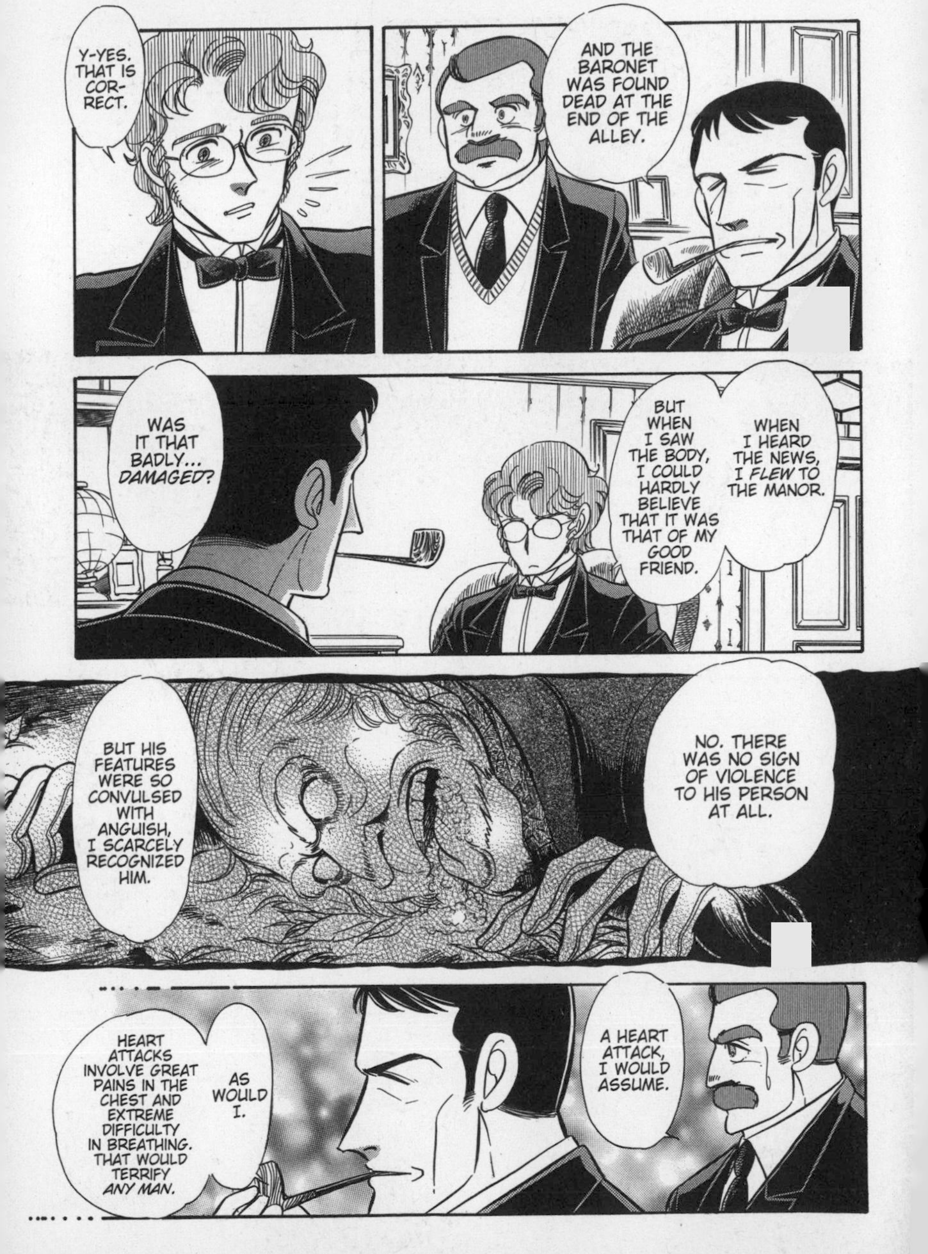
AND THE BARONET WAS FOUND DEAD AT THE END OF THE ALLEY.
Y-YES. THAT IS CORRECT.
WHEN I HEARD THE NEWS, I *FLEW* TO THE MANOR.
BUT WHEN I SAW THE BODY, I COULD HARDLY BELIEVE THAT IT WAS THAT OF MY GOOD FRIEND.
WAS IT THAT BADLY... *DAMAGED?*
NO. THERE WAS NO SIGN OF VIOLENCE TO HIS PERSON AT ALL.
BUT HIS FEATURES WERE SO CONVULSED WITH ANGUISH, I SCARCELY RECOGNIZED HIM.
A HEART ATTACK, I WOULD ASSUME.
AS WOULD I.
HEART ATTACKS INVOLVE GREAT PAINS IN THE CHEST AND EXTREME DIFFICULTY IN BREATHING. THAT WOULD TERRIFY *ANY MAN.*

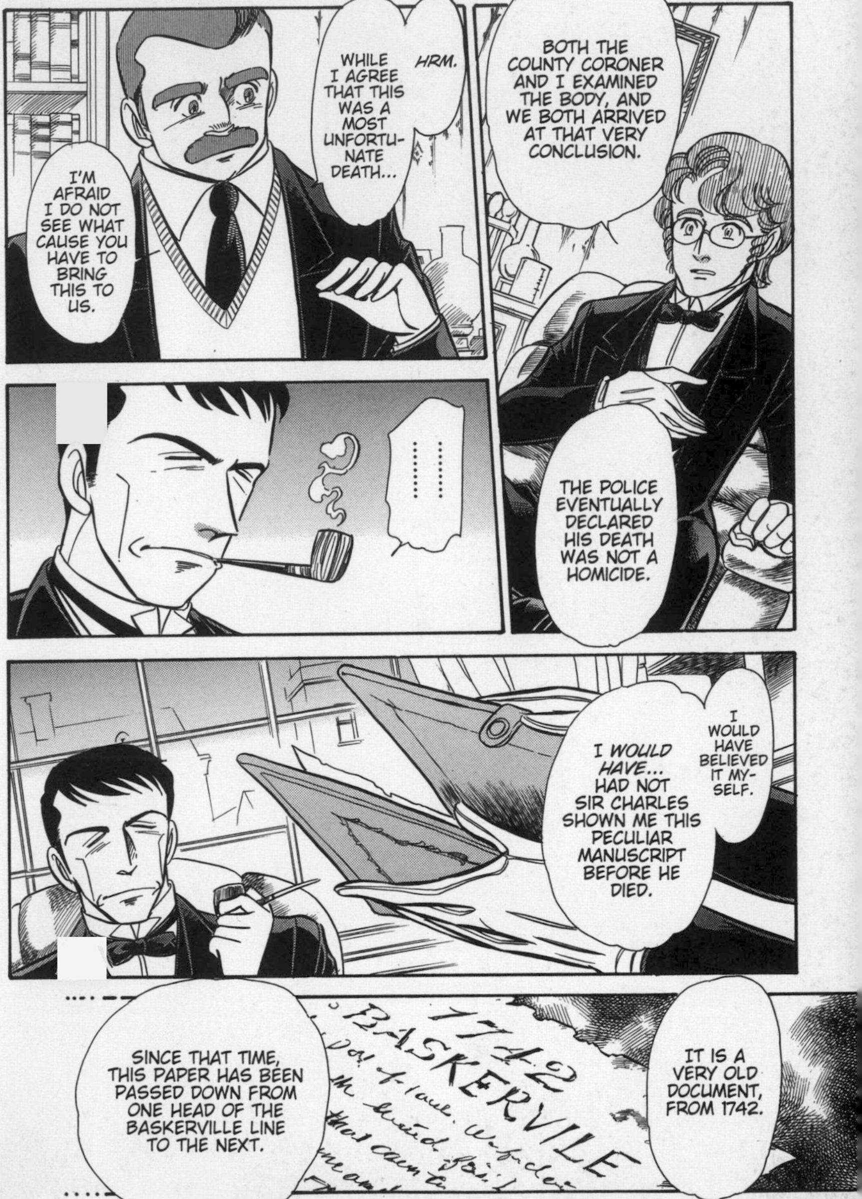
BOTH THE COUNTY CORONER AND I EXAMINED THE BODY, AND WE BOTH ARRIVED AT THAT VERY CONCLUSION.
THE POLICE EVENTUALLY DECLARED HIS DEATH WAS NOT A HOMICIDE.
HRM.
WHILE I AGREE THAT THIS WAS A MOST UNFORTU-NATE DEATH...
I'M AFRAID I DO NOT SEE WHAT CAUSE YOU HAVE TO BRING THIS TO US.
......
I WOULD HAVE BELIEVED IT MY-SELF.
I *WOULD HAVE*... HAD NOT SIR CHARLES SHOWN ME THIS PECULIAR MANUSCRIPT BEFORE HE DIED.
IT IS A VERY OLD DOCUMENT, FROM 1742.
1742
BASKERVILE
SINCE THAT TIME, THIS PAPER HAS BEEN PASSED DOWN FROM ONE HEAD OF THE BASKERVILLE LINE TO THE NEXT.

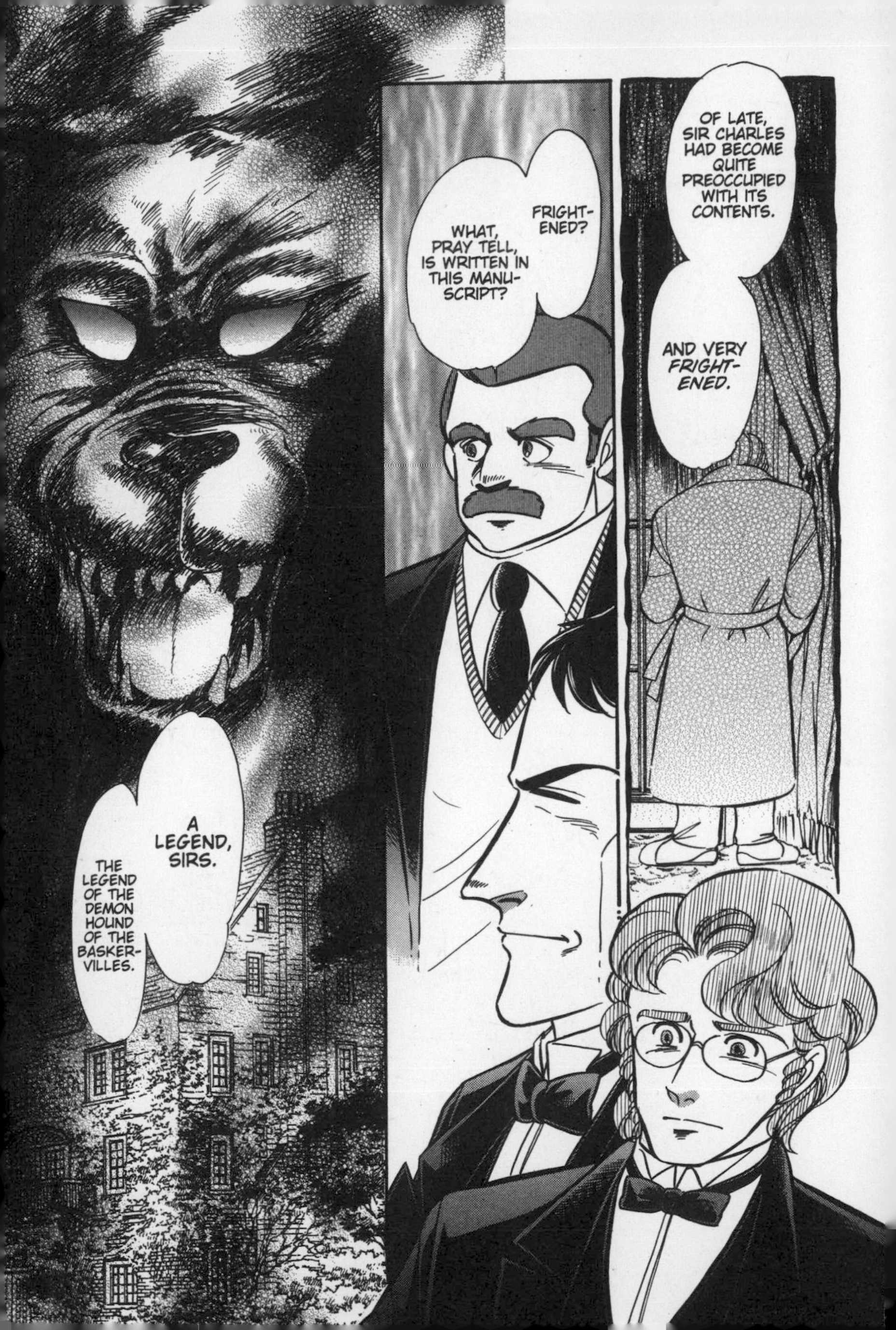
OF LATE, SIR CHARLES HAD BECOME QUITE PREOCCUPIED WITH ITS CONTENTS.
AND VERY *FRIGHTENED.*
FRIGHTENED?
WHAT, PRAY TELL, IS WRITTEN IN THIS MANUSCRIPT?
A LEGEND, SIRS.
THE LEGEND OF THE DEMON HOUND OF THE BASKERVILLES.

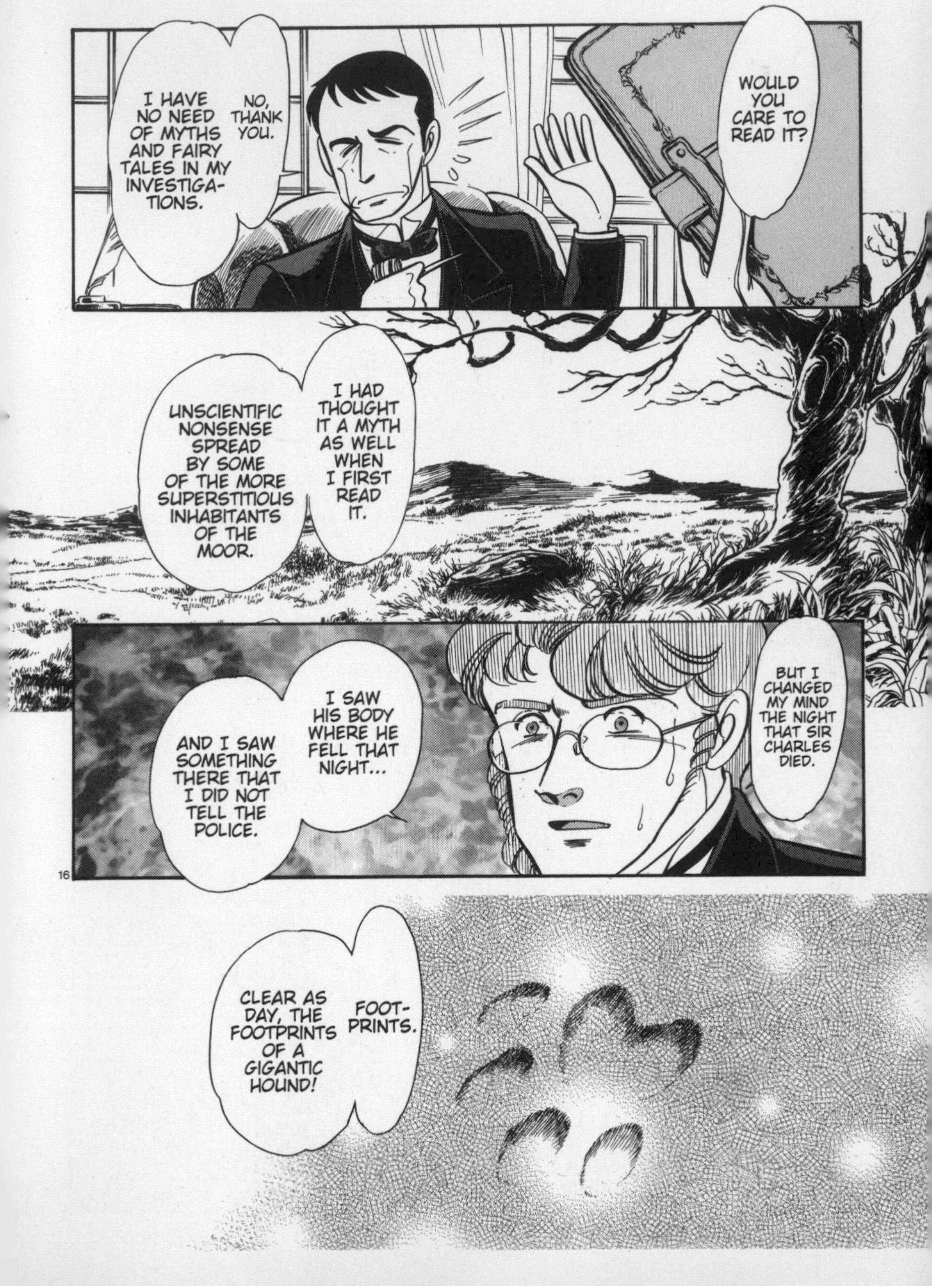
WOULD YOU CARE TO READ IT?
NO, THANK YOU.
I HAVE NO NEED OF MYTHS AND FAIRY TALES IN MY INVESTIGA-TIONS.
I HAD THOUGHT IT A MYTH AS WELL WHEN I FIRST READ IT.
UNSCIENTIFIC NONSENSE SPREAD BY SOME OF THE MORE SUPERSTITIOUS INHABITANTS OF THE MOOR.
BUT I CHANGED MY MIND THE NIGHT THAT SIR CHARLES DIED.
I SAW HIS BODY WHERE HE FELL THAT NIGHT...
AND I SAW SOMETHING THERE THAT I DID NOT TELL THE POLICE.
FOOT-PRINTS.
CLEAR AS DAY, THE FOOTPRINTS OF A GIGANTIC HOUND!

The Hound of the Baskervilles (3)

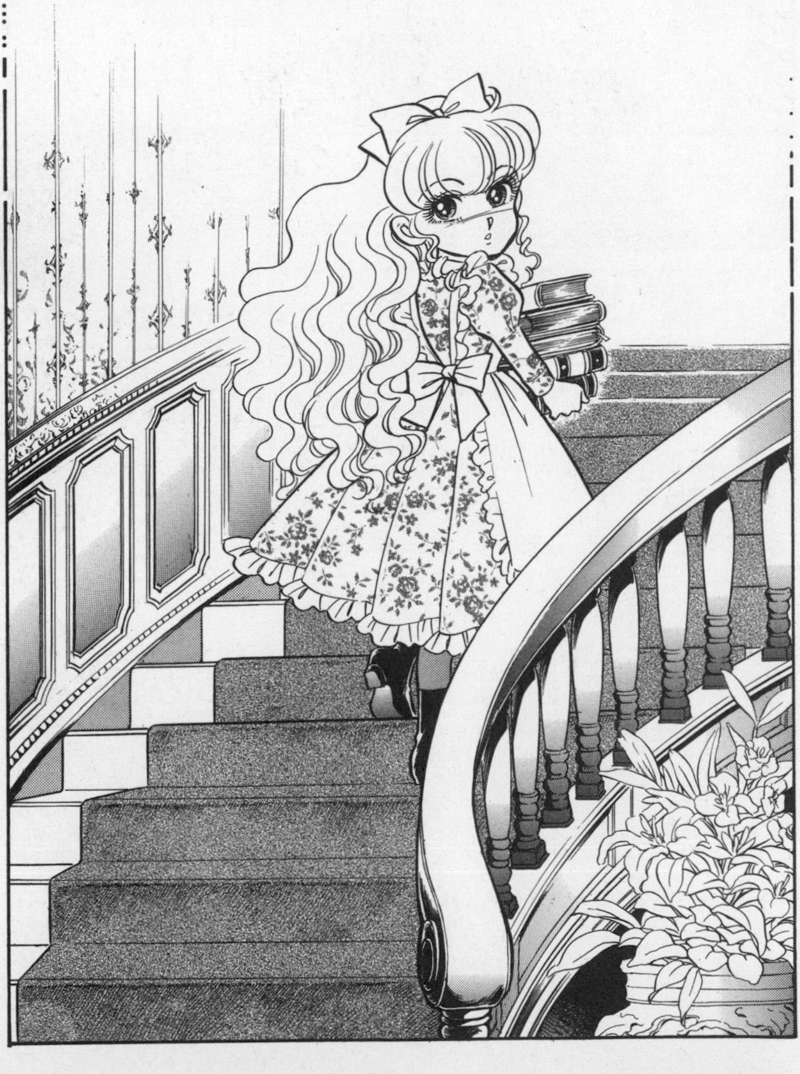

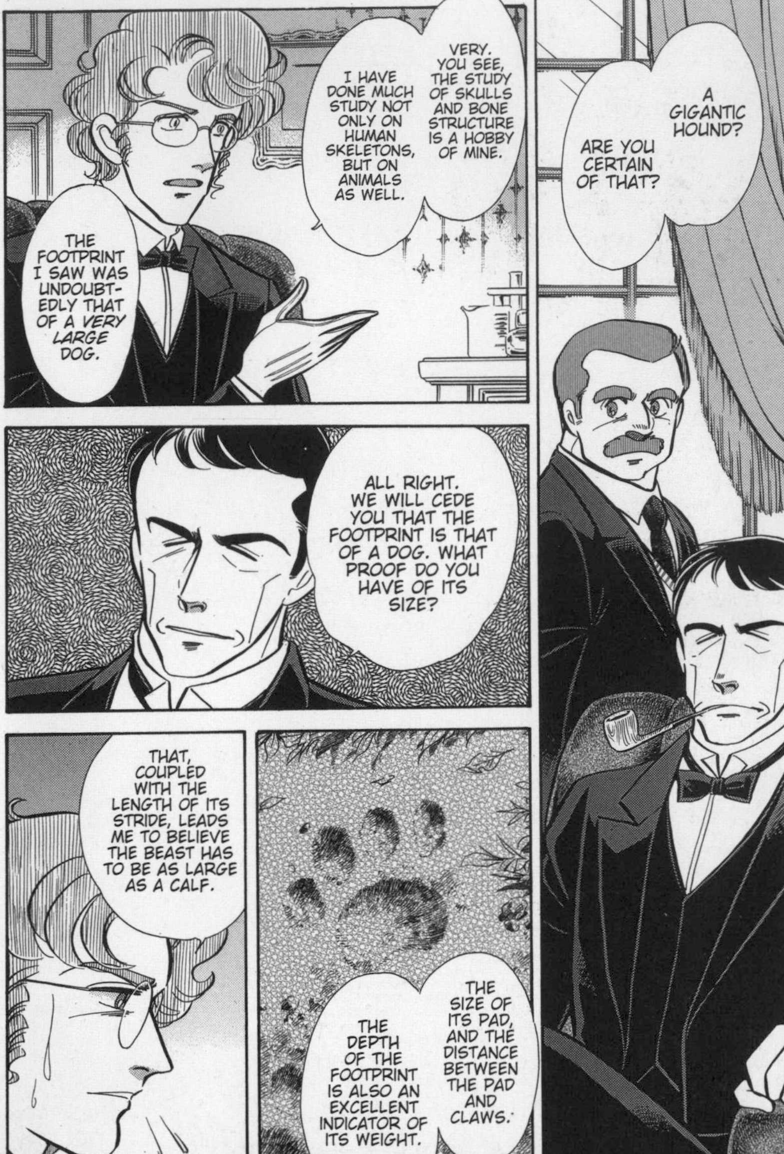
A GIGANTIC HOUND?
ARE YOU CERTAIN OF THAT?
VERY. YOU SEE, THE STUDY OF SKULLS AND BONE STRUCTURE IS A HOBBY OF MINE.
I HAVE DONE MUCH STUDY NOT ONLY ON HUMAN SKELETONS, BUT ON ANIMALS AS WELL.
THE FOOTPRINT I SAW WAS UNDOUBTEDLY THAT OF A *VERY LARGE* DOG.
ALL RIGHT. WE WILL CEDE YOU THAT THE FOOTPRINT IS THAT OF A DOG. WHAT PROOF DO YOU HAVE OF ITS SIZE?
THE SIZE OF ITS PAD, AND THE DISTANCE BETWEEN THE PAD AND CLAWS.
THE DEPTH OF THE FOOTPRINT IS ALSO AN EXCELLENT INDICATOR OF ITS WEIGHT.
THAT, COUPLED WITH THE LENGTH OF ITS STRIDE, LEADS ME TO BELIEVE THE BEAST HAS TO BE AS LARGE AS A CALF.

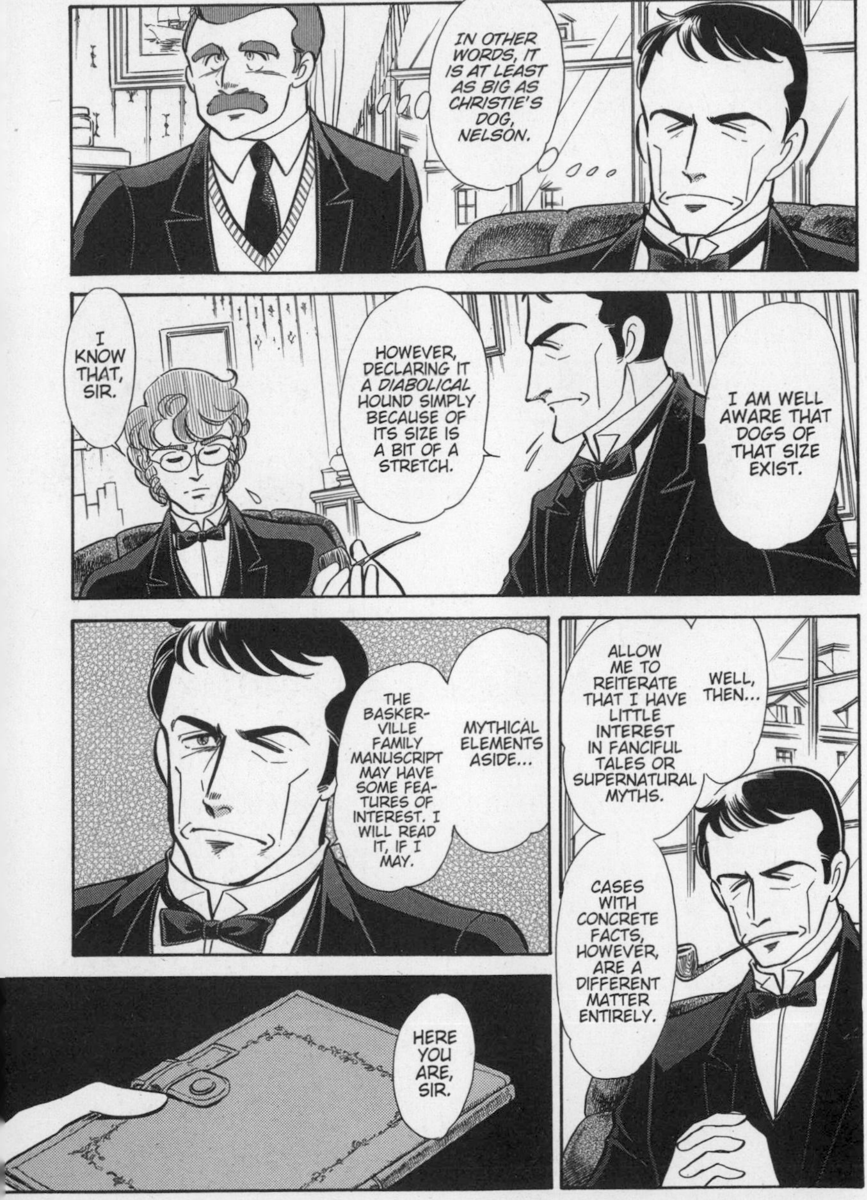
IN OTHER WORDS, IT IS AT LEAST AS BIG AS CHRISTIE'S DOG, NELSON.
I AM WELL AWARE THAT DOGS OF THAT SIZE EXIST.
HOWEVER, DECLARING IT A *DIABOLICAL* HOUND SIMPLY BECAUSE OF ITS SIZE IS A BIT OF A STRETCH.
I KNOW THAT, SIR.
WELL, THEN...
ALLOW ME TO REITERATE THAT I HAVE LITTLE INTEREST IN FANCIFUL TALES OR SUPERNATURAL MYTHS.
CASES WITH CONCRETE FACTS, HOWEVER, ARE A DIFFERENT MATTER ENTIRELY.
MYTHICAL ELEMENTS ASIDE...
THE BASKER-VILLE FAMILY MANUSCRIPT MAY HAVE SOME FEA-TURES OF INTEREST. I WILL READ IT, IF I MAY.
HERE YOU ARE, SIR.

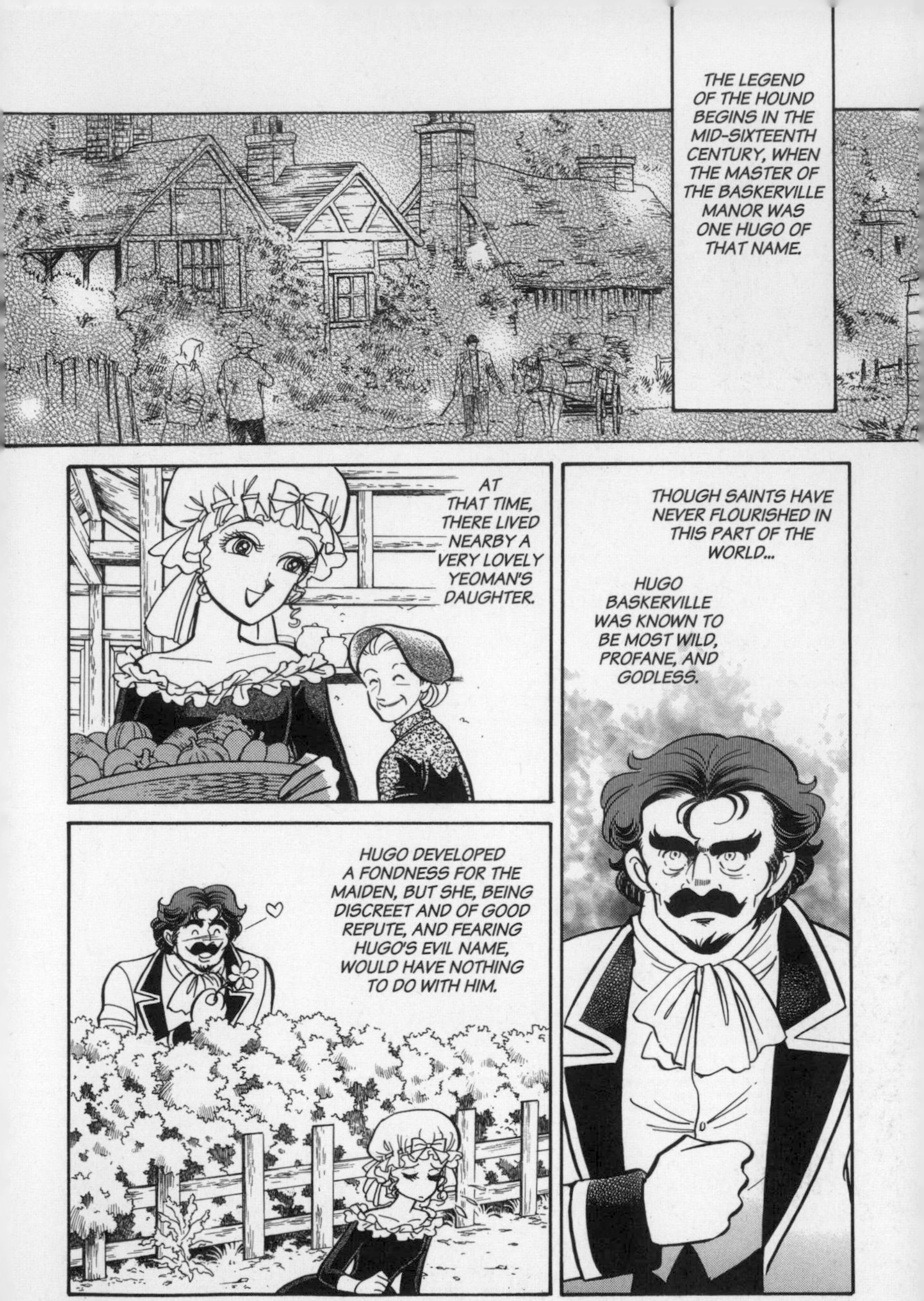
THE LEGEND OF THE HOUND BEGINS IN THE MID-SIXTEENTH CENTURY, WHEN THE MASTER OF THE BASKERVILLE MANOR WAS ONE HUGO OF THAT NAME.
THOUGH SAINTS HAVE NEVER FLOURISHED IN THIS PART OF THE WORLD...
HUGO BASKERVILLE WAS KNOWN TO BE MOST WILD, PROFANE, AND GODLESS.
AT THAT TIME, THERE LIVED NEARBY A VERY LOVELY YEOMAN'S DAUGHTER.
HUGO DEVELOPED A FONDNESS FOR THE MAIDEN, BUT SHE, BEING DISCREET AND OF GOOD REPUTE, AND FEARING HUGO'S EVIL NAME, WOULD HAVE NOTHING TO DO WITH HIM.

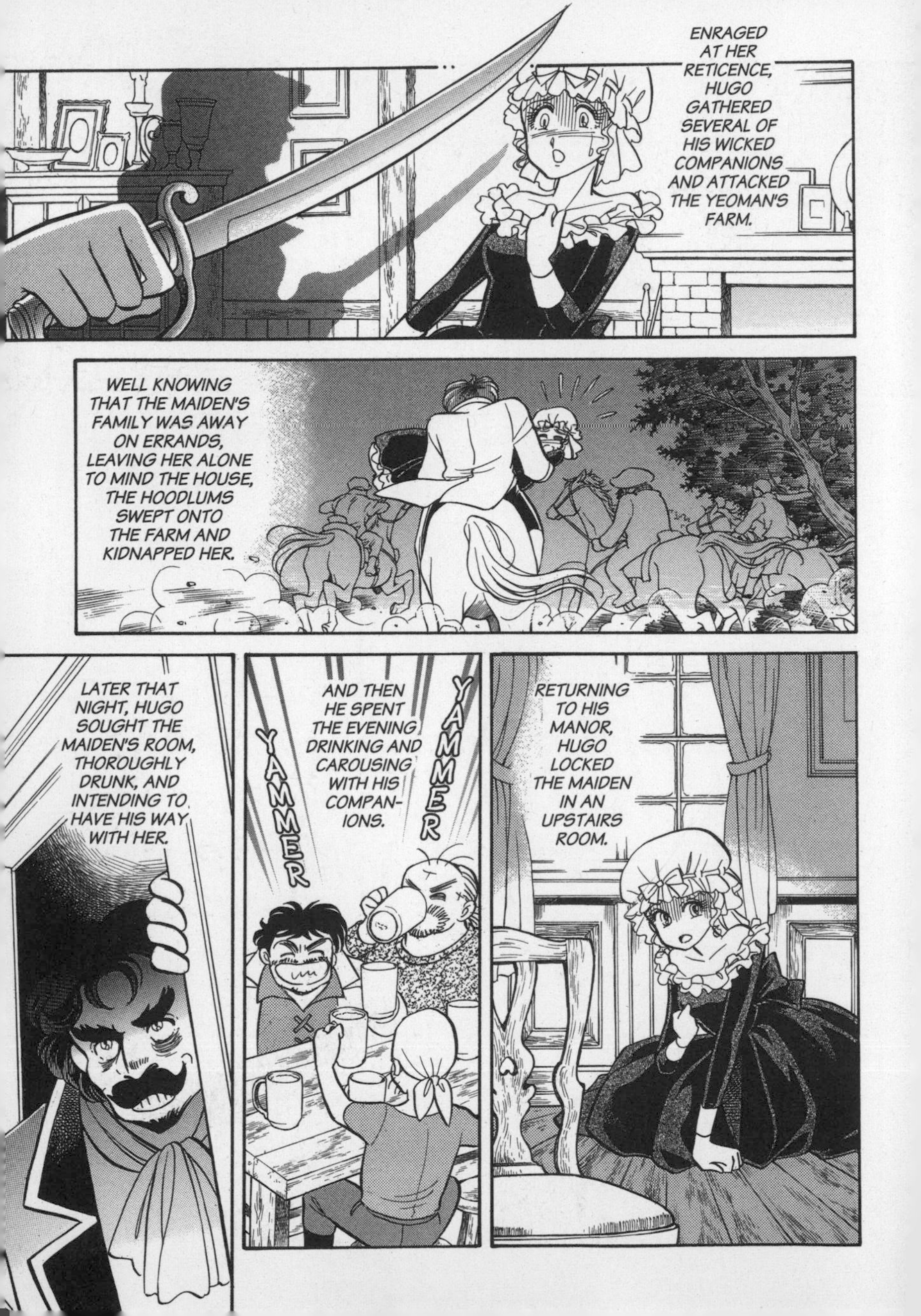

ENRAGED AT HER RETICENCE, HUGO GATHERED SEVERAL OF HIS WICKED COMPANIONS AND ATTACKED THE YEOMAN'S FARM.
WELL KNOWING THAT THE MAIDEN'S FAMILY WAS AWAY ON ERRANDS, LEAVING HER ALONE TO MIND THE HOUSE, THE HOODLUMS SWEPT ONTO THE FARM AND KIDNAPPED HER.
RETURNING TO HIS MANOR, HUGO LOCKED THE MAIDEN IN AN UPSTAIRS ROOM.
YAMMER
AND THEN HE SPENT THE EVENING DRINKING AND CAROUSING WITH HIS COMPANIONS.
YAMMER
LATER THAT NIGHT, HUGO SOUGHT THE MAIDEN'S ROOM, THOROUGHLY DRUNK, AND INTENDING TO HAVE HIS WAY WITH HER.

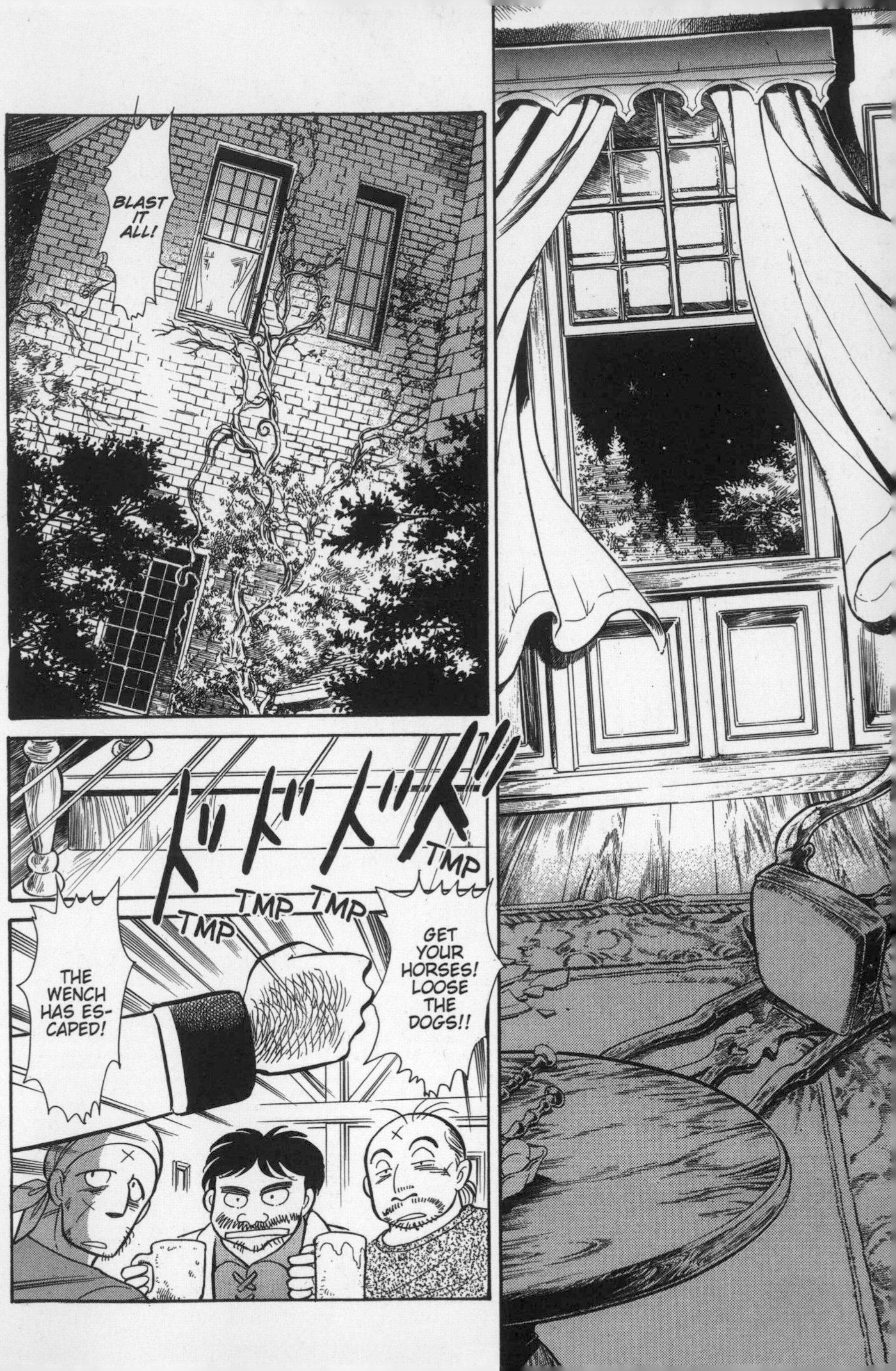
BLAST IT ALL!
TMP TMP TMP TMP
GET YOUR HORSES! LOOSE THE DOGS!!
THE WENCH HAS ES-CAPED!

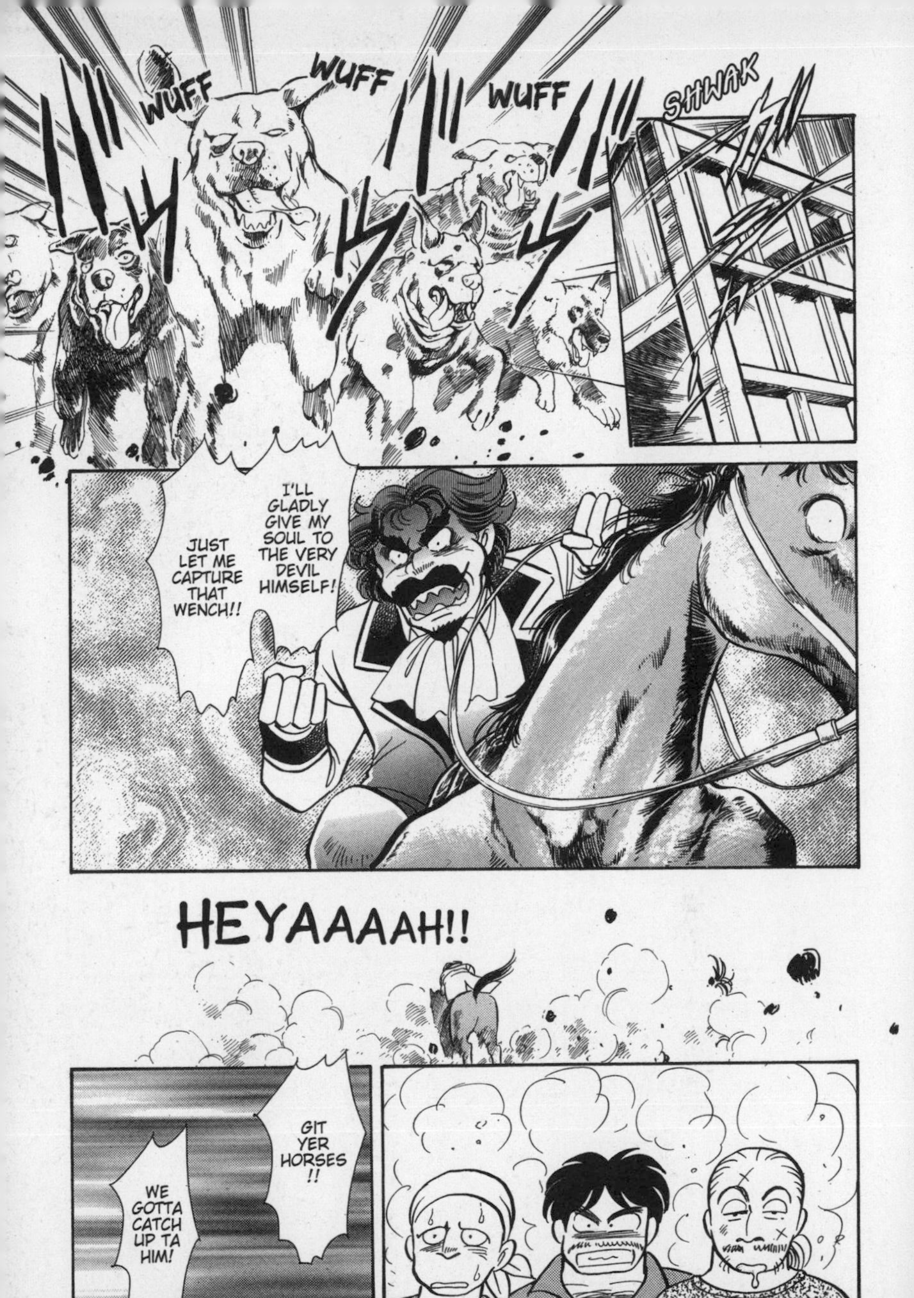
SHWAK
WUFF
WUFF
WUFF
I'LL GLADLY GIVE MY SOUL TO THE VERY DEVIL HIMSELF!
JUST LET ME CAPTURE THAT WENCH!!
HEYAAAAH!!
GIT YER HORSES !!
WE GOTTA CATCH UP TA HIM!

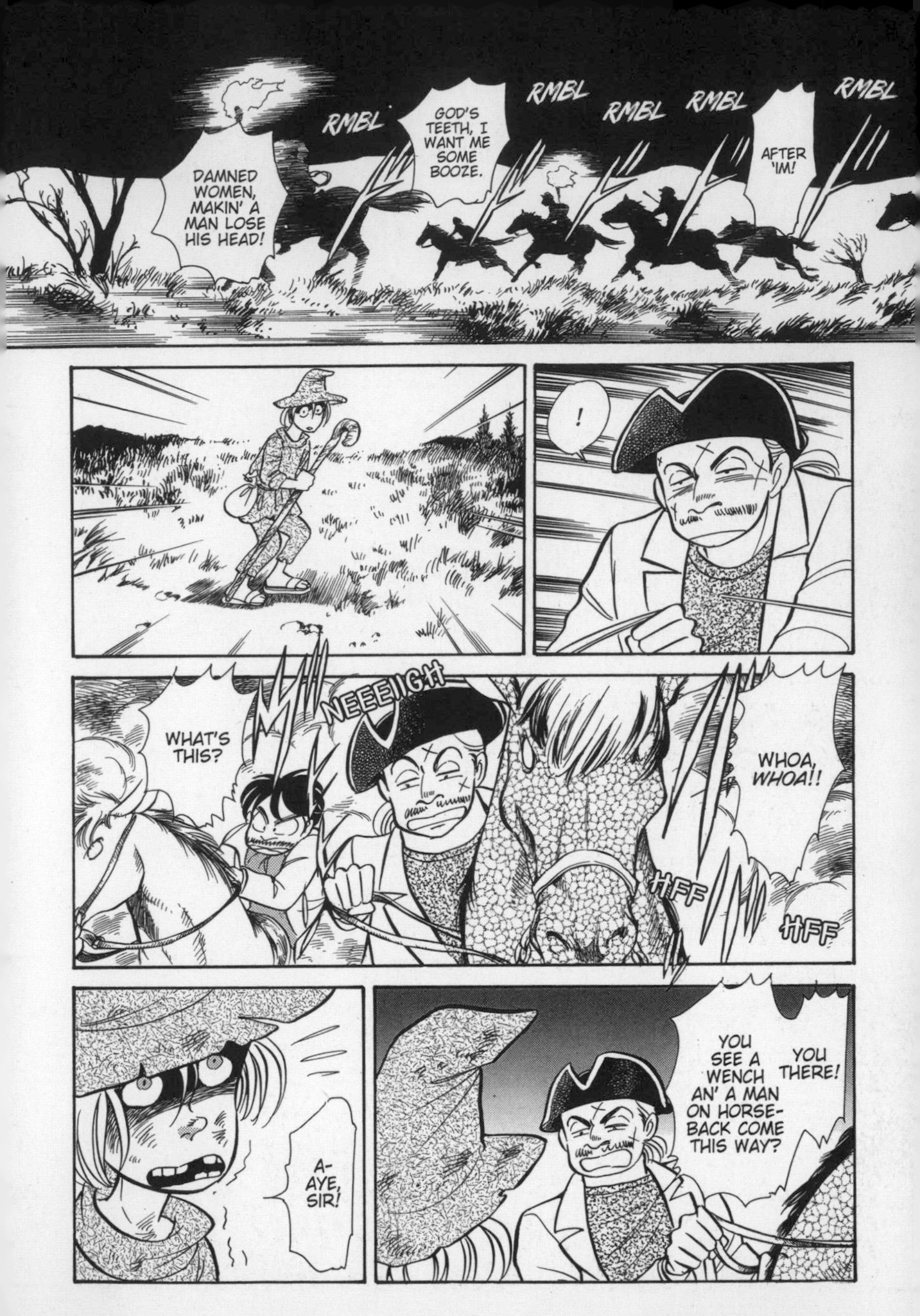
RMBL
AFTER 'IM!
RMBL
RMBL
RMBL
GOD'S TEETH, I WANT ME SOME BOOZE.
RMBL
DAMNED WOMEN, MAKIN' A MAN LOSE HIS HEAD!
!
WHOA, WHOA!!
HFF
HFF
NEEEIGH
WHAT'S THIS?
YOU THERE!
YOU SEE A WENCH AN' A MAN ON HORSE-BACK COME THIS WAY?
A-AYE, SIR!

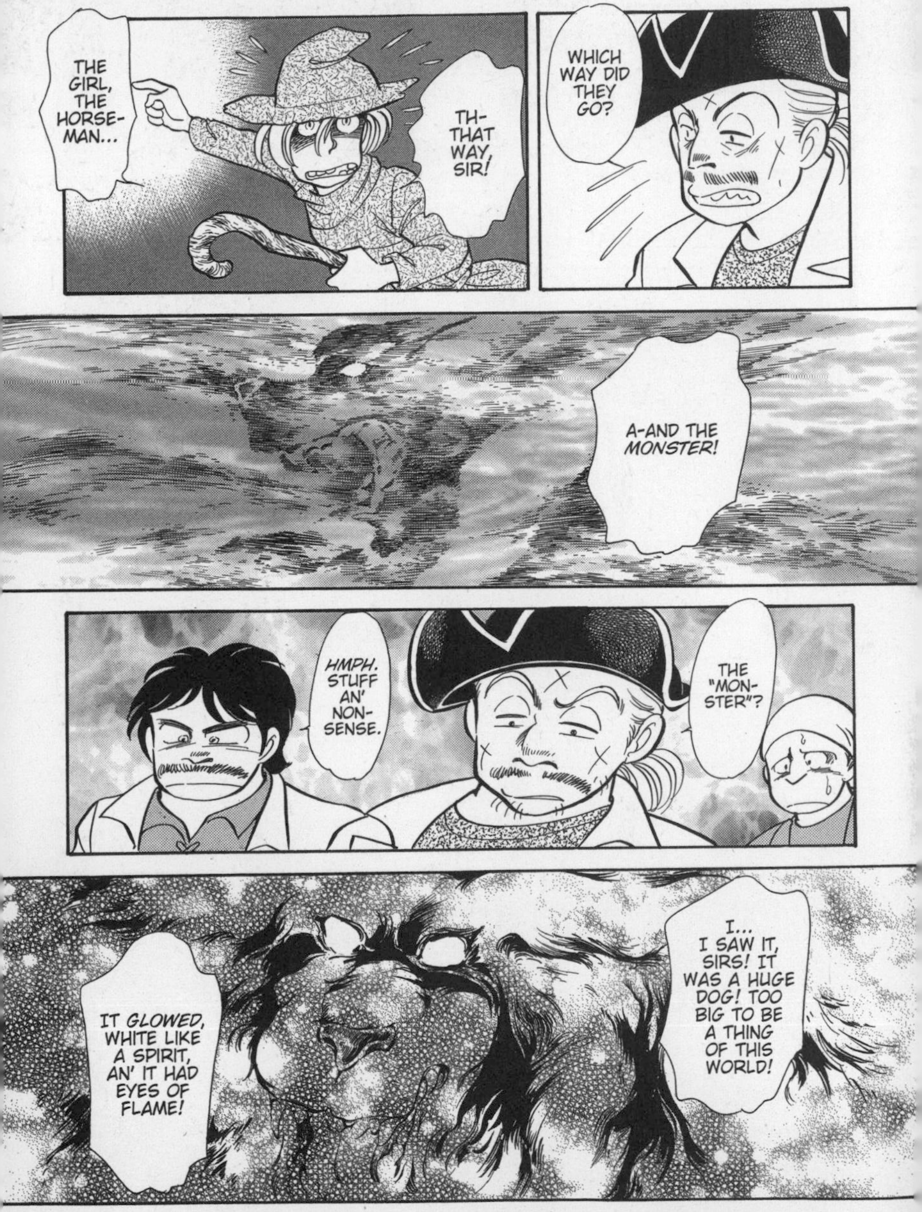
WHICH WAY DID THEY GO?
TH-THAT WAY, SIR!
THE GIRL, THE HORSEMAN...
A-AND THE *MONSTER!*
THE "MONSTER"?
HMPH. STUFF AN' NONSENSE.
I... I SAW IT, SIRS! IT WAS A HUGE DOG! TOO BIG TO BE A THING OF THIS WORLD!
IT *GLOWED,* WHITE LIKE A SPIRIT, AN' IT HAD EYES OF FLAME!

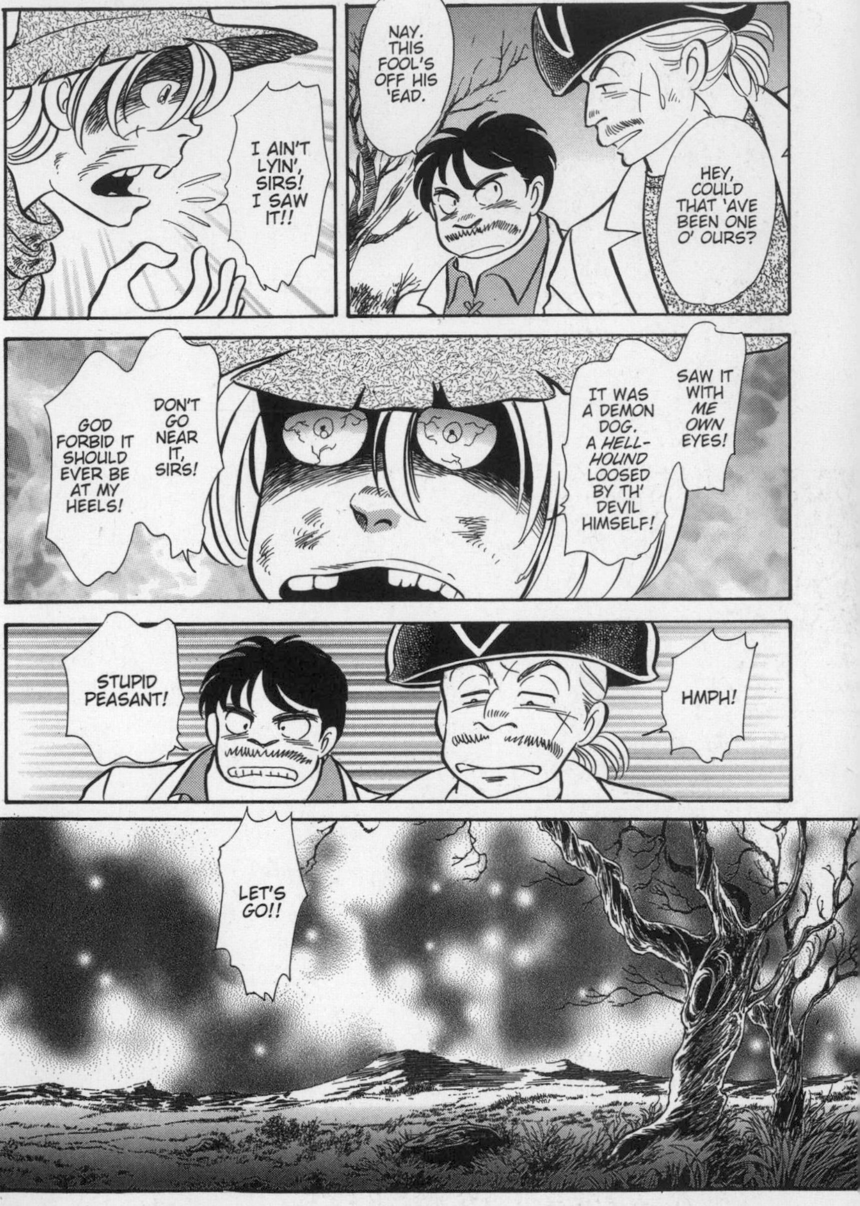
HEY, COULD THAT 'AVE BEEN ONE O' OURS?
NAY. THIS FOOL'S OFF HIS 'EAD.
I AIN'T LYIN', SIRS! I SAW IT!!
SAW IT WITH *ME OWN* EYES!
IT WAS A DEMON DOG. A *HELL-HOUND* LOOSED BY TH' DEVIL HIMSELF!
DON'T GO NEAR IT, SIRS!
GOD FORBID IT SHOULD EVER BE AT MY HEELS!
HMPH!
STUPID PEASANT!
LET'S GO!!

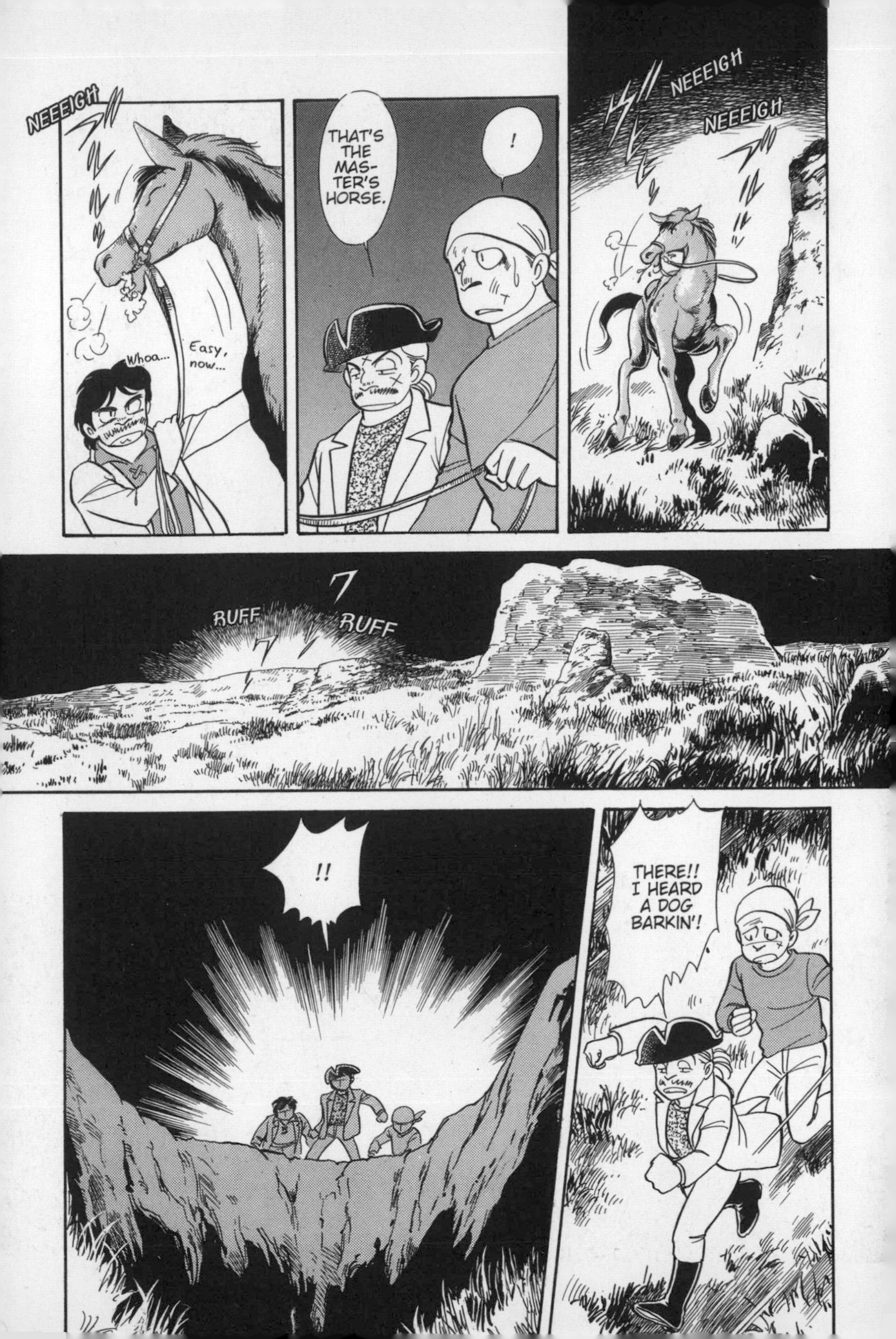
NEEEIGH
NEEEIGH
!
THAT'S THE MAS-TER'S HORSE.
NEEEIGH
Easy, now...
Whoa...
RUFF
RUFF
THERE!! I HEARD A DOG BARKIN'!
!!

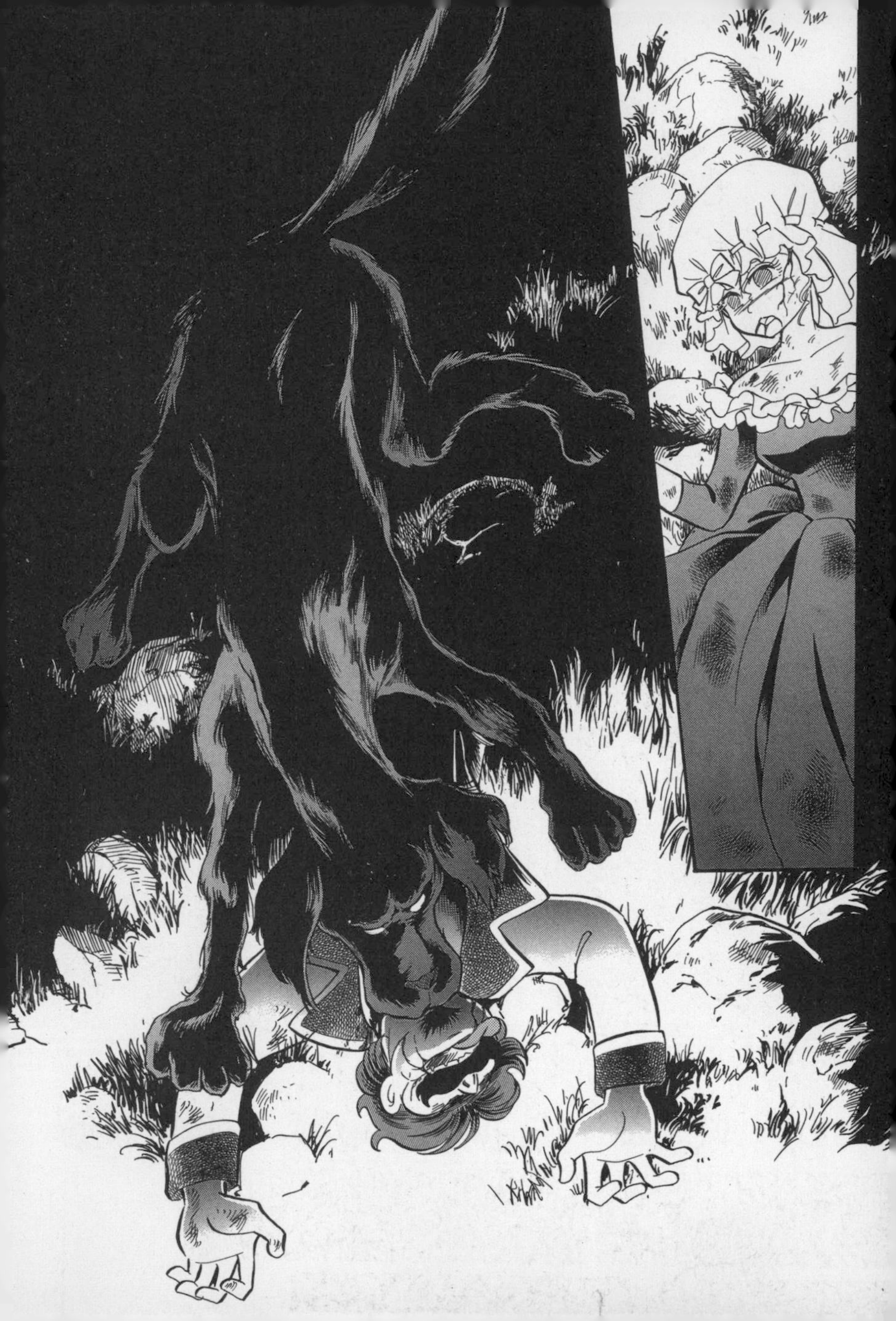

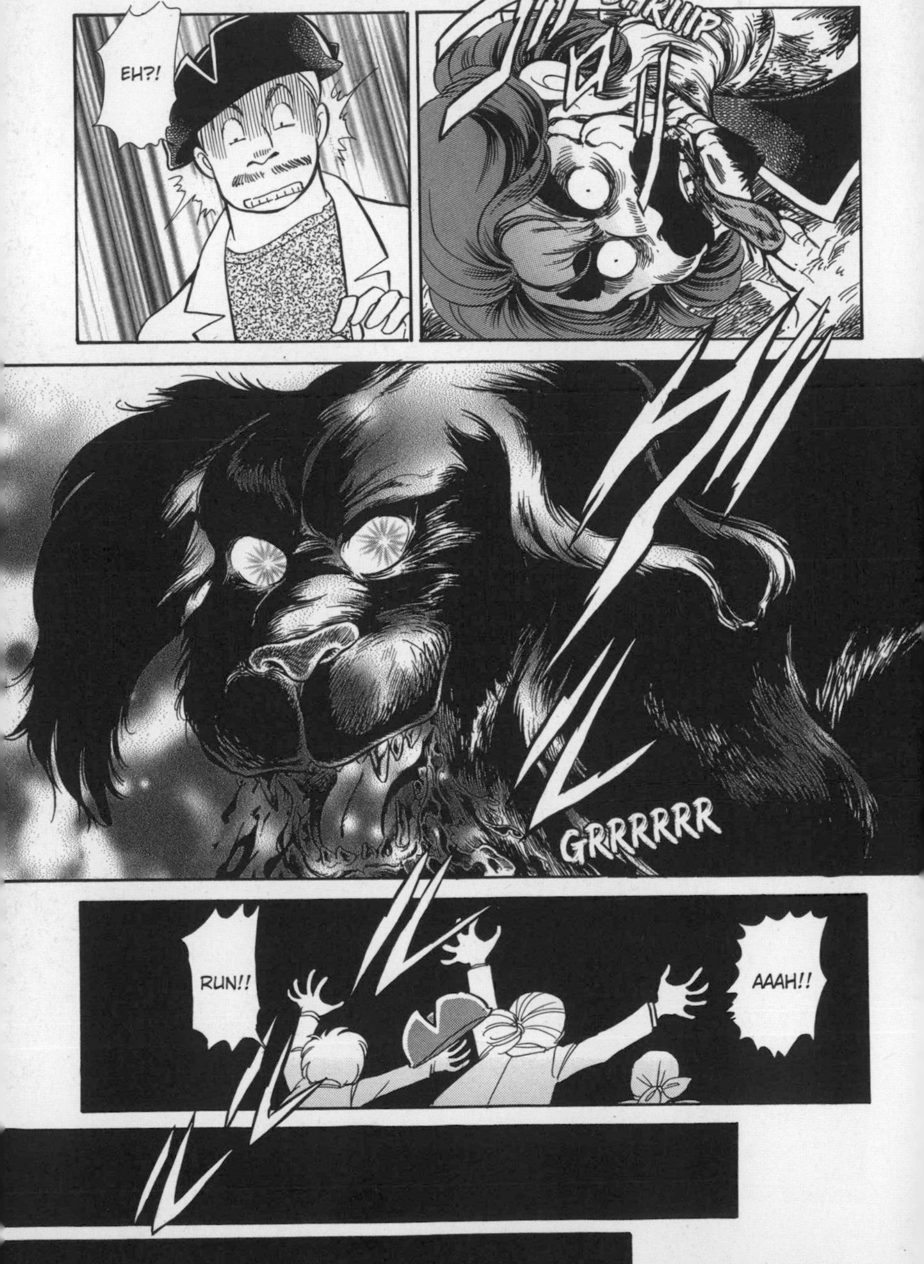
SHRIIIP
EH?!
GRRRRRR
AAAH!!
RUN!!

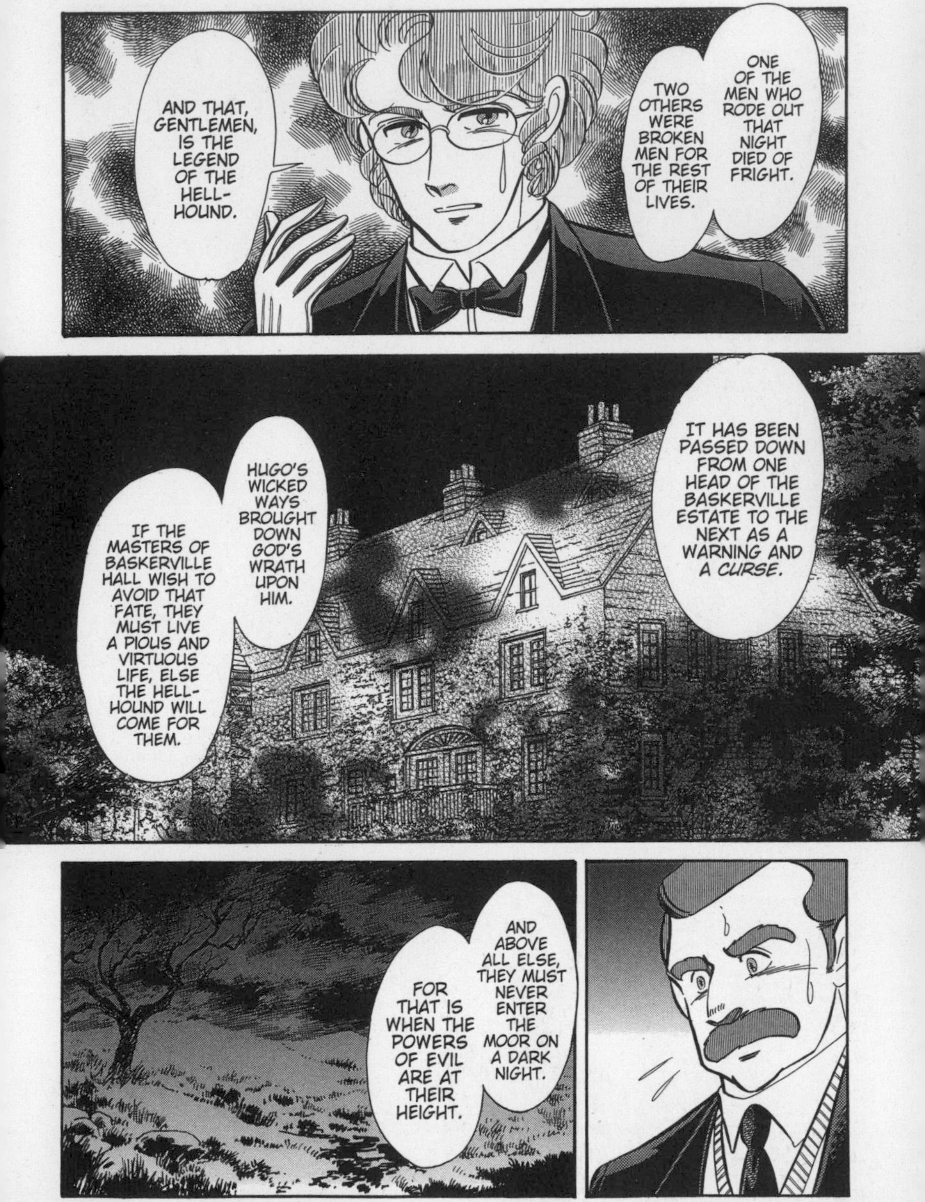
ONE OF THE MEN WHO RODE OUT THAT NIGHT DIED OF FRIGHT.
TWO OTHERS WERE BROKEN MEN FOR THE REST OF THEIR LIVES.
AND THAT, GENTLEMEN, IS THE LEGEND OF THE HELL-HOUND.
IT HAS BEEN PASSED DOWN FROM ONE HEAD OF THE BASKERVILLE ESTATE TO THE NEXT AS A WARNING AND A *CURSE*.
HUGO'S WICKED WAYS BROUGHT DOWN GOD'S WRATH UPON HIM.
IF THE MASTERS OF BASKERVILLE HALL WISH TO AVOID THAT FATE, THEY MUST LIVE A PIOUS AND VIRTUOUS LIFE, ELSE THE HELL-HOUND WILL COME FOR THEM.
AND ABOVE ALL ELSE, THEY MUST NEVER ENTER THE MOOR ON A DARK NIGHT.
FOR THAT IS WHEN THE POWERS OF EVIL ARE AT THEIR HEIGHT.

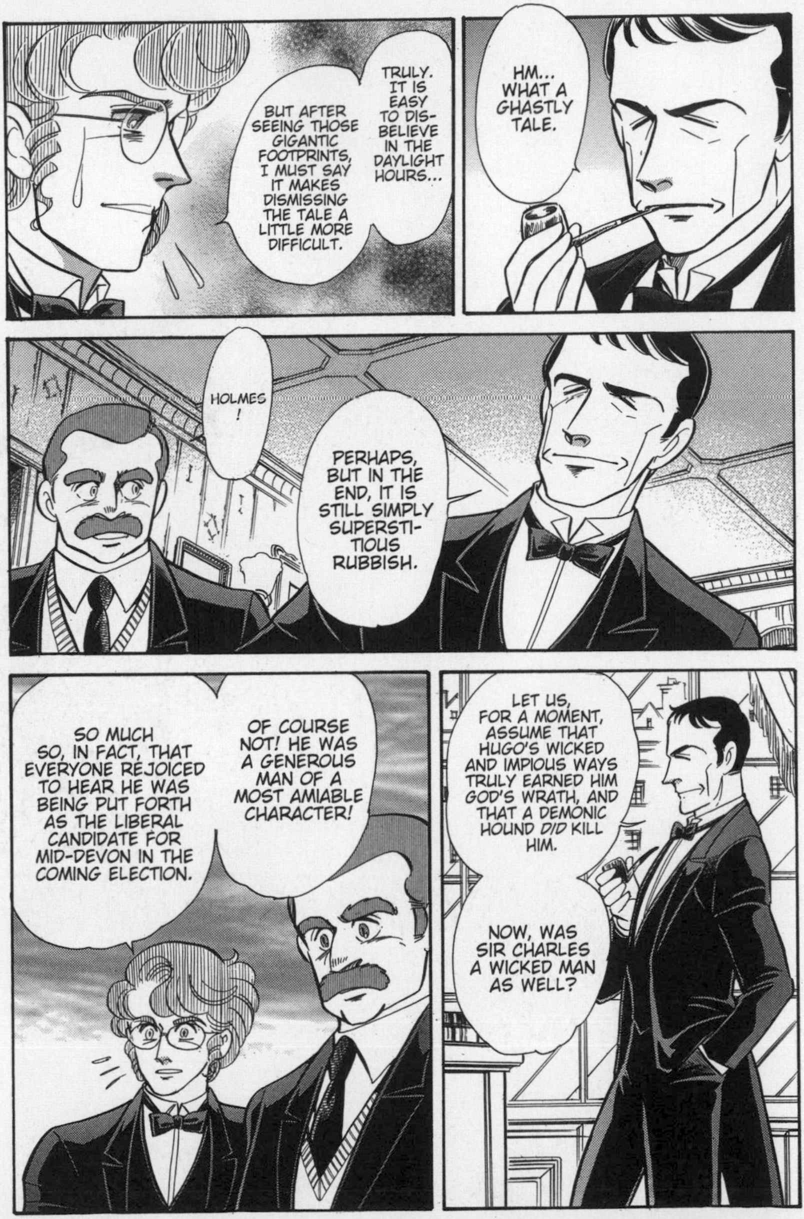
HM... WHAT A GHASTLY TALE.
TRULY. IT IS EASY TO DIS- BELIEVE IN THE DAYLIGHT HOURS...
BUT AFTER SEEING THOSE GIGANTIC FOOTPRINTS, I MUST SAY IT MAKES DISMISSING THE TALE A LITTLE MORE DIFFICULT.
PERHAPS, BUT IN THE END, IT IS STILL SIMPLY SUPERSTI- TIOUS RUBBISH.
HOLMES!
LET US, FOR A MOMENT, ASSUME THAT HUGO'S WICKED AND IMPIOUS WAYS TRULY EARNED HIM GOD'S WRATH, AND THAT A DEMONIC HOUND *DID* KILL HIM.
NOW, WAS SIR CHARLES A WICKED MAN AS WELL?
OF COURSE NOT! HE WAS A GENEROUS MAN OF A MOST AMIABLE CHARACTER!
SO MUCH SO, IN FACT, THAT EVERYONE REJOICED TO HEAR HE WAS BEING PUT FORTH AS THE LIBERAL CANDIDATE FOR MID-DEVON IN THE COMING ELECTION.

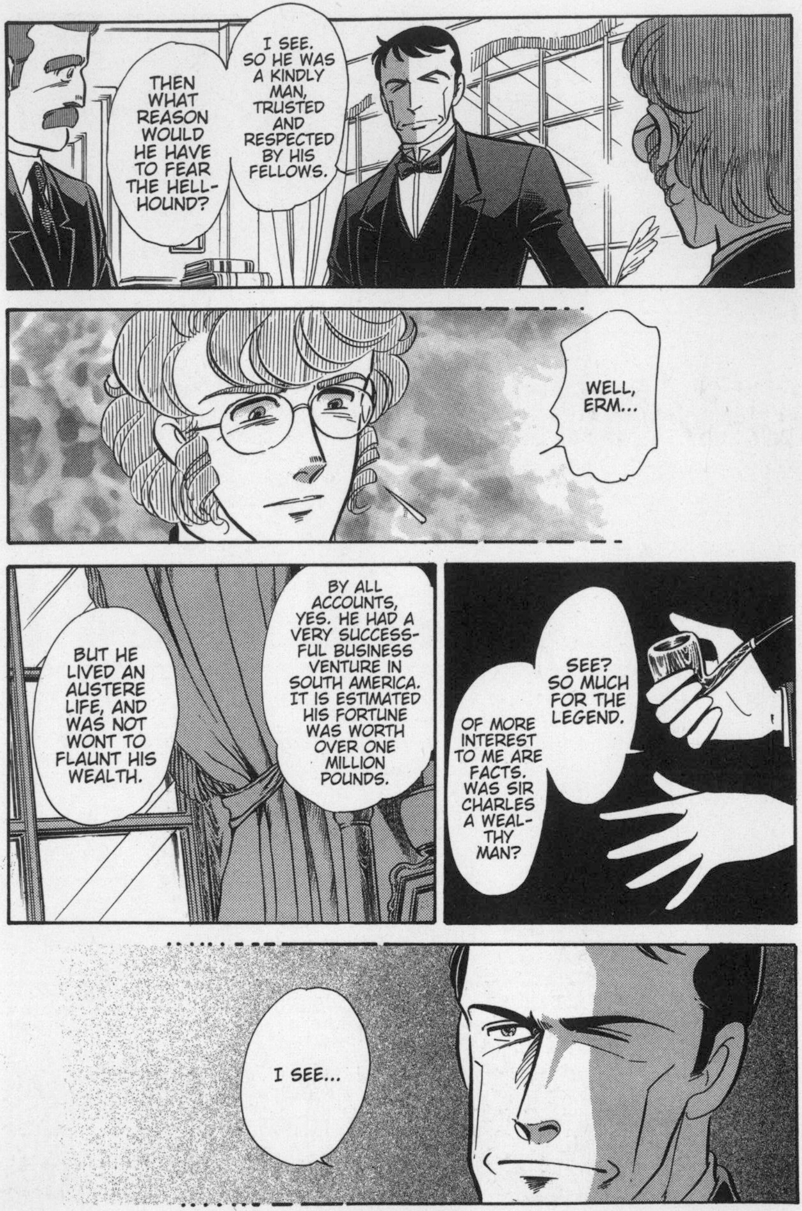
I SEE. SO HE WAS A KINDLY MAN, TRUSTED AND RESPECTED BY HIS FELLOWS.
THEN WHAT REASON WOULD HE HAVE TO FEAR THE HELL-HOUND?
WELL, ERM...
SEE? SO MUCH FOR THE LEGEND.
OF MORE INTEREST TO ME ARE FACTS. WAS SIR CHARLES A WEAL-THY MAN?
BY ALL ACCOUNTS, YES. HE HAD A VERY SUCCESS-FUL BUSINESS VENTURE IN SOUTH AMERICA. IT IS ESTIMATED HIS FORTUNE WAS WORTH OVER ONE MILLION POUNDS.
BUT HE LIVED AN AUSTERE LIFE, AND WAS NOT WONT TO FLAUNT HIS WEALTH.
I SEE...

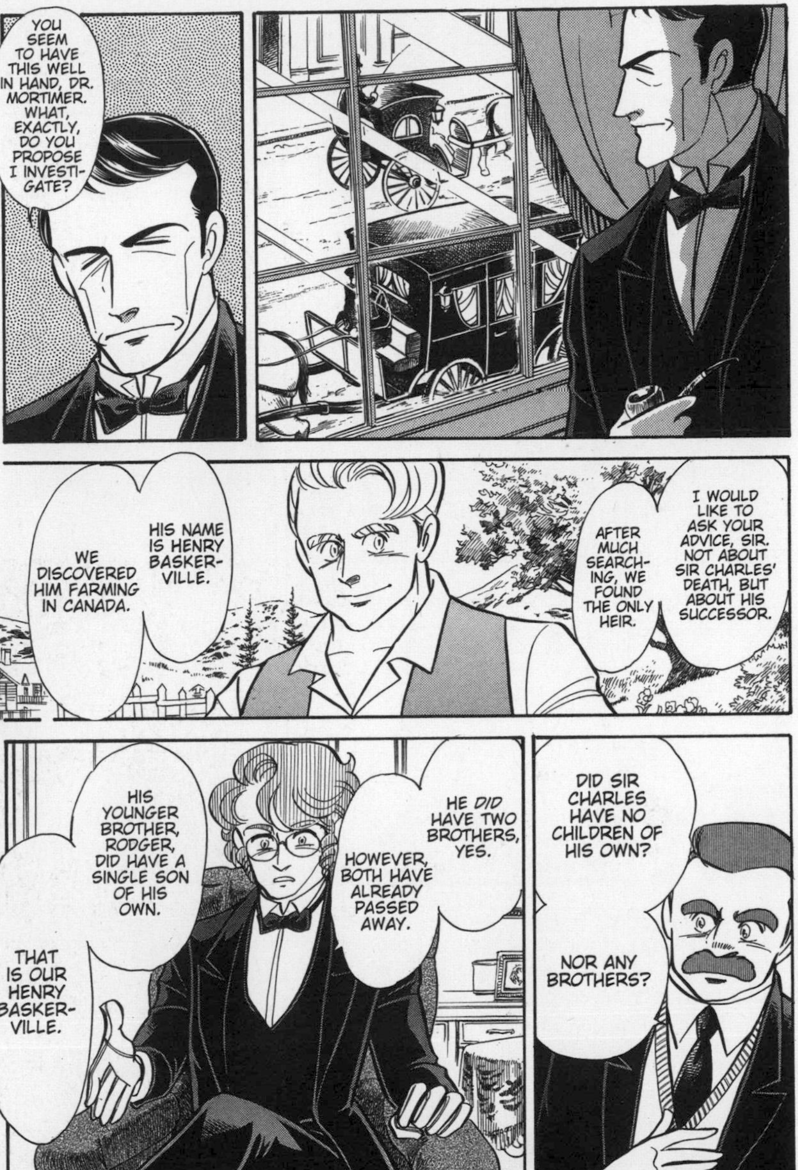
YOU SEEM TO HAVE THIS WELL IN HAND, DR. MORTIMER. WHAT, EXACTLY, DO YOU PROPOSE I INVESTIGATE?
I WOULD LIKE TO ASK YOUR ADVICE, SIR. NOT ABOUT SIR CHARLES' DEATH, BUT ABOUT HIS SUCCESSOR.
AFTER MUCH SEARCHING, WE FOUND THE ONLY HEIR.
HIS NAME IS HENRY BASKERVILLE.
WE DISCOVERED HIM FARMING IN CANADA.
DID SIR CHARLES HAVE NO CHILDREN OF HIS OWN?
NOR ANY BROTHERS?
HE *DID* HAVE TWO BROTHERS, YES.
HOWEVER, BOTH HAVE ALREADY PASSED AWAY.
HIS YOUNGER BROTHER, RODGER, DID HAVE A SINGLE SON OF HIS OWN.
THAT IS OUR HENRY BASKERVILLE.

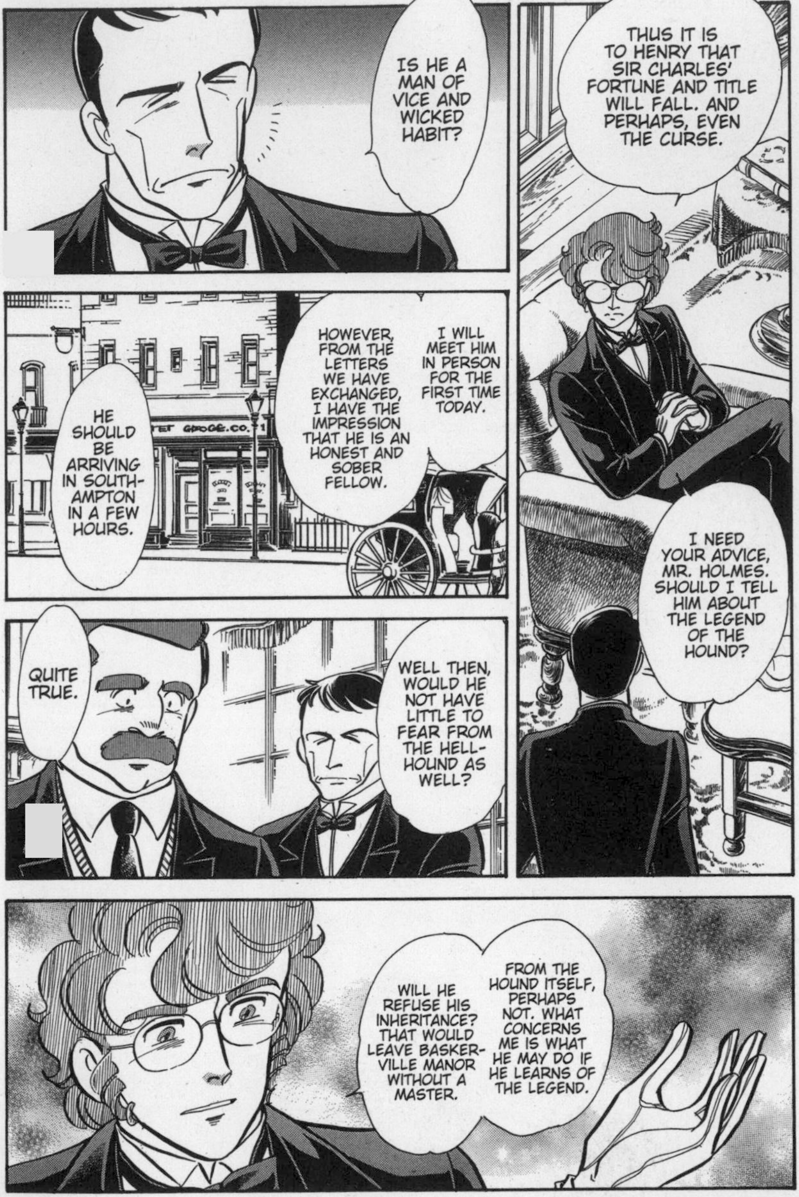
THUS IT IS TO HENRY THAT SIR CHARLES' FORTUNE AND TITLE WILL FALL. AND PERHAPS, EVEN THE CURSE.
I NEED YOUR ADVICE, MR. HOLMES. SHOULD I TELL HIM ABOUT THE LEGEND OF THE HOUND?
IS HE A MAN OF VICE AND WICKED HABIT?
I WILL MEET HIM IN PERSON FOR THE FIRST TIME TODAY.
HOWEVER, FROM THE LETTERS WE HAVE EXCHANGED, I HAVE THE IMPRESSION THAT HE IS AN HONEST AND SOBER FELLOW.
HE SHOULD BE ARRIVING IN SOUTH-AMPTON IN A FEW HOURS.
WELL THEN, WOULD HE NOT HAVE LITTLE TO FEAR FROM THE HELL-HOUND AS WELL?
QUITE TRUE.
FROM THE HOUND ITSELF, PERHAPS NOT. WHAT CONCERNS ME IS WHAT HE MAY DO IF HE LEARNS OF THE LEGEND.
WILL HE REFUSE HIS INHERITANCE? THAT WOULD LEAVE BASKER-VILLE MANOR WITHOUT A MASTER.

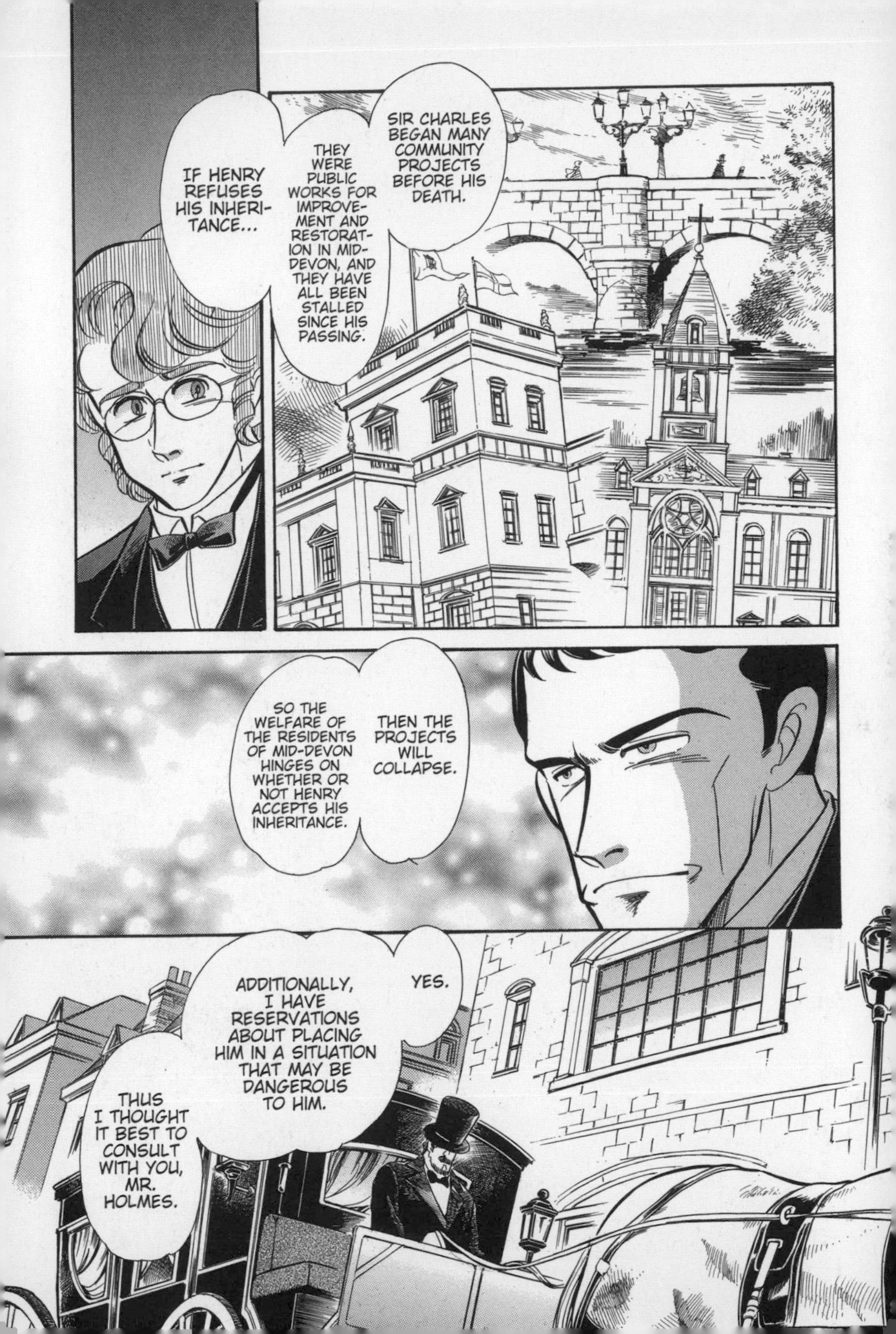

SIR CHARLES BEGAN MANY COMMUNITY PROJECTS BEFORE HIS DEATH.
THEY WERE PUBLIC WORKS FOR IMPROVEMENT AND RESTORATION IN MID-DEVON, AND THEY HAVE ALL BEEN STALLED SINCE HIS PASSING.
IF HENRY REFUSES HIS INHERITANCE...
THEN THE PROJECTS WILL COLLAPSE.
SO THE WELFARE OF THE RESIDENTS OF MID-DEVON HINGES ON WHETHER OR NOT HENRY ACCEPTS HIS INHERITANCE.
YES.
ADDITIONALLY, I HAVE RESERVATIONS ABOUT PLACING HIM IN A SITUATION THAT MAY BE DANGEROUS TO HIM.
THUS I THOUGHT IT BEST TO CONSULT WITH YOU, MR. HOLMES.

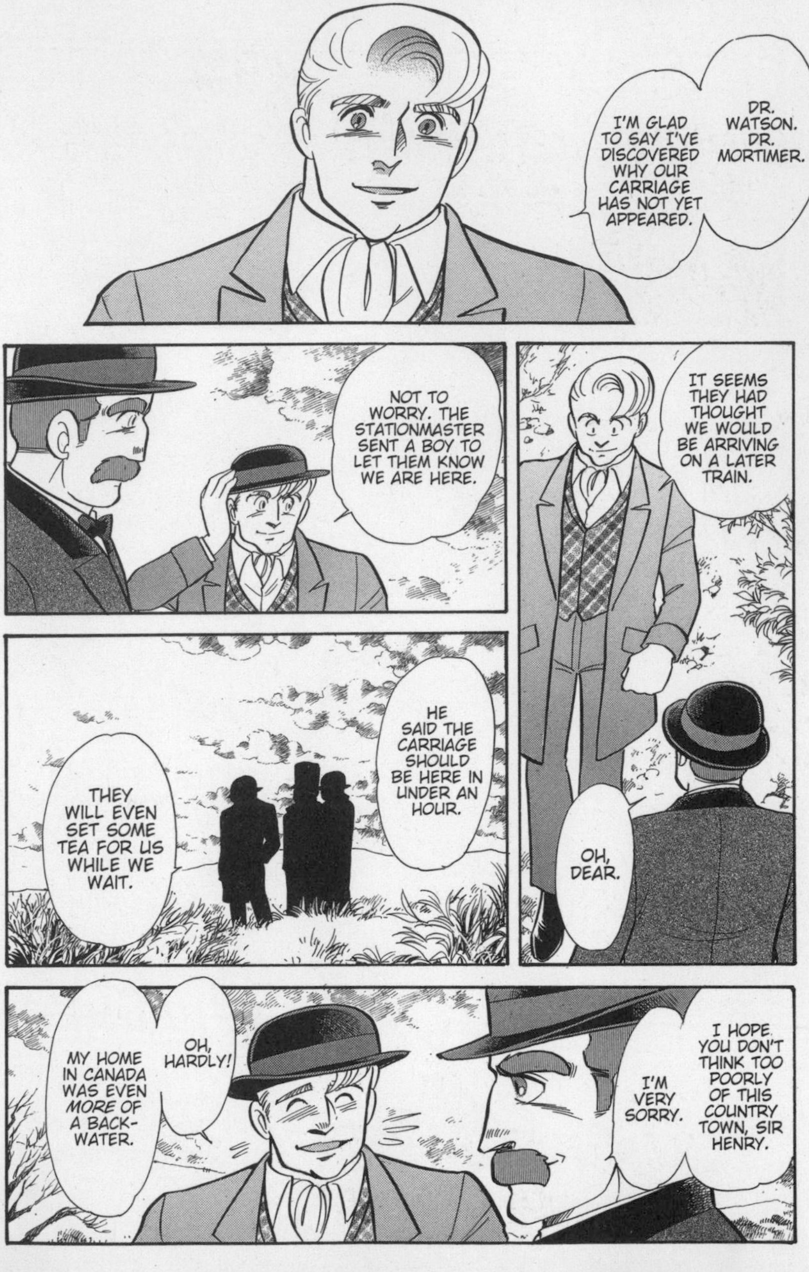
DR. WATSON. DR. MORTIMER.
I'M GLAD TO SAY I'VE DISCOVERED WHY OUR CARRIAGE HAS NOT YET APPEARED.
IT SEEMS THEY HAD THOUGHT WE WOULD BE ARRIVING ON A LATER TRAIN.
OH, DEAR.
NOT TO WORRY. THE STATIONMASTER SENT A BOY TO LET THEM KNOW WE ARE HERE.
HE SAID THE CARRIAGE SHOULD BE HERE IN UNDER AN HOUR.
THEY WILL EVEN SET SOME TEA FOR US WHILE WE WAIT.
I HOPE YOU DON'T THINK TOO POORLY OF THIS COUNTRY TOWN, SIR HENRY.
I'M VERY SORRY.
OH, HARDLY!
MY HOME IN CANADA WAS EVEN *MORE OF A* BACK-WATER.

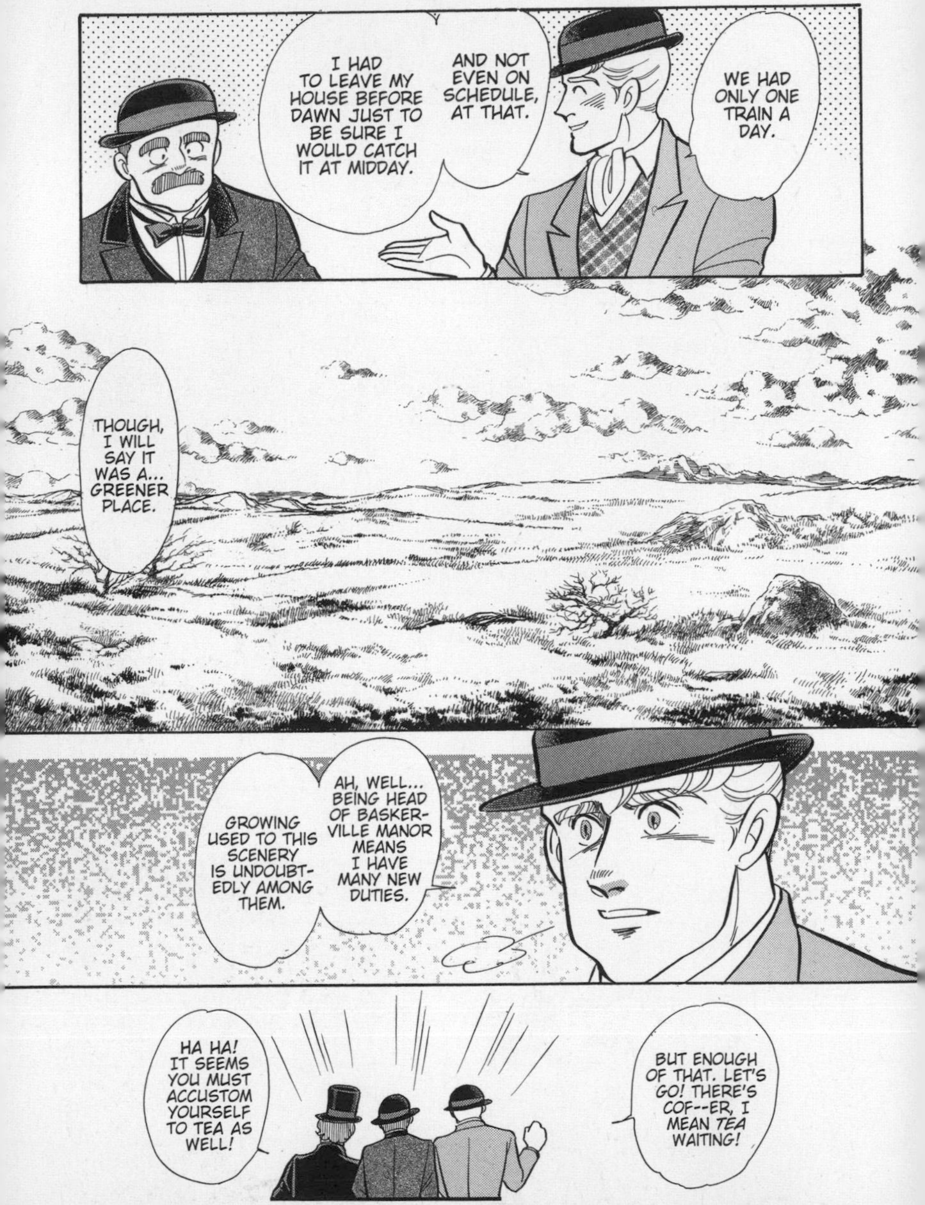
WE HAD ONLY ONE TRAIN A DAY.
AND NOT EVEN ON SCHEDULE, AT THAT.
I HAD TO LEAVE MY HOUSE BEFORE DAWN JUST TO BE SURE I WOULD CATCH IT AT MIDDAY.
THOUGH, I WILL SAY IT WAS A... GREENER PLACE.
AH, WELL... BEING HEAD OF BASKERVILLE MANOR MEANS I HAVE MANY NEW DUTIES.
GROWING USED TO THIS SCENERY IS UNDOUBTEDLY AMONG THEM.
BUT ENOUGH OF THAT. LET'S GO! THERE'S COF--ER, I MEAN *TEA* WAITING!
HA HA! IT SEEMS YOU MUST ACCUSTOM YOURSELF TO TEA AS WELL!

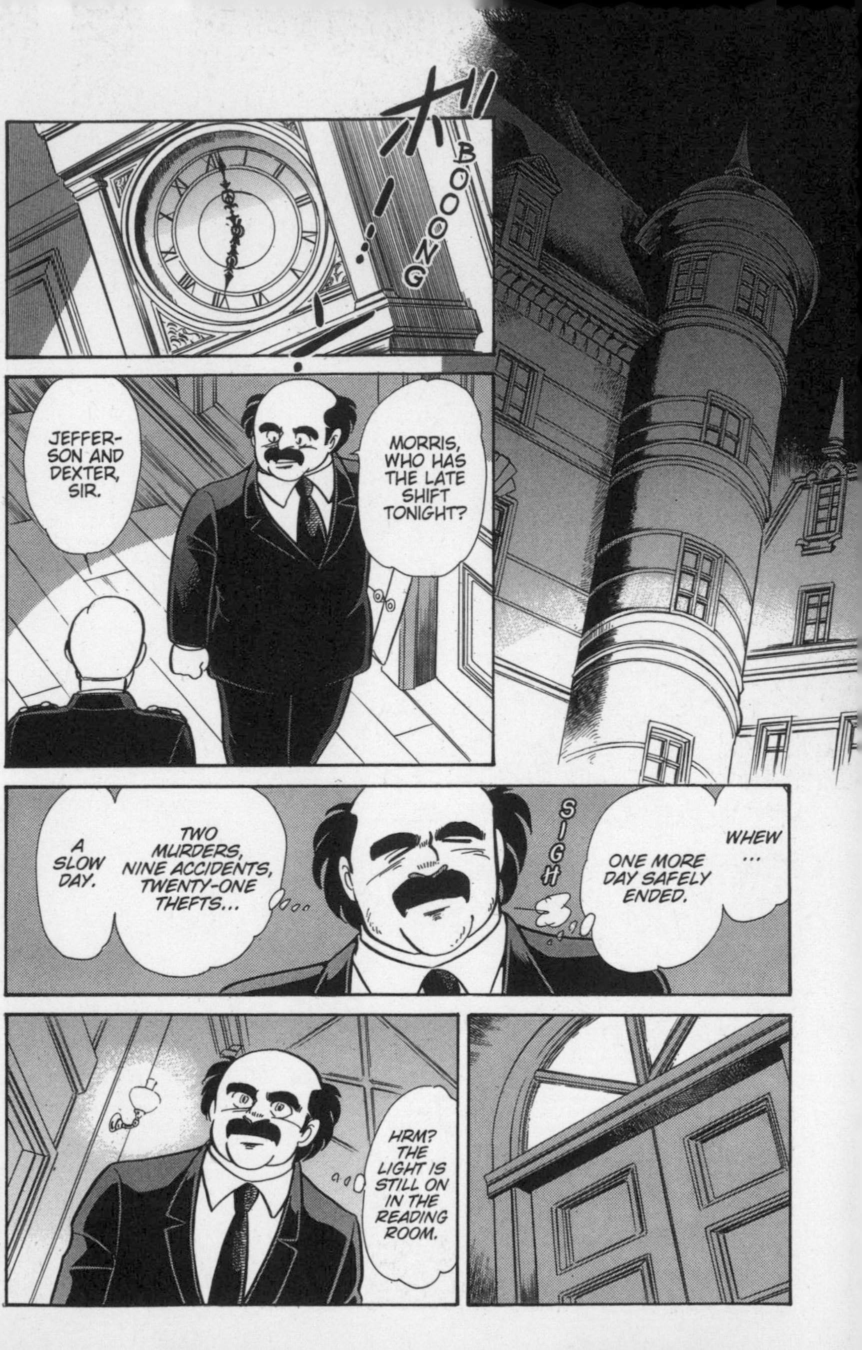
BOOOONG
MORRIS, WHO HAS THE LATE SHIFT TONIGHT?
JEFFER-SON AND DEXTER, SIR.
WHEW ...
ONE MORE DAY SAFELY ENDED.
SIGH
TWO MURDERS, NINE ACCIDENTS, TWENTY-ONE THEFTS...
A SLOW DAY.
HRM? THE LIGHT IS STILL ON IN THE READING ROOM.

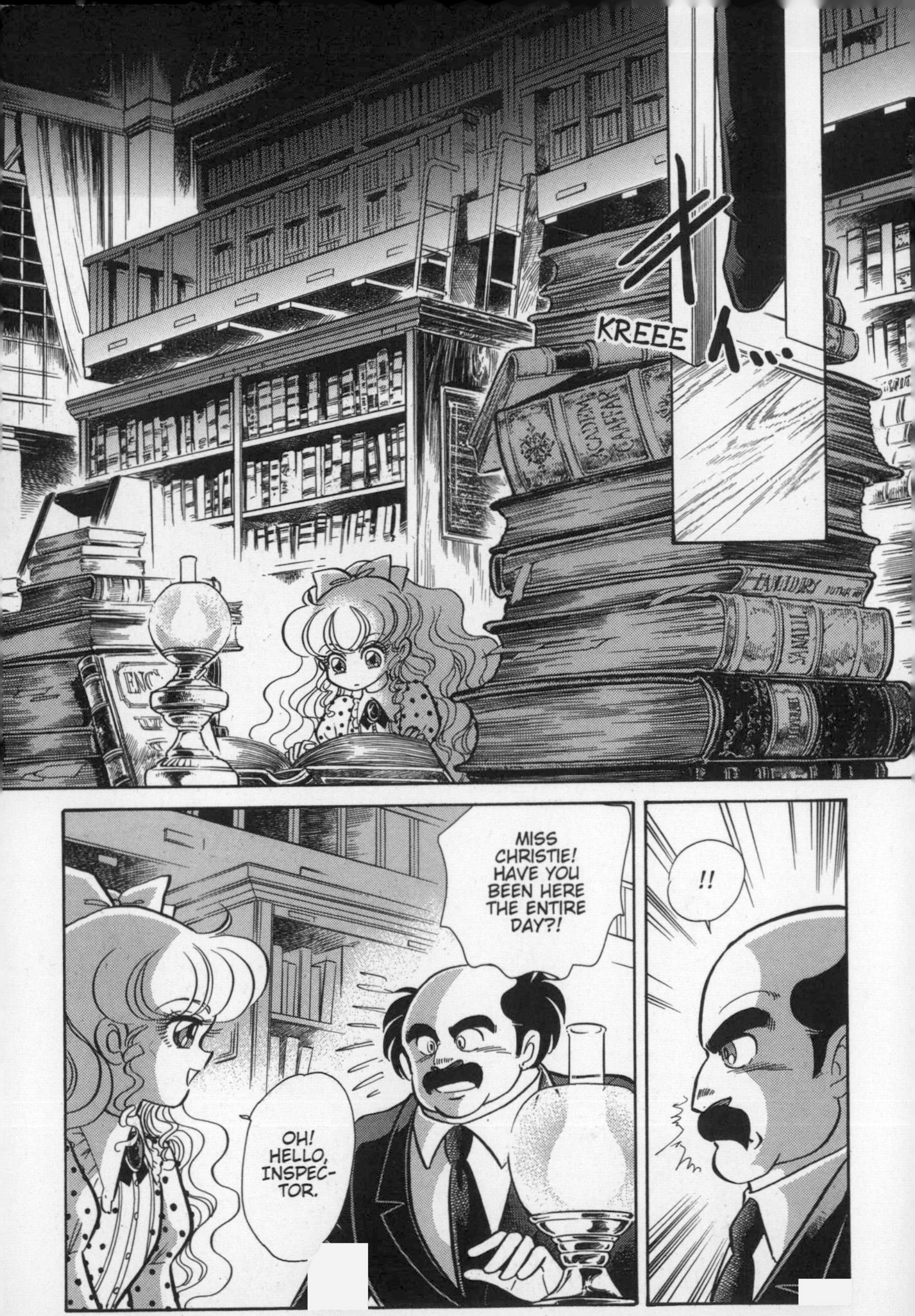
KREEE
!!
MISS CHRISTIE! HAVE YOU BEEN HERE THE ENTIRE DAY?!
OH! HELLO, INSPECTOR.

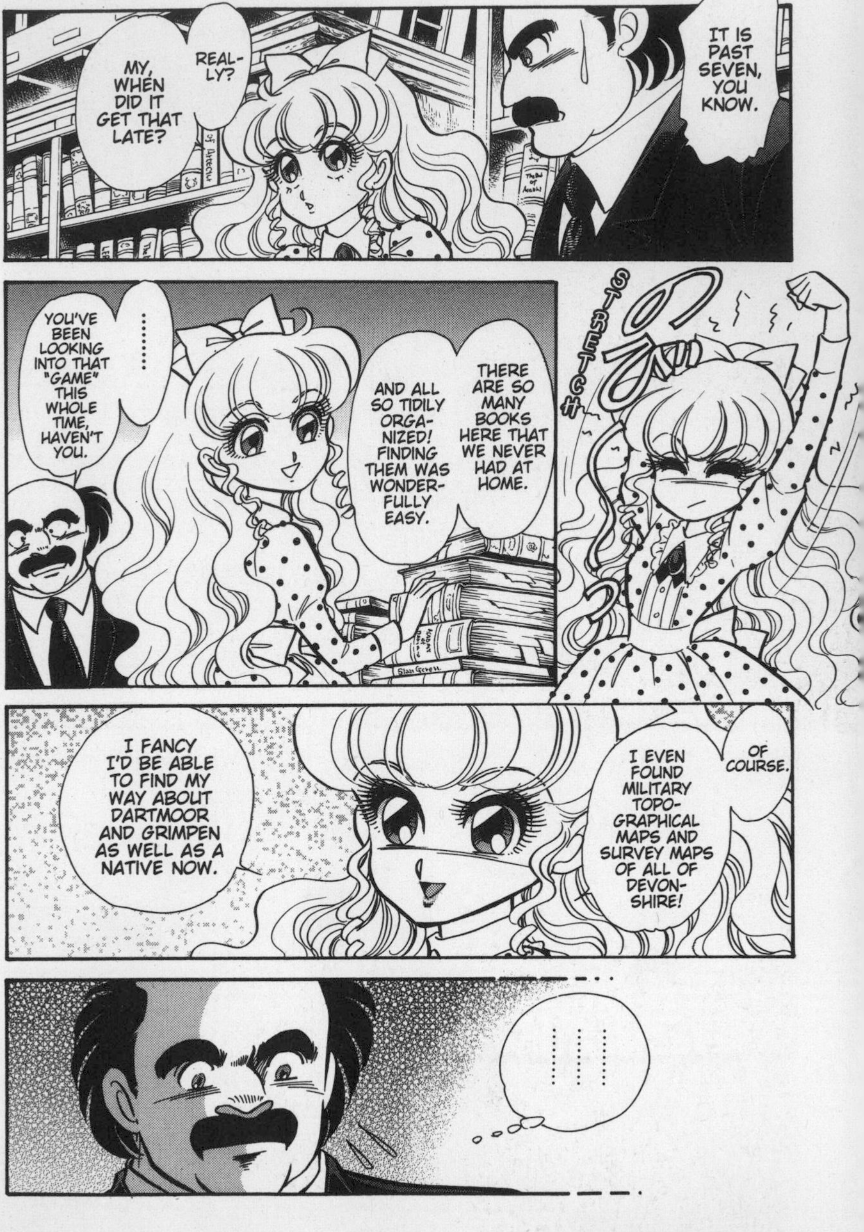
IT IS PAST SEVEN, YOU KNOW.
REAL-LY?
MY, WHEN DID IT GET THAT LATE?
STRETCH
THERE ARE SO MANY BOOKS HERE THAT WE NEVER HAD AT HOME.
AND ALL SO TIDILY ORGA-NIZED! FINDING THEM WAS WONDER-FULLY EASY.
......
YOU'VE BEEN LOOKING INTO THAT "GAME" THIS WHOLE TIME, HAVEN'T YOU.
OF COURSE.
I EVEN FOUND MILITARY TOPO-GRAPHICAL MAPS AND SURVEY MAPS OF ALL OF DEVON-SHIRE!
I FANCY I'D BE ABLE TO FIND MY WAY ABOUT DARTMOOR AND GRIMPEN AS WELL AS A NATIVE NOW.
......

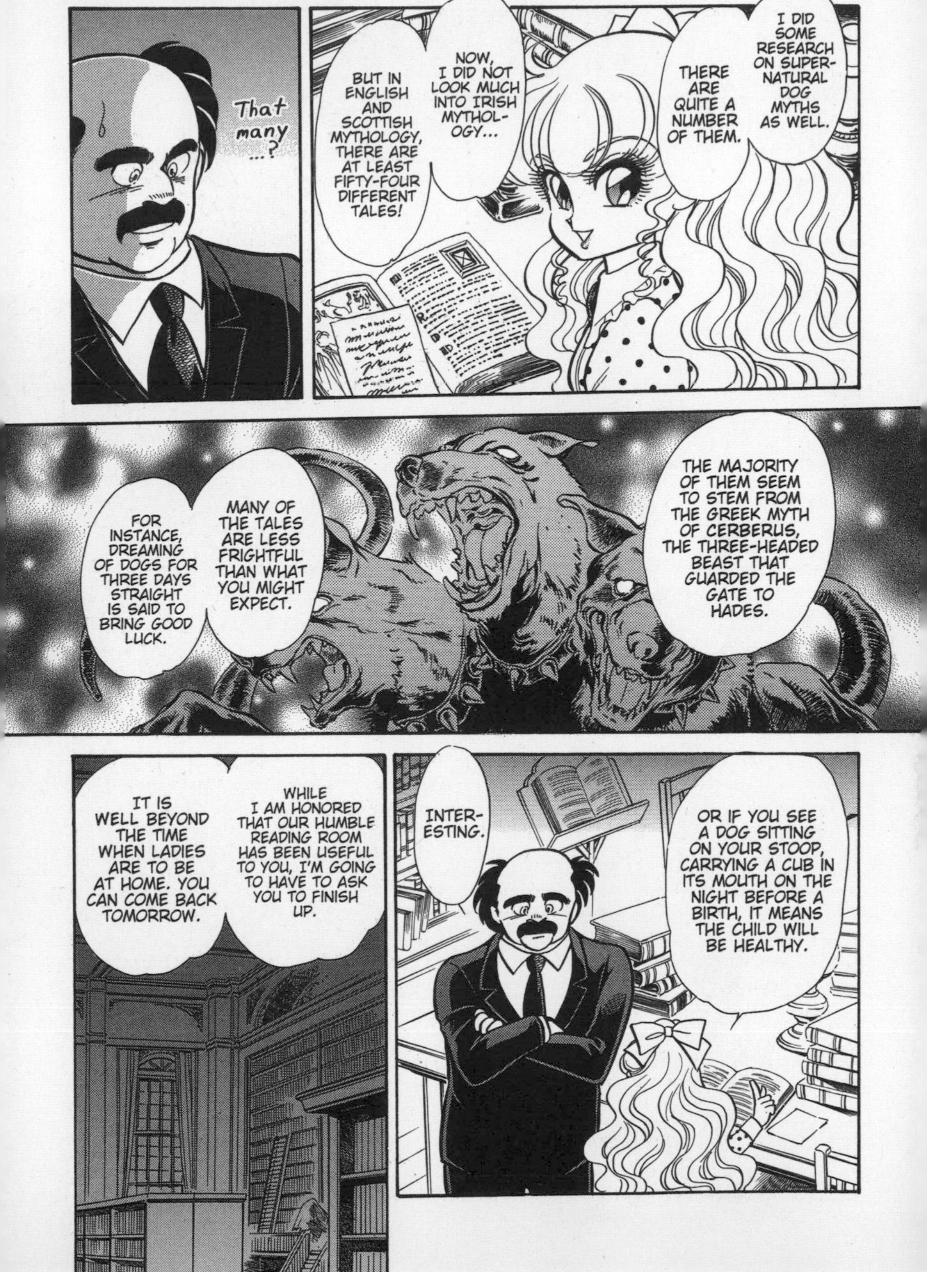
I DID SOME RESEARCH ON SUPER-NATURAL DOG MYTHS AS WELL.
THERE ARE QUITE A NUMBER OF THEM.
NOW, I DID NOT LOOK MUCH INTO IRISH MYTHOL-OGY...
BUT IN ENGLISH AND SCOTTISH MYTHOLOGY, THERE ARE AT LEAST FIFTY-FOUR DIFFERENT TALES!
That many ...?
THE MAJORITY OF THEM SEEM TO STEM FROM THE GREEK MYTH OF CERBERUS, THE THREE-HEADED BEAST THAT GUARDED THE GATE TO HADES.
MANY OF THE TALES ARE LESS FRIGHTFUL THAN WHAT YOU MIGHT EXPECT.
FOR INSTANCE, DREAMING OF DOGS FOR THREE DAYS STRAIGHT IS SAID TO BRING GOOD LUCK.
OR IF YOU SEE A DOG SITTING ON YOUR STOOP, CARRYING A CUB IN ITS MOUTH ON THE NIGHT BEFORE A BIRTH, IT MEANS THE CHILD WILL BE HEALTHY.
INTER-ESTING.
WHILE I AM HONORED THAT OUR HUMBLE READING ROOM HAS BEEN USEFUL TO YOU, I'M GOING TO HAVE TO ASK YOU TO FINISH UP.
IT IS WELL BEYOND THE TIME WHEN LADIES ARE TO BE AT HOME. YOU CAN COME BACK TOMORROW.

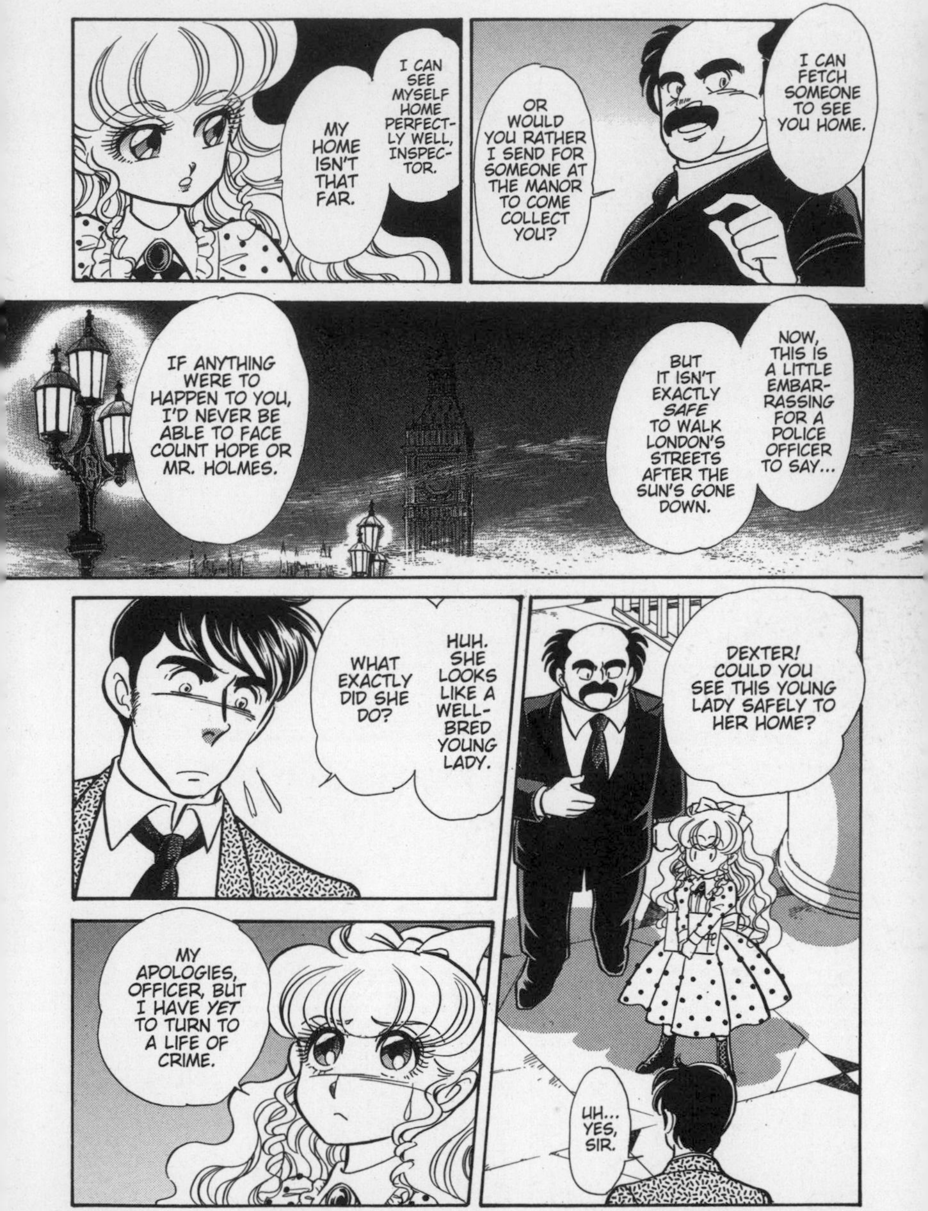
I CAN FETCH SOMEONE TO SEE YOU HOME.
OR WOULD YOU RATHER I SEND FOR SOMEONE AT THE MANOR TO COME COLLECT YOU?
I CAN SEE MYSELF HOME PERFECTLY WELL, INSPECTOR.
MY HOME ISN'T THAT FAR.
NOW, THIS IS A LITTLE EMBARRASSING FOR A POLICE OFFICER TO SAY...
BUT IT ISN'T EXACTLY *SAFE* TO WALK LONDON'S STREETS AFTER THE SUN'S GONE DOWN.
IF ANYTHING WERE TO HAPPEN TO YOU, I'D NEVER BE ABLE TO FACE COUNT HOPE OR MR. HOLMES.
DEXTER! COULD YOU SEE THIS YOUNG LADY SAFELY TO HER HOME?
UH... YES, SIR.
HUH. SHE LOOKS LIKE A WELL-BRED YOUNG LADY.
WHAT EXACTLY DID SHE DO?
MY APOLOGIES, OFFICER, BUT I HAVE *YET* TO TURN TO A LIFE OF CRIME.

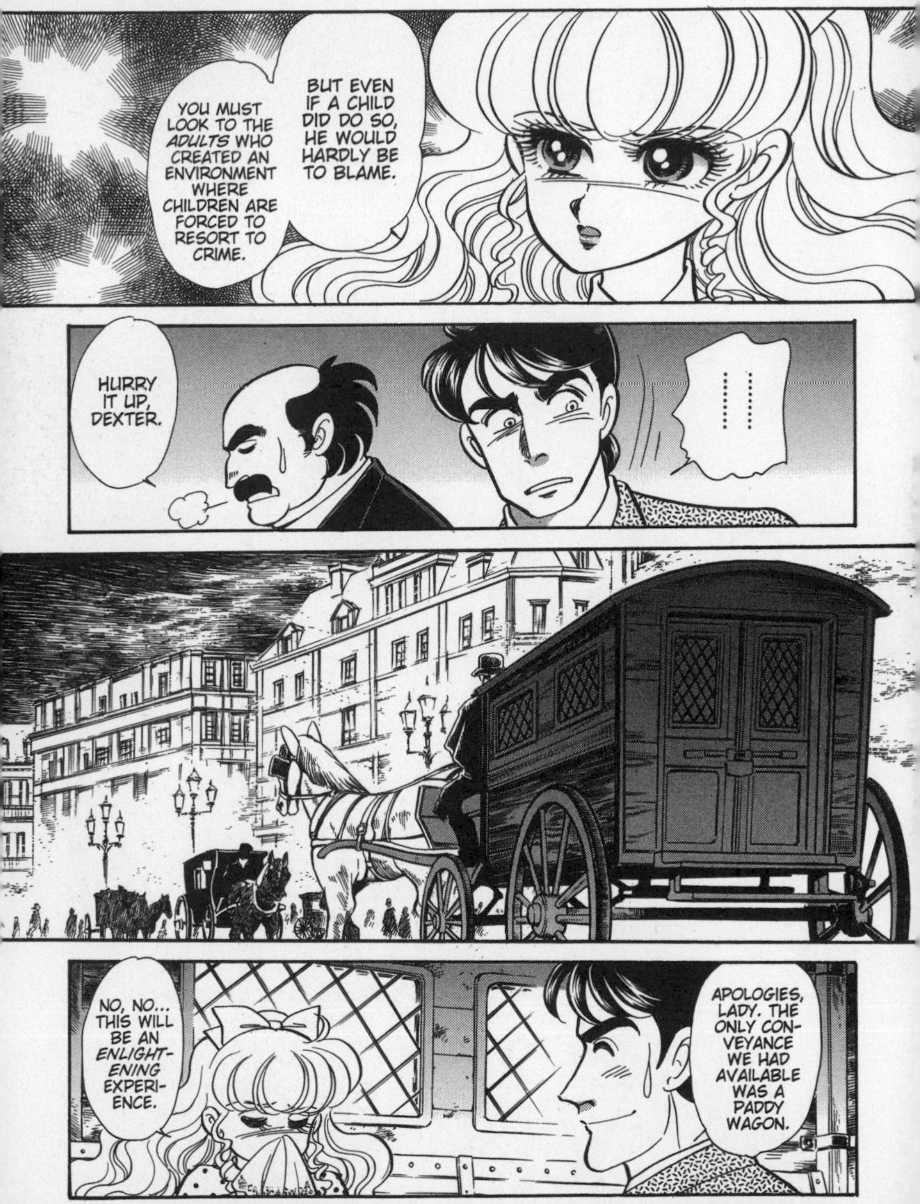
BUT EVEN IF A CHILD DID DO SO, HE WOULD HARDLY BE TO BLAME.
YOU MUST LOOK TO THE *ADULTS* WHO CREATED AN ENVIRONMENT WHERE CHILDREN ARE FORCED TO RESORT TO CRIME.
......
HURRY IT UP, DEXTER.
APOLOGIES, LADY. THE ONLY CONVEYANCE WE HAD AVAILABLE WAS A PADDY WAGON.
NO, NO... THIS WILL BE AN *ENLIGHTENING* EXPERIENCE.

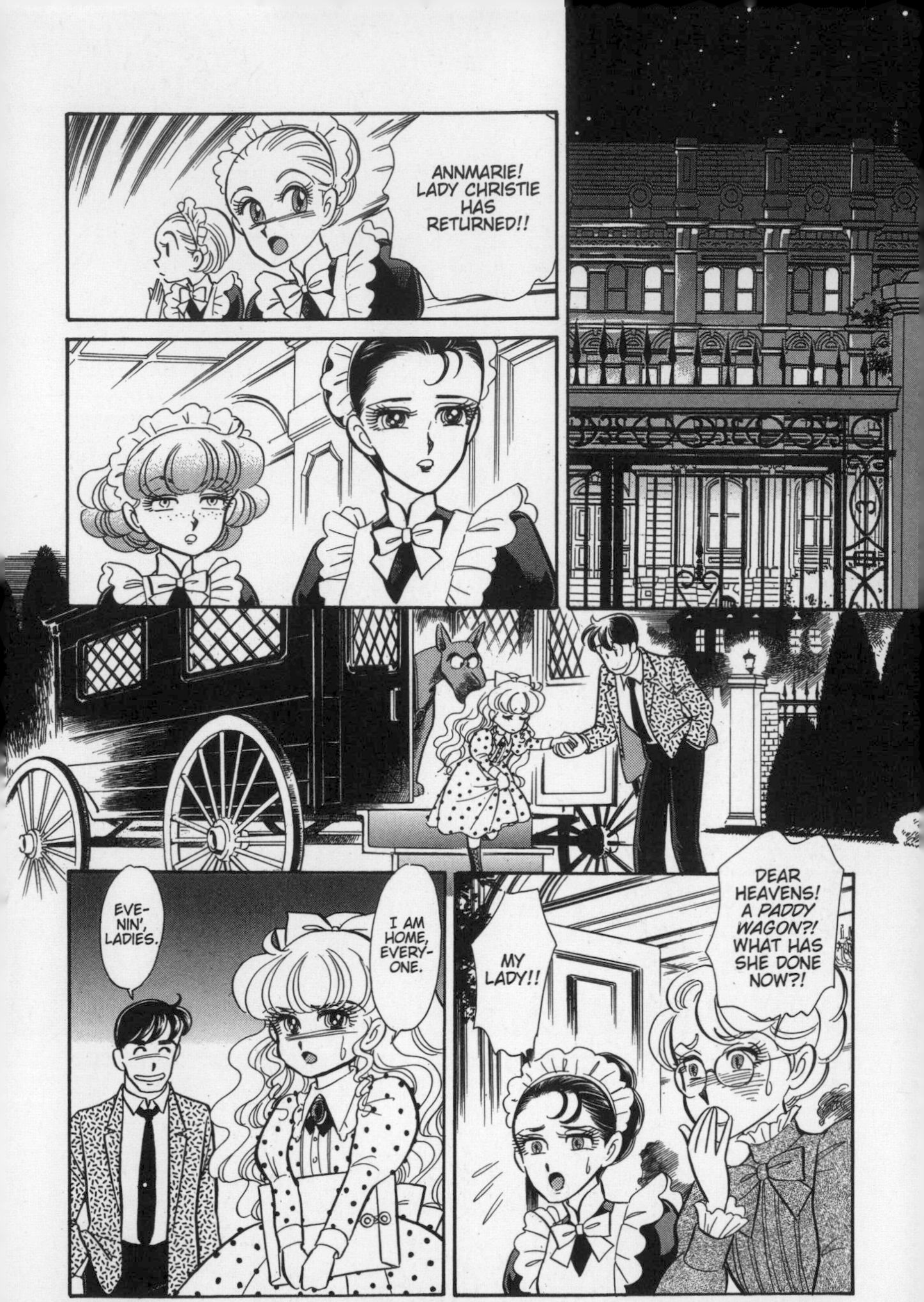
ANNMARIE! LADY CHRISTIE HAS RETURNED!!
DEAR HEAVENS! A *PADDY WAGON*?! WHAT HAS SHE DONE NOW?!
MY LADY!!
I AM HOME, EVERY-ONE.
EVE-NIN', LADIES.

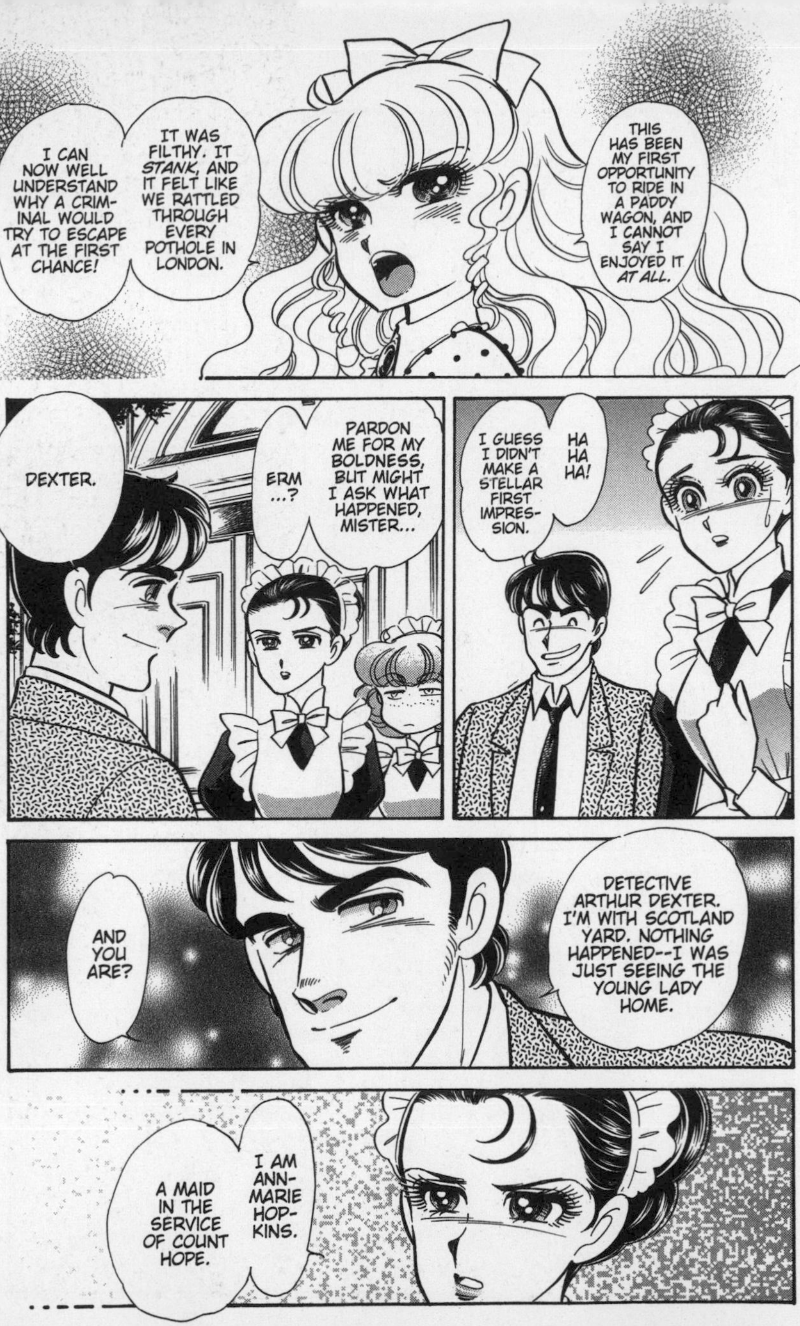
THIS HAS BEEN MY FIRST OPPORTUNITY TO RIDE IN A PADDY WAGON, AND I CANNOT SAY I ENJOYED IT *AT ALL.*
IT WAS FILTHY. IT *STANK,* AND IT FELT LIKE WE RATTLED THROUGH EVERY POTHOLE IN LONDON.
I CAN NOW WELL UNDERSTAND WHY A CRIMINAL WOULD TRY TO ESCAPE AT THE FIRST CHANCE!
HA HA HA!
I GUESS I DIDN'T MAKE A STELLAR FIRST IMPRESSION.
PARDON ME FOR MY BOLDNESS, BUT MIGHT I ASK WHAT HAPPENED, MISTER...
ERM ...?
DEXTER.
DETECTIVE ARTHUR DEXTER. I'M WITH SCOTLAND YARD. NOTHING HAPPENED--I WAS JUST SEEING THE YOUNG LADY HOME.
AND YOU ARE?
I AM ANN-MARIE HOP-KINS.
A MAID IN THE SERVICE OF COUNT HOPE.

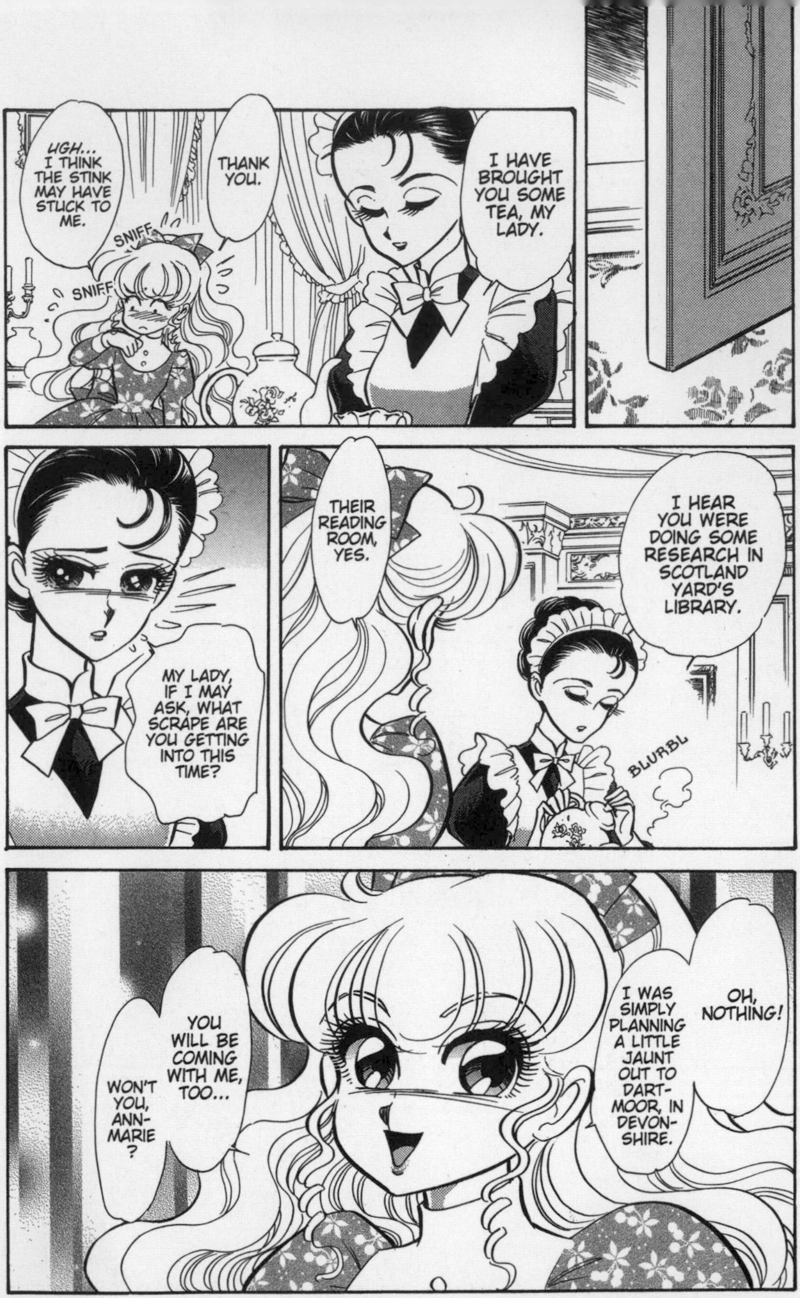
I HAVE BROUGHT YOU SOME TEA, MY LADY.
THANK YOU.
UGH... I THINK THE STINK MAY HAVE STUCK TO ME.
SNIFF
SNIFF
I HEAR YOU WERE DOING SOME RESEARCH IN SCOTLAND YARD'S LIBRARY.
THEIR READING ROOM, YES.
BLURBL
MY LADY, IF I MAY ASK, WHAT SCRAPE ARE YOU GETTING INTO THIS TIME?
OH, NOTHING!
I WAS SIMPLY PLANNING A LITTLE JAUNT OUT TO DART-MOOR, IN DEVON-SHIRE.
YOU WILL BE COMING WITH ME, TOO...
WON'T YOU, ANN-MARIE?

The Hound of the Baskervilles (4)

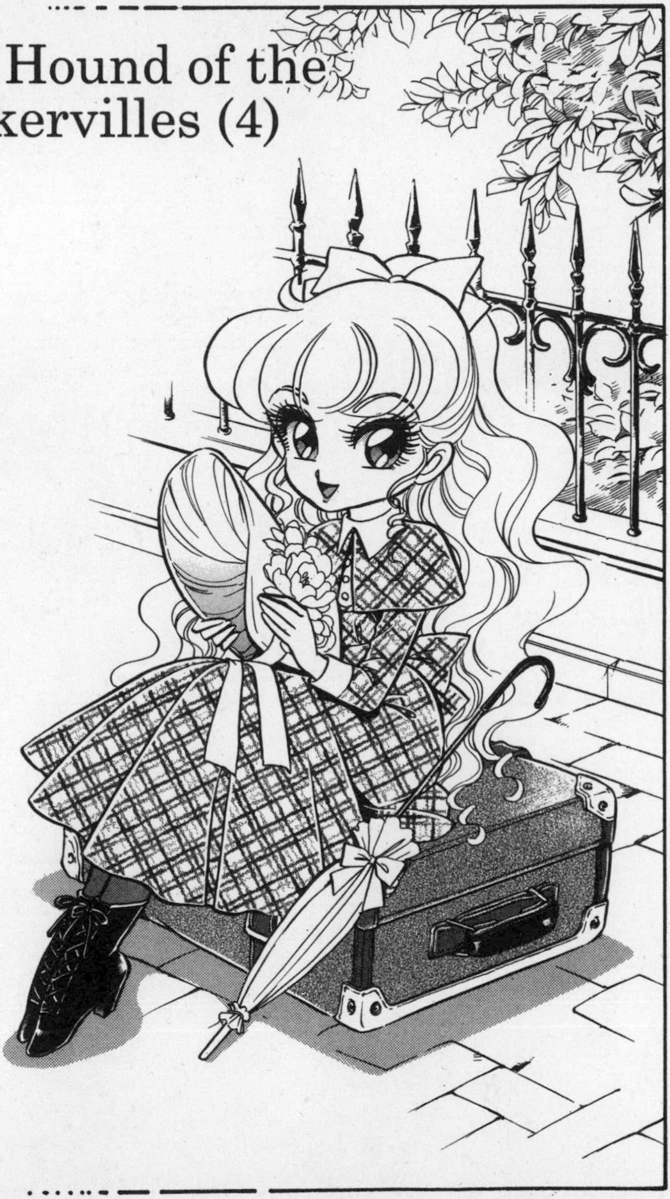

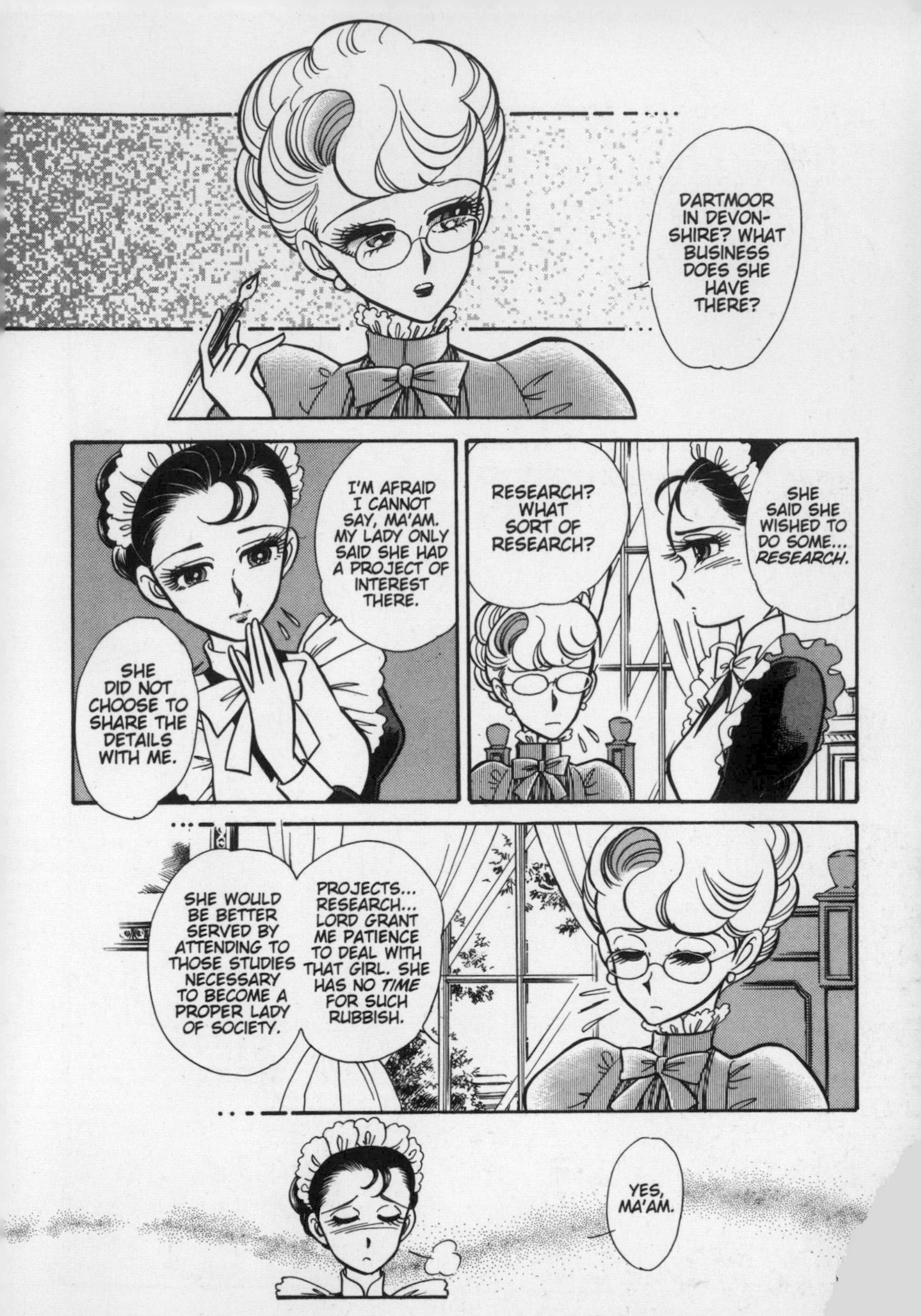
DARTMOOR IN DEVONSHIRE? WHAT BUSINESS DOES SHE HAVE THERE?
SHE SAID SHE WISHED TO DO SOME... *RESEARCH.*
RESEARCH? WHAT SORT OF RESEARCH?
I'M AFRAID I CANNOT SAY, MA'AM. MY LADY ONLY SAID SHE HAD A PROJECT OF INTEREST THERE.
SHE DID NOT CHOOSE TO SHARE THE DETAILS WITH ME.
PROJECTS... RESEARCH... LORD GRANT ME PATIENCE TO DEAL WITH THAT GIRL. SHE HAS NO *TIME* FOR SUCH RUBBISH.
SHE WOULD BE BETTER SERVED BY ATTENDING TO THOSE STUDIES NECESSARY TO BECOME A PROPER LADY OF SOCIETY.
YES, MA'AM.

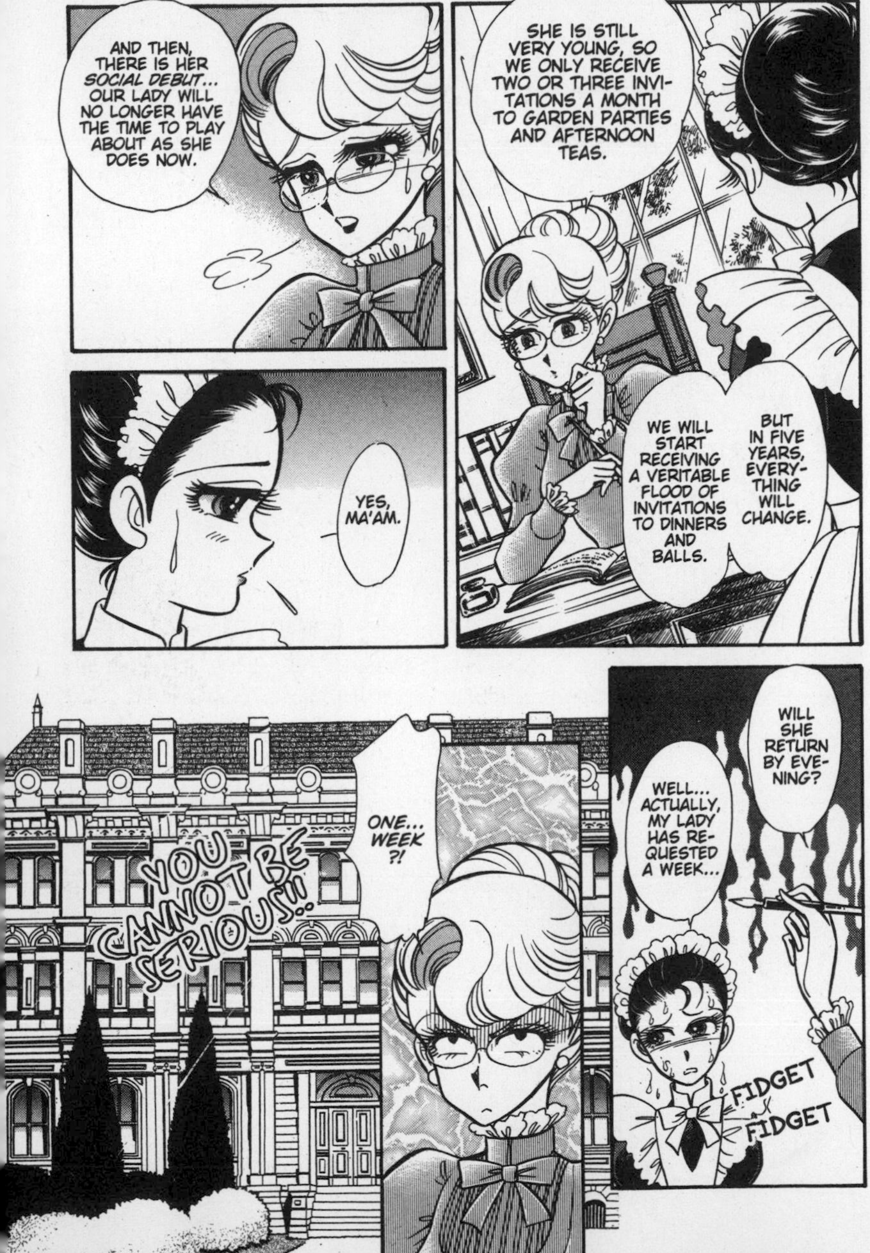
SHE IS STILL VERY YOUNG, SO WE ONLY RECEIVE TWO OR THREE INVITATIONS A MONTH TO GARDEN PARTIES AND AFTERNOON TEAS.
BUT IN FIVE YEARS, EVERYTHING WILL CHANGE.
WE WILL START RECEIVING A VERITABLE FLOOD OF INVITATIONS TO DINNERS AND BALLS.
AND THEN, THERE IS HER *SOCIAL DEBUT*... OUR LADY WILL NO LONGER HAVE THE TIME TO PLAY ABOUT AS SHE DOES NOW.
YES, MA'AM.
WILL SHE RETURN BY EVENING?
WELL... ACTUALLY, MY LADY HAS REQUESTED A WEEK...
FIDGET FIDGET
ONE... WEEK?!
YOU CANNOT BE SERIOUS!!

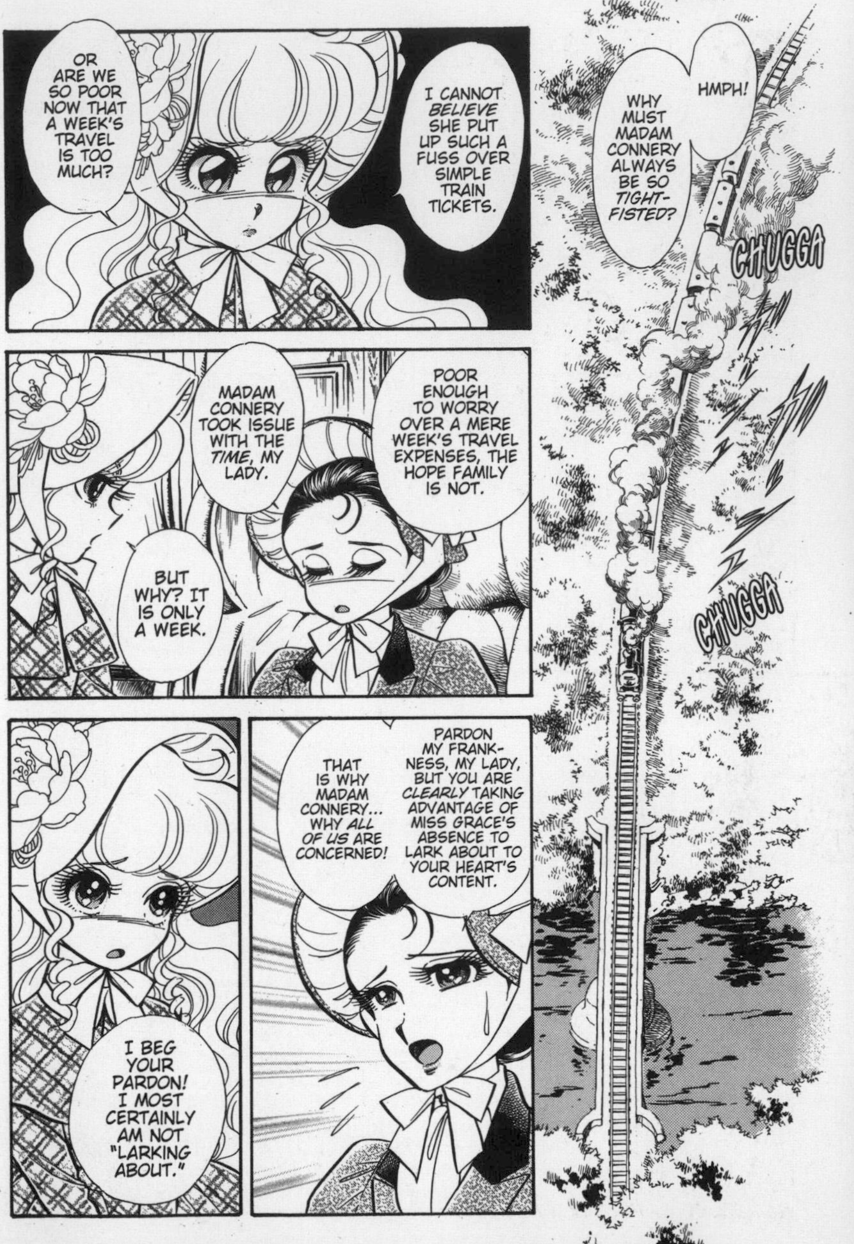
HMPH!
WHY MUST MADAM CONNERY ALWAYS BE SO *TIGHT-FISTED?*
CHUGGA
CHUGGA
I CANNOT *BELIEVE* SHE PUT UP SUCH A FUSS OVER SIMPLE TRAIN TICKETS.
OR ARE WE SO POOR NOW THAT A WEEK'S TRAVEL IS TOO MUCH?
POOR ENOUGH TO WORRY OVER A MERE WEEK'S TRAVEL EXPENSES, THE HOPE FAMILY IS NOT.
MADAM CONNERY TOOK ISSUE WITH THE *TIME*, MY LADY.
BUT WHY? IT IS ONLY A WEEK.
PARDON MY FRANK-NESS, MY LADY, BUT YOU ARE *CLEARLY* TAKING ADVANTAGE OF MISS GRACE'S ABSENCE TO LARK ABOUT TO YOUR HEART'S CONTENT.
THAT IS WHY MADAM CONNERY... WHY *ALL OF US* ARE CONCERNED!
I BEG YOUR PARDON! I MOST CERTAINLY AM NOT "LARKING ABOUT."

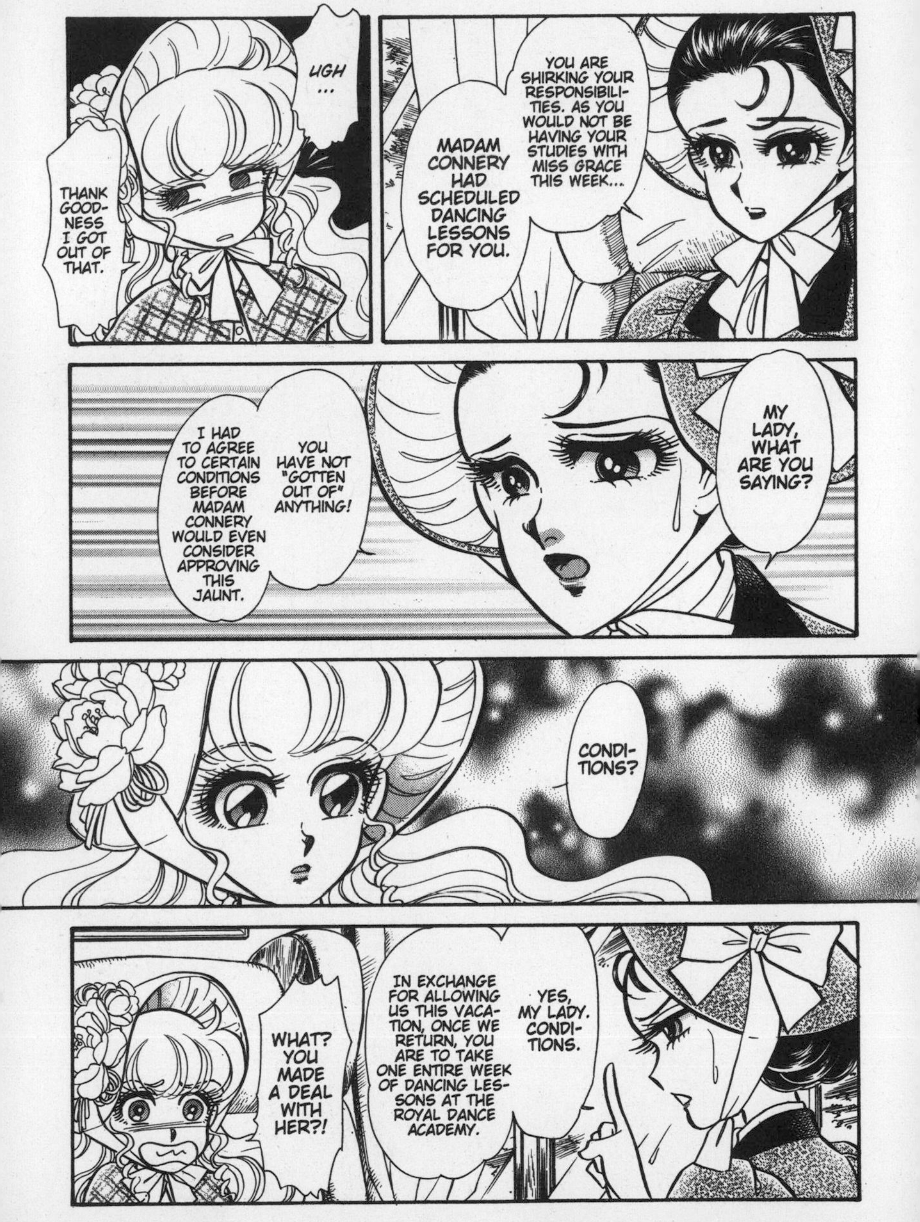
YOU ARE SHIRKING YOUR RESPONSIBILITIES. AS YOU WOULD NOT BE HAVING YOUR STUDIES WITH MISS GRACE THIS WEEK...
MADAM CONNERY HAD SCHEDULED DANCING LESSONS FOR YOU.
UGH ...
THANK GOODNESS I GOT OUT OF THAT.
MY LADY, WHAT ARE YOU SAYING?
YOU HAVE NOT "GOTTEN OUT OF" ANYTHING!
I HAD TO AGREE TO CERTAIN CONDITIONS BEFORE MADAM CONNERY WOULD EVEN CONSIDER APPROVING THIS JAUNT.
CONDITIONS?
YES, MY LADY. CONDITIONS.
IN EXCHANGE FOR ALLOWING US THIS VACATION, ONCE WE RETURN, YOU ARE TO TAKE ONE ENTIRE WEEK OF DANCING LESSONS AT THE ROYAL DANCE ACADEMY.
WHAT? YOU MADE A DEAL WITH HER?!

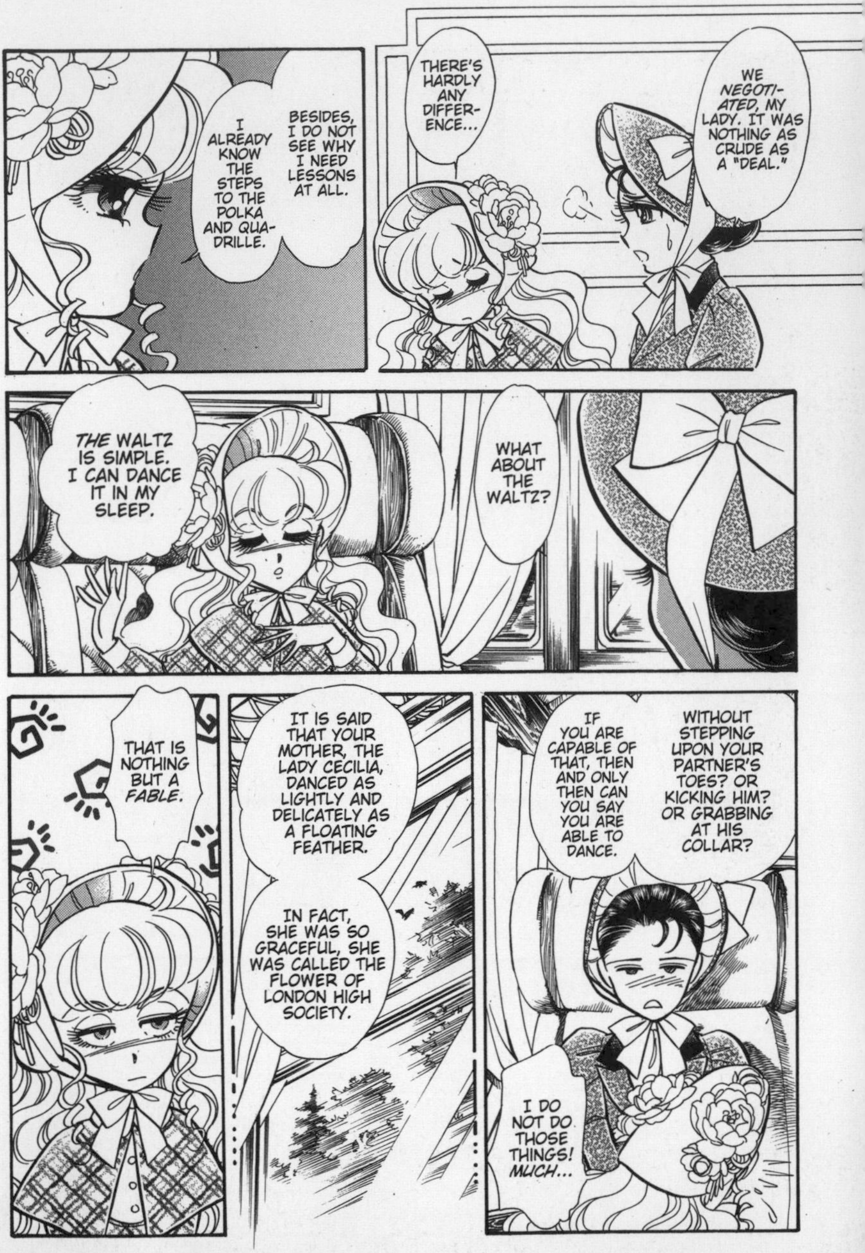
WE NEGOTIATED, MY LADY. IT WAS NOTHING AS CRUDE AS A "DEAL."
THERE'S HARDLY ANY DIFFERENCE...
BESIDES, I DO NOT SEE WHY I NEED LESSONS AT ALL.
I ALREADY KNOW THE STEPS TO THE POLKA AND QUADRILLE.
WHAT ABOUT THE WALTZ?
THE WALTZ IS SIMPLE. I CAN DANCE IT IN MY SLEEP.
WITHOUT STEPPING UPON YOUR PARTNER'S TOES? OR KICKING HIM? OR GRABBING AT HIS COLLAR?
IF YOU ARE CAPABLE OF THAT, THEN AND ONLY THEN CAN YOU SAY YOU ARE ABLE TO DANCE.
I DO NOT DO THOSE THINGS! MUCH...
IT IS SAID THAT YOUR MOTHER, THE LADY CECILIA, DANCED AS LIGHTLY AND DELICATELY AS A FLOATING FEATHER.
IN FACT, SHE WAS SO GRACEFUL, SHE WAS CALLED THE FLOWER OF LONDON HIGH SOCIETY.
THAT IS NOTHING BUT A FABLE.

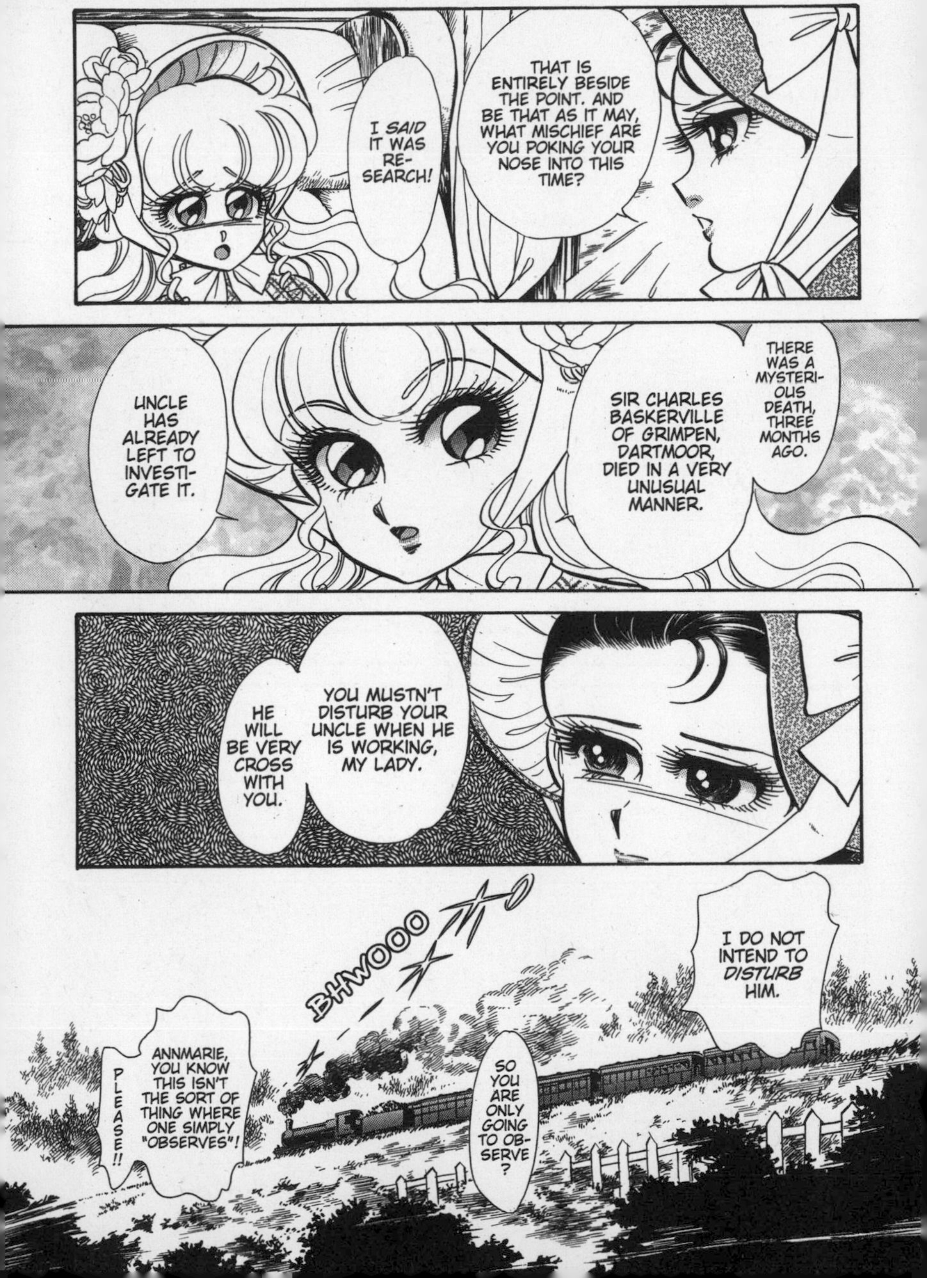
THAT IS ENTIRELY BESIDE THE POINT. AND BE THAT AS IT MAY, WHAT MISCHIEF ARE YOU POKING YOUR NOSE INTO THIS TIME?
I *SAID* IT WAS RE-SEARCH!
THERE WAS A MYSTERIOUS DEATH, THREE MONTHS AGO.
SIR CHARLES BASKERVILLE OF GRIMPEN, DARTMOOR, DIED IN A VERY UNUSUAL MANNER.
UNCLE HAS ALREADY LEFT TO INVESTI-GATE IT.
YOU MUSTN'T DISTURB YOUR UNCLE WHEN HE IS WORKING, MY LADY.
HE WILL BE VERY CROSS WITH YOU.
I DO NOT INTEND TO *DISTURB* HIM.
BHWOOO
SO YOU ARE ONLY GOING TO OB-SERVE?
ANNMARIE, YOU KNOW THIS ISN'T THE SORT OF THING WHERE ONE SIMPLY "OBSERVES"!
PLEASE!!

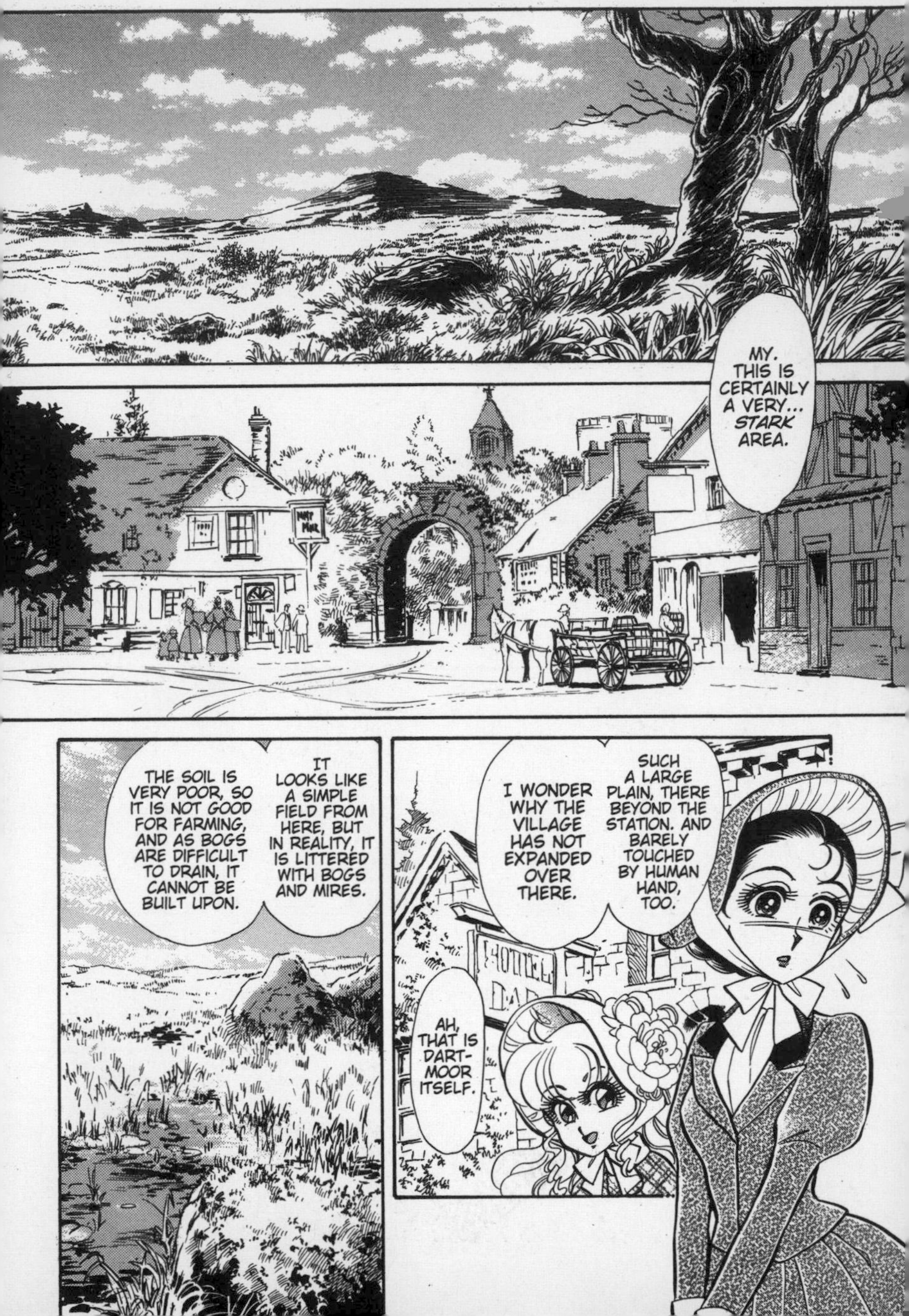
MY. THIS IS CERTAINLY A VERY... STARK AREA.
SUCH A LARGE PLAIN, THERE BEYOND THE STATION. AND BARELY TOUCHED BY HUMAN HAND, TOO.
I WONDER WHY THE VILLAGE HAS NOT EXPANDED OVER THERE.
AH, THAT IS DART-MOOR ITSELF.
IT LOOKS LIKE A SIMPLE FIELD FROM HERE, BUT IN REALITY, IT IS LITTERED WITH BOGS AND MIRES.
THE SOIL IS VERY POOR, SO IT IS NOT GOOD FOR FARMING, AND AS BOGS ARE DIFFICULT TO DRAIN, IT CANNOT BE BUILT UPON.

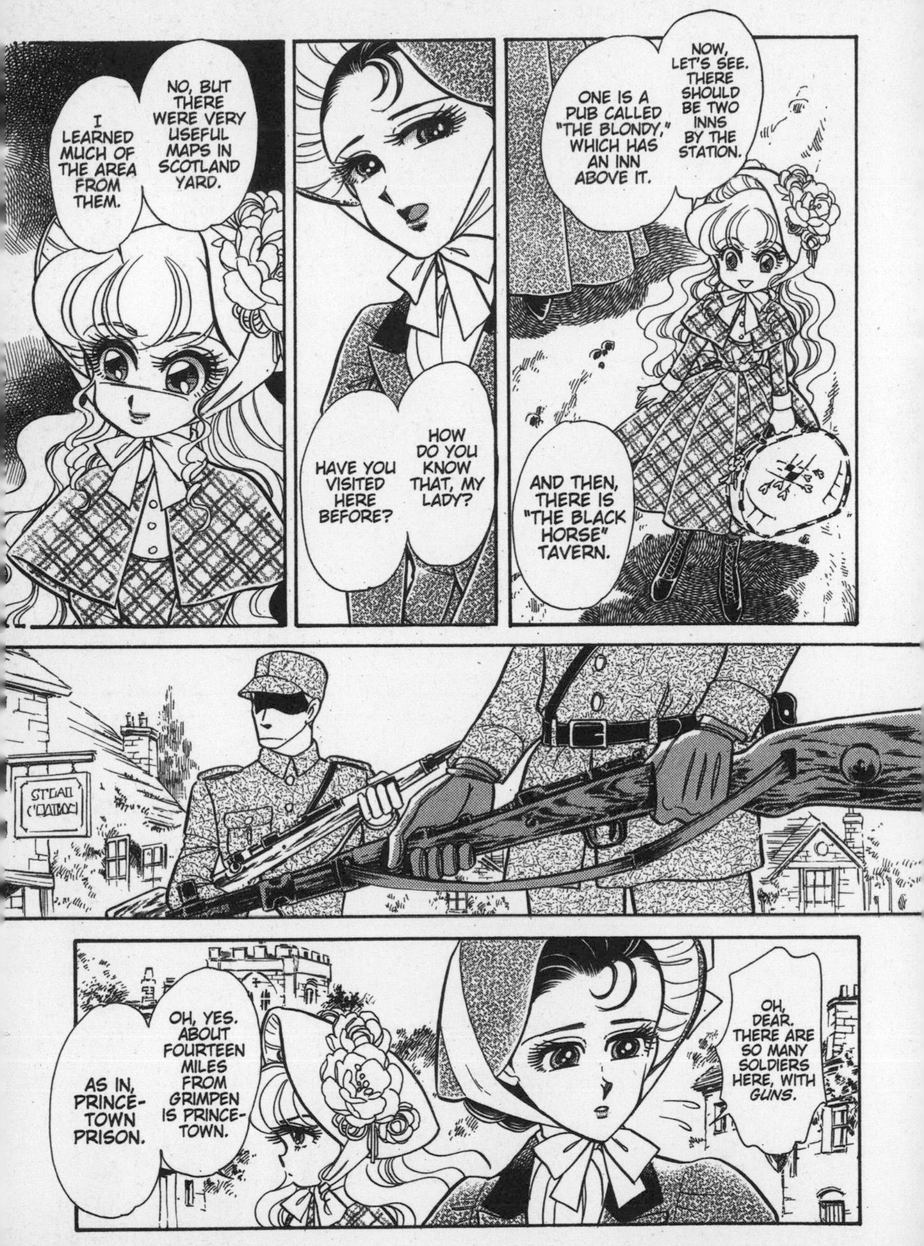
NOW, LET'S SEE. THERE SHOULD BE TWO INNS BY THE STATION.
ONE IS A PUB CALLED "THE BLONDY," WHICH HAS AN INN ABOVE IT.
AND THEN, THERE IS "THE BLACK HORSE" TAVERN.
HOW DO YOU KNOW THAT, MY LADY?
HAVE YOU VISITED HERE BEFORE?
NO, BUT THERE WERE VERY USEFUL MAPS IN SCOTLAND YARD.
I LEARNED MUCH OF THE AREA FROM THEM.
OH, DEAR. THERE ARE SO MANY SOLDIERS HERE, WITH *GUNS*.
OH, YES. ABOUT FOURTEEN MILES FROM GRIMPEN IS PRINCE-TOWN.
AS IN, PRINCE-TOWN PRISON.

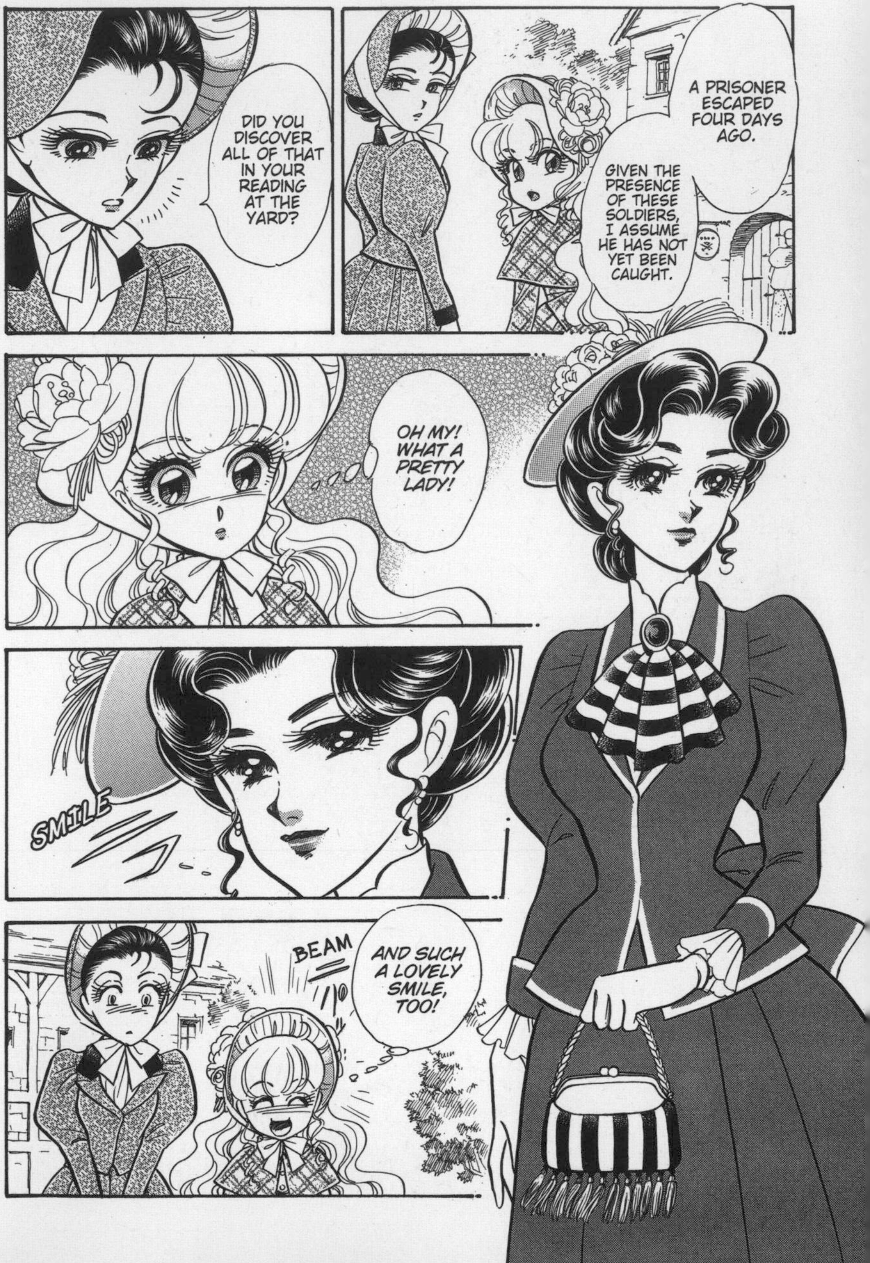
A PRISONER ESCAPED FOUR DAYS AGO.
GIVEN THE PRESENCE OF THESE SOLDIERS, I ASSUME HE HAS NOT YET BEEN CAUGHT.
DID YOU DISCOVER ALL OF THAT IN YOUR READING AT THE YARD?
OH MY! WHAT A PRETTY LADY!
SMILE
BEAM
AND SUCH A LOVELY SMILE, TOO!

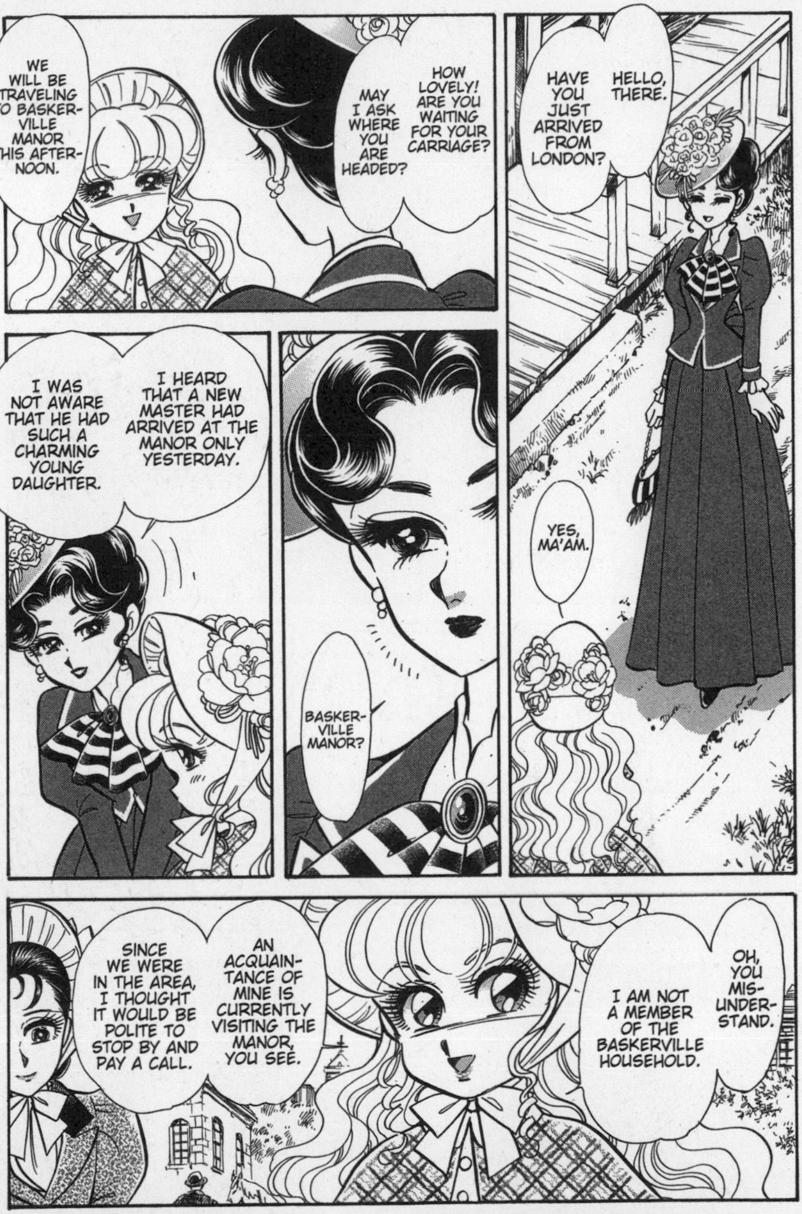
HELLO, THERE.
HAVE YOU JUST ARRIVED FROM LONDON?
YES, MA'AM.
HOW LOVELY! ARE YOU WAITING FOR YOUR CARRIAGE?
MAY I ASK WHERE YOU ARE HEADED?
WE WILL BE TRAVELING TO BASKER-VILLE MANOR THIS AFTER-NOON.
BASKER-VILLE MANOR?
I HEARD THAT A NEW MASTER HAD ARRIVED AT THE MANOR ONLY YESTERDAY.
I WAS NOT AWARE THAT HE HAD SUCH A CHARMING YOUNG DAUGHTER.
OH, YOU MIS-UNDER-STAND.
I AM NOT A MEMBER OF THE BASKERVILLE HOUSEHOLD.
AN ACQUAIN-TANCE OF MINE IS CURRENTLY VISITING THE MANOR, YOU SEE.
SINCE WE WERE IN THE AREA, I THOUGHT IT WOULD BE POLITE TO STOP BY AND PAY A CALL.

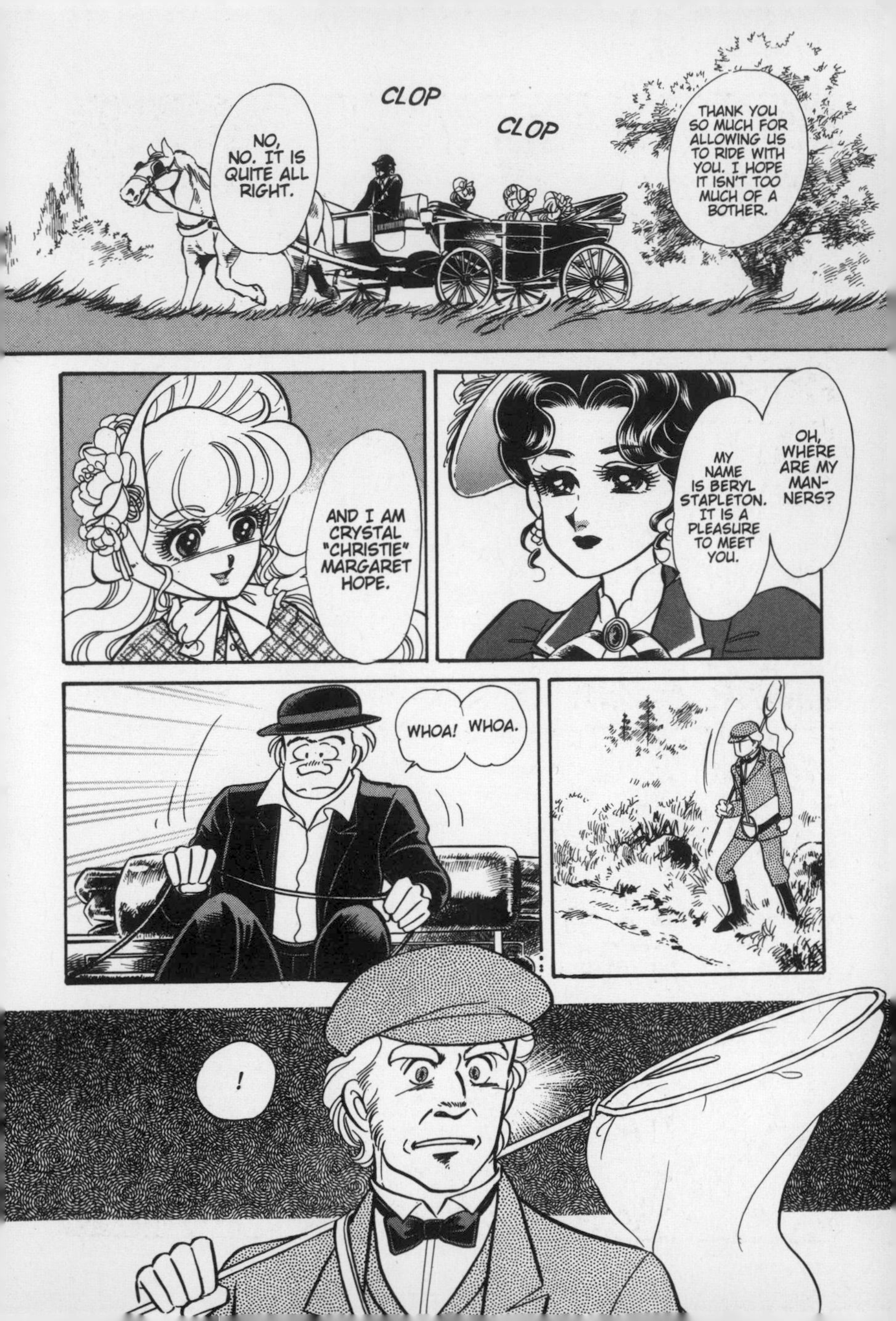
THANK YOU SO MUCH FOR ALLOWING US TO RIDE WITH YOU. I HOPE IT ISN'T TOO MUCH OF A BOTHER.
CLOP
CLOP
NO, NO. IT IS QUITE ALL RIGHT.
OH, WHERE ARE MY MAN-NERS?
MY NAME IS BERYL STAPLETON. IT IS A PLEASURE TO MEET YOU.
AND I AM CRYSTAL "CHRISTIE" MARGARET HOPE.
WHOA! WHOA.
!

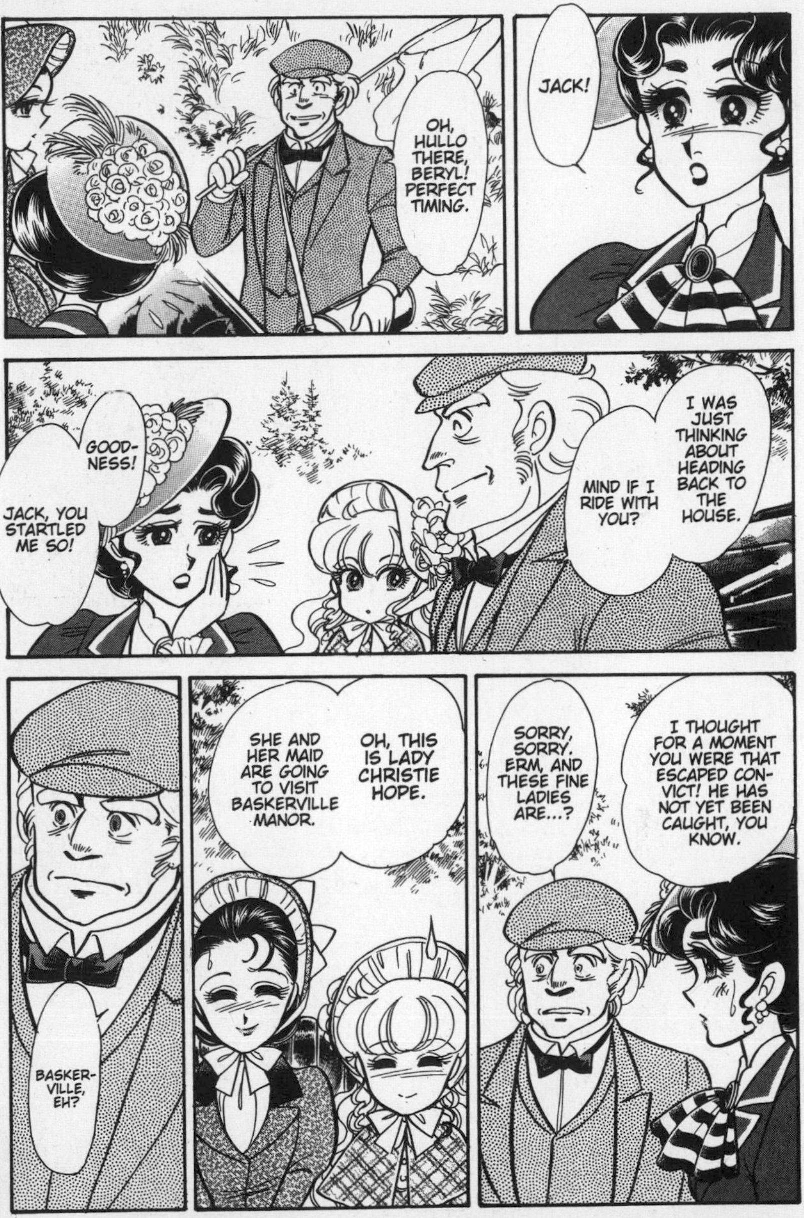
JACK!
OH, HULLO THERE, BERYL! PERFECT TIMING.
I WAS JUST THINKING ABOUT HEADING BACK TO THE HOUSE.
MIND IF I RIDE WITH YOU?
GOODNESS!
JACK, YOU STARTLED ME SO!
I THOUGHT FOR A MOMENT YOU WERE THAT ESCAPED CONVICT! HE HAS NOT YET BEEN CAUGHT, YOU KNOW.
SORRY, SORRY. ERM, AND THESE FINE LADIES ARE...?
OH, THIS IS LADY CHRISTIE HOPE.
SHE AND HER MAID ARE GOING TO VISIT BASKERVILLE MANOR.
BASKERVILLE, EH?

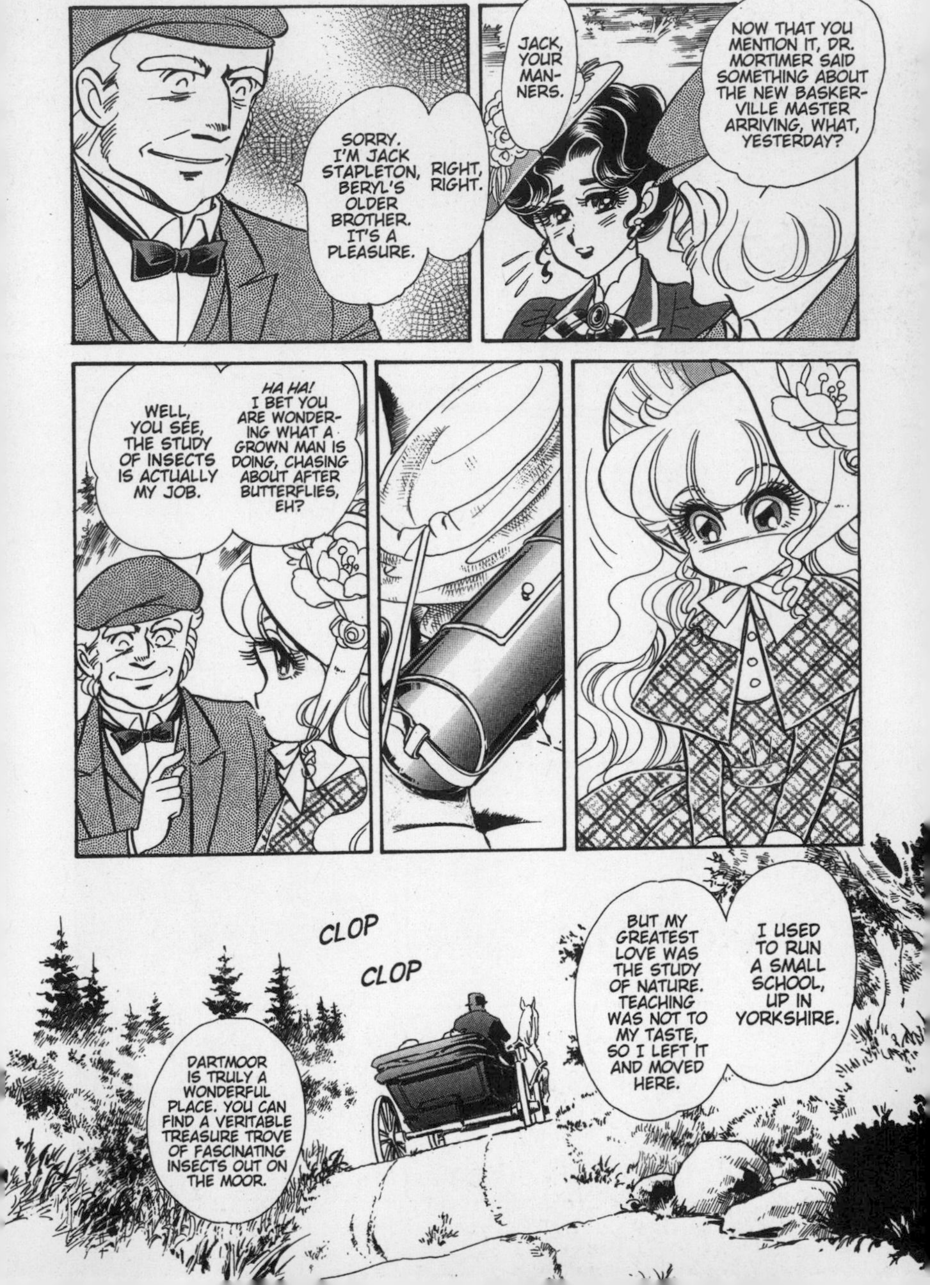
NOW THAT YOU MENTION IT, DR. MORTIMER SAID SOMETHING ABOUT THE NEW BASKERVILLE MASTER ARRIVING, WHAT, YESTERDAY?
JACK, YOUR MANNERS.
RIGHT, RIGHT.
SORRY. I'M JACK STAPLETON, BERYL'S OLDER BROTHER. IT'S A PLEASURE.
HA HA! I BET YOU ARE WONDERING WHAT A GROWN MAN IS DOING, CHASING ABOUT AFTER BUTTERFLIES, EH?
WELL, YOU SEE, THE STUDY OF INSECTS IS ACTUALLY MY JOB.
I USED TO RUN A SMALL SCHOOL, UP IN YORKSHIRE.
BUT MY GREATEST LOVE WAS THE STUDY OF NATURE. TEACHING WAS NOT TO MY TASTE, SO I LEFT IT AND MOVED HERE.
CLOP
CLOP
DARTMOOR IS TRULY A WONDERFUL PLACE. YOU CAN FIND A VERITABLE TREASURE TROVE OF FASCINATING INSECTS OUT ON THE MOOR.

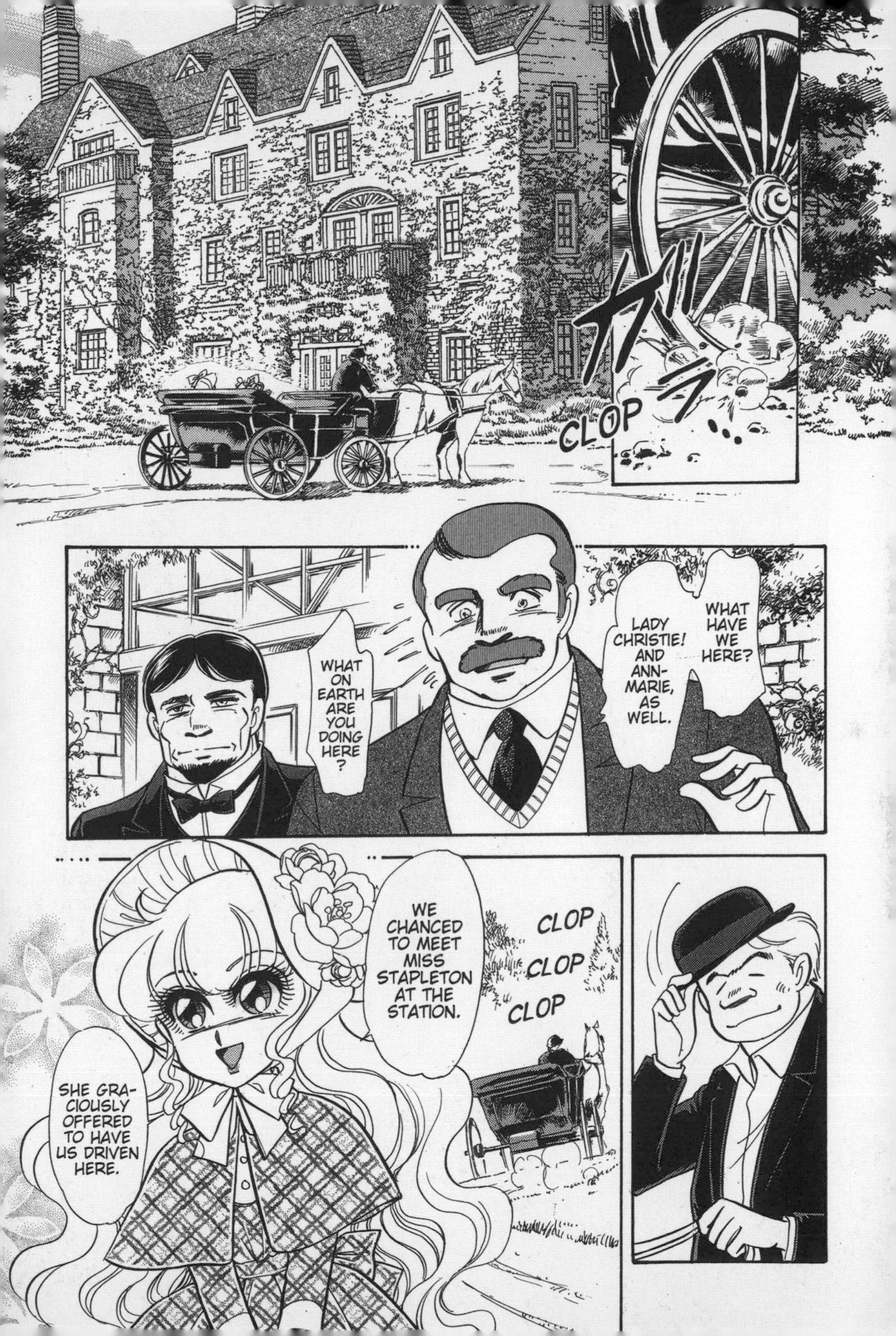
CLOP
WHAT HAVE WE HERE?
LADY CHRISTIE! AND ANN-MARIE, AS WELL.
WHAT ON EARTH ARE YOU DOING HERE?
CLOP
CLOP
CLOP
WE CHANCED TO MEET MISS STAPLETON AT THE STATION.
SHE GRACIOUSLY OFFERED TO HAVE US DRIVEN HERE.

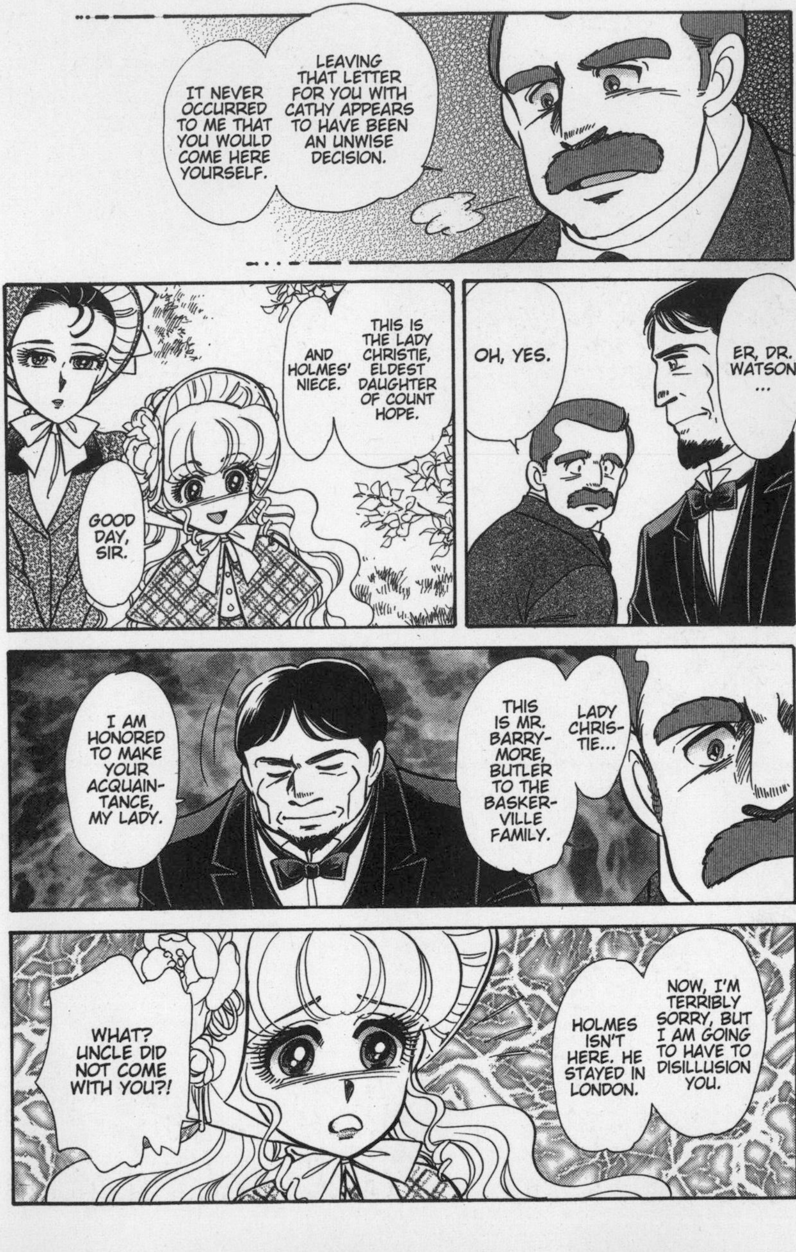
LEAVING THAT LETTER FOR YOU WITH CATHY APPEARS TO HAVE BEEN AN UNWISE DECISION.
IT NEVER OCCURRED TO ME THAT YOU WOULD COME HERE YOURSELF.
ER, DR. WATSON ...
OH, YES.
THIS IS THE LADY CHRISTIE, ELDEST DAUGHTER OF COUNT HOPE.
AND HOLMES' NIECE.
GOOD DAY, SIR.
LADY CHRIS-TIE...
THIS IS MR. BARRY-MORE, BUTLER TO THE BASKER-VILLE FAMILY.
I AM HONORED TO MAKE YOUR ACQUAIN-TANCE, MY LADY.
NOW, I'M TERRIBLY SORRY, BUT I AM GOING TO HAVE TO DISILLUSION YOU.
HOLMES ISN'T HERE. HE STAYED IN LONDON.
WHAT? UNCLE DID NOT COME WITH YOU?!

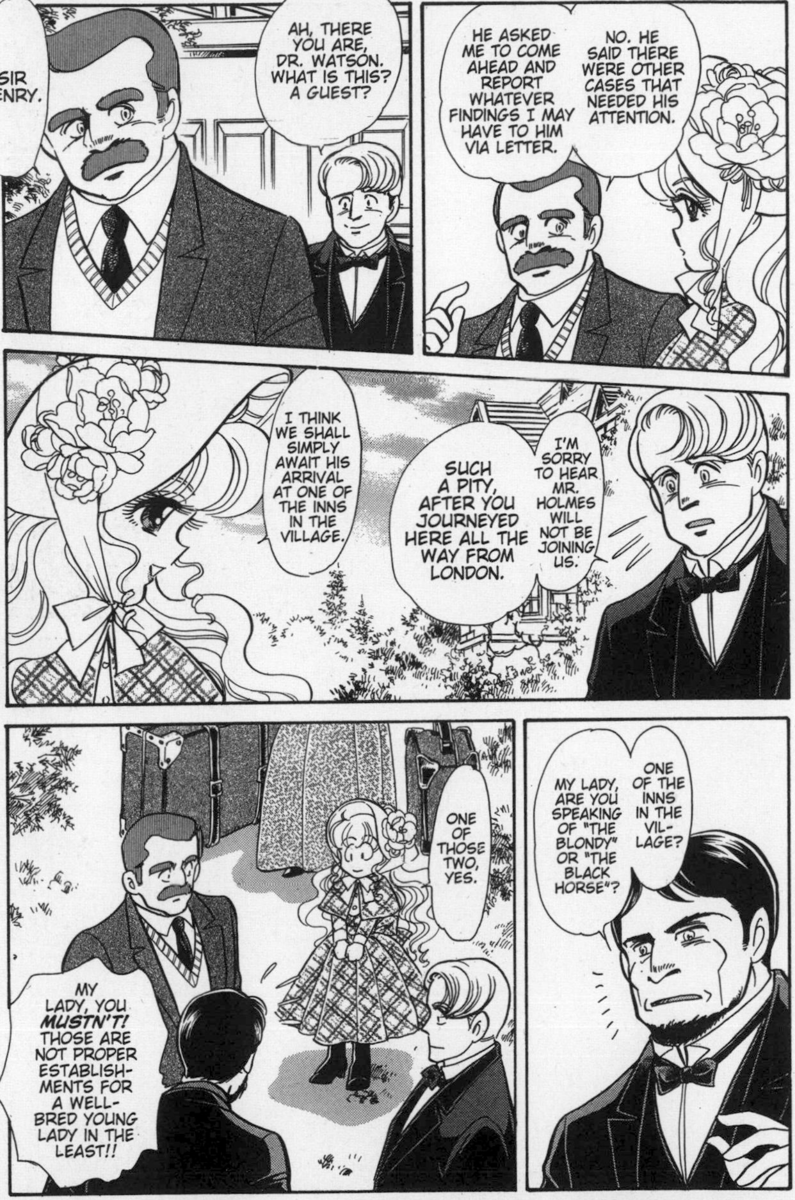
NO. HE SAID THERE WERE OTHER CASES THAT NEEDED HIS ATTENTION.
HE ASKED ME TO COME AHEAD AND REPORT WHATEVER FINDINGS I MAY HAVE TO HIM VIA LETTER.
AH, THERE YOU ARE, DR. WATSON. WHAT IS THIS? A GUEST?
SIR HENRY.
I'M SORRY TO HEAR MR. HOLMES WILL NOT BE JOINING US.
SUCH A PITY, AFTER YOU JOURNEYED HERE ALL THE WAY FROM LONDON.
I THINK WE SHALL SIMPLY AWAIT HIS ARRIVAL AT ONE OF THE INNS IN THE VILLAGE.
ONE OF THE INNS IN THE VIL-LAGE?
MY LADY, ARE YOU SPEAKING OF "THE BLONDY" OR "THE BLACK HORSE"?
ONE OF THOSE TWO, YES.
MY LADY, YOU ***MUSTN'T!*** THOSE ARE NOT PROPER ESTABLISH-MENTS FOR A WELL-BRED YOUNG LADY IN THE LEAST!!

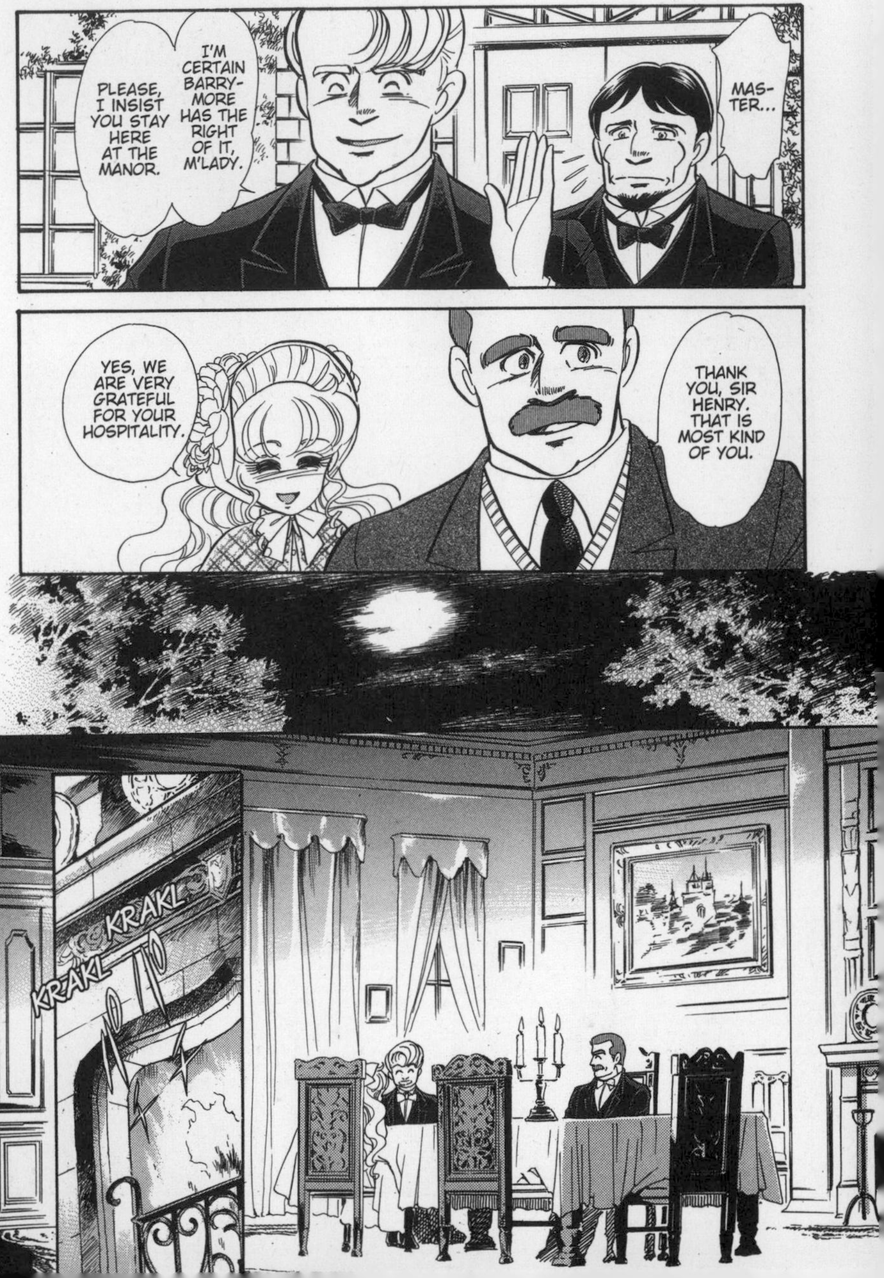
MAS-TER...
I'M CERTAIN BARRY-MORE HAS THE RIGHT OF IT, M'LADY.
PLEASE, I INSIST YOU STAY HERE AT THE MANOR.
THANK YOU, SIR HENRY. THAT IS MOST KIND OF YOU.
YES, WE ARE VERY GRATEFUL FOR YOUR HOSPITALITY.
KRAKL
KRAKL

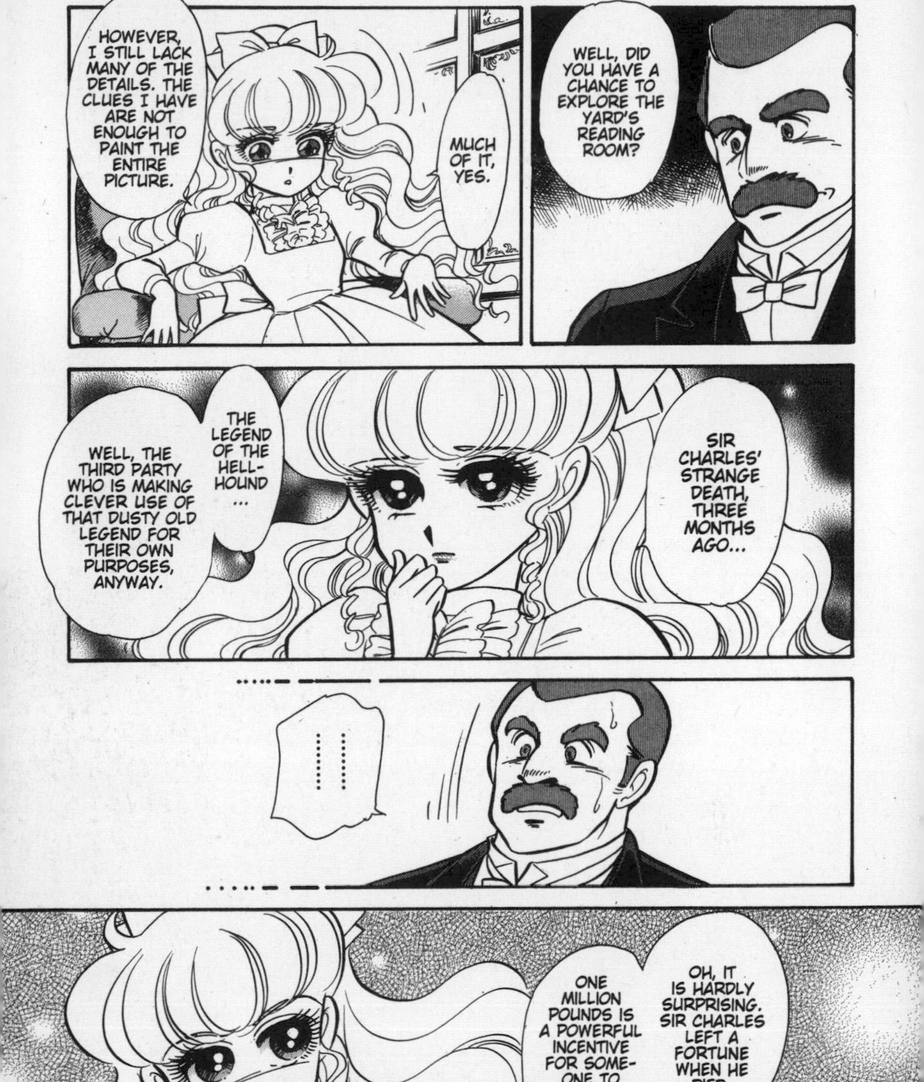
WELL, DID YOU HAVE A CHANCE TO EXPLORE THE YARD'S READING ROOM?
MUCH OF IT, YES.
HOWEVER, I STILL LACK MANY OF THE DETAILS. THE CLUES I HAVE ARE NOT ENOUGH TO PAINT THE ENTIRE PICTURE.
SIR CHARLES' STRANGE DEATH, THREE MONTHS AGO...
THE LEGEND OF THE HELL-HOUND ...
WELL, THE THIRD PARTY WHO IS MAKING CLEVER USE OF THAT DUSTY OLD LEGEND FOR THEIR OWN PURPOSES, ANYWAY.
OH, IT IS HARDLY SURPRISING. SIR CHARLES LEFT A FORTUNE WHEN HE DIED.
ONE MILLION POUNDS IS A POWERFUL INCENTIVE FOR SOME-ONE TO SUMMON "DEVILS."

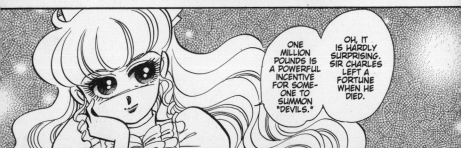

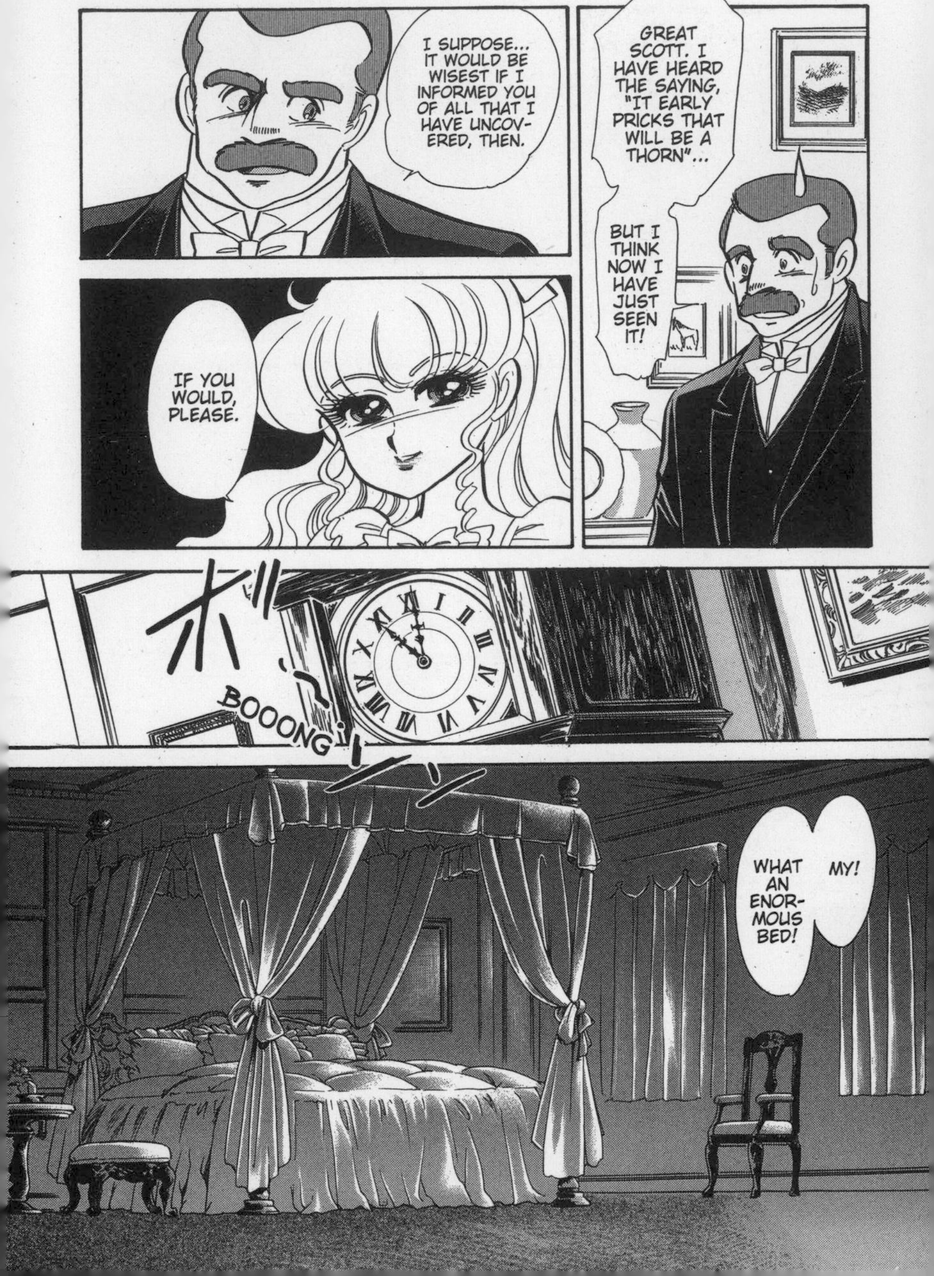
GREAT SCOTT. I HAVE HEARD THE SAYING, "IT EARLY PRICKS THAT WILL BE A THORN"...
BUT I THINK NOW I HAVE JUST SEEN IT!
I SUPPOSE... IT WOULD BE WISEST IF I INFORMED YOU OF ALL THAT I HAVE UNCOV-ERED, THEN.
IF YOU WOULD, PLEASE.
BOOONG
MY!
WHAT AN ENOR-MOUS BED!

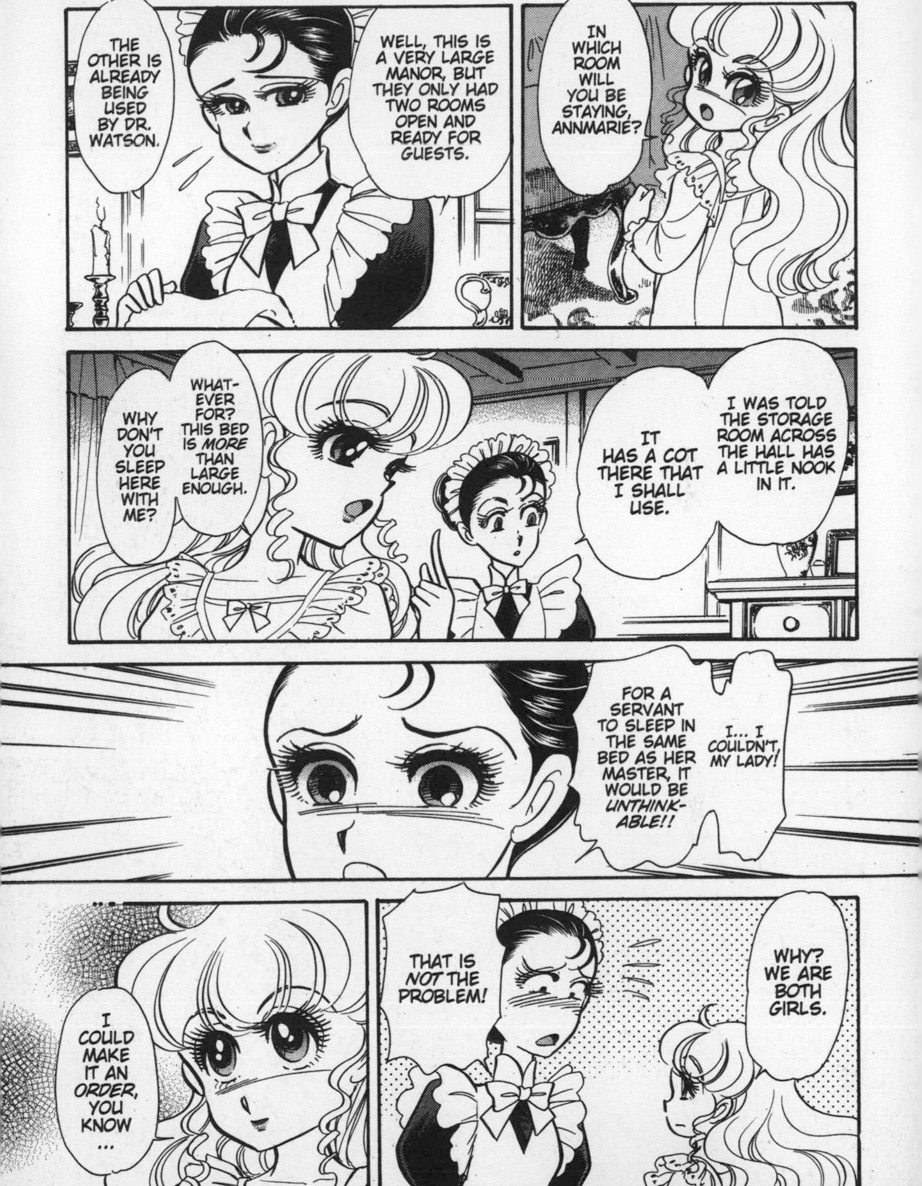

IN WHICH ROOM WILL YOU BE STAYING, ANNMARIE?
WELL, THIS IS A VERY LARGE MANOR, BUT THEY ONLY HAD TWO ROOMS OPEN AND READY FOR GUESTS.
THE OTHER IS ALREADY BEING USED BY DR. WATSON.
I WAS TOLD THE STORAGE ROOM ACROSS THE HALL HAS A LITTLE NOOK IN IT.
IT HAS A COT THERE THAT I SHALL USE.
WHAT-EVER FOR? THIS BED IS *MORE* THAN LARGE ENOUGH.
WHY DON'T YOU SLEEP HERE WITH ME?
I... I COULDN'T, MY LADY!
FOR A SERVANT TO SLEEP IN THE SAME BED AS HER MASTER, IT WOULD BE *UNTHINK-ABLE!!*
WHY? WE ARE BOTH GIRLS.
THAT IS *NOT* THE PROBLEM!
I COULD MAKE IT AN *ORDER*, YOU KNOW ...

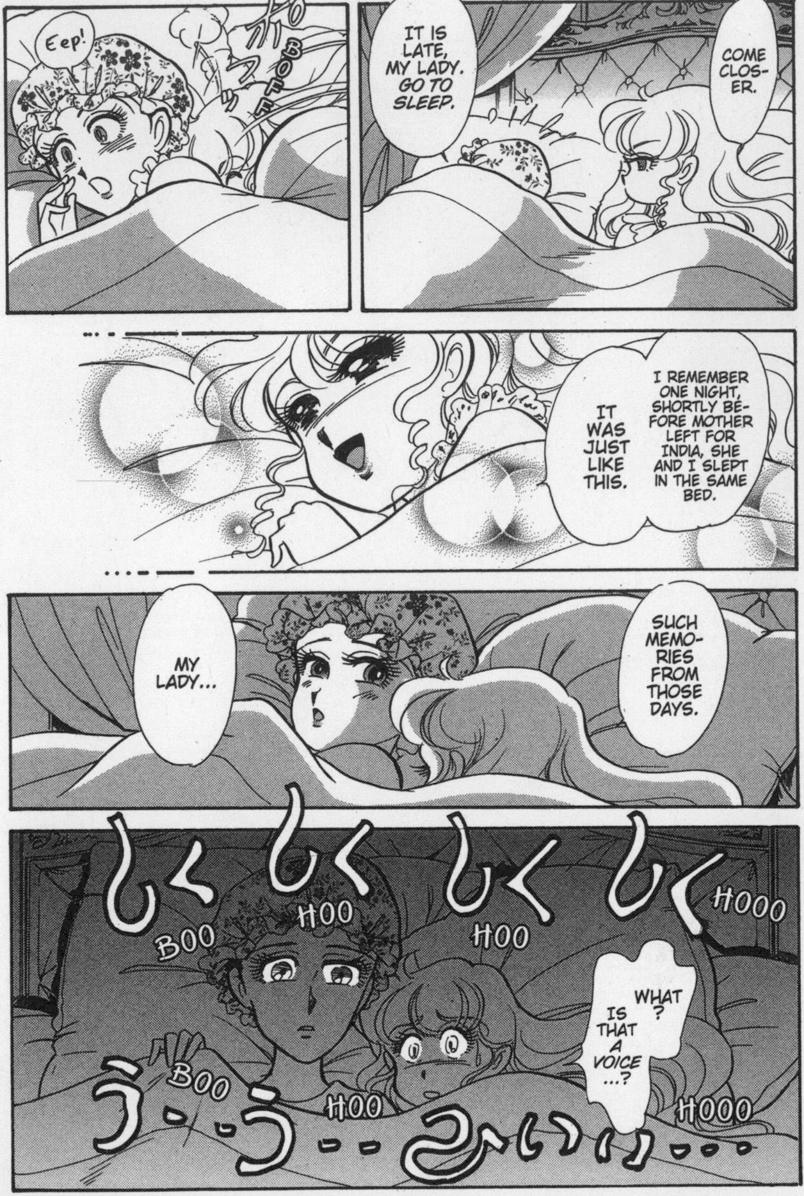
COME CLOSER.
IT IS LATE, MY LADY. GO TO SLEEP.
BOFF
Eep!
I REMEMBER ONE NIGHT, SHORTLY BEFORE MOTHER LEFT FOR INDIA, SHE AND I SLEPT IN THE SAME BED.
IT WAS JUST LIKE THIS.
SUCH MEMORIES FROM THOSE DAYS.
MY LADY...
HOOO
HOO
HOO
BOO
WHAT?
IS THAT A VOICE...?
HOOO
HOO
BOO

The Hound of the Baskervilles (5)

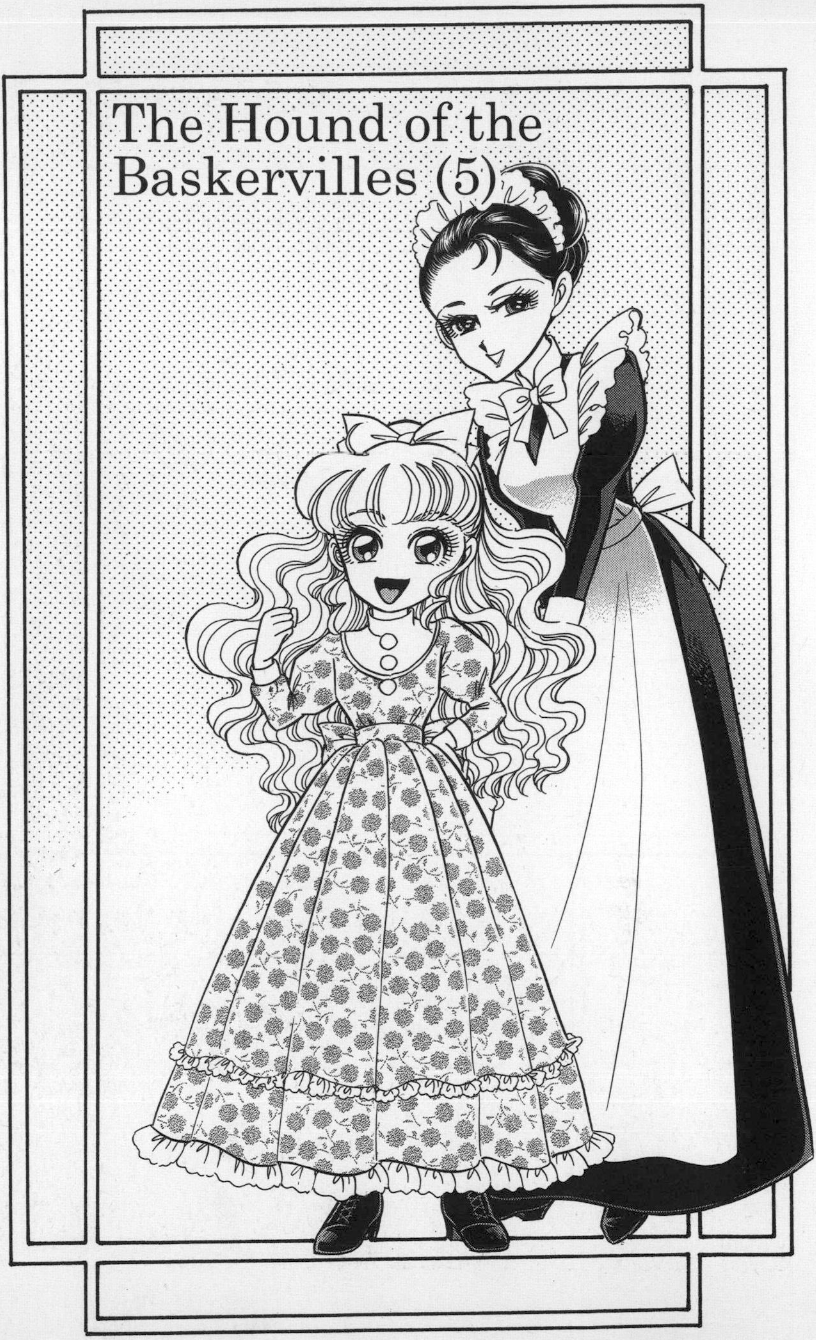

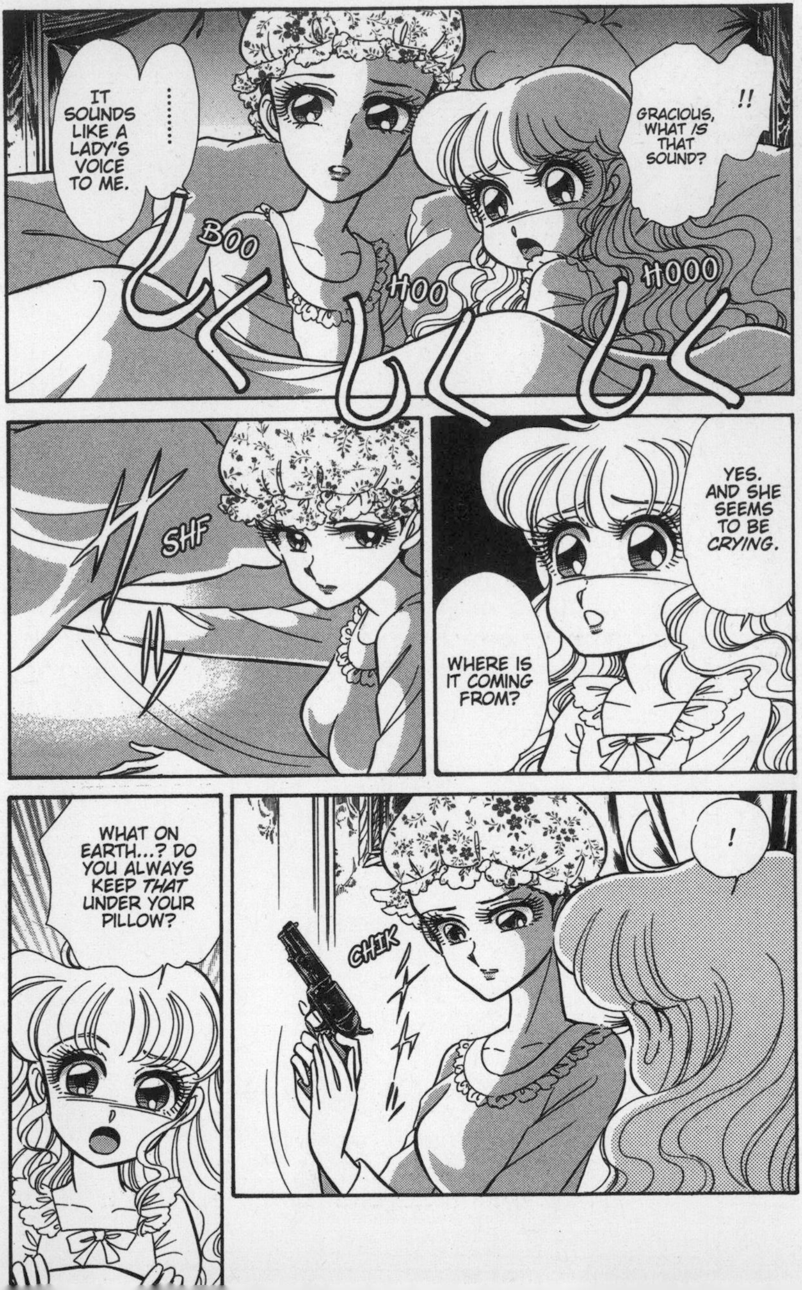
!!
GRACIOUS, WHAT *IS* THAT SOUND?
....
IT SOUNDS LIKE A LADY'S VOICE TO ME.
BOO
HOO
HOOO
YES. AND SHE SEEMS TO BE *CRYING*.
WHERE IS IT COMING FROM?
SHF
!
CHIK
WHAT ON EARTH...? DO YOU ALWAYS KEEP *THAT* UNDER YOUR PILLOW?

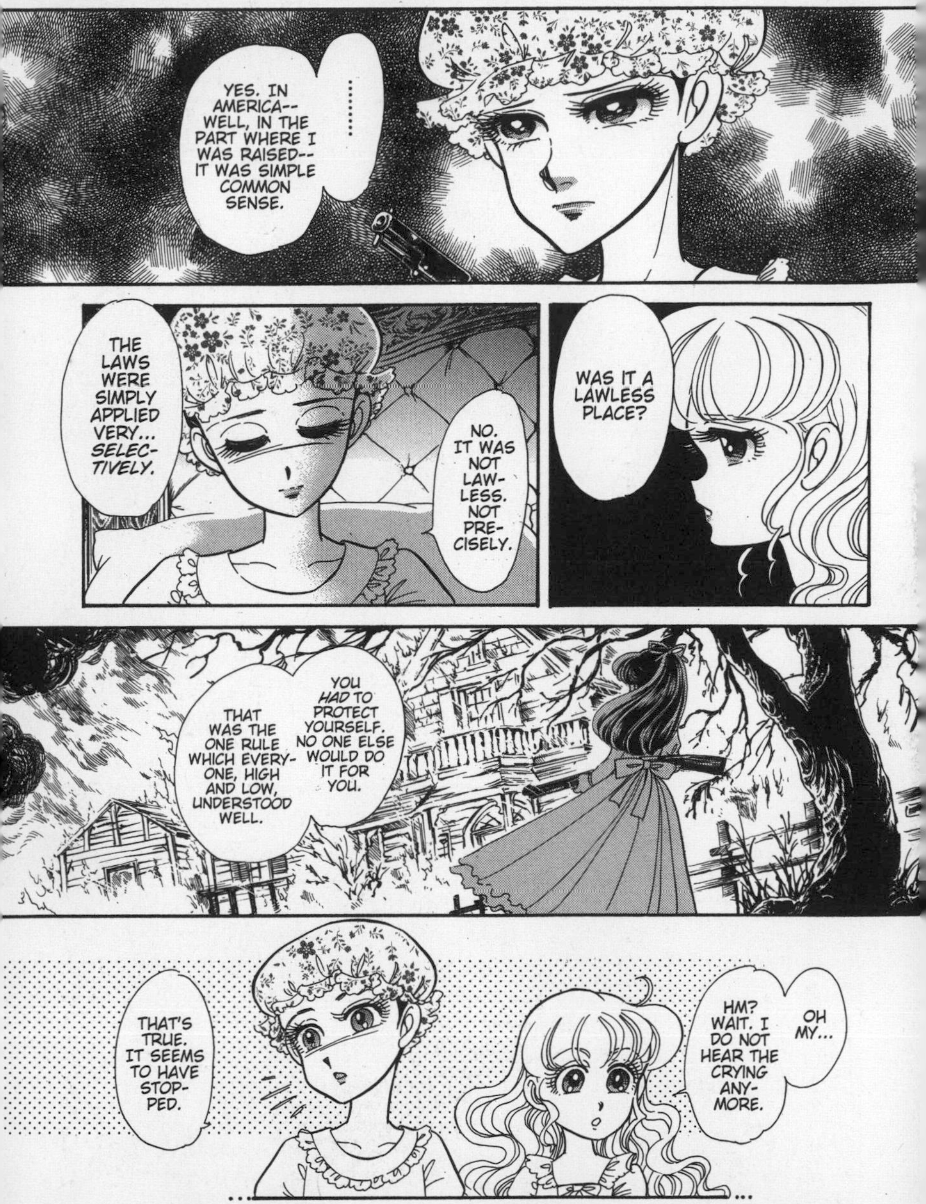
……
YES. IN AMERICA-- WELL, IN THE PART WHERE I WAS RAISED-- IT WAS SIMPLE COMMON SENSE.
WAS IT A LAWLESS PLACE?
NO. IT WAS NOT LAW-LESS. NOT PRE-CISELY.
THE LAWS WERE SIMPLY APPLIED VERY... SELEC-TIVELY.
YOU *HAD* TO PROTECT YOURSELF. NO ONE ELSE WOULD DO IT FOR YOU.
THAT WAS THE ONE RULE WHICH EVERY-ONE, HIGH AND LOW, UNDERSTOOD WELL.
OH MY...
HM? WAIT. I DO NOT HEAR THE CRYING ANY-MORE.
THAT'S TRUE. IT SEEMS TO HAVE STOP-PED.
…… ……

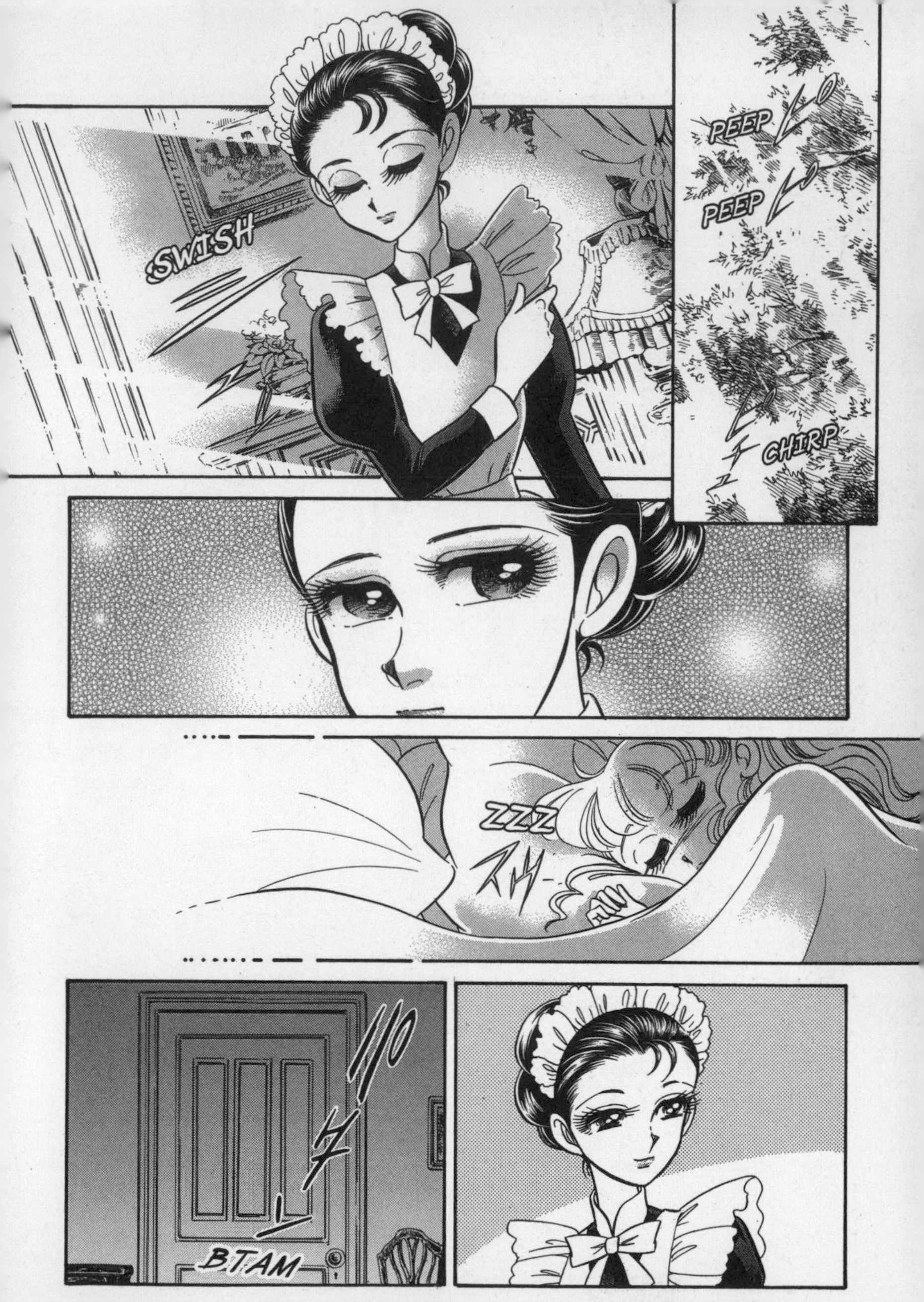
PEEP
PEEP
CHIRP
SWISH
ZZZ
BTAM

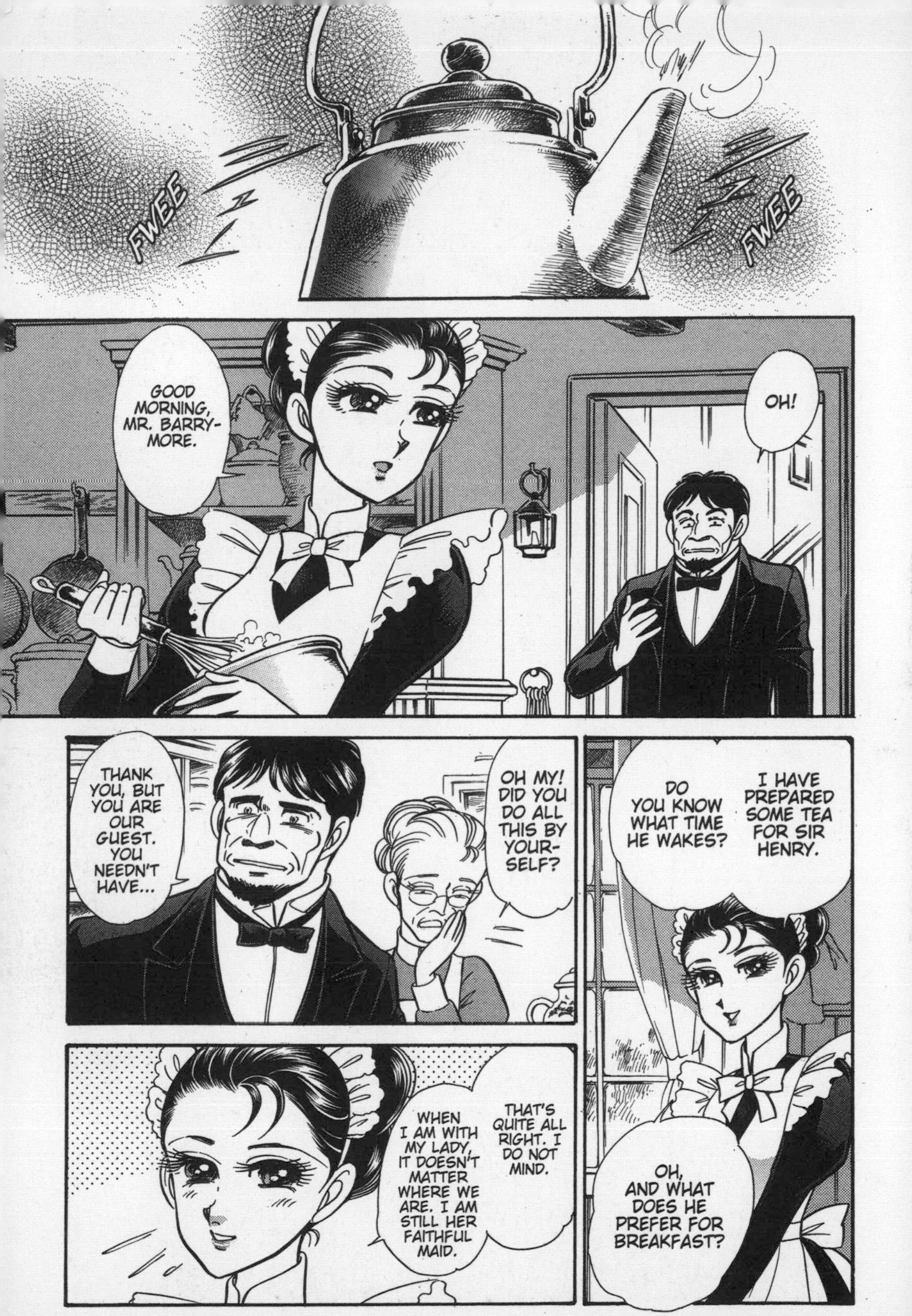
FWEE
FWEE
OH!
GOOD MORNING, MR. BARRY-MORE.
I HAVE PREPARED SOME TEA FOR SIR HENRY.
DO YOU KNOW WHAT TIME HE WAKES?
OH, AND WHAT DOES HE PREFER FOR BREAKFAST?
OH MY! DID YOU DO ALL THIS BY YOUR-SELF?
THANK YOU, BUT YOU ARE OUR GUEST. YOU NEEDN'T HAVE...
THAT'S QUITE ALL RIGHT. I DO NOT MIND.
WHEN I AM WITH MY LADY, IT DOESN'T MATTER WHERE WE ARE. I AM STILL HER FAITHFUL MAID.

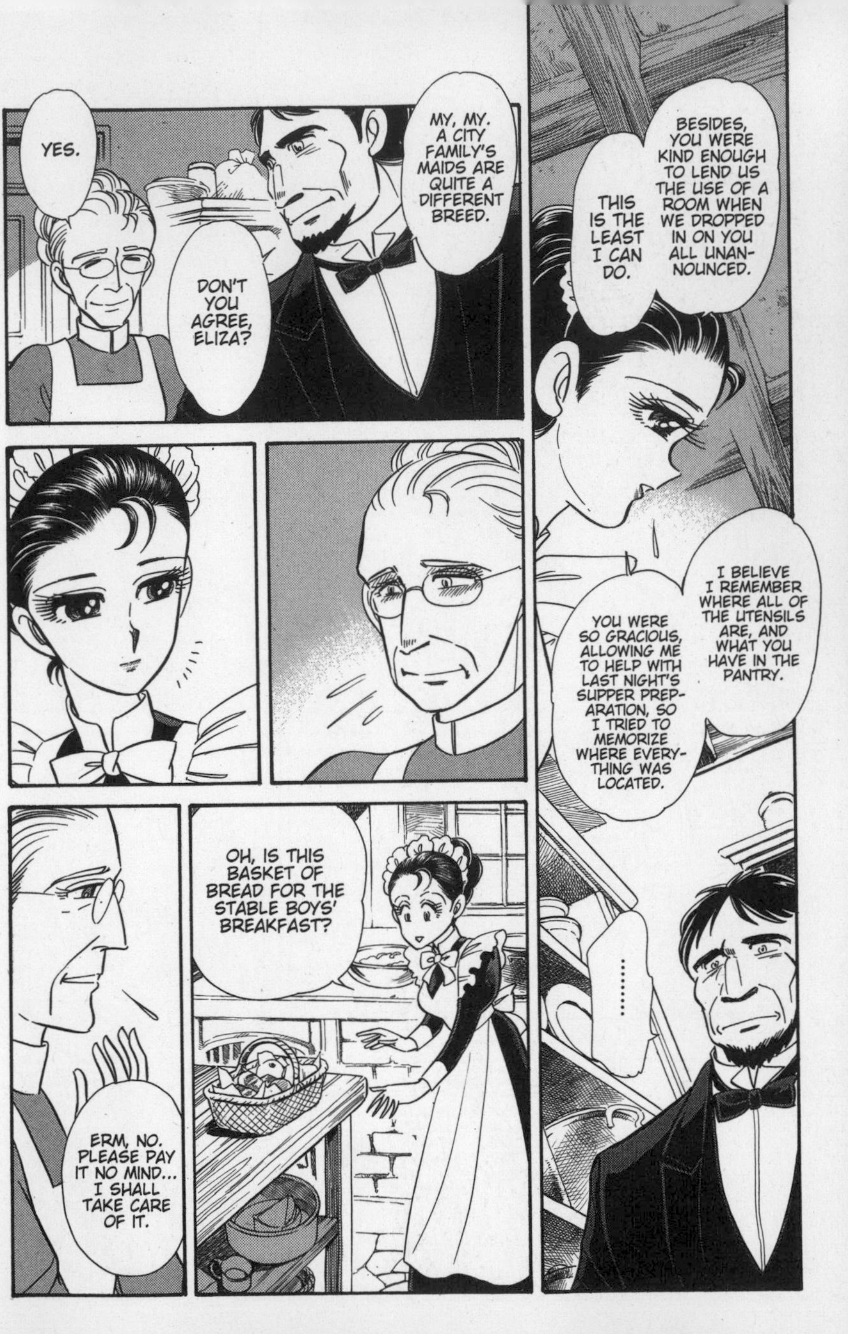
BESIDES, YOU WERE KIND ENOUGH TO LEND US THE USE OF A ROOM WHEN WE DROPPED IN ON YOU ALL UNANNOUNCED.
THIS IS THE LEAST I CAN DO.
I BELIEVE I REMEMBER WHERE ALL OF THE UTENSILS ARE, AND WHAT YOU HAVE IN THE PANTRY.
YOU WERE SO GRACIOUS, ALLOWING ME TO HELP WITH LAST NIGHT'S SUPPER PREPARATION, SO I TRIED TO MEMORIZE WHERE EVERYTHING WAS LOCATED.
......
MY, MY. A CITY FAMILY'S MAIDS ARE QUITE A DIFFERENT BREED.
DON'T YOU AGREE, ELIZA?
YES.
OH, IS THIS BASKET OF BREAD FOR THE STABLE BOYS' BREAKFAST?
ERM, NO. PLEASE PAY IT NO MIND... I SHALL TAKE CARE OF IT.

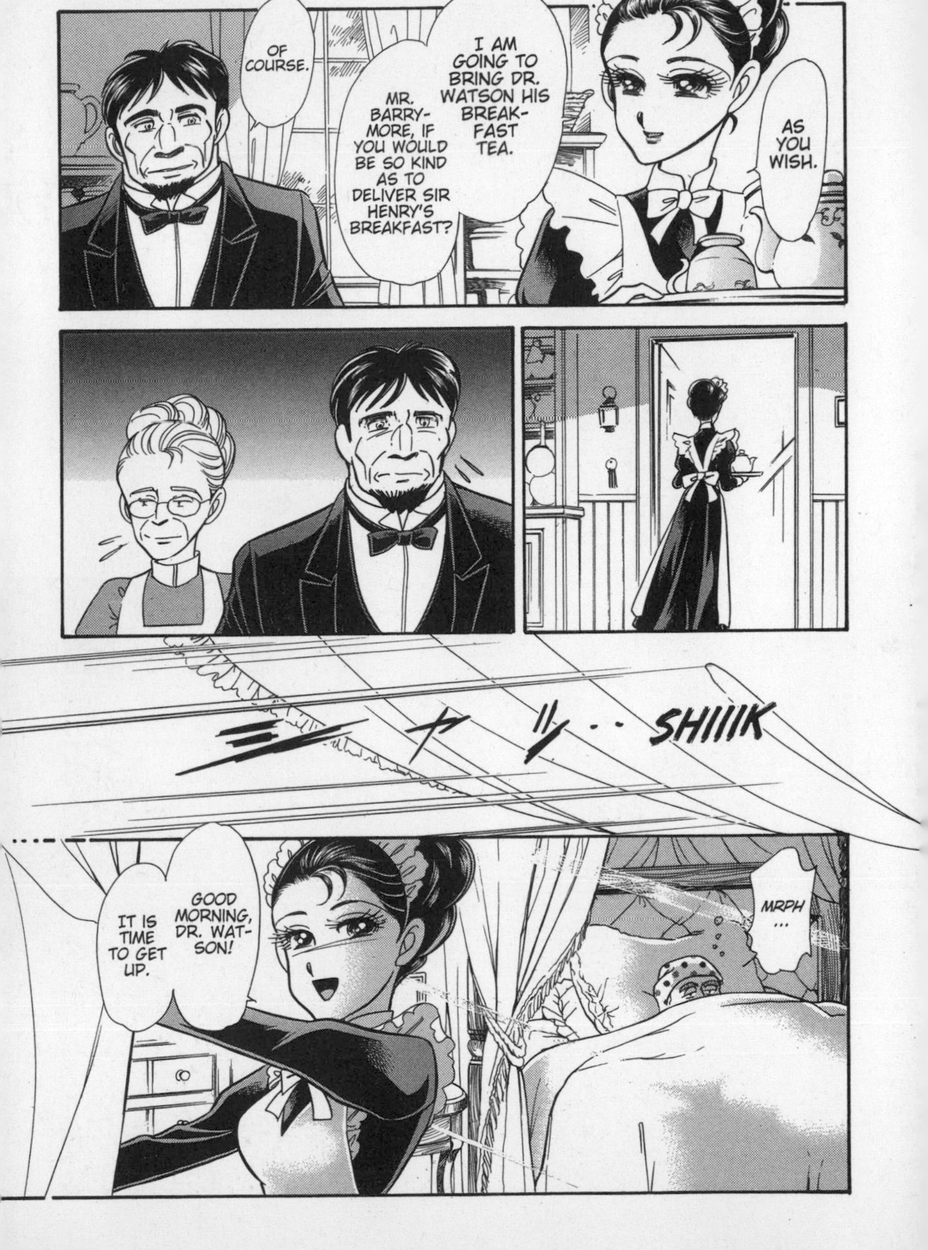
AS YOU WISH.
I AM GOING TO BRING DR. WATSON HIS BREAKFAST TEA.
MR. BARRYMORE, IF YOU WOULD BE SO KIND AS TO DELIVER SIR HENRY'S BREAKFAST?
OF COURSE.
SHIIIK
MRPH ...
GOOD MORNING, DR. WATSON!
IT IS TIME TO GET UP.

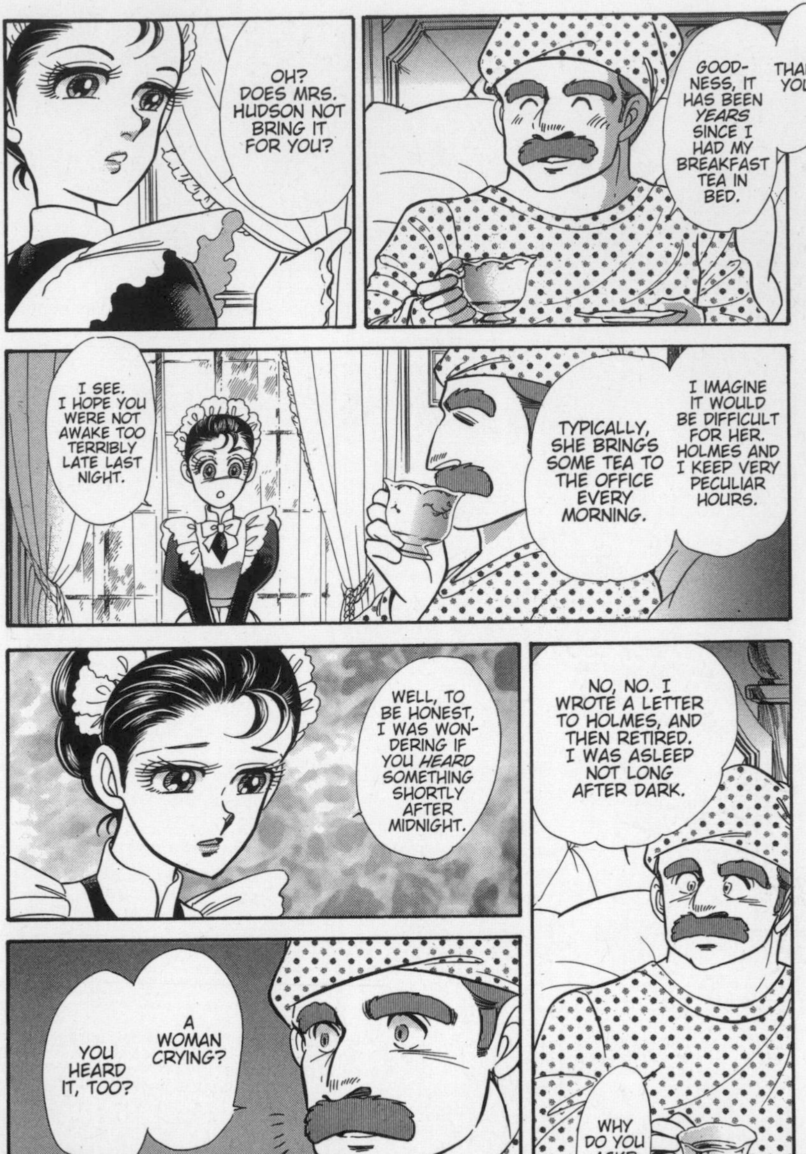
THANK YOU!
GOODNESS, IT HAS BEEN *YEARS* SINCE I HAD MY BREAKFAST TEA IN BED.
OH? DOES MRS. HUDSON NOT BRING IT FOR YOU?
I IMAGINE IT WOULD BE DIFFICULT FOR HER. HOLMES AND I KEEP VERY PECULIAR HOURS.
TYPICALLY, SHE BRINGS SOME TEA TO THE OFFICE EVERY MORNING.
I SEE. I HOPE YOU WERE NOT AWAKE TOO TERRIBLY LATE LAST NIGHT.
NO, NO. I WROTE A LETTER TO HOLMES, AND THEN RETIRED. I WAS ASLEEP NOT LONG AFTER DARK.
WHY DO YOU ASK?
WELL, TO BE HONEST, I WAS WON-DERING IF YOU *HEARD* SOMETHING SHORTLY AFTER MIDNIGHT.
A WOMAN CRYING?
YOU HEARD IT, TOO?

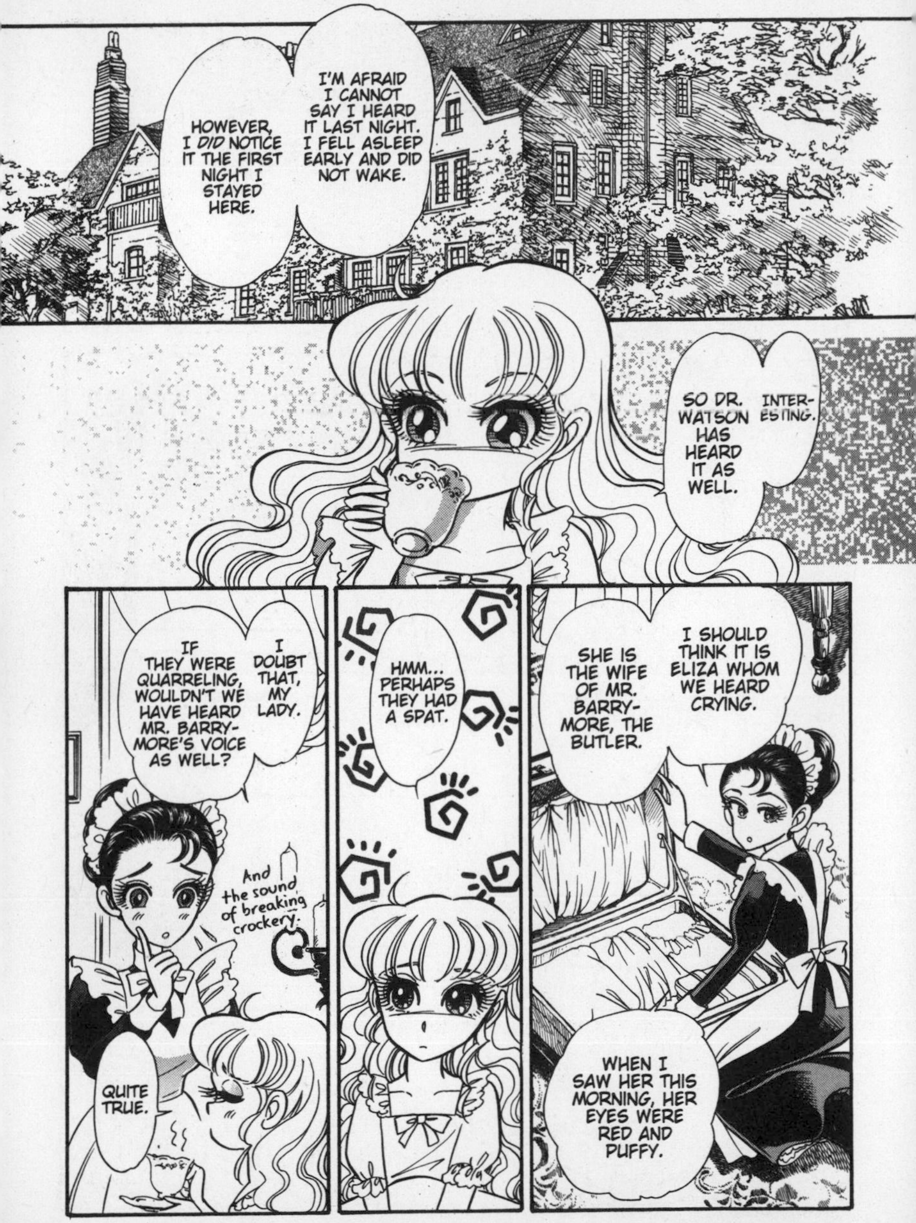
I'M AFRAID I CANNOT SAY I HEARD IT LAST NIGHT. I FELL ASLEEP EARLY AND DID NOT WAKE.
HOWEVER, I *DID* NOTICE IT THE FIRST NIGHT I STAYED HERE.
INTERESTING.
SO DR. WATSON HAS HEARD IT AS WELL.
I SHOULD THINK IT IS ELIZA WHOM WE HEARD CRYING.
SHE IS THE WIFE OF MR. BARRYMORE, THE BUTLER.
WHEN I SAW HER THIS MORNING, HER EYES WERE RED AND PUFFY.
HMM... PERHAPS THEY HAD A SPAT.
I DOUBT THAT, MY LADY.
IF THEY WERE QUARRELING, WOULDN'T WE HAVE HEARD MR. BARRYMORE'S VOICE AS WELL?
And the sound of breaking crockery.
QUITE TRUE.

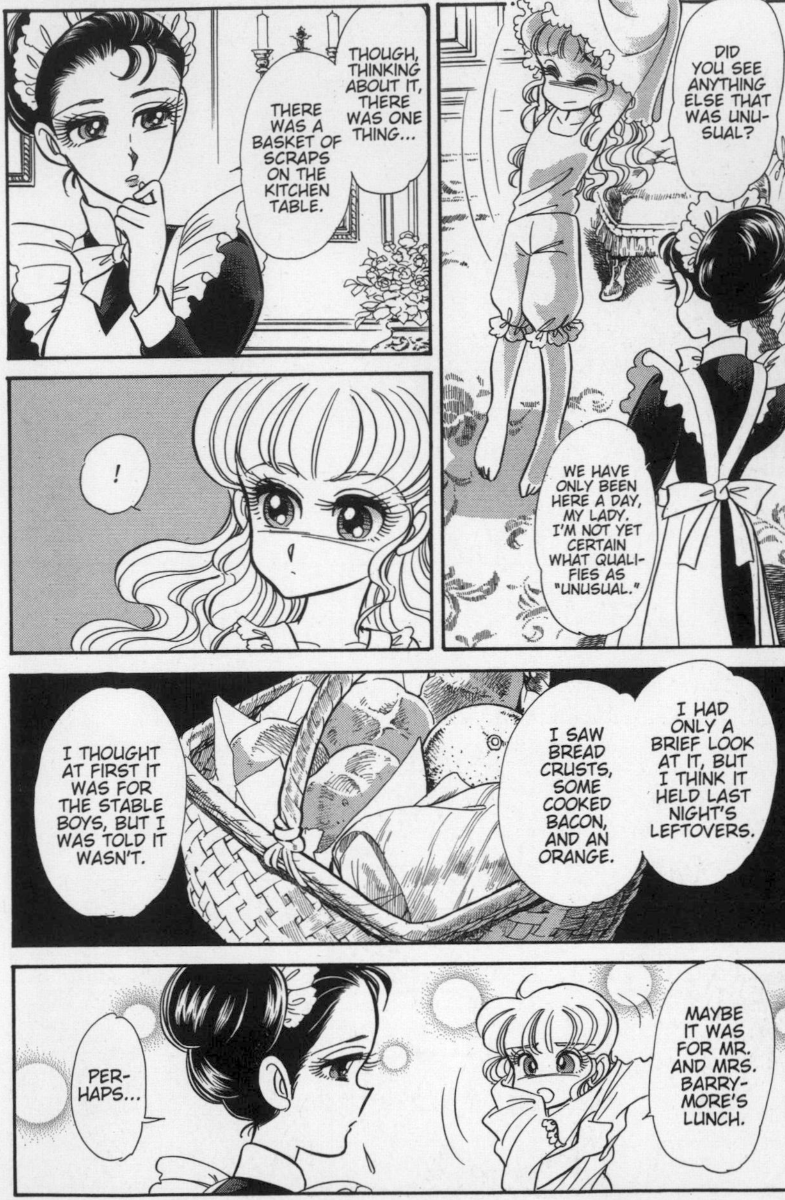
DID YOU SEE ANYTHING ELSE THAT WAS UNU-SUAL?
WE HAVE ONLY BEEN HERE A DAY, MY LADY. I'M NOT YET CERTAIN WHAT QUALI-FIES AS "UNUSUAL."
THOUGH, THINKING ABOUT IT, THERE WAS ONE THING...
THERE WAS A BASKET OF SCRAPS ON THE KITCHEN TABLE.
!
I HAD ONLY A BRIEF LOOK AT IT, BUT I THINK IT HELD LAST NIGHT'S LEFTOVERS.
I SAW BREAD CRUSTS, SOME COOKED BACON, AND AN ORANGE.
I THOUGHT AT FIRST IT WAS FOR THE STABLE BOYS, BUT I WAS TOLD IT WASN'T.
MAYBE IT WAS FOR MR. AND MRS. BARRY-MORE'S LUNCH.
PER-HAPS...

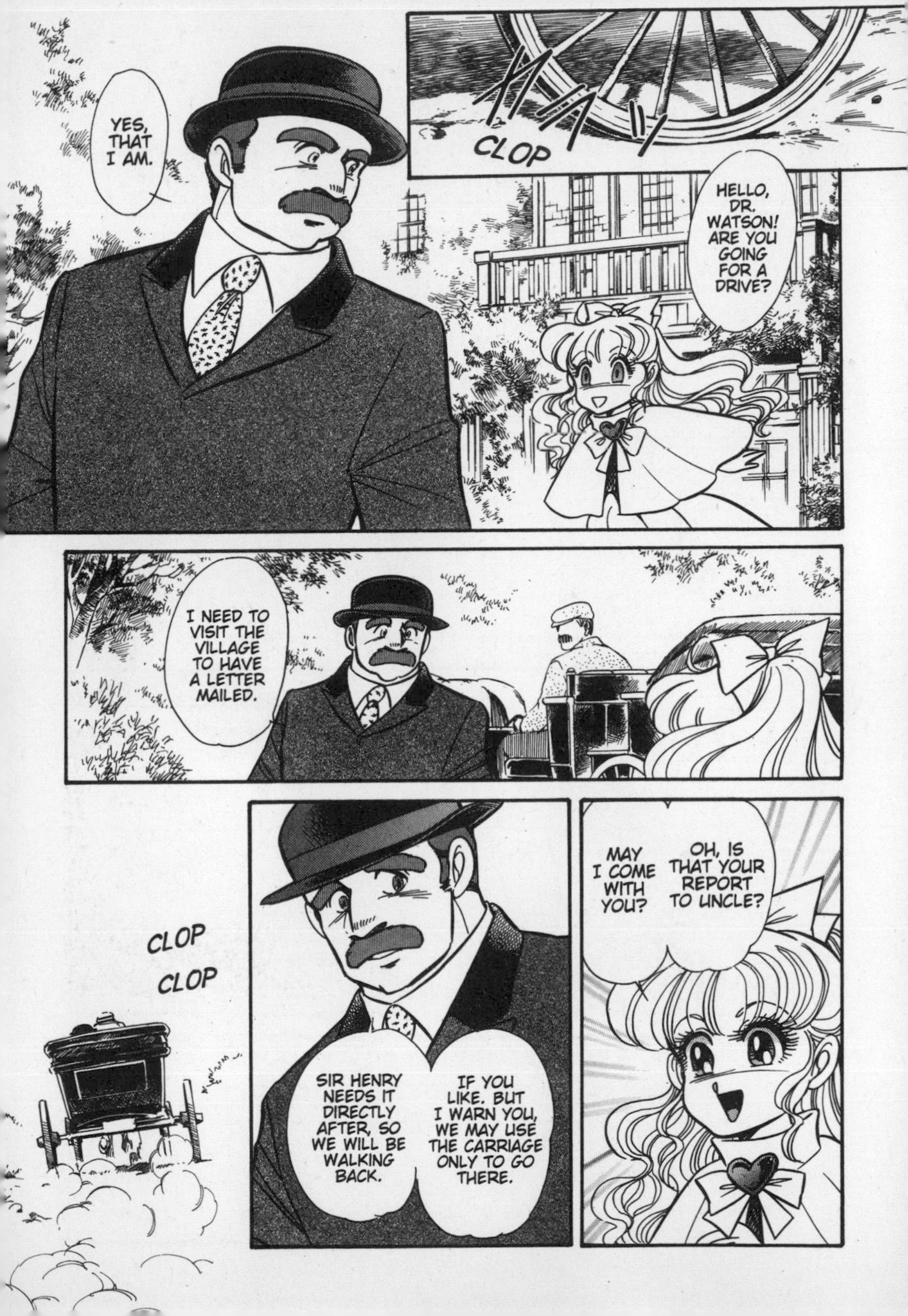
CLOP
HELLO, DR. WATSON! ARE YOU GOING FOR A DRIVE?
YES, THAT I AM.
I NEED TO VISIT THE VILLAGE TO HAVE A LETTER MAILED.
OH, IS THAT YOUR REPORT TO UNCLE?
MAY I COME WITH YOU?
IF YOU LIKE. BUT I WARN YOU, WE MAY USE THE CARRIAGE ONLY TO GO THERE.
SIR HENRY NEEDS IT DIRECTLY AFTER, SO WE WILL BE WALKING BACK.
CLOP
CLOP

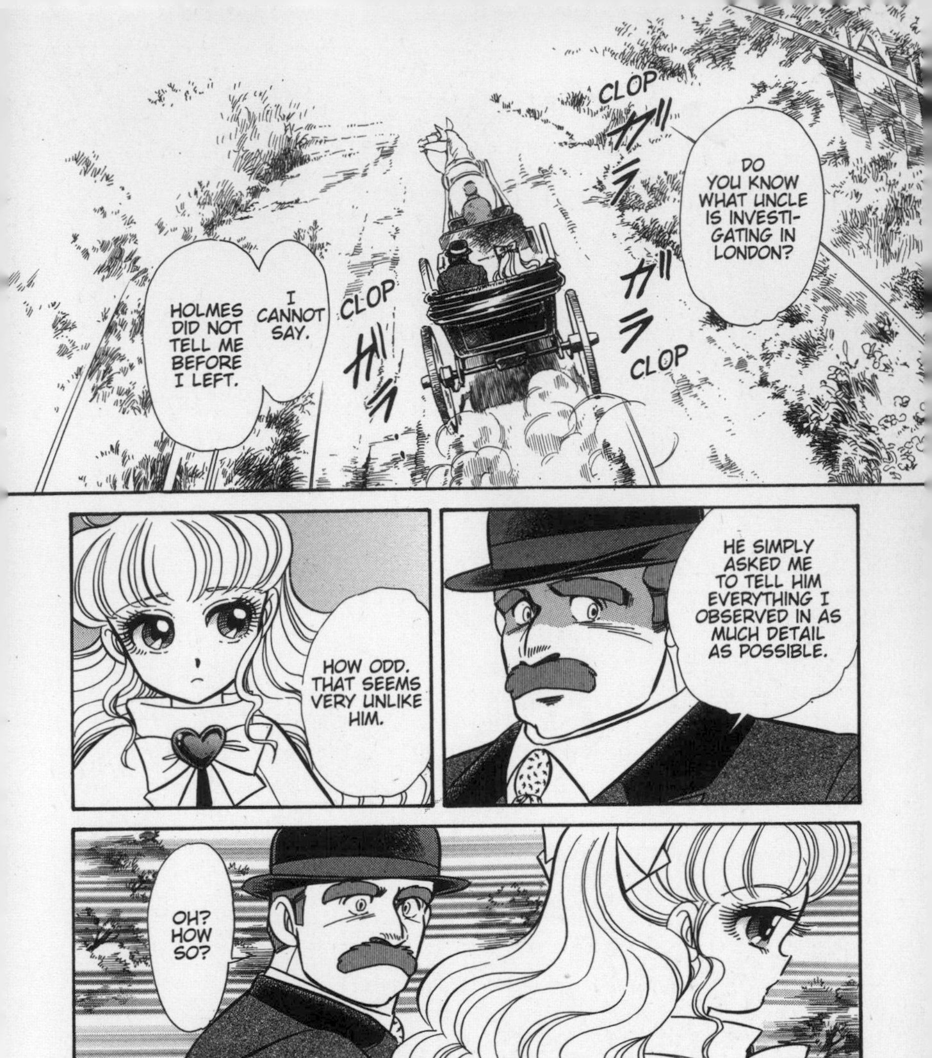
CLOP
DO YOU KNOW WHAT UNCLE IS INVESTIGATING IN LONDON?
CLOP
CLOP
I CANNOT SAY.
HOLMES DID NOT TELL ME BEFORE I LEFT.
HE SIMPLY ASKED ME TO TELL HIM EVERYTHING I OBSERVED IN AS MUCH DETAIL AS POSSIBLE.
HOW ODD. THAT SEEMS VERY UNLIKE HIM.
OH? HOW SO?
UNCLE HAS ACCEPTED THIS CASE, YES?
BUT HE HAS YET TO VISIT THE SCENE OF THE CRIME.
IT FEELS...LAX. AS THOUGH HE IS NOT ENTIRELY ENGAGED.

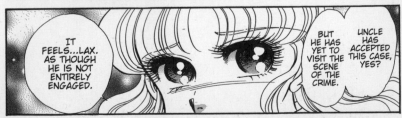

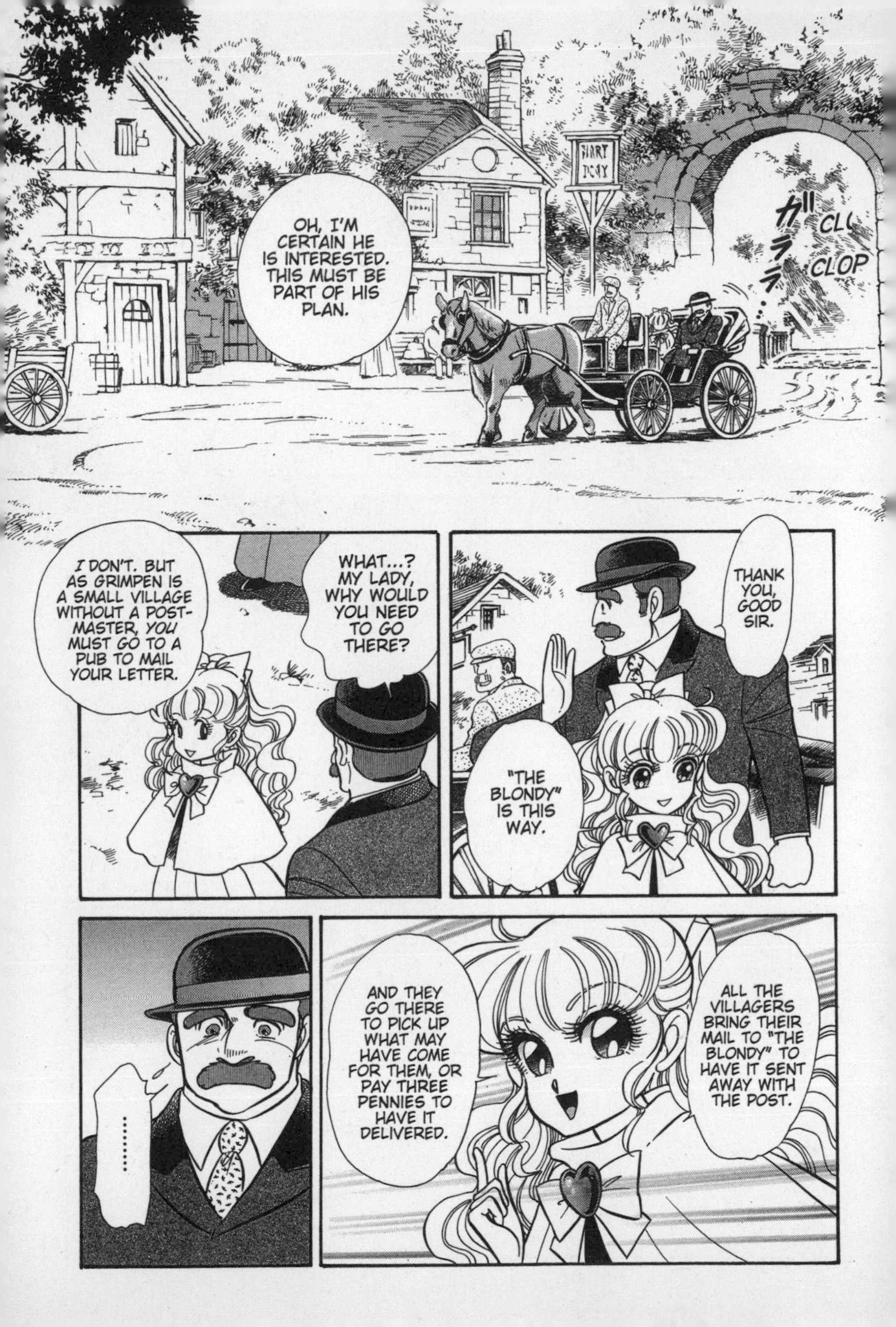
CLOP
OH, I'M CERTAIN HE IS INTERESTED. THIS MUST BE PART OF HIS PLAN.
THANK YOU, GOOD SIR.
"THE BLONDY" IS THIS WAY.
WHAT...? MY LADY, WHY WOULD YOU NEED TO GO THERE?
I DON'T. BUT AS GRIMPEN IS A SMALL VILLAGE WITHOUT A POST-MASTER, YOU MUST GO TO A PUB TO MAIL YOUR LETTER.
ALL THE VILLAGERS BRING THEIR MAIL TO "THE BLONDY" TO HAVE IT SENT AWAY WITH THE POST.
AND THEY GO THERE TO PICK UP WHAT MAY HAVE COME FOR THEM, OR PAY THREE PENNIES TO HAVE IT DELIVERED.
......

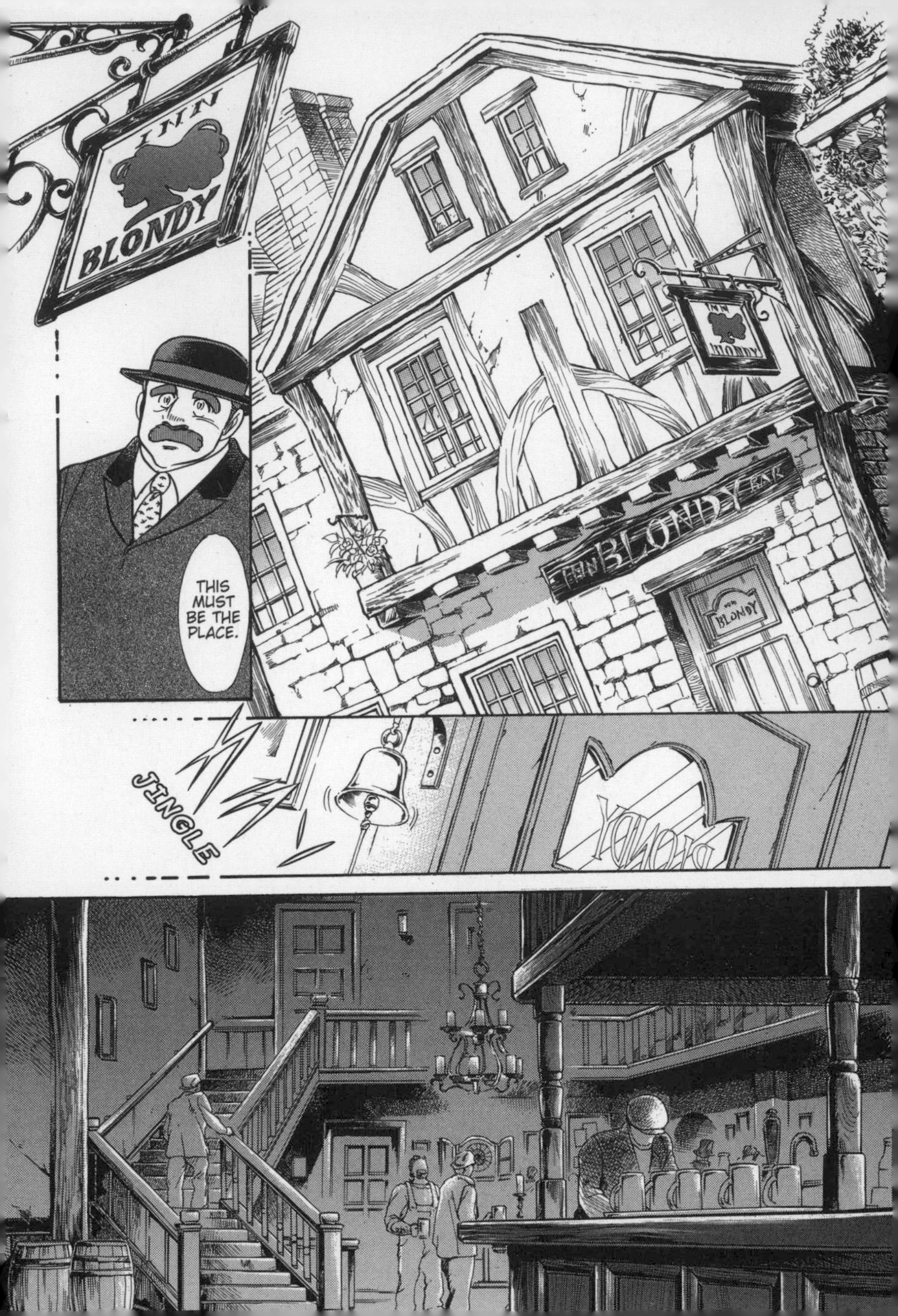
INN BLONDY
BLONDY
THIS MUST BE THE PLACE.
JINGLE

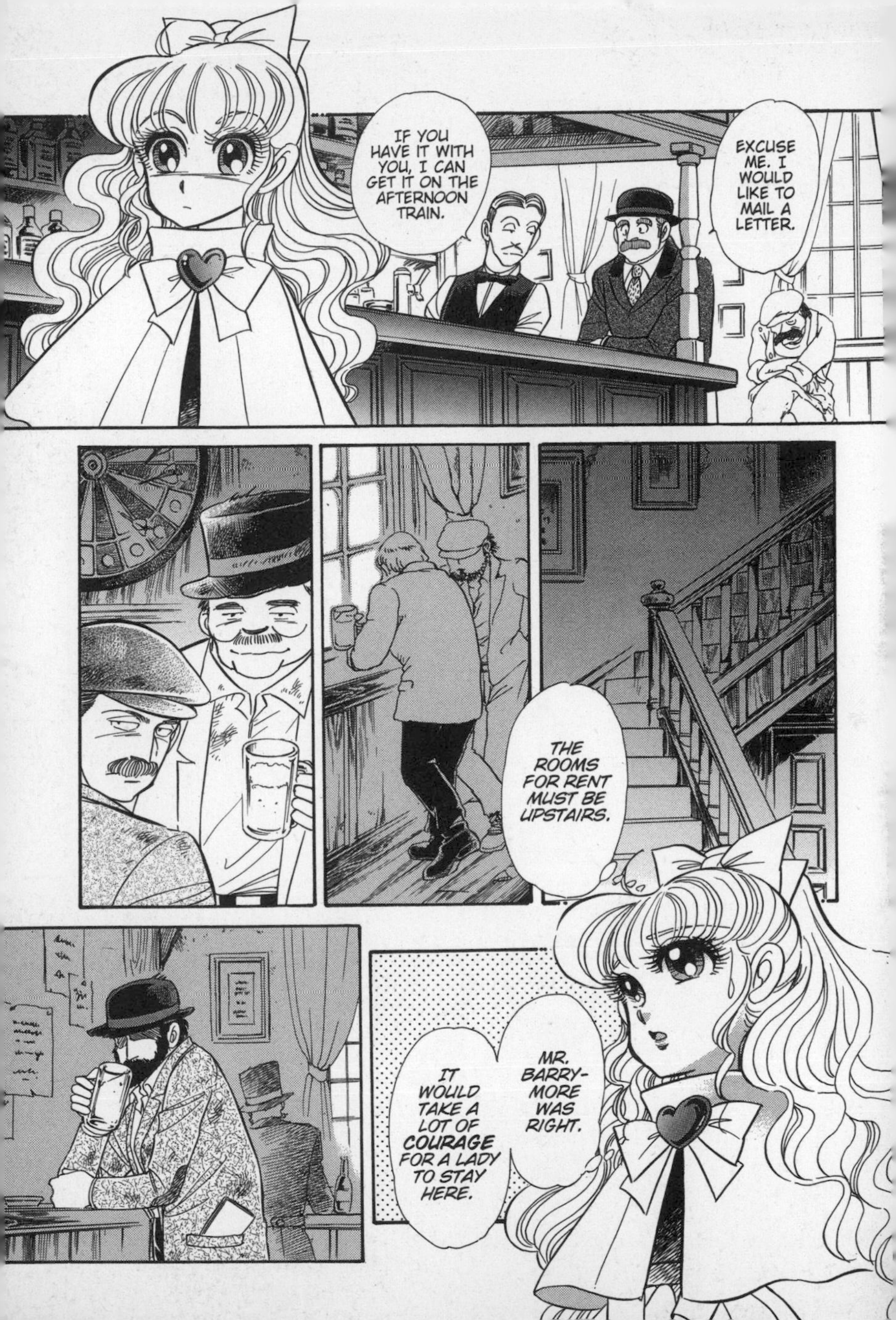
EXCUSE ME. I WOULD LIKE TO MAIL A LETTER.
IF YOU HAVE IT WITH YOU, I CAN GET IT ON THE AFTERNOON TRAIN.
THE ROOMS FOR RENT MUST BE UPSTAIRS.
MR. BARRY-MORE WAS RIGHT.
IT WOULD TAKE A LOT OF **COURAGE** FOR A LADY TO STAY HERE.

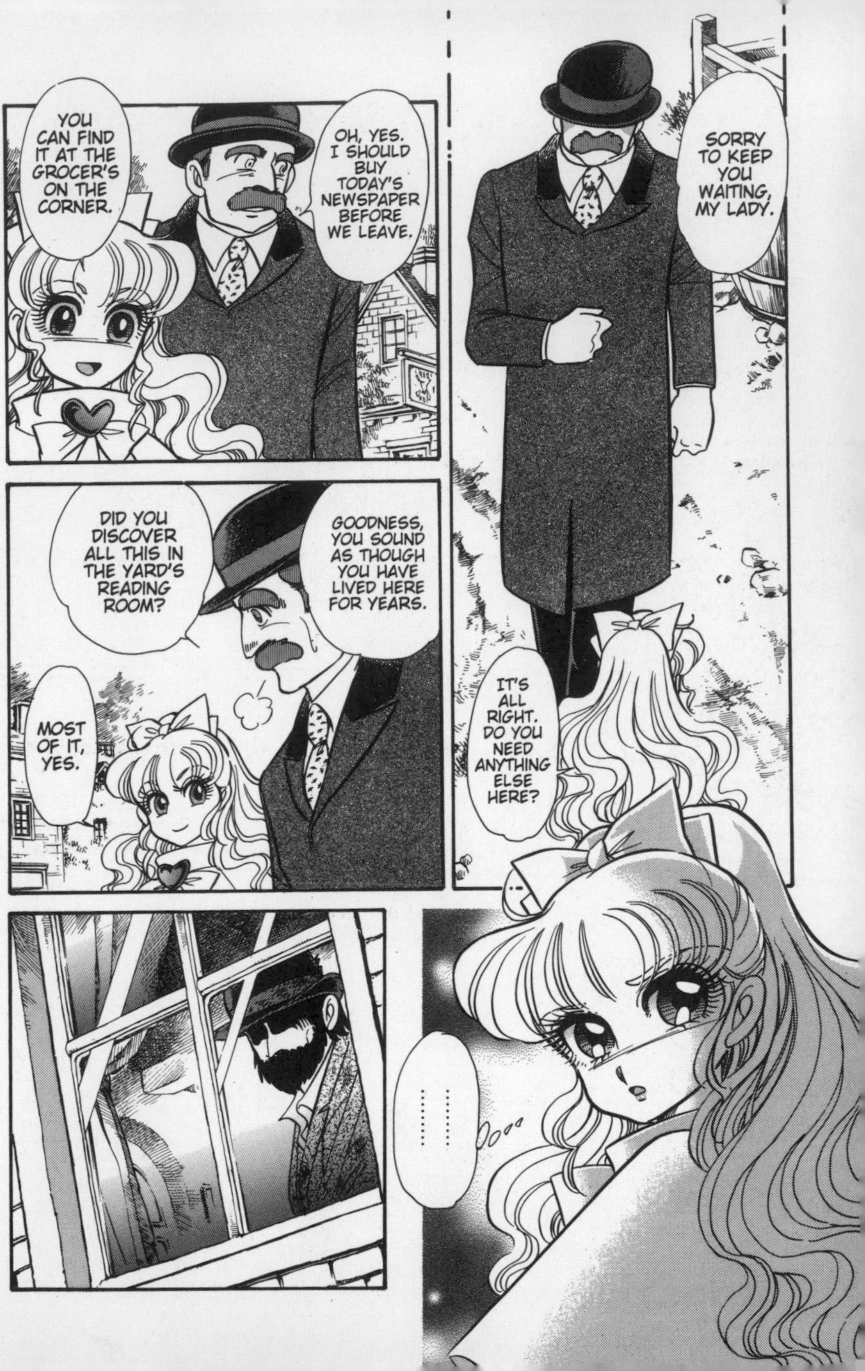
SORRY TO KEEP YOU WAITING, MY LADY.
IT'S ALL RIGHT. DO YOU NEED ANYTHING ELSE HERE?
OH, YES. I SHOULD BUY TODAY'S NEWSPAPER BEFORE WE LEAVE.
YOU CAN FIND IT AT THE GROCER'S ON THE CORNER.
GOODNESS, YOU SOUND AS THOUGH YOU HAVE LIVED HERE FOR YEARS.
DID YOU DISCOVER ALL THIS IN THE YARD'S READING ROOM?
MOST OF IT, YES.
......

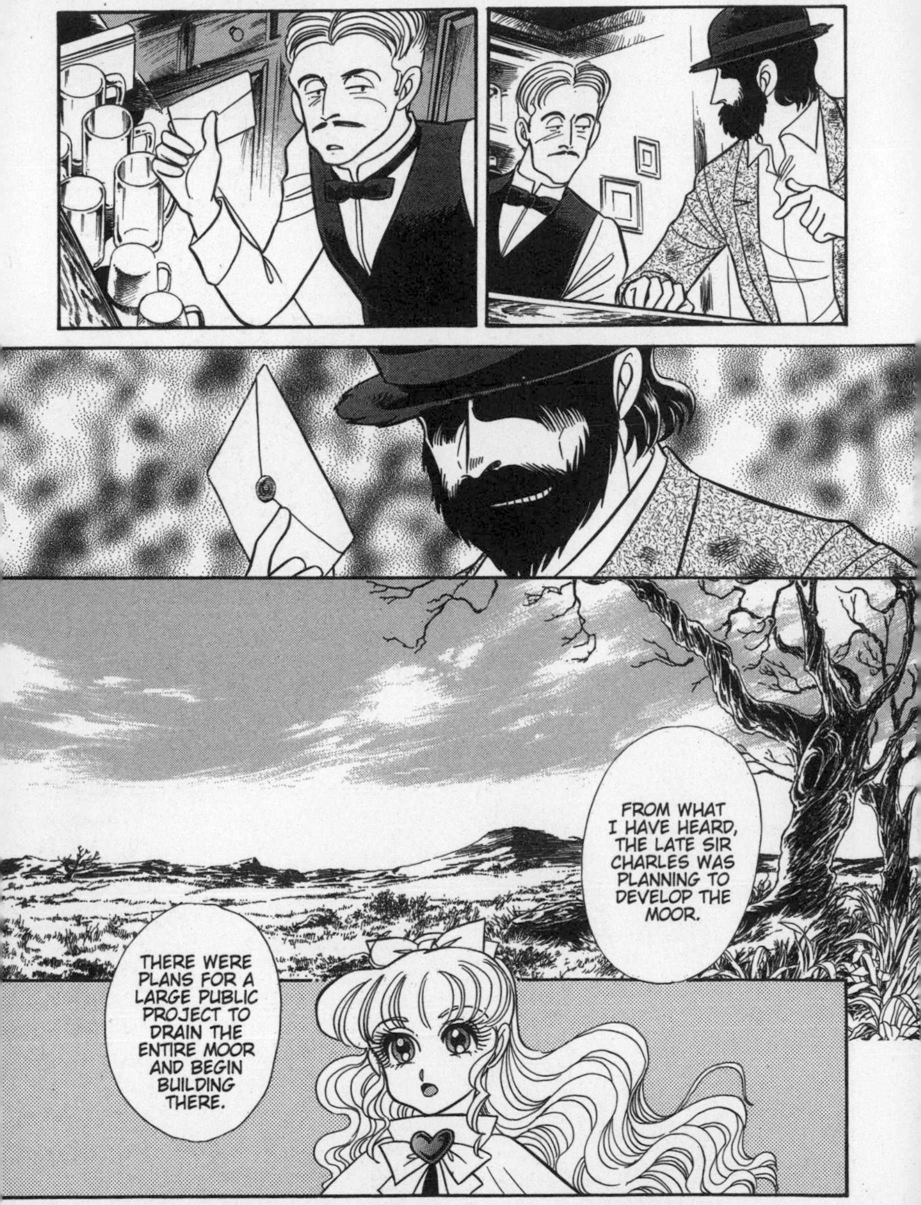
FROM WHAT I HAVE HEARD, THE LATE SIR CHARLES WAS PLANNING TO DEVELOP THE MOOR.
THERE WERE PLANS FOR A LARGE PUBLIC PROJECT TO DRAIN THE ENTIRE MOOR AND BEGIN BUILDING THERE.

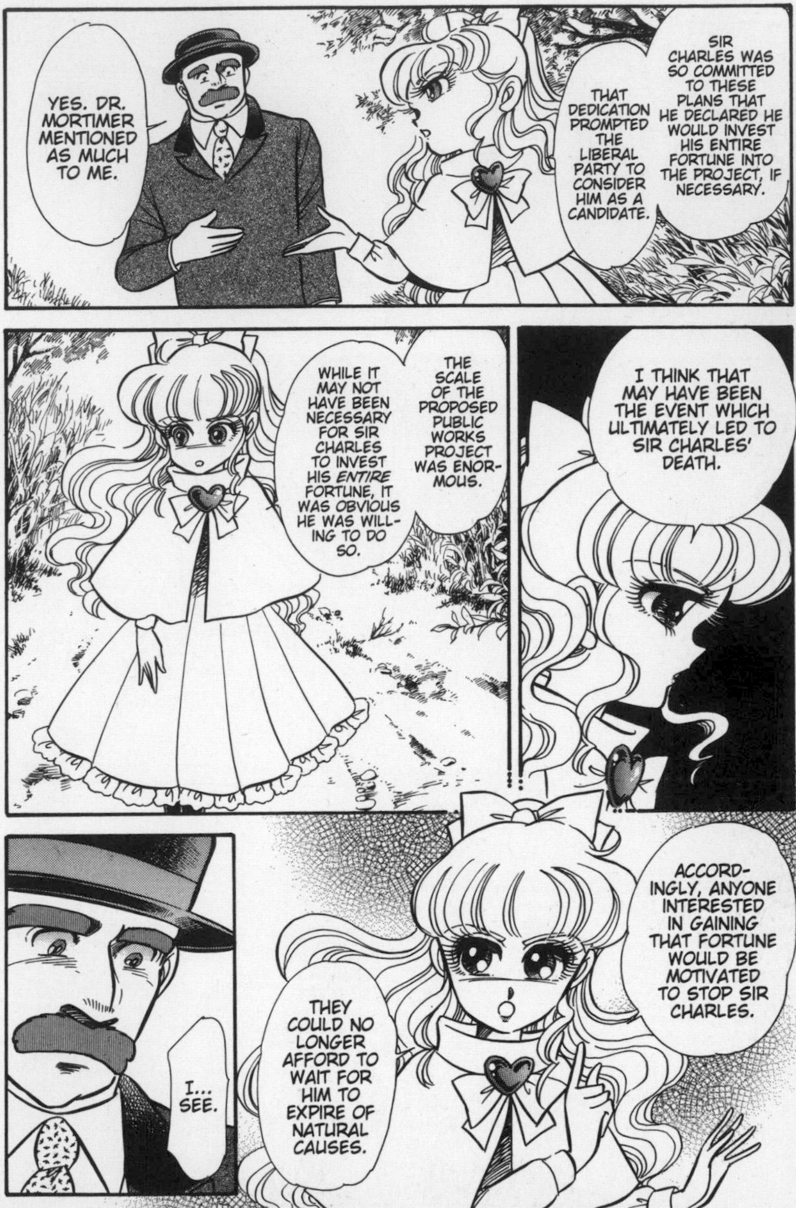
SIR CHARLES WAS SO COMMITTED TO THESE PLANS THAT HE DECLARED HE WOULD INVEST HIS ENTIRE FORTUNE INTO THE PROJECT, IF NECESSARY.
THAT DEDICATION PROMPTED THE LIBERAL PARTY TO CONSIDER HIM AS A CANDIDATE.
YES. DR. MORTIMER MENTIONED AS MUCH TO ME.
I THINK THAT MAY HAVE BEEN THE EVENT WHICH ULTIMATELY LED TO SIR CHARLES' DEATH.
THE SCALE OF THE PROPOSED PUBLIC WORKS PROJECT WAS ENORMOUS.
WHILE IT MAY NOT HAVE BEEN NECESSARY FOR SIR CHARLES TO INVEST HIS *ENTIRE* FORTUNE, IT WAS OBVIOUS HE WAS WILLING TO DO SO.
ACCORDINGLY, ANYONE INTERESTED IN GAINING THAT FORTUNE WOULD BE MOTIVATED TO STOP SIR CHARLES.
THEY COULD NO LONGER AFFORD TO WAIT FOR HIM TO EXPIRE OF NATURAL CAUSES.
I... SEE.

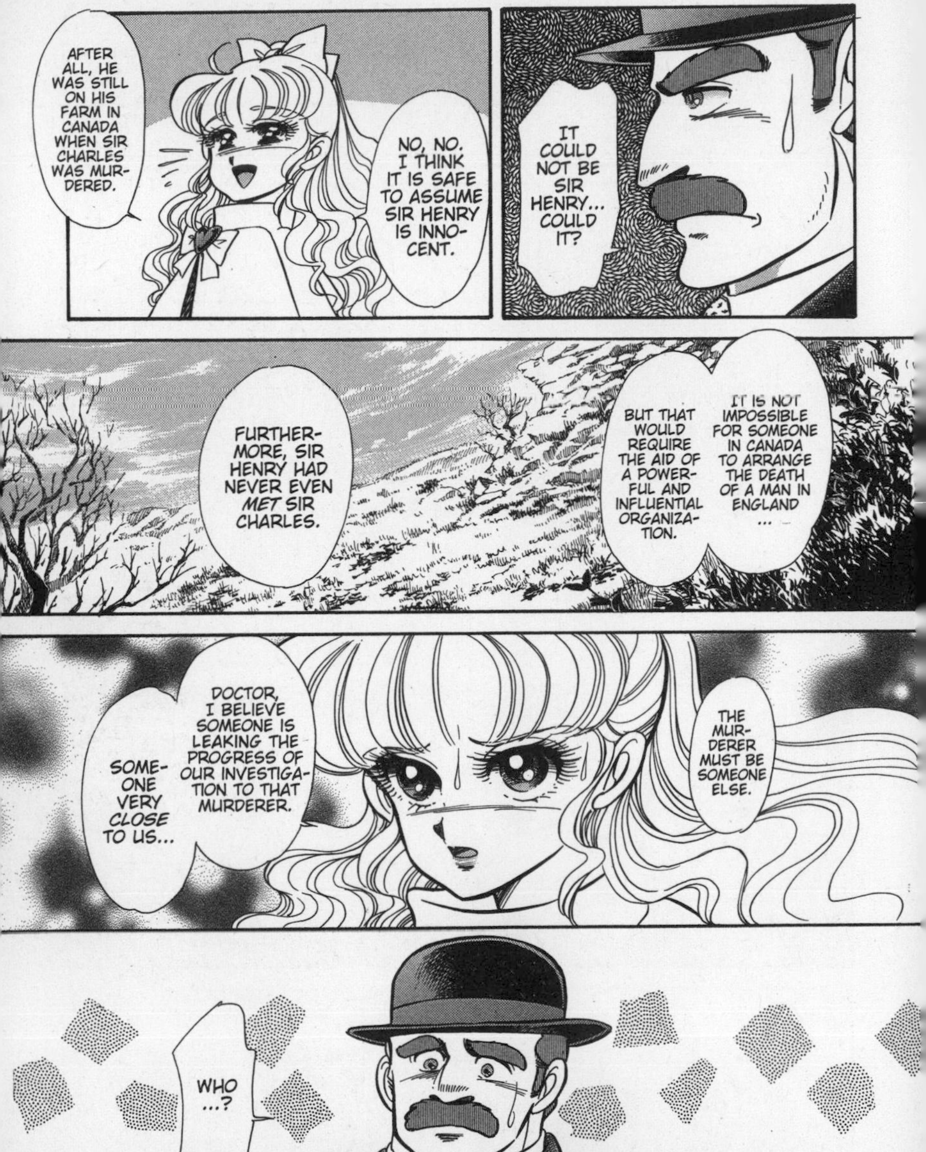
IT COULD NOT BE SIR HENRY... COULD IT?
NO, NO. I THINK IT IS SAFE TO ASSUME SIR HENRY IS INNOCENT.
AFTER ALL, HE WAS STILL ON HIS FARM IN CANADA WHEN SIR CHARLES WAS MURDERED.
IT IS NOT IMPOSSIBLE FOR SOMEONE IN CANADA TO ARRANGE THE DEATH OF A MAN IN ENGLAND ...
BUT THAT WOULD REQUIRE THE AID OF A POWERFUL AND INFLUENTIAL ORGANIZATION.
FURTHERMORE, SIR HENRY HAD NEVER EVEN *MET* SIR CHARLES.
THE MURDERER MUST BE SOMEONE ELSE.
DOCTOR, I BELIEVE SOMEONE IS LEAKING THE PROGRESS OF OUR INVESTIGATION TO THAT MURDERER.
SOMEONE VERY *CLOSE* TO US...
WHO ...?

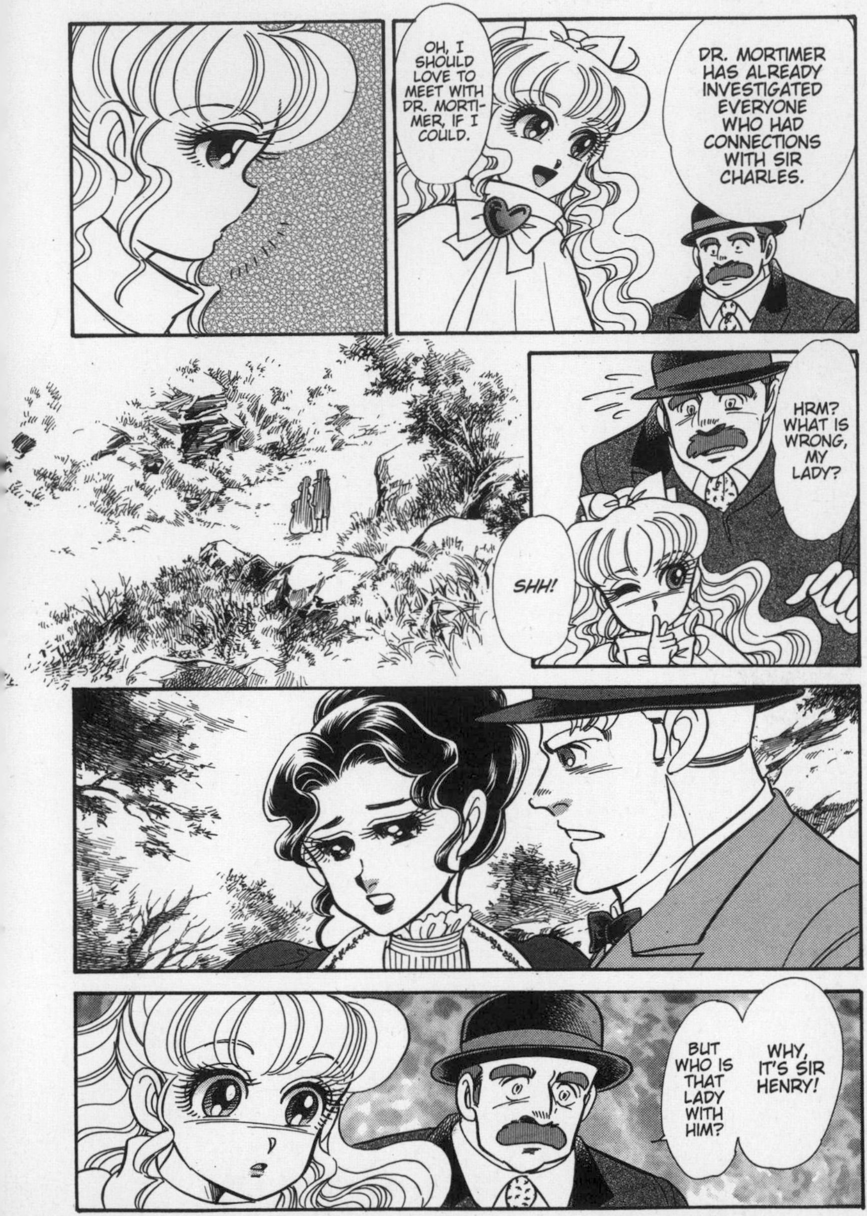
DR. MORTIMER HAS ALREADY INVESTIGATED EVERYONE WHO HAD CONNECTIONS WITH SIR CHARLES.
OH, I SHOULD LOVE TO MEET WITH DR. MORTI-MER, IF I COULD.
HRM? WHAT IS WRONG, MY LADY?
SHH!
WHY, IT'S SIR HENRY!
BUT WHO IS THAT LADY WITH HIM?

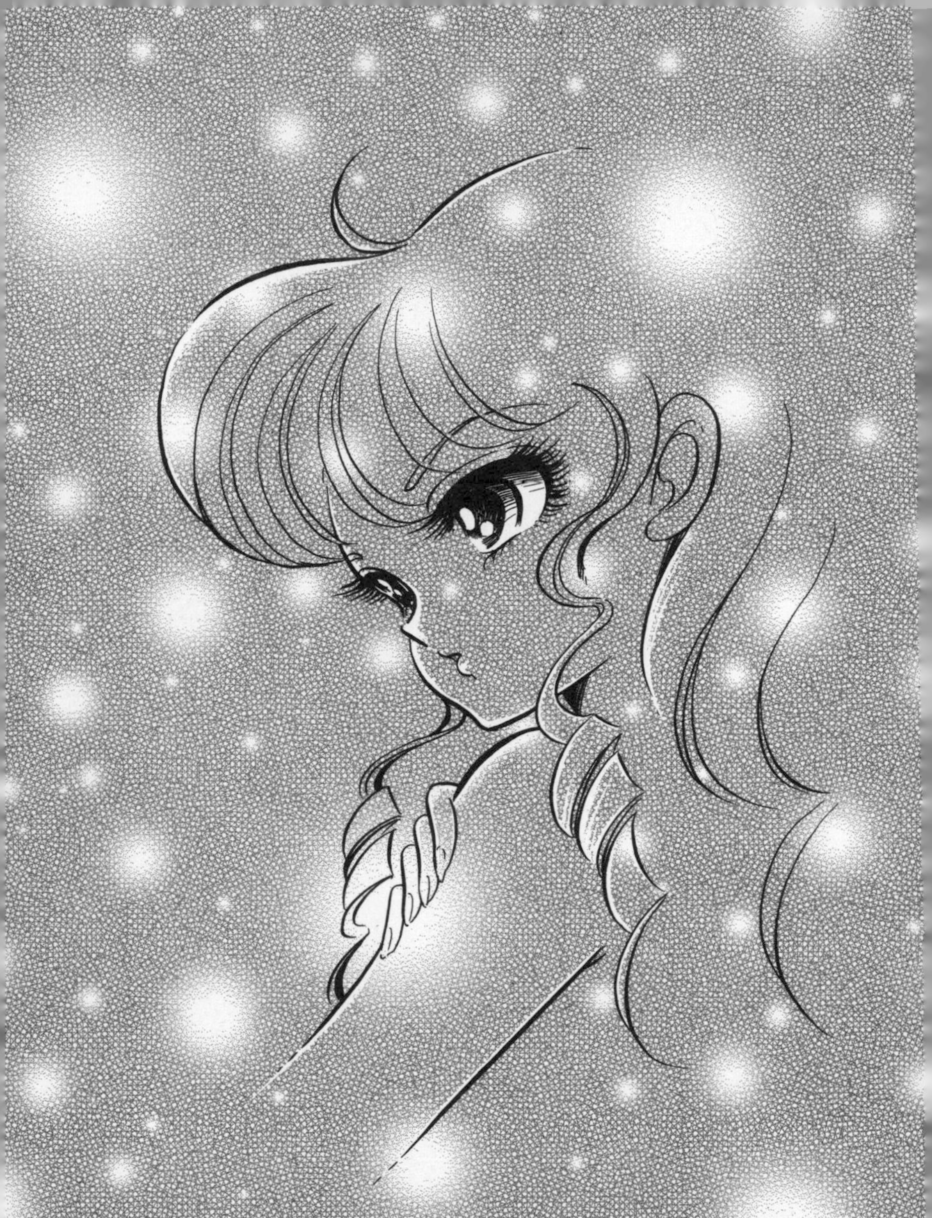

The Hound of the Baskervilles (6)

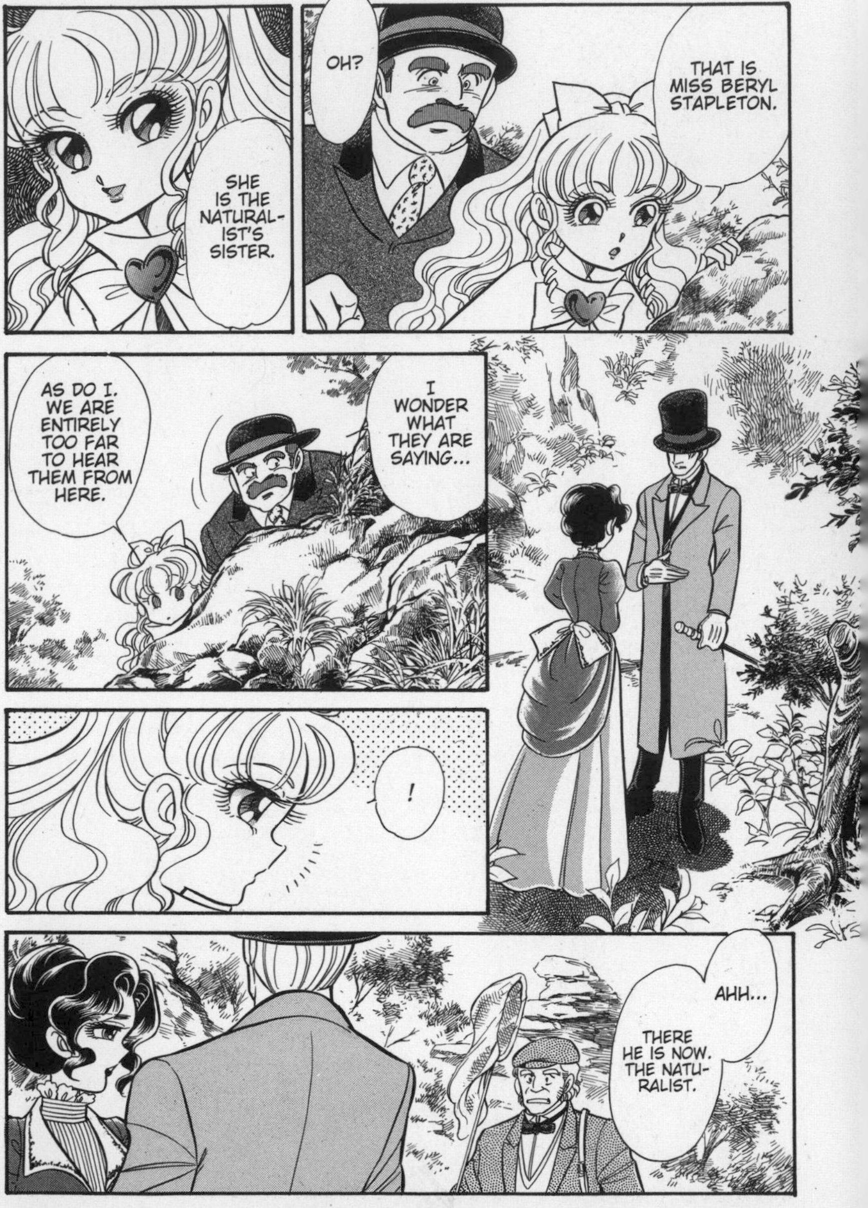
THAT IS MISS BERYL STAPLETON.
OH?
SHE IS THE NATURAL-IST'S SISTER.
I WONDER WHAT THEY ARE SAYING...
AS DO I. WE ARE ENTIRELY TOO FAR TO HEAR THEM FROM HERE.
!
AHH...
THERE HE IS NOW. THE NATU-RALIST.

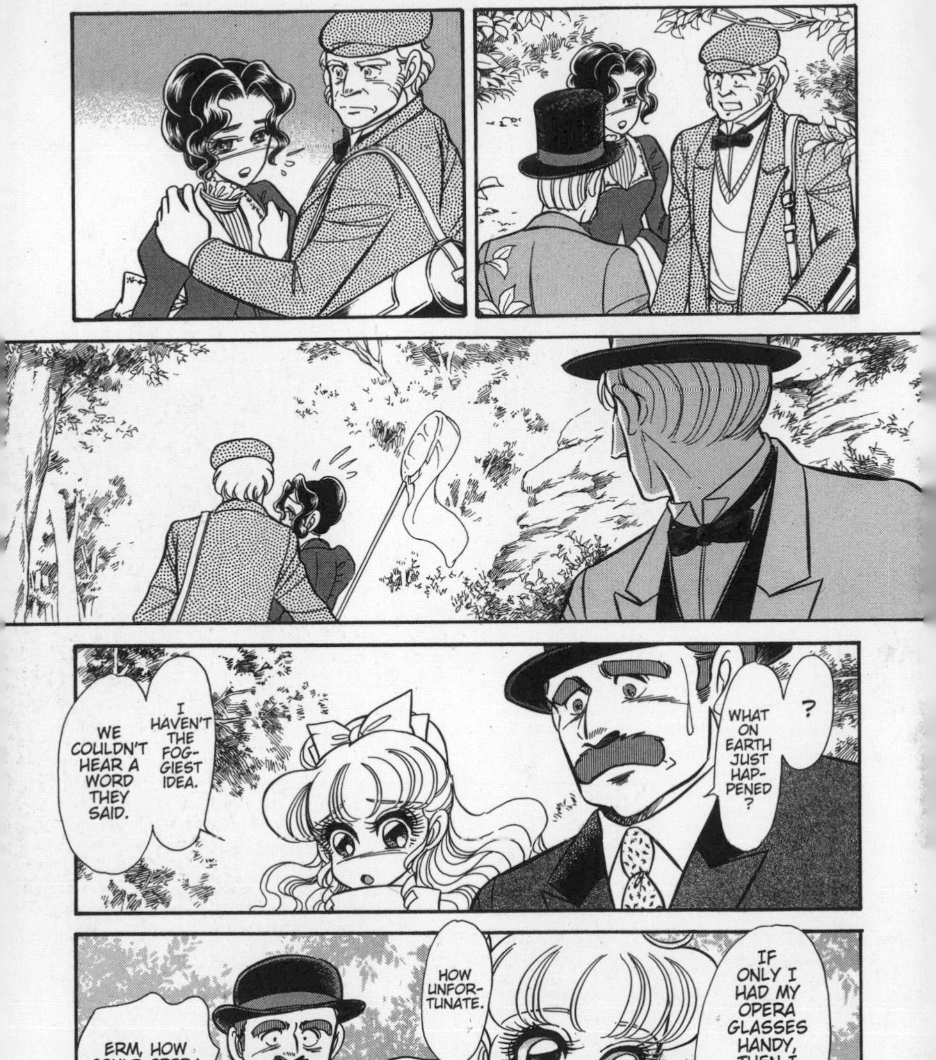
?
WHAT ON EARTH JUST HAPPENED?
I HAVEN'T THE FOGGIEST IDEA.
WE COULDN'T HEAR A WORD THEY SAID.
IF ONLY I HAD MY OPERA GLASSES HANDY, THEN I COULD HAVE MADE IT OUT.
HOW UNFORTUNATE.
ERM, HOW COULD OPERA GLASSES HELP YOU TO HEAR THEIR CONVERSATION?

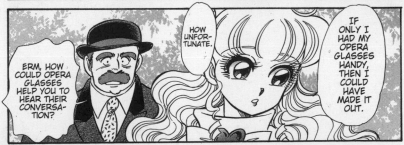

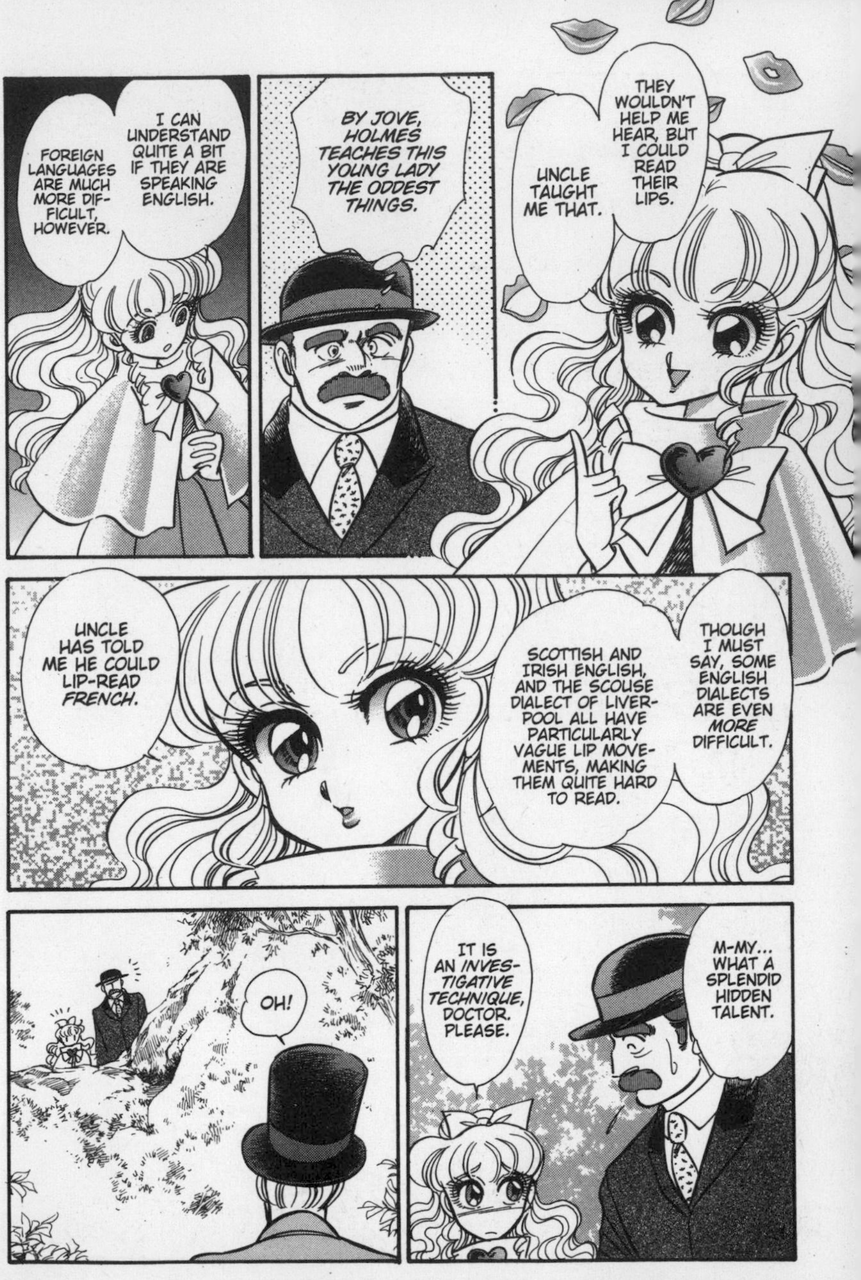
THEY WOULDN'T HELP ME HEAR, BUT I COULD READ THEIR LIPS.
UNCLE TAUGHT ME THAT.
BY JOVE, HOLMES TEACHES THIS YOUNG LADY THE ODDEST THINGS.
I CAN UNDERSTAND QUITE A BIT IF THEY ARE SPEAKING ENGLISH.
FOREIGN LANGUAGES ARE MUCH MORE DIFFICULT, HOWEVER.
THOUGH I MUST SAY, SOME ENGLISH DIALECTS ARE EVEN MORE DIFFICULT.
SCOTTISH AND IRISH ENGLISH, AND THE SCOUSE DIALECT OF LIVERPOOL ALL HAVE PARTICULARLY VAGUE LIP MOVEMENTS, MAKING THEM QUITE HARD TO READ.
UNCLE HAS TOLD ME HE COULD LIP-READ FRENCH.
M-MY... WHAT A SPLENDID HIDDEN TALENT.
IT IS AN INVESTIGATIVE TECHNIQUE, DOCTOR. PLEASE.
OH!

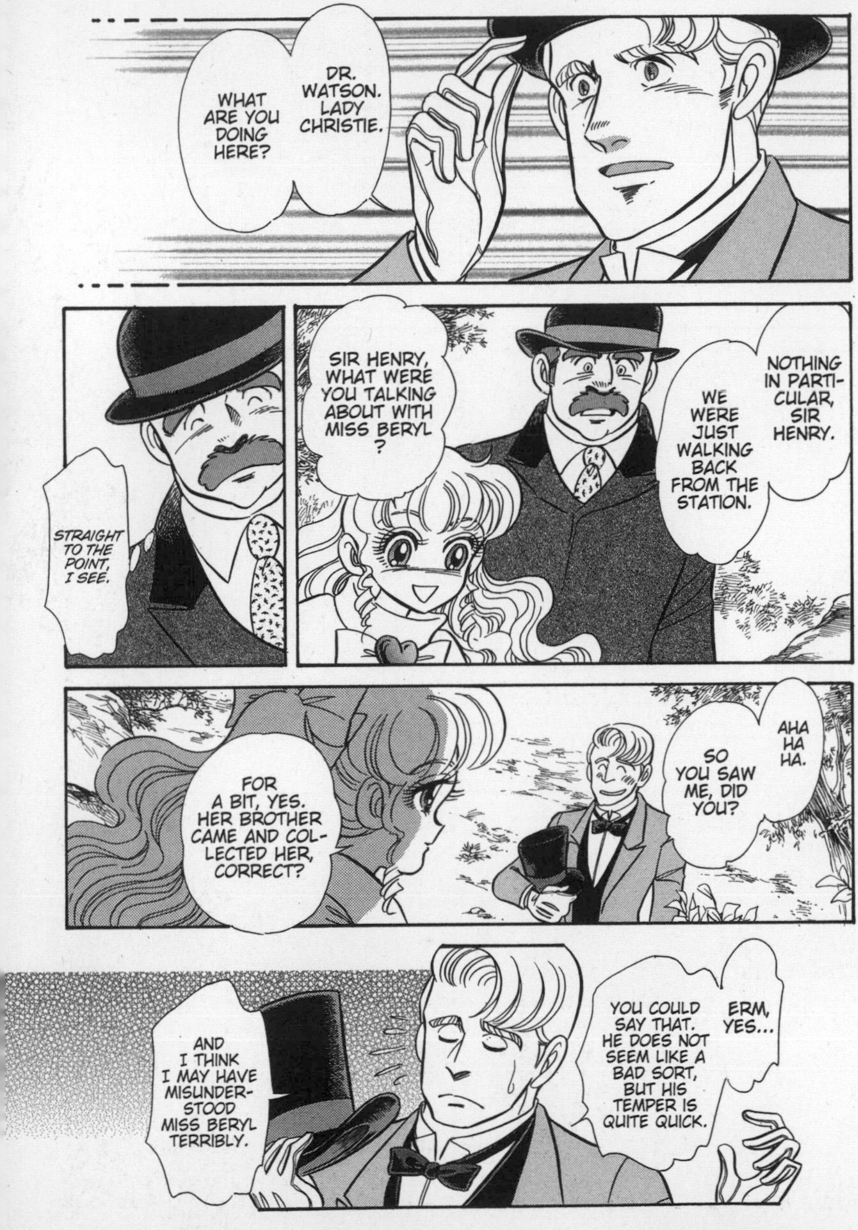
DR. WATSON. LADY CHRISTIE.
WHAT ARE YOU DOING HERE?
NOTHING IN PARTICULAR, SIR HENRY.
WE WERE JUST WALKING BACK FROM THE STATION.
SIR HENRY, WHAT WERE YOU TALKING ABOUT WITH MISS BERYL?
STRAIGHT TO THE POINT, I SEE.
AHA HA HA.
SO YOU SAW ME, DID YOU?
FOR A BIT, YES. HER BROTHER CAME AND COLLECTED HER, CORRECT?
ERM, YES...
YOU COULD SAY THAT. HE DOES NOT SEEM LIKE A BAD SORT, BUT HIS TEMPER IS QUITE QUICK.
AND I THINK I MAY HAVE MISUNDERSTOOD MISS BERYL TERRIBLY.

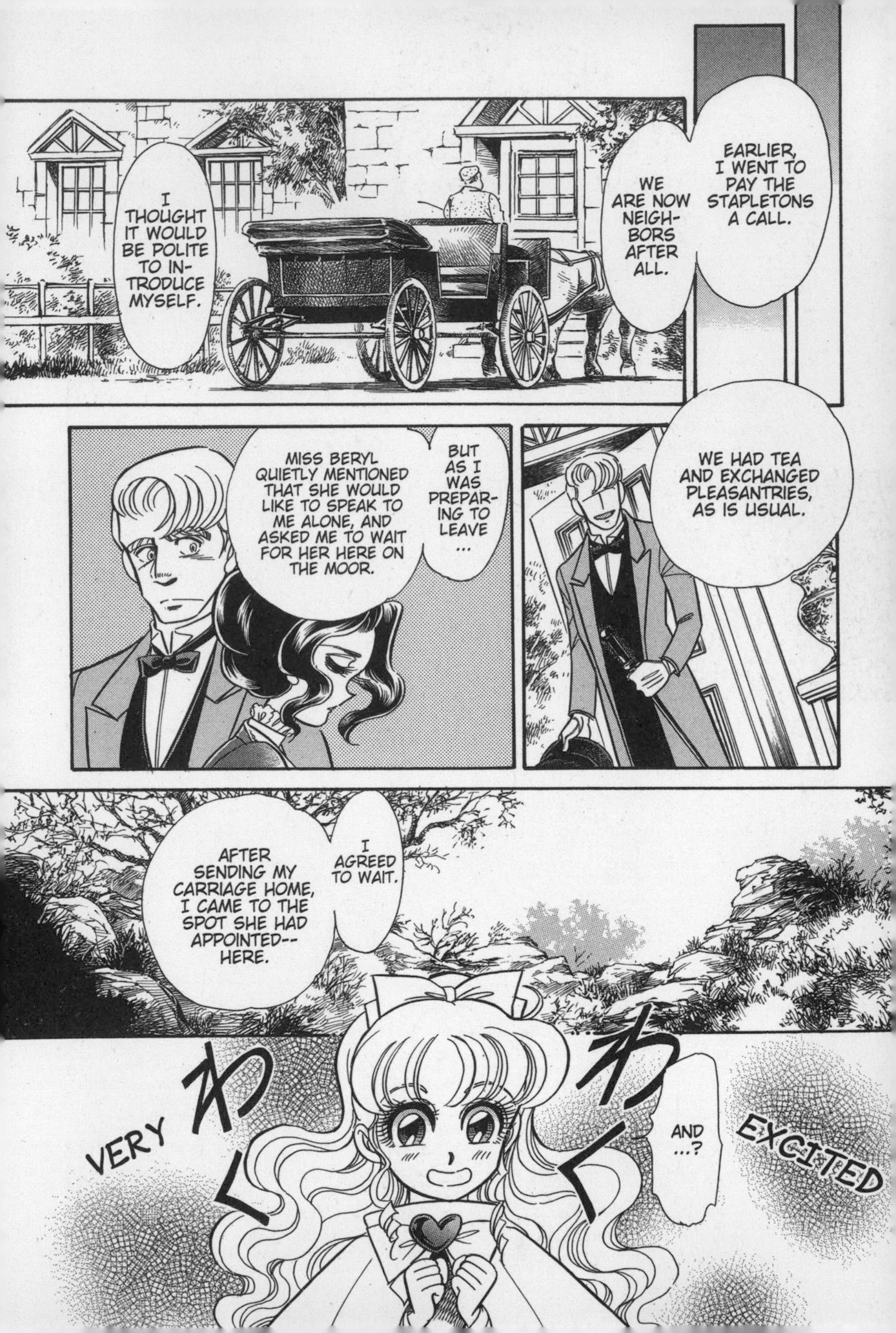
EARLIER, I WENT TO PAY THE STAPLETONS A CALL.
WE ARE NOW NEIGHBORS AFTER ALL.
I THOUGHT IT WOULD BE POLITE TO INTRODUCE MYSELF.
WE HAD TEA AND EXCHANGED PLEASANTRIES, AS IS USUAL.
BUT AS I WAS PREPARING TO LEAVE ...
MISS BERYL QUIETLY MENTIONED THAT SHE WOULD LIKE TO SPEAK TO ME ALONE, AND ASKED ME TO WAIT FOR HER HERE ON THE MOOR.
I AGREED TO WAIT.
AFTER SENDING MY CARRIAGE HOME, I CAME TO THE SPOT SHE HAD APPOINTED--HERE.
AND ...?
VERY EXCITED

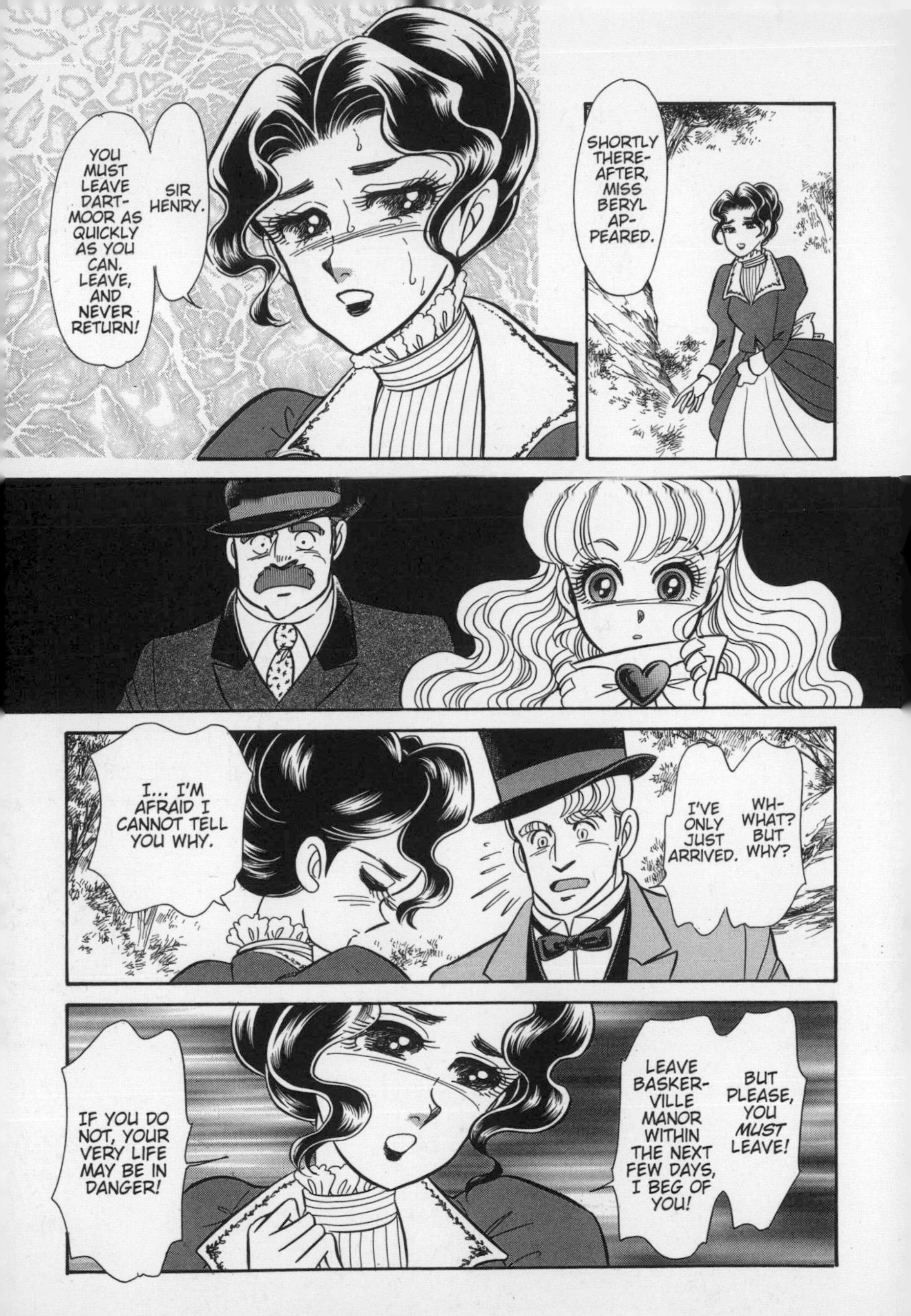
SHORTLY THERE-AFTER, MISS BERYL AP-PEARED.
SIR HENRY.
YOU MUST LEAVE DART-MOOR AS QUICKLY AS YOU CAN. LEAVE, AND NEVER RETURN!
WH- WHAT? BUT WHY?
I'VE ONLY JUST ARRIVED.
I... I'M AFRAID I CANNOT TELL YOU WHY.
BUT PLEASE, YOU *MUST* LEAVE!
LEAVE BASKER-VILLE MANOR WITHIN THE NEXT FEW DAYS, I BEG OF YOU!
IF YOU DO NOT, YOUR VERY LIFE MAY BE IN DANGER!

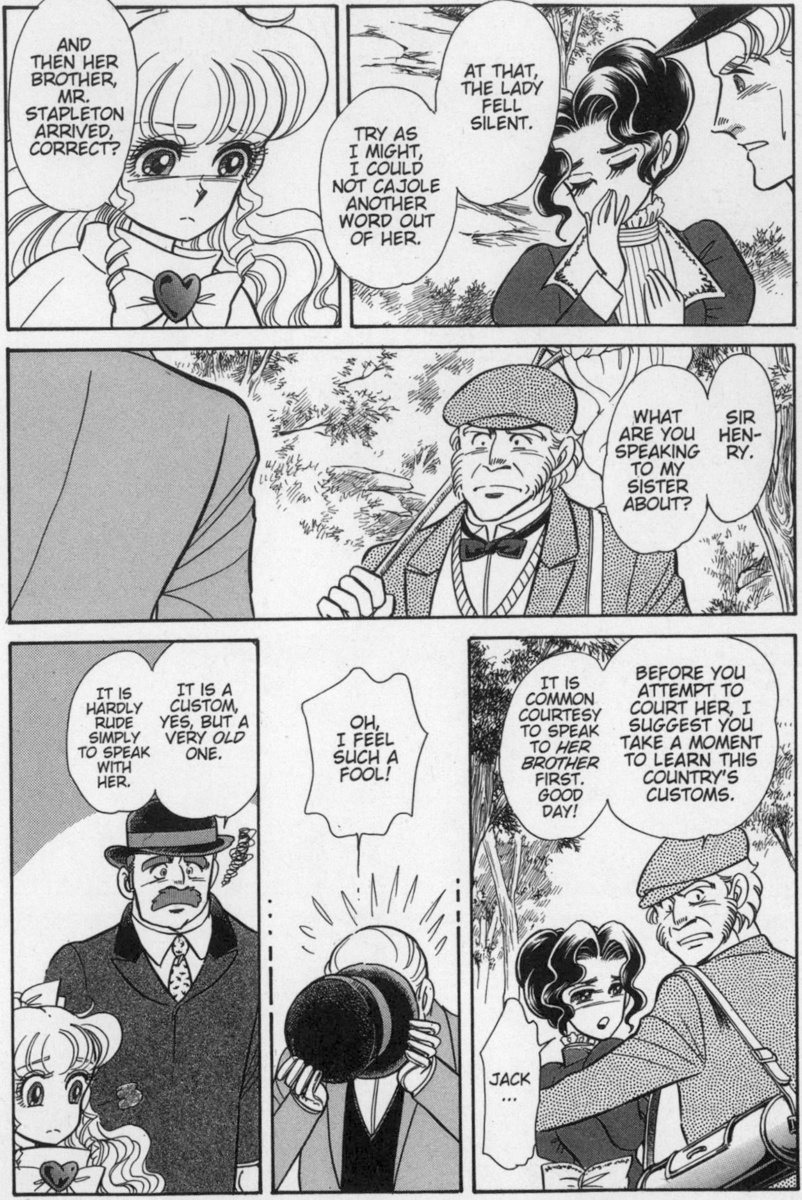
AT THAT, THE LADY FELL SILENT.
TRY AS I MIGHT, I COULD NOT CAJOLE ANOTHER WORD OUT OF HER.
AND THEN HER BROTHER, MR. STAPLETON ARRIVED, CORRECT?
SIR HENRY.
WHAT ARE YOU SPEAKING TO MY SISTER ABOUT?
BEFORE YOU ATTEMPT TO COURT HER, I SUGGEST YOU TAKE A MOMENT TO LEARN THIS COUNTRY'S CUSTOMS.
IT IS COMMON COURTESY TO SPEAK TO *HER BROTHER* FIRST. GOOD DAY!
JACK ...
OH, I FEEL SUCH A FOOL!
IT IS A CUSTOM, YES, BUT A VERY *OLD* ONE.
IT IS HARDLY RUDE SIMPLY TO SPEAK WITH HER.

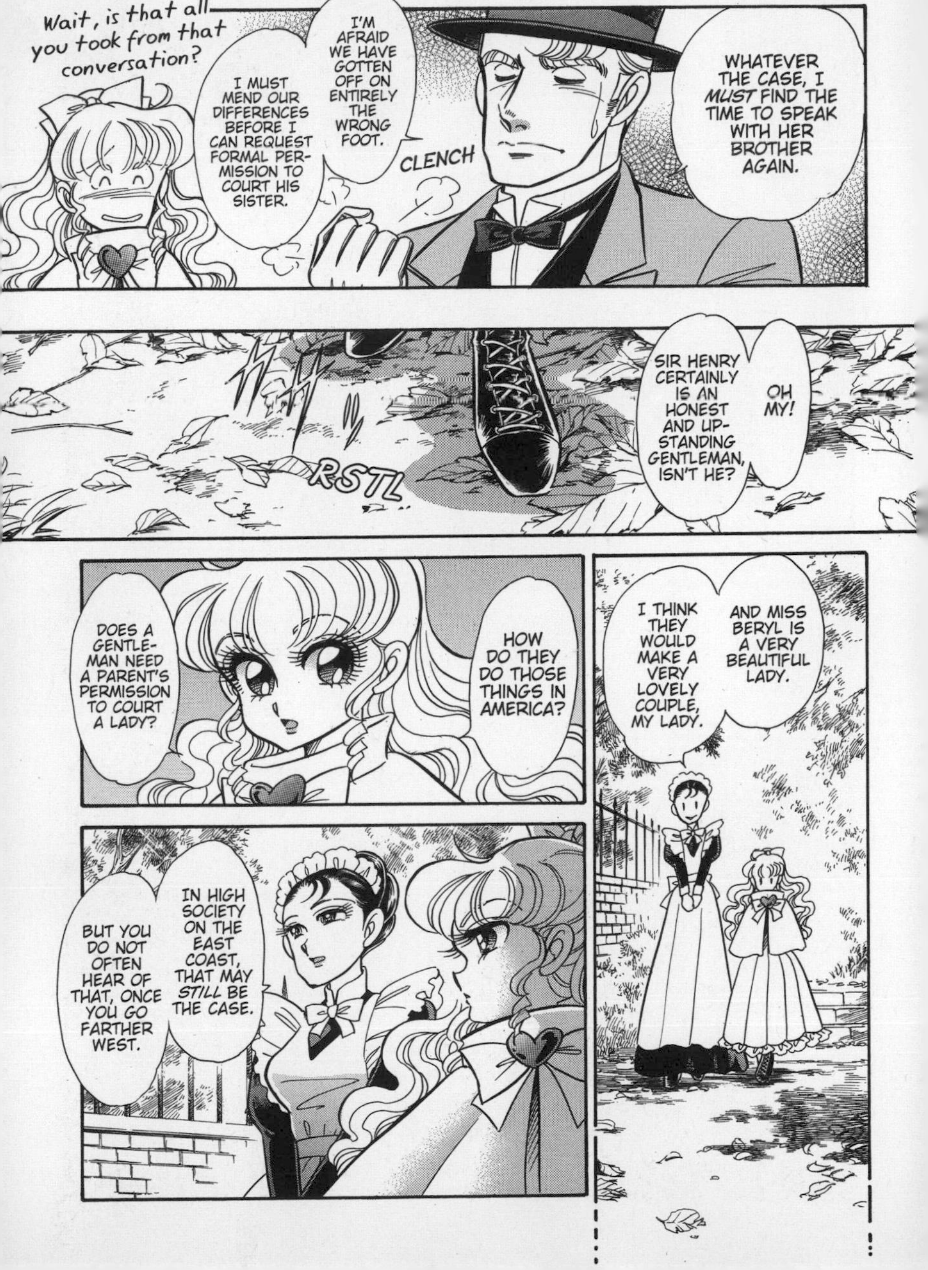
WHATEVER THE CASE, I MUST FIND THE TIME TO SPEAK WITH HER BROTHER AGAIN.
I'M AFRAID WE HAVE GOTTEN OFF ON ENTIRELY THE WRONG FOOT.
I MUST MEND OUR DIFFERENCES BEFORE I CAN REQUEST FORMAL PERMISSION TO COURT HIS SISTER.
CLENCH
Wait, is that all you took from that conversation?
OH MY!
SIR HENRY CERTAINLY IS AN HONEST AND UPSTANDING GENTLEMAN, ISN'T HE?
RSTL
AND MISS BERYL IS A VERY BEAUTIFUL LADY.
I THINK THEY WOULD MAKE A VERY LOVELY COUPLE, MY LADY.
HOW DO THEY DO THOSE THINGS IN AMERICA?
DOES A GENTLEMAN NEED A PARENT'S PERMISSION TO COURT A LADY?
IN HIGH SOCIETY ON THE EAST COAST, THAT MAY STILL BE THE CASE.
BUT YOU DO NOT OFTEN HEAR OF THAT, ONCE YOU GO FARTHER WEST.

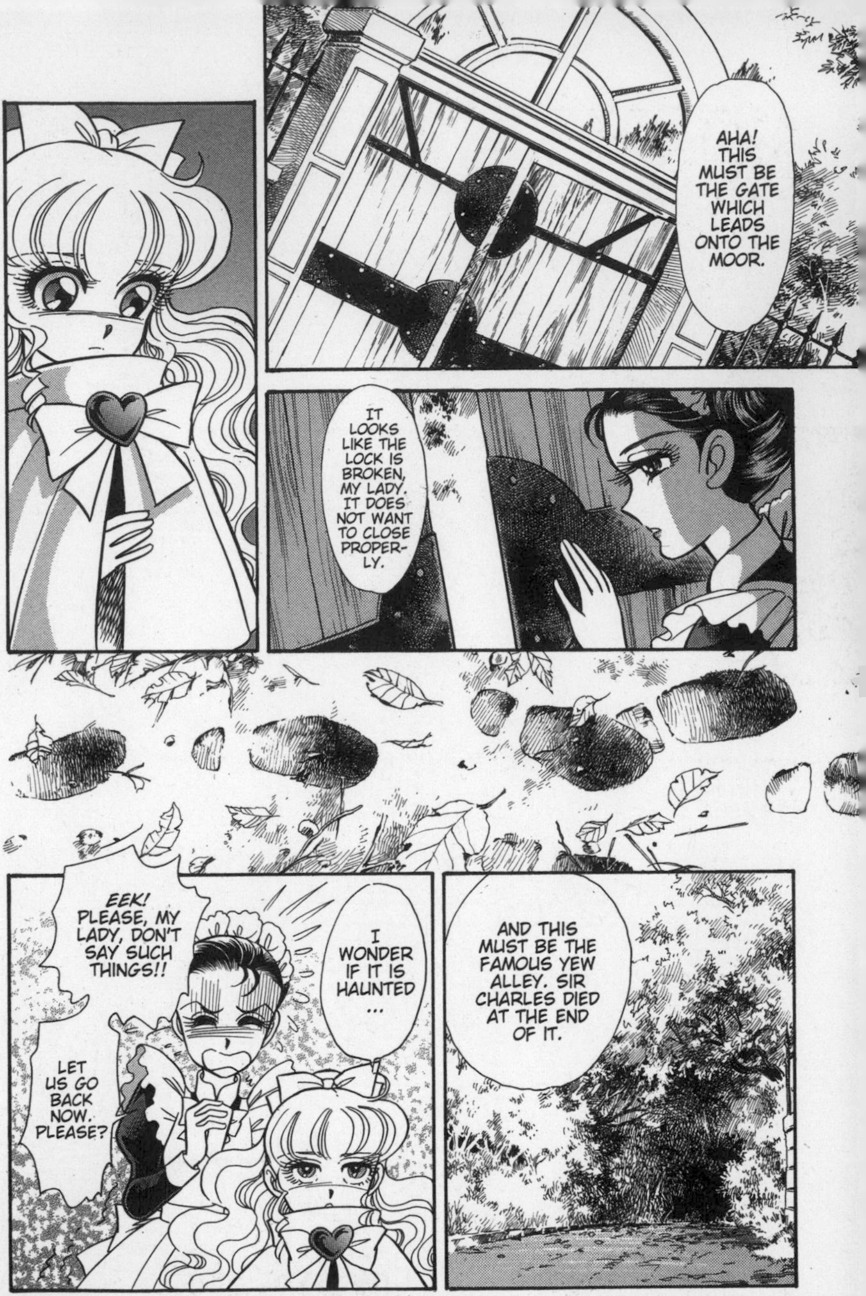
AHA! THIS MUST BE THE GATE WHICH LEADS ONTO THE MOOR.
IT LOOKS LIKE THE LOCK IS BROKEN, MY LADY. IT DOES NOT WANT TO CLOSE PROPER-LY.
AND THIS MUST BE THE FAMOUS YEW ALLEY. SIR CHARLES DIED AT THE END OF IT.
I WONDER IF IT IS HAUNTED ...
EEK! PLEASE, MY LADY, DON'T SAY SUCH THINGS!!
LET US GO BACK NOW. PLEASE?

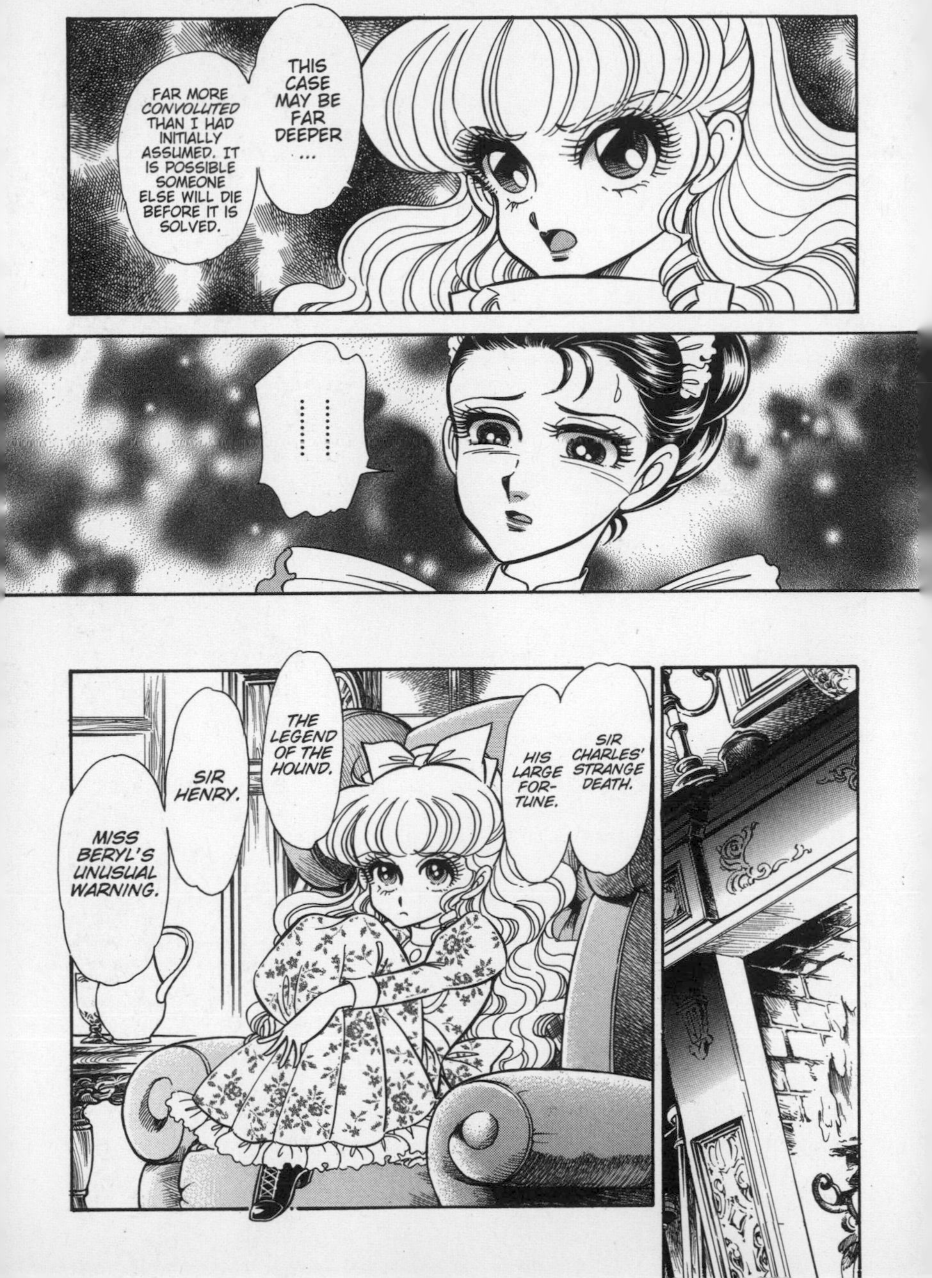
THIS CASE MAY BE FAR DEEPER ...
FAR MORE CONVOLUTED THAN I HAD INITIALLY ASSUMED. IT IS POSSIBLE SOMEONE ELSE WILL DIE BEFORE IT IS SOLVED.
......
SIR CHARLES' STRANGE DEATH.
HIS LARGE FOR-TUNE.
THE LEGEND OF THE HOUND.
SIR HENRY.
MISS BERYL'S UNUSUAL WARNING.

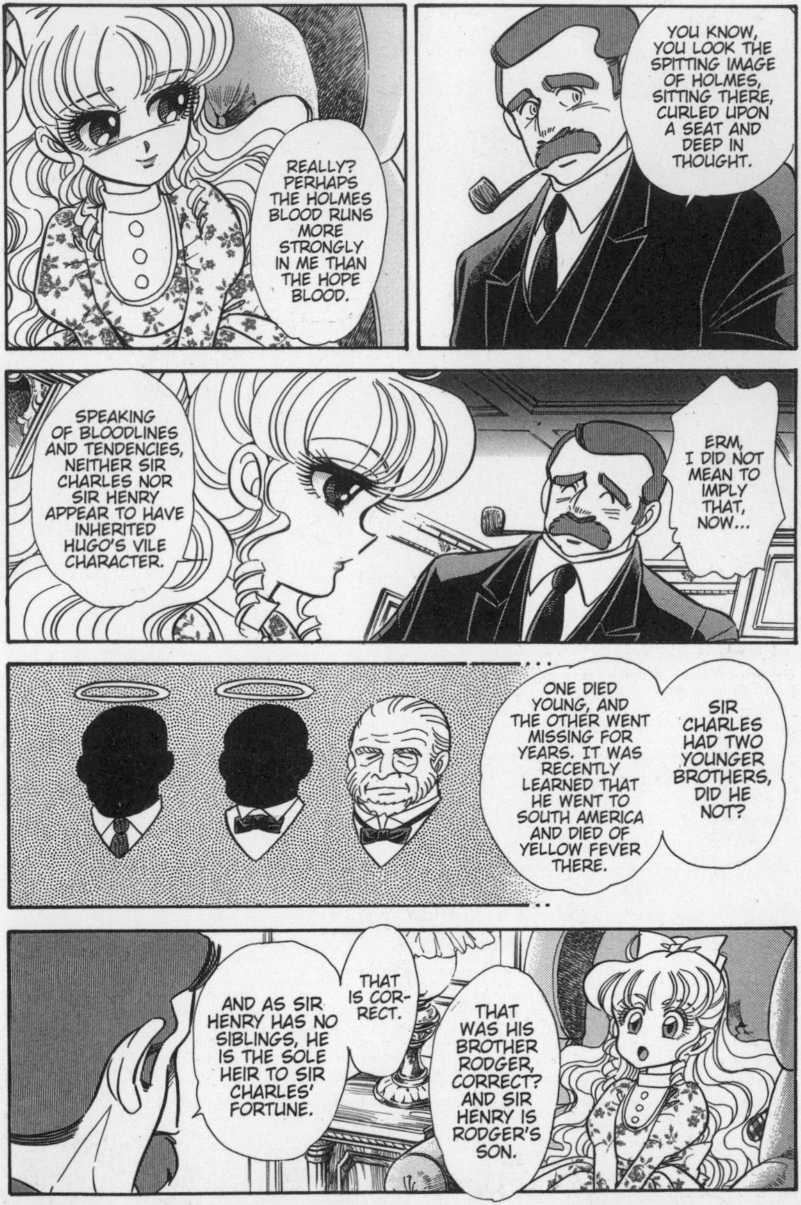
YOU KNOW, YOU LOOK THE SPITTING IMAGE OF HOLMES, SITTING THERE, CURLED UPON A SEAT AND DEEP IN THOUGHT.
REALLY? PERHAPS THE HOLMES BLOOD RUNS MORE STRONGLY IN ME THAN THE HOPE BLOOD.
ERM, I DID NOT MEAN TO IMPLY THAT, NOW...
SPEAKING OF BLOODLINES AND TENDENCIES, NEITHER SIR CHARLES NOR SIR HENRY APPEAR TO HAVE INHERITED HUGO'S VILE CHARACTER.
SIR CHARLES HAD TWO YOUNGER BROTHERS, DID HE NOT?
ONE DIED YOUNG, AND THE OTHER WENT MISSING FOR YEARS. IT WAS RECENTLY LEARNED THAT HE WENT TO SOUTH AMERICA AND DIED OF YELLOW FEVER THERE.
THAT WAS HIS BROTHER RODGER, CORRECT? AND SIR HENRY IS RODGER'S SON.
THAT IS COR-RECT.
AND AS SIR HENRY HAS NO SIBLINGS, HE IS THE SOLE HEIR TO SIR CHARLES' FORTUNE.

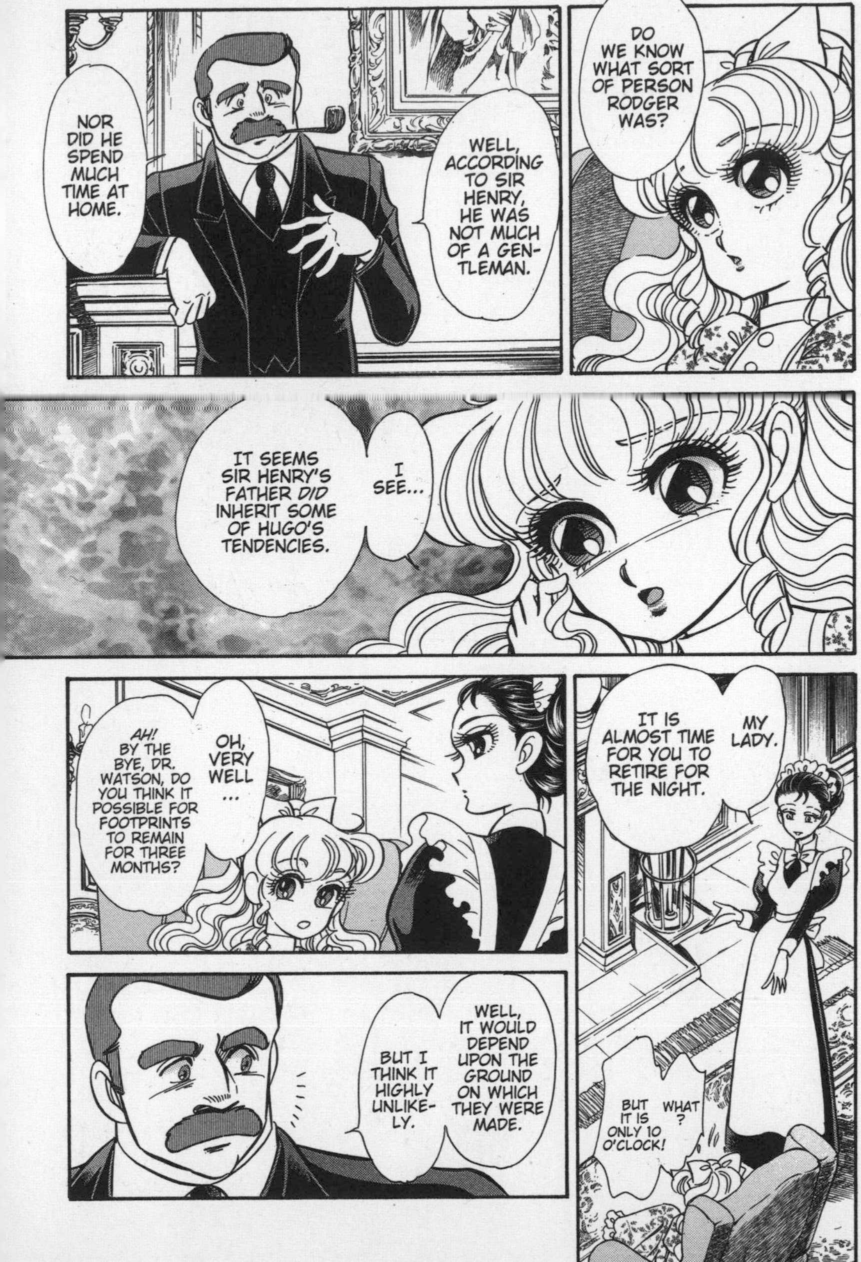
DO WE KNOW WHAT SORT OF PERSON RODGER WAS?
WELL, ACCORDING TO SIR HENRY, HE WAS NOT MUCH OF A GENTLEMAN.
NOR DID HE SPEND MUCH TIME AT HOME.
I SEE...
IT SEEMS SIR HENRY'S FATHER *DID* INHERIT SOME OF HUGO'S TENDENCIES.
MY LADY.
IT IS ALMOST TIME FOR YOU TO RETIRE FOR THE NIGHT.
WHAT?
BUT IT IS ONLY 10 O'CLOCK!
OH, VERY WELL ...
AH! BY THE BYE, DR. WATSON, DO YOU THINK IT POSSIBLE FOR FOOTPRINTS TO REMAIN FOR THREE MONTHS?
WELL, IT WOULD DEPEND UPON THE GROUND ON WHICH THEY WERE MADE.
BUT I THINK IT HIGHLY UNLIKE-LY.

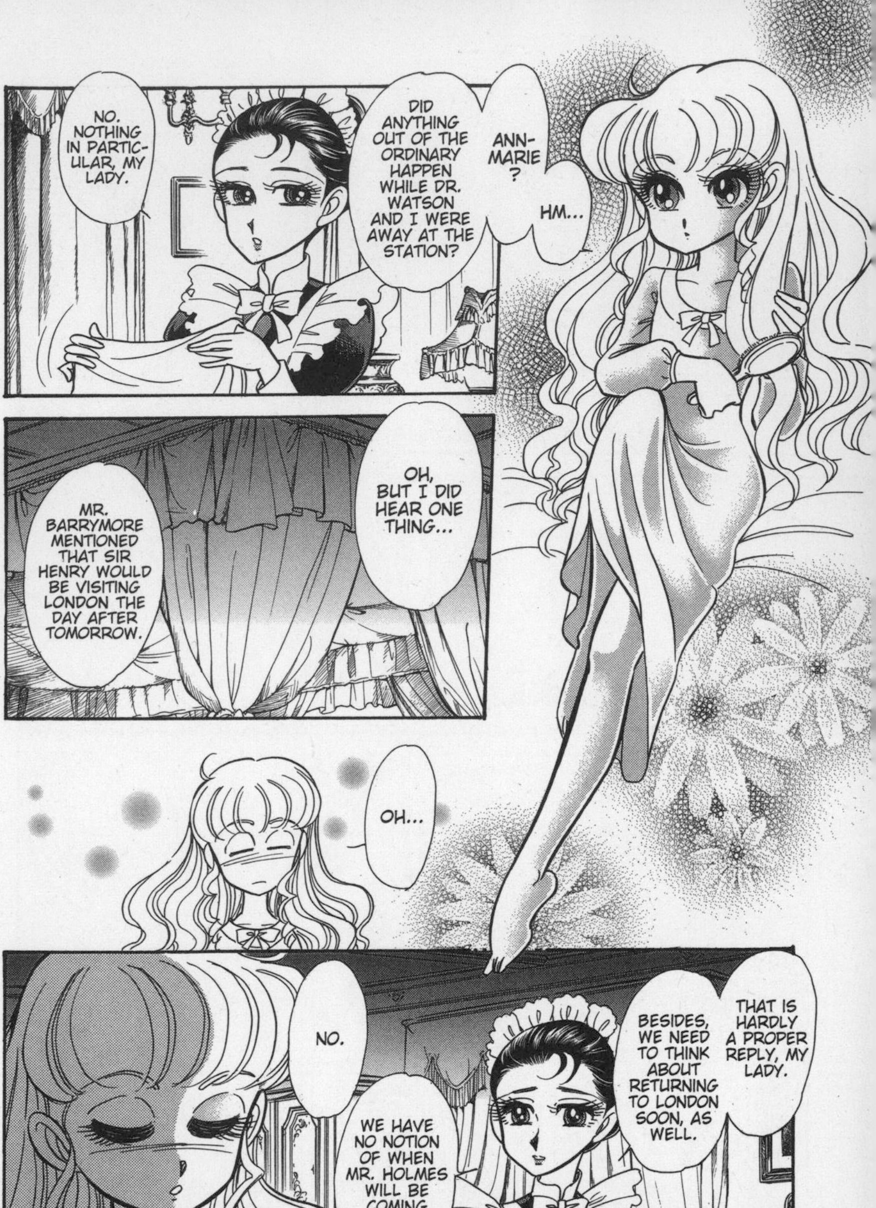
ANN-MARIE?
HM...
DID ANYTHING OUT OF THE ORDINARY HAPPEN WHILE DR. WATSON AND I WERE AWAY AT THE STATION?
NO. NOTHING IN PARTICULAR, MY LADY.
OH, BUT I DID HEAR ONE THING...
MR. BARRYMORE MENTIONED THAT SIR HENRY WOULD BE VISITING LONDON THE DAY AFTER TOMORROW.
OH...
THAT IS HARDLY A PROPER REPLY, MY LADY.
BESIDES, WE NEED TO THINK ABOUT RETURNING TO LONDON SOON, AS WELL.
NO.
WE HAVE NO NOTION OF WHEN MR. HOLMES WILL BE COMING HERE, IF AT ALL.

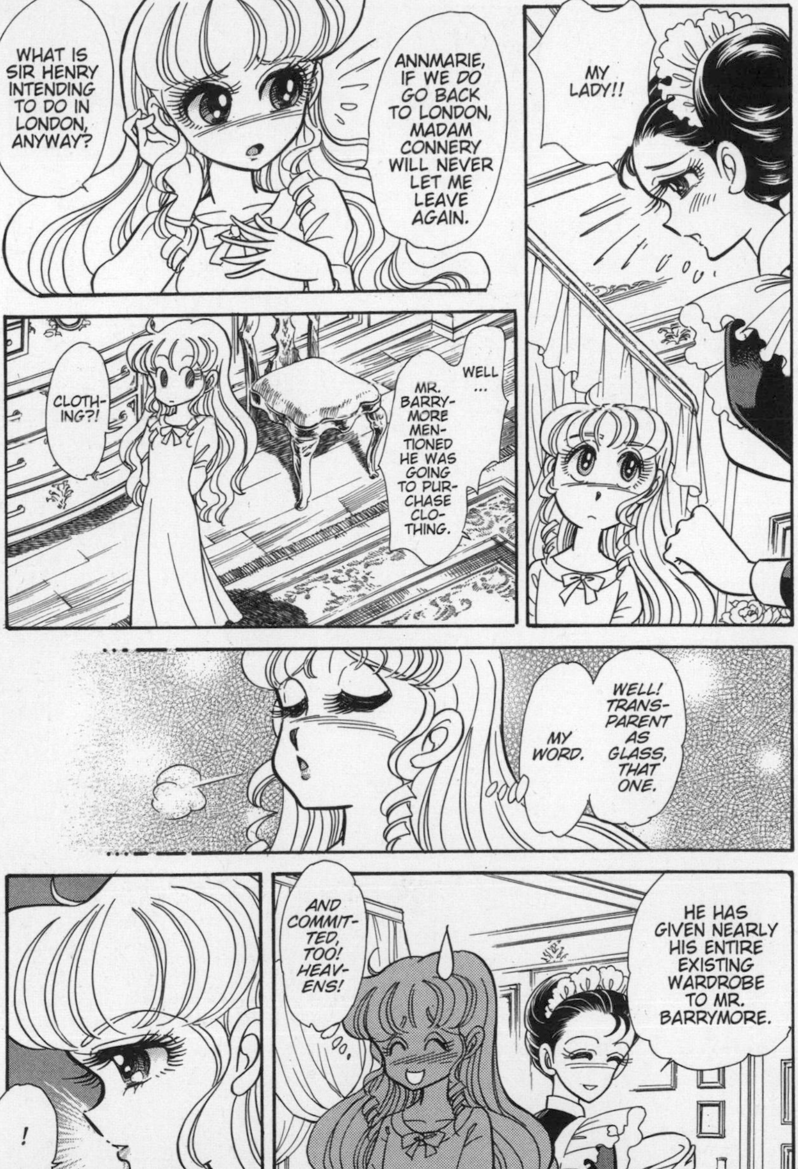
MY LADY!!
ANNMARIE, IF WE DO GO BACK TO LONDON, MADAM CONNERY WILL NEVER LET ME LEAVE AGAIN.
WHAT IS SIR HENRY INTENDING TO DO IN LONDON, ANYWAY?
WELL ...
MR. BARRYMORE MENTIONED HE WAS GOING TO PURCHASE CLOTHING.
CLOTHING?!
WELL! TRANSPARENT AS GLASS, THAT ONE.
MY WORD.
HE HAS GIVEN NEARLY HIS ENTIRE EXISTING WARDROBE TO MR. BARRYMORE.
AND COMMITTED, TOO! HEAVENS!
!

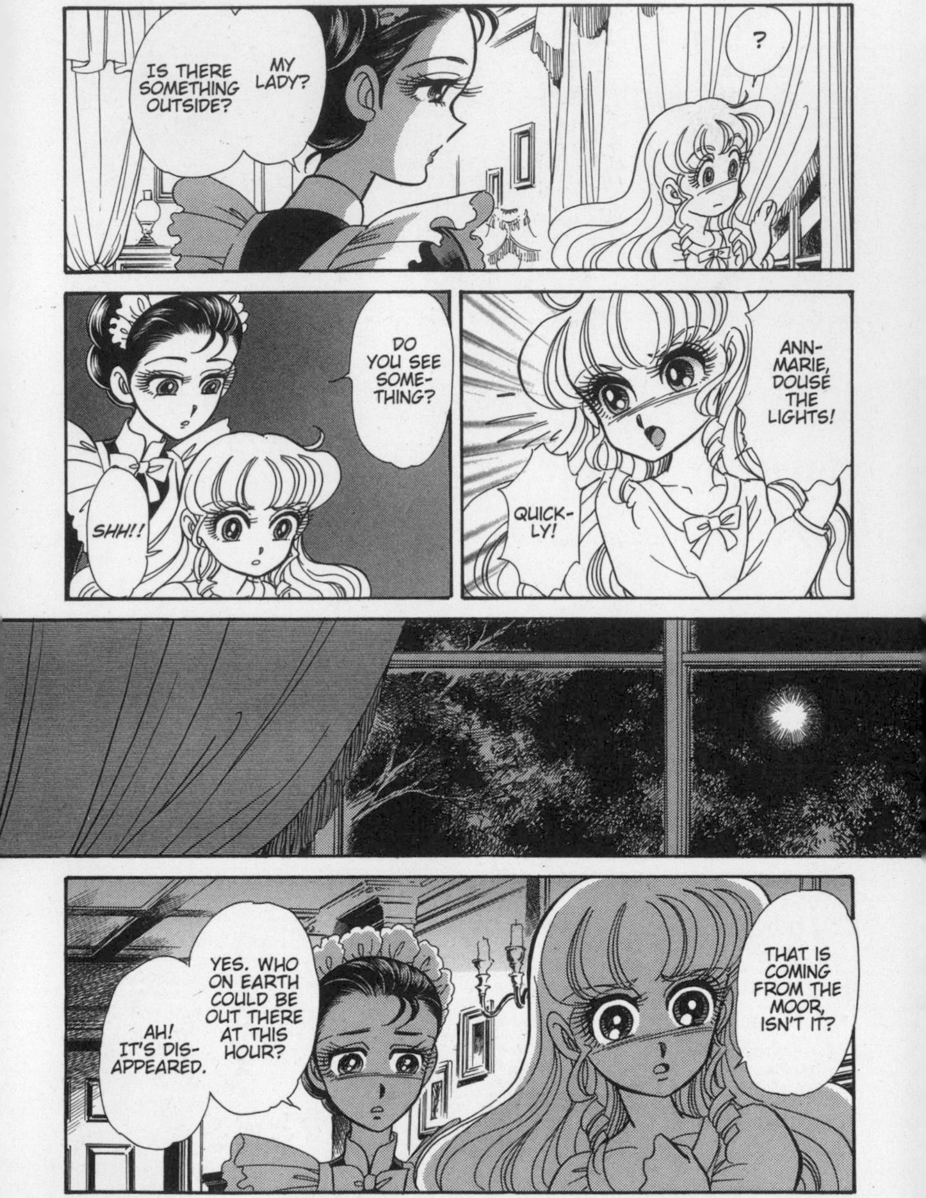
?
MY LADY?
IS THERE SOMETHING OUTSIDE?
ANN-MARIE, DOUSE THE LIGHTS!
QUICKLY!
DO YOU SEE SOMETHING?
SHH!!
THAT IS COMING FROM THE MOOR, ISN'T IT?
YES. WHO ON EARTH COULD BE OUT THERE AT THIS HOUR?
AH! IT'S DISAPPEARED.

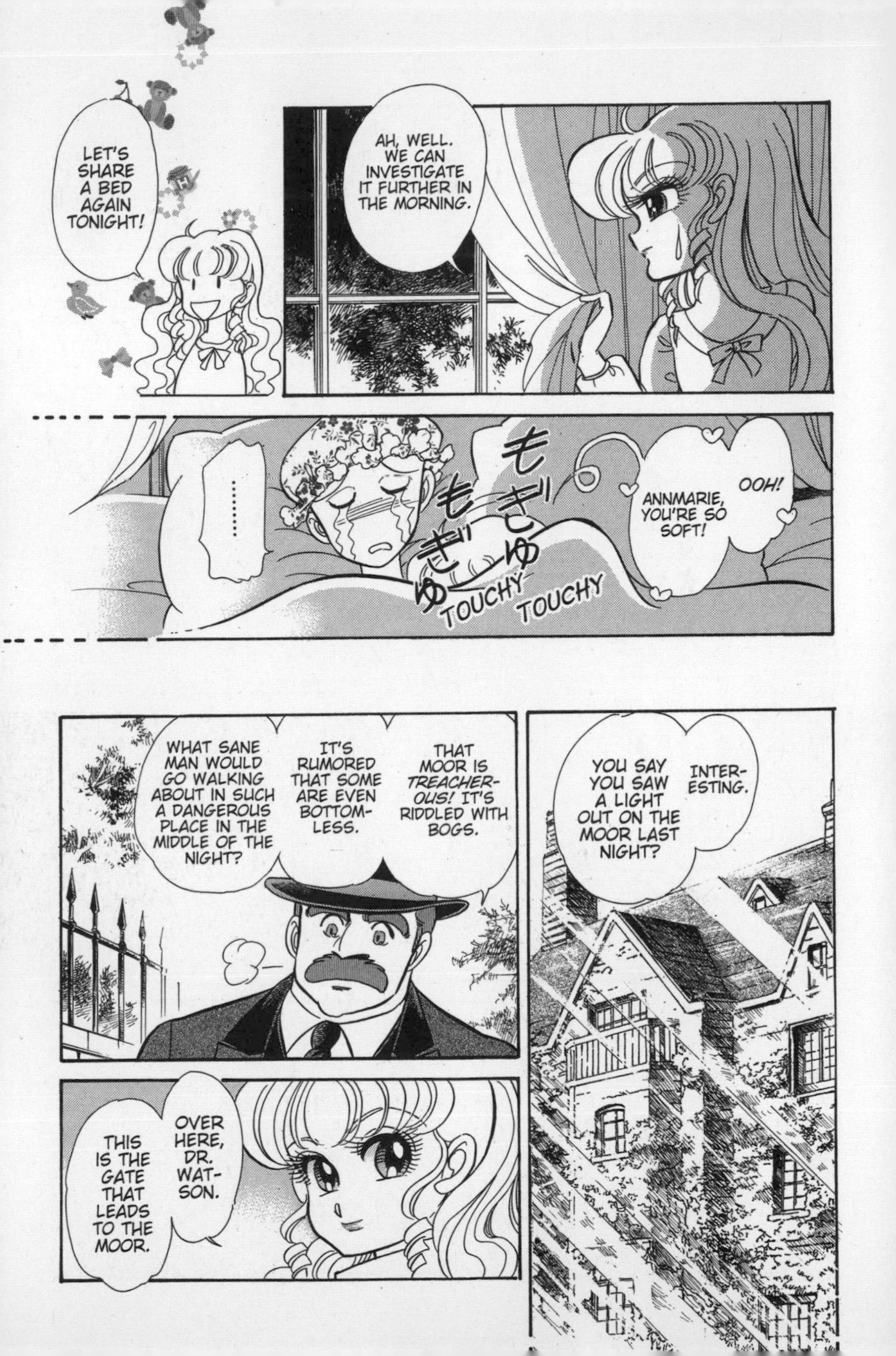

AH, WELL. WE CAN INVESTIGATE IT FURTHER IN THE MORNING.
LET'S SHARE A BED AGAIN TONIGHT!
OOH!
ANNMARIE, YOU'RE SO SOFT!
もぎゅ
もぎゅ
TOUCHY TOUCHY
......
INTERESTING.
YOU SAY YOU SAW A LIGHT OUT ON THE MOOR LAST NIGHT?
THAT MOOR IS *TREACHEROUS!* IT'S RIDDLED WITH BOGS.
IT'S RUMORED THAT SOME ARE EVEN BOTTOMLESS.
WHAT SANE MAN WOULD GO WALKING ABOUT IN SUCH A DANGEROUS PLACE IN THE MIDDLE OF THE NIGHT?
OVER HERE, DR. WATSON.
THIS IS THE GATE THAT LEADS TO THE MOOR.

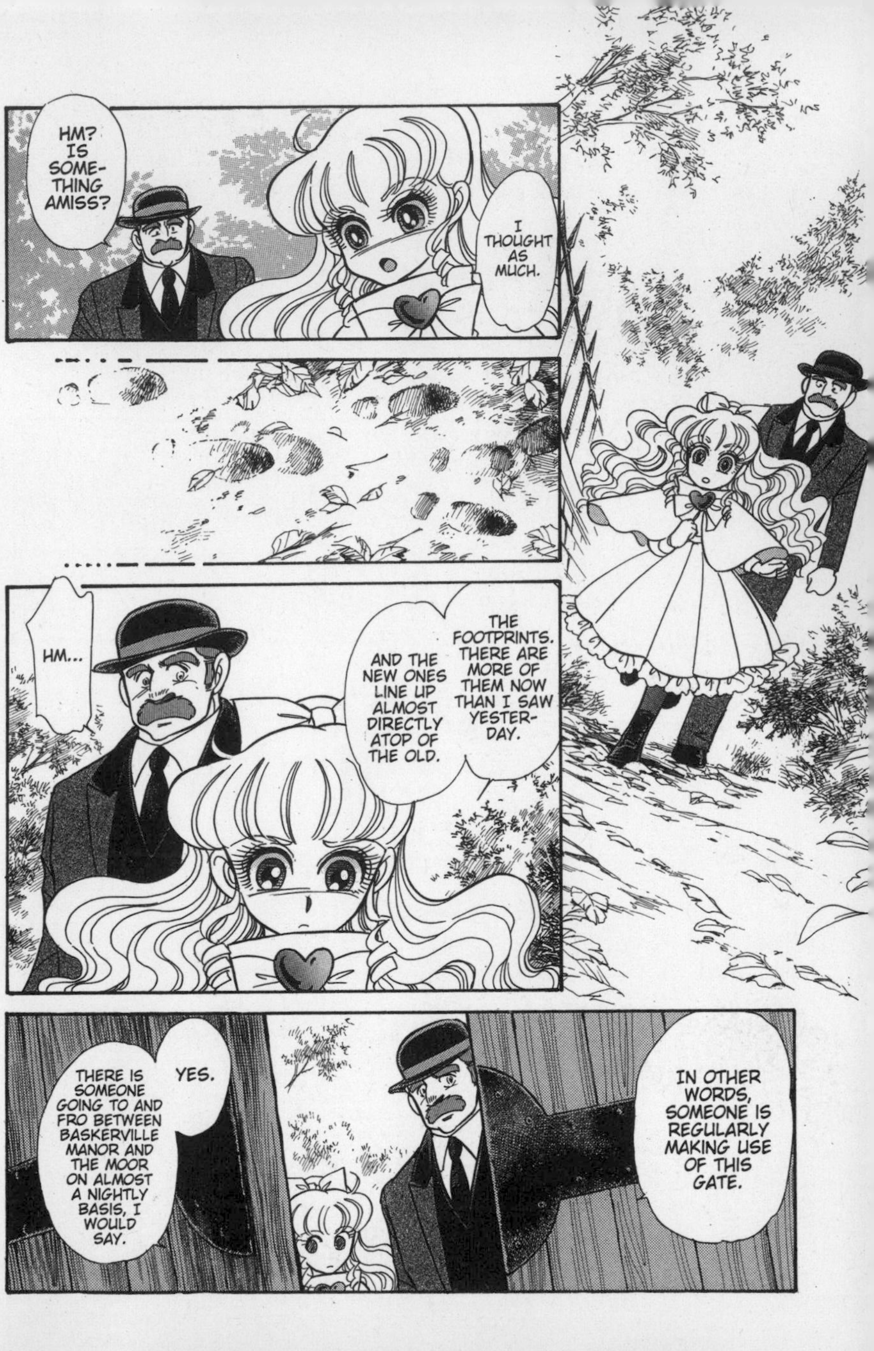
I THOUGHT AS MUCH.
HM? IS SOME-THING AMISS?
THE FOOTPRINTS. THERE ARE MORE OF THEM NOW THAN I SAW YESTER-DAY.
AND THE NEW ONES LINE UP ALMOST DIRECTLY ATOP OF THE OLD.
HM...
IN OTHER WORDS, SOMEONE IS REGULARLY MAKING USE OF THIS GATE.
YES.
THERE IS SOMEONE GOING TO AND FRO BETWEEN BASKERVILLE MANOR AND THE MOOR ON ALMOST A NIGHTLY BASIS, I WOULD SAY.

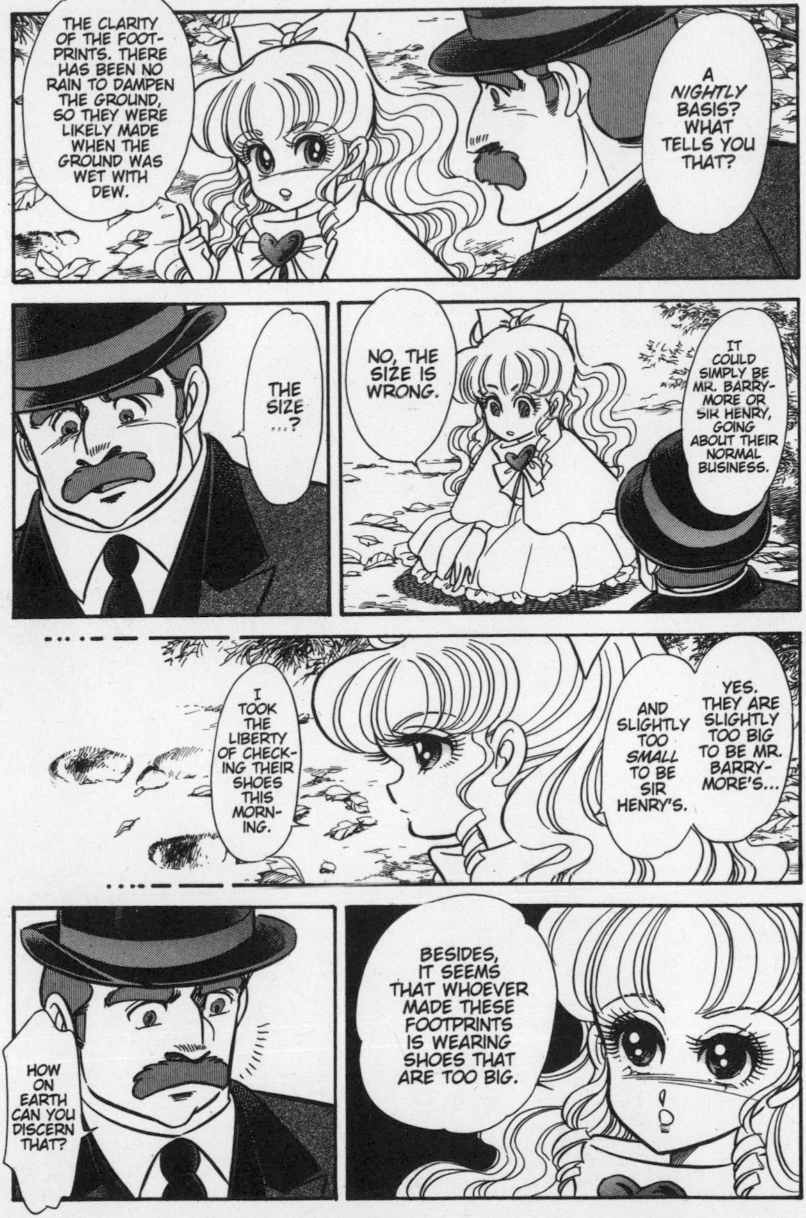
A *NIGHTLY* BASIS? WHAT TELLS YOU THAT?
THE CLARITY OF THE FOOTPRINTS. THERE HAS BEEN NO RAIN TO DAMPEN THE GROUND, SO THEY WERE LIKELY MADE WHEN THE GROUND WAS WET WITH DEW.
IT COULD SIMPLY BE MR. BARRYMORE OR SIR HENRY, GOING ABOUT THEIR NORMAL BUSINESS.
NO, THE SIZE IS WRONG.
THE SIZE ...?
YES. THEY ARE SLIGHTLY TOO BIG TO BE MR. BARRYMORE'S...
AND SLIGHTLY TOO *SMALL* TO BE SIR HENRY'S.
I TOOK THE LIBERTY OF CHECKING THEIR SHOES THIS MORNING.
BESIDES, IT SEEMS THAT WHOEVER MADE THESE FOOTPRINTS IS WEARING SHOES THAT ARE TOO BIG.
HOW ON EARTH CAN YOU DISCERN THAT?

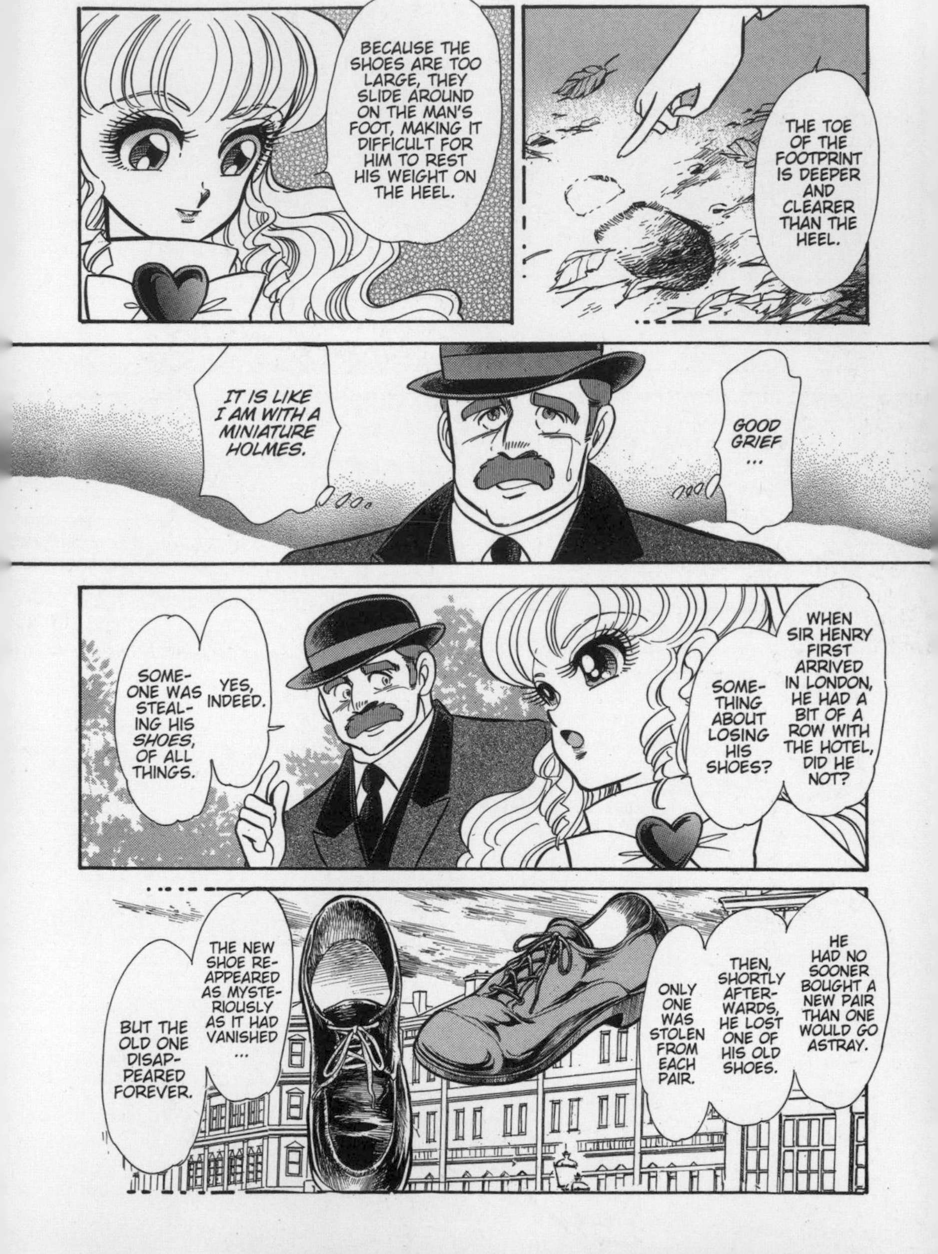
THE TOE OF THE FOOTPRINT IS DEEPER AND CLEARER THAN THE HEEL.
BECAUSE THE SHOES ARE TOO LARGE, THEY SLIDE AROUND ON THE MAN'S FOOT, MAKING IT DIFFICULT FOR HIM TO REST HIS WEIGHT ON THE HEEL.
GOOD GRIEF ...
IT IS LIKE I AM WITH A MINIATURE HOLMES.
WHEN SIR HENRY FIRST ARRIVED IN LONDON, HE HAD A BIT OF A ROW WITH THE HOTEL, DID HE NOT?
SOME-THING ABOUT LOSING HIS SHOES?
YES, INDEED.
SOME-ONE WAS STEAL-ING HIS SHOES, OF ALL THINGS.
HE HAD NO SOONER BOUGHT A NEW PAIR THAN ONE WOULD GO ASTRAY.
THEN, SHORTLY AFTER-WARDS, HE LOST ONE OF HIS OLD SHOES.
ONLY ONE WAS STOLEN FROM EACH PAIR.
THE NEW SHOE RE-APPEARED AS MYSTE-RIOUSLY AS IT HAD VANISHED ...
BUT THE OLD ONE DISAP-PEARED FOREVER.

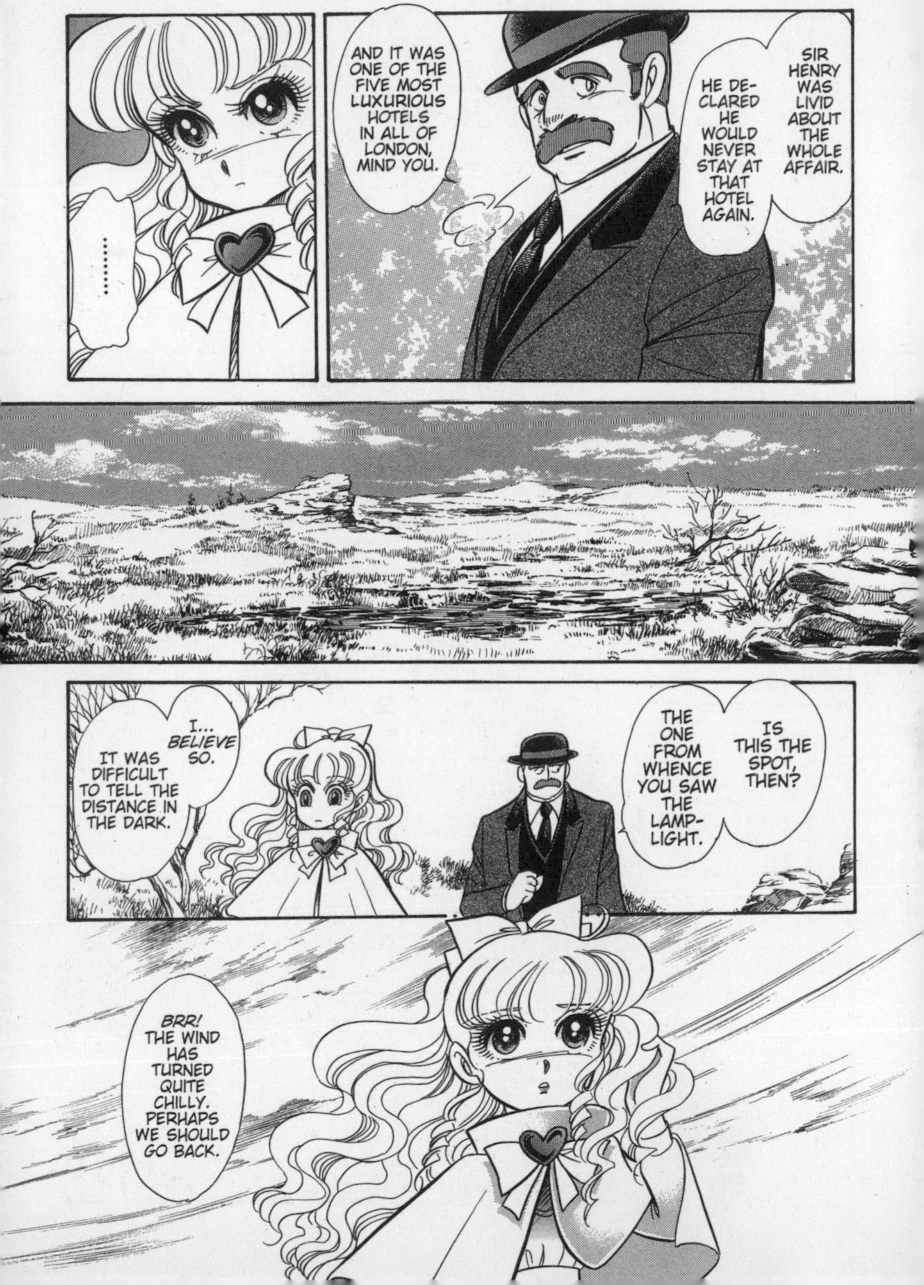

SIR HENRY WAS LIVID ABOUT THE WHOLE AFFAIR.
HE DECLARED HE WOULD NEVER STAY AT THAT HOTEL AGAIN.
AND IT WAS ONE OF THE FIVE MOST LUXURIOUS HOTELS IN ALL OF LONDON, MIND YOU.
....
IS THIS THE SPOT, THEN?
THE ONE FROM WHENCE YOU SAW THE LAMPLIGHT.
I... *BELIEVE* SO.
IT WAS DIFFICULT TO TELL THE DISTANCE IN THE DARK.
BRR! THE WIND HAS TURNED QUITE CHILLY. PERHAPS WE SHOULD GO BACK.

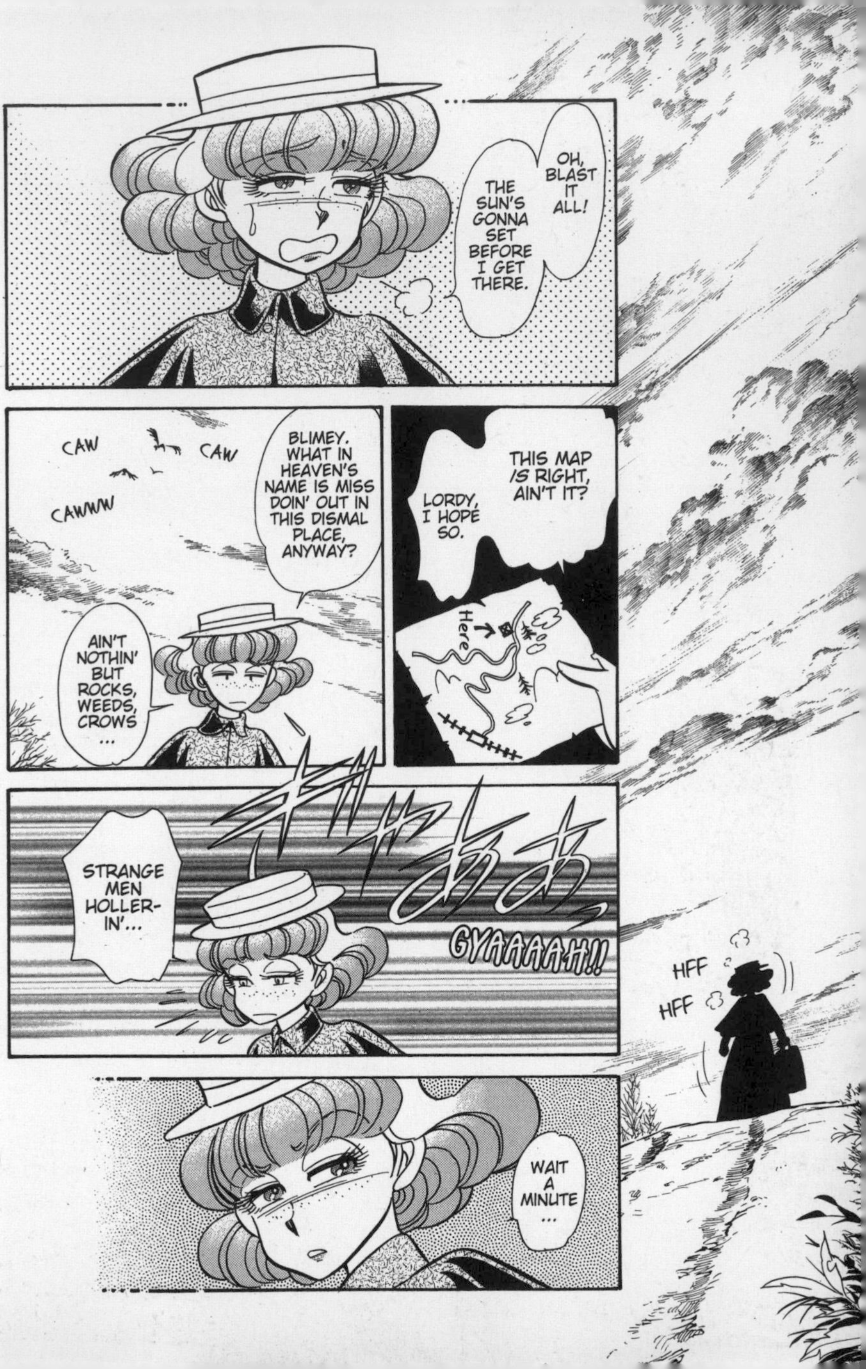
HFF
HFF
OH, BLAST IT ALL!
THE SUN'S GONNA SET BEFORE I GET THERE.
THIS MAP IS RIGHT, AIN'T IT?
LORDY, I HOPE SO.
Here
BLIMEY. WHAT IN HEAVEN'S NAME IS MISS DOIN' OUT IN THIS DISMAL PLACE, ANYWAY?
CAW
CAW
CAWWW
AIN'T NOTHIN' BUT ROCKS, WEEDS, CROWS ...
GYAAAAH!!
STRANGE MEN HOLLER-IN'...
WAIT A MINUTE ...

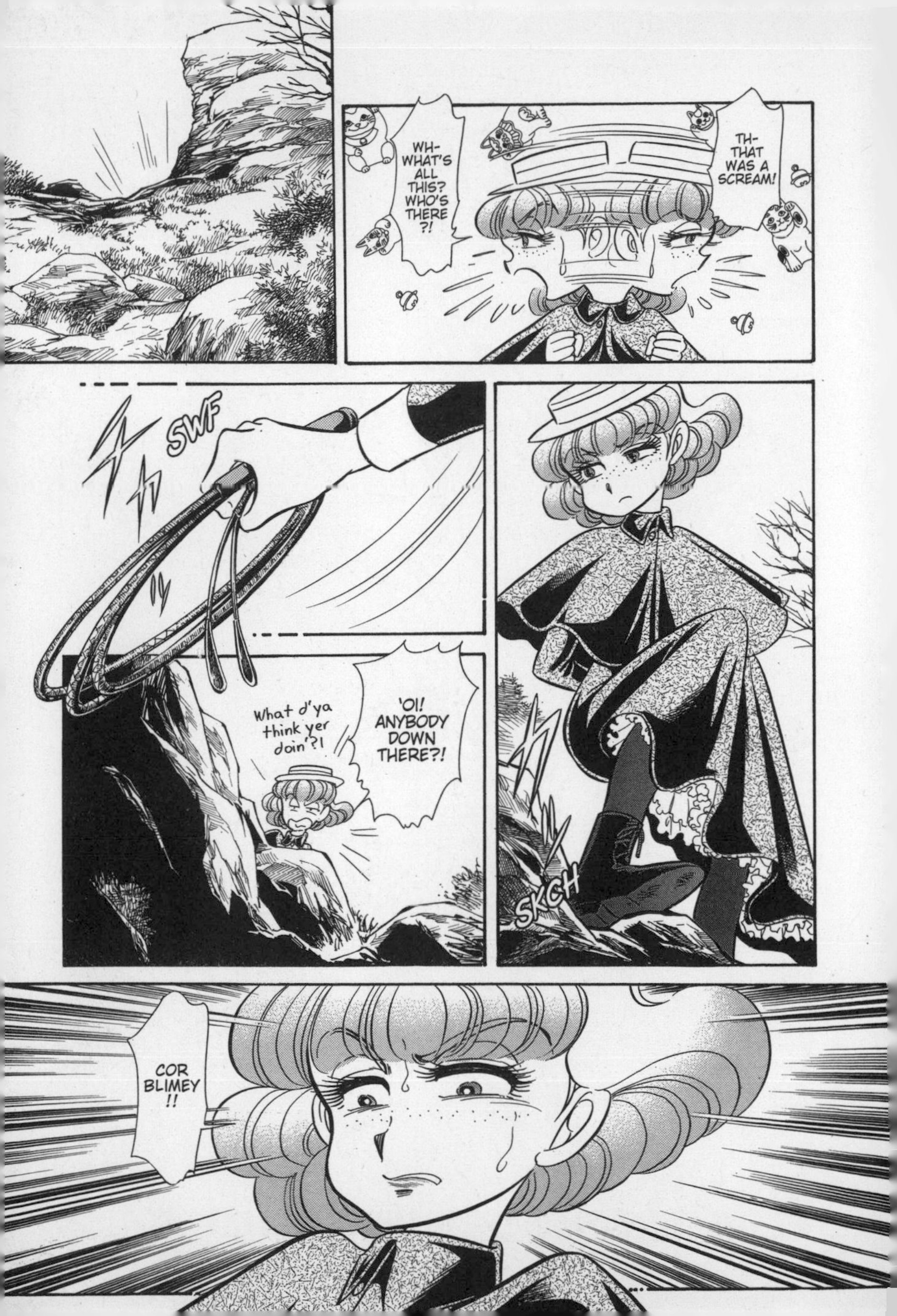
TH-THAT WAS A SCREAM!
WH-WHAT'S ALL THIS? WHO'S THERE?!
SKCH
SWF
'OI! ANYBODY DOWN THERE?!
What d'ya think yer doin'?!
COR BLIMEY!!

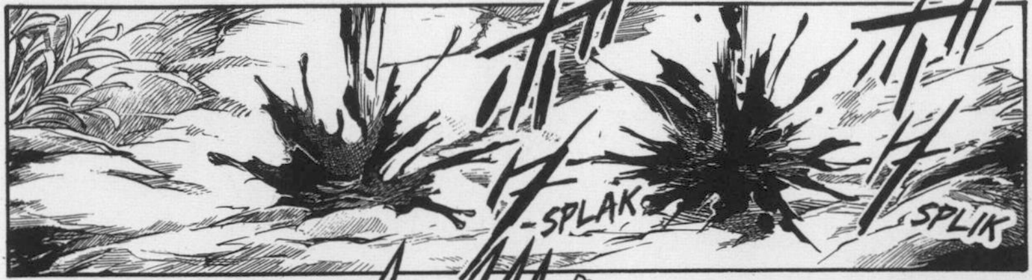
SPLAK
SPLIK
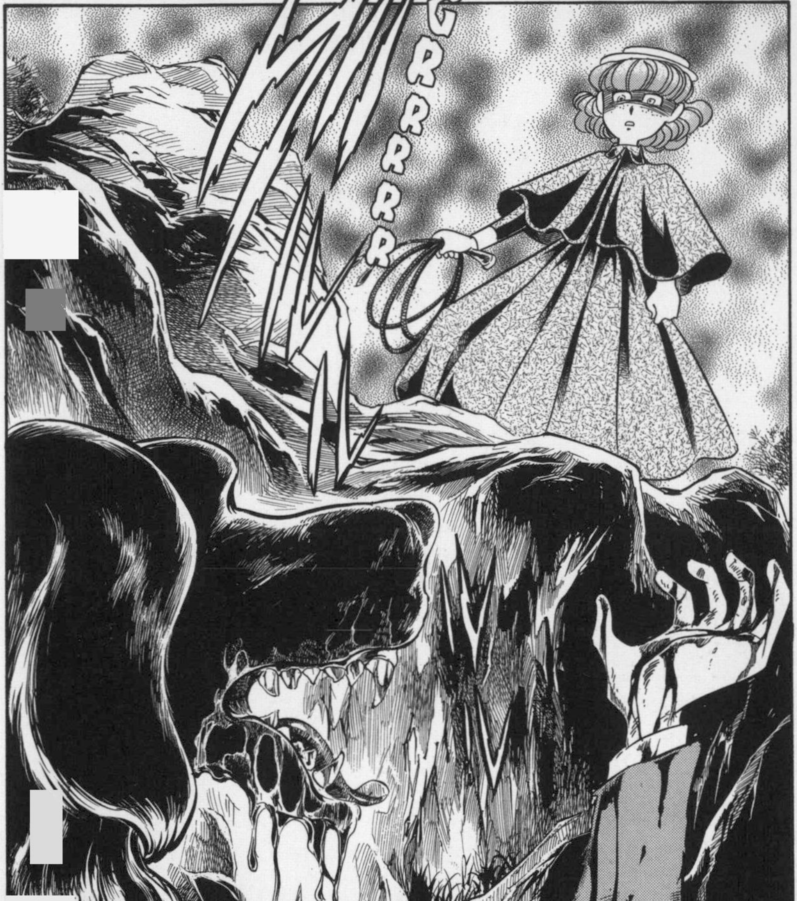
GRRRRRRR

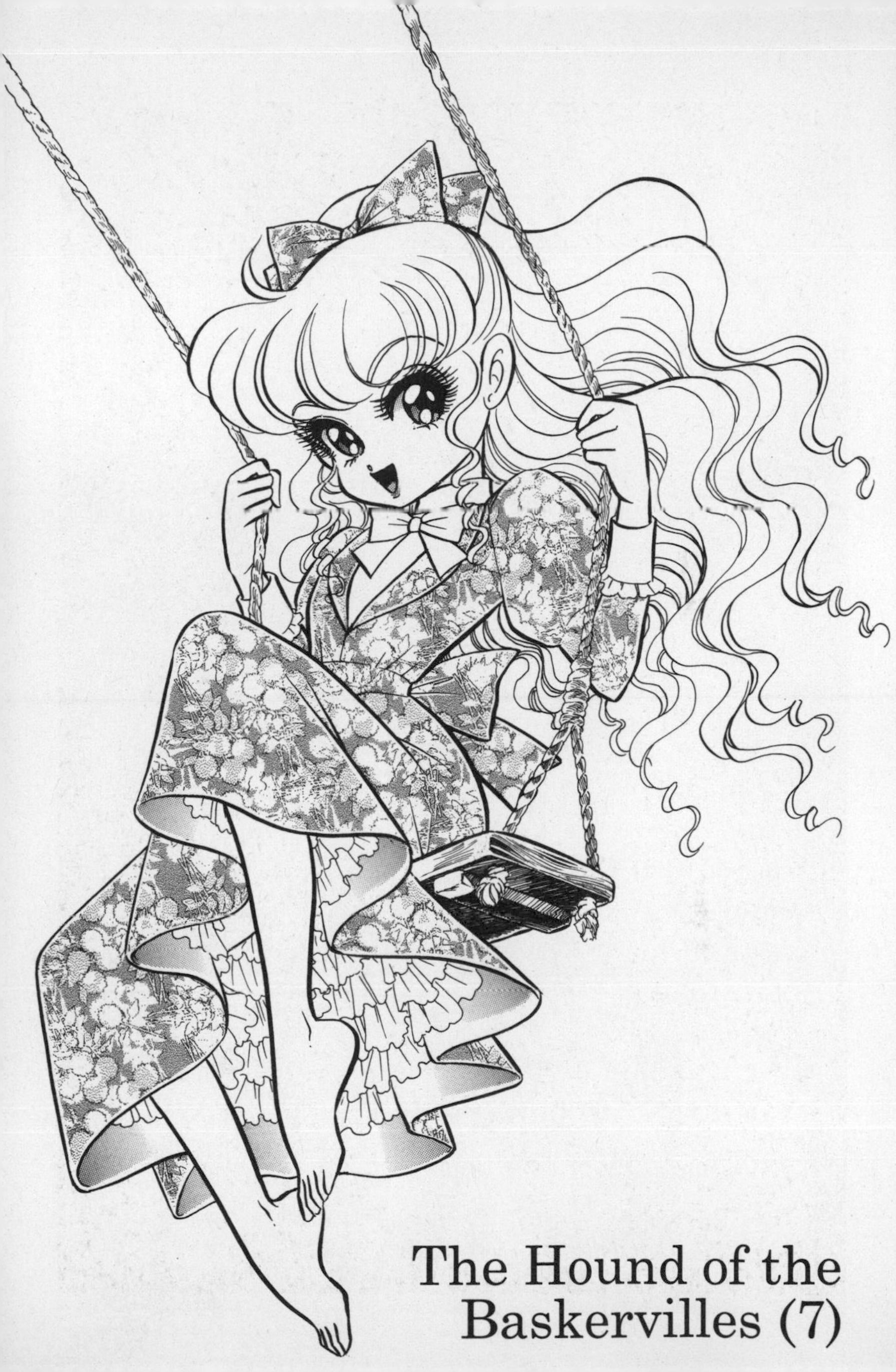

The Hound of the Baskervilles (7)

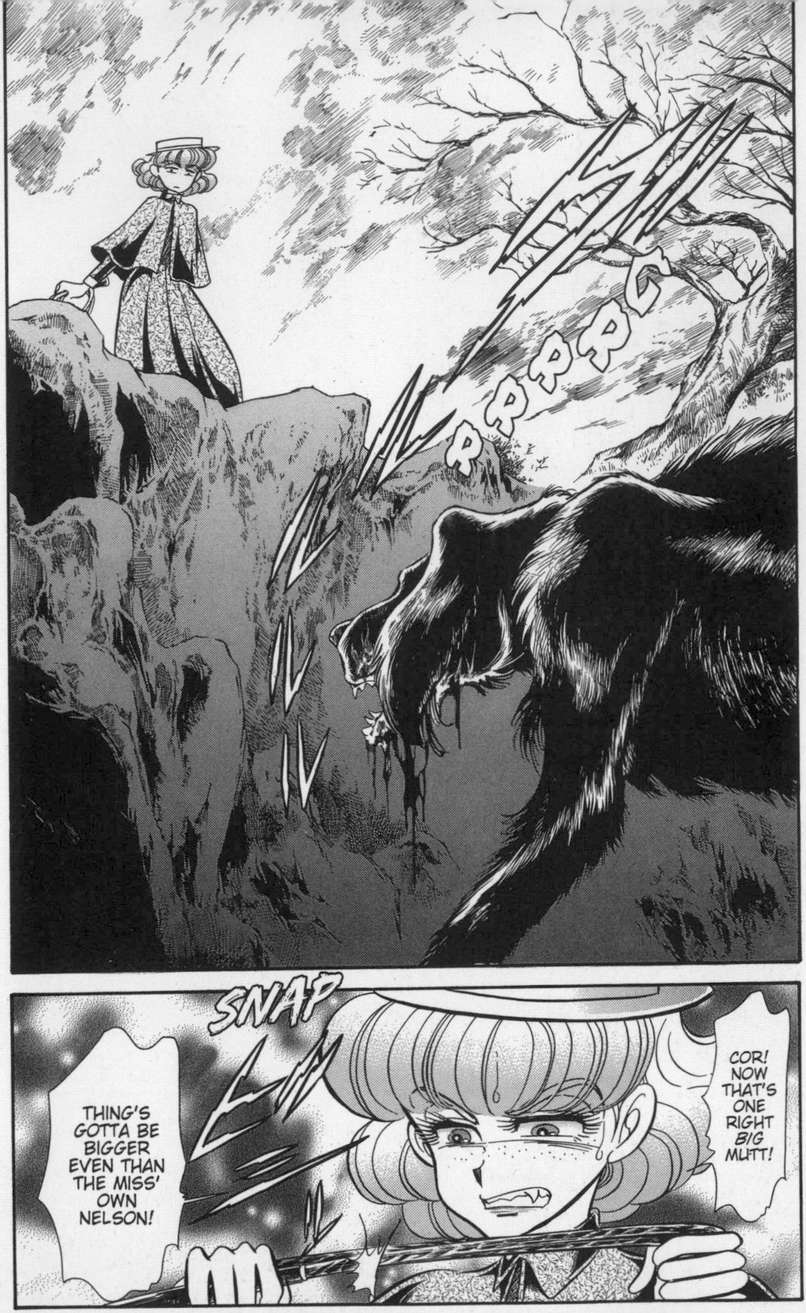
RRRRG
COR! NOW THAT'S ONE RIGHT *BIG* MUTT!
SNAP
THING'S GOTTA BE BIGGER EVEN THAN THE MISS' OWN NELSON!

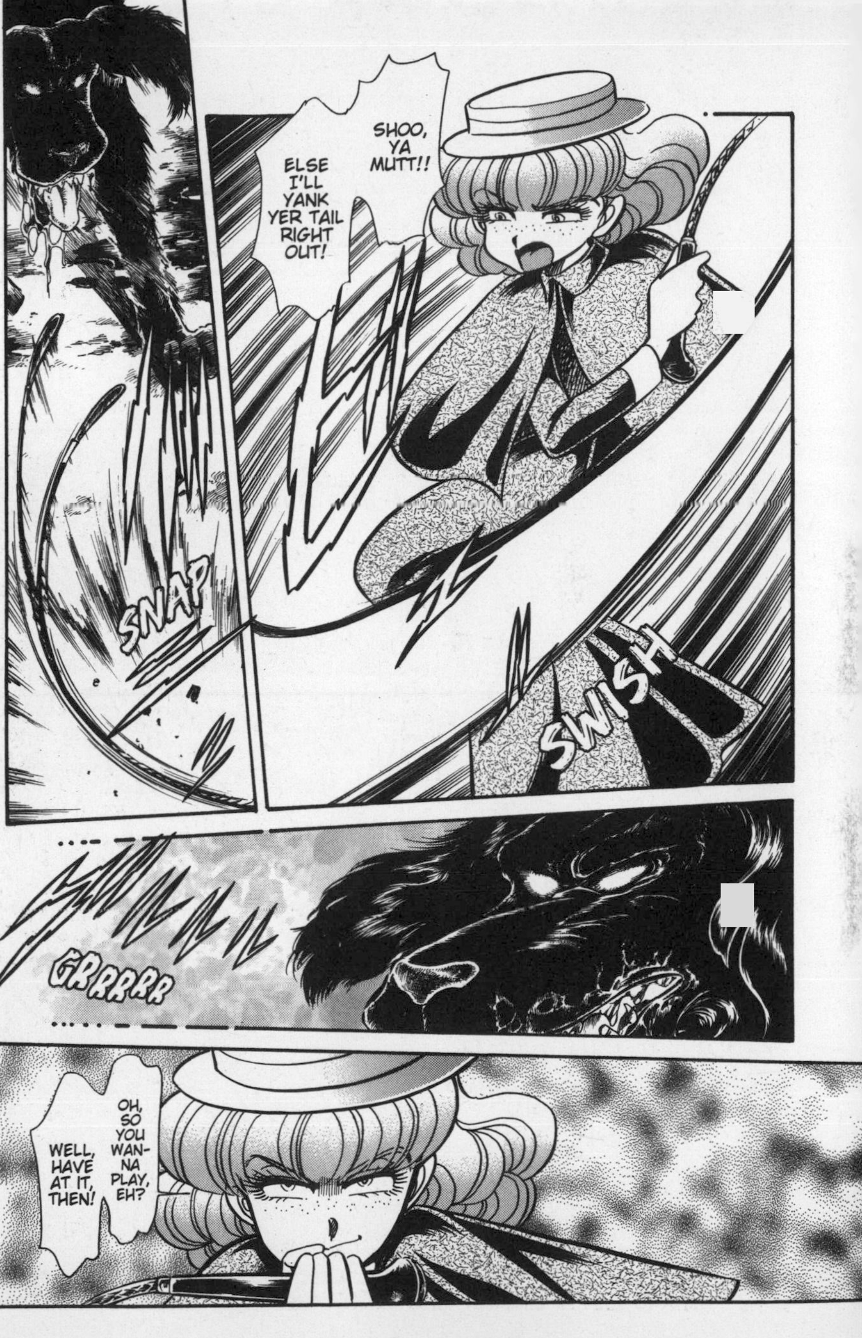
SHOO, YA MUTT!!
ELSE I'LL YANK YER TAIL RIGHT OUT!
SWISH
SNAP
GRRRRR
OH, SO YOU WAN-NA PLAY, EH?
WELL, HAVE AT IT, THEN!

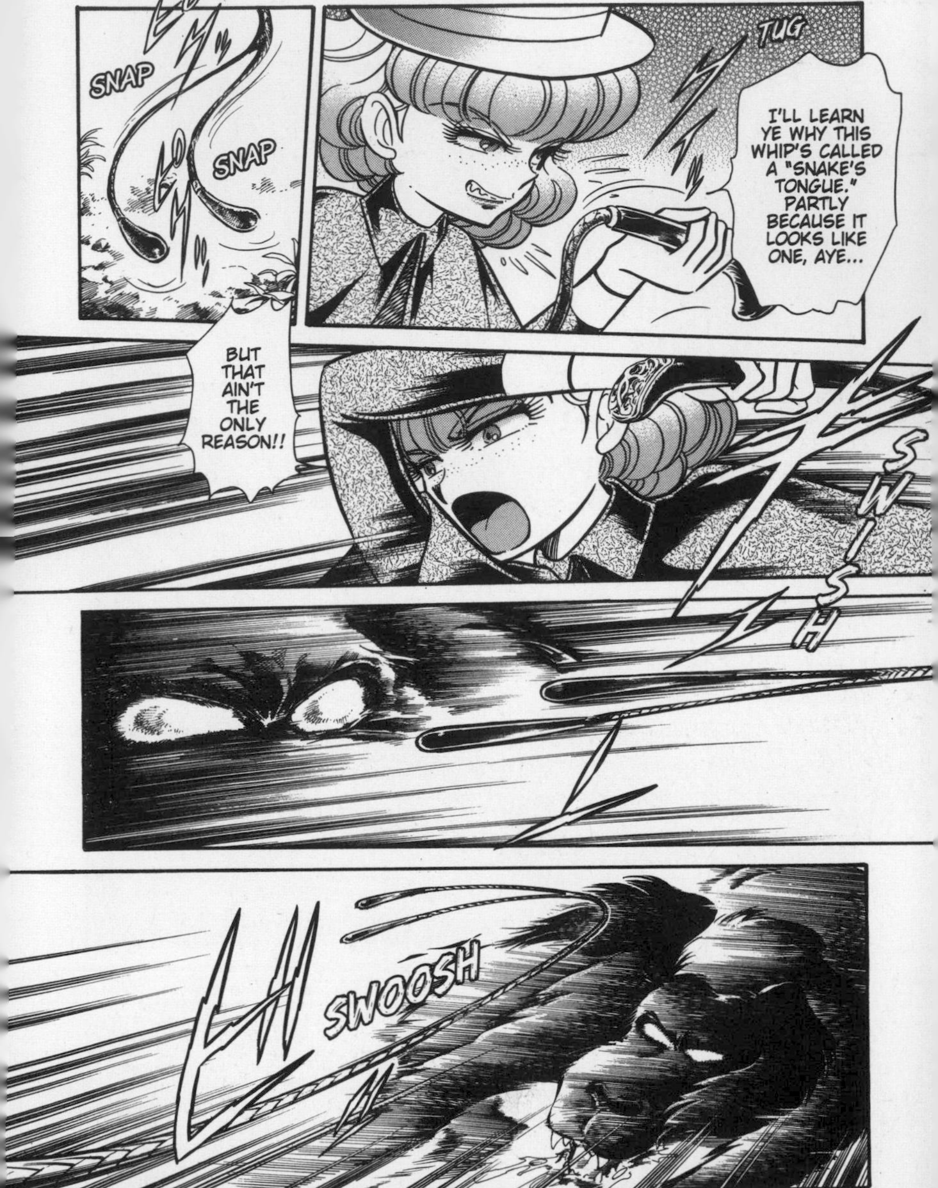
TUG
I'LL LEARN YE WHY THIS WHIP'S CALLED A "SNAKE'S TONGUE." PARTLY BECAUSE IT LOOKS LIKE ONE, AYE...
SNAP
SNAP
BUT THAT AIN'T THE ONLY REASON!!
SWISH
SWOOSH

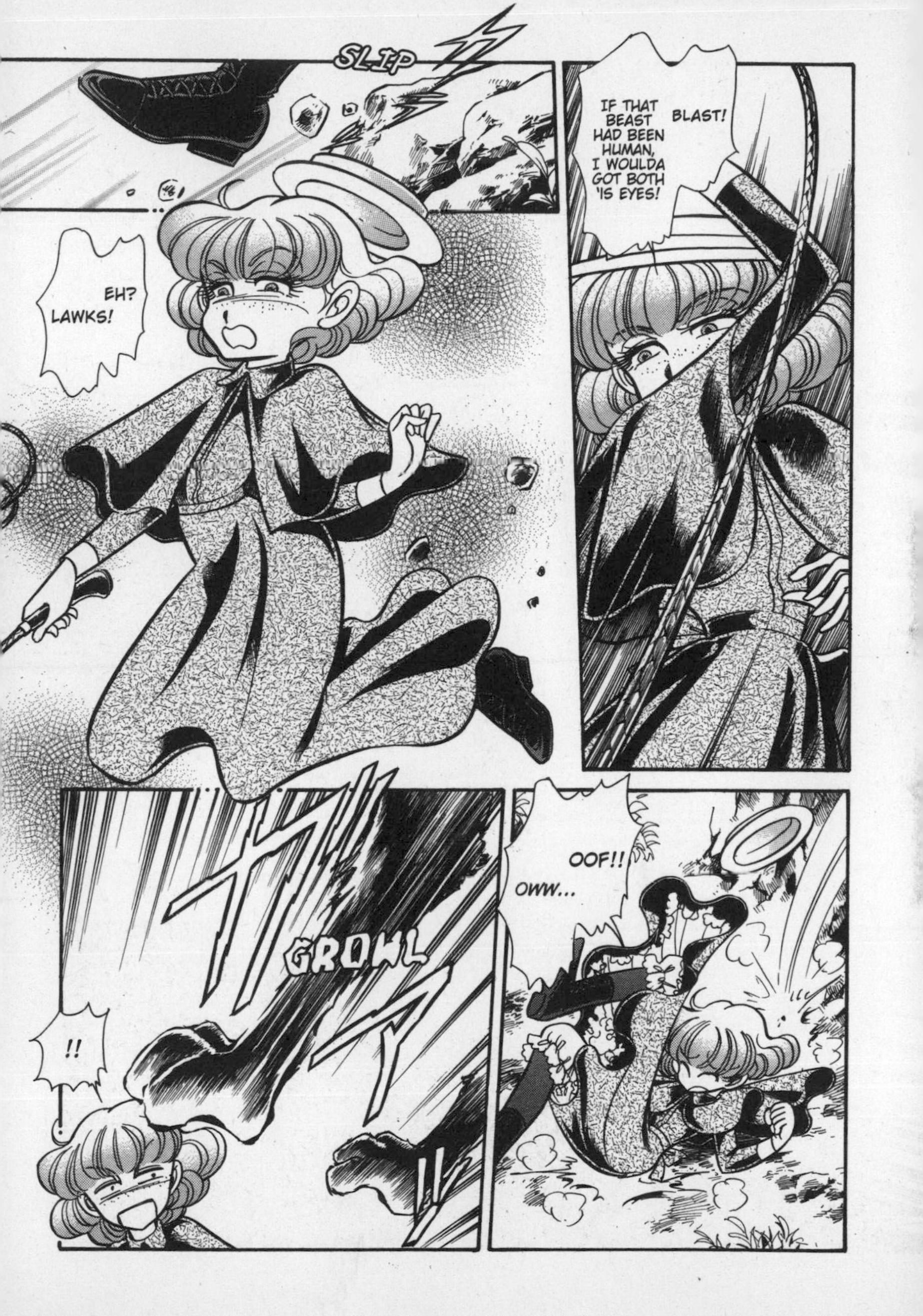
BLAST!
IF THAT BEAST HAD BEEN HUMAN, I WOULDA GOT BOTH 'IS EYES!
SLIP
EH? LAWKS!
OOF!!
OWW...
GROWL
!!

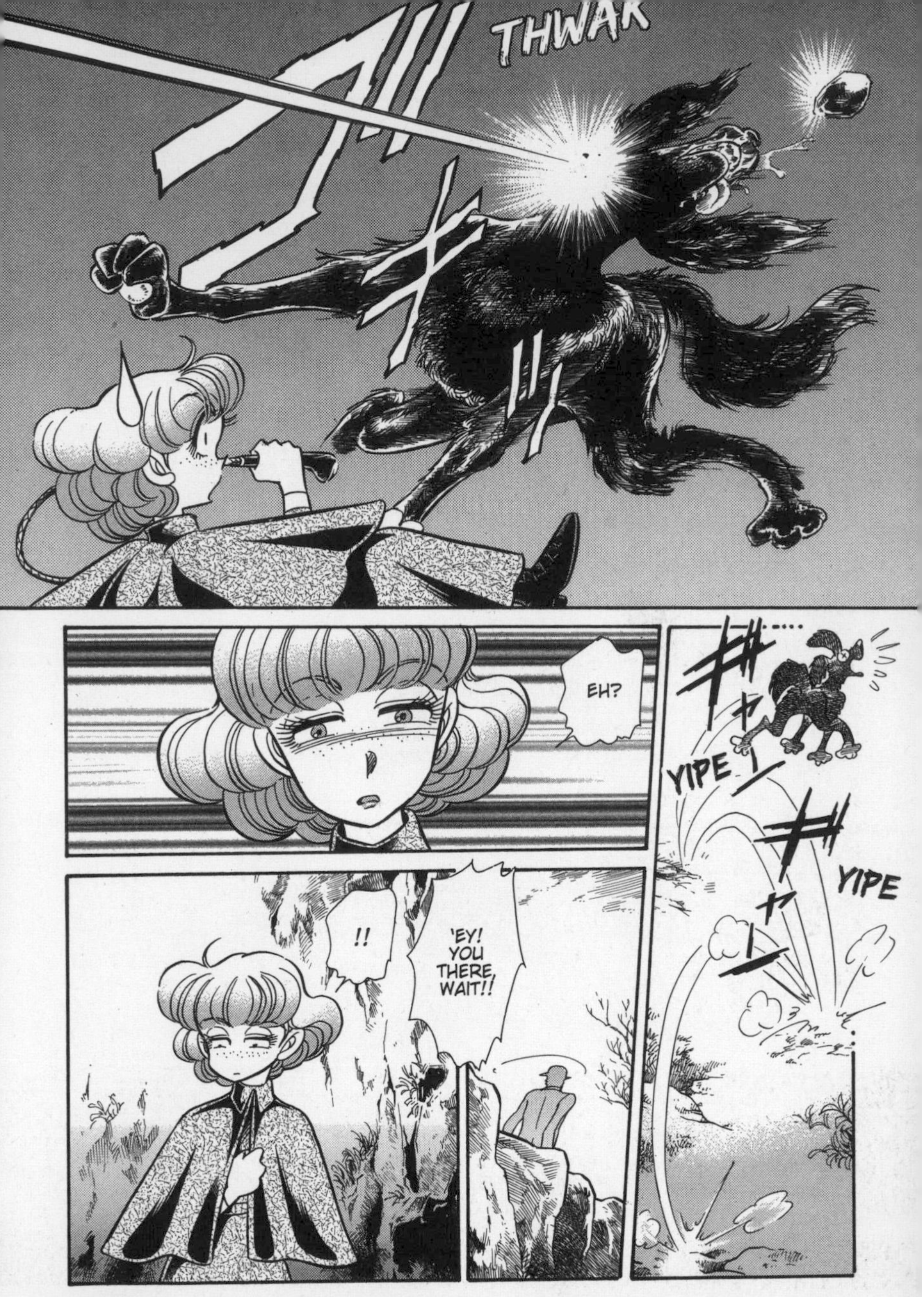
THWAK
YIPE
YIPE
EH?
'EY! YOU THERE WAIT!!
!!

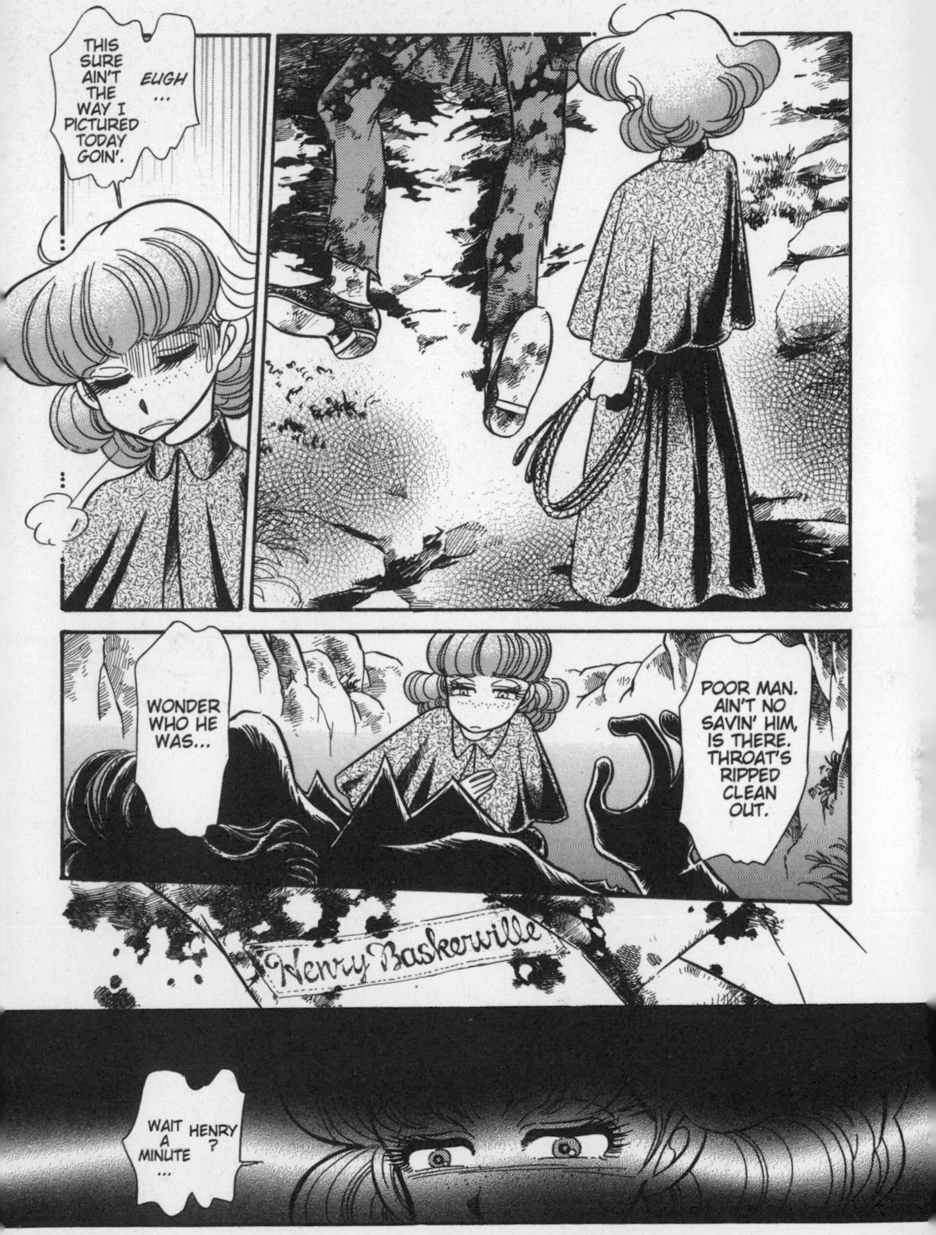
THIS SURE AIN'T THE WAY I PICTURED TODAY GOIN'.
EUGH ...
POOR MAN. AIN'T NO SAVIN' HIM, IS THERE. THROAT'S RIPPED CLEAN OUT.
WONDER WHO HE WAS...
Henry Baskerville
HENRY ?
WAIT A MINUTE ...

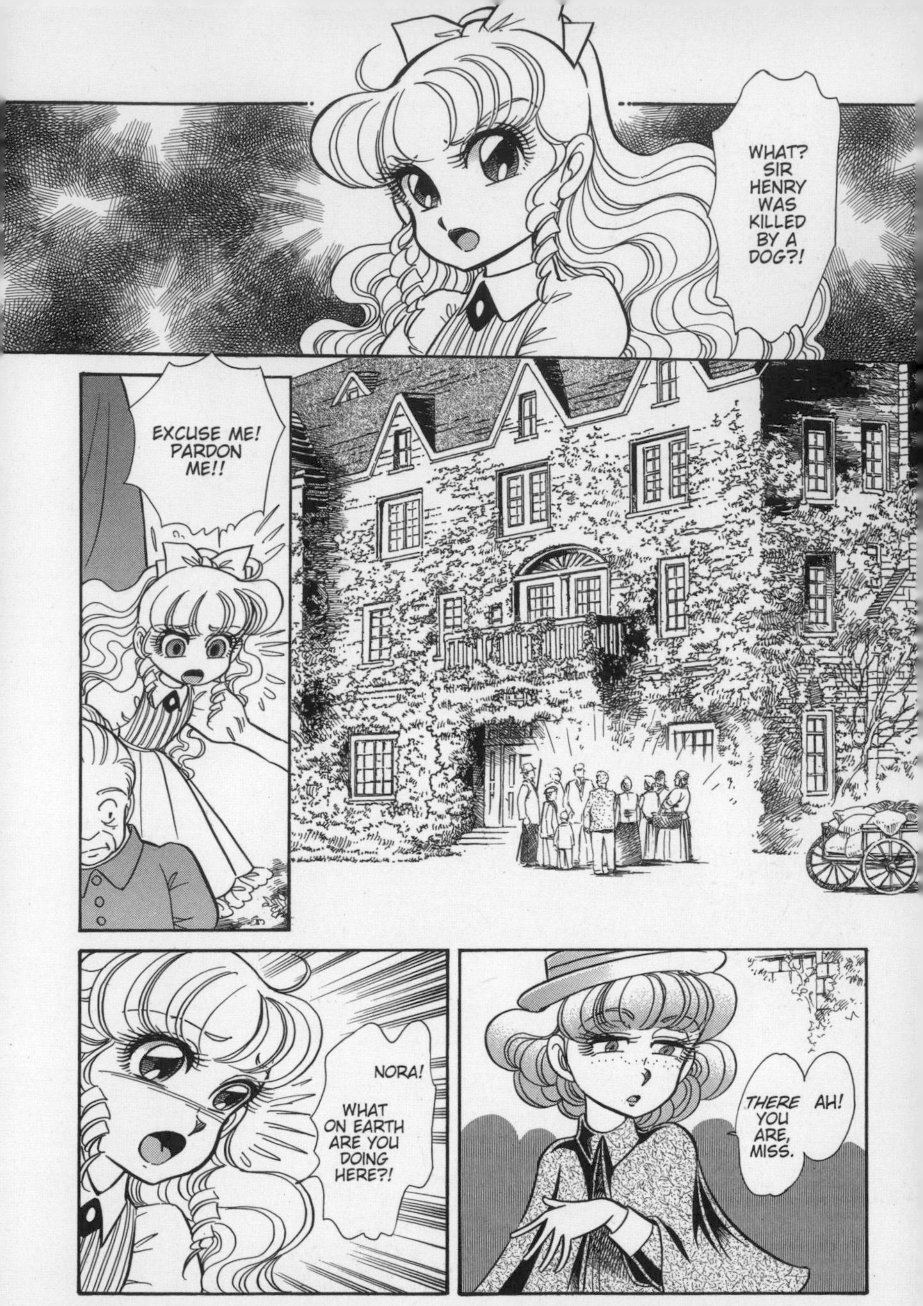
WHAT? SIR HENRY WAS KILLED BY A DOG?!
EXCUSE ME! PARDON ME!!
AH!
THERE YOU ARE, MISS.
NORA!
WHAT ON EARTH ARE YOU DOING HERE?!

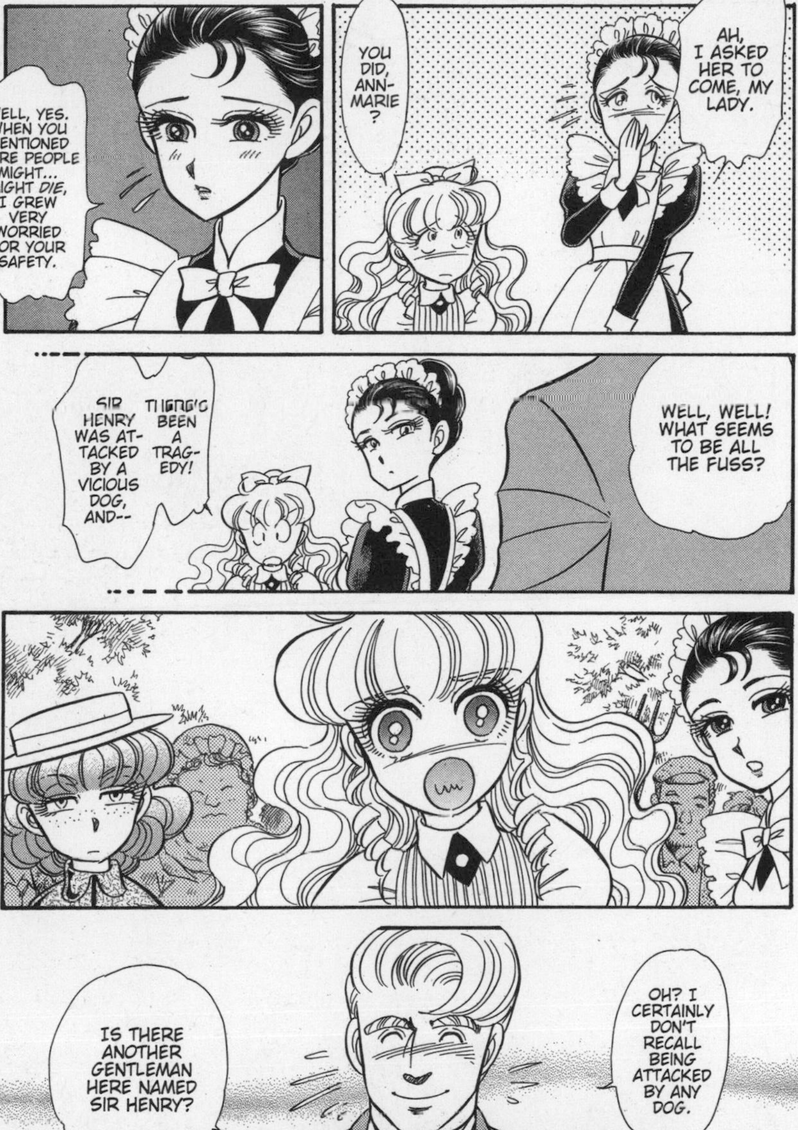
AH, I ASKED HER TO COME, MY LADY.
YOU DID, ANN-MARIE?
WELL, YES. WHEN YOU MENTIONED MORE PEOPLE MIGHT... MIGHT *DIE*, I GREW VERY WORRIED FOR YOUR SAFETY.
WELL, WELL! WHAT SEEMS TO BE ALL THE FUSS?
THERE'S BEEN A TRAG-EDY! SIR HENRY WAS AT-TACKED BY A VICIOUS DOG, AND--
OH? I CERTAINLY DON'T RECALL BEING ATTACKED BY ANY DOG.
IS THERE ANOTHER GENTLEMAN HERE NAMED SIR HENRY?

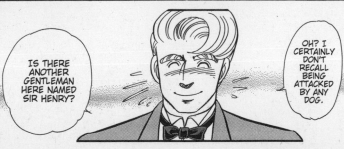

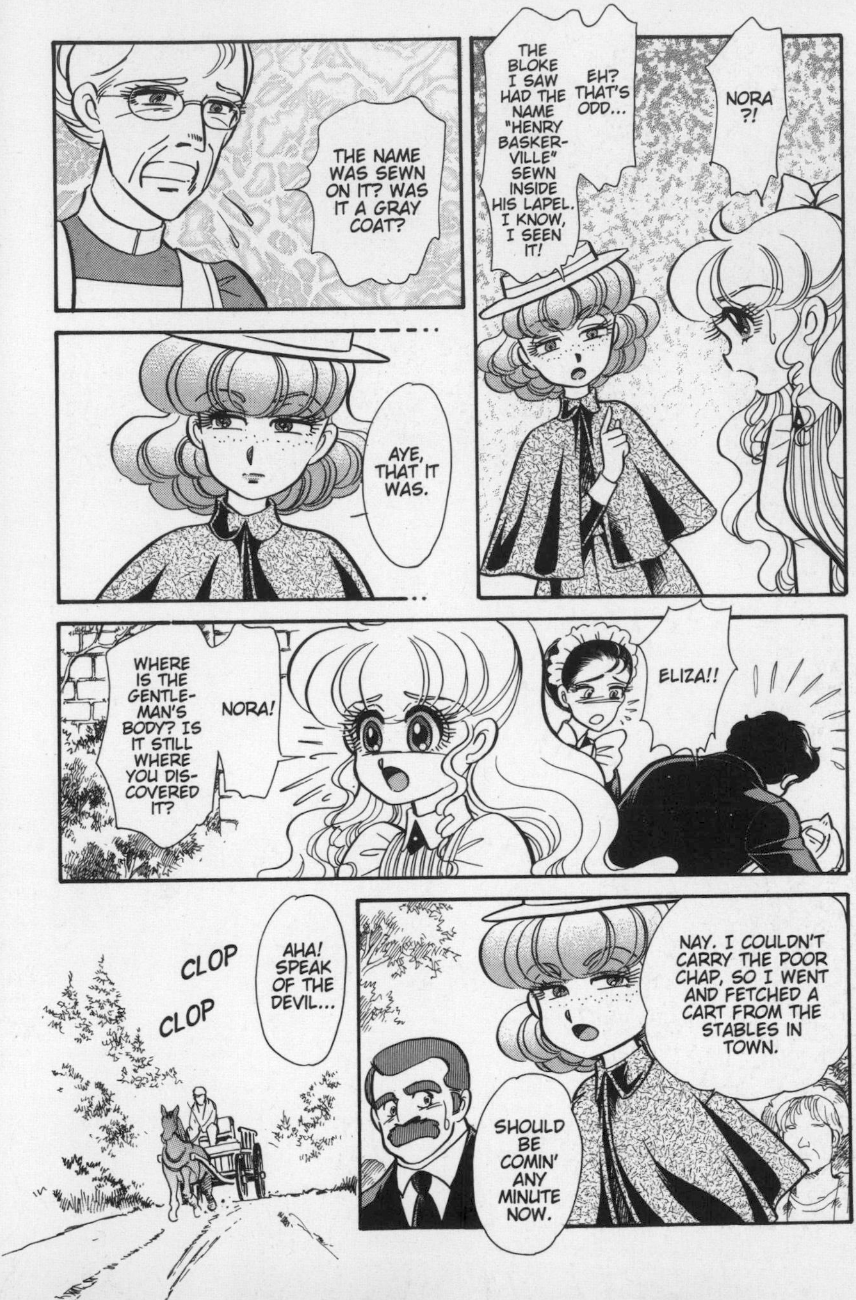
NORA ?!
EH? THAT'S ODD...
THE BLOKE I SAW HAD THE NAME "HENRY BASKER-VILLE" SEWN INSIDE HIS LAPEL. I KNOW, I SEEN IT!
THE NAME WAS SEWN ON IT? WAS IT A GRAY COAT?
AYE, THAT IT WAS.
ELIZA!!
NORA!
WHERE IS THE GENTLE-MAN'S BODY? IS IT STILL WHERE YOU DIS-COVERED IT?
NAY. I COULDN'T CARRY THE POOR CHAP, SO I WENT AND FETCHED A CART FROM THE STABLES IN TOWN.
SHOULD BE COMIN' ANY MINUTE NOW.
AHA! SPEAK OF THE DEVIL...
CLOP
CLOP

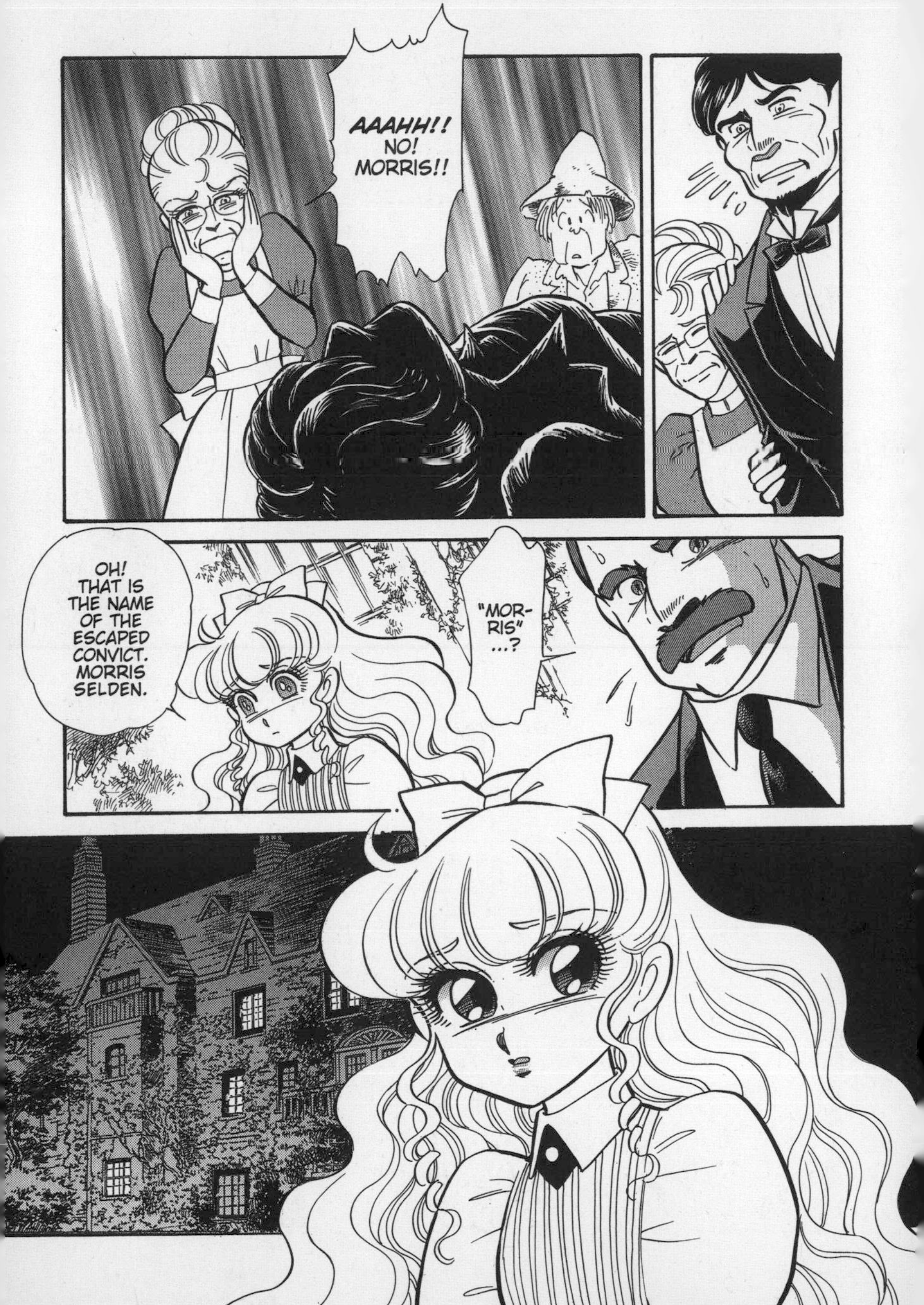
AAAHH!! NO! MORRIS!!
"MOR-RIS" ...?
OH! THAT IS THE NAME OF THE ESCAPED CONVICT. MORRIS SELDEN.

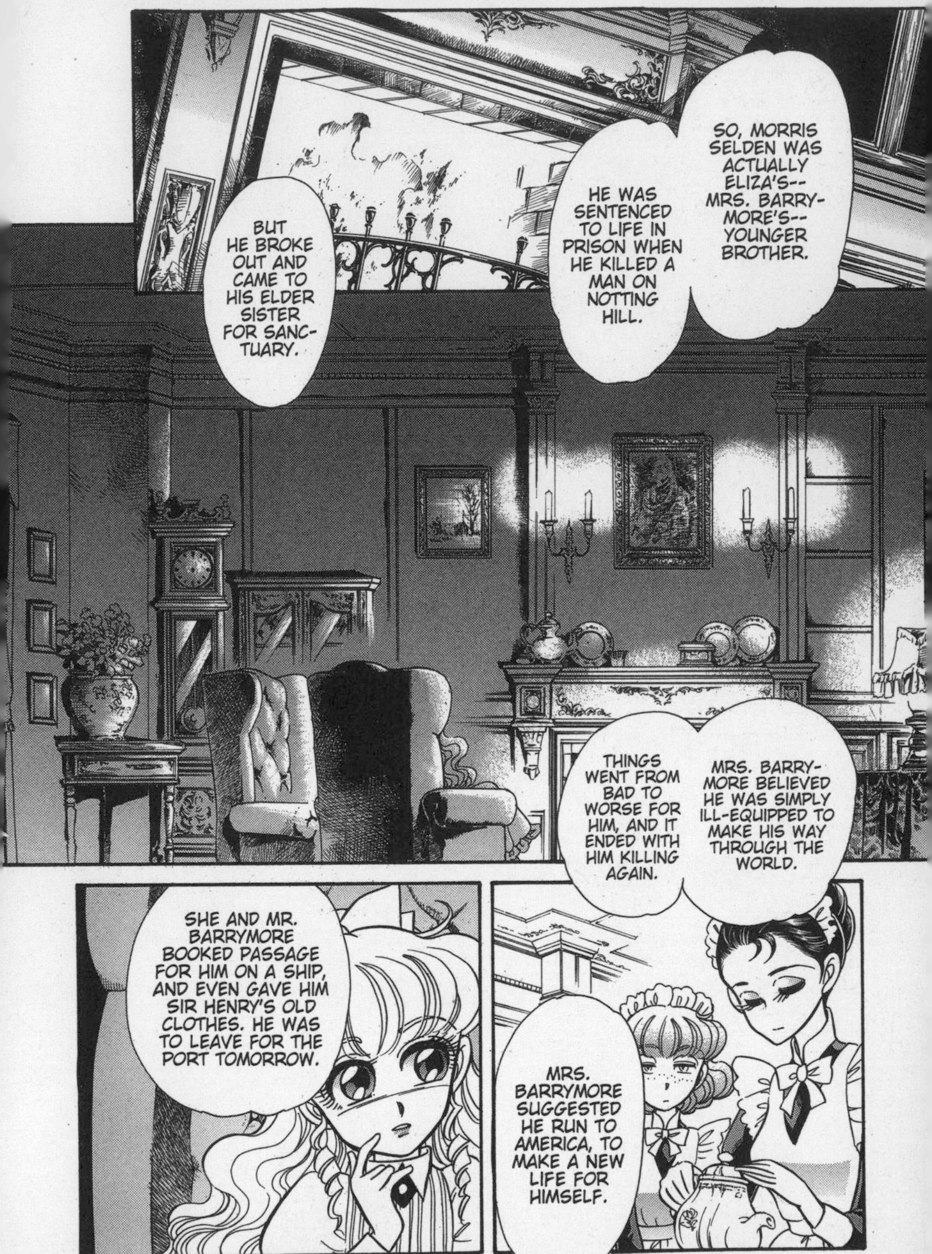
SO, MORRIS SELDEN WAS ACTUALLY ELIZA'S-- MRS. BARRYMORE'S-- YOUNGER BROTHER.
HE WAS SENTENCED TO LIFE IN PRISON WHEN HE KILLED A MAN ON NOTTING HILL.
BUT HE BROKE OUT AND CAME TO HIS ELDER SISTER FOR SANCTUARY.
MRS. BARRYMORE BELIEVED HE WAS SIMPLY ILL-EQUIPPED TO MAKE HIS WAY THROUGH THE WORLD.
THINGS WENT FROM BAD TO WORSE FOR HIM, AND IT ENDED WITH HIM KILLING AGAIN.
MRS. BARRYMORE SUGGESTED HE RUN TO AMERICA, TO MAKE A NEW LIFE FOR HIMSELF.
SHE AND MR. BARRYMORE BOOKED PASSAGE FOR HIM ON A SHIP, AND EVEN GAVE HIM SIR HENRY'S OLD CLOTHES. HE WAS TO LEAVE FOR THE PORT TOMORROW.

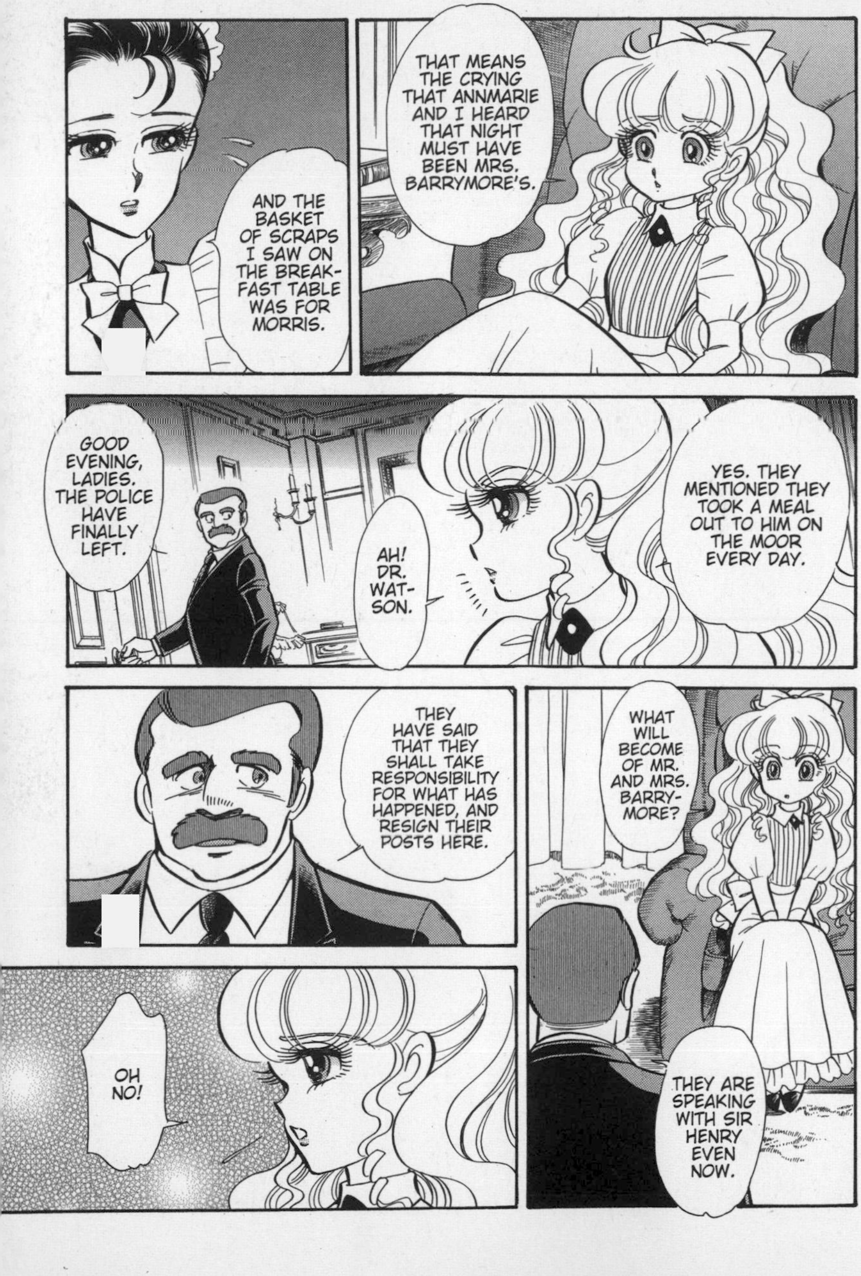
THAT MEANS THE CRYING THAT ANNMARIE AND I HEARD THAT NIGHT MUST HAVE BEEN MRS. BARRYMORE'S.
AND THE BASKET OF SCRAPS I SAW ON THE BREAK-FAST TABLE WAS FOR MORRIS.
YES. THEY MENTIONED THEY TOOK A MEAL OUT TO HIM ON THE MOOR EVERY DAY.
AH! DR. WAT-SON.
GOOD EVENING, LADIES. THE POLICE HAVE FINALLY LEFT.
WHAT WILL BECOME OF MR. AND MRS. BARRY-MORE?
THEY ARE SPEAKING WITH SIR HENRY EVEN NOW.
THEY HAVE SAID THAT THEY SHALL TAKE RESPONSIBILITY FOR WHAT HAS HAPPENED, AND RESIGN THEIR POSTS HERE.
OH NO!

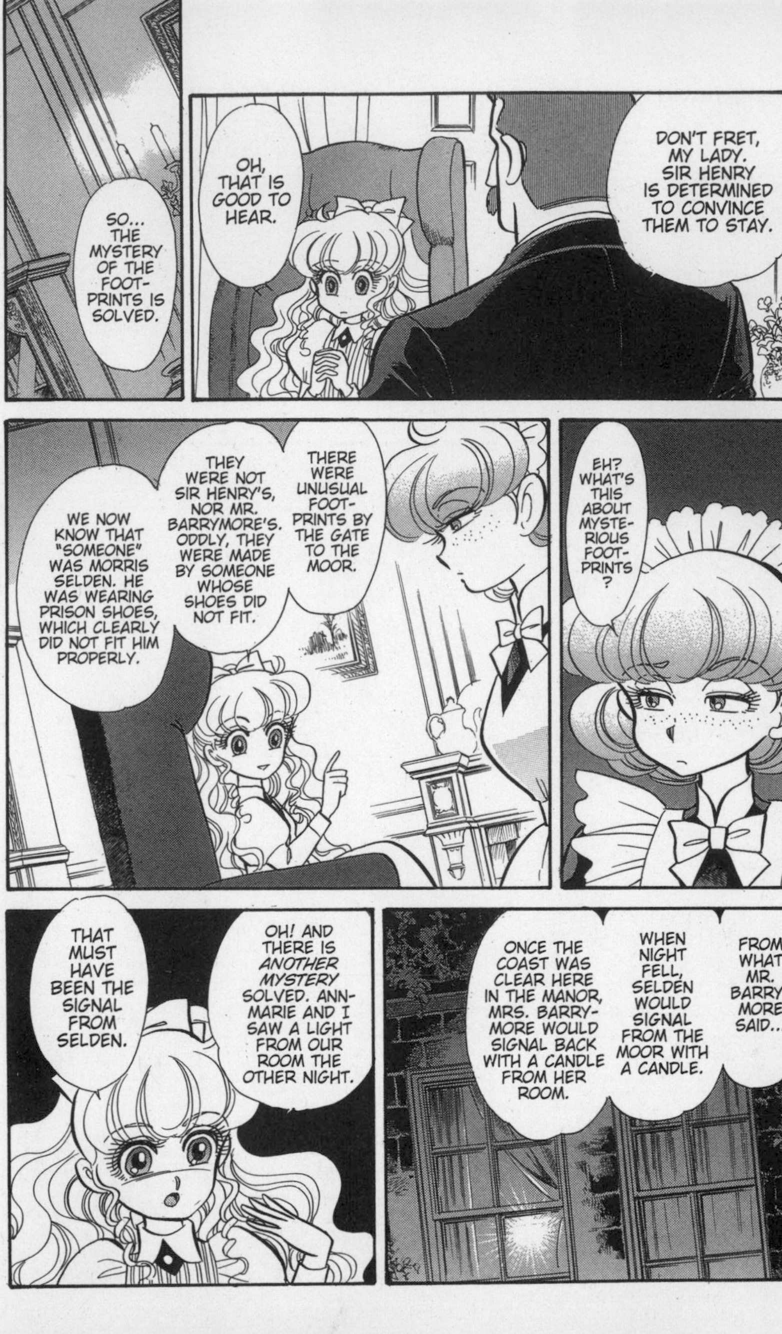
DON'T FRET, MY LADY. SIR HENRY IS DETERMINED TO CONVINCE THEM TO STAY.
OH, THAT IS GOOD TO HEAR.
SO... THE MYSTERY OF THE FOOTPRINTS IS SOLVED.
EH? WHAT'S THIS ABOUT MYSTERIOUS FOOTPRINTS?
THERE WERE UNUSUAL FOOTPRINTS BY THE GATE TO THE MOOR.
THEY WERE NOT SIR HENRY'S, NOR MR. BARRYMORE'S. ODDLY, THEY WERE MADE BY SOMEONE WHOSE SHOES DID NOT FIT.
WE NOW KNOW THAT "SOMEONE" WAS MORRIS SELDEN. HE WAS WEARING PRISON SHOES, WHICH CLEARLY DID NOT FIT HIM PROPERLY.
FROM WHAT MR. BARRYMORE SAID...
WHEN NIGHT FELL, SELDEN WOULD SIGNAL FROM THE MOOR WITH A CANDLE.
ONCE THE COAST WAS CLEAR HERE IN THE MANOR, MRS. BARRYMORE WOULD SIGNAL BACK WITH A CANDLE FROM HER ROOM.
OH! AND THERE IS *ANOTHER MYSTERY* SOLVED. ANN-MARIE AND I SAW A LIGHT FROM OUR ROOM THE OTHER NIGHT.
THAT MUST HAVE BEEN THE SIGNAL FROM SELDEN.

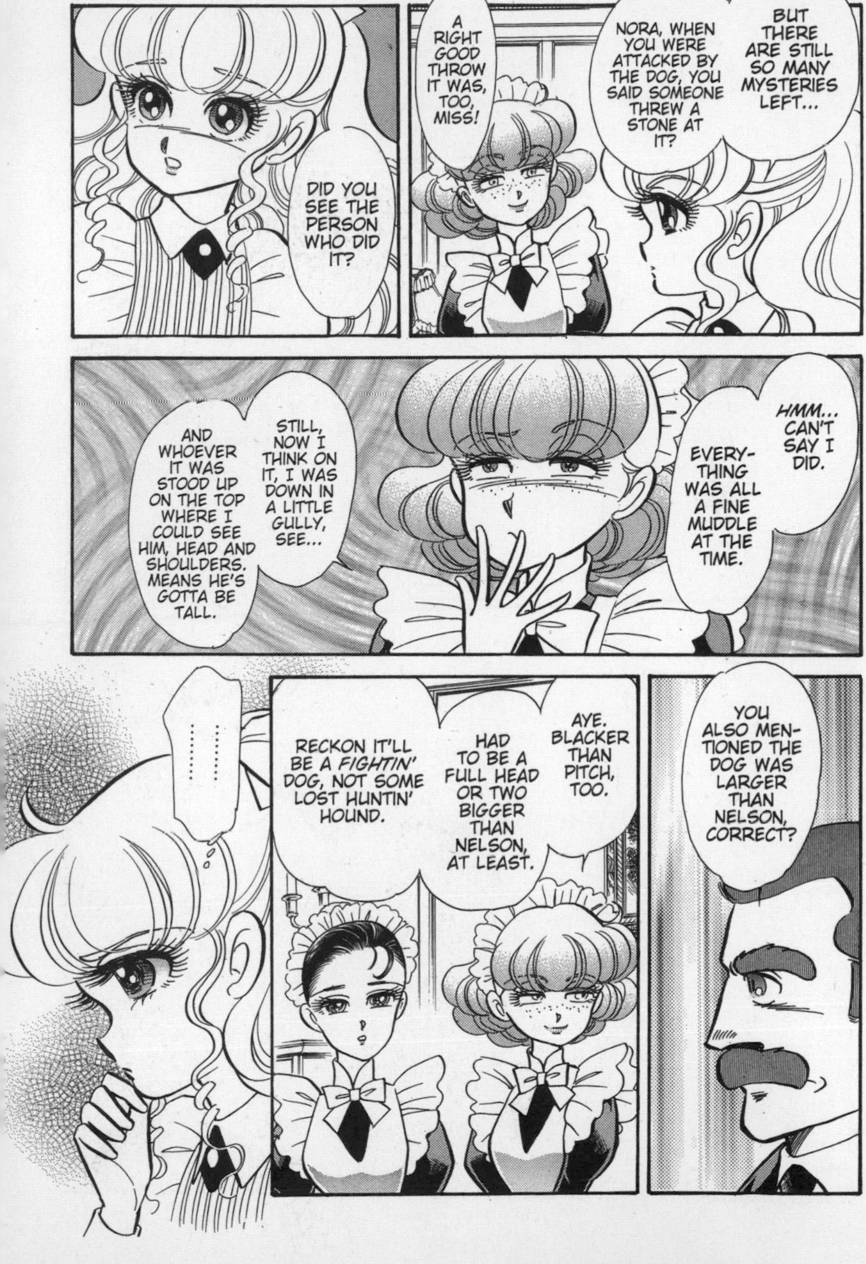
BUT THERE ARE STILL SO MANY MYSTERIES LEFT...
NORA, WHEN YOU WERE ATTACKED BY THE DOG, YOU SAID SOMEONE THREW A STONE AT IT?
A RIGHT GOOD THROW IT WAS, TOO, MISS!
DID YOU SEE THE PERSON WHO DID IT?
HMM... CAN'T SAY I DID.
EVERYTHING WAS ALL A FINE MUDDLE AT THE TIME.
STILL, NOW I THINK ON IT, I WAS DOWN IN A LITTLE GULLY, SEE...
AND WHOEVER IT WAS STOOD UP ON THE TOP WHERE I COULD SEE HIM, HEAD AND SHOULDERS. MEANS HE'S GOTTA BE TALL.
YOU ALSO MENTIONED THE DOG WAS LARGER THAN NELSON, CORRECT?
AYE. BLACKER THAN PITCH, TOO.
HAD TO BE A FULL HEAD OR TWO BIGGER THAN NELSON, AT LEAST.
RECKON IT'LL BE A *FIGHTIN'* DOG, NOT SOME LOST HUNTIN' HOUND.
......

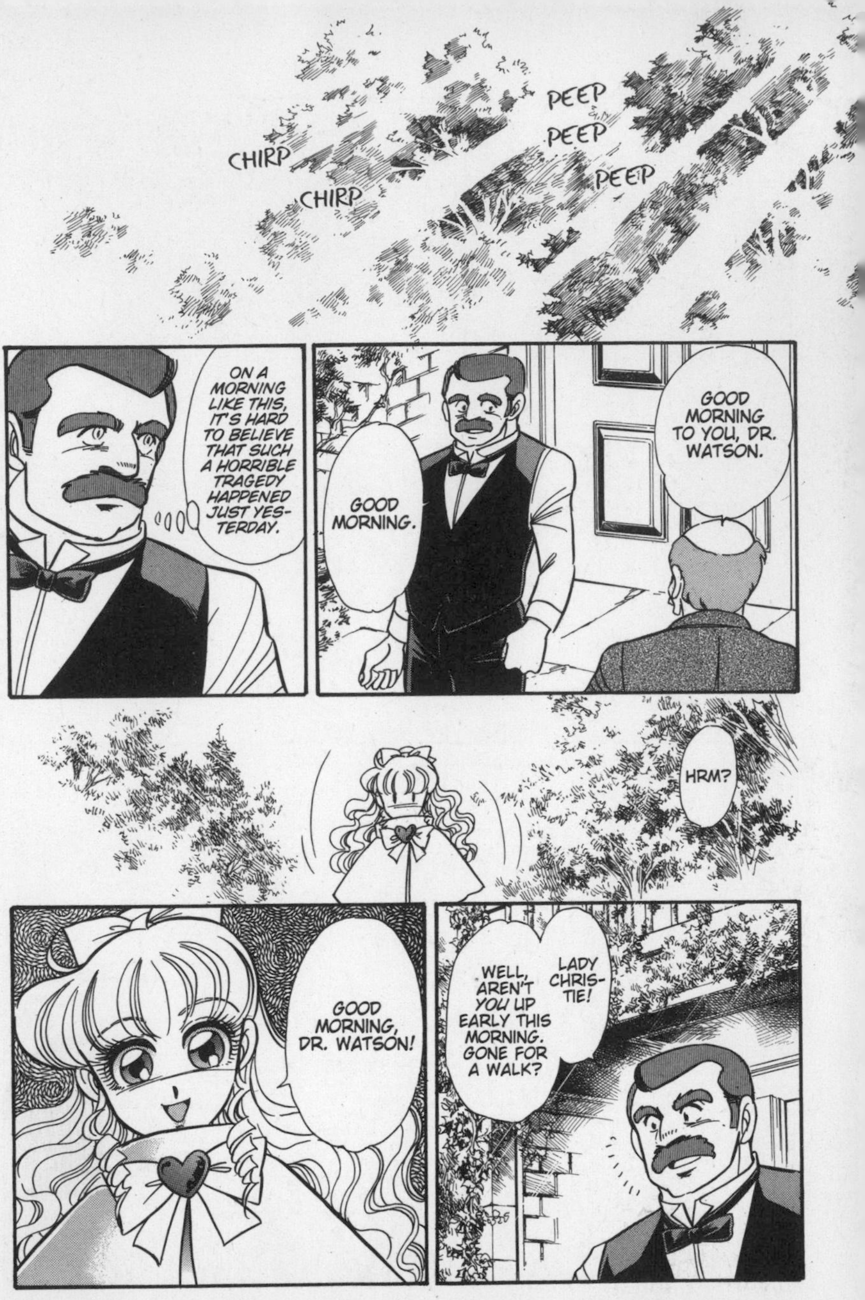
PEEP
PEEP
PEEP
CHIRP
CHIRP
GOOD MORNING TO YOU, DR. WATSON.
GOOD MORNING.
ON A MORNING LIKE THIS, IT'S HARD TO BELIEVE THAT SUCH A HORRIBLE TRAGEDY HAPPENED JUST YESTERDAY.
HRM?
LADY CHRISTIE!
WELL, AREN'T YOU UP EARLY THIS MORNING. GONE FOR A WALK?
GOOD MORNING, DR. WATSON!

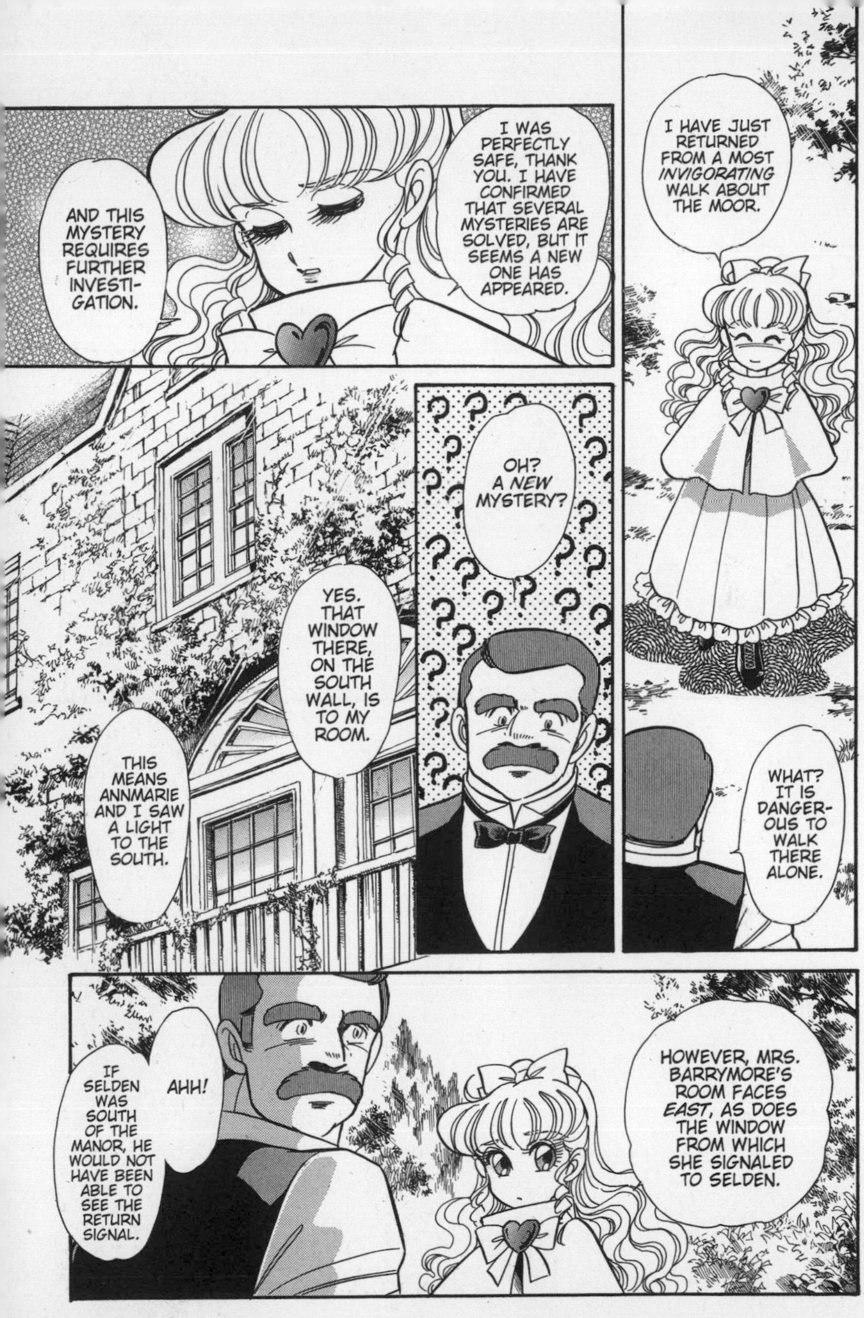
I HAVE JUST RETURNED FROM A MOST *INVIGORATING* WALK ABOUT THE MOOR.
WHAT? IT IS DANGEROUS TO WALK THERE ALONE.
I WAS PERFECTLY SAFE, THANK YOU. I HAVE CONFIRMED THAT SEVERAL MYSTERIES ARE SOLVED, BUT IT SEEMS A NEW ONE HAS APPEARED.
AND THIS MYSTERY REQUIRES FURTHER INVESTIGATION.
OH? A *NEW* MYSTERY?
YES. THAT WINDOW THERE, ON THE SOUTH WALL, IS TO MY ROOM.
THIS MEANS ANNMARIE AND I SAW A LIGHT TO THE SOUTH.
HOWEVER, MRS. BARRYMORE'S ROOM FACES *EAST*, AS DOES THE WINDOW FROM WHICH SHE SIGNALED TO SELDEN.
AHH!
IF SELDEN WAS SOUTH OF THE MANOR, HE WOULD NOT HAVE BEEN ABLE TO SEE THE RETURN SIGNAL.

THEN ... WHAT WAS THE LIGHT THAT YOU AND ANNMARIE SAW?

IT SEEMS IT COULD NOT HAVE BEEN SELDEN'S AFTER ALL.

THAT IS *PRECISELY* WHAT I WISH TO INVESTIGATE THIS AFTERNOON!

HOWEVER, GOING THAT FAR INTO THE MOOR ALONE IS BEYOND MY MEAGER COURAGE.

WOULD YOU BE SO KIND AS TO ACCOMPANY ME, DR. WATSON?

YES, OF COURSE!

I WOULD BE DELIGHTED.

THAT IS A MOST WISE IDEA, IF I DO SAY SO MYSELF.

THE MATTER OF THE DOG IS MORE DIFFICULT, HOWEVER.

THAT I WILL NOT BE ABLE TO INVESTIGATE WITHOUT RETURNING TO LONDON.

OH? AND WHY NOT?

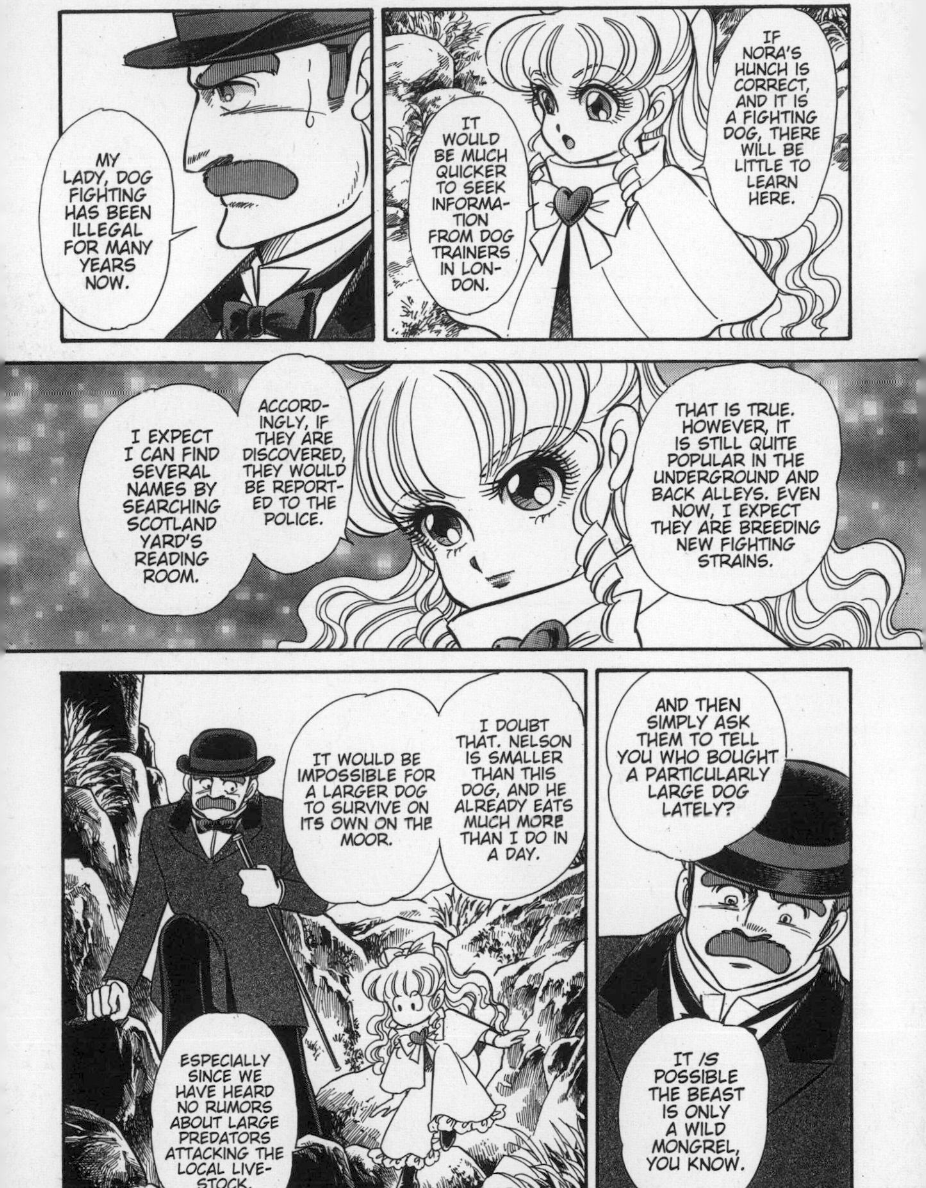
IF NORA'S HUNCH IS CORRECT, AND IT IS A FIGHTING DOG, THERE WILL BE LITTLE TO LEARN HERE.
IT WOULD BE MUCH QUICKER TO SEEK INFORMATION FROM DOG TRAINERS IN LONDON.
MY LADY, DOG FIGHTING HAS BEEN ILLEGAL FOR MANY YEARS NOW.
THAT IS TRUE. HOWEVER, IT IS STILL QUITE POPULAR IN THE UNDERGROUND AND BACK ALLEYS. EVEN NOW, I EXPECT THEY ARE BREEDING NEW FIGHTING STRAINS.
ACCORDINGLY, IF THEY ARE DISCOVERED, THEY WOULD BE REPORTED TO THE POLICE.
I EXPECT I CAN FIND SEVERAL NAMES BY SEARCHING SCOTLAND YARD'S READING ROOM.
AND THEN SIMPLY ASK THEM TO TELL YOU WHO BOUGHT A PARTICULARLY LARGE DOG LATELY?
IT *IS* POSSIBLE THE BEAST IS ONLY A WILD MONGREL, YOU KNOW.
I DOUBT THAT. NELSON IS SMALLER THAN THIS DOG, AND HE ALREADY EATS MUCH MORE THAN I DO IN A DAY.
IT WOULD BE IMPOSSIBLE FOR A LARGER DOG TO SURVIVE ON ITS OWN ON THE MOOR.
ESPECIALLY SINCE WE HAVE HEARD NO RUMORS ABOUT LARGE PREDATORS ATTACKING THE LOCAL LIVESTOCK.

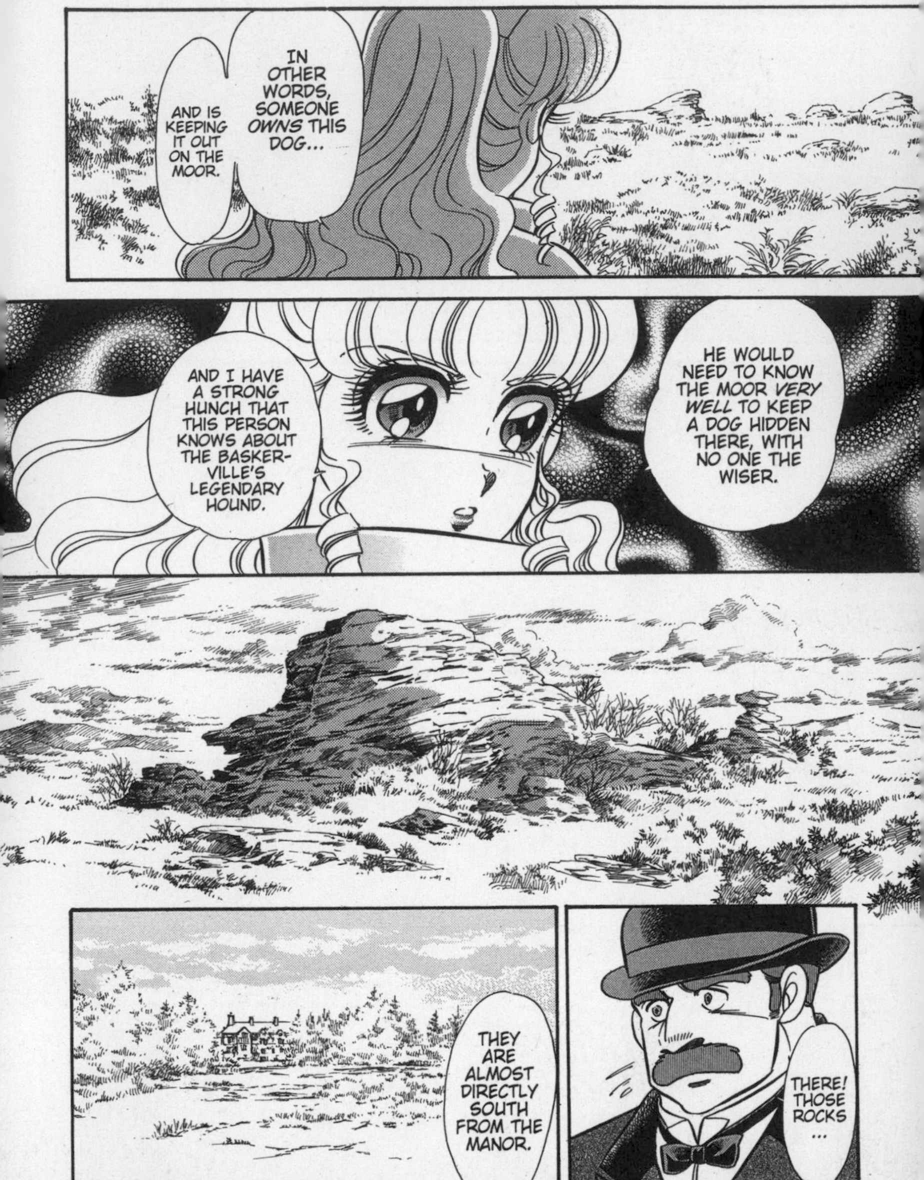
IN OTHER WORDS, SOMEONE OWNS THIS DOG...
AND IS KEEPING IT OUT ON THE MOOR.
HE WOULD NEED TO KNOW THE MOOR VERY WELL TO KEEP A DOG HIDDEN THERE, WITH NO ONE THE WISER.
AND I HAVE A STRONG HUNCH THAT THIS PERSON KNOWS ABOUT THE BASKER-VILLE'S LEGENDARY HOUND.
THERE! THOSE ROCKS ...
THEY ARE ALMOST DIRECTLY SOUTH FROM THE MANOR.

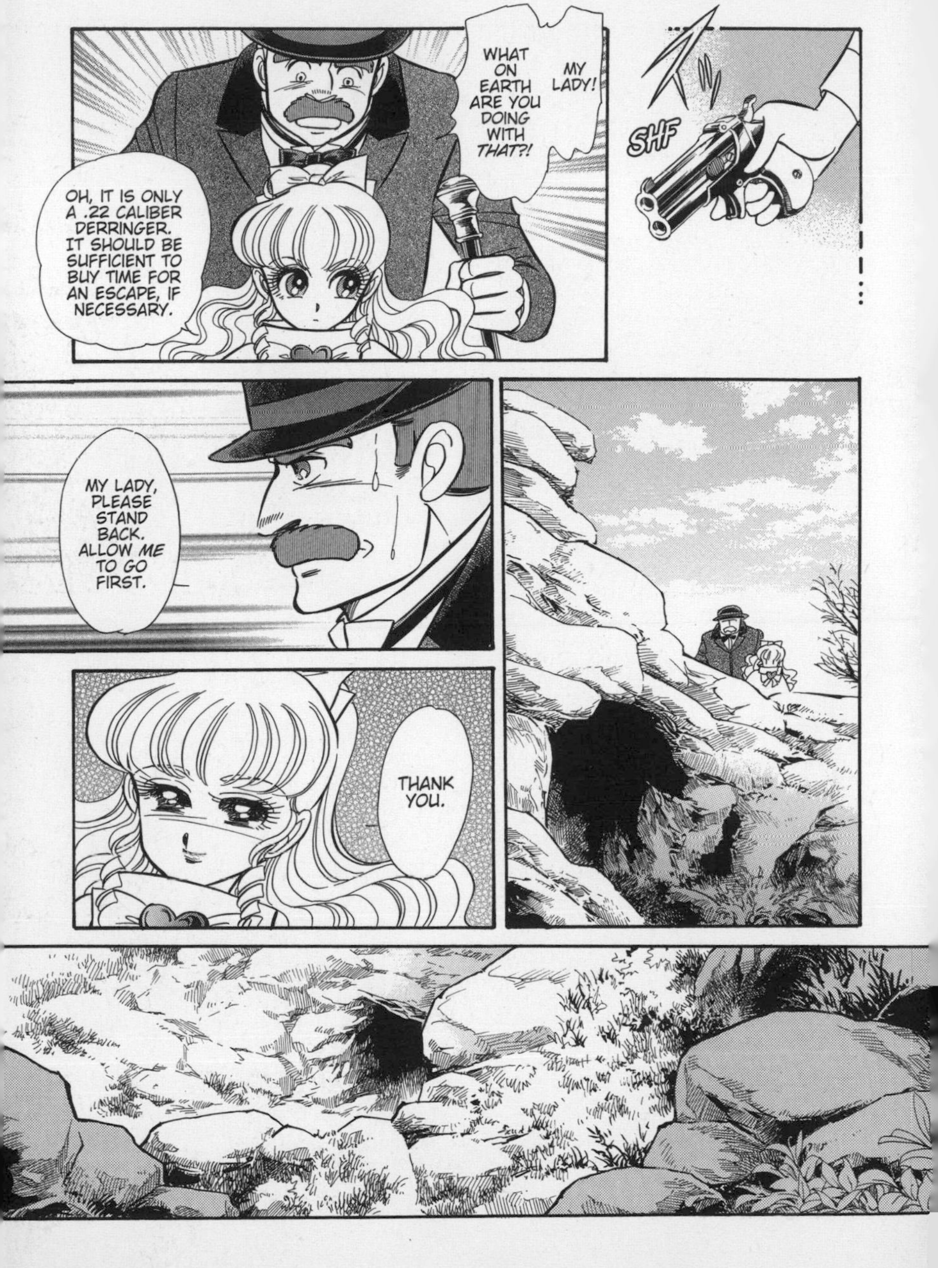
SHF
MY LADY!
WHAT ON EARTH ARE YOU DOING WITH *THAT?!*
OH, IT IS ONLY A .22 CALIBER DERRINGER. IT SHOULD BE SUFFICIENT TO BUY TIME FOR AN ESCAPE, IF NECESSARY.
MY LADY, PLEASE STAND BACK. ALLOW *ME* TO GO FIRST.
THANK YOU.

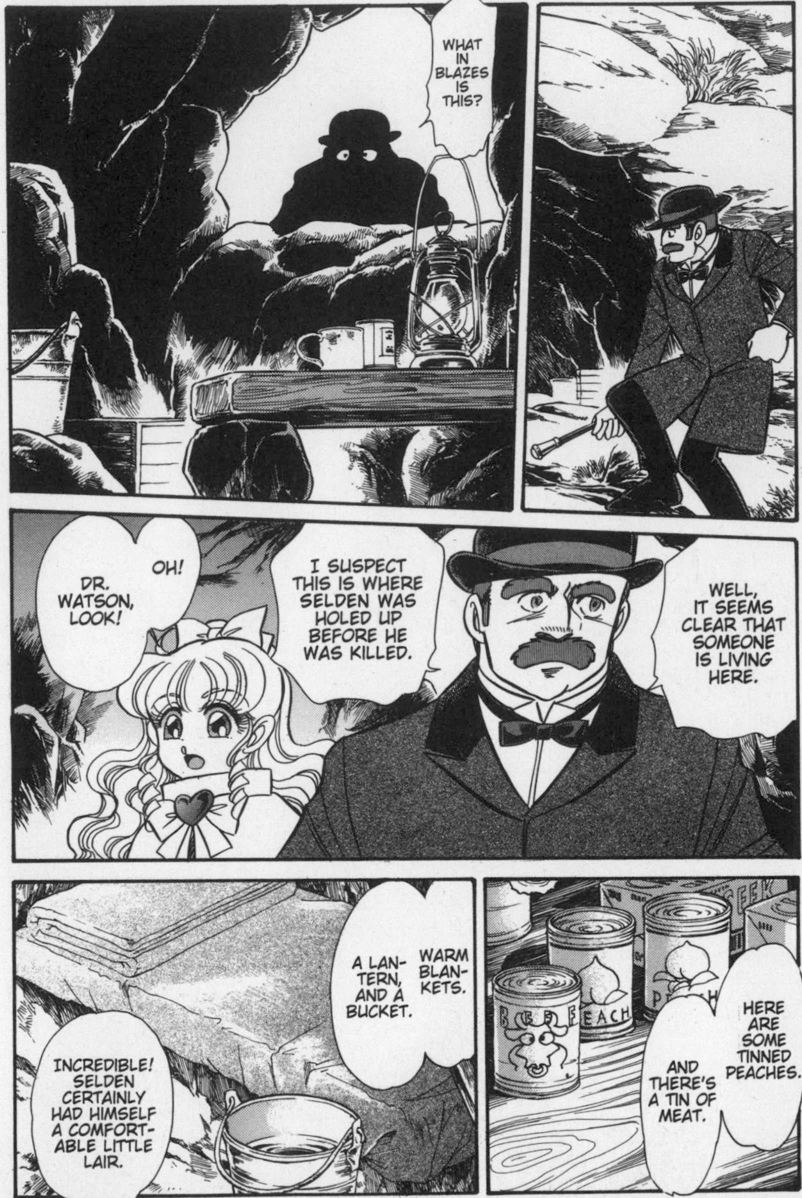
WHAT IN BLAZES IS THIS?
WELL, IT SEEMS CLEAR THAT SOMEONE IS LIVING HERE.
I SUSPECT THIS IS WHERE SELDEN WAS HOLED UP BEFORE HE WAS KILLED.
OH! DR. WATSON, LOOK!
HERE ARE SOME TINNED PEACHES.
AND THERE'S A TIN OF MEAT.
WARM BLANKETS.
A LANTERN, AND A BUCKET.
INCREDIBLE! SELDEN CERTAINLY HAD HIMSELF A COMFORTABLE LITTLE LAIR.

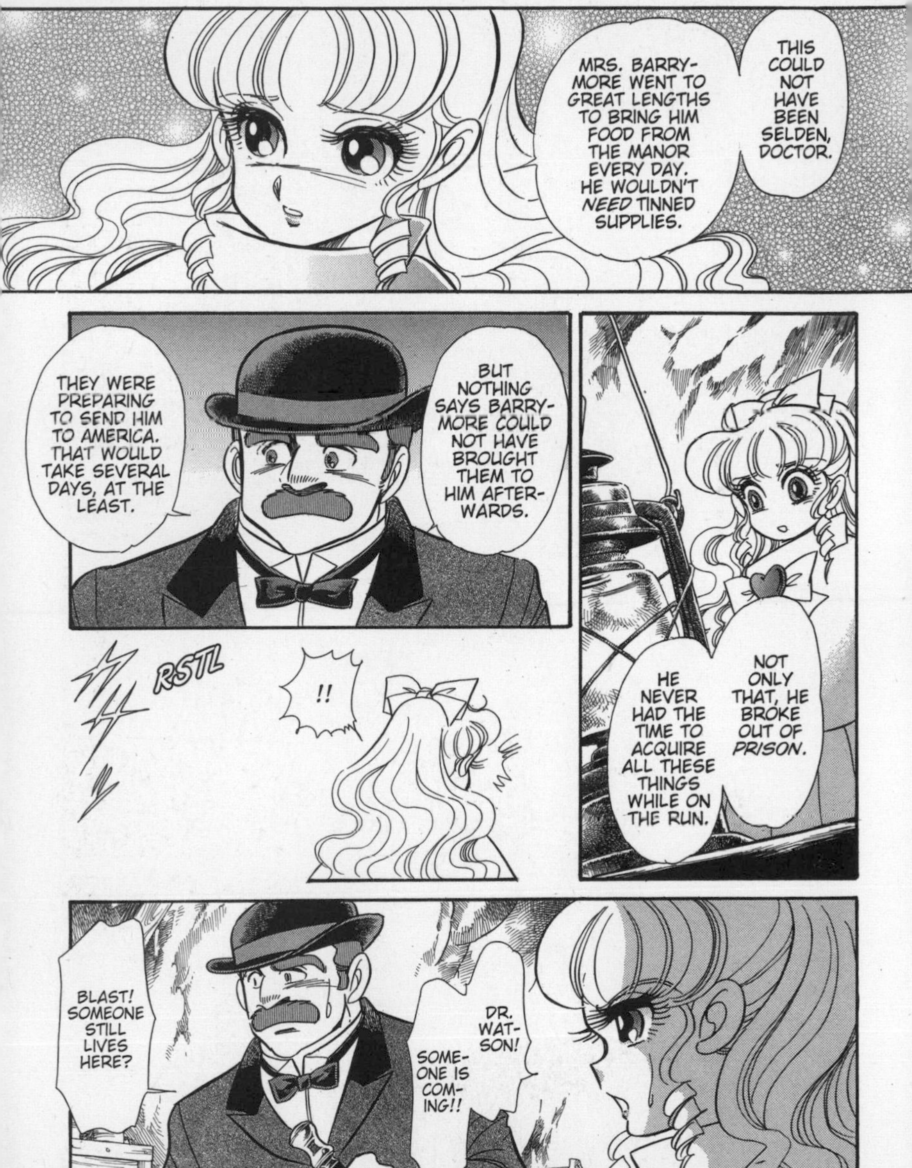
THIS COULD NOT HAVE BEEN SELDEN, DOCTOR.
MRS. BARRYMORE WENT TO GREAT LENGTHS TO BRING HIM FOOD FROM THE MANOR EVERY DAY. HE WOULDN'T *NEED* TINNED SUPPLIES.
NOT ONLY THAT, HE BROKE OUT OF *PRISON*.
HE NEVER HAD THE TIME TO ACQUIRE ALL THESE THINGS WHILE ON THE RUN.
BUT NOTHING SAYS BARRYMORE COULD NOT HAVE BROUGHT THEM TO HIM AFTERWARDS.
THEY WERE PREPARING TO SEND HIM TO AMERICA. THAT WOULD TAKE SEVERAL DAYS, AT THE LEAST.
!!
RSTL
DR. WATSON!
SOMEONE IS COMING!!
BLAST! SOMEONE STILL LIVES HERE?

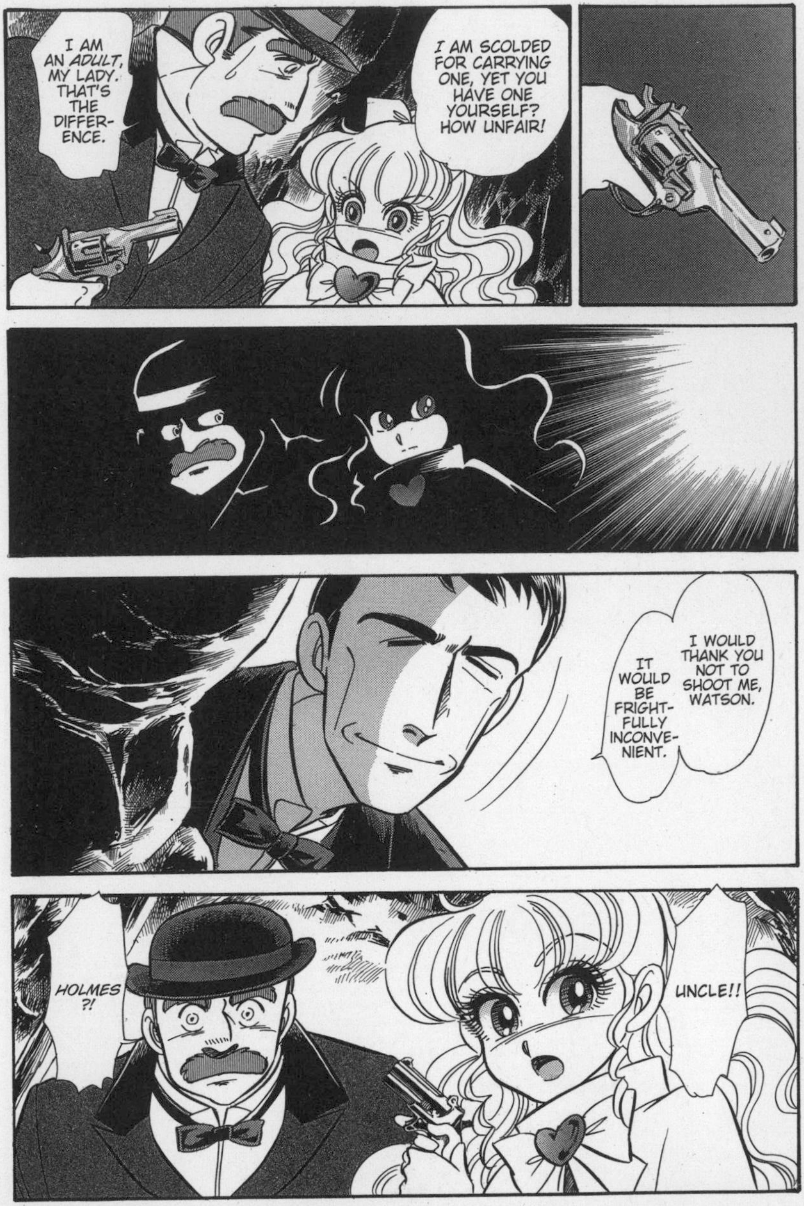
I AM SCOLDED FOR CARRYING ONE, YET YOU HAVE ONE YOURSELF? HOW UNFAIR!
I AM AN *ADULT*, MY LADY. THAT'S THE DIFFERENCE.
I WOULD THANK YOU NOT TO SHOOT ME, WATSON.
IT WOULD BE FRIGHTFULLY INCONVENIENT.
UNCLE!!
HOLMES?!

The Hound of the Baskervilles (8)

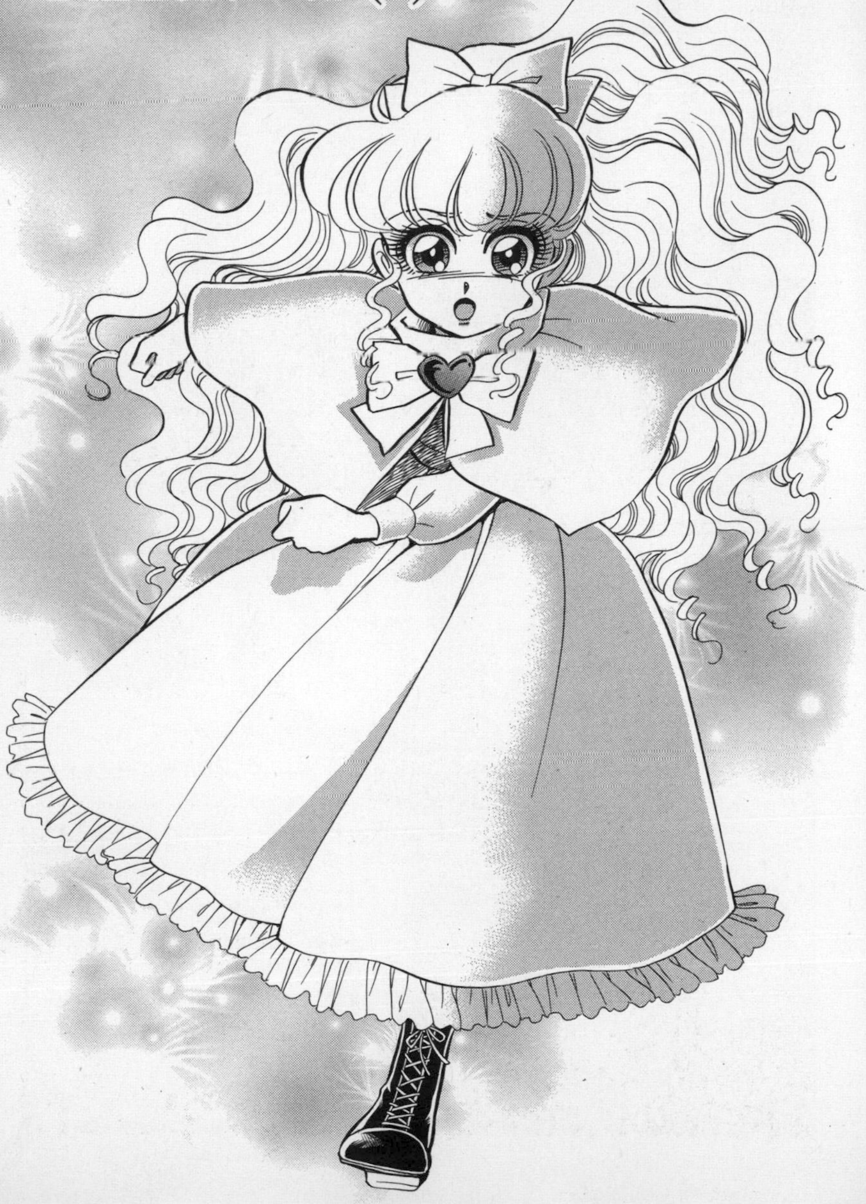

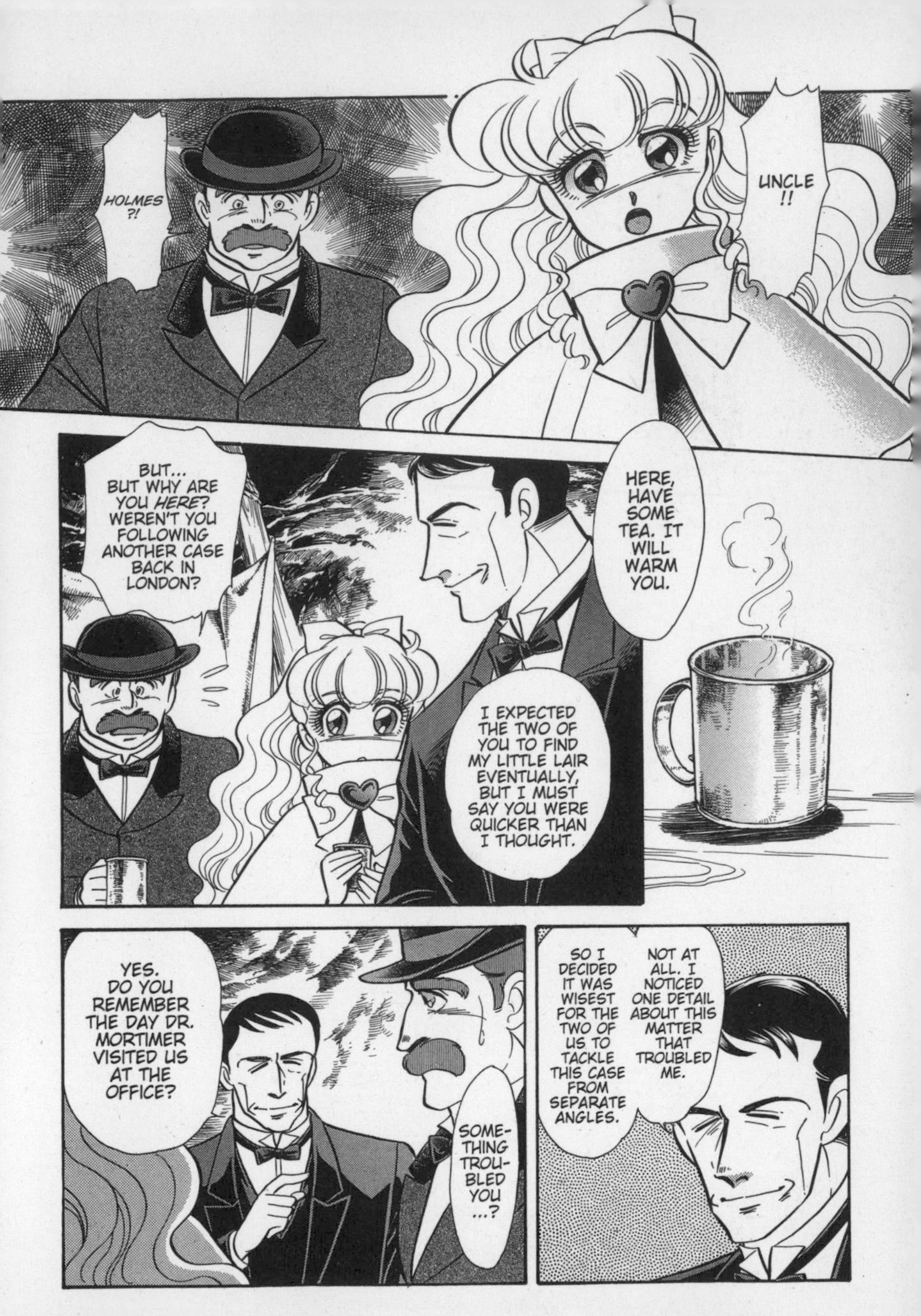
HOLMES ?!
UNCLE !!
BUT... BUT WHY ARE YOU *HERE*? WEREN'T YOU FOLLOWING ANOTHER CASE BACK IN LONDON?
HERE, HAVE SOME TEA. IT WILL WARM YOU.
I EXPECTED THE TWO OF YOU TO FIND MY LITTLE LAIR EVENTUALLY, BUT I MUST SAY YOU WERE QUICKER THAN I THOUGHT.
YES. DO YOU REMEMBER THE DAY DR. MORTIMER VISITED US AT THE OFFICE?
SOME-THING TROU-BLED YOU ...?
NOT AT ALL. I NOTICED ONE DETAIL ABOUT THIS MATTER THAT TROUBLED ME.
SO I DECIDED IT WAS WISEST FOR THE TWO OF US TO TACKLE THIS CASE FROM SEPARATE ANGLES.

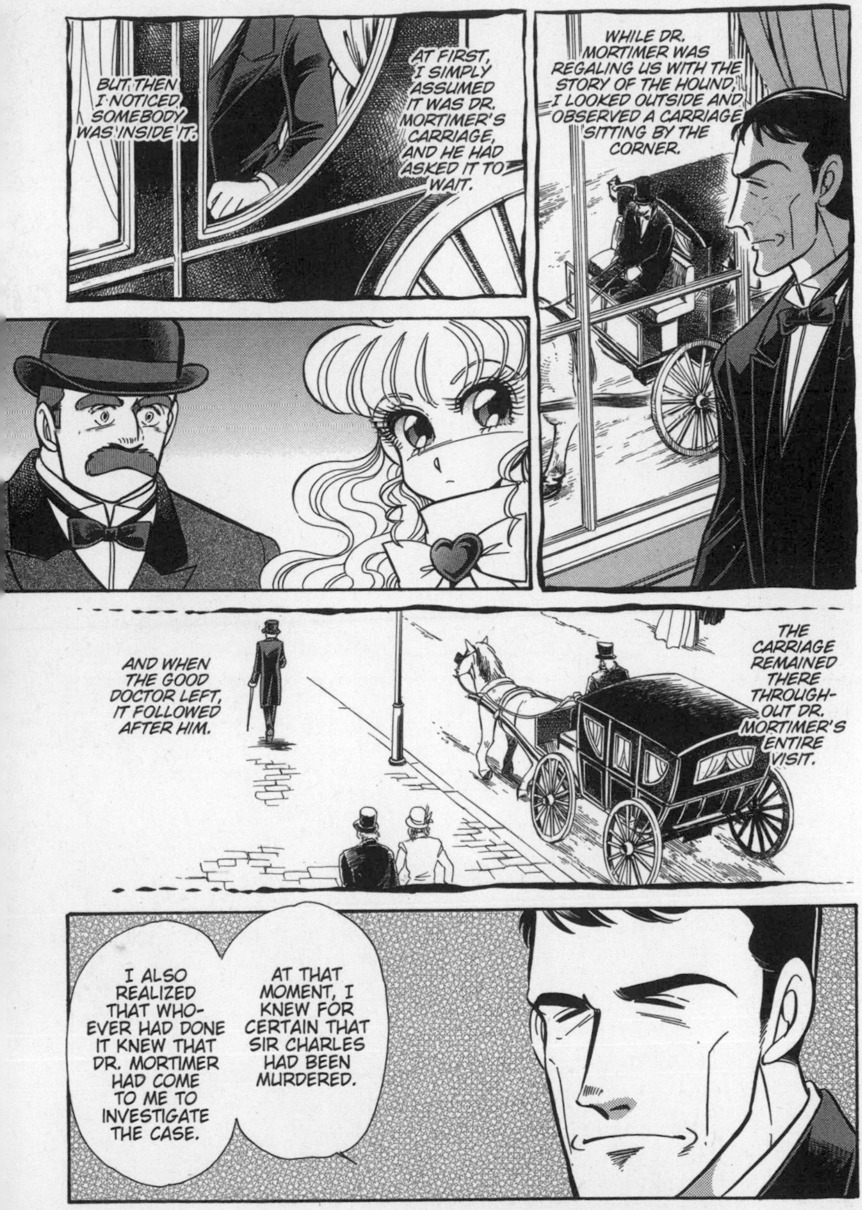
WHILE DR. MORTIMER WAS REGALING US WITH THE STORY OF THE HOUND, I LOOKED OUTSIDE AND OBSERVED A CARRIAGE SITTING BY THE CORNER.
AT FIRST, I SIMPLY ASSUMED IT WAS DR. MORTIMER'S CARRIAGE, AND HE HAD ASKED IT TO WAIT.
BUT THEN I NOTICED SOMEBODY WAS INSIDE IT.
THE CARRIAGE REMAINED THERE THROUGH-OUT DR. MORTIMER'S ENTIRE VISIT.
AND WHEN THE GOOD DOCTOR LEFT, IT FOLLOWED AFTER HIM.
AT THAT MOMENT, I KNEW FOR CERTAIN THAT SIR CHARLES HAD BEEN MURDERED.
I ALSO REALIZED THAT WHO-EVER HAD DONE IT KNEW THAT DR. MORTIMER HAD COME TO ME TO INVESTIGATE THE CASE.

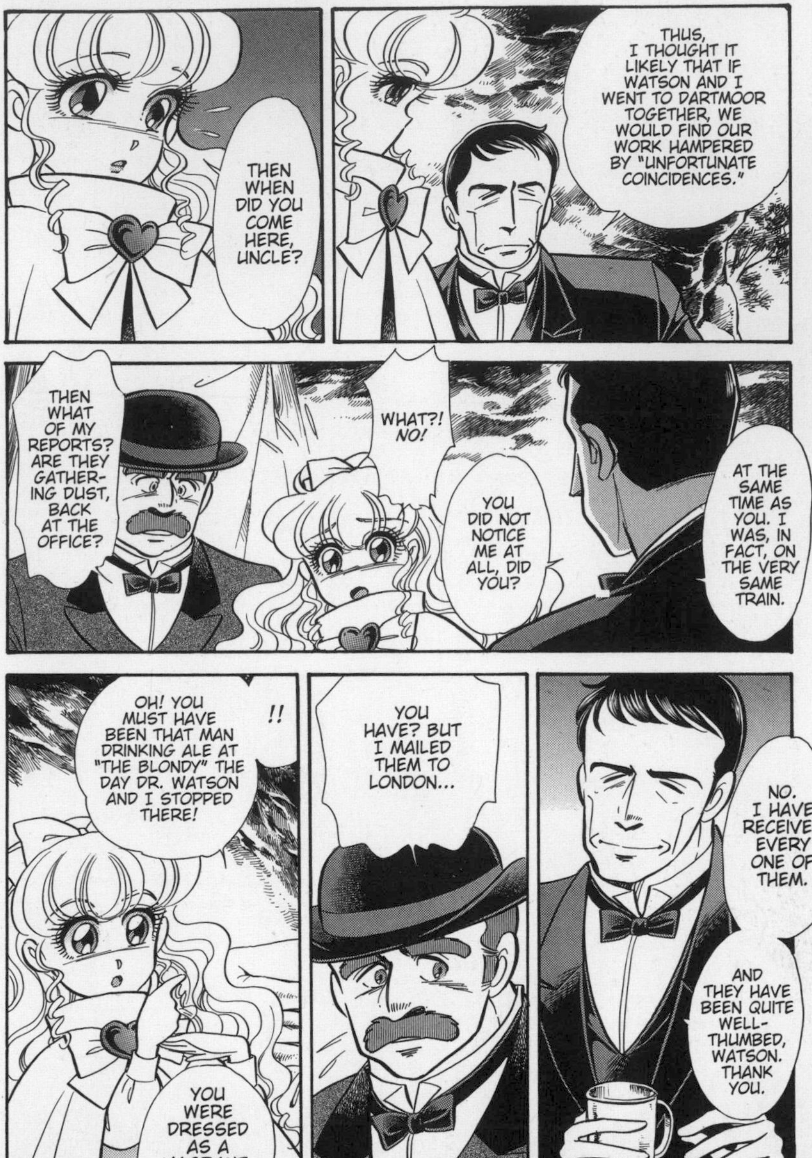
THUS, I THOUGHT IT LIKELY THAT IF WATSON AND I WENT TO DARTMOOR TOGETHER, WE WOULD FIND OUR WORK HAMPERED BY "UNFORTUNATE COINCIDENCES."
THEN WHEN DID YOU COME HERE, UNCLE?
AT THE SAME TIME AS YOU. I WAS, IN FACT, ON THE VERY SAME TRAIN.
YOU DID NOT NOTICE ME AT ALL, DID YOU?
WHAT?! NO!
THEN WHAT OF MY REPORTS? ARE THEY GATHERING DUST, BACK AT THE OFFICE?
NO. I HAVE RECEIVED EVERY ONE OF THEM.
AND THEY HAVE BEEN QUITE WELL-THUMBED, WATSON. THANK YOU.
YOU HAVE? BUT I MAILED THEM TO LONDON...
!!
OH! YOU MUST HAVE BEEN THAT MAN DRINKING ALE AT "THE BLONDY" THE DAY DR. WATSON AND I STOPPED THERE!
YOU WERE DRESSED AS A VAGRANT. A FILTHY ONE, AT THAT.

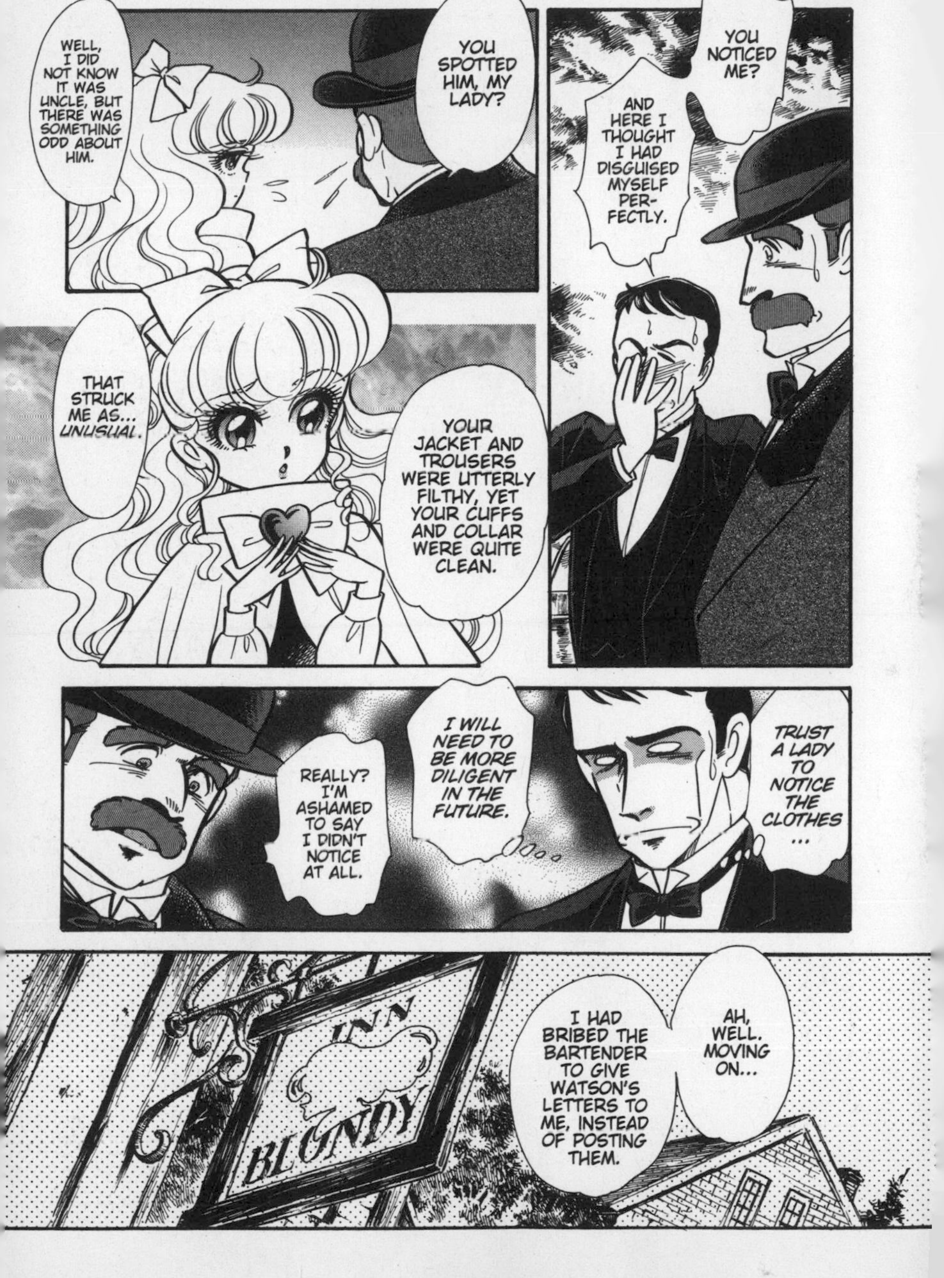
YOU NOTICED ME?
AND HERE I THOUGHT I HAD DISGUISED MYSELF PER-FECTLY.
YOU SPOTTED HIM, MY LADY?
WELL, I DID NOT KNOW IT WAS UNCLE, BUT THERE WAS SOMETHING ODD ABOUT HIM.
YOUR JACKET AND TROUSERS WERE UTTERLY FILTHY, YET YOUR CUFFS AND COLLAR WERE QUITE CLEAN.
THAT STRUCK ME AS... *UNUSUAL*.
TRUST A LADY TO NOTICE THE CLOTHES...
I WILL NEED TO BE MORE DILIGENT IN THE FUTURE.
REALLY? I'M ASHAMED TO SAY I DIDN'T NOTICE AT ALL.
AH, WELL. MOVING ON...
I HAD BRIBED THE BARTENDER TO GIVE WATSON'S LETTERS TO ME, INSTEAD OF POSTING THEM.
INN
BLONDY

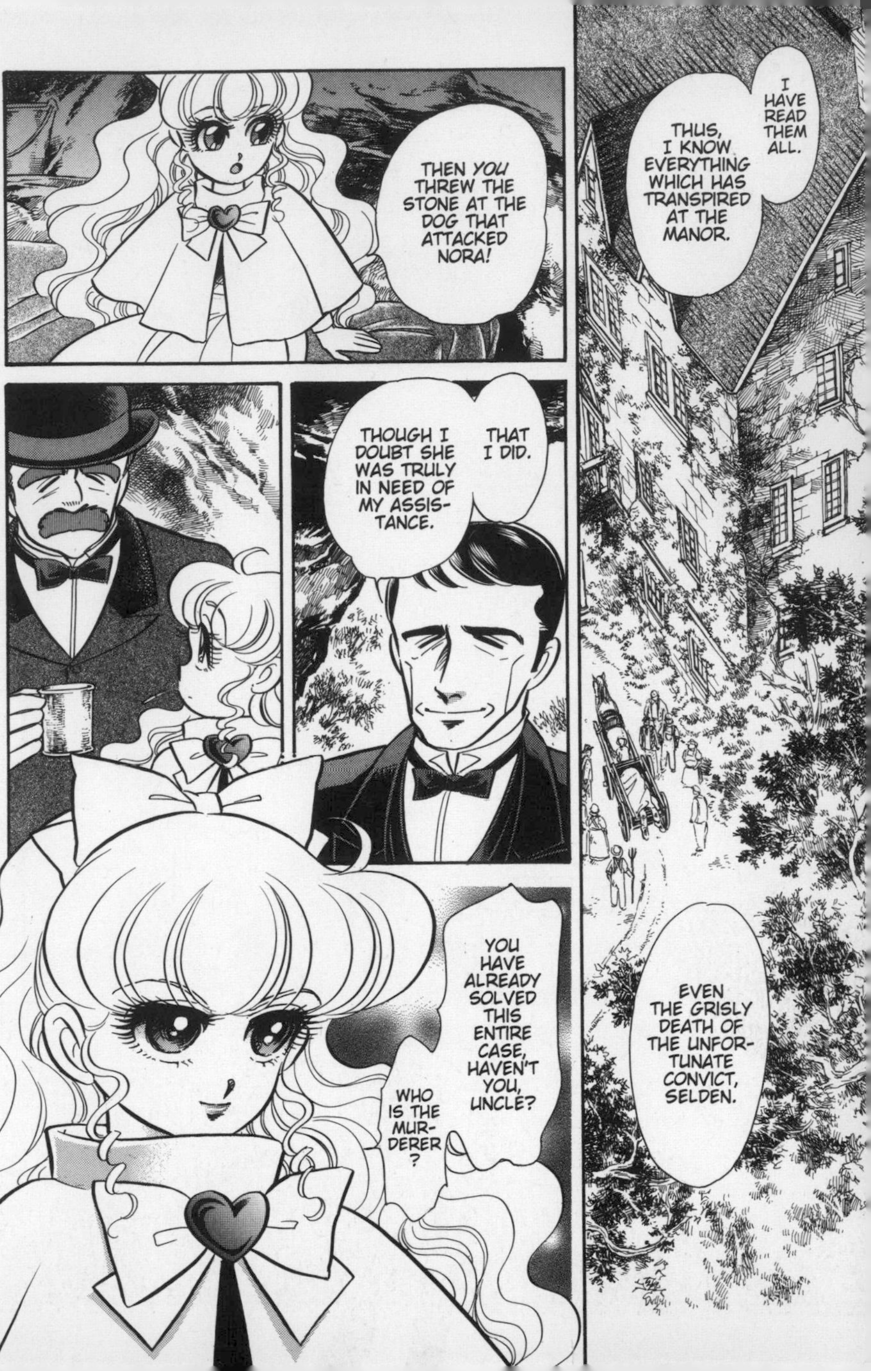
I HAVE READ THEM ALL.
THUS, I KNOW EVERYTHING WHICH HAS TRANSPIRED AT THE MANOR.
EVEN THE GRISLY DEATH OF THE UNFORTUNATE CONVICT, SELDEN.
THEN *YOU* THREW THE STONE AT THE DOG THAT ATTACKED NORA!
THAT I DID.
THOUGH I DOUBT SHE WAS TRULY IN NEED OF MY ASSISTANCE.
YOU HAVE ALREADY SOLVED THIS ENTIRE CASE, HAVEN'T YOU, UNCLE?
WHO IS THE MURDERER?

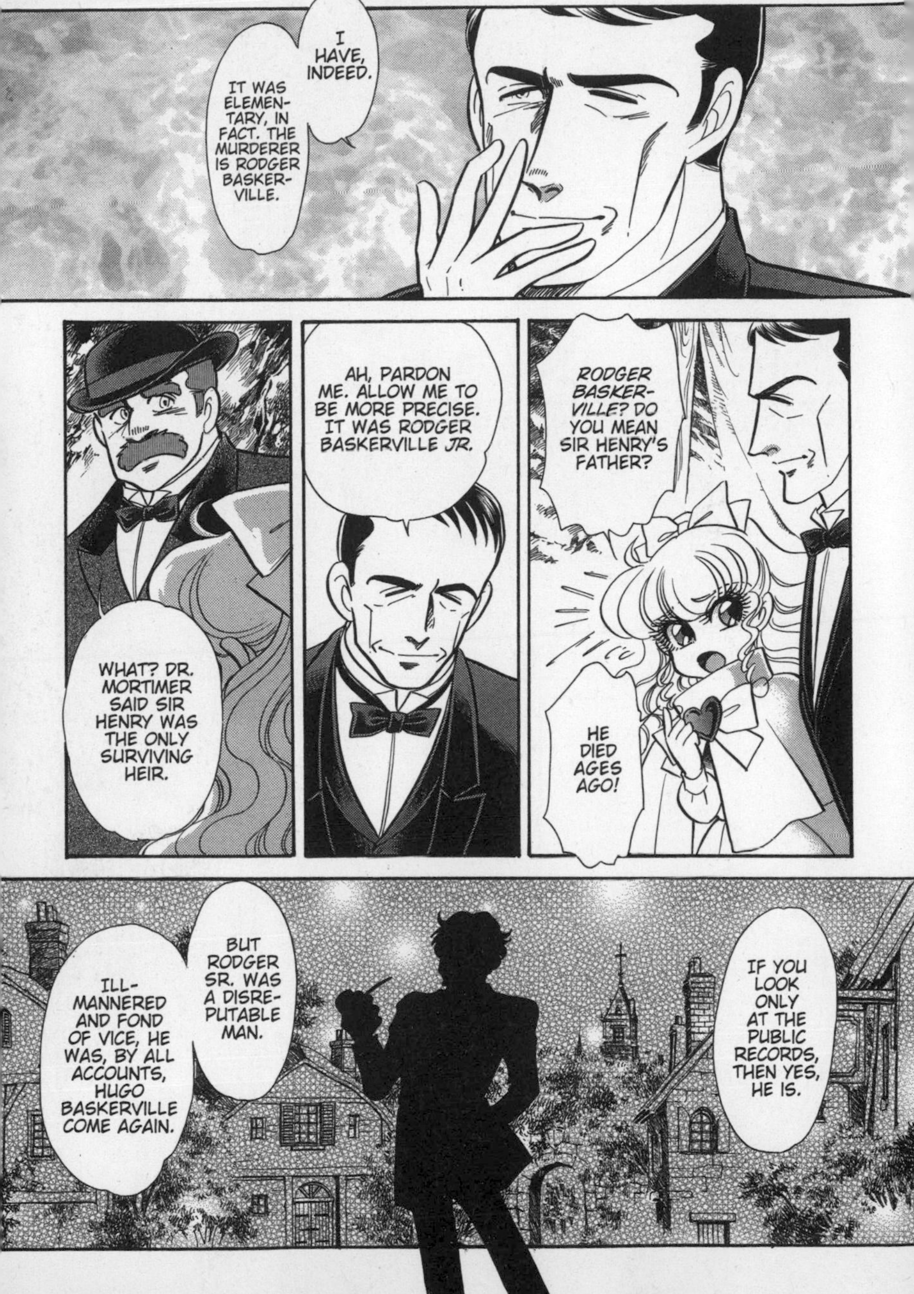
I HAVE, INDEED.
IT WAS ELEMENTARY, IN FACT. THE MURDERER IS RODGER BASKERVILLE.
RODGER BASKERVILLE? DO YOU MEAN SIR HENRY'S FATHER?
HE DIED AGES AGO!
AH, PARDON ME. ALLOW ME TO BE MORE PRECISE. IT WAS RODGER BASKERVILLE *JR.*
WHAT? DR. MORTIMER SAID SIR HENRY WAS THE ONLY SURVIVING HEIR.
IF YOU LOOK ONLY AT THE PUBLIC RECORDS, THEN YES, HE IS.
BUT RODGER SR. WAS A DISREPUTABLE MAN.
ILL-MANNERED AND FOND OF VICE, HE WAS, BY ALL ACCOUNTS, HUGO BASKERVILLE COME AGAIN.

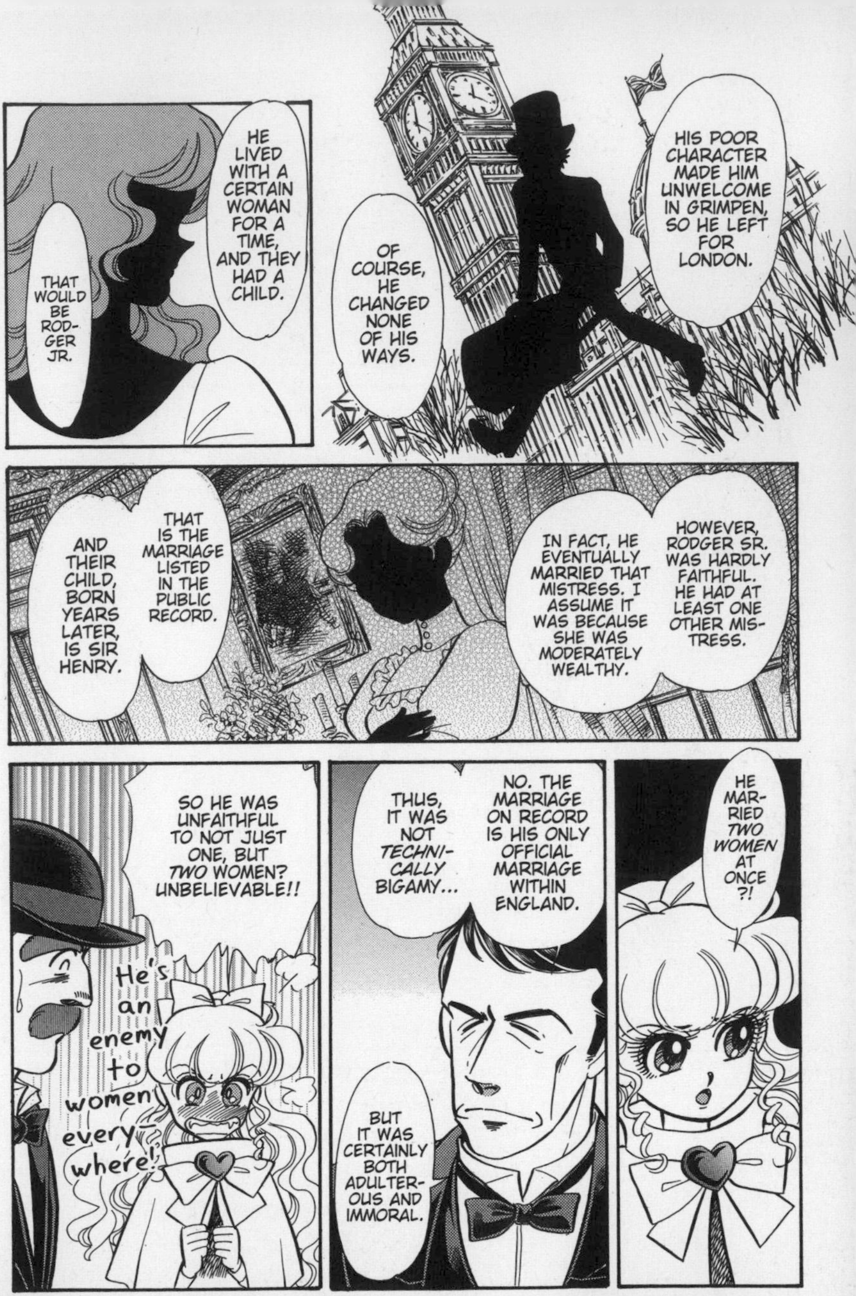
HIS POOR CHARACTER MADE HIM UNWELCOME IN GRIMPEN, SO HE LEFT FOR LONDON.
OF COURSE, HE CHANGED NONE OF HIS WAYS.
HE LIVED WITH A CERTAIN WOMAN FOR A TIME, AND THEY HAD A CHILD.
THAT WOULD BE RODGER JR.
HOWEVER, RODGER SR. WAS HARDLY FAITHFUL. HE HAD AT LEAST ONE OTHER MISTRESS.
IN FACT, HE EVENTUALLY MARRIED THAT MISTRESS. I ASSUME IT WAS BECAUSE SHE WAS MODERATELY WEALTHY.
THAT IS THE MARRIAGE LISTED IN THE PUBLIC RECORD.
AND THEIR CHILD, BORN YEARS LATER, IS SIR HENRY.
HE MARRIED *TWO WOMEN* AT ONCE?!
NO. THE MARRIAGE ON RECORD IS HIS ONLY OFFICIAL MARRIAGE WITHIN ENGLAND.
THUS, IT WAS NOT *TECHNICALLY* BIGAMY...
BUT IT WAS CERTAINLY BOTH ADULTEROUS AND IMMORAL.
SO HE WAS UNFAITHFUL TO NOT JUST ONE, BUT *TWO* WOMEN? UNBELIEVABLE!!
He's an enemy to women everywhere!

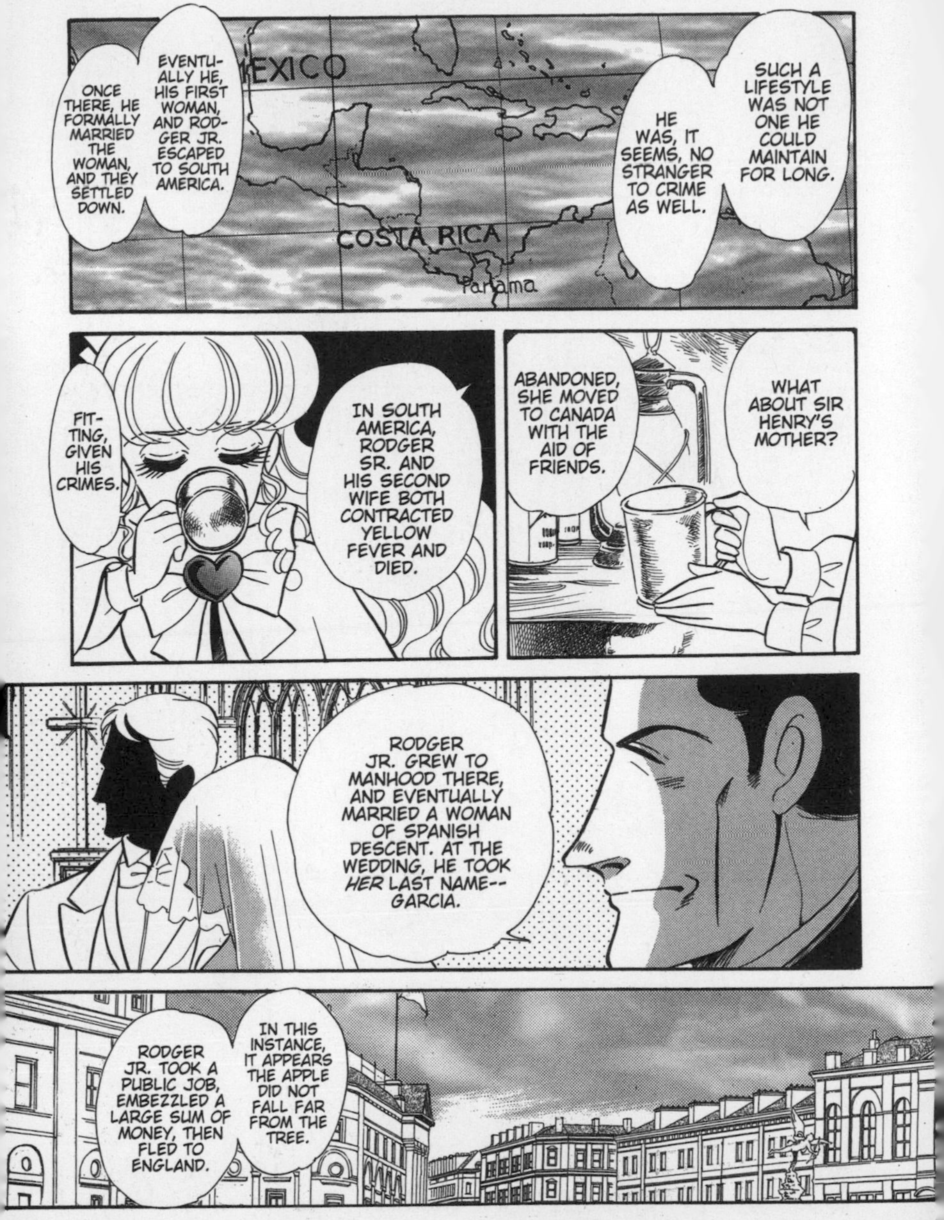
SUCH A LIFESTYLE WAS NOT ONE HE COULD MAINTAIN FOR LONG.
HE WAS, IT SEEMS, NO STRANGER TO CRIME AS WELL.
EVENTUALLY HE, HIS FIRST WOMAN, AND RODGER JR. ESCAPED TO SOUTH AMERICA.
ONCE THERE, HE FORMALLY MARRIED THE WOMAN, AND THEY SETTLED DOWN.
EXICO
COSTA RICA
Panama
WHAT ABOUT SIR HENRY'S MOTHER?
ABANDONED, SHE MOVED TO CANADA WITH THE AID OF FRIENDS.
IN SOUTH AMERICA, RODGER SR. AND HIS SECOND WIFE BOTH CONTRACTED YELLOW FEVER AND DIED.
FITTING, GIVEN HIS CRIMES.
RODGER JR. GREW TO MANHOOD THERE, AND EVENTUALLY MARRIED A WOMAN OF SPANISH DESCENT. AT THE WEDDING, HE TOOK *HER* LAST NAME--GARCIA.
IN THIS INSTANCE, IT APPEARS THE APPLE DID NOT FALL FAR FROM THE TREE.
RODGER JR. TOOK A PUBLIC JOB, EMBEZZLED A LARGE SUM OF MONEY, THEN FLED TO ENGLAND.

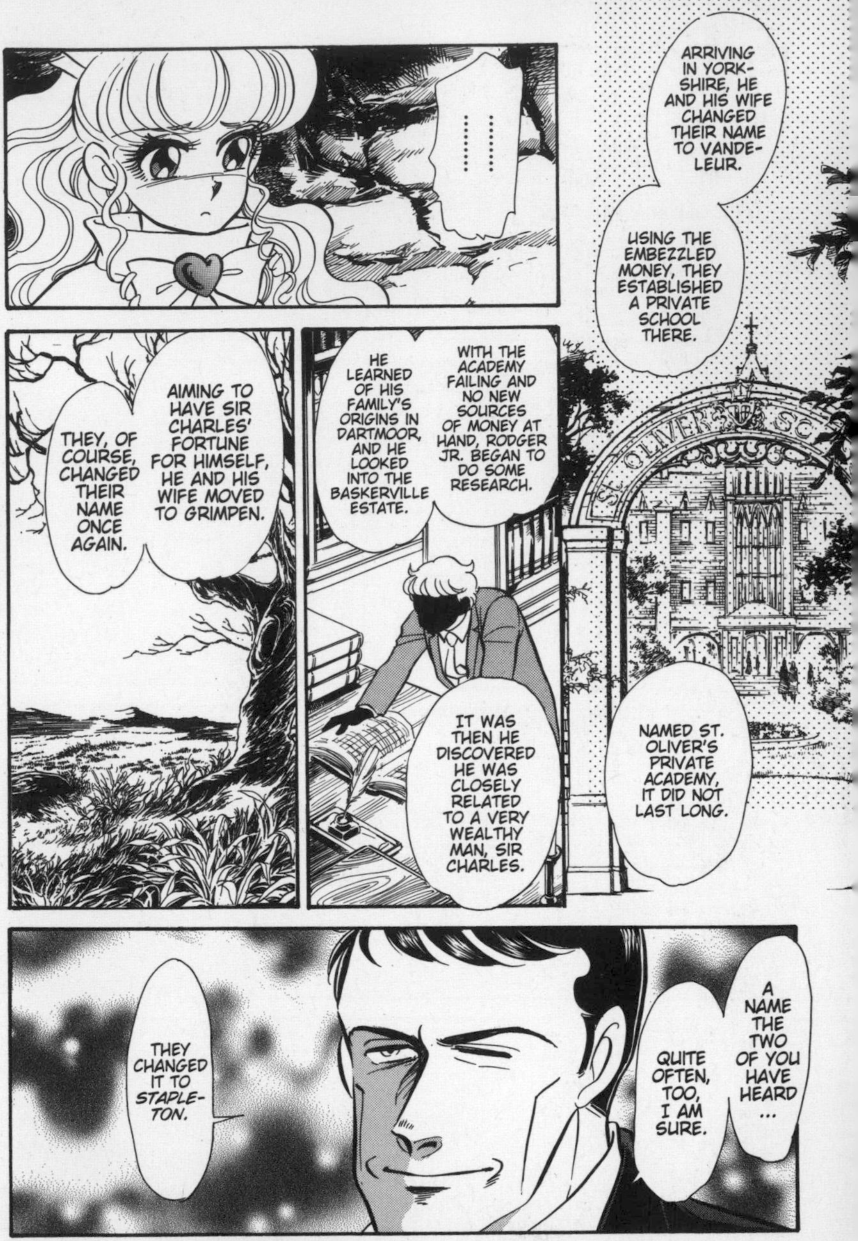
ARRIVING IN YORKSHIRE, HE AND HIS WIFE CHANGED THEIR NAME TO VANDELEUR.
USING THE EMBEZZLED MONEY, THEY ESTABLISHED A PRIVATE SCHOOL THERE.
ST. OLIVER'S SC
NAMED ST. OLIVER'S PRIVATE ACADEMY, IT DID NOT LAST LONG.
......
WITH THE ACADEMY FAILING AND NO NEW SOURCES OF MONEY AT HAND, RODGER JR. BEGAN TO DO SOME RESEARCH.
HE LEARNED OF HIS FAMILY'S ORIGINS IN DARTMOOR, AND HE LOOKED INTO THE BASKERVILLE ESTATE.
IT WAS THEN HE DISCOVERED HE WAS CLOSELY RELATED TO A VERY WEALTHY MAN, SIR CHARLES.
AIMING TO HAVE SIR CHARLES' FORTUNE FOR HIMSELF, HE AND HIS WIFE MOVED TO GRIMPEN.
THEY, OF COURSE, CHANGED THEIR NAME ONCE AGAIN.
A NAME THE TWO OF YOU HAVE HEARD ...
QUITE OFTEN, TOO, I AM SURE.
THEY CHANGED IT TO *STAPLETON.*

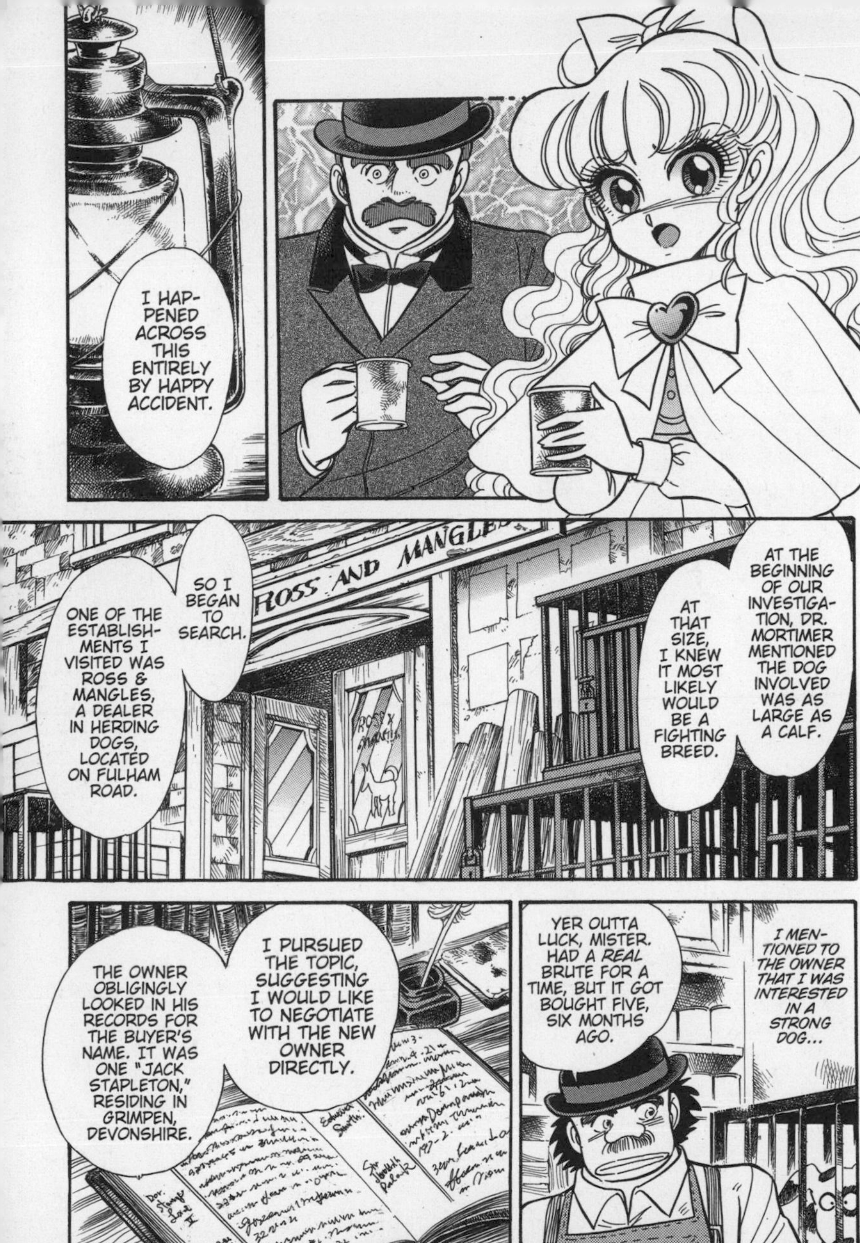
I HAPPENED ACROSS THIS ENTIRELY BY HAPPY ACCIDENT.
AT THE BEGINNING OF OUR INVESTIGATION, DR. MORTIMER MENTIONED THE DOG INVOLVED WAS AS LARGE AS A CALF.
AT THAT SIZE, I KNEW IT MOST LIKELY WOULD BE A FIGHTING BREED.
ROSS AND MANGLE
SO I BEGAN TO SEARCH.
ONE OF THE ESTABLISHMENTS I VISITED WAS ROSS & MANGLES, A DEALER IN HERDING DOGS, LOCATED ON FULHAM ROAD.
I MENTIONED TO THE OWNER THAT I WAS INTERESTED IN A STRONG DOG...
YER OUTTA LUCK, MISTER. HAD A *REAL* BRUTE FOR A TIME, BUT IT GOT BOUGHT FIVE, SIX MONTHS AGO.
I PURSUED THE TOPIC, SUGGESTING I WOULD LIKE TO NEGOTIATE WITH THE NEW OWNER DIRECTLY.
THE OWNER OBLIGINGLY LOOKED IN HIS RECORDS FOR THE BUYER'S NAME. IT WAS ONE "JACK STAPLETON," RESIDING IN GRIMPEN, DEVONSHIRE.

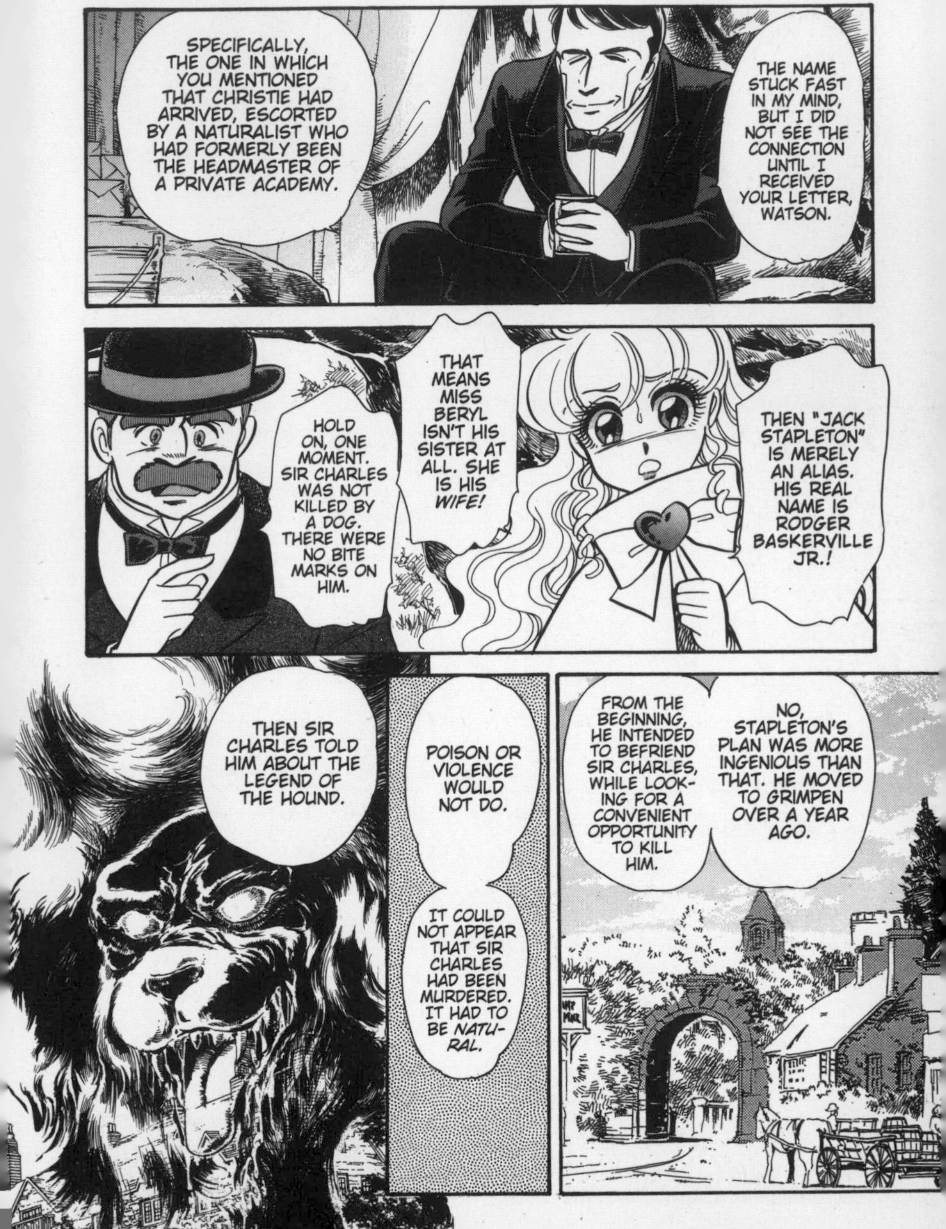
THE NAME STUCK FAST IN MY MIND, BUT I DID NOT SEE THE CONNECTION UNTIL I RECEIVED YOUR LETTER, WATSON.
SPECIFICALLY, THE ONE IN WHICH YOU MENTIONED THAT CHRISTIE HAD ARRIVED, ESCORTED BY A NATURALIST WHO HAD FORMERLY BEEN THE HEADMASTER OF A PRIVATE ACADEMY.
THEN "JACK STAPLETON" IS MERELY AN ALIAS. HIS REAL NAME IS RODGER BASKERVILLE JR.!
THAT MEANS MISS BERYL ISN'T HIS SISTER AT ALL. SHE IS HIS *WIFE!*
HOLD ON, ONE MOMENT. SIR CHARLES WAS NOT KILLED BY A DOG. THERE WERE NO BITE MARKS ON HIM.
NO, STAPLETON'S PLAN WAS MORE INGENIOUS THAN THAT. HE MOVED TO GRIMPEN OVER A YEAR AGO.
FROM THE BEGINNING, HE INTENDED TO BEFRIEND SIR CHARLES, WHILE LOOK-ING FOR A CONVENIENT OPPORTUNITY TO KILL HIM.
POISON OR VIOLENCE WOULD NOT DO.
IT COULD NOT APPEAR THAT SIR CHARLES HAD BEEN MURDERED. IT HAD TO BE *NATU-RAL.*
THEN SIR CHARLES TOLD HIM ABOUT THE LEGEND OF THE HOUND.

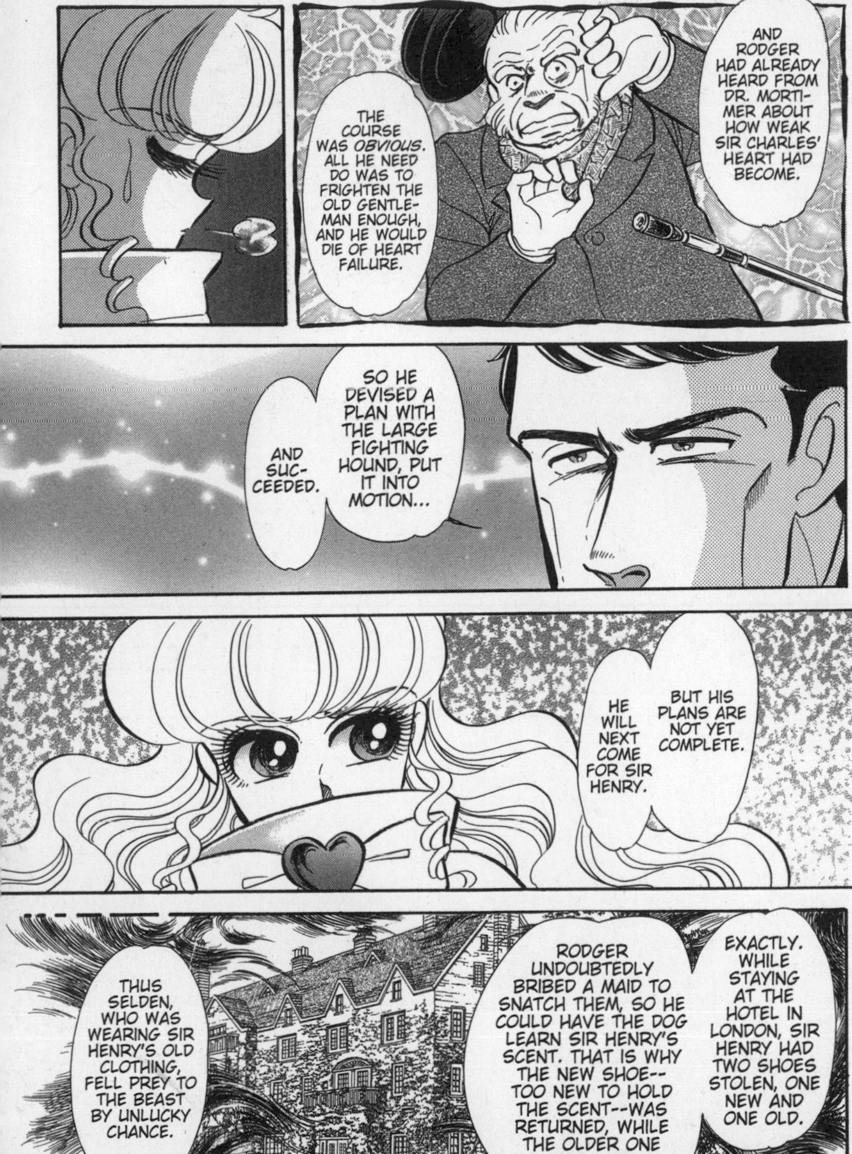
AND RODGER HAD ALREADY HEARD FROM DR. MORTIMER ABOUT HOW WEAK SIR CHARLES' HEART HAD BECOME.
THE COURSE WAS *OBVIOUS*. ALL HE NEED DO WAS TO FRIGHTEN THE OLD GENTLEMAN ENOUGH, AND HE WOULD DIE OF HEART FAILURE.
SO HE DEVISED A PLAN WITH THE LARGE FIGHTING HOUND, PUT IT INTO MOTION...
AND SUCCEEDED.
BUT HIS PLANS ARE NOT YET COMPLETE.
HE WILL NEXT COME FOR SIR HENRY.
EXACTLY. WHILE STAYING AT THE HOTEL IN LONDON, SIR HENRY HAD TWO SHOES STOLEN, ONE NEW AND ONE OLD.
RODGER UNDOUBTEDLY BRIBED A MAID TO SNATCH THEM, SO HE COULD HAVE THE DOG LEARN SIR HENRY'S SCENT. THAT IS WHY THE NEW SHOE--TOO NEW TO HOLD THE SCENT--WAS RETURNED, WHILE THE OLDER ONE WAS *NOT*.
THUS SELDEN, WHO WAS WEARING SIR HENRY'S OLD CLOTHING, FELL PREY TO THE BEAST BY UNLUCKY CHANCE.

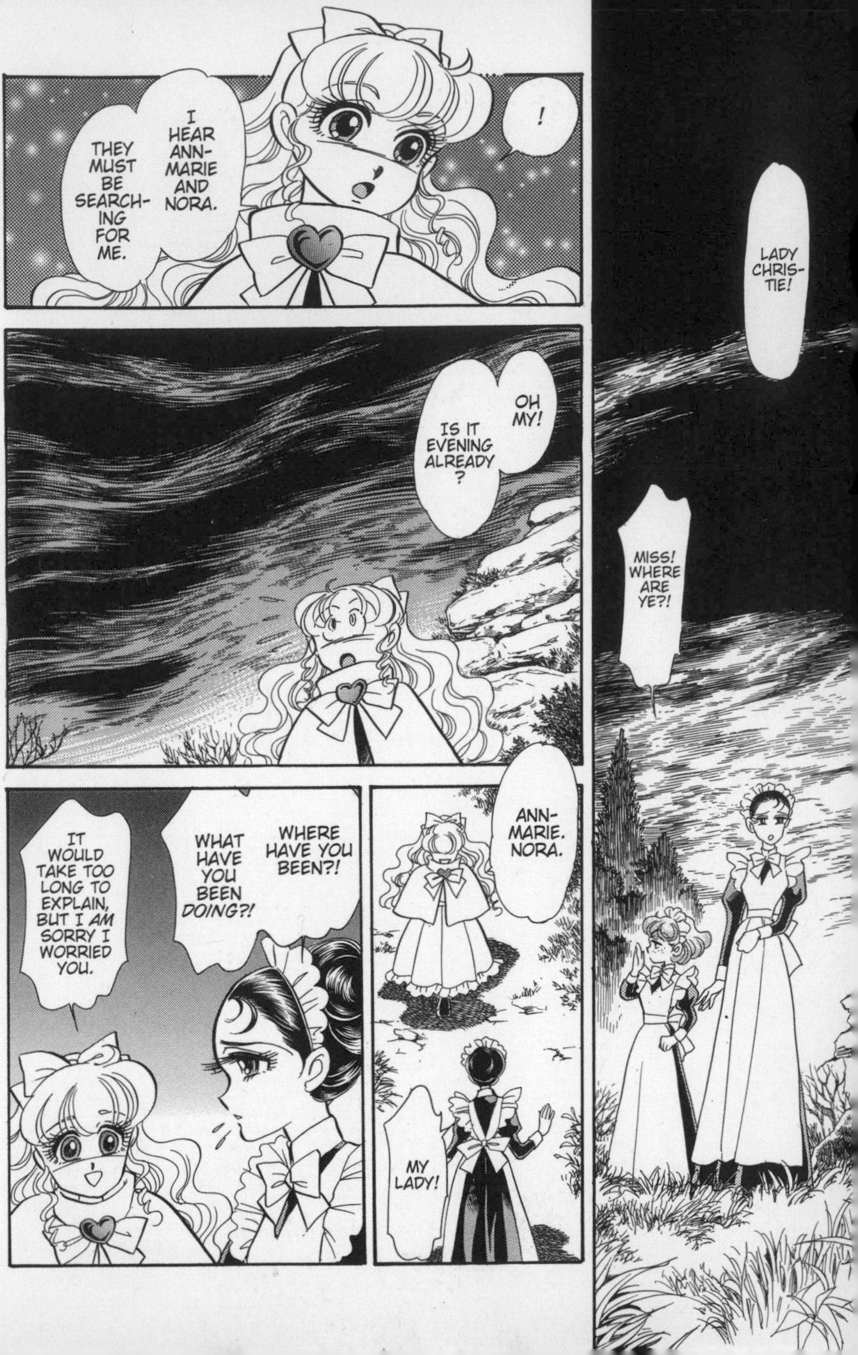
LADY CHRIS-TIE!
MISS! WHERE ARE YE?!
!
I HEAR ANN-MARIE AND NORA.
THEY MUST BE SEARCH-ING FOR ME.
OH MY!
IS IT EVENING ALREADY?
ANN-MARIE. NORA.
MY LADY!
WHERE HAVE YOU BEEN?!
WHAT HAVE YOU BEEN *DOING*?!
IT WOULD TAKE TOO LONG TO EXPLAIN, BUT I *AM* SORRY I WORRIED YOU.

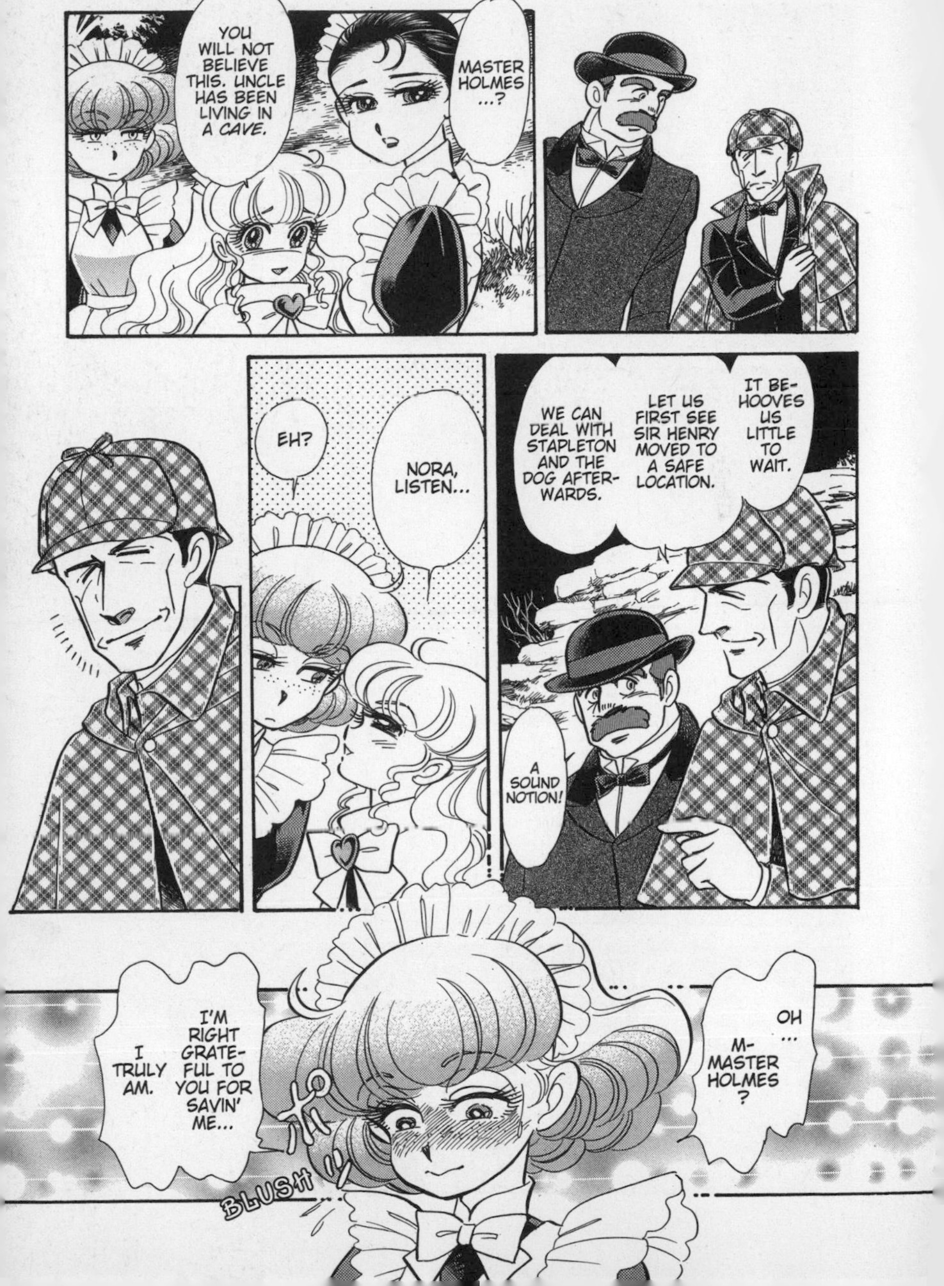
MASTER HOLMES ...?
YOU WILL NOT BELIEVE THIS. UNCLE HAS BEEN LIVING IN A CAVE.
IT BE-HOOVES US LITTLE TO WAIT.
LET US FIRST SEE SIR HENRY MOVED TO A SAFE LOCATION.
WE CAN DEAL WITH STAPLETON AND THE DOG AFTER-WARDS.
A SOUND NOTION!
NORA, LISTEN...
EH?
OH ... M-MASTER HOLMES ?
I'M RIGHT GRATE-FUL TO YOU FOR SAVIN' ME...
I TRULY AM.
BLUSH

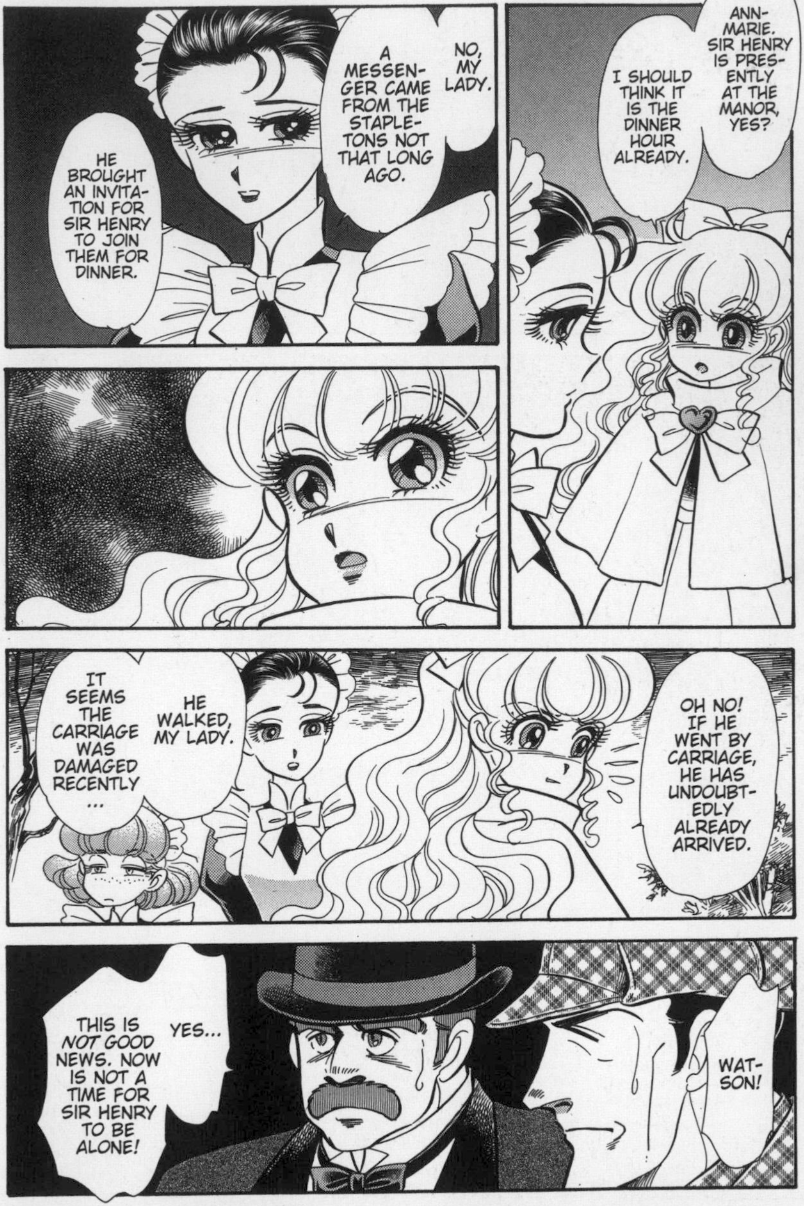
ANN-MARIE. SIR HENRY IS PRESENTLY AT THE MANOR, YES?
I SHOULD THINK IT IS THE DINNER HOUR ALREADY.
NO, MY LADY.
A MESSENGER CAME FROM THE STAPLETONS NOT THAT LONG AGO.
HE BROUGHT AN INVITATION FOR SIR HENRY TO JOIN THEM FOR DINNER.
OH NO! IF HE WENT BY CARRIAGE, HE HAS UNDOUBTEDLY ALREADY ARRIVED.
HE WALKED, MY LADY.
IT SEEMS THE CARRIAGE WAS DAMAGED RECENTLY ...
WATSON!
YES...
THIS IS NOT GOOD NEWS. NOW IS NOT A TIME FOR SIR HENRY TO BE ALONE!

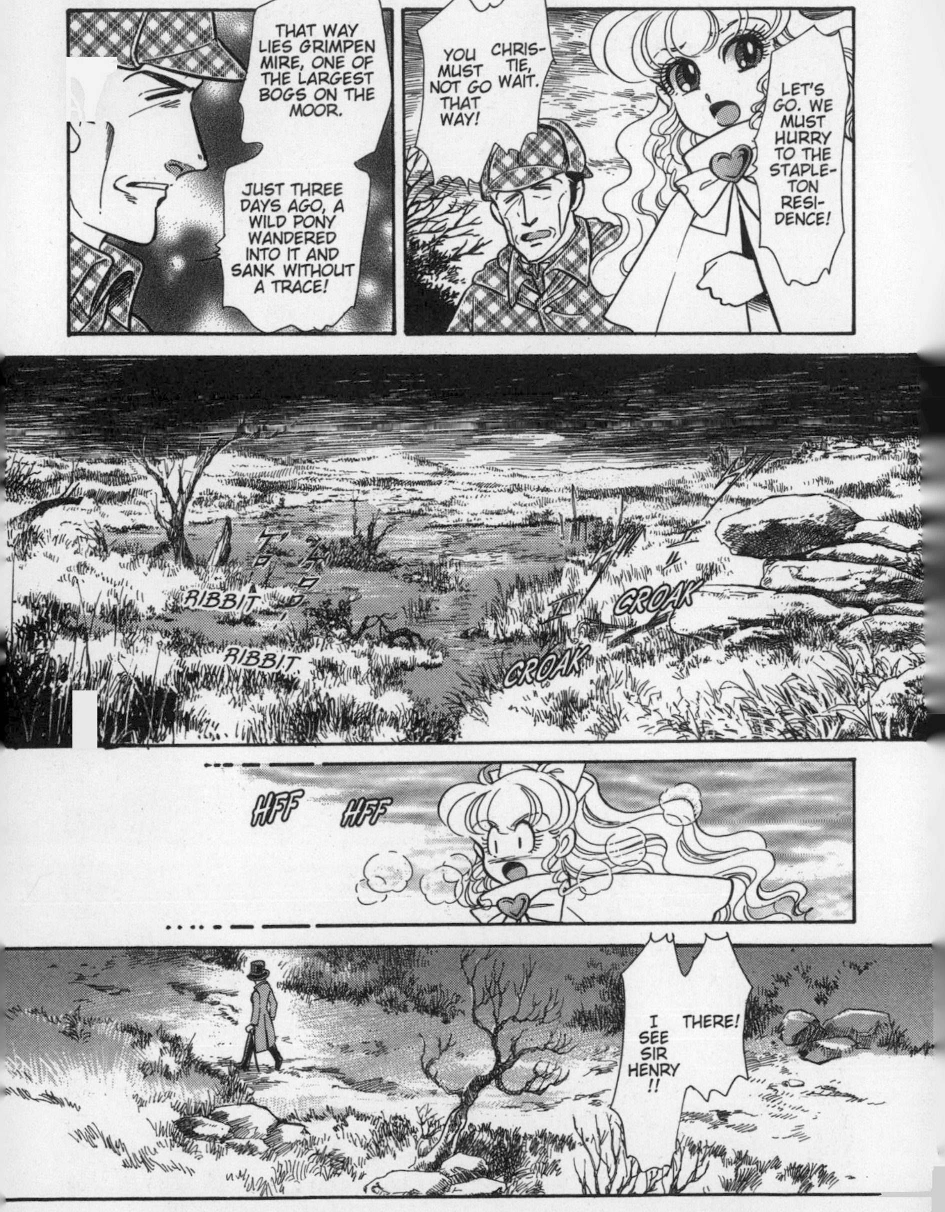
LET'S GO. WE MUST HURRY TO THE STAPLE-TON RESI-DENCE!
CHRIS-TIE, WAIT. YOU MUST NOT GO THAT WAY!
THAT WAY LIES GRIMPEN MIRE, ONE OF THE LARGEST BOGS ON THE MOOR.
JUST THREE DAYS AGO, A WILD PONY WANDERED INTO IT AND SANK WITHOUT A TRACE!
CROAK
CROAK
RIBBIT
RIBBIT
HFF
HFF
THERE! I SEE SIR HENRY!!

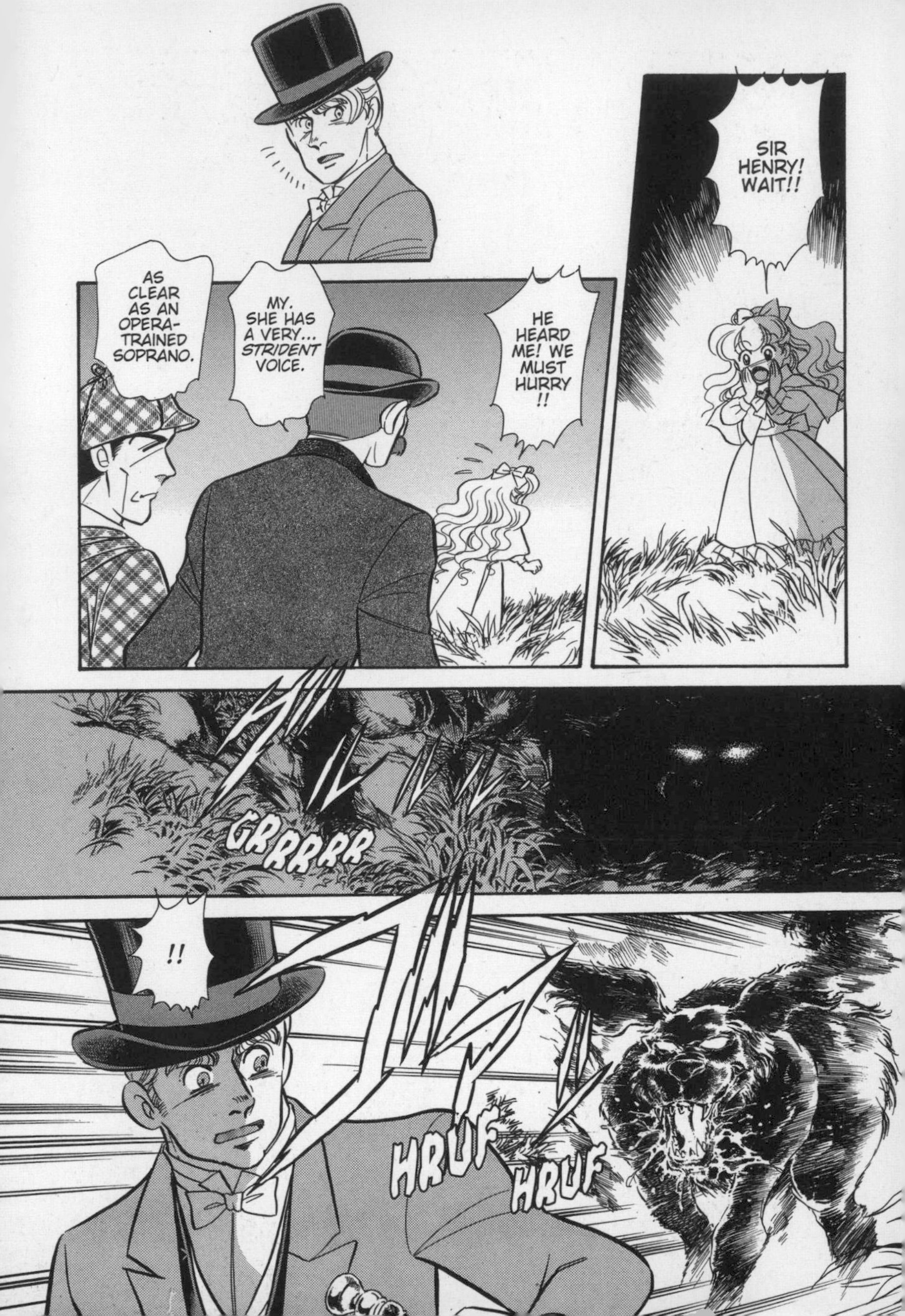
SIR HENRY! WAIT!!
HE HEARD ME! WE MUST HURRY!!
MY. SHE HAS A VERY... STRIDENT VOICE.
AS CLEAR AS AN OPERA-TRAINED SOPRANO.
GRRRRR
!!
HRUF HRUF

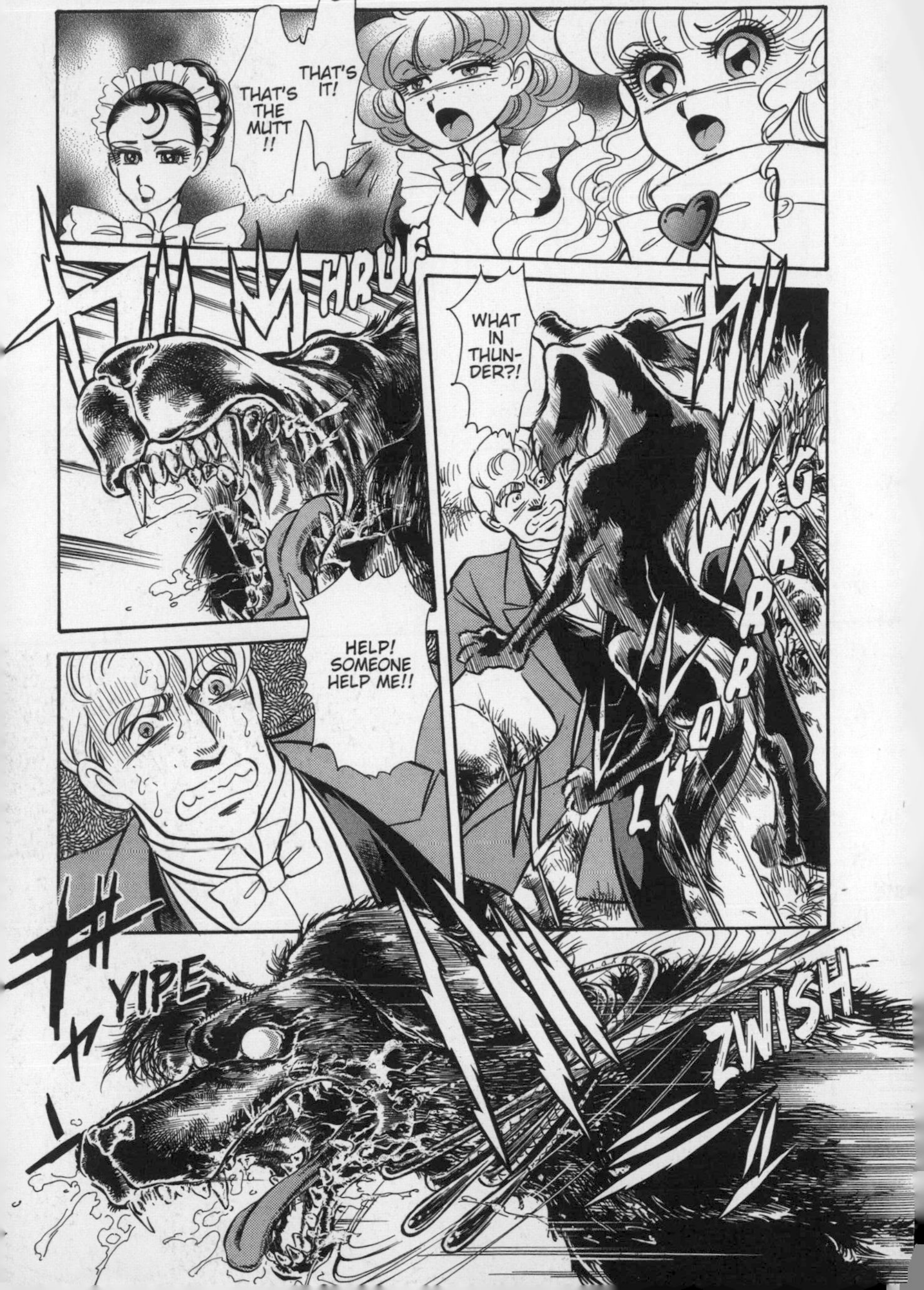
THAT'S IT!
THAT'S THE MUTT!!
WHAT IN THUNDER?!
GRRROWL
HRUF
HELP! SOMEONE HELP ME!!
ZWISH
YIPE

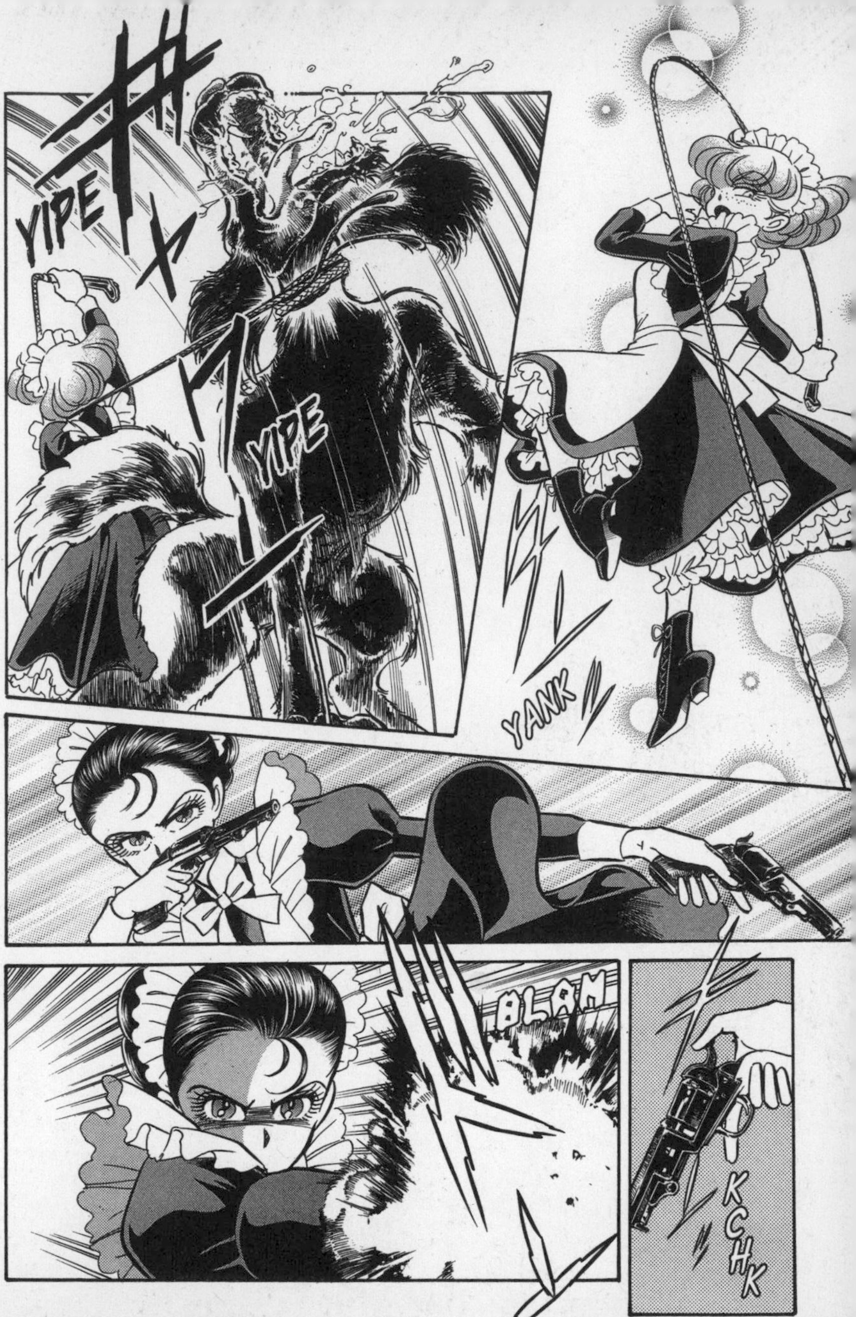
YANK
YIPE
YIPE
KCHK
BLAM

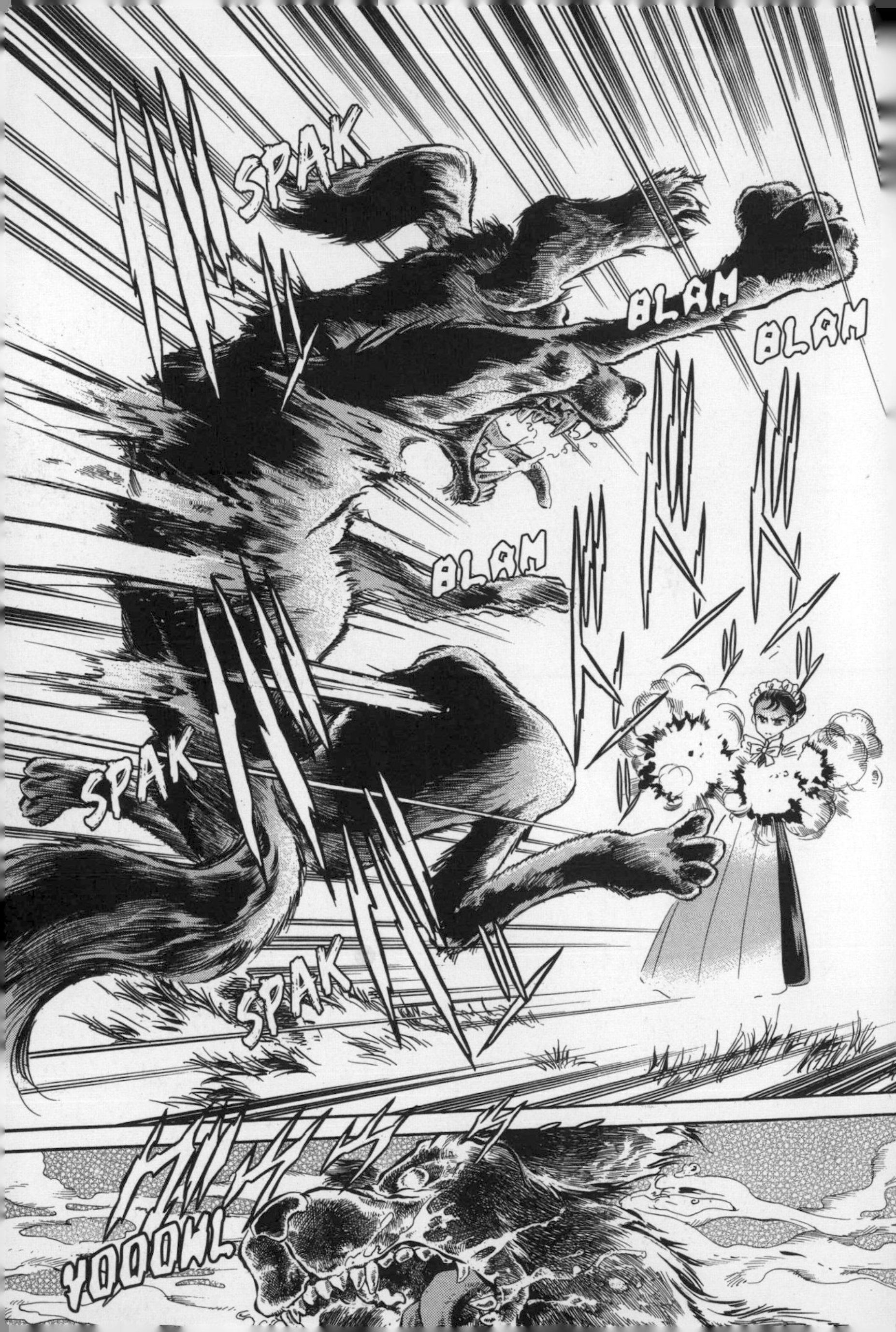
BLAM
BLAM
SPAK
BLAM
SPAK
SPAK
YOOOWL

WHUD
SIR HENRY!
WATSON!!
STAPLETON!
HE'S HERE!!
ANNMARIE!
HELP DR. WATSON WITH SIR HENRY, WOULD YOU?
HOLD, STAPLETON! COME BACK HERE!!

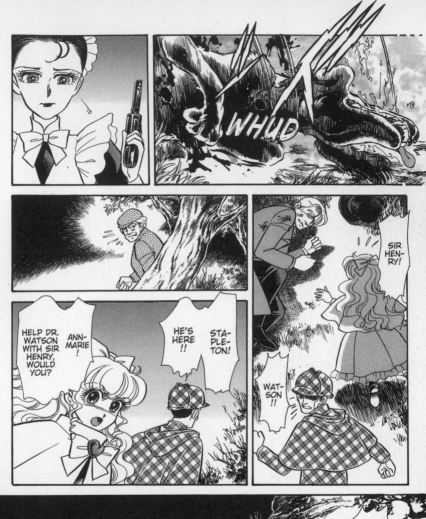

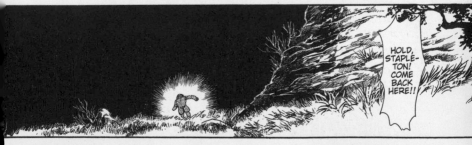

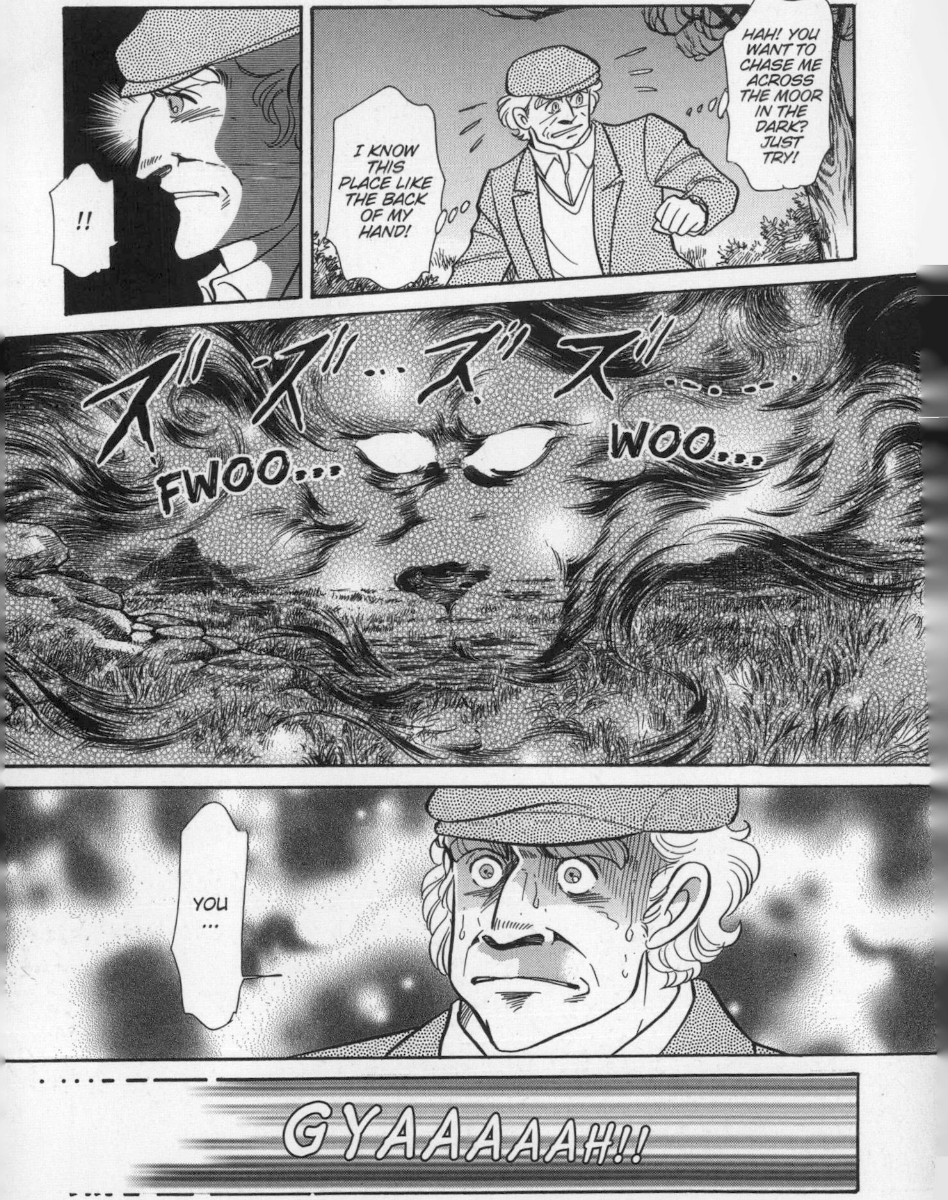
HAH! YOU WANT TO CHASE ME ACROSS THE MOOR IN THE DARK? JUST TRY!
I KNOW THIS PLACE LIKE THE BACK OF MY HAND!
!!
ズズ…ズズ…
WOO...
FWOO...
YOU ...
GYAAAAAAH!!

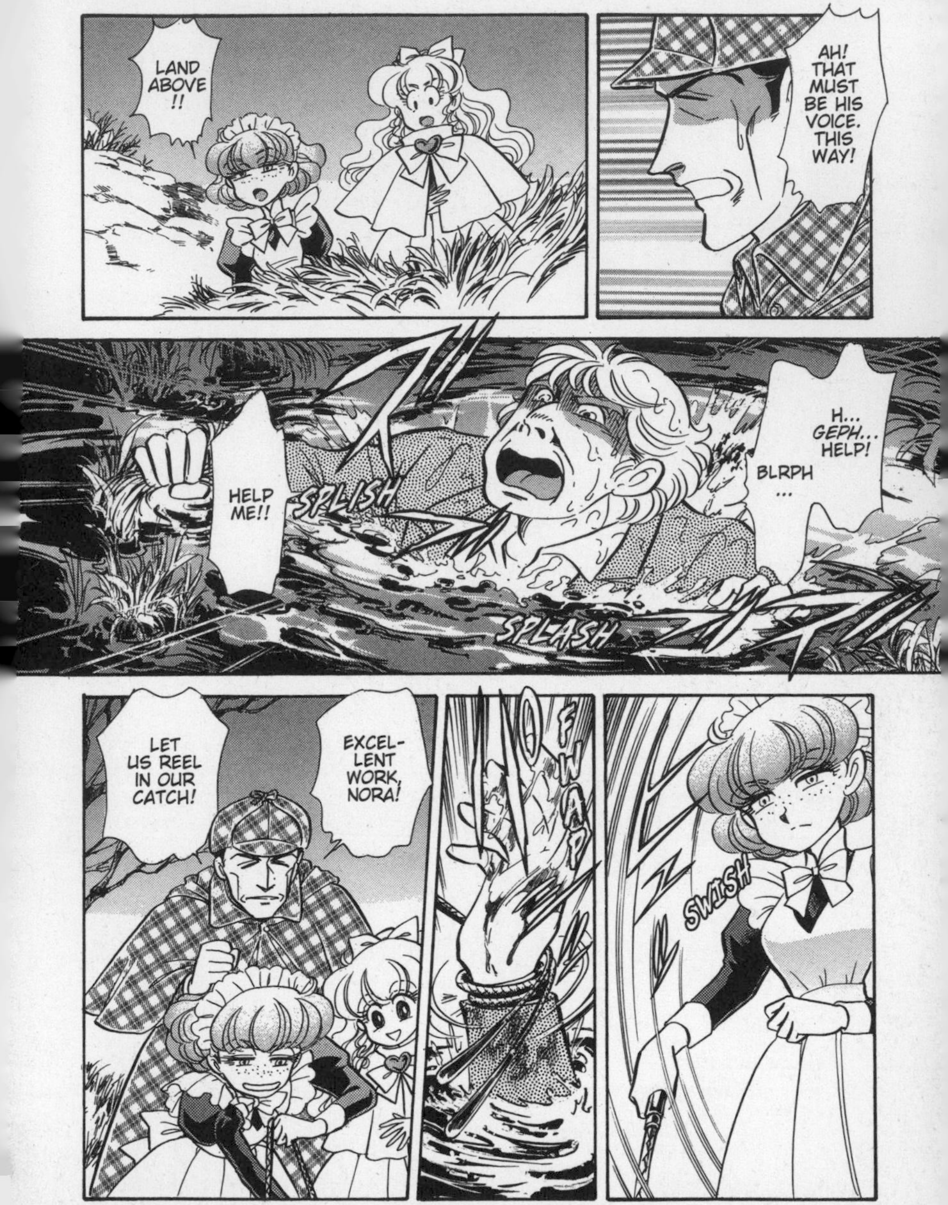
AH! THAT MUST BE HIS VOICE. THIS WAY!
LAND ABOVE !!
H... GEPH... HELP!
BLRPH ...
SPLISH
HELP ME!!
SPLASH
SWISH
FWAP
EXCEL-LENT WORK, NORA!
LET US REEL IN OUR CATCH!

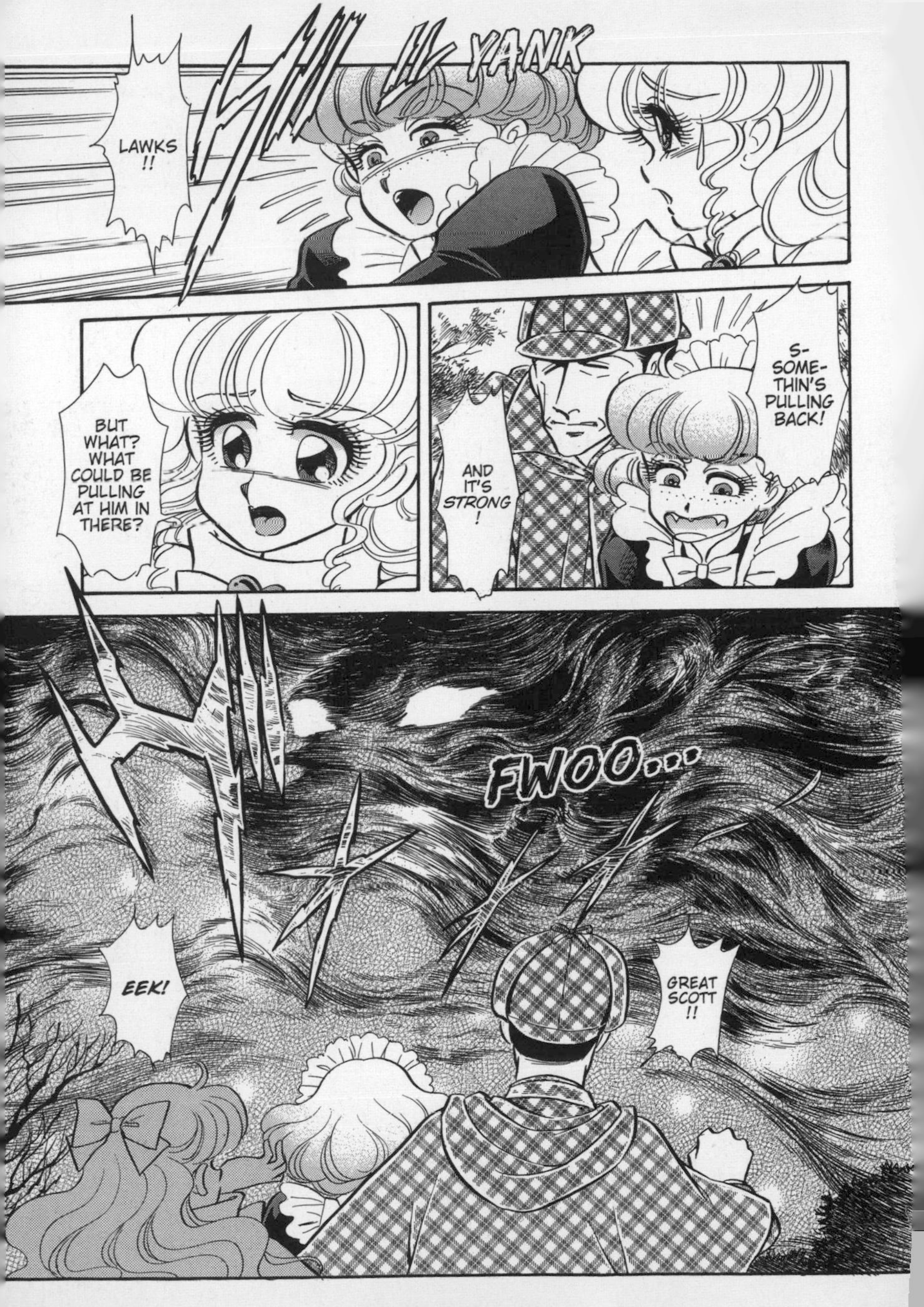
YANK
LAWKS !!
S-SOMETHIN'S PULLING BACK!
AND IT'S STRONG!
BUT WHAT? WHAT COULD BE PULLING AT HIM IN THERE?
FWOO...
GREAT SCOTT !!
EEK!

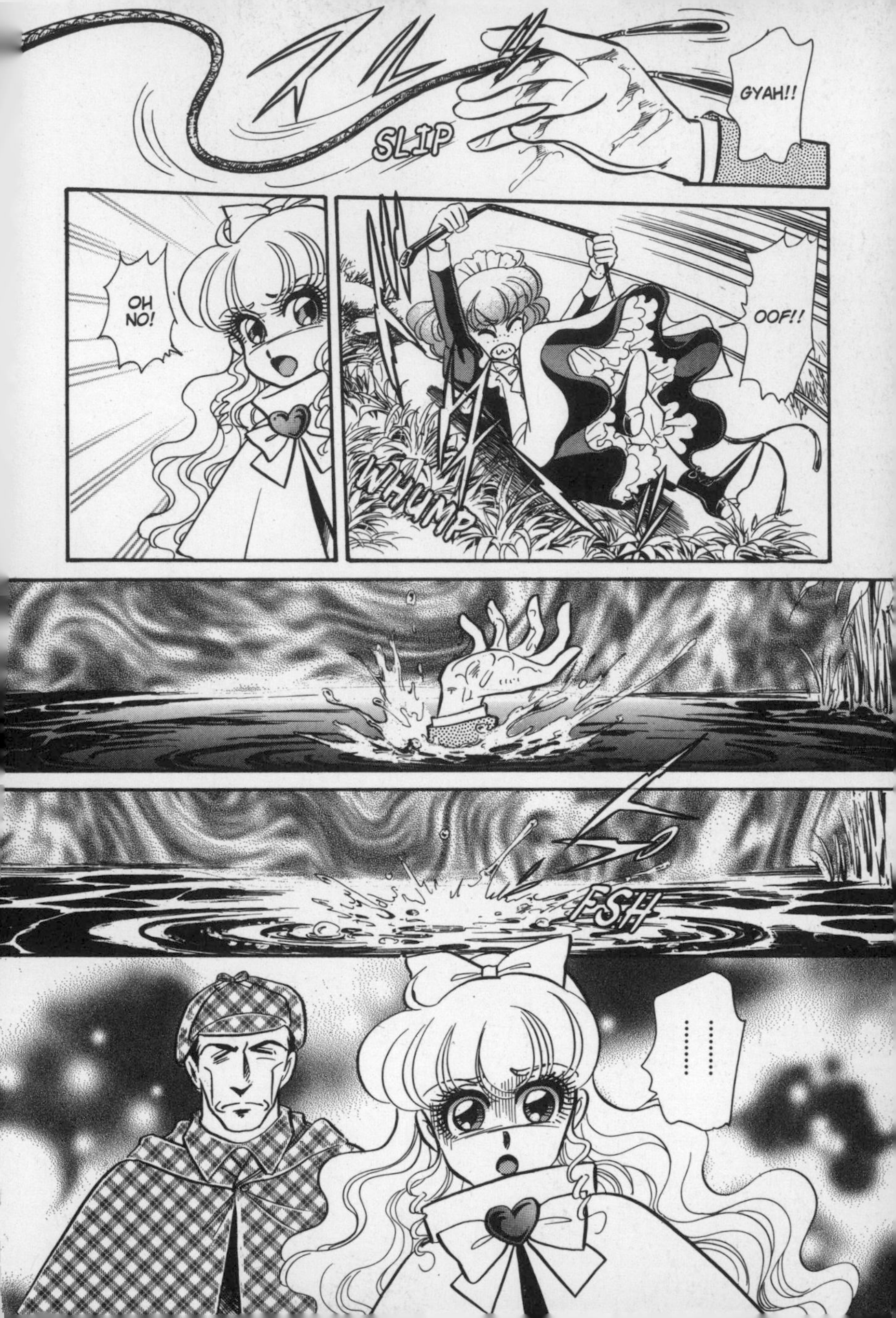
GYAH!!
SLIP
OOF!!
WHUMP
OH NO!
FSH
......

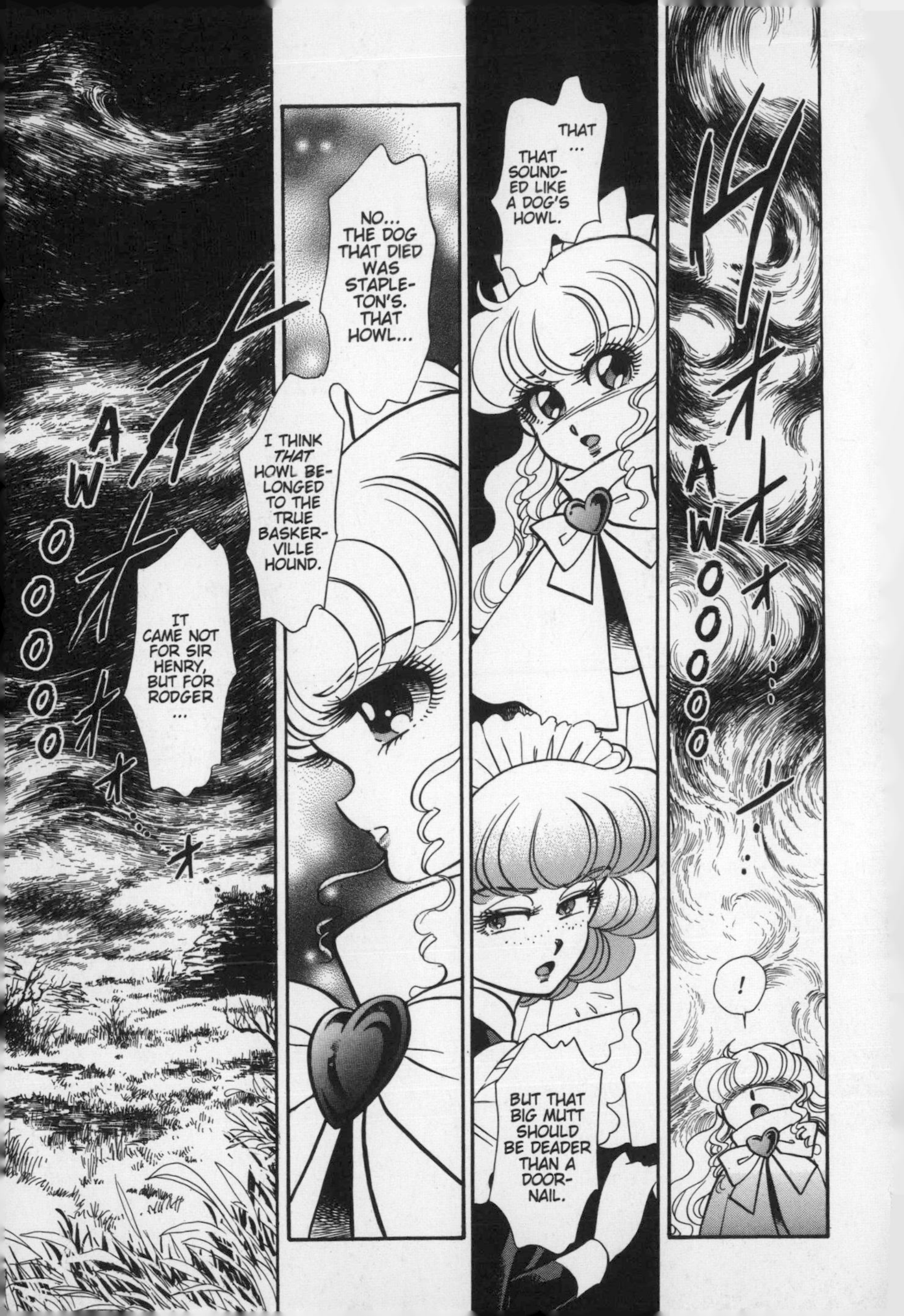
AWOOOOOO
!
THAT... THAT SOUNDED LIKE A DOG'S HOWL.
BUT THAT BIG MUTT SHOULD BE DEADER THAN A DOORNAIL.
NO... THE DOG THAT DIED WAS STAPLETON'S. THAT HOWL...
I THINK *THAT* HOWL BELONGED TO THE TRUE BASKERVILLE HOUND.
AWOOOOOOO
IT CAME NOT FOR SIR HENRY, BUT FOR RODGER...

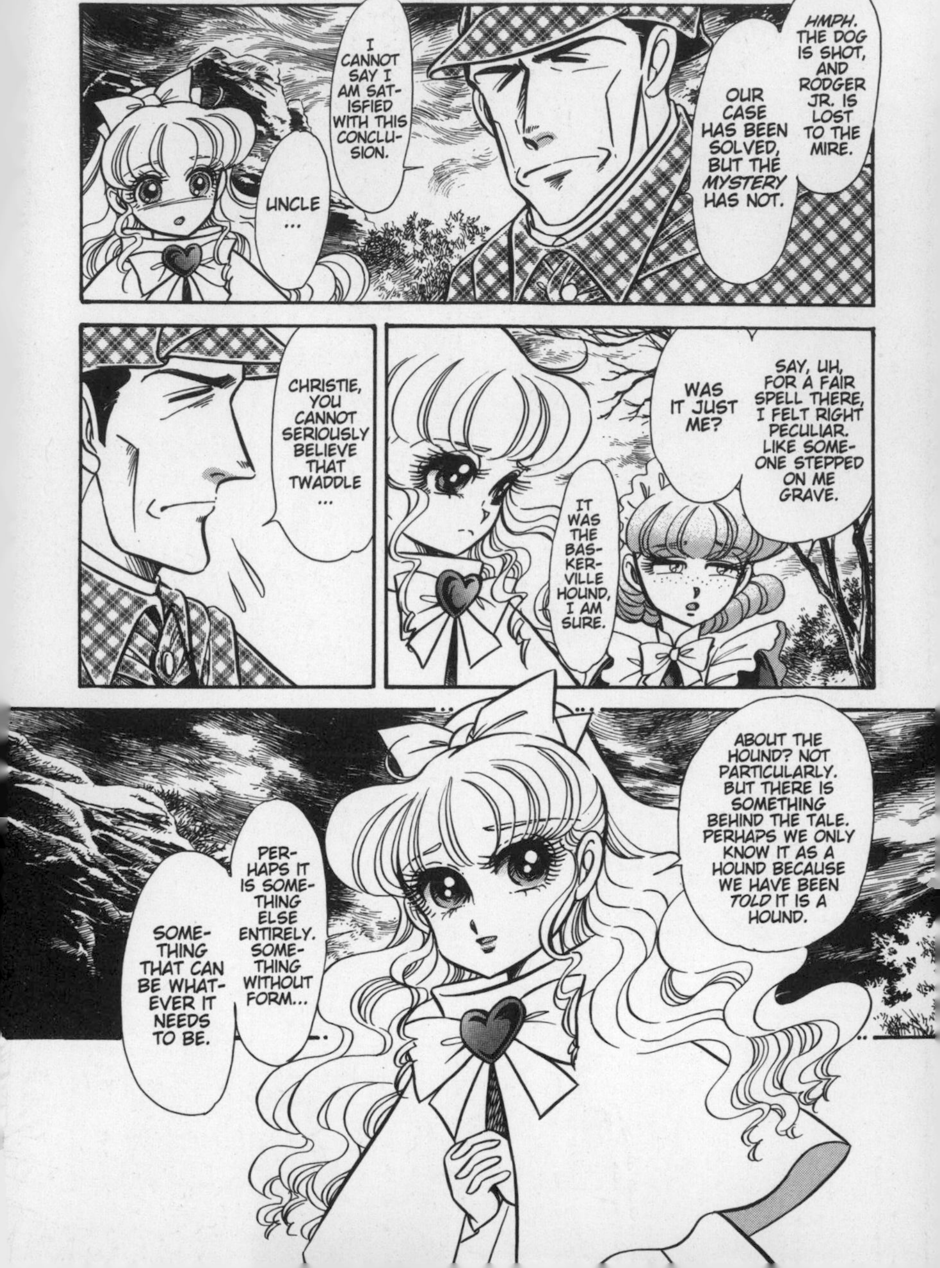
HMPH. THE DOG IS SHOT, AND RODGER JR. IS LOST TO THE MIRE.
OUR CASE HAS BEEN SOLVED, BUT THE *MYSTERY* HAS NOT.
I CANNOT SAY I AM SATISFIED WITH THIS CONCLUSION.
UNCLE ...
SAY, UH, FOR A FAIR SPELL THERE, I FELT RIGHT PECULIAR. LIKE SOMEONE STEPPED ON ME GRAVE.
WAS IT JUST ME?
IT WAS THE BASKERVILLE HOUND, I AM SURE.
CHRISTIE, YOU CANNOT SERIOUSLY BELIEVE THAT TWADDLE ...
ABOUT THE HOUND? NOT PARTICULARLY. BUT THERE IS SOMETHING BEHIND THE TALE. PERHAPS WE ONLY KNOW IT AS A HOUND BECAUSE WE HAVE BEEN *TOLD* IT IS A HOUND.
PERHAPS IT IS SOMETHING ELSE ENTIRELY. SOMETHING WITHOUT FORM...
SOMETHING THAT CAN BE WHATEVER IT NEEDS TO BE.

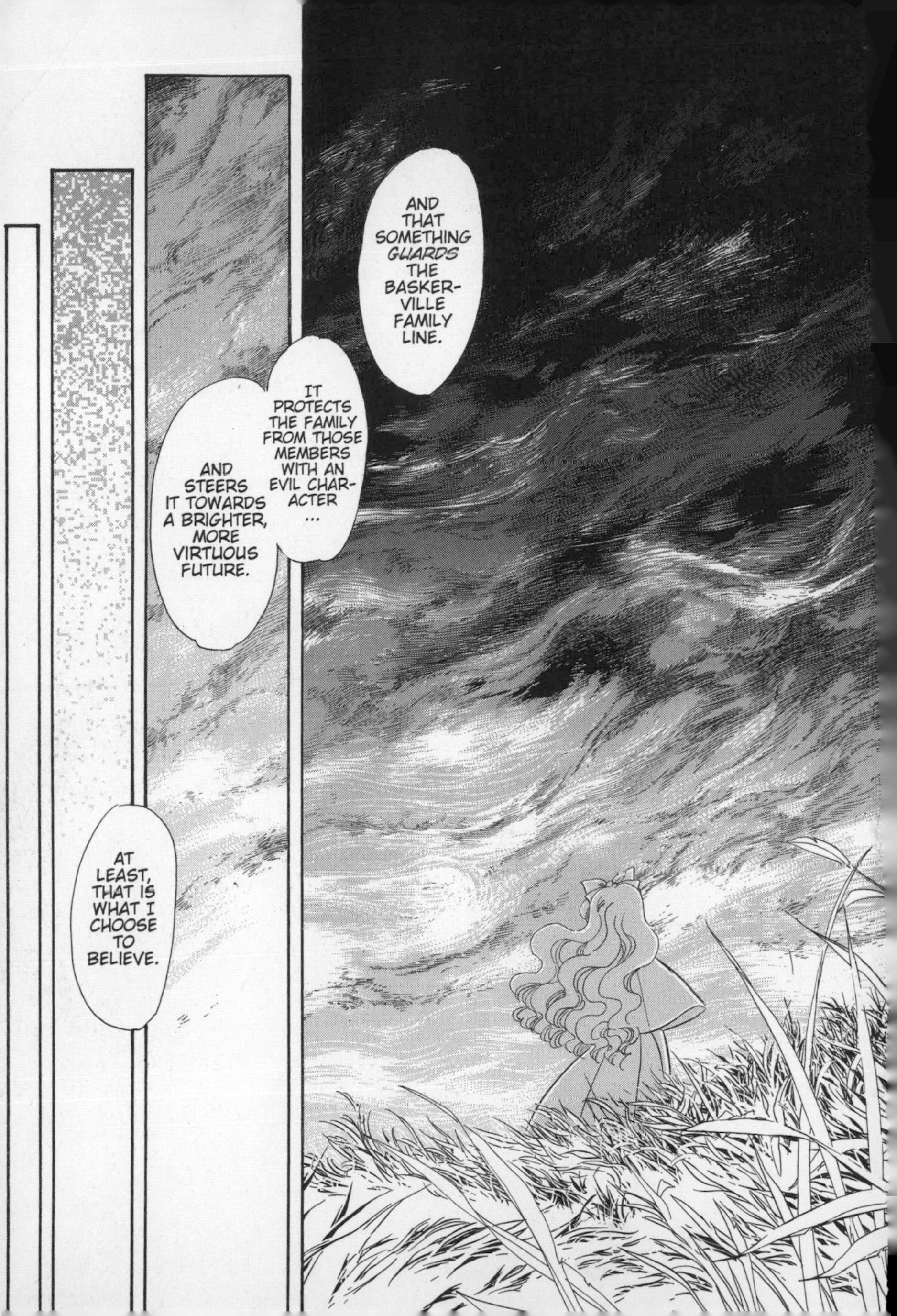
AND THAT SOMETHING *GUARDS* THE BASKER-VILLE FAMILY LINE.
IT PROTECTS THE FAMILY FROM THOSE MEMBERS WITH AN EVIL CHAR-ACTER ...
AND STEERS IT TOWARDS A BRIGHTER, MORE VIRTUOUS FUTURE.
AT LEAST, THAT IS WHAT I CHOOSE TO BELIEVE.

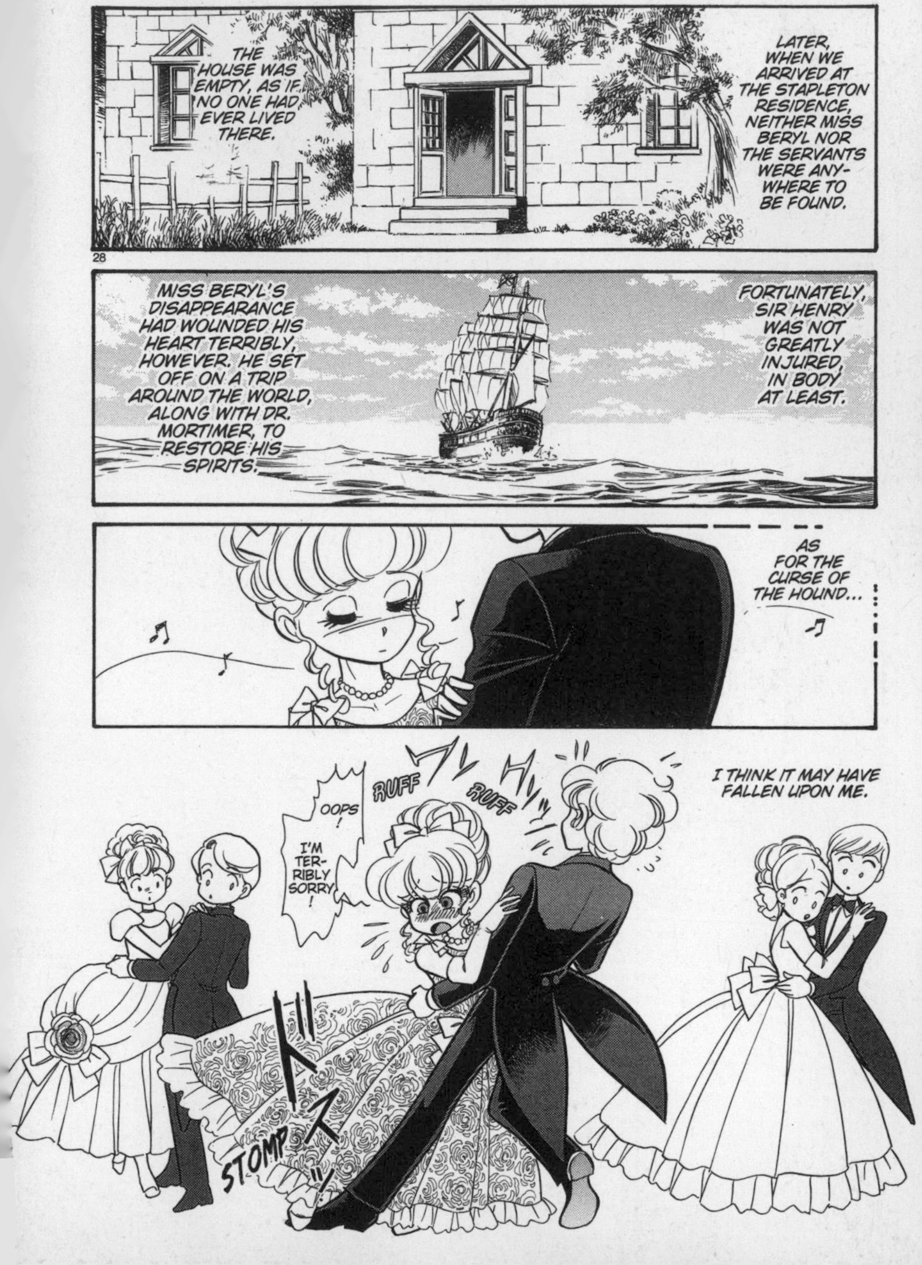
LATER, WHEN WE ARRIVED AT THE STAPLETON RESIDENCE, NEITHER MISS BERYL NOR THE SERVANTS WERE ANY-WHERE TO BE FOUND.
THE HOUSE WAS EMPTY, AS IF NO ONE HAD EVER LIVED THERE.
FORTUNATELY, SIR HENRY WAS NOT GREATLY INJURED, IN BODY AT LEAST.
MISS BERYL'S DISAPPEARANCE HAD WOUNDED HIS HEART TERRIBLY, HOWEVER. HE SET OFF ON A TRIP AROUND THE WORLD, ALONG WITH DR. MORTIMER, TO RESTORE HIS SPIRITS.
AS FOR THE CURSE OF THE HOUND...
I THINK IT MAY HAVE FALLEN UPON ME.
RUFF
RUFF
OOPS!
I'M TER-RIBLY SORRY!
STOMP

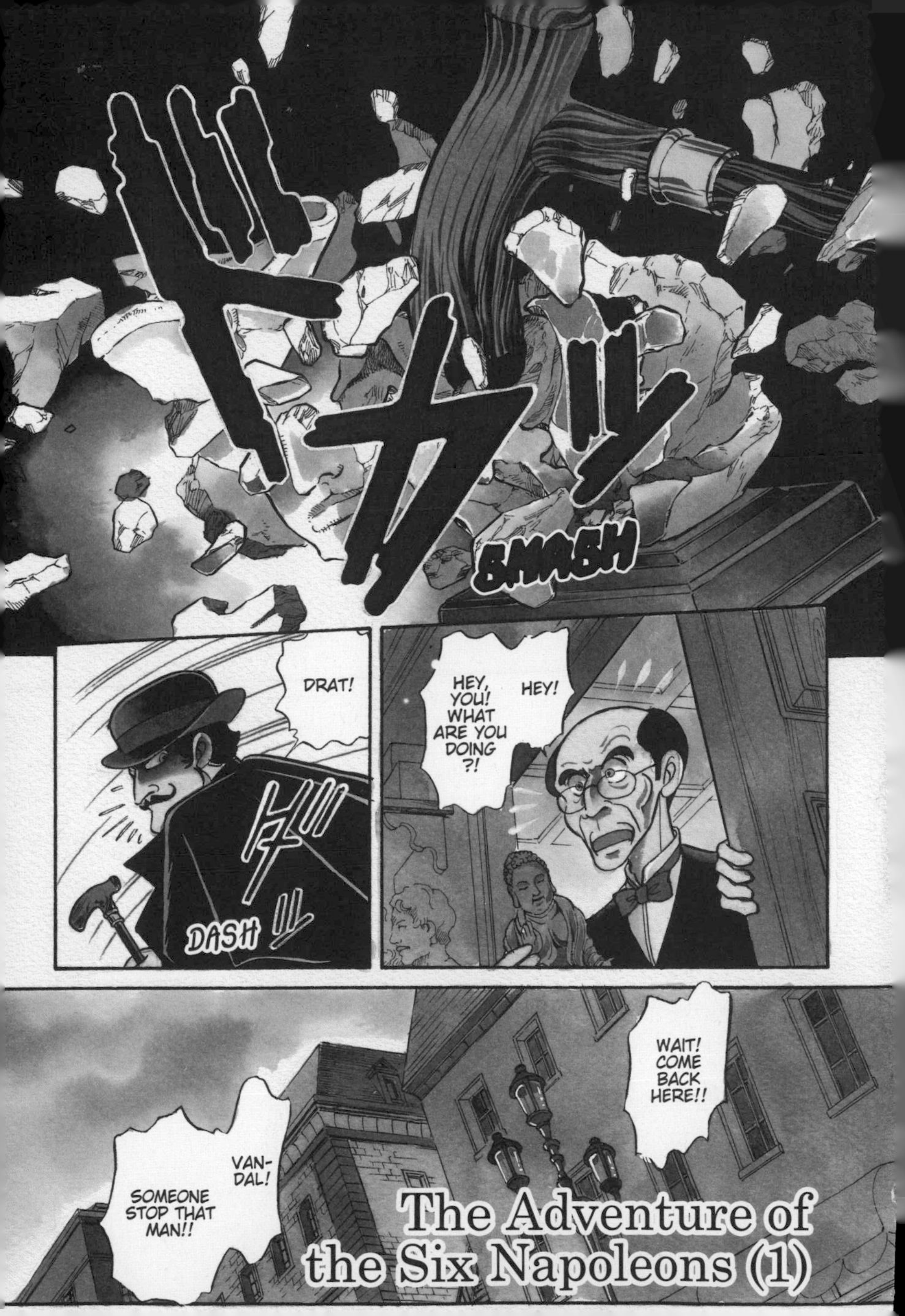
SMASH
HEY!
HEY, YOU! WHAT ARE YOU DOING?!
DRAT!
DASH
WAIT! COME BACK HERE!!
VAN-DAL!
SOMEONE STOP THAT MAN!!
The Adventure of the Six Napoleons (1)

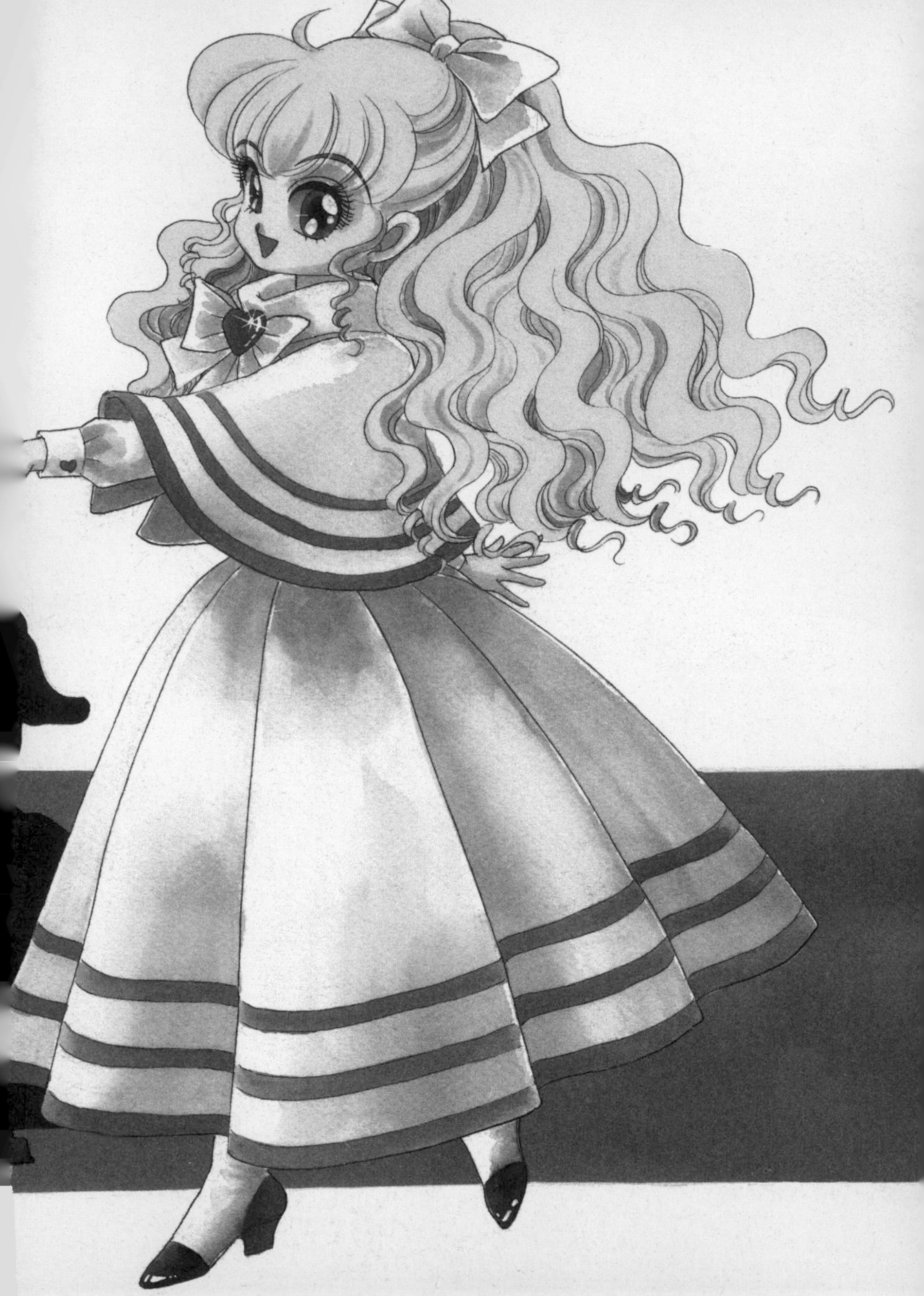

Young Miss HOLMES

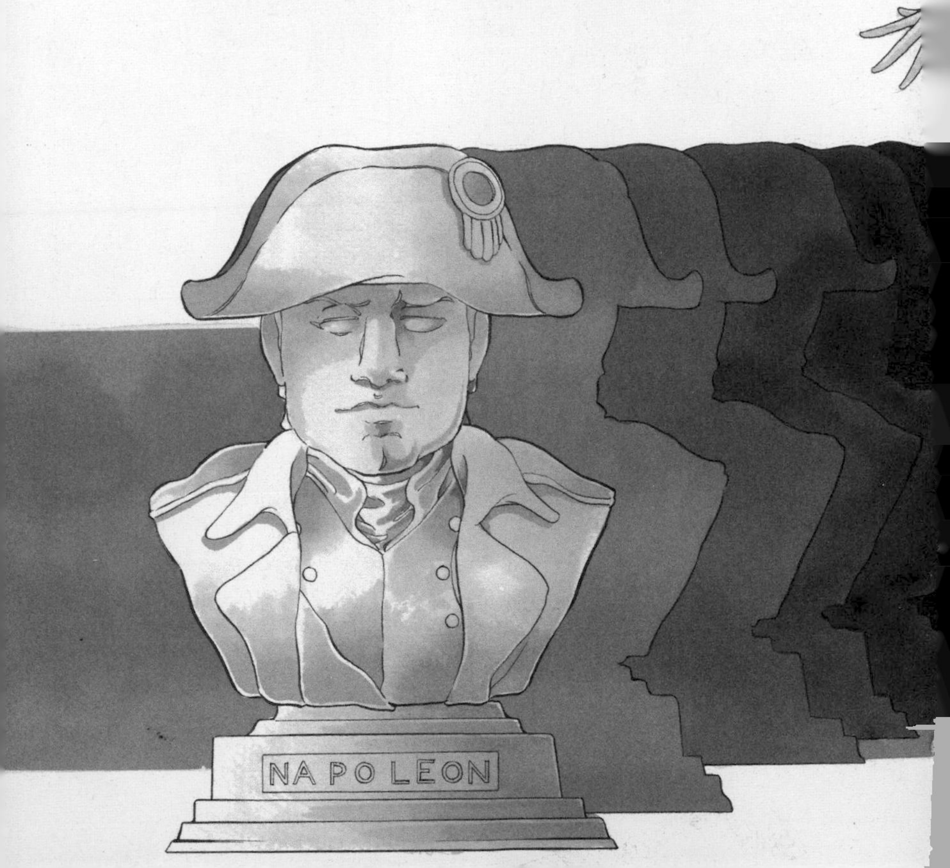
NAPOLEON

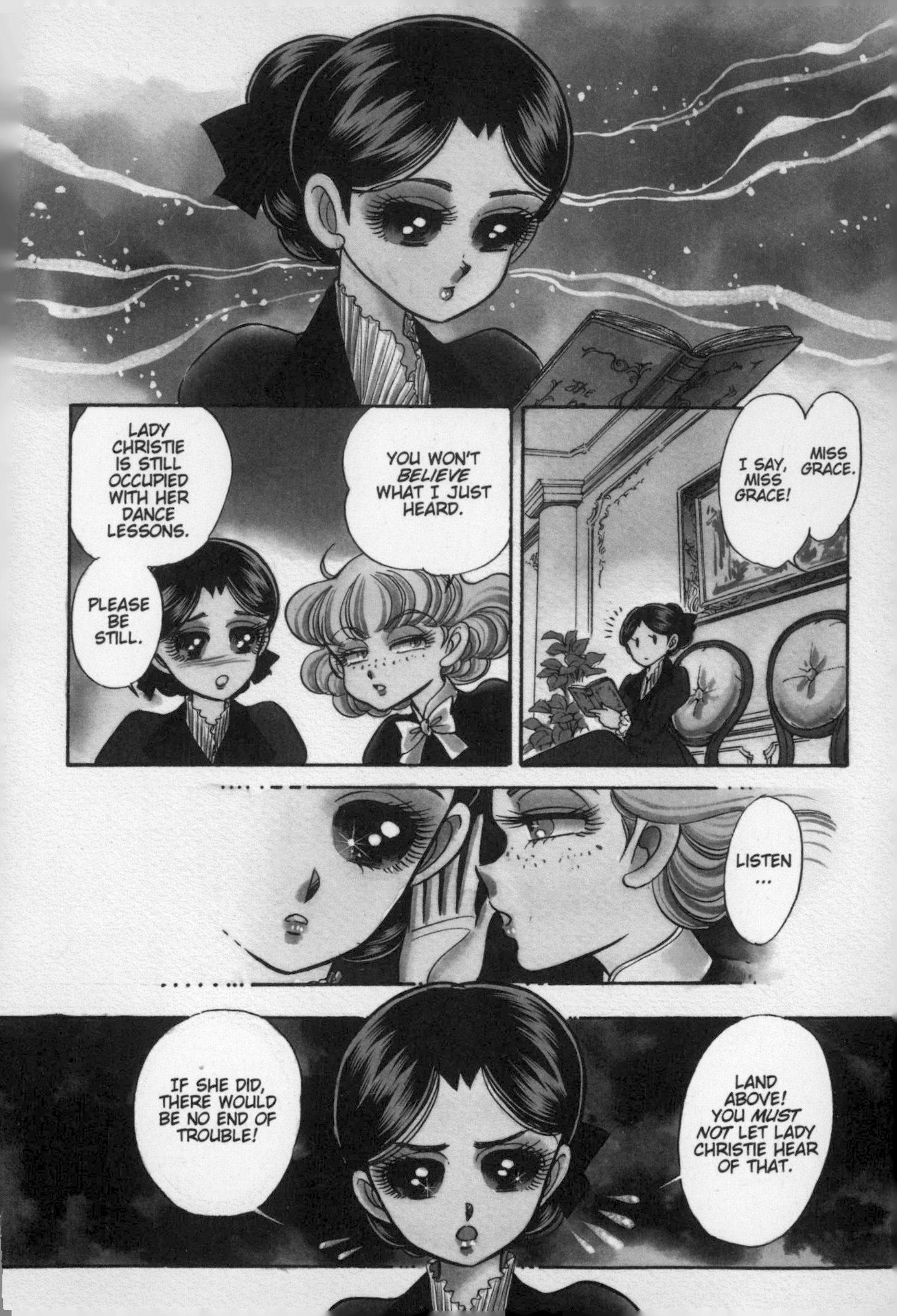
MISS GRACE.
I SAY, MISS GRACE!
YOU WON'T *BELIEVE* WHAT I JUST HEARD.
LADY CHRISTIE IS STILL OCCUPIED WITH HER DANCE LESSONS.
PLEASE BE STILL.
LISTEN ...
LAND ABOVE! YOU *MUST NOT* LET LADY CHRISTIE HEAR OF THAT.
IF SHE DID, THERE WOULD BE NO END OF TROUBLE!

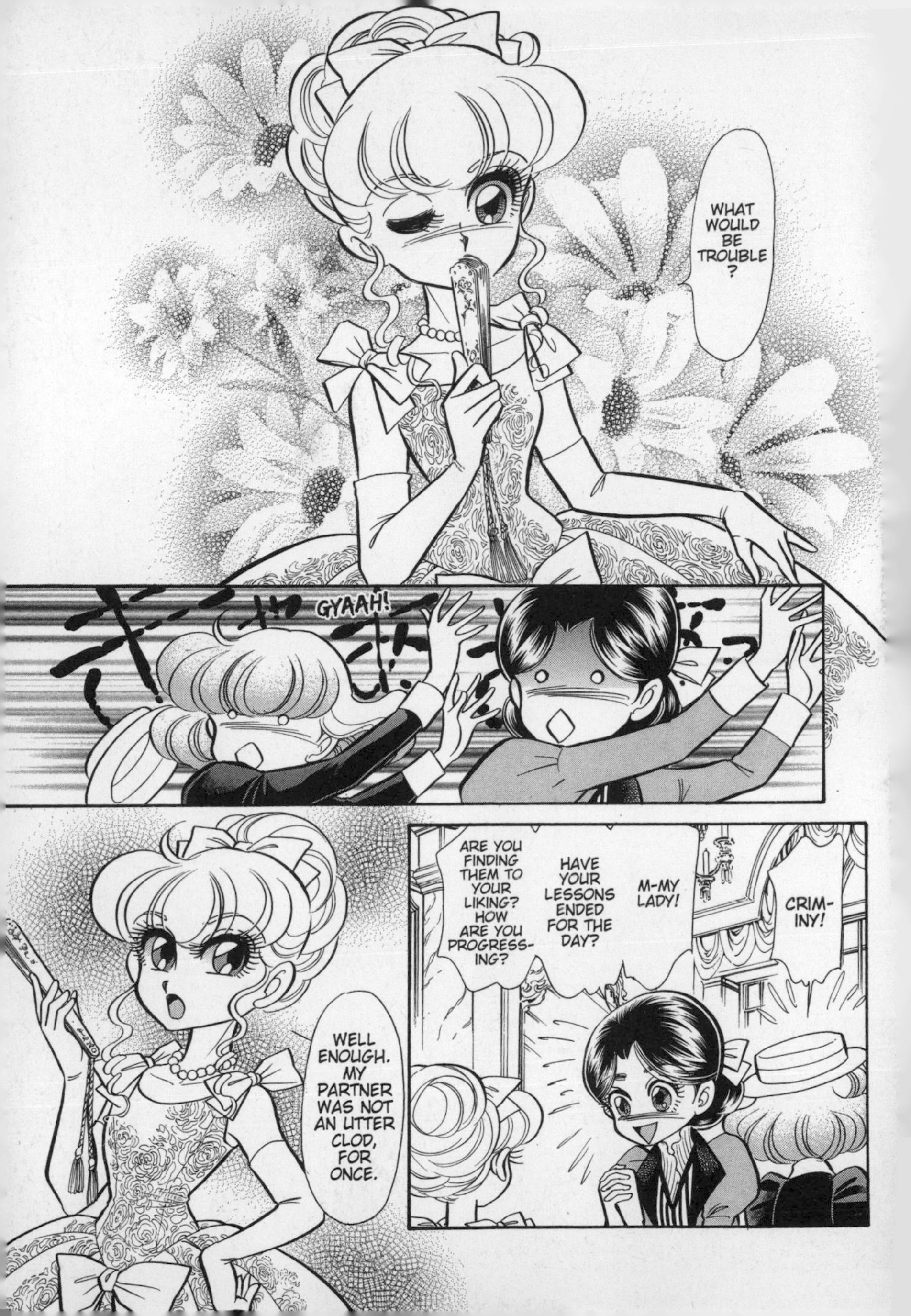
WHAT WOULD BE TROUBLE?
GYAAH!
CRIM-INY!
M-MY LADY!
HAVE YOUR LESSONS ENDED FOR THE DAY?
ARE YOU FINDING THEM TO YOUR LIKING? HOW ARE YOU PROGRESS-ING?
WELL ENOUGH. MY PARTNER WAS NOT AN UTTER CLOD, FOR ONCE.

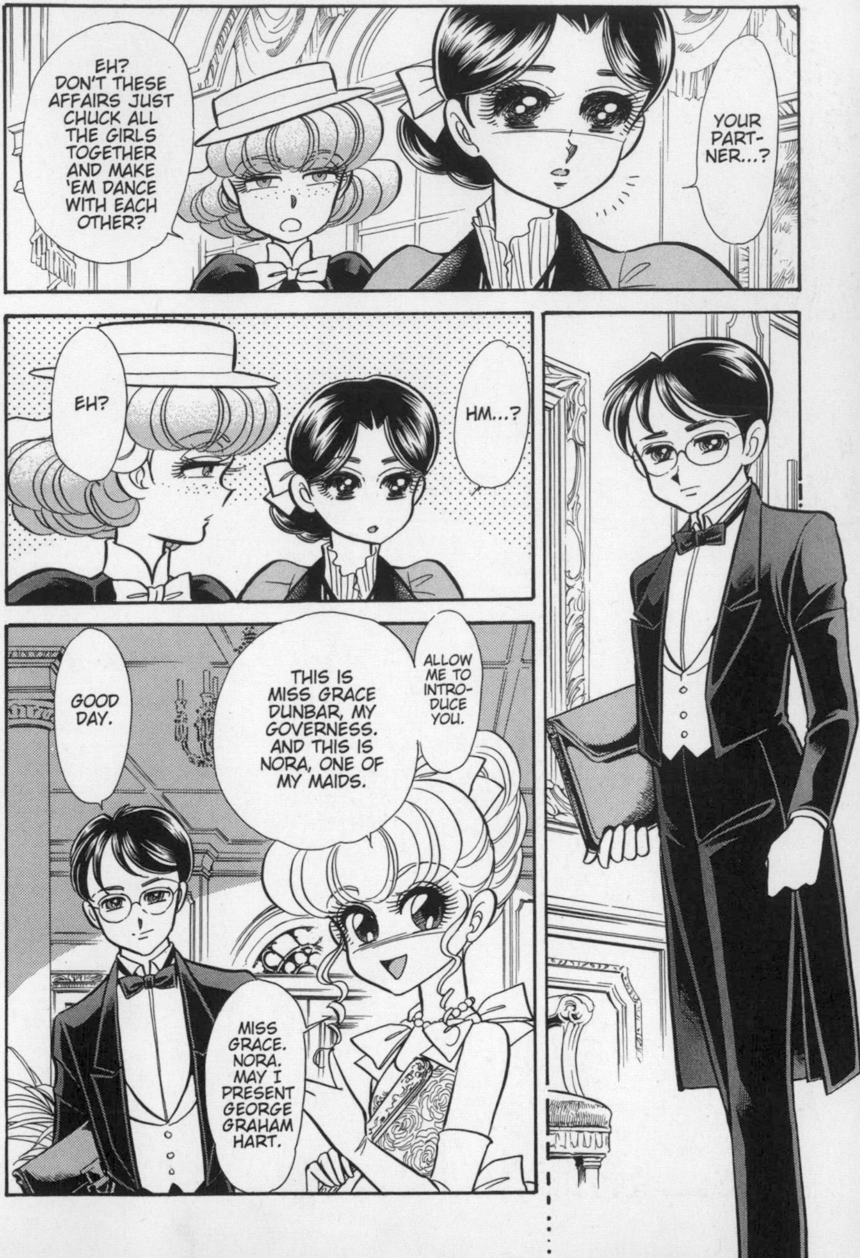
YOUR PARTNER...?
EH? DON'T THESE AFFAIRS JUST CHUCK ALL THE GIRLS TOGETHER AND MAKE 'EM DANCE WITH EACH OTHER?
HM...?
EH?
ALLOW ME TO INTRODUCE YOU.
THIS IS MISS GRACE DUNBAR, MY GOVERNESS. AND THIS IS NORA, ONE OF MY MAIDS.
GOOD DAY.
MISS GRACE. NORA. MAY I PRESENT GEORGE GRAHAM HART.

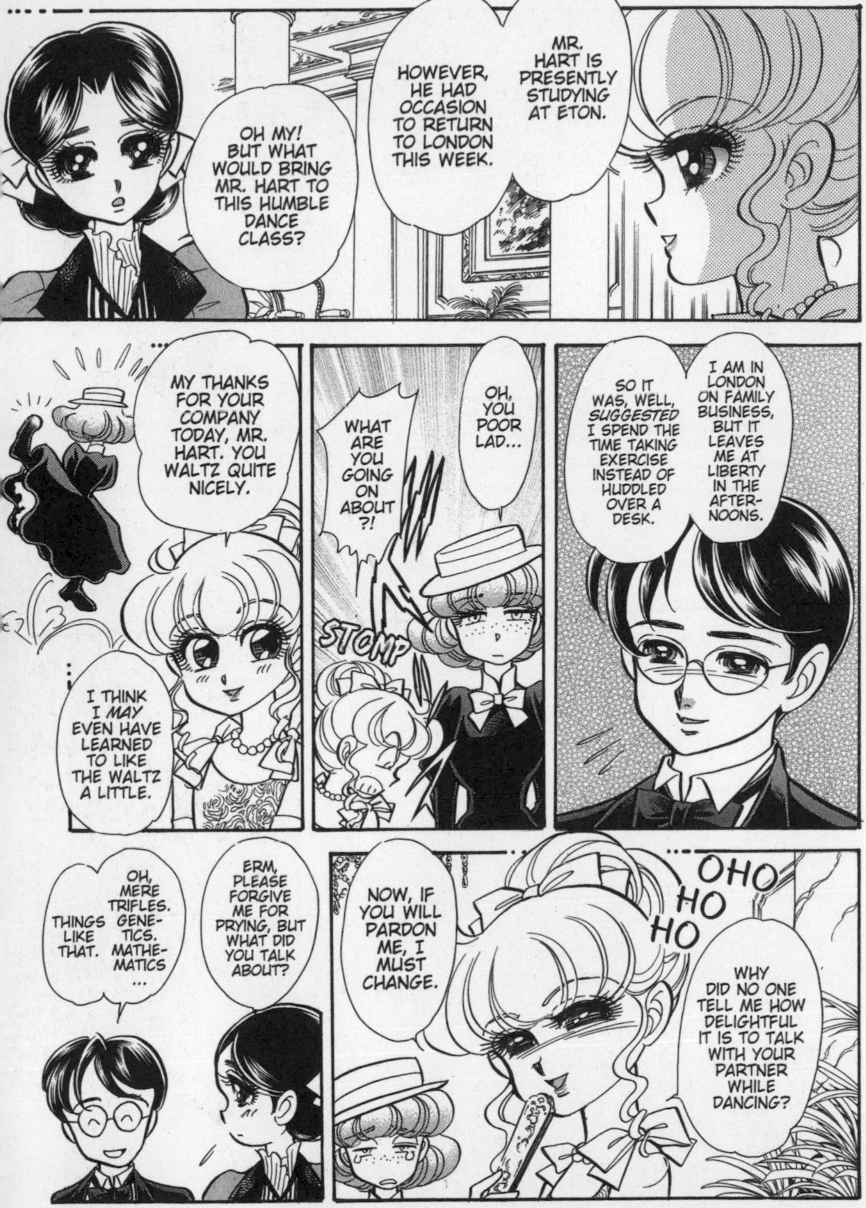
MR. HART IS PRESENTLY STUDYING AT ETON.
HOWEVER, HE HAD OCCASION TO RETURN TO LONDON THIS WEEK.
OH MY! BUT WHAT WOULD BRING MR. HART TO THIS HUMBLE DANCE CLASS?
I AM IN LONDON ON FAMILY BUSINESS, BUT IT LEAVES ME AT LIBERTY IN THE AFTERNOONS.
SO IT WAS, WELL, *SUGGESTED* I SPEND THE TIME TAKING EXERCISE INSTEAD OF HUDDLED OVER A DESK.
OH, YOU POOR LAD...
WHAT ARE YOU GOING ON ABOUT?!
STOMP
MY THANKS FOR YOUR COMPANY TODAY, MR. HART. YOU WALTZ QUITE NICELY.
I THINK I *MAY* EVEN HAVE LEARNED TO LIKE THE WALTZ A LITTLE.
OHO HO HO
WHY DID NO ONE TELL ME HOW DELIGHTFUL IT IS TO TALK WITH YOUR PARTNER WHILE DANCING?
NOW, IF YOU WILL PARDON ME, I MUST CHANGE.
ERM, PLEASE FORGIVE ME FOR PRYING, BUT WHAT DID YOU TALK ABOUT?
OH, MERE TRIFLES. GENETICS. MATHEMATICS ...
THINGS LIKE THAT.

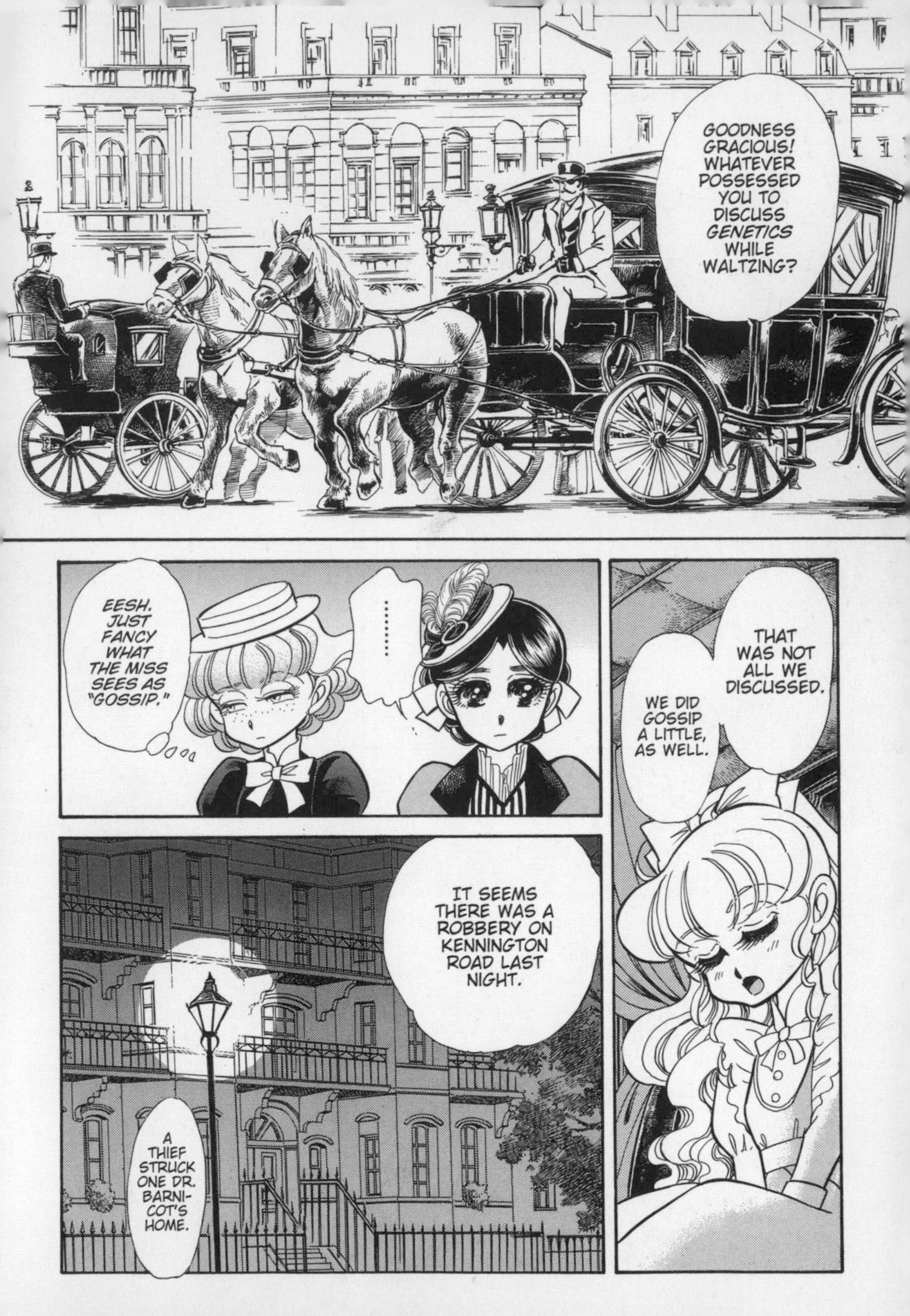
GOODNESS GRACIOUS! WHATEVER POSSESSED YOU TO DISCUSS GENETICS WHILE WALTZING?
THAT WAS NOT ALL WE DISCUSSED.
WE DID GOSSIP A LITTLE, AS WELL.
......
EESH. JUST FANCY WHAT THE MISS SEES AS "GOSSIP."
IT SEEMS THERE WAS A ROBBERY ON KENNINGTON ROAD LAST NIGHT.
A THIEF STRUCK ONE DR. BARNI-COT'S HOME.

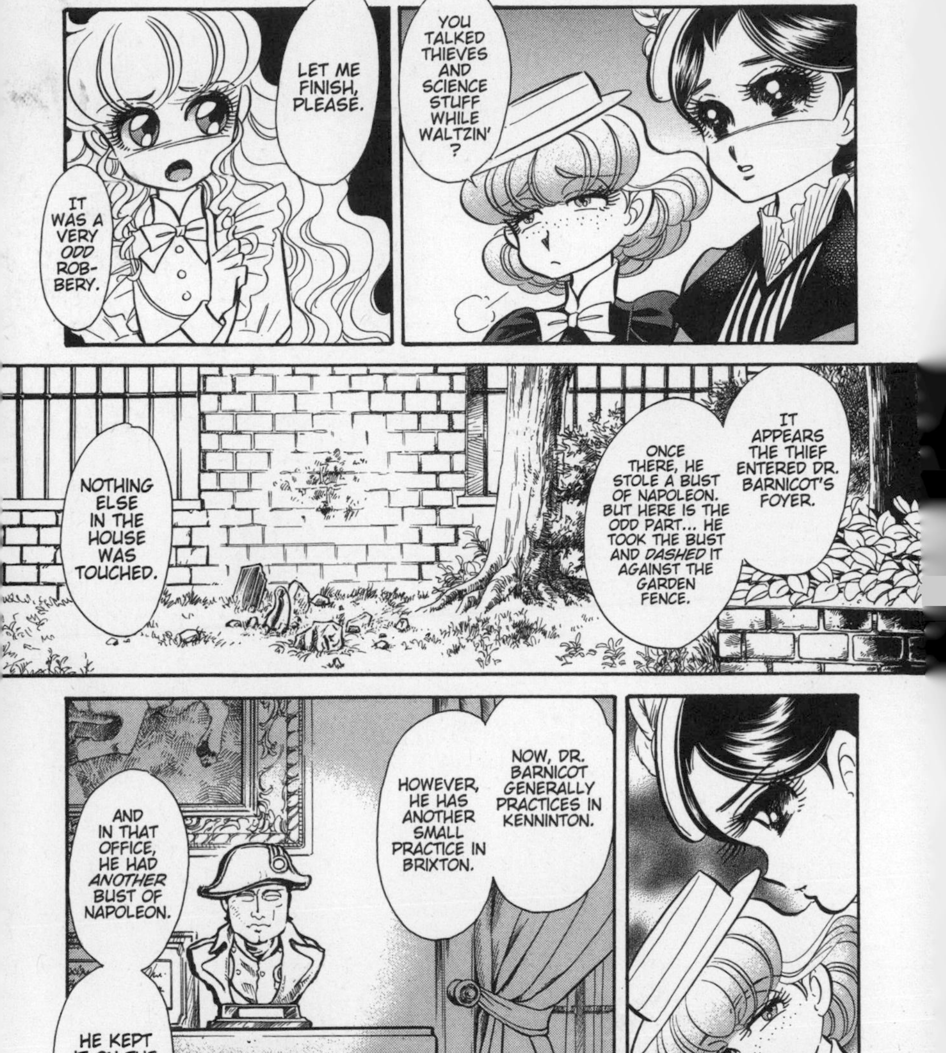
YOU TALKED THIEVES AND SCIENCE STUFF WHILE WALTZIN'?
LET ME FINISH, PLEASE.
IT WAS A VERY *ODD* ROBBERY.
IT APPEARS THE THIEF ENTERED DR. BARNICOT'S FOYER.
ONCE THERE, HE STOLE A BUST OF NAPOLEON. BUT HERE IS THE ODD PART... HE TOOK THE BUST AND *DASHED* IT AGAINST THE GARDEN FENCE.
NOTHING ELSE IN THE HOUSE WAS TOUCHED.
NOW, DR. BARNICOT GENERALLY PRACTICES IN KENNINTON.
HOWEVER, HE HAS ANOTHER SMALL PRACTICE IN BRIXTON.
AND IN THAT OFFICE, HE HAD *ANOTHER* BUST OF NAPOLEON.
HE KEPT IT ON THE MANTEL-PIECE.

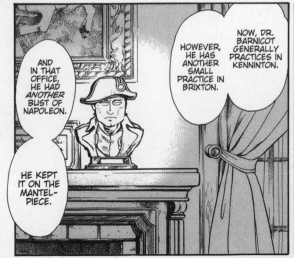

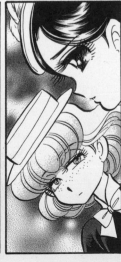

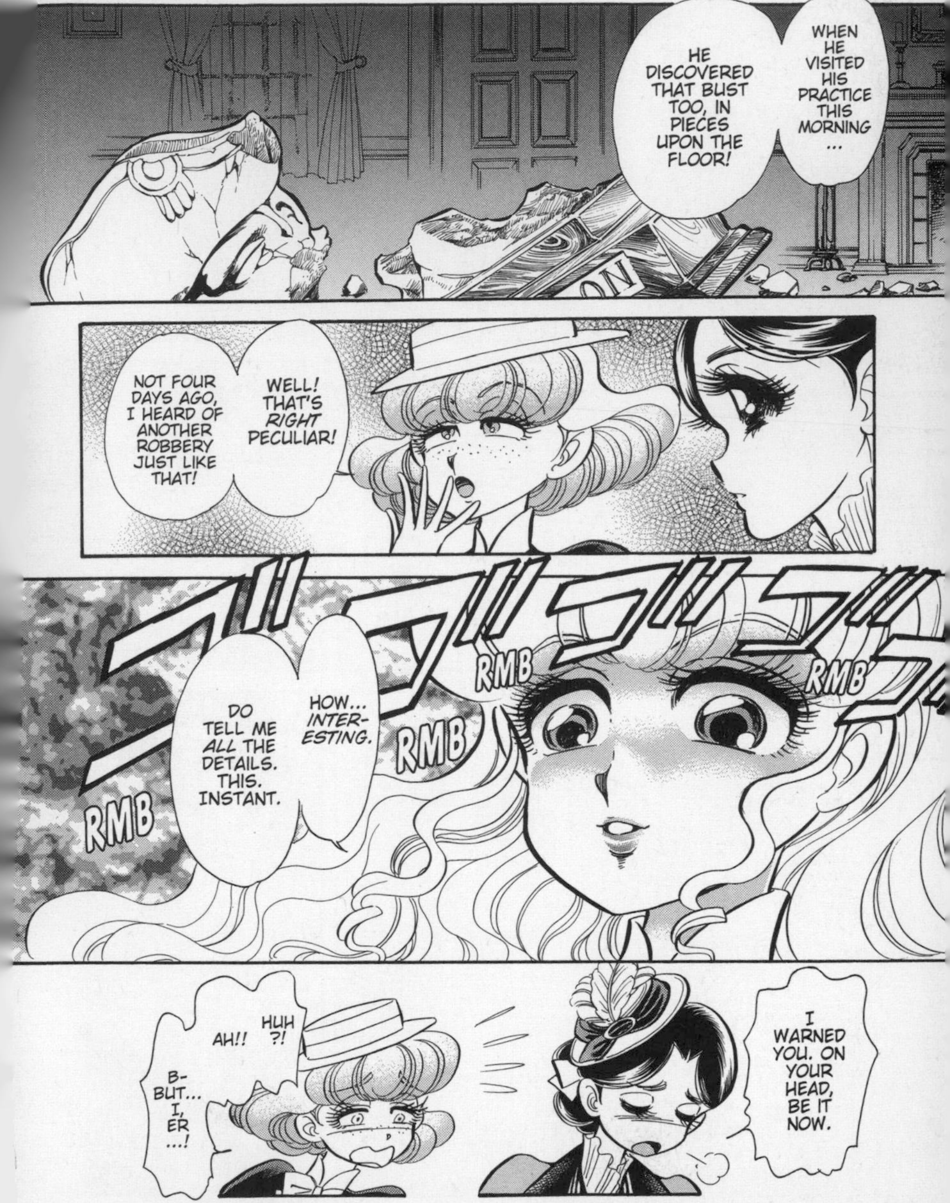
WHEN HE VISITED HIS PRACTICE THIS MORNING ...
HE DISCOVERED THAT BUST TOO, IN PIECES UPON THE FLOOR!
WELL! THAT'S *RIGHT* PECULIAR!
NOT FOUR DAYS AGO, I HEARD OF ANOTHER ROBBERY JUST LIKE THAT!
RMB
RMB
HOW... *INTERESTING.*
DO TELL ME *ALL* THE DETAILS. THIS. INSTANT.
RMB
RMB
I WARNED YOU. ON YOUR HEAD, BE IT NOW.
HUH ?!
AH!!
B-BUT... I, ER ...!

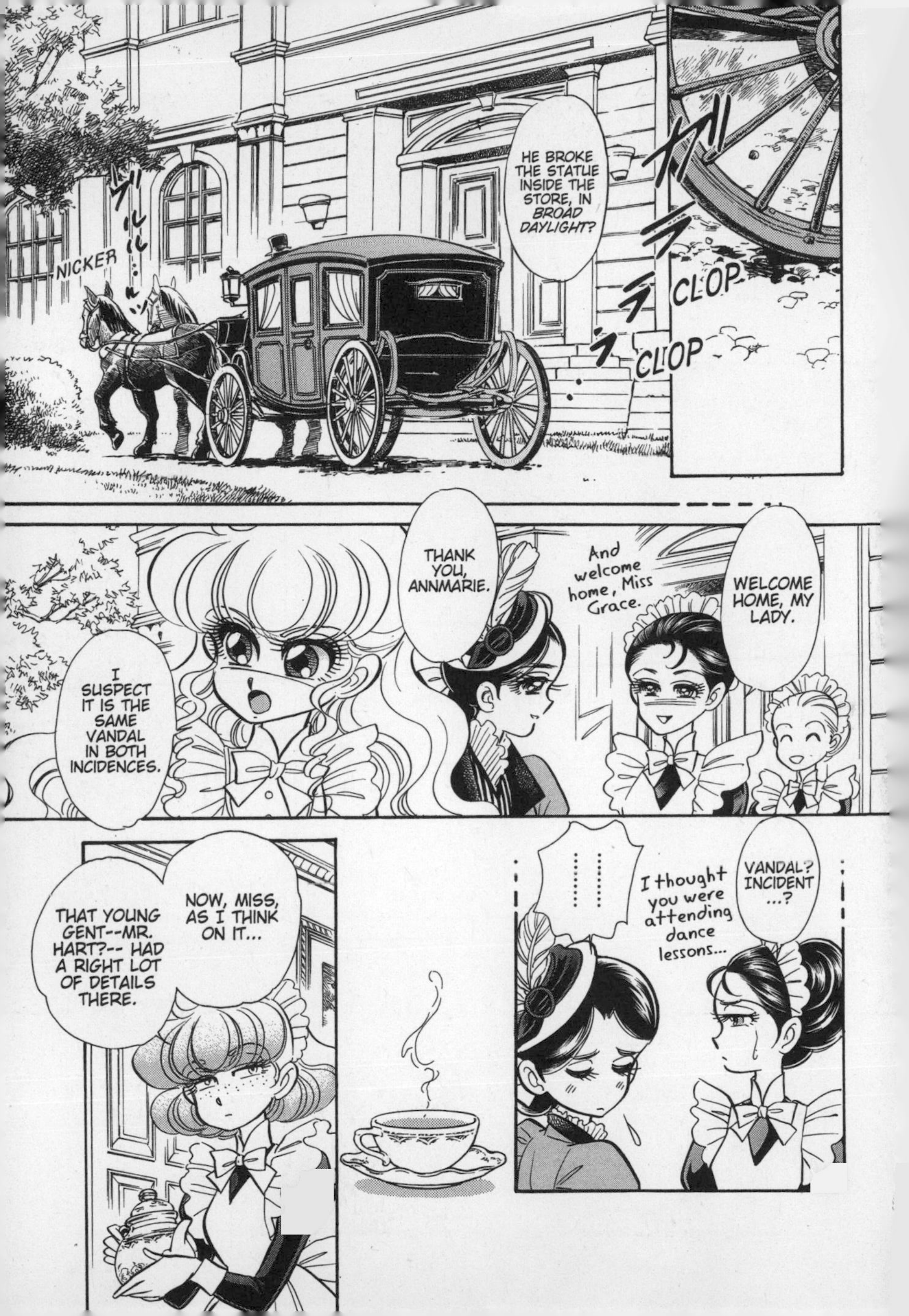
CLOP
CLOP
HE BROKE THE STATUE INSIDE THE STORE, IN *BROAD DAYLIGHT*?
NICKER
WELCOME HOME, MY LADY.
And welcome home, Miss Grace.
THANK YOU, ANNMARIE.
I SUSPECT IT IS THE SAME VANDAL IN BOTH INCIDENCES.
VANDAL? INCIDENT ...?
I thought you were attending dance lessons...
......
NOW, MISS, AS I THINK ON IT...
THAT YOUNG GENT--MR. HART?-- HAD A RIGHT LOT OF DETAILS THERE.

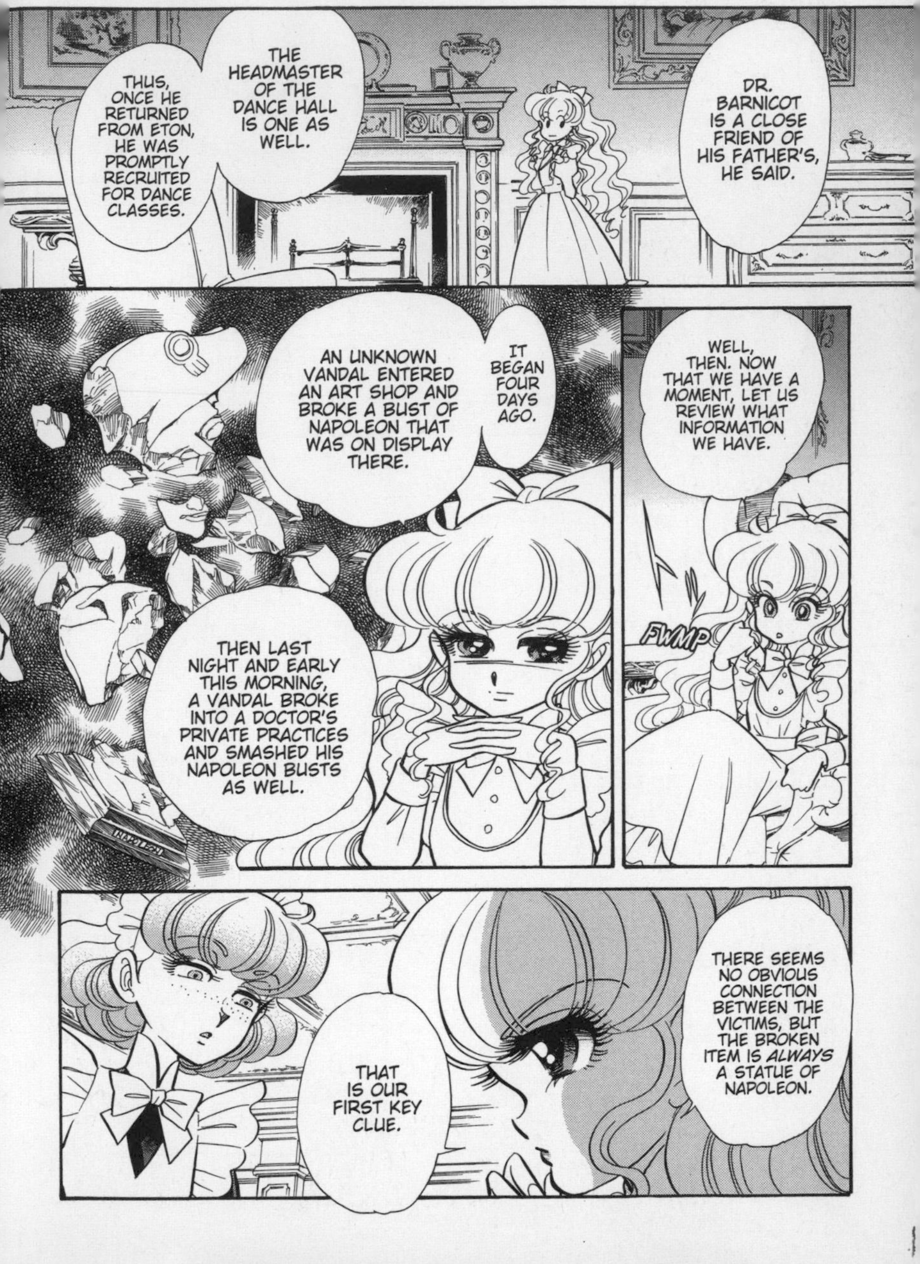
DR. BARNICOT IS A CLOSE FRIEND OF HIS FATHER'S, HE SAID.
THE HEADMASTER OF THE DANCE HALL IS ONE AS WELL.
THUS, ONCE HE RETURNED FROM ETON, HE WAS PROMPTLY RECRUITED FOR DANCE CLASSES.
WELL, THEN. NOW THAT WE HAVE A MOMENT, LET US REVIEW WHAT INFORMATION WE HAVE.
FWMP
IT BEGAN FOUR DAYS AGO.
AN UNKNOWN VANDAL ENTERED AN ART SHOP AND BROKE A BUST OF NAPOLEON THAT WAS ON DISPLAY THERE.
THEN LAST NIGHT AND EARLY THIS MORNING, A VANDAL BROKE INTO A DOCTOR'S PRIVATE PRACTICES AND SMASHED HIS NAPOLEON BUSTS AS WELL.
THERE SEEMS NO OBVIOUS CONNECTION BETWEEN THE VICTIMS, BUT THE BROKEN ITEM IS *ALWAYS* A STATUE OF NAPOLEON.
THAT IS OUR FIRST KEY CLUE.

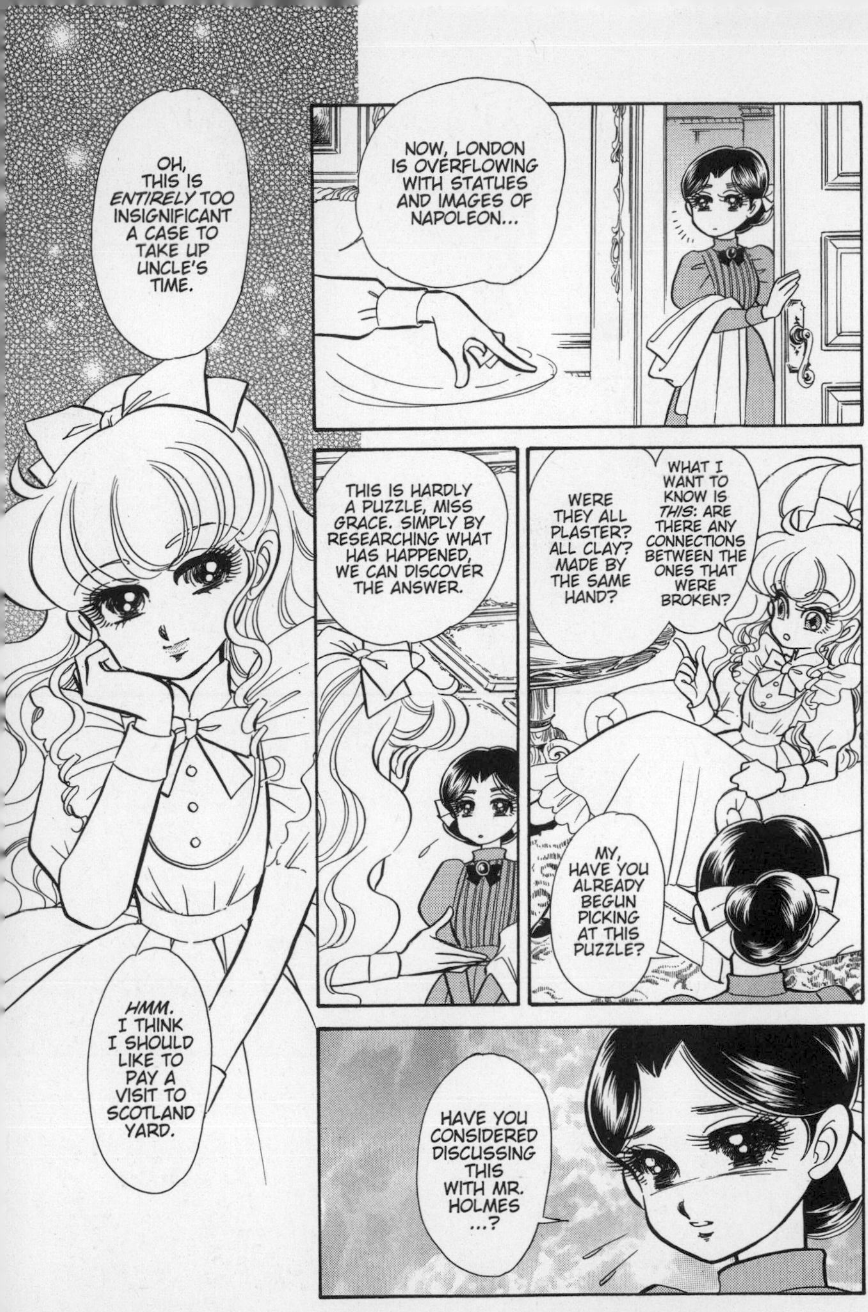
NOW, LONDON IS OVERFLOWING WITH STATUES AND IMAGES OF NAPOLEON...
WHAT I WANT TO KNOW IS *THIS*: ARE THERE ANY CONNECTIONS BETWEEN THE ONES THAT WERE BROKEN?
WERE THEY ALL PLASTER? ALL CLAY? MADE BY THE SAME HAND?
MY, HAVE YOU ALREADY BEGUN PICKING AT THIS PUZZLE?
THIS IS HARDLY A PUZZLE, MISS GRACE. SIMPLY BY RESEARCHING WHAT HAS HAPPENED, WE CAN DISCOVER THE ANSWER.
HAVE YOU CONSIDERED DISCUSSING THIS WITH MR. HOLMES ...?
OH, THIS IS *ENTIRELY* TOO INSIGNIFICANT A CASE TO TAKE UP UNCLE'S TIME.
HMM. I THINK I SHOULD LIKE TO PAY A VISIT TO SCOTLAND YARD.

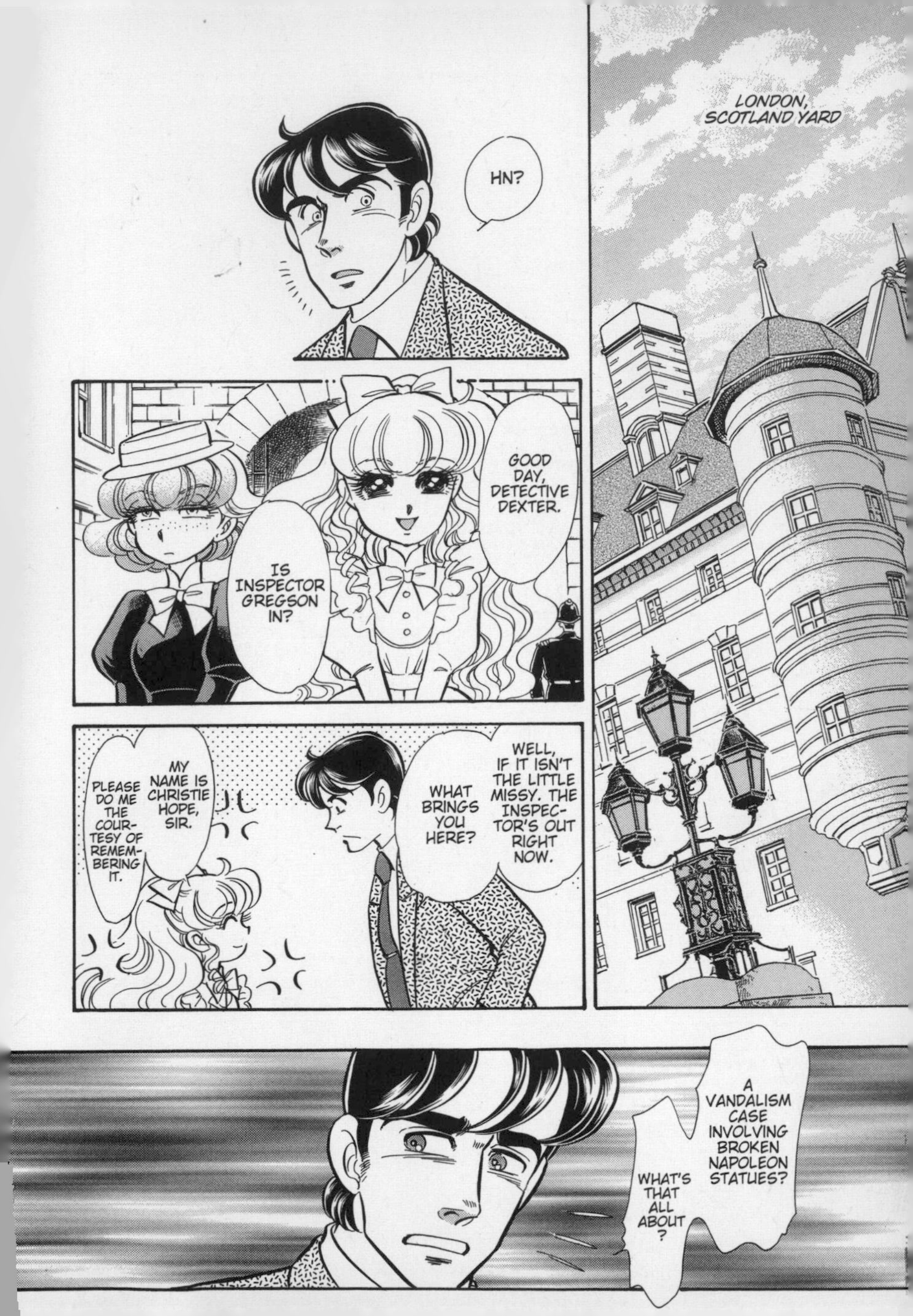
LONDON, SCOTLAND YARD
HN?
GOOD DAY, DETECTIVE DEXTER.
IS INSPECTOR GREGSON IN?
WELL, IF IT ISN'T THE LITTLE MISSY. THE INSPEC-TOR'S OUT RIGHT NOW.
WHAT BRINGS YOU HERE?
MY NAME IS CHRISTIE HOPE, SIR.
PLEASE DO ME THE COUR-TESY OF REMEM-BERING IT.
A VANDALISM CASE INVOLVING BROKEN NAPOLEON STATUES?
WHAT'S THAT ALL ABOUT?

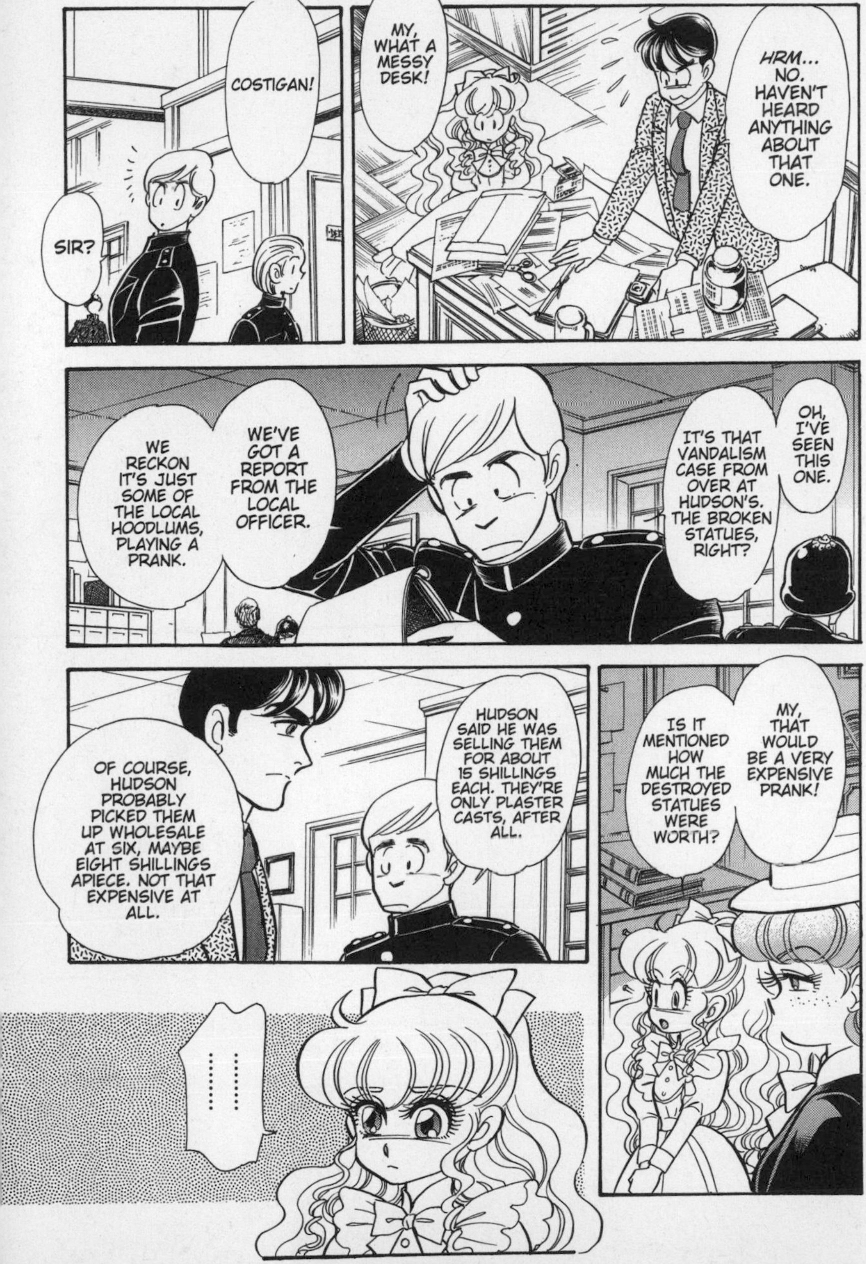
HRM... NO. HAVEN'T HEARD ANYTHING ABOUT THAT ONE.
MY, WHAT A MESSY DESK!
COSTIGAN!
SIR?
OH, I'VE SEEN THIS ONE.
IT'S THAT VANDALISM CASE FROM OVER AT HUDSON'S. THE BROKEN STATUES, RIGHT?
WE'VE GOT A REPORT FROM THE LOCAL OFFICER.
WE RECKON IT'S JUST SOME OF THE LOCAL HOODLUMS, PLAYING A PRANK.
MY, THAT WOULD BE A VERY EXPENSIVE PRANK!
IS IT MENTIONED HOW MUCH THE DESTROYED STATUES WERE WORTH?
HUDSON SAID HE WAS SELLING THEM FOR ABOUT 15 SHILLINGS EACH. THEY'RE ONLY PLASTER CASTS, AFTER ALL.
OF COURSE, HUDSON PROBABLY PICKED THEM UP WHOLESALE AT SIX, MAYBE EIGHT SHILLINGS APIECE. NOT THAT EXPENSIVE AT ALL.
......

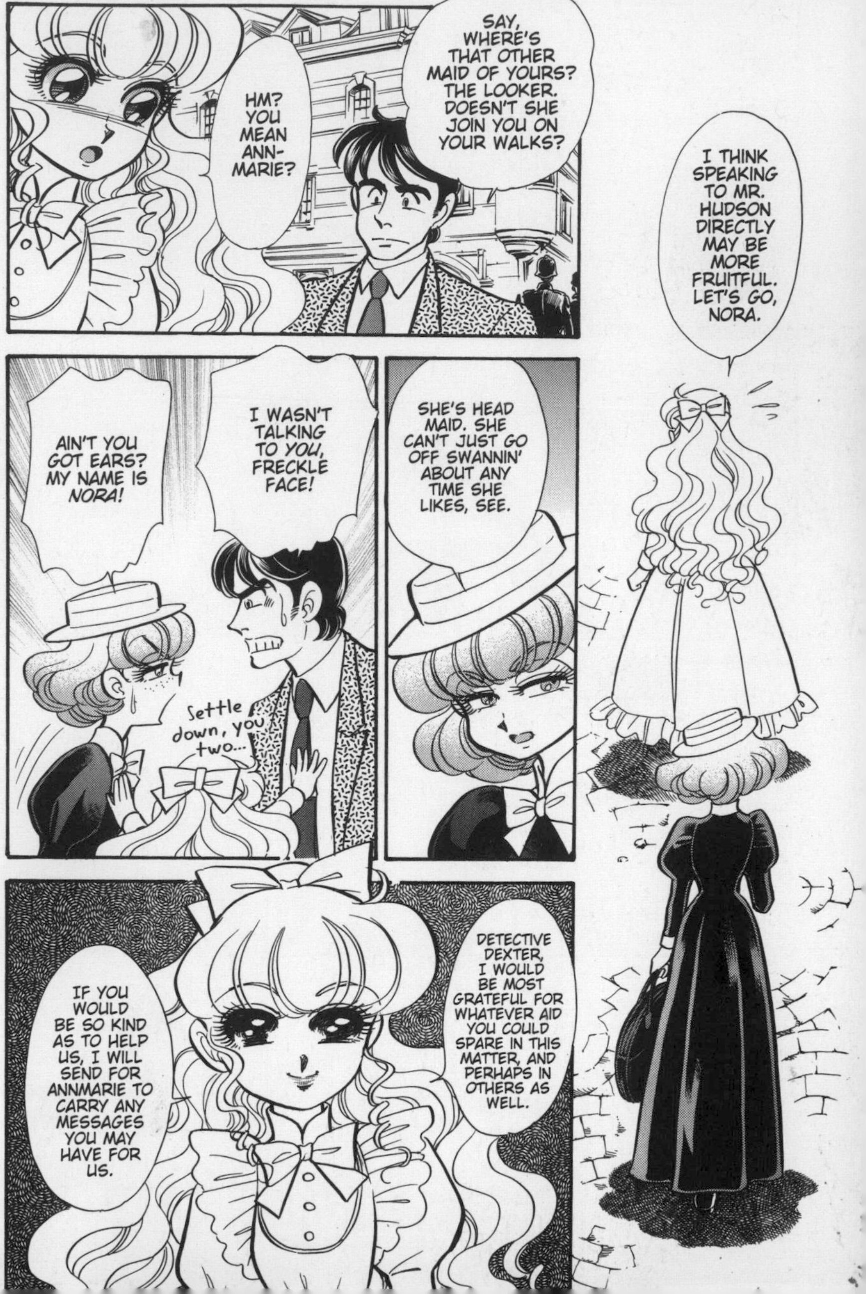
I THINK SPEAKING TO MR. HUDSON DIRECTLY MAY BE MORE FRUITFUL. LET'S GO, NORA.
SAY, WHERE'S THAT OTHER MAID OF YOURS? THE LOOKER. DOESN'T SHE JOIN YOU ON YOUR WALKS?
HM? YOU MEAN ANN-MARIE?
SHE'S HEAD MAID. SHE CAN'T JUST GO OFF SWANNIN' ABOUT ANY TIME SHE LIKES, SEE.
I WASN'T TALKING TO *YOU*, FRECKLE FACE!
AIN'T YOU GOT EARS? MY NAME IS *NORA*!
Settle down, you two...
DETECTIVE DEXTER, I WOULD BE MOST GRATEFUL FOR WHATEVER AID YOU COULD SPARE IN THIS MATTER, AND PERHAPS IN OTHERS AS WELL.
IF YOU WOULD BE SO KIND AS TO HELP US, I WILL SEND FOR ANNMARIE TO CARRY ANY MESSAGES YOU MAY HAVE FOR US.

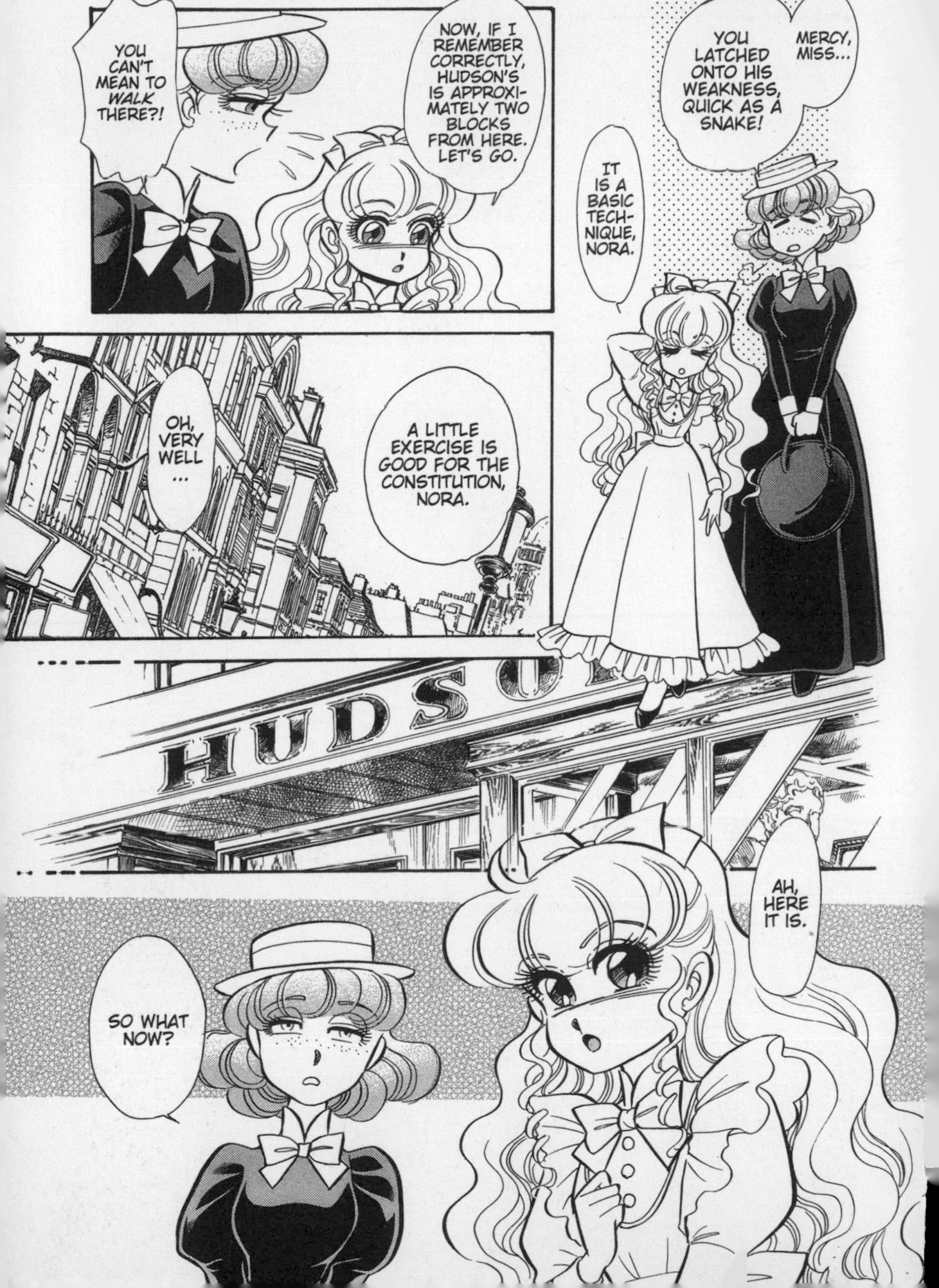
MERCY, MISS...
YOU LATCHED ONTO HIS WEAKNESS, QUICK AS A SNAKE!
IT IS A BASIC TECHNIQUE, NORA.
NOW, IF I REMEMBER CORRECTLY, HUDSON'S IS APPROXIMATELY TWO BLOCKS FROM HERE. LET'S GO.
YOU CAN'T MEAN TO *WALK* THERE?!
A LITTLE EXERCISE IS GOOD FOR THE CONSTITUTION, NORA.
OH, VERY WELL ...
HUDS
AH, HERE IT IS.
SO WHAT NOW?

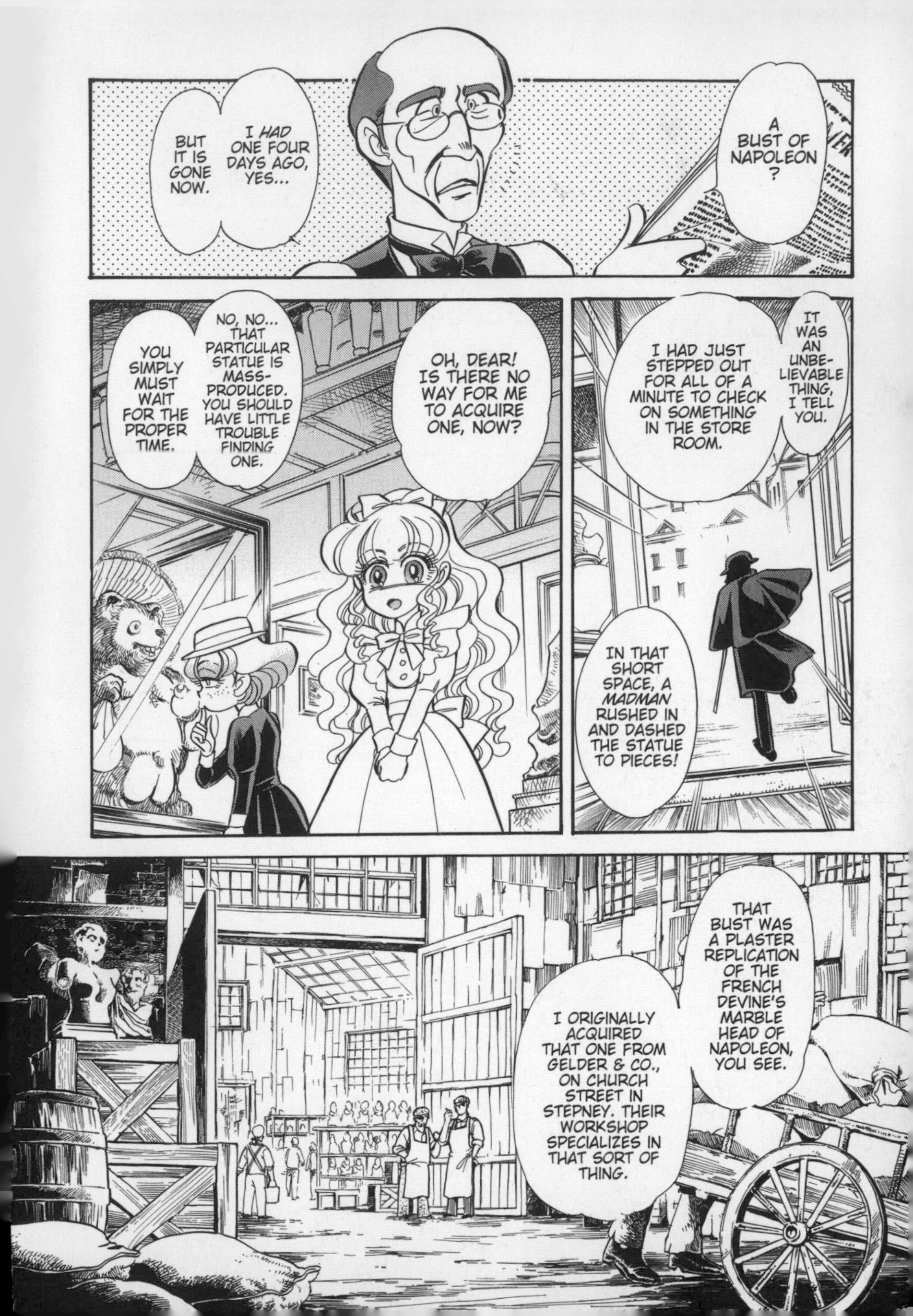
A BUST OF NAPOLEON?
I *HAD* ONE FOUR DAYS AGO, YES...
BUT IT IS GONE NOW.
IT WAS AN UNBELIEVABLE THING, I TELL YOU.
I HAD JUST STEPPED OUT FOR ALL OF A MINUTE TO CHECK ON SOMETHING IN THE STORE ROOM.
IN THAT SHORT SPACE, A *MADMAN* RUSHED IN AND DASHED THE STATUE TO PIECES!
OH, DEAR! IS THERE NO WAY FOR ME TO ACQUIRE ONE, NOW?
NO, NO... THAT PARTICULAR STATUE IS MASS-PRODUCED. YOU SHOULD HAVE LITTLE TROUBLE FINDING ONE.
YOU SIMPLY MUST WAIT FOR THE PROPER TIME.
THAT BUST WAS A PLASTER REPLICATION OF THE FRENCH DEVINE'S MARBLE HEAD OF NAPOLEON, YOU SEE.
I ORIGINALLY ACQUIRED THAT ONE FROM GELDER & CO., ON CHURCH STREET IN STEPNEY. THEIR WORKSHOP SPECIALIZES IN THAT SORT OF THING.

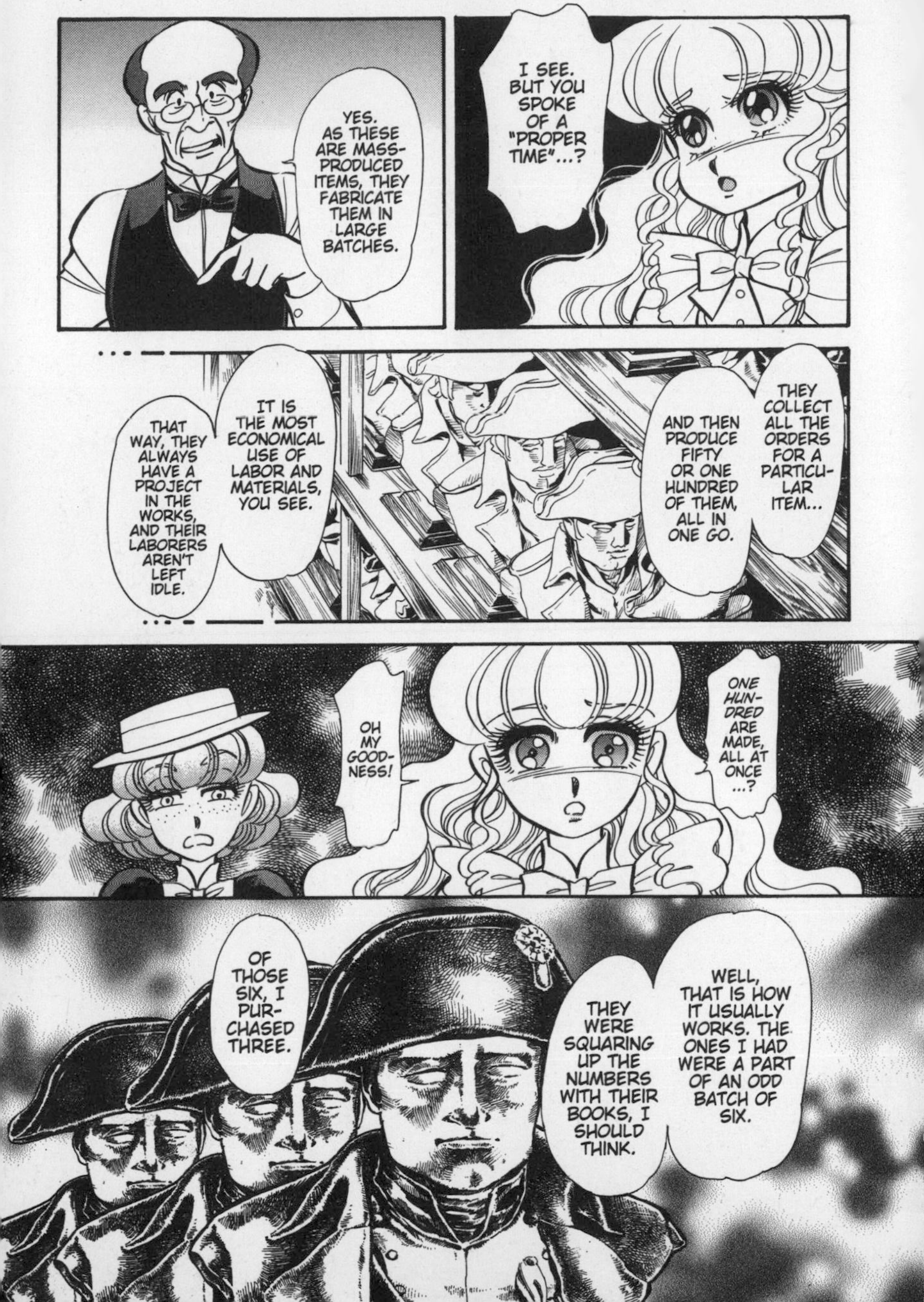
I SEE. BUT YOU SPOKE OF A "PROPER TIME"...?
YES. AS THESE ARE MASS-PRODUCED ITEMS, THEY FABRICATE THEM IN LARGE BATCHES.
THEY COLLECT ALL THE ORDERS FOR A PARTICULAR ITEM...
AND THEN PRODUCE FIFTY OR ONE HUNDRED OF THEM, ALL IN ONE GO.
IT IS THE MOST ECONOMICAL USE OF LABOR AND MATERIALS, YOU SEE.
THAT WAY, THEY ALWAYS HAVE A PROJECT IN THE WORKS, AND THEIR LABORERS AREN'T LEFT IDLE.
ONE HUNDRED ARE MADE, ALL AT ONCE...?
OH MY GOODNESS!
WELL, THAT IS HOW IT USUALLY WORKS. THE ONES I HAD WERE A PART OF AN ODD BATCH OF SIX.
THEY WERE SQUARING UP THE NUMBERS WITH THEIR BOOKS, I SHOULD THINK.
OF THOSE SIX, I PURCHASED THREE.

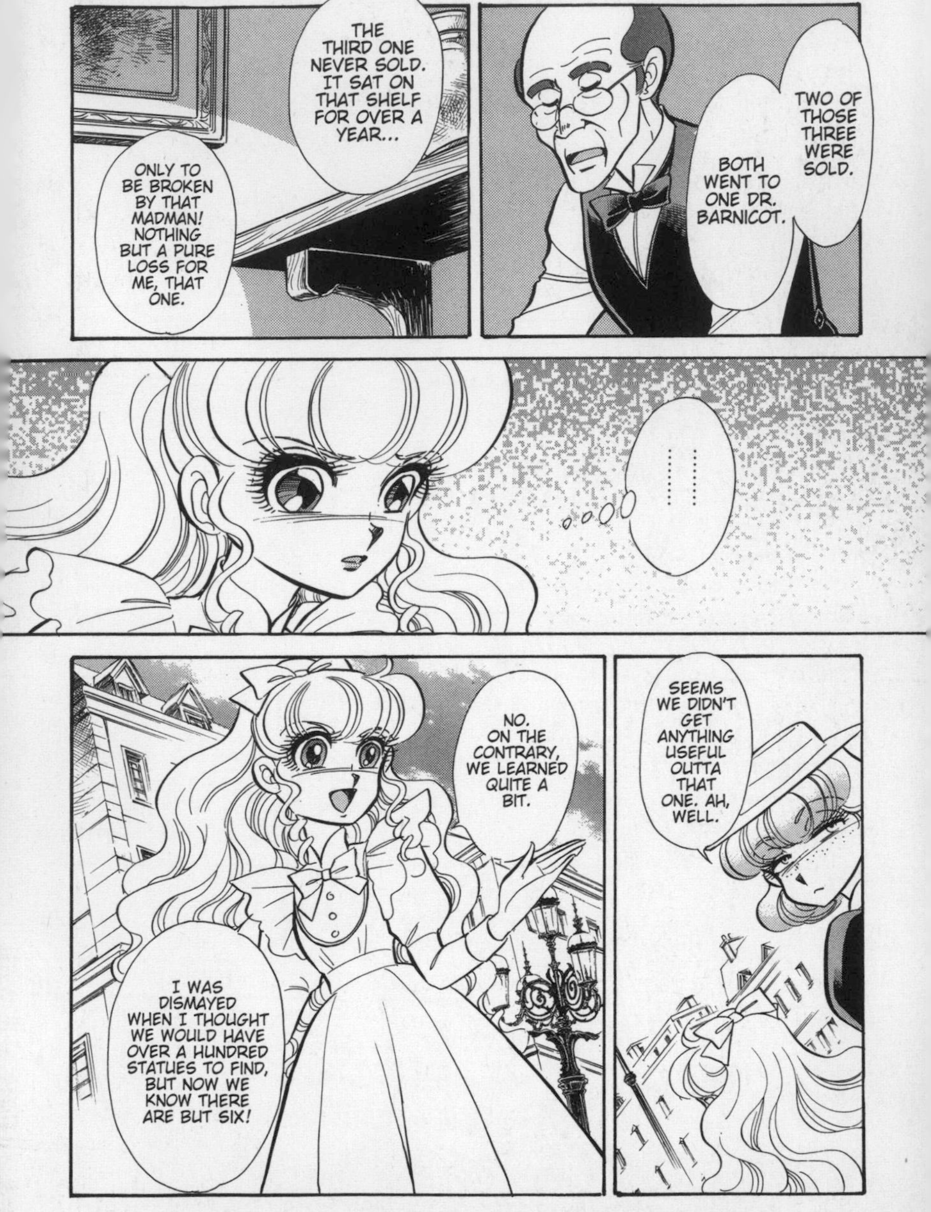
TWO OF THOSE THREE WERE SOLD.
BOTH WENT TO ONE DR. BARNICOT.
THE THIRD ONE NEVER SOLD. IT SAT ON THAT SHELF FOR OVER A YEAR...
ONLY TO BE BROKEN BY THAT MADMAN! NOTHING BUT A PURE LOSS FOR ME, THAT ONE.
......
SEEMS WE DIDN'T GET ANYTHING USEFUL OUTTA THAT ONE. AH, WELL.
NO. ON THE CONTRARY, WE LEARNED QUITE A BIT.
I WAS DISMAYED WHEN I THOUGHT WE WOULD HAVE OVER A HUNDRED STATUES TO FIND, BUT NOW WE KNOW THERE ARE BUT SIX!

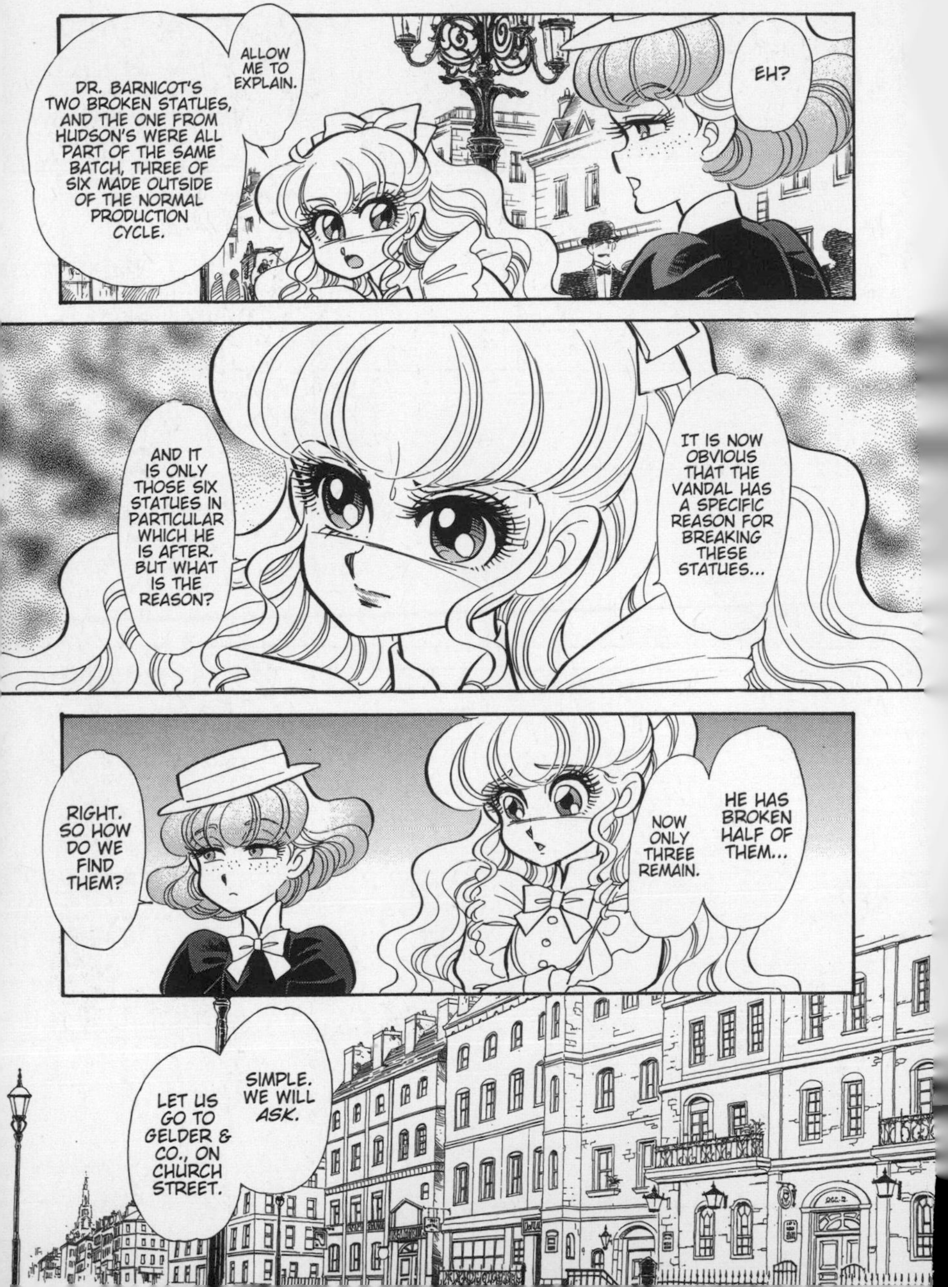
EH?
ALLOW ME TO EXPLAIN.
DR. BARNICOT'S TWO BROKEN STATUES, AND THE ONE FROM HUDSON'S WERE ALL PART OF THE SAME BATCH, THREE OF SIX MADE OUTSIDE OF THE NORMAL PRODUCTION CYCLE.
IT IS NOW OBVIOUS THAT THE VANDAL HAS A SPECIFIC REASON FOR BREAKING THESE STATUES...
AND IT IS ONLY THOSE SIX STATUES IN PARTICULAR WHICH HE IS AFTER. BUT WHAT IS THE REASON?
HE HAS BROKEN HALF OF THEM...
NOW ONLY THREE REMAIN.
RIGHT. SO HOW DO WE FIND THEM?
SIMPLE. WE WILL ASK.
LET US GO TO GELDER & CO., ON CHURCH STREET.

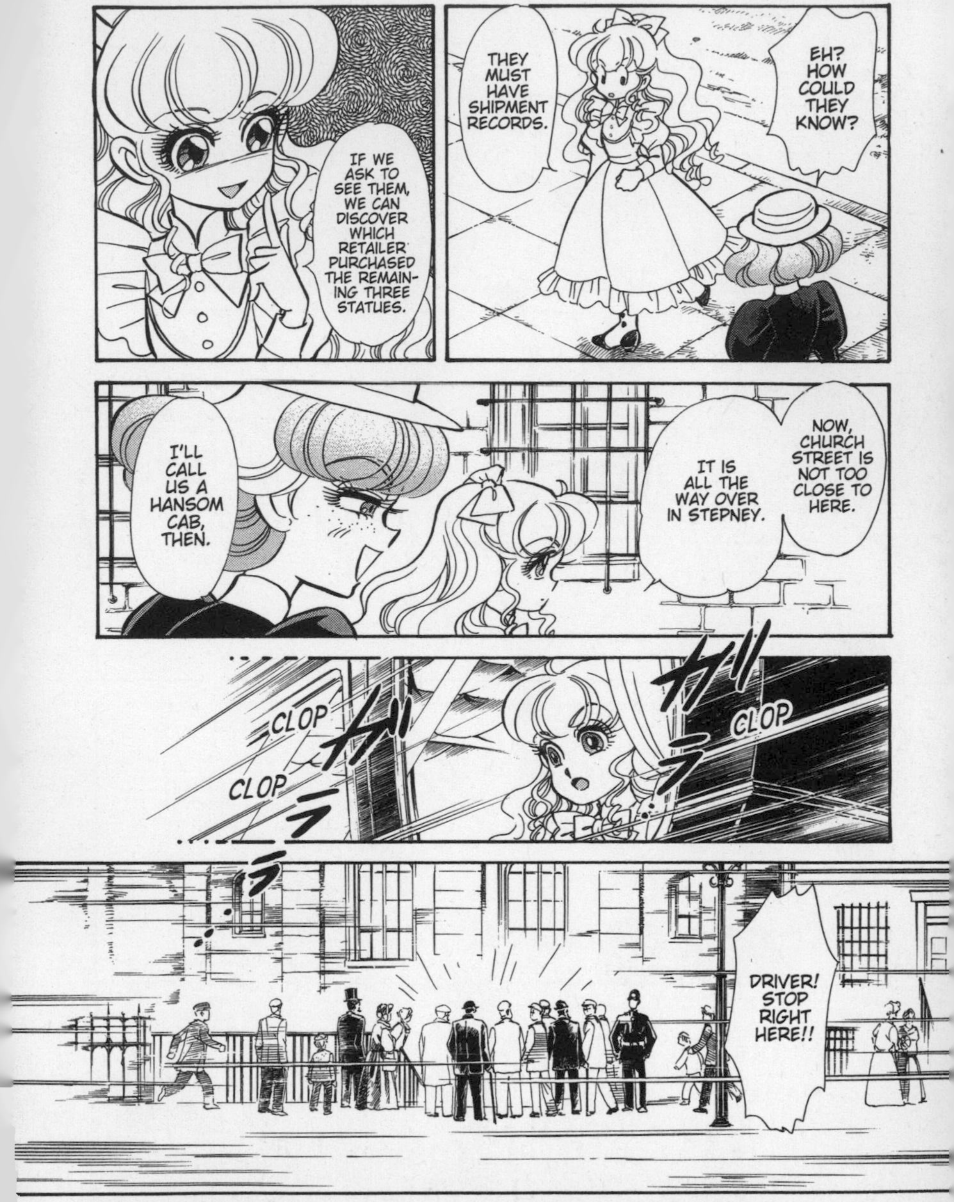
EH? HOW COULD THEY KNOW?
THEY MUST HAVE SHIPMENT RECORDS.
IF WE ASK TO SEE THEM, WE CAN DISCOVER WHICH RETAILER PURCHASED THE REMAINING THREE STATUES.
NOW, CHURCH STREET IS NOT TOO CLOSE TO HERE.
IT IS ALL THE WAY OVER IN STEPNEY.
I'LL CALL US A HANSOM CAB, THEN.
CLOP
CLOP
CLOP
DRIVER! STOP RIGHT HERE!!

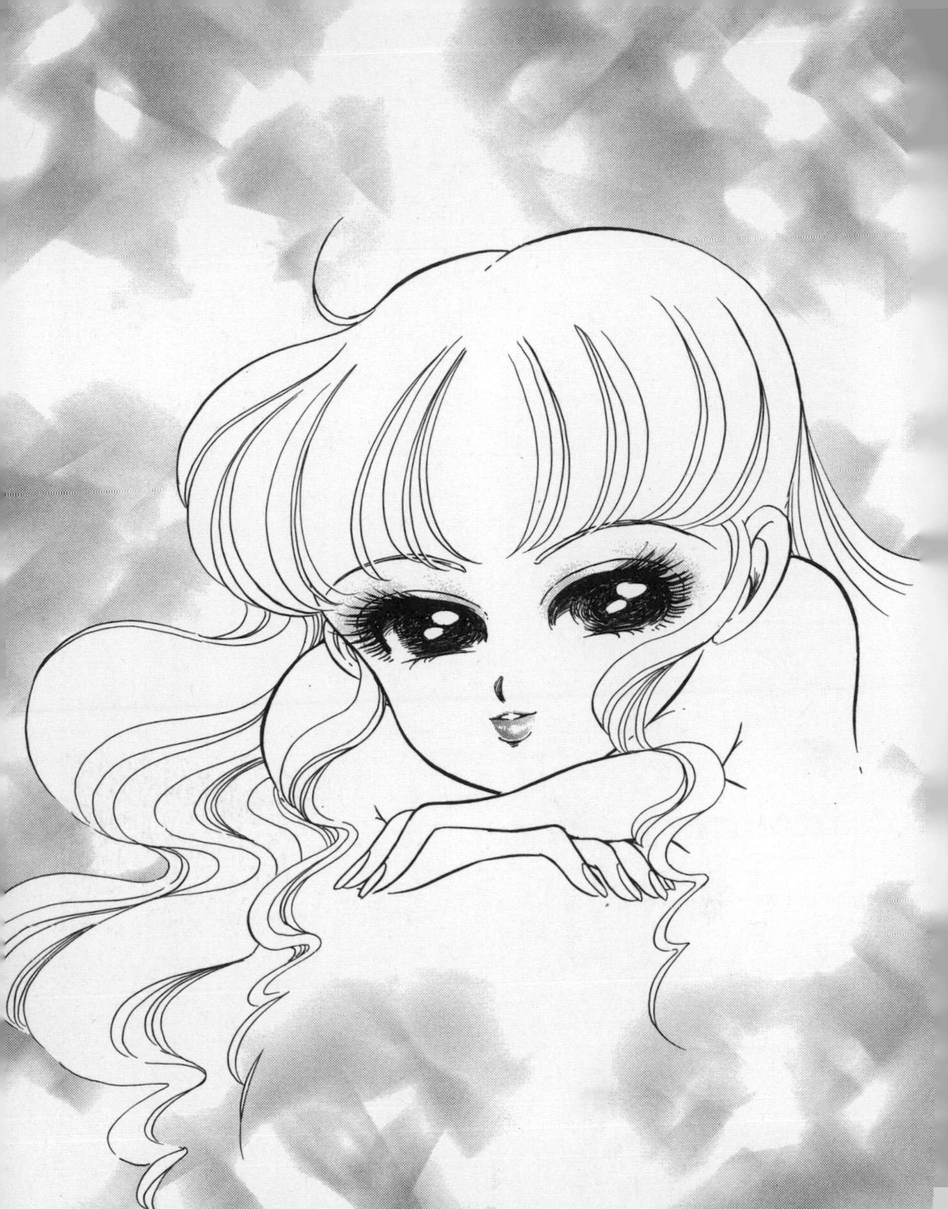

The Adventure of the Six Napoleons (2)

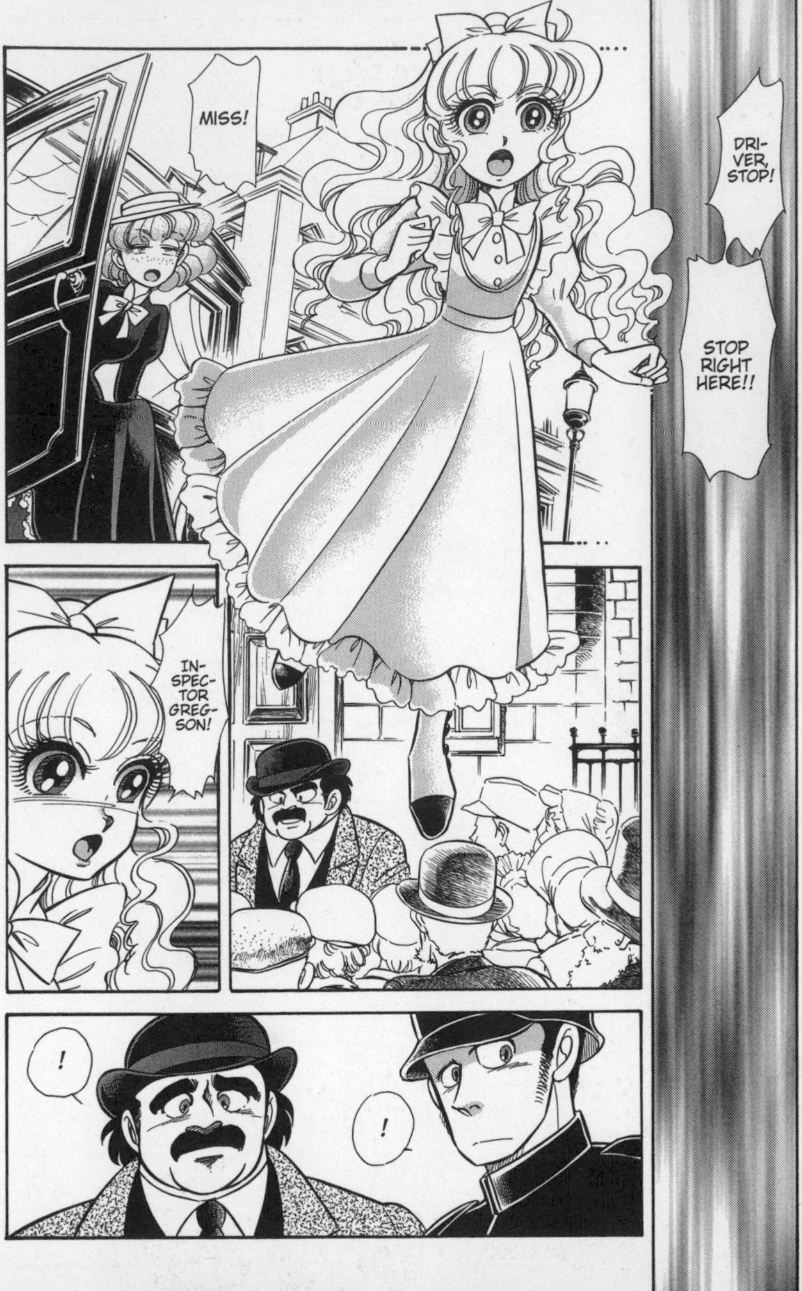
DRI-VER, STOP!
STOP RIGHT HERE!!
MISS!
IN-SPEC-TOR GREG-SON!
!
!

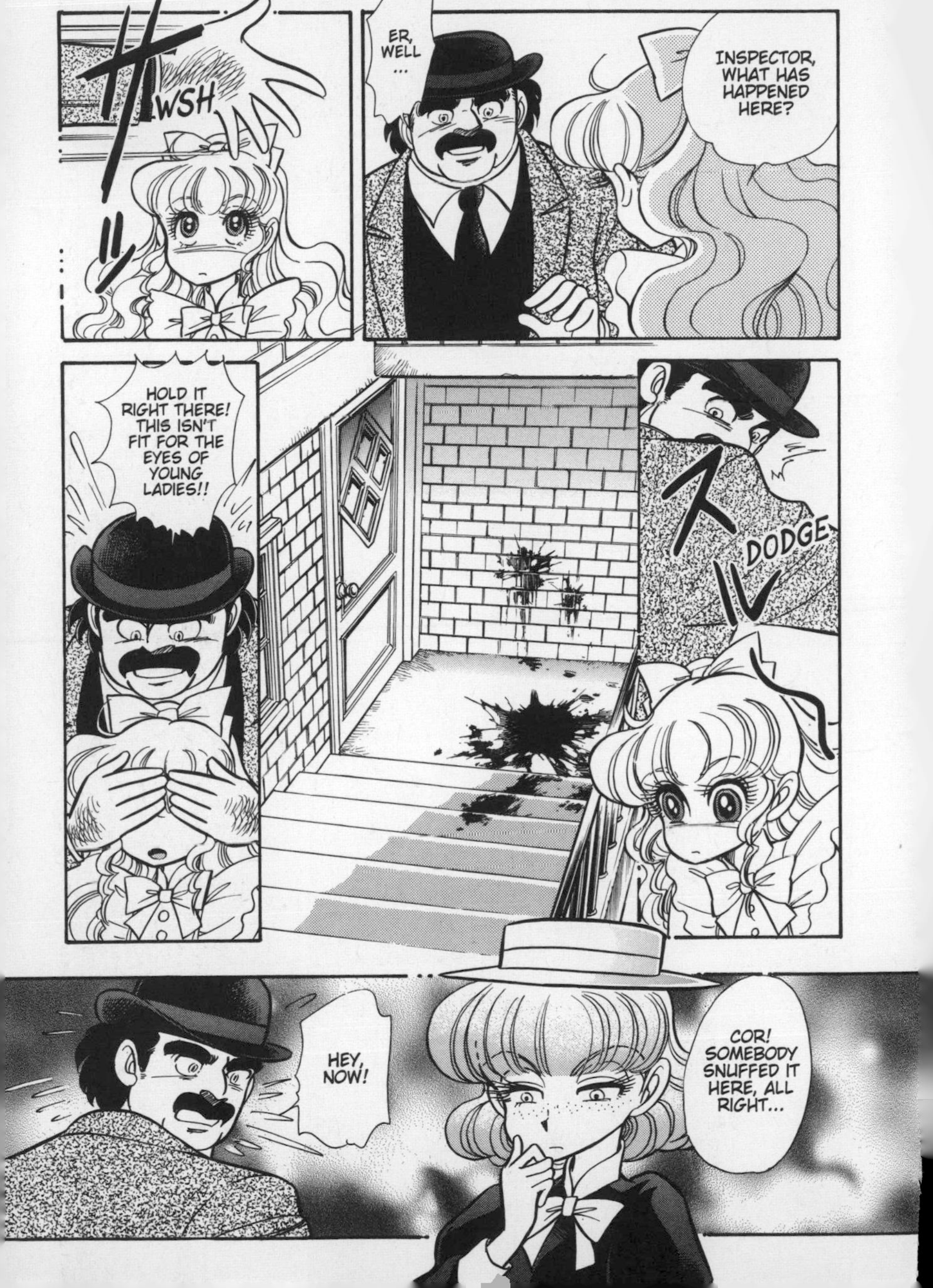
INSPECTOR, WHAT HAS HAPPENED HERE?
ER, WELL ...
WSH
DODGE
HOLD IT RIGHT THERE! THIS ISN'T FIT FOR THE EYES OF YOUNG LADIES!!
COR! SOMEBODY SNUFFED IT HERE, ALL RIGHT...
HEY, NOW!

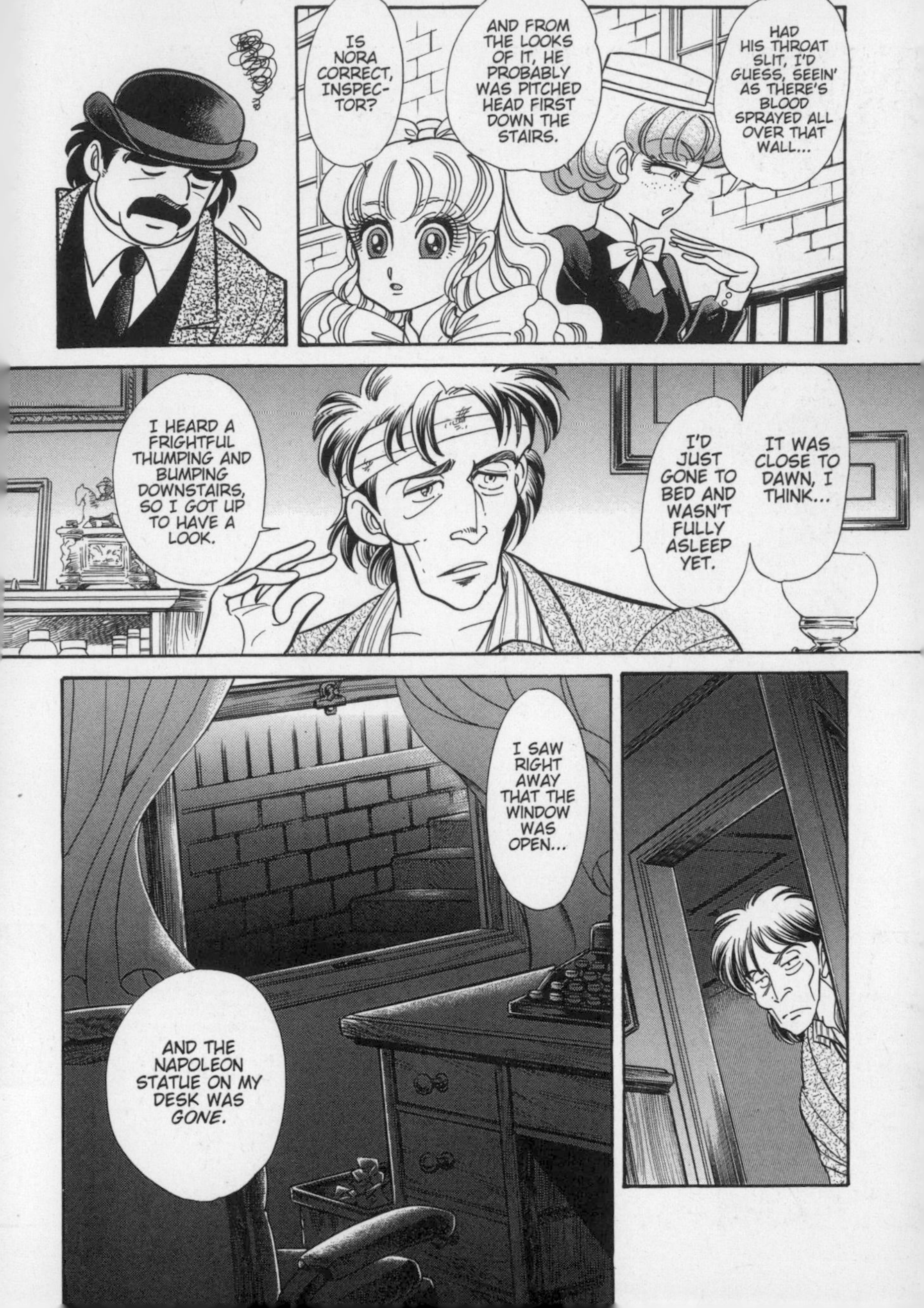
HAD HIS THROAT SLIT, I'D GUESS, SEEIN' AS THERE'S BLOOD SPRAYED ALL OVER THAT WALL...
AND FROM THE LOOKS OF IT, HE PROBABLY WAS PITCHED HEAD FIRST DOWN THE STAIRS.
IS NORA CORRECT, INSPECTOR?
IT WAS CLOSE TO DAWN, I THINK...
I'D JUST GONE TO BED AND WASN'T FULLY ASLEEP YET.
I HEARD A FRIGHTFUL THUMPING AND BUMPING DOWNSTAIRS, SO I GOT UP TO HAVE A LOOK.
I SAW RIGHT AWAY THAT THE WINDOW WAS OPEN...
AND THE NAPOLEON STATUE ON MY DESK WAS GONE.

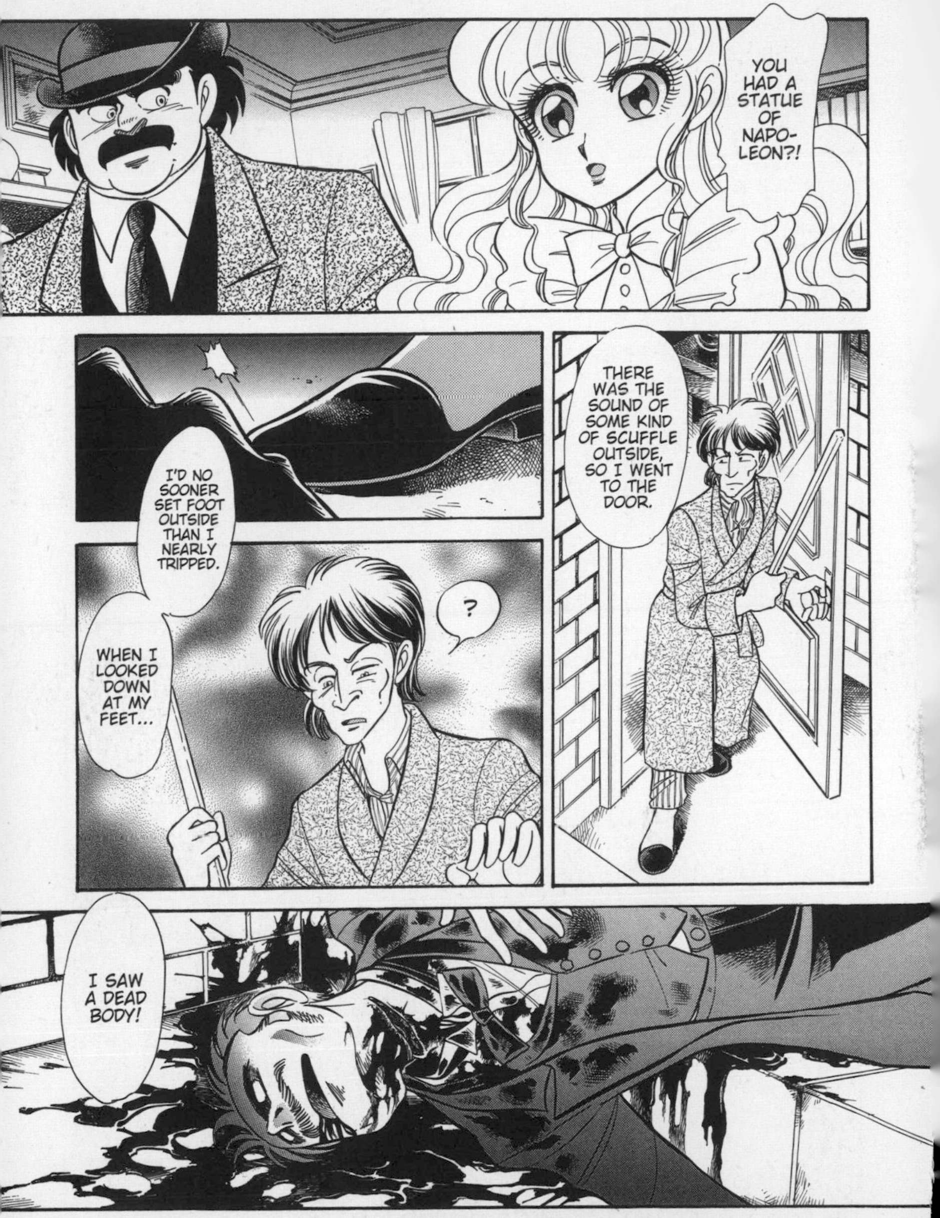
YOU HAD A STATUE OF NAPO-LEON?!
THERE WAS THE SOUND OF SOME KIND OF SCUFFLE OUTSIDE, SO I WENT TO THE DOOR.
I'D NO SOONER SET FOOT OUTSIDE THAN I NEARLY TRIPPED.
?
WHEN I LOOKED DOWN AT MY FEET...
I SAW A DEAD BODY!

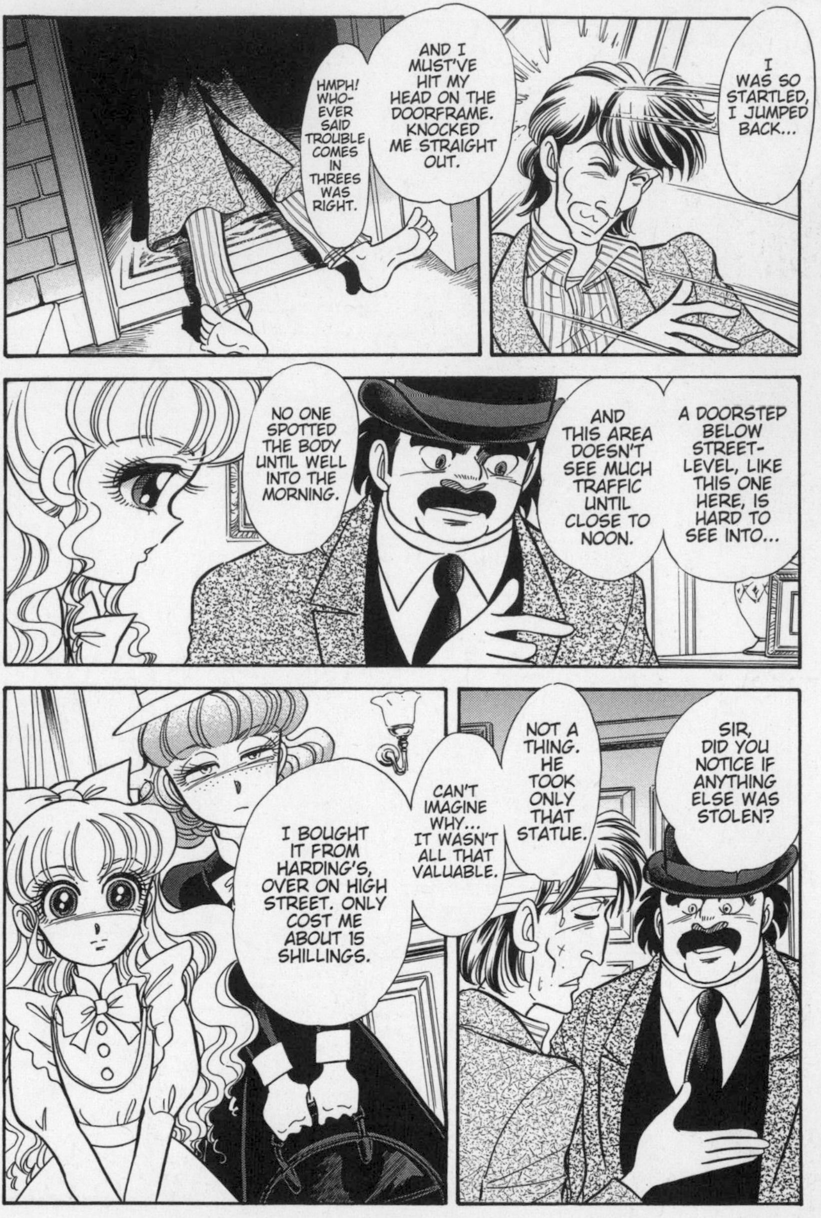
I WAS SO STARTLED, I JUMPED BACK...
AND I MUST'VE HIT MY HEAD ON THE DOORFRAME. KNOCKED ME STRAIGHT OUT.
HMPH! WHO-EVER SAID TROUBLE COMES IN THREES WAS RIGHT.
A DOORSTEP BELOW STREET-LEVEL, LIKE THIS ONE HERE, IS HARD TO SEE INTO...
AND THIS AREA DOESN'T SEE MUCH TRAFFIC UNTIL CLOSE TO NOON.
NO ONE SPOTTED THE BODY UNTIL WELL INTO THE MORNING.
SIR, DID YOU NOTICE IF ANYTHING ELSE WAS STOLEN?
NOT A THING. HE TOOK ONLY THAT STATUE.
CAN'T IMAGINE WHY... IT WASN'T ALL THAT VALUABLE.
I BOUGHT IT FROM HARDING'S, OVER ON HIGH STREET. ONLY COST ME ABOUT 15 SHILLINGS.

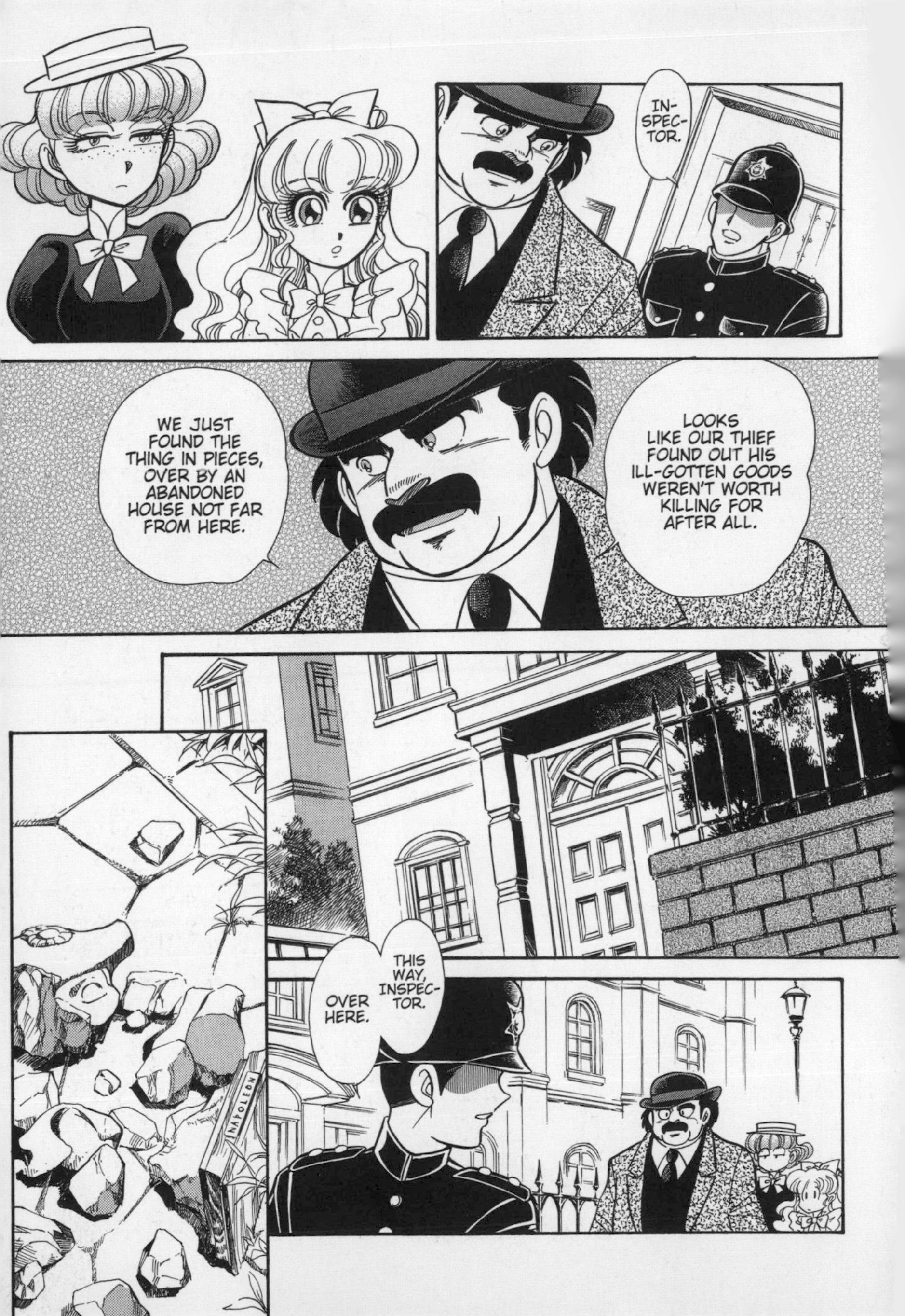
IN-SPECTOR.
LOOKS LIKE OUR THIEF FOUND OUT HIS ILL-GOTTEN GOODS WEREN'T WORTH KILLING FOR AFTER ALL.
WE JUST FOUND THE THING IN PIECES, OVER BY AN ABANDONED HOUSE NOT FAR FROM HERE.
THIS WAY, INSPEC-TOR.
OVER HERE.
NAPOLEON

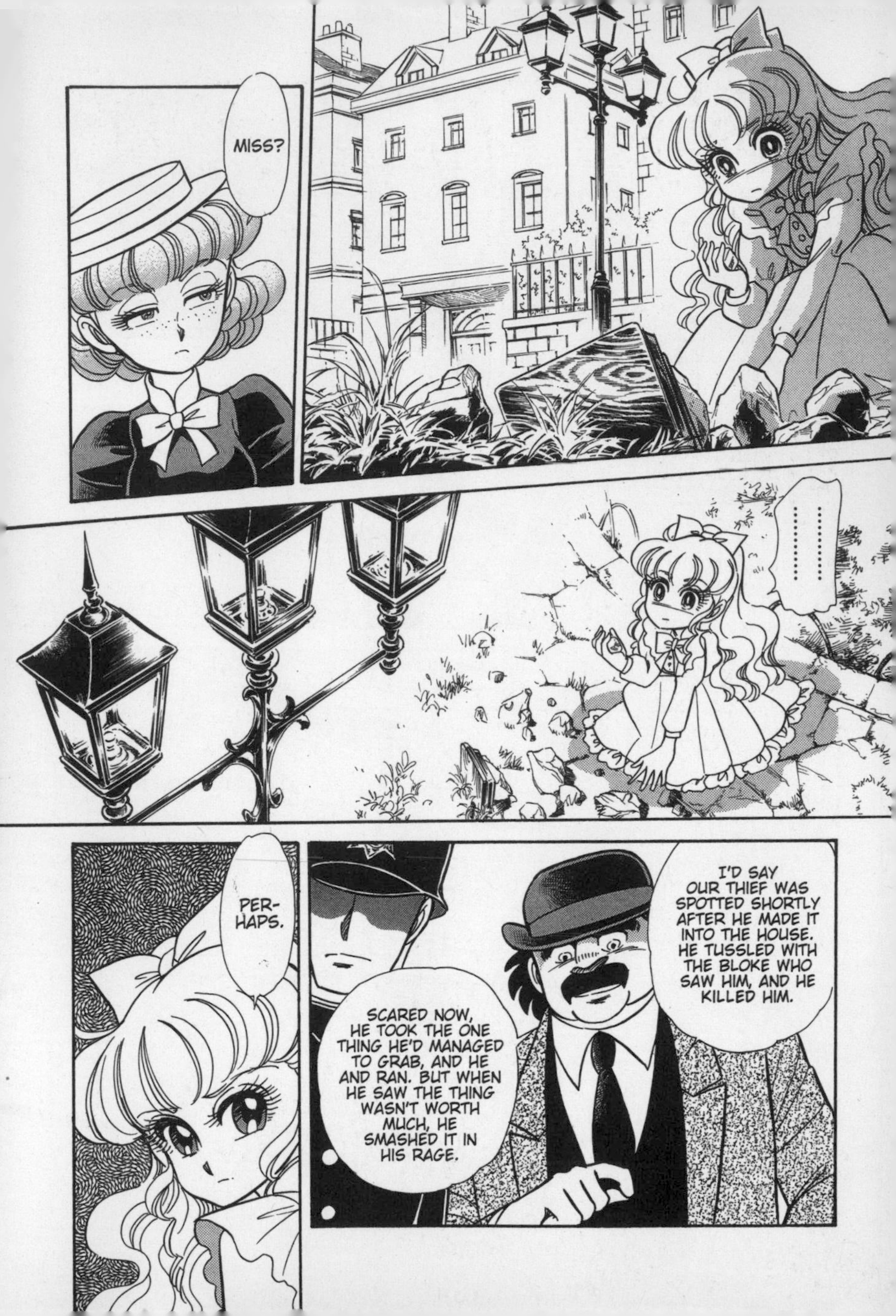
MISS?
......
I'D SAY OUR THIEF WAS SPOTTED SHORTLY AFTER HE MADE IT INTO THE HOUSE. HE TUSSLED WITH THE BLOKE WHO SAW HIM, AND HE KILLED HIM.
SCARED NOW, HE TOOK THE ONE THING HE'D MANAGED TO GRAB, AND HE AND RAN. BUT WHEN HE SAW THE THING WASN'T WORTH MUCH, HE SMASHED IT IN HIS RAGE.
PER-HAPS.

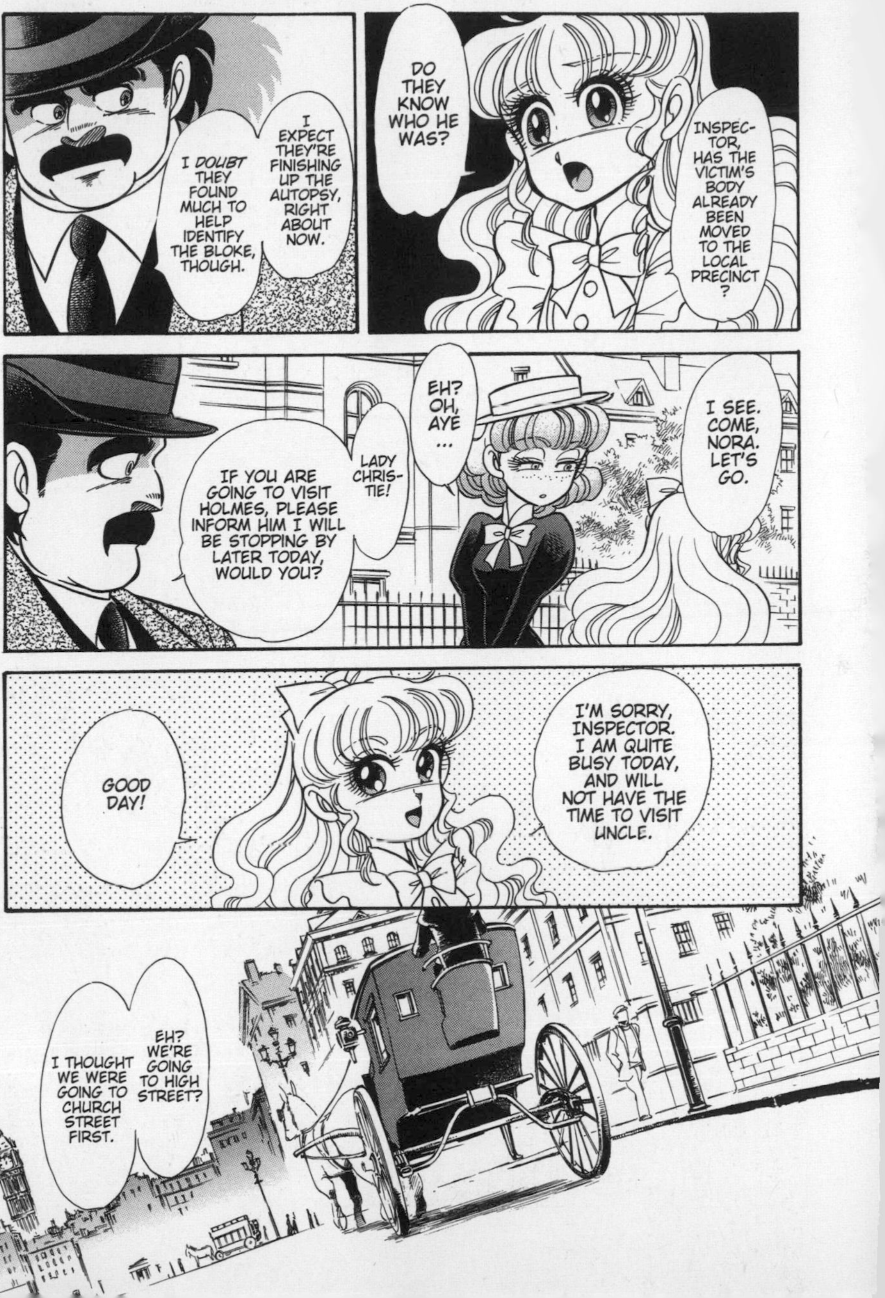
INSPECTOR, HAS THE VICTIM'S BODY ALREADY BEEN MOVED TO THE LOCAL PRECINCT?
DO THEY KNOW WHO HE WAS?
I EXPECT THEY'RE FINISHING UP THE AUTOPSY, RIGHT ABOUT NOW.
I *DOUBT* THEY FOUND MUCH TO HELP IDENTIFY THE BLOKE, THOUGH.
I SEE. COME, NORA. LET'S GO.
EH? OH, AYE ...
LADY CHRISTIE!
IF YOU ARE GOING TO VISIT HOLMES, PLEASE INFORM HIM I WILL BE STOPPING BY LATER TODAY, WOULD YOU?
I'M SORRY, INSPECTOR. I AM QUITE BUSY TODAY, AND WILL NOT HAVE THE TIME TO VISIT UNCLE.
GOOD DAY!
EH? WE'RE GOING TO HIGH STREET?
I THOUGHT WE WERE GOING TO CHURCH STREET FIRST.

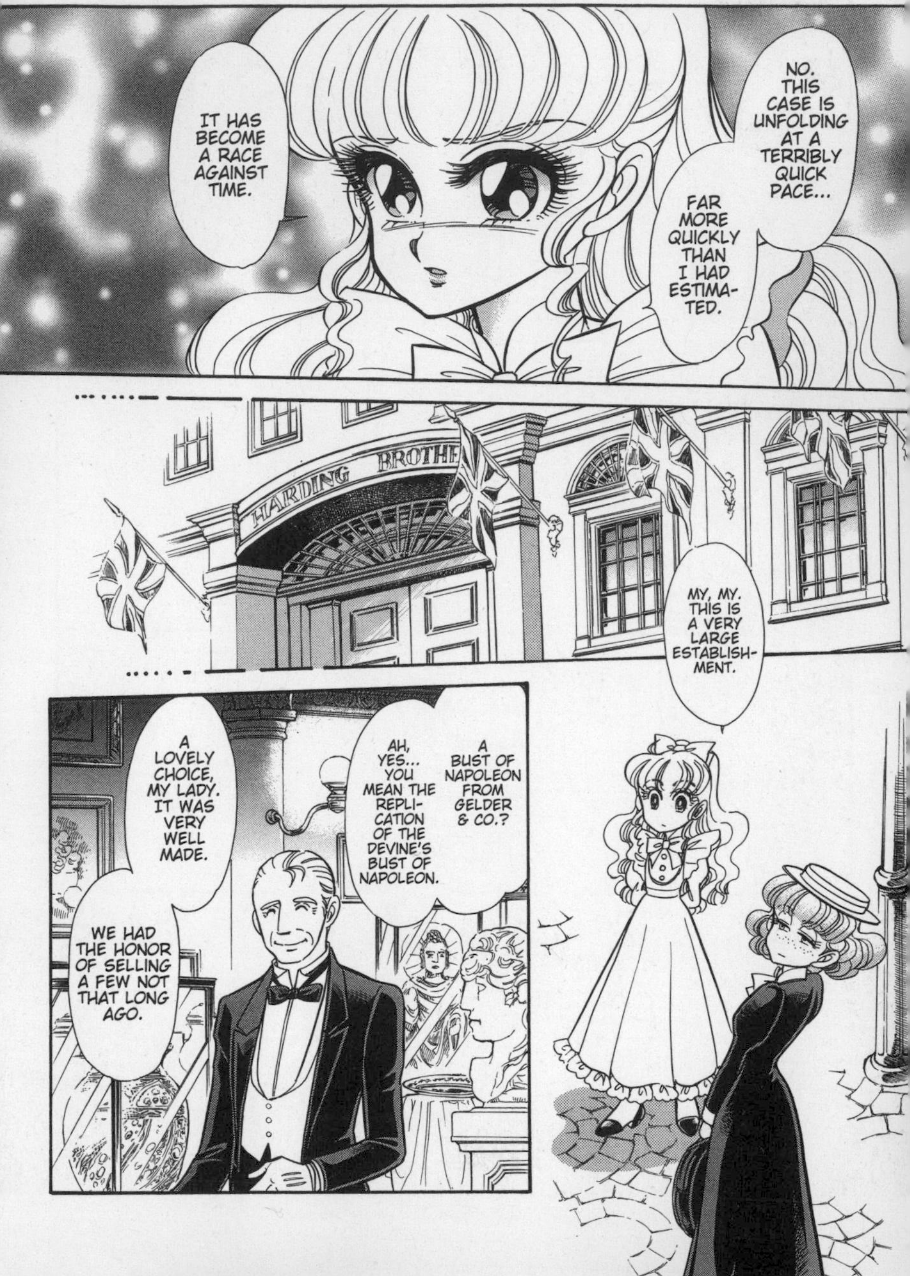
NO. THIS CASE IS UNFOLDING AT A TERRIBLY QUICK PACE...
FAR MORE QUICKLY THAN I HAD ESTIMA-TED.
IT HAS BECOME A RACE AGAINST TIME.
HARDING BROTHE
MY, MY. THIS IS A VERY LARGE ESTABLISH-MENT.
A BUST OF NAPOLEON FROM GELDER & CO.?
AH, YES... YOU MEAN THE REPLI-CATION OF THE DEVINE'S BUST OF NAPOLEON.
A LOVELY CHOICE, MY LADY. IT WAS VERY WELL MADE.
WE HAD THE HONOR OF SELLING A FEW NOT THAT LONG AGO.

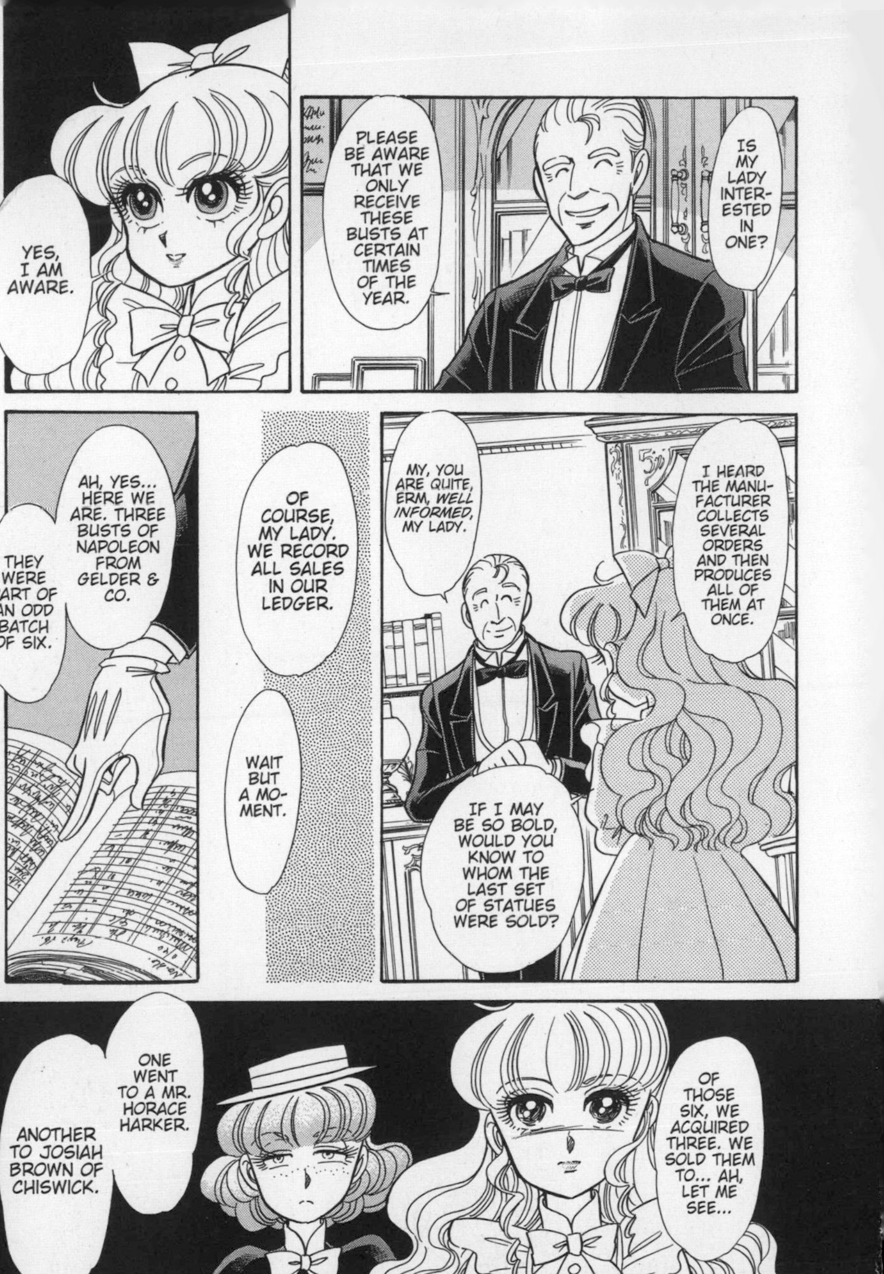
IS MY LADY INTERESTED IN ONE?
PLEASE BE AWARE THAT WE ONLY RECEIVE THESE BUSTS AT CERTAIN TIMES OF THE YEAR.
YES, I AM AWARE.
I HEARD THE MANUFACTURER COLLECTS SEVERAL ORDERS AND THEN PRODUCES ALL OF THEM AT ONCE.
MY, YOU ARE QUITE, ERM, *WELL INFORMED*, MY LADY.
IF I MAY BE SO BOLD, WOULD YOU KNOW TO WHOM THE LAST SET OF STATUES WERE SOLD?
OF COURSE, MY LADY. WE RECORD ALL SALES IN OUR LEDGER.
WAIT BUT A MOMENT.
AH, YES... HERE WE ARE. THREE BUSTS OF NAPOLEON FROM GELDER & CO.
THEY WERE PART OF AN ODD BATCH OF SIX.
OF THOSE SIX, WE ACQUIRED THREE. WE SOLD THEM TO... AH, LET ME SEE...
ONE WENT TO A MR. HORACE HARKER.
ANOTHER TO JOSIAH BROWN OF CHISWICK.

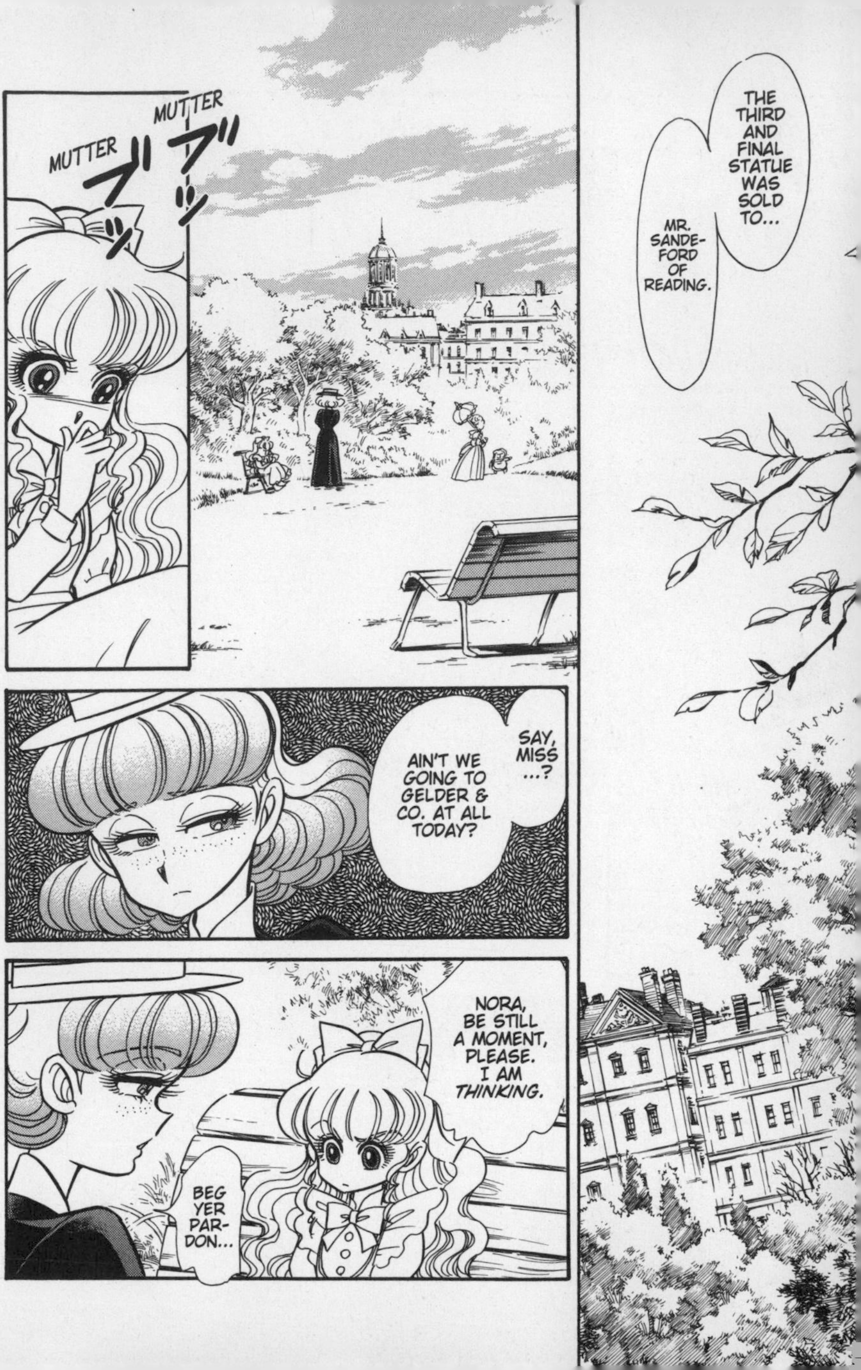
THE THIRD AND FINAL STATUE WAS SOLD TO...
MR. SANDEFORD OF READING.
MUTTER
MUTTER
ブツ
ブツ
SAY, MISS ...?
AIN'T WE GOING TO GELDER & CO. AT ALL TODAY?
NORA, BE STILL A MOMENT, PLEASE. I AM *THINKING*.
BEG YER PARDON...

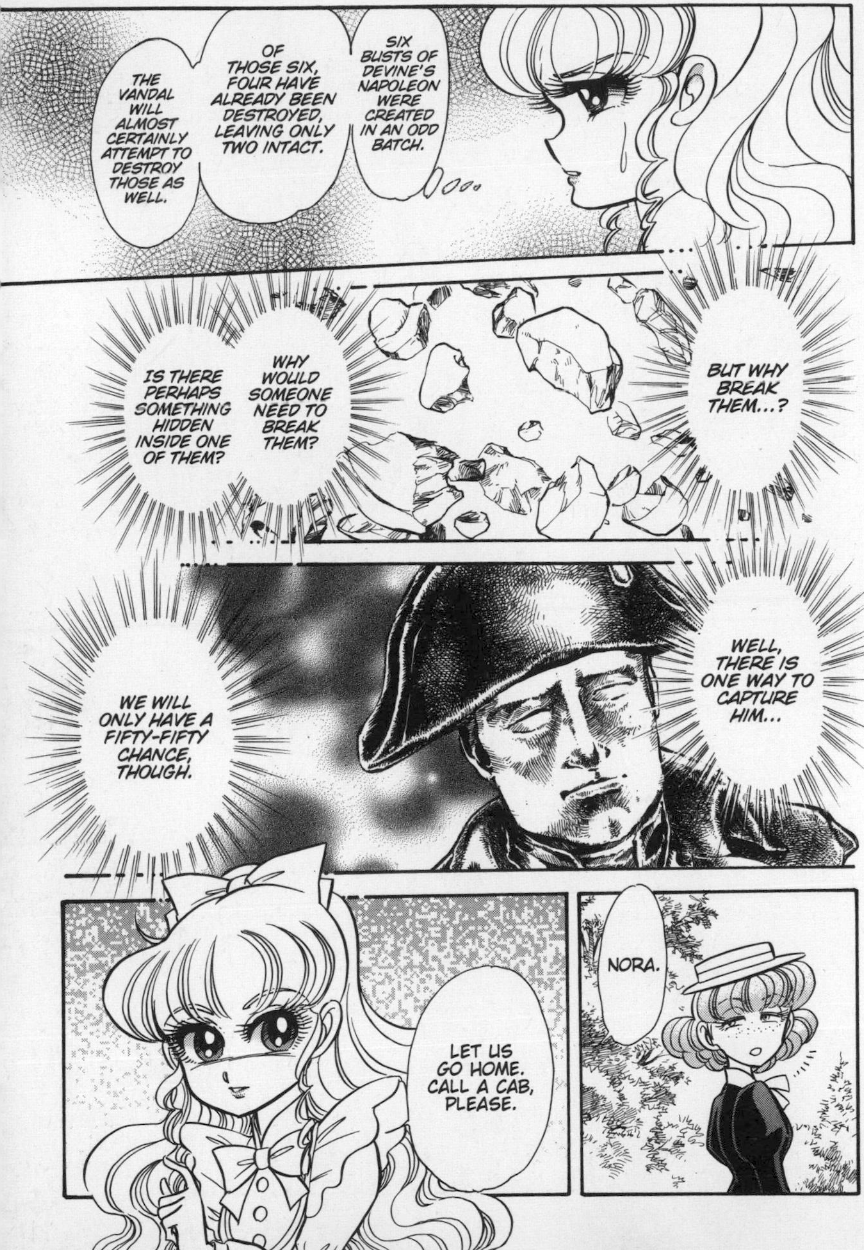
SIX BUSTS OF DEVINE'S NAPOLEON WERE CREATED IN AN ODD BATCH.
OF THOSE SIX, FOUR HAVE ALREADY BEEN DESTROYED, LEAVING ONLY TWO INTACT.
THE VANDAL WILL ALMOST CERTAINLY ATTEMPT TO DESTROY THOSE AS WELL.
BUT WHY BREAK THEM...?
WHY WOULD SOMEONE NEED TO BREAK THEM?
IS THERE PERHAPS SOMETHING HIDDEN INSIDE ONE OF THEM?
WELL, THERE IS ONE WAY TO CAPTURE HIM...
WE WILL ONLY HAVE A FIFTY-FIFTY CHANCE, THOUGH.
NORA.
LET US GO HOME. CALL A CAB, PLEASE.

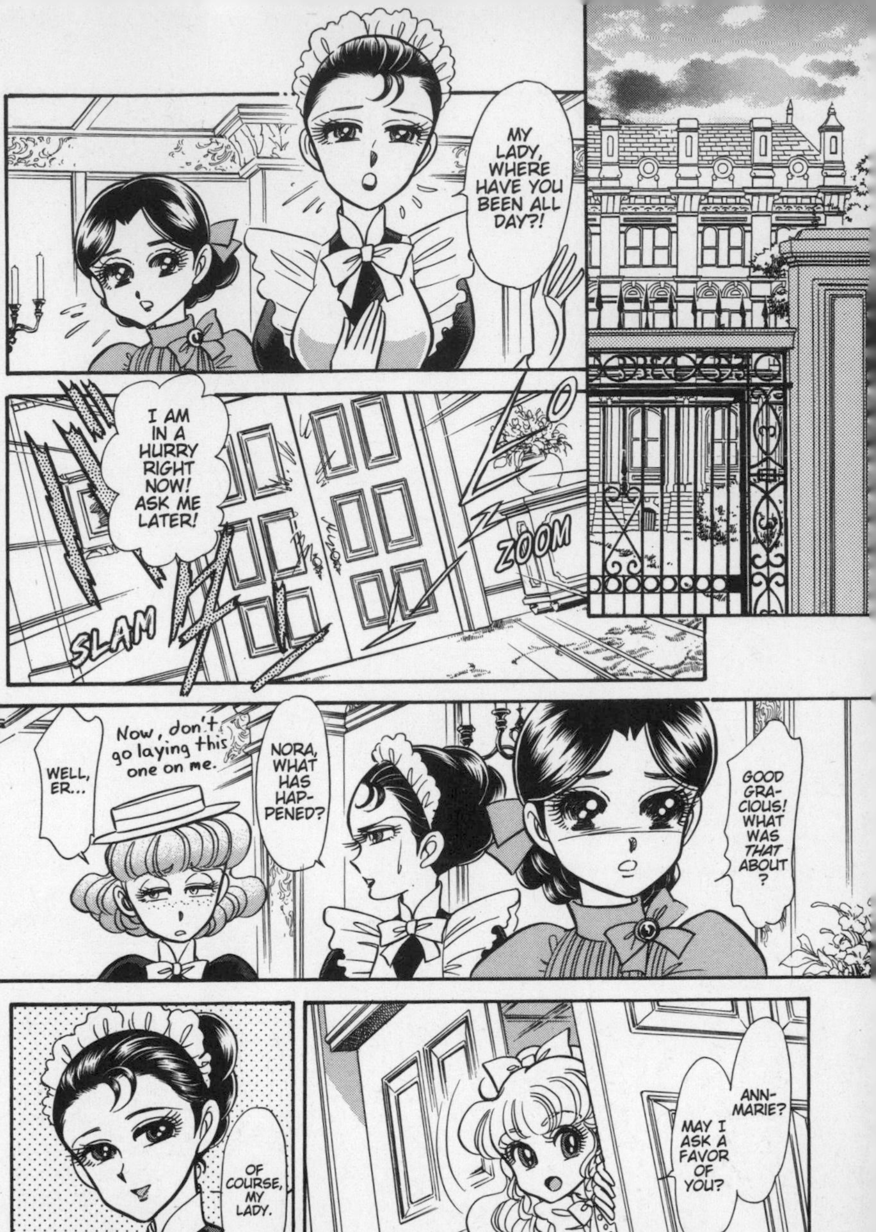
MY LADY, WHERE HAVE YOU BEEN ALL DAY?!
I AM IN A HURRY RIGHT NOW! ASK ME LATER!
ZOOM
SLAM
GOOD GRACIOUS! WHAT WAS *THAT* ABOUT?
NORA, WHAT HAS HAPPENED?
Now, don't go laying this one on me.
WELL, ER...
ANN-MARIE? MAY I ASK A FAVOR OF YOU?
OF COURSE, MY LADY.

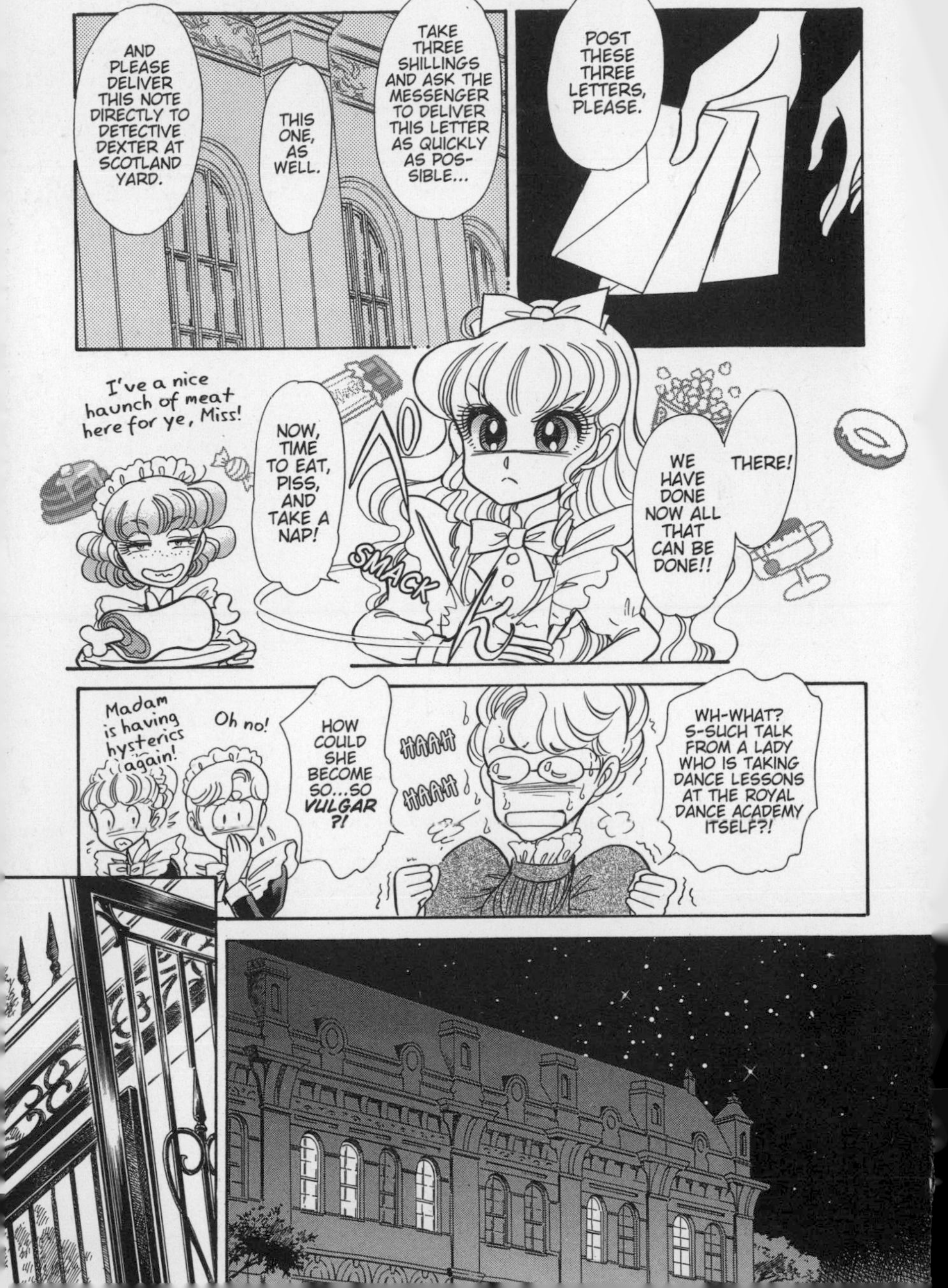
POST THESE THREE LETTERS, PLEASE.
TAKE THREE SHILLINGS AND ASK THE MESSENGER TO DELIVER THIS LETTER AS QUICKLY AS POS-SIBLE...
THIS ONE, AS WELL.
AND PLEASE DELIVER THIS NOTE DIRECTLY TO DETECTIVE DEXTER AT SCOTLAND YARD.
THERE!
WE HAVE DONE NOW ALL THAT CAN BE DONE!!
NOW, TIME TO EAT, PISS, AND TAKE A NAP!
SMACK
I've a nice haunch of meat here for ye, Miss!
WH-WHAT? S-SUCH TALK FROM A LADY WHO IS TAKING DANCE LESSONS AT THE ROYAL DANCE ACADEMY ITSELF?!
HAAH
HAAH
HOW COULD SHE BECOME SO...SO VULGAR?!
Oh no!
Madam is having hysterics again!

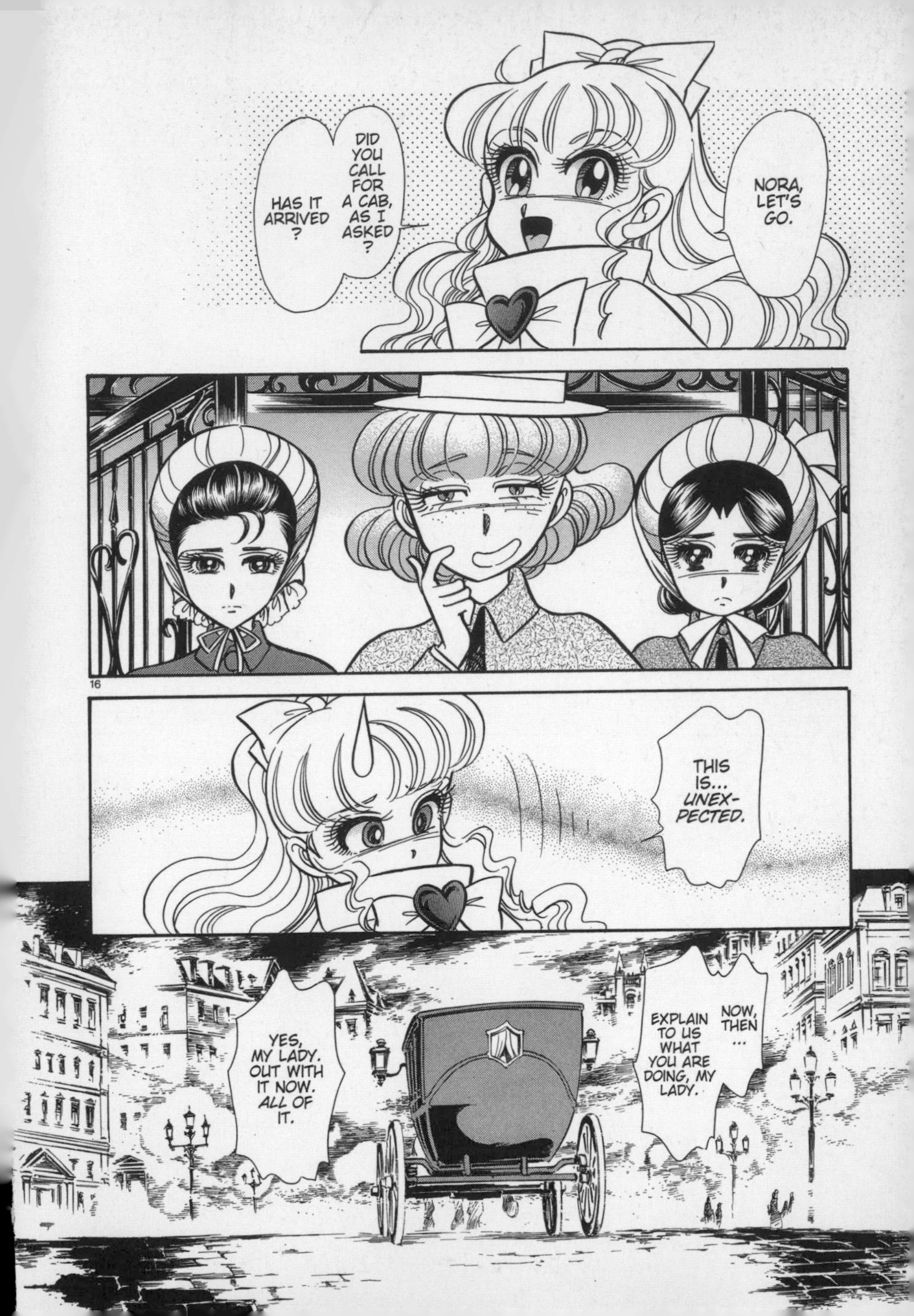
NORA, LET'S GO.
DID YOU CALL FOR A CAB, AS I ASKED?
HAS IT ARRIVED?
THIS IS... *UNEXPECTED.*
NOW, THEN...
EXPLAIN TO US WHAT YOU ARE DOING, MY LADY.
YES, MY LADY. OUT WITH IT NOW. *ALL OF IT.*

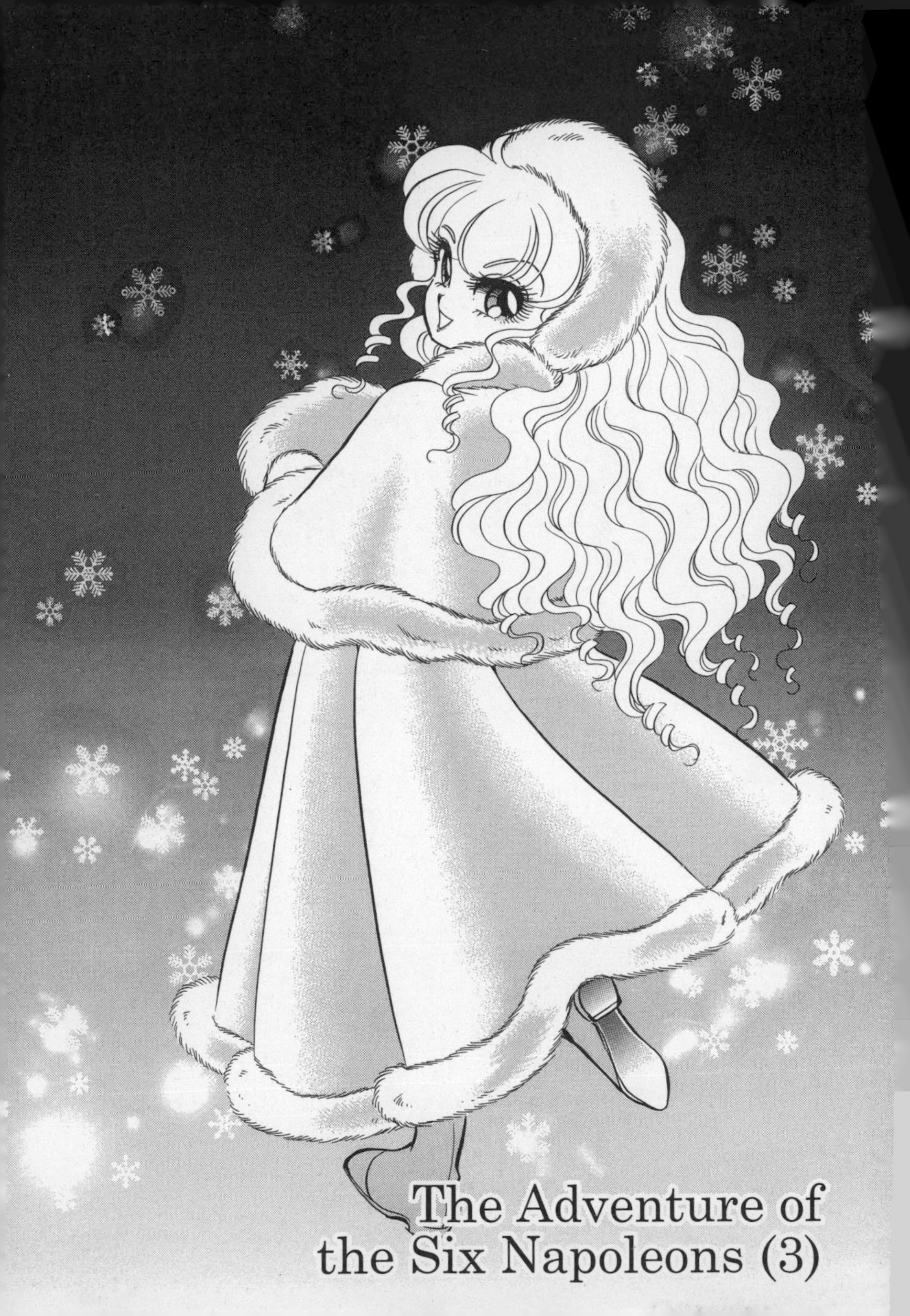

The Adventure of the Six Napoleons (3)

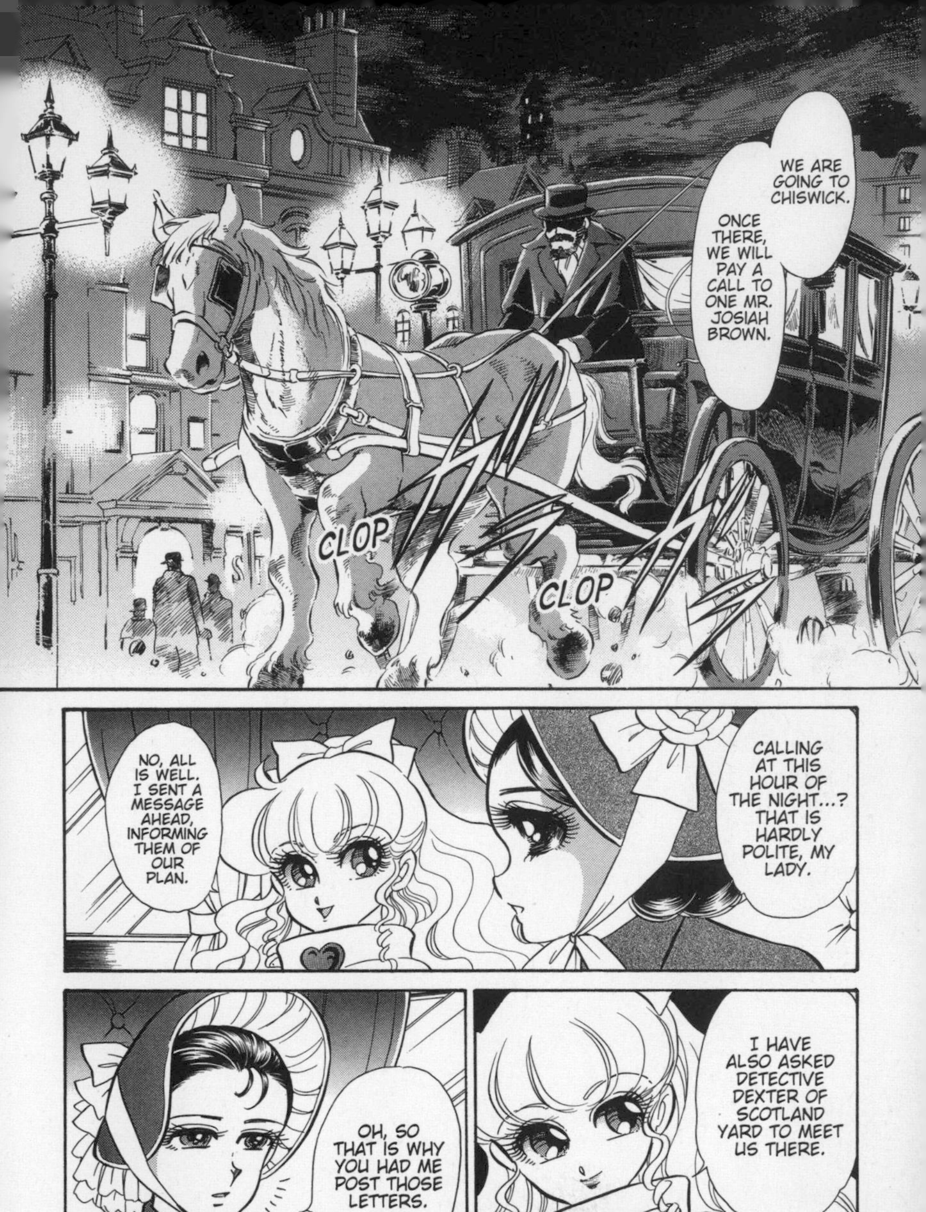
WE ARE GOING TO CHISWICK.
ONCE THERE, WE WILL PAY A CALL TO ONE MR. JOSIAH BROWN.
CLOP
CLOP
CALLING AT THIS HOUR OF THE NIGHT...? THAT IS HARDLY POLITE, MY LADY.
NO, ALL IS WELL. I SENT A MESSAGE AHEAD, INFORMING THEM OF OUR PLAN.
I HAVE ALSO ASKED DETECTIVE DEXTER OF SCOTLAND YARD TO MEET US THERE.
OH, SO THAT IS WHY YOU HAD ME POST THOSE LETTERS.

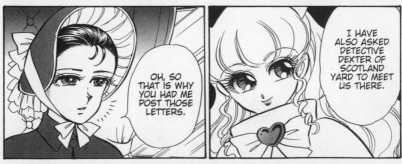

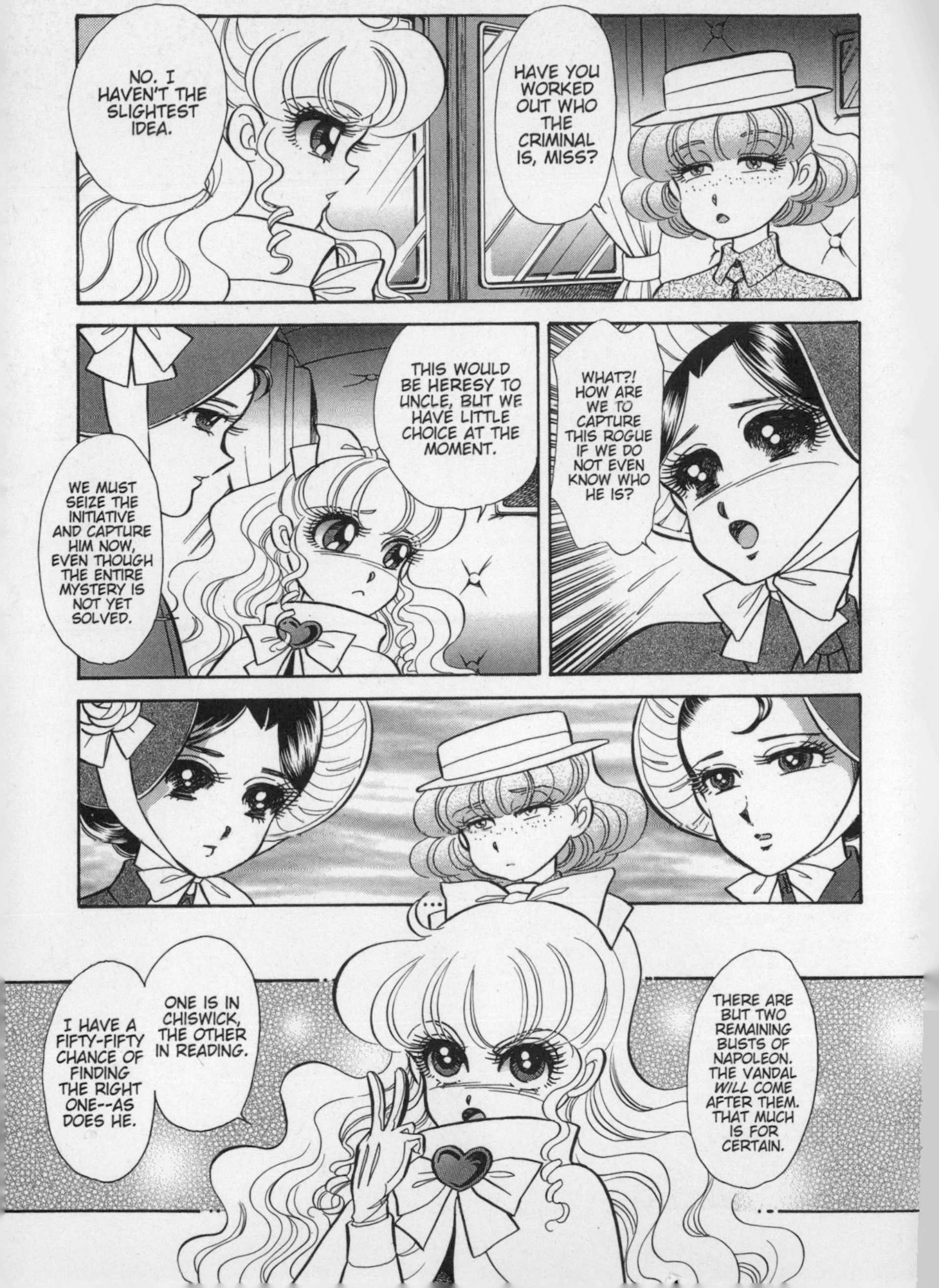
HAVE YOU WORKED OUT WHO THE CRIMINAL IS, MISS?
NO. I HAVEN'T THE SLIGHTEST IDEA.
WHAT?! HOW ARE WE TO CAPTURE THIS ROGUE IF WE DO NOT EVEN KNOW WHO HE IS?
THIS WOULD BE HERESY TO UNCLE, BUT WE HAVE LITTLE CHOICE AT THE MOMENT.
WE MUST SEIZE THE INITIATIVE AND CAPTURE HIM NOW, EVEN THOUGH THE ENTIRE MYSTERY IS NOT YET SOLVED.
....
THERE ARE BUT TWO REMAINING BUSTS OF NAPOLEON. THE VANDAL *WILL* COME AFTER THEM. THAT MUCH IS FOR CERTAIN.
ONE IS IN CHISWICK, THE OTHER IN READING.
I HAVE A FIFTY-FIFTY CHANCE OF FINDING THE RIGHT ONE--AS DOES HE.

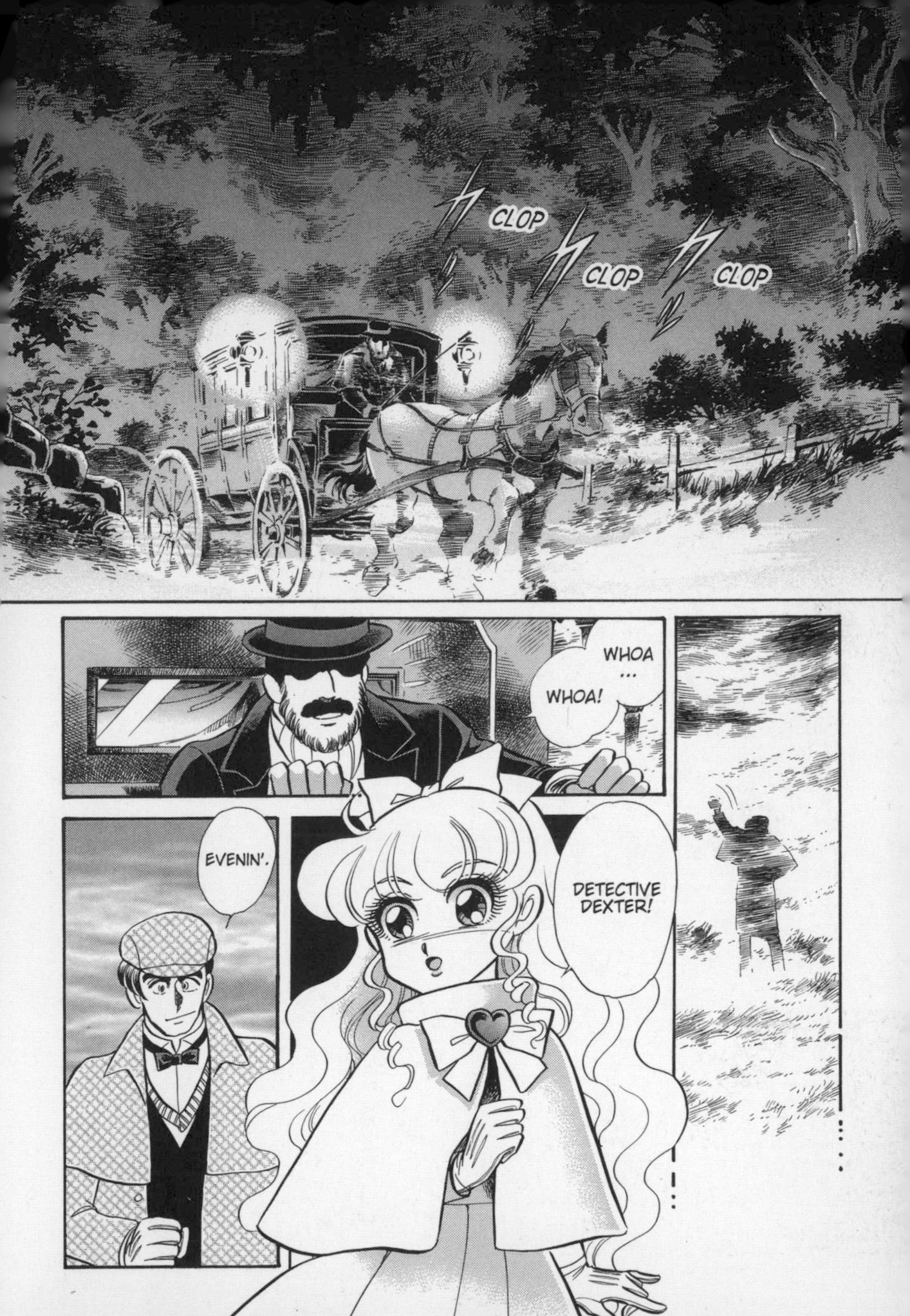
CLOP
CLOP
CLOP
WHOA ... WHOA!
DETECTIVE DEXTER!
EVENIN'.

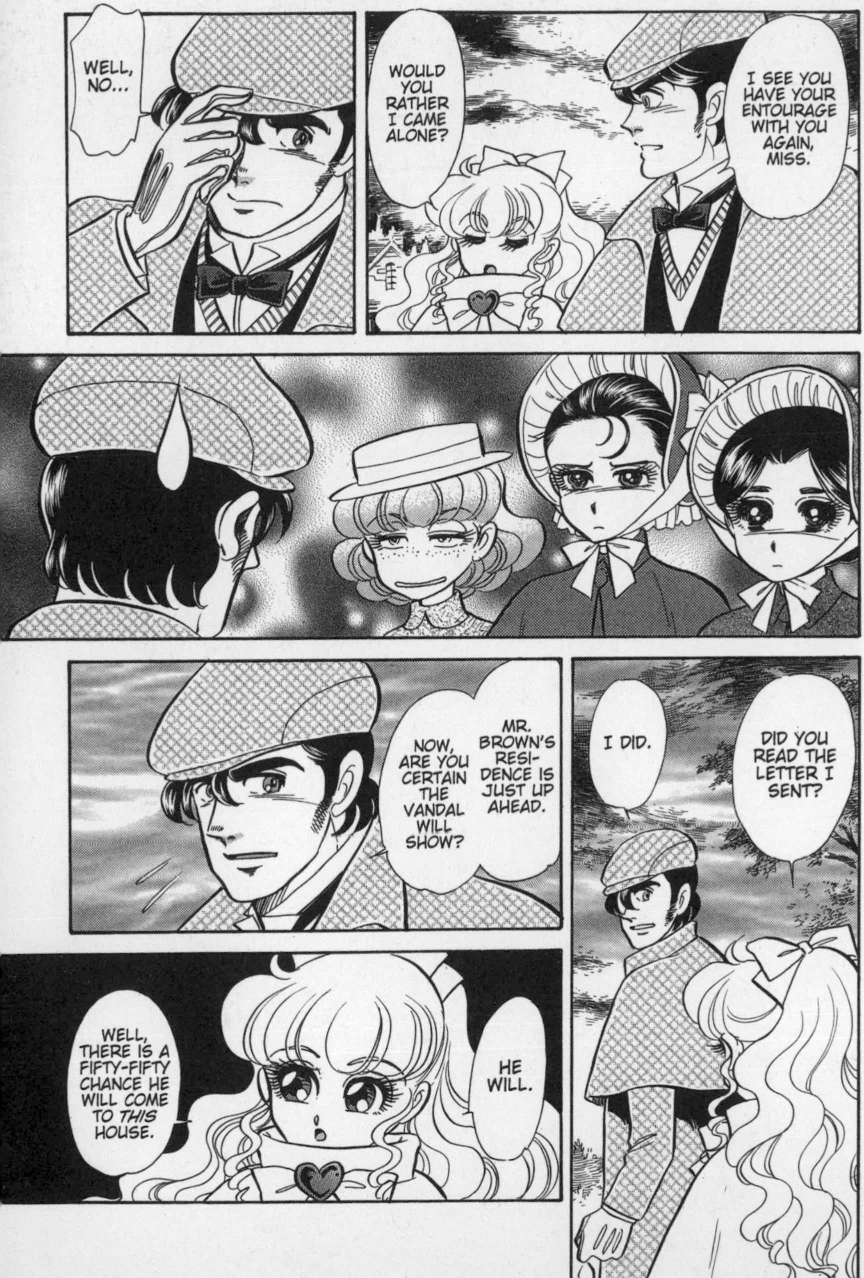
I SEE YOU HAVE YOUR ENTOURAGE WITH YOU AGAIN, MISS.
WOULD YOU RATHER I CAME ALONE?
WELL, NO...
DID YOU READ THE LETTER I SENT?
I DID.
MR. BROWN'S RESI-DENCE IS JUST UP AHEAD.
NOW, ARE YOU CERTAIN THE VANDAL WILL SHOW?
HE WILL.
WELL, THERE IS A FIFTY-FIFTY CHANCE HE WILL COME TO *THIS* HOUSE.

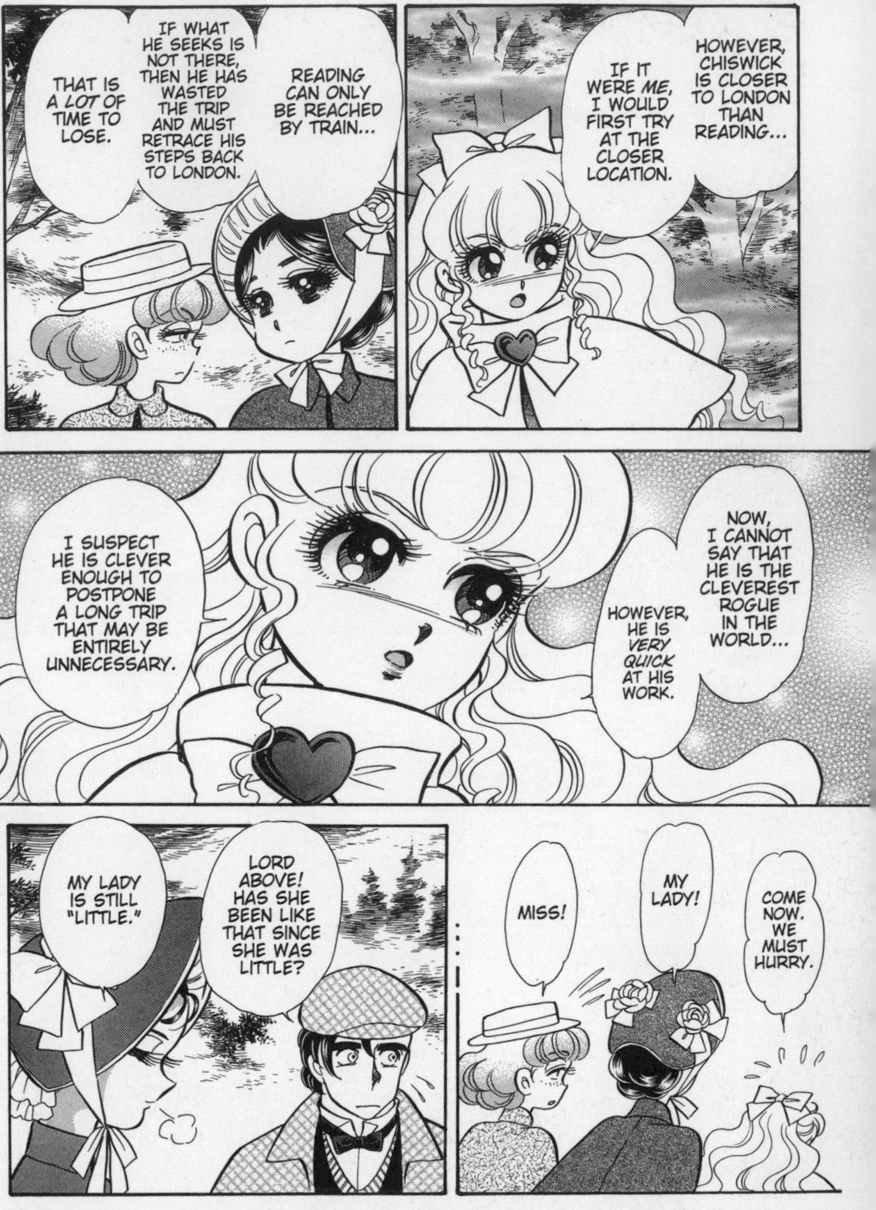
HOWEVER, CHISWICK IS CLOSER TO LONDON THAN READING...
IF IT WERE *ME*, I WOULD FIRST TRY AT THE CLOSER LOCATION.
READING CAN ONLY BE REACHED BY TRAIN...
IF WHAT HE SEEKS IS NOT THERE, THEN HE HAS WASTED THE TRIP AND MUST RETRACE HIS STEPS BACK TO LONDON.
THAT IS A *LOT* OF TIME TO LOSE.
NOW, I CANNOT SAY THAT HE IS THE CLEVEREST ROGUE IN THE WORLD...
HOWEVER, HE IS *VERY QUICK* AT HIS WORK.
I SUSPECT HE IS CLEVER ENOUGH TO POSTPONE A LONG TRIP THAT MAY BE ENTIRELY UNNECESSARY.
COME NOW. WE MUST HURRY.
MY LADY!
MISS!
...
LORD ABOVE! HAS SHE BEEN LIKE THAT SINCE SHE WAS LITTLE?
MY LADY IS STILL "LITTLE."

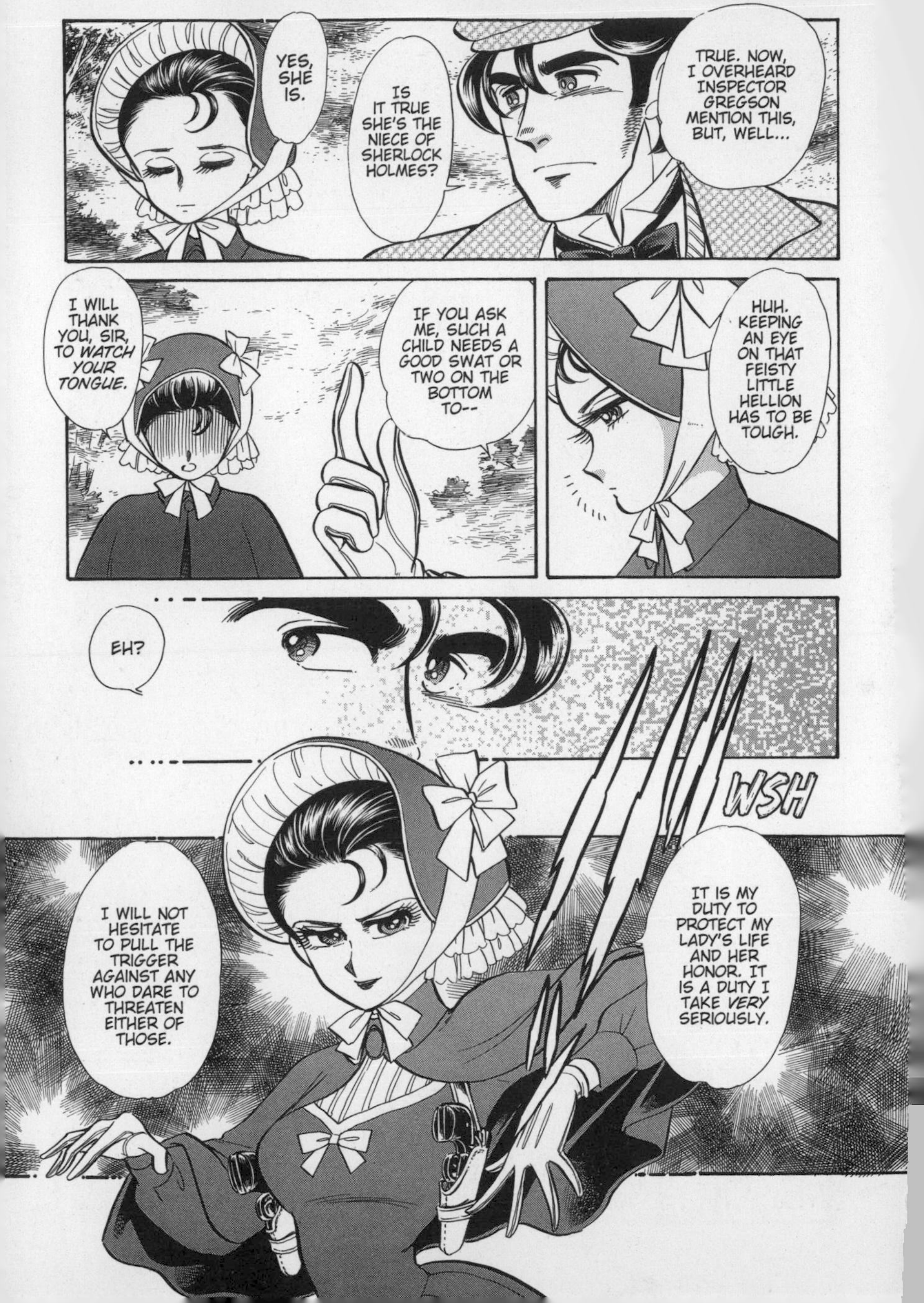
TRUE. NOW, I OVERHEARD INSPECTOR GREGSON MENTION THIS, BUT, WELL...
IS IT TRUE SHE'S THE NIECE OF SHERLOCK HOLMES?
YES, SHE IS.
HUH. KEEPING AN EYE ON THAT FEISTY LITTLE HELLION HAS TO BE TOUGH.
IF YOU ASK ME, SUCH A CHILD NEEDS A GOOD SWAT OR TWO ON THE BOTTOM TO--
I WILL THANK YOU, SIR, TO *WATCH YOUR TONGUE.*
EH?
WSH
IT IS MY DUTY TO PROTECT MY LADY'S LIFE AND HER HONOR. IT IS A DUTY I TAKE *VERY* SERIOUSLY.
I WILL NOT HESITATE TO PULL THE TRIGGER AGAINST ANY WHO DARE TO THREATEN EITHER OF THOSE.

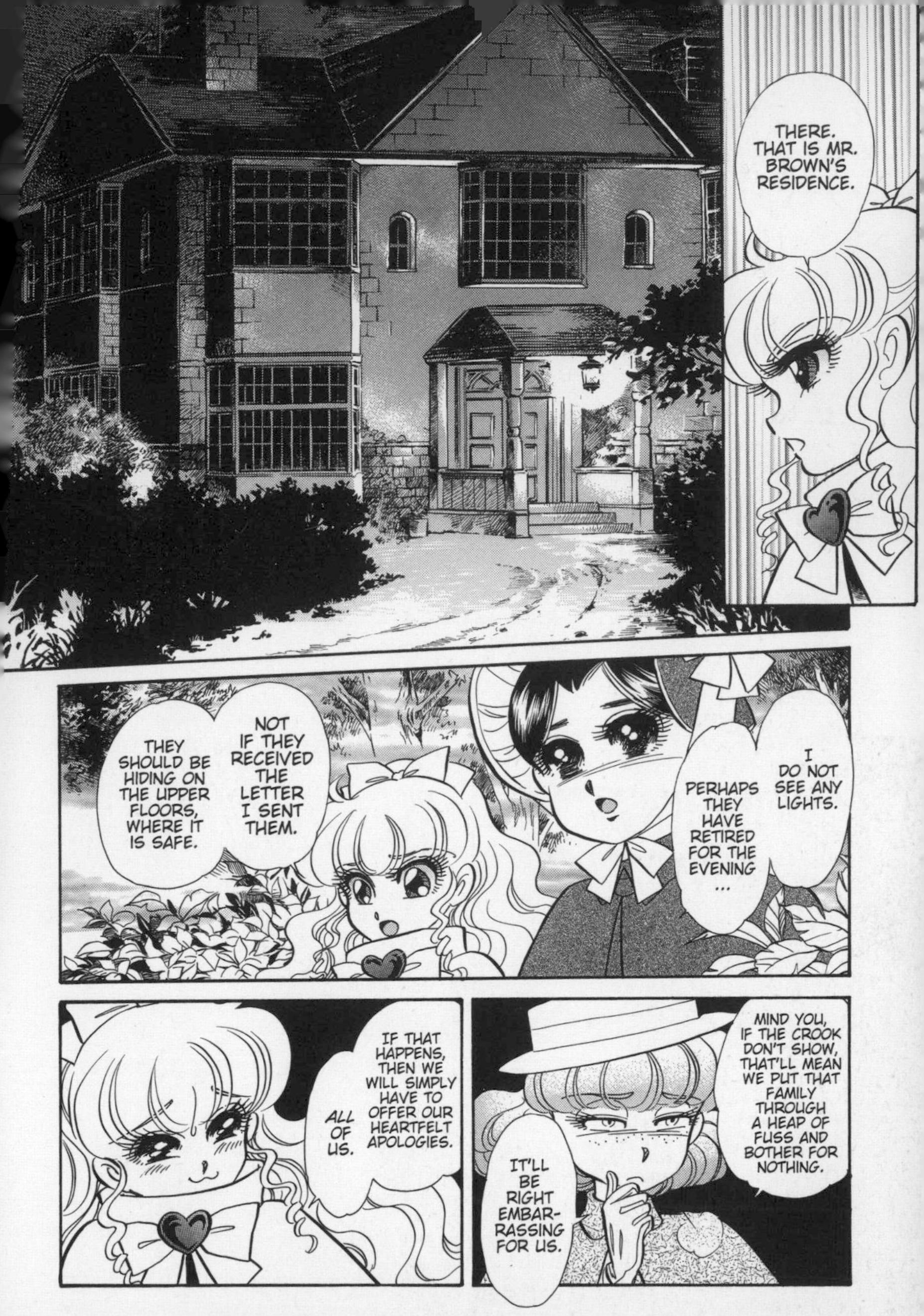
THERE. THAT IS MR. BROWN'S RESIDENCE.
I DO NOT SEE ANY LIGHTS.
PERHAPS THEY HAVE RETIRED FOR THE EVENING ...
NOT IF THEY RECEIVED THE LETTER I SENT THEM.
THEY SHOULD BE HIDING ON THE UPPER FLOORS, WHERE IT IS SAFE.
MIND YOU, IF THE CROOK DON'T SHOW, THAT'LL MEAN WE PUT THAT FAMILY THROUGH A HEAP OF FUSS AND BOTHER FOR NOTHING.
IT'LL BE RIGHT EMBARRASSING FOR US.
IF THAT HAPPENS, THEN WE WILL SIMPLY HAVE TO OFFER OUR HEARTFELT APOLOGIES.
ALL OF US.

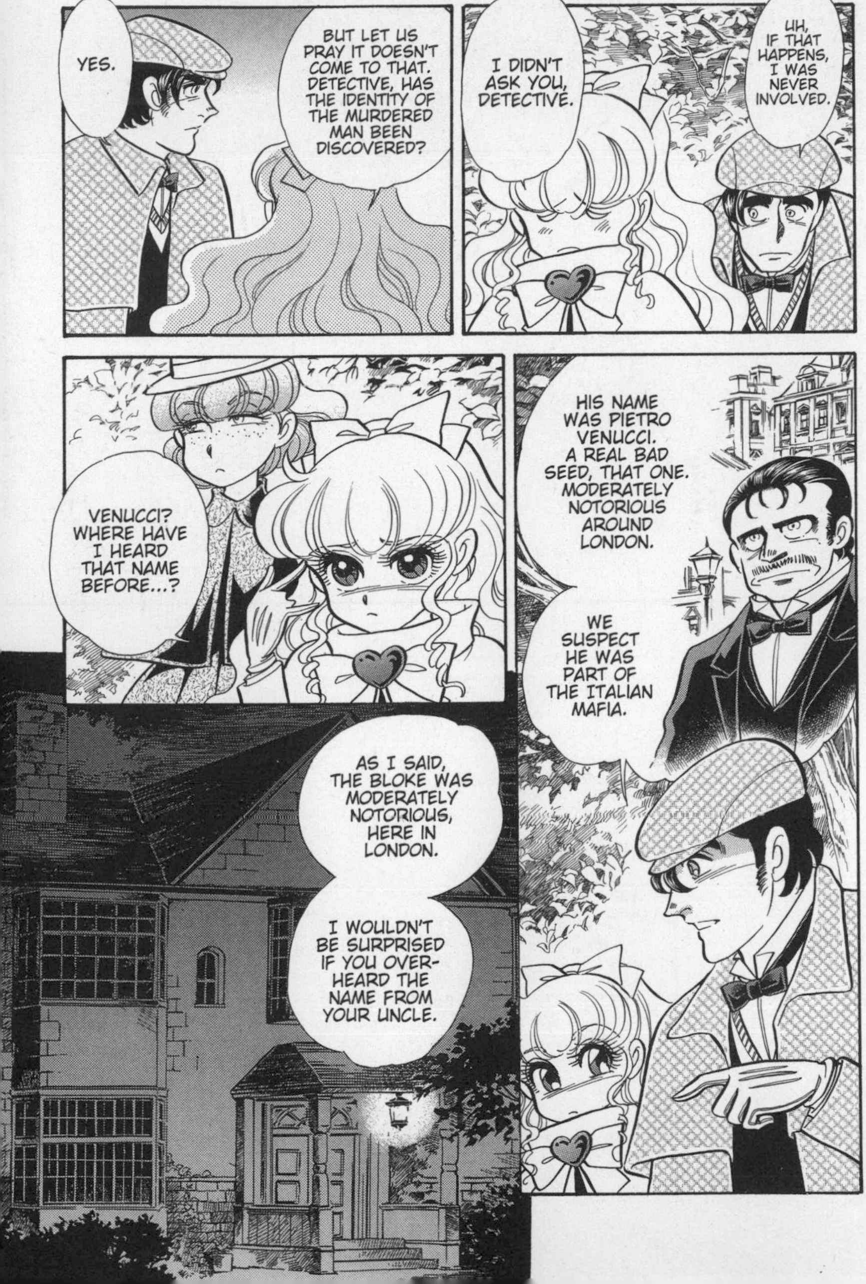
UH, IF THAT HAPPENS, I WAS NEVER INVOLVED.
I DIDN'T ASK YOU, DETECTIVE.
BUT LET US PRAY IT DOESN'T COME TO THAT. DETECTIVE, HAS THE IDENTITY OF THE MURDERED MAN BEEN DISCOVERED?
YES.
HIS NAME WAS PIETRO VENUCCI. A REAL BAD SEED, THAT ONE. MODERATELY NOTORIOUS AROUND LONDON.
WE SUSPECT HE WAS PART OF THE ITALIAN MAFIA.
VENUCCI? WHERE HAVE I HEARD THAT NAME BEFORE...?
AS I SAID, THE BLOKE WAS MODERATELY NOTORIOUS, HERE IN LONDON.
I WOULDN'T BE SURPRISED IF YOU OVER-HEARD THE NAME FROM YOUR UNCLE.

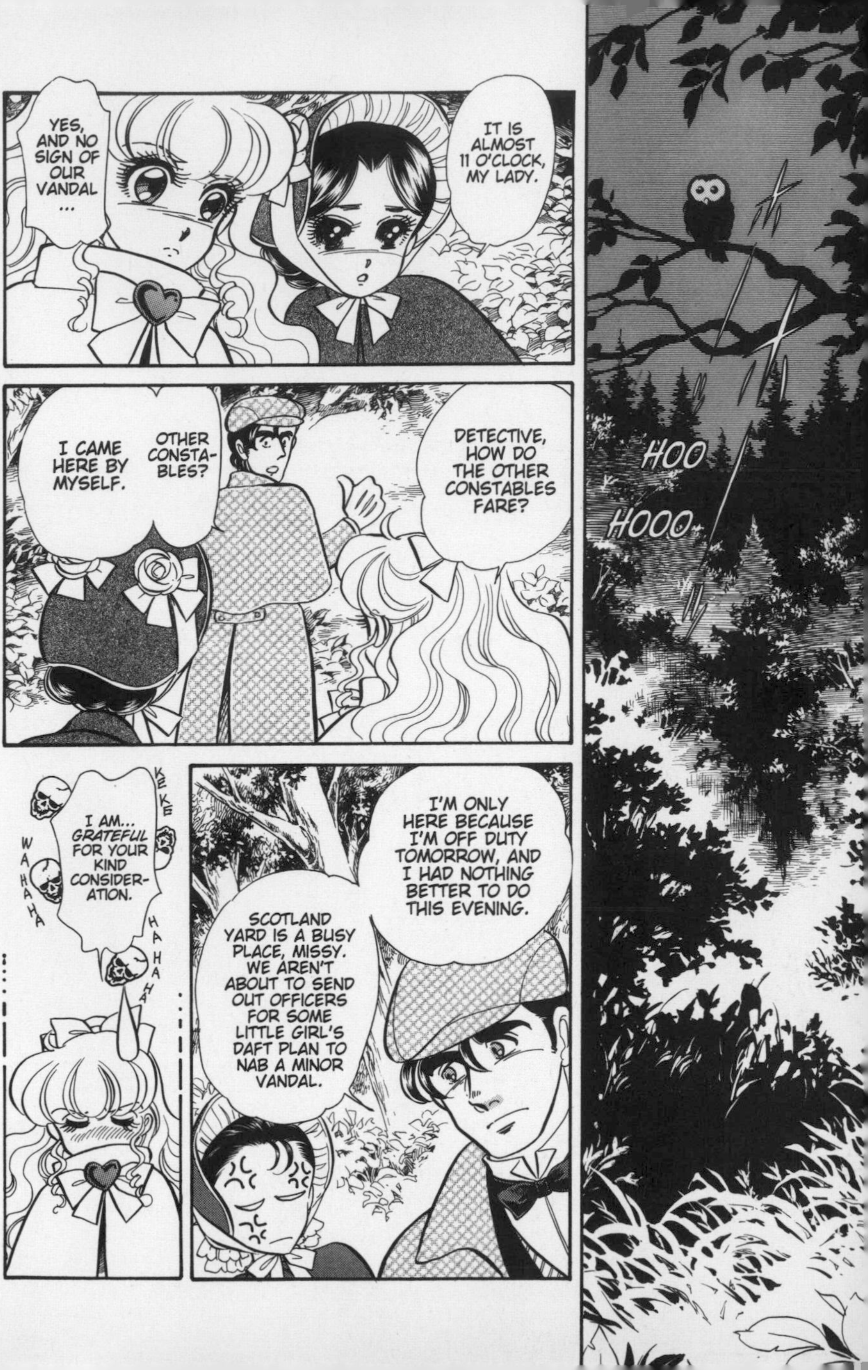
HOO
HOOO
IT IS ALMOST 11 O'CLOCK, MY LADY.
YES, AND NO SIGN OF OUR VANDAL ...
DETECTIVE, HOW DO THE OTHER CONSTABLES FARE?
OTHER CONSTA-BLES?
I CAME HERE BY MYSELF.
I'M ONLY HERE BECAUSE I'M OFF DUTY TOMORROW, AND I HAD NOTHING BETTER TO DO THIS EVENING.
SCOTLAND YARD IS A BUSY PLACE, MISSY. WE AREN'T ABOUT TO SEND OUT OFFICERS FOR SOME LITTLE GIRL'S DAFT PLAN TO NAB A MINOR VANDAL.
KE KE
I AM... GRATEFUL FOR YOUR KIND CONSIDER-ATION.
WAHAHA
HAHAHAHA

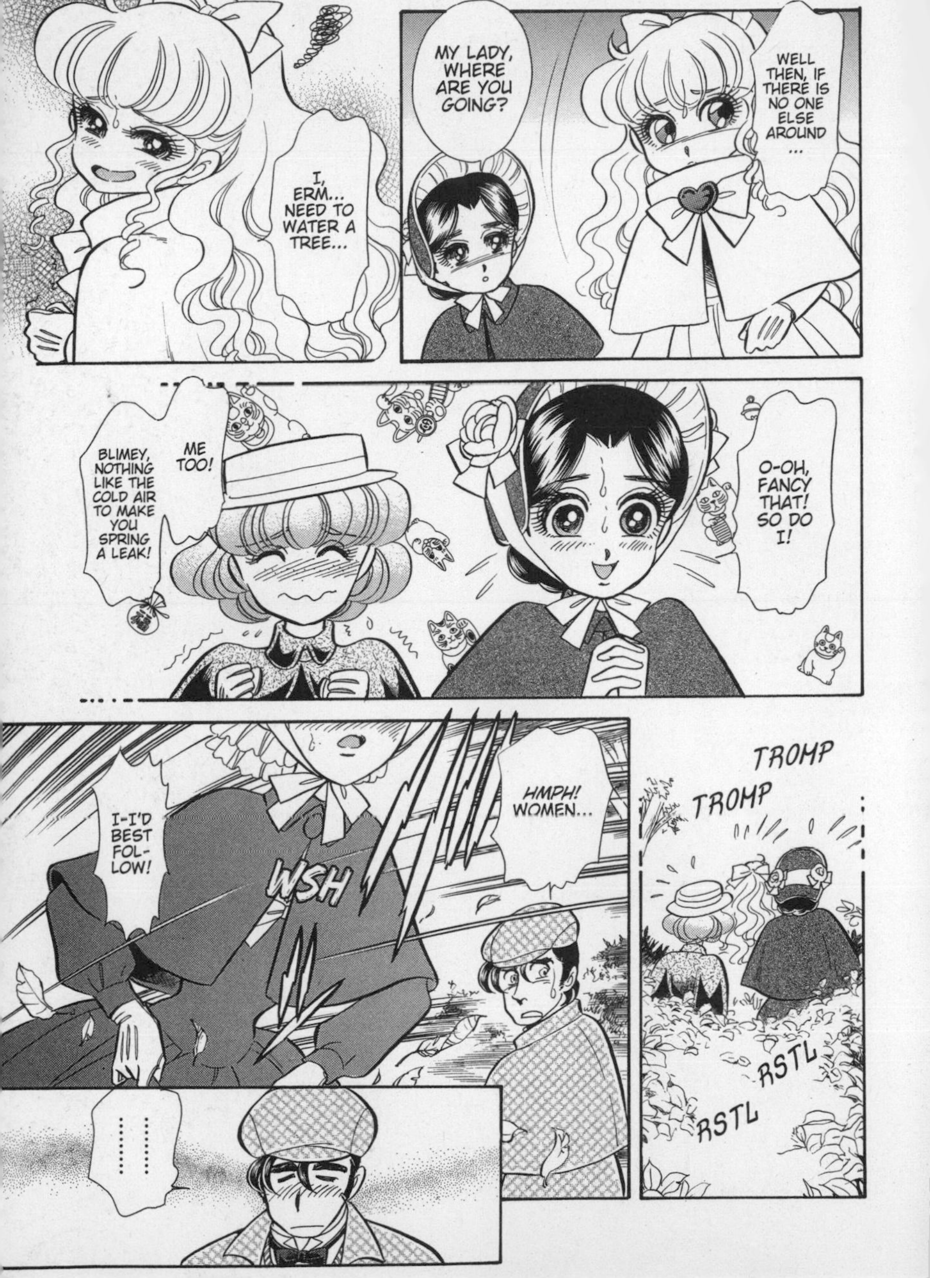
WELL THEN, IF THERE IS NO ONE ELSE AROUND ...
MY LADY, WHERE ARE YOU GOING?
I, ERM... NEED TO WATER A TREE...
O-OH, FANCY THAT! SO DO I!
ME TOO!
BLIMEY, NOTHING LIKE THE COLD AIR TO MAKE YOU SPRING A LEAK!
TROMP
TROMP
RSTL
RSTL
HMPH! WOMEN...
WSH
I-I'D BEST FOL-LOW!
......

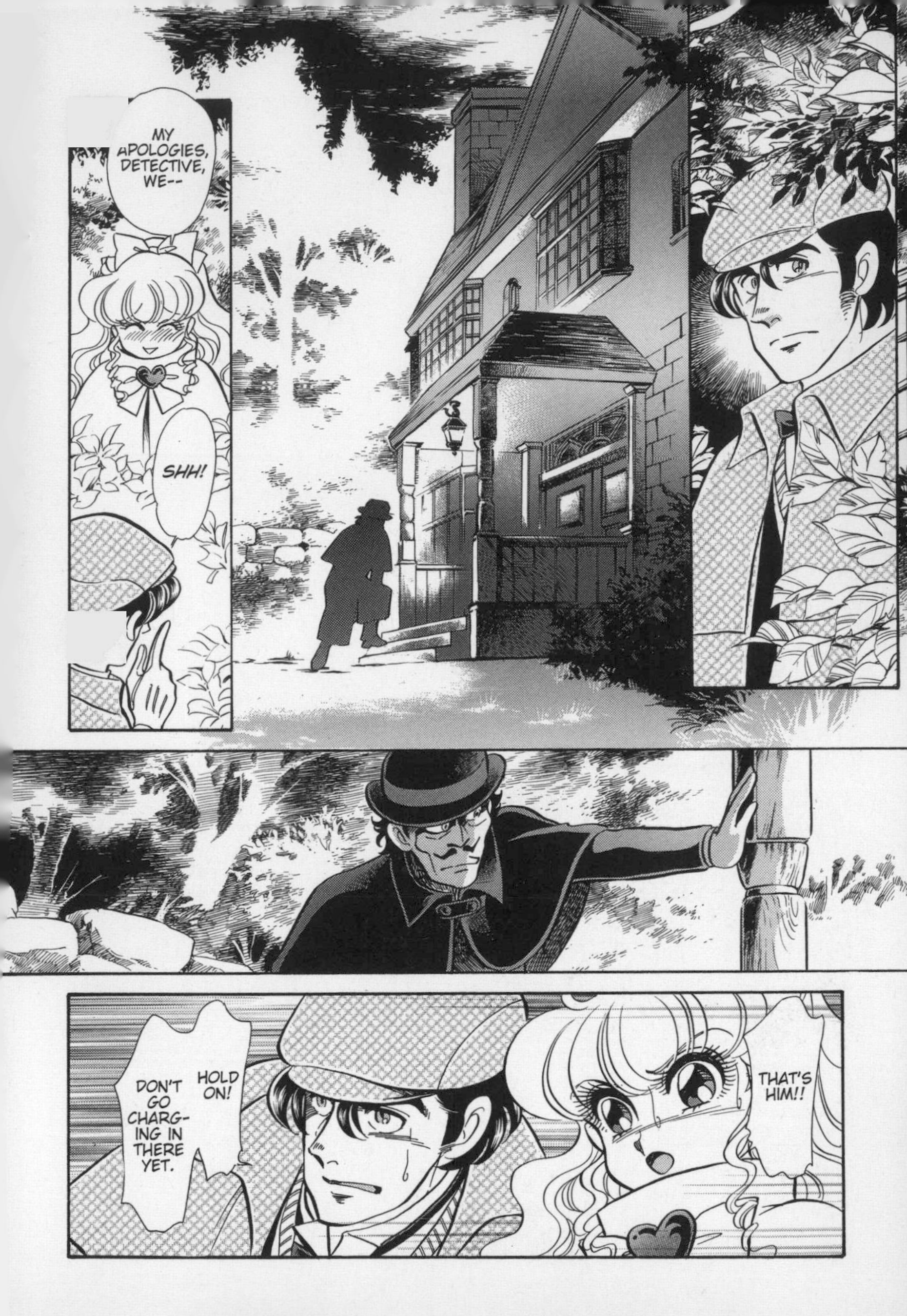
MY APOLOGIES, DETECTIVE, WE--
SHH!
THAT'S HIM!!
HOLD ON!
DON'T GO CHARGING IN THERE YET.

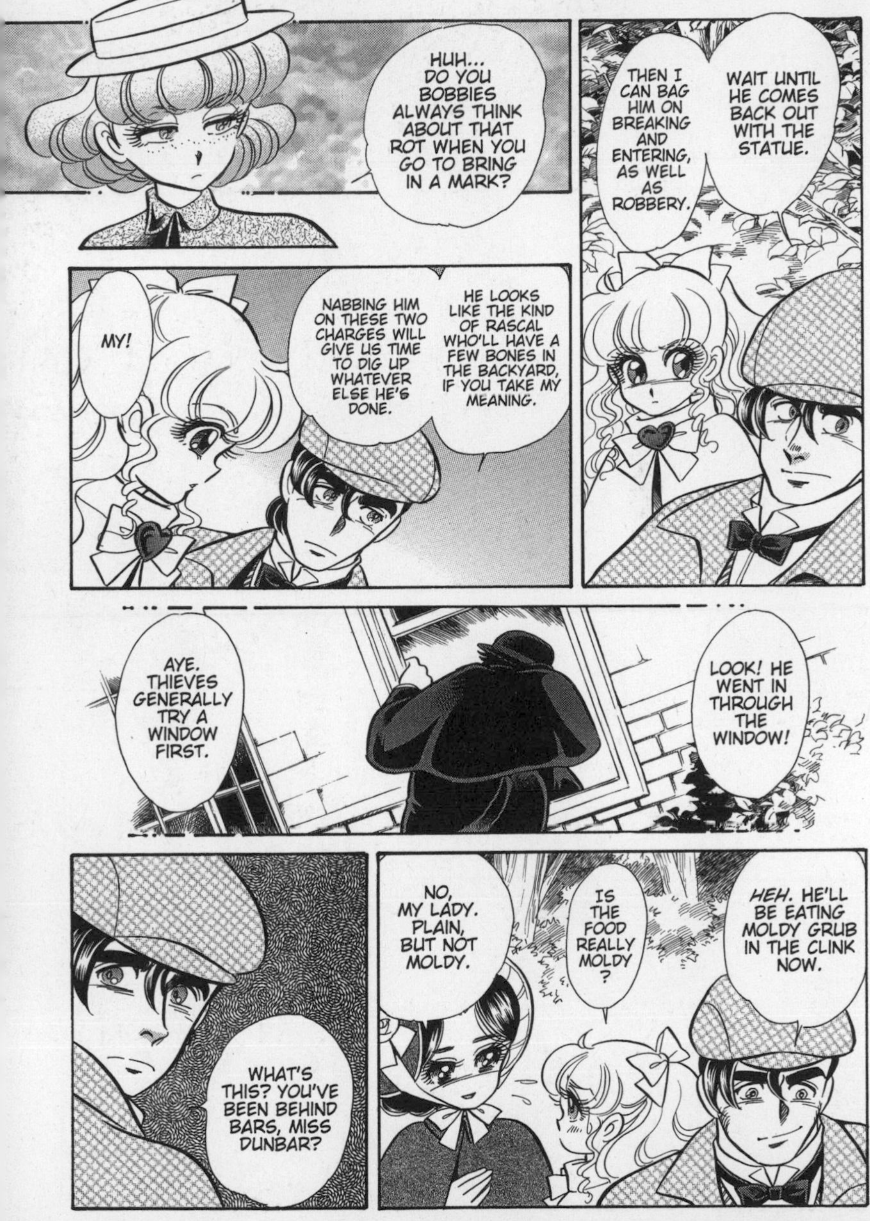
WAIT UNTIL HE COMES BACK OUT WITH THE STATUE.
THEN I CAN BAG HIM ON BREAKING AND ENTERING, AS WELL AS ROBBERY.
HUH... DO YOU BOBBIES ALWAYS THINK ABOUT THAT ROT WHEN YOU GO TO BRING IN A MARK?
HE LOOKS LIKE THE KIND OF RASCAL WHO'LL HAVE A FEW BONES IN THE BACKYARD, IF YOU TAKE MY MEANING.
NABBING HIM ON THESE TWO CHARGES WILL GIVE US TIME TO DIG UP WHATEVER ELSE HE'S DONE.
MY!
LOOK! HE WENT IN THROUGH THE WINDOW!
AYE. THIEVES GENERALLY TRY A WINDOW FIRST.
HEH. HE'LL BE EATING MOLDY GRUB IN THE CLINK NOW.
IS THE FOOD REALLY MOLDY?
NO, MY LADY. PLAIN, BUT NOT MOLDY.
WHAT'S THIS? YOU'VE BEEN BEHIND BARS, MISS DUNBAR?

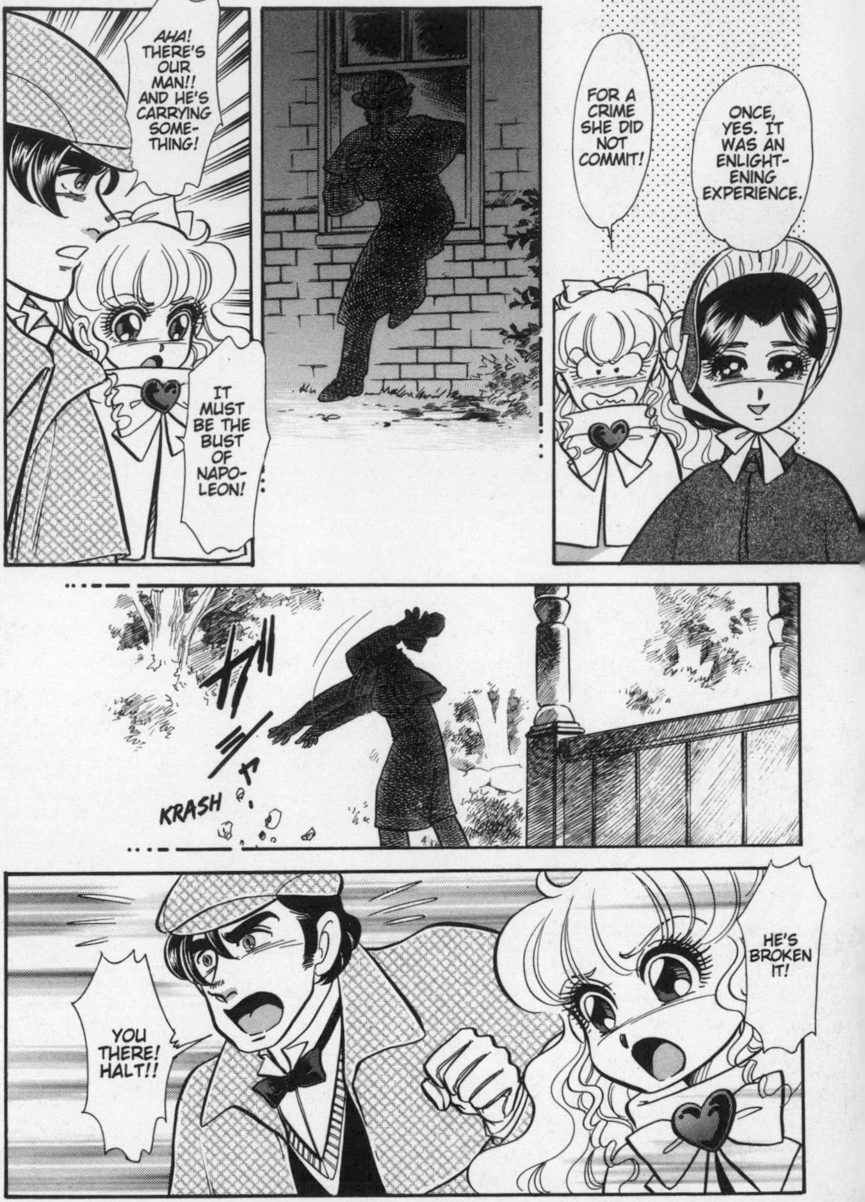
ONCE, YES. IT WAS AN ENLIGHTENING EXPERIENCE.
FOR A CRIME SHE DID NOT COMMIT!
AHA! THERE'S OUR MAN!! AND HE'S CARRYING SOMETHING!
IT MUST BE THE BUST OF NAPOLEON!
KRASH
HE'S BROKEN IT!
YOU THERE! HALT!!

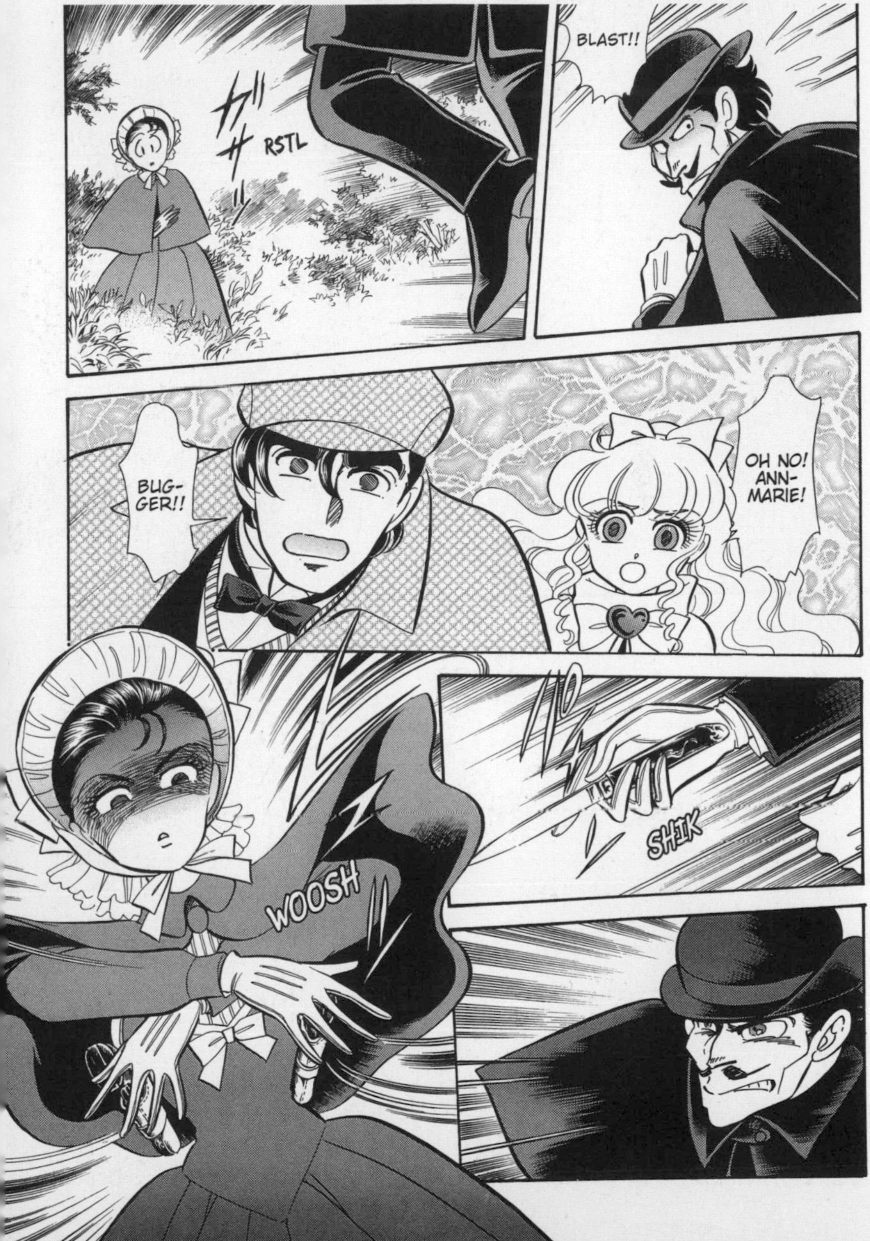
BLAST!!
RSTL
OH NO! ANN-MARIE!
BUG-GER!!
SHIK
WOOSH

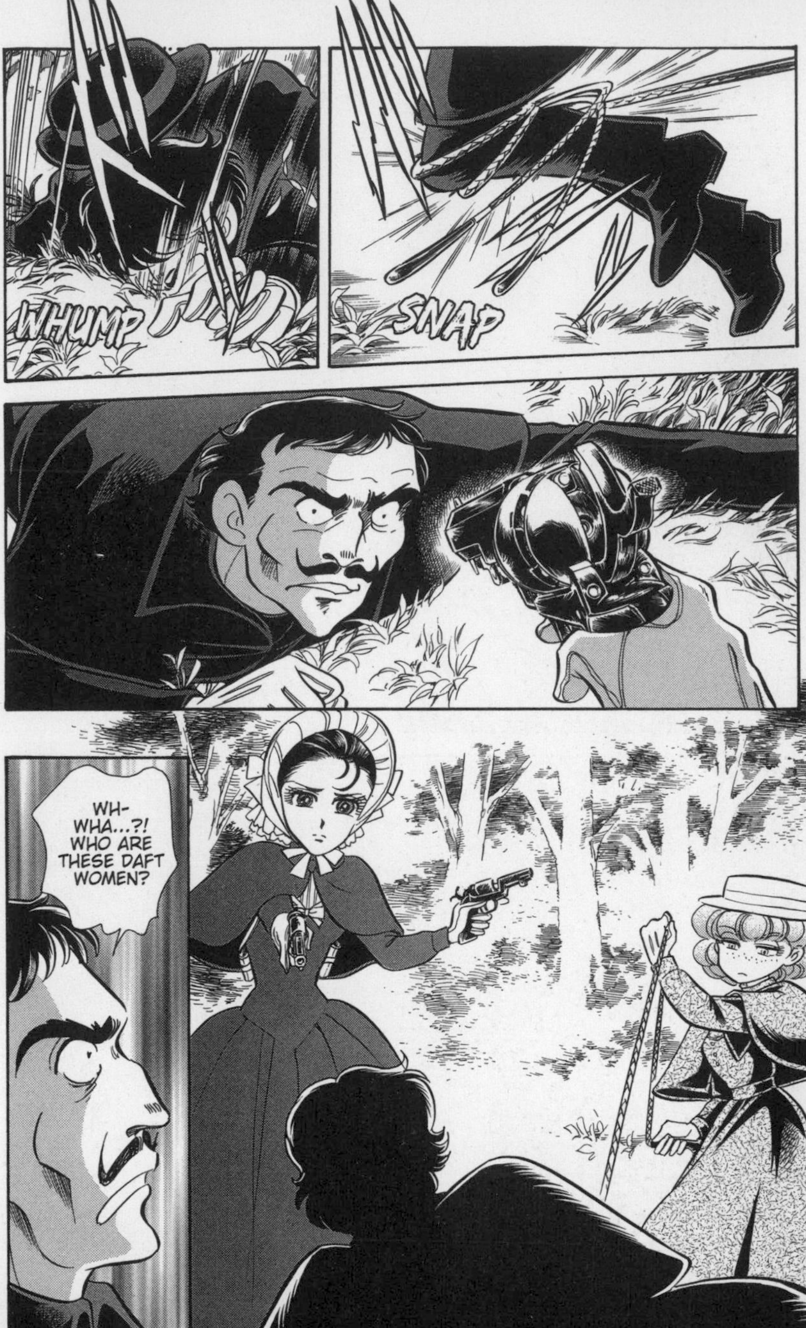
SNAP
WHUMP
WH- WHA...?! WHO ARE THESE DAFT WOMEN?

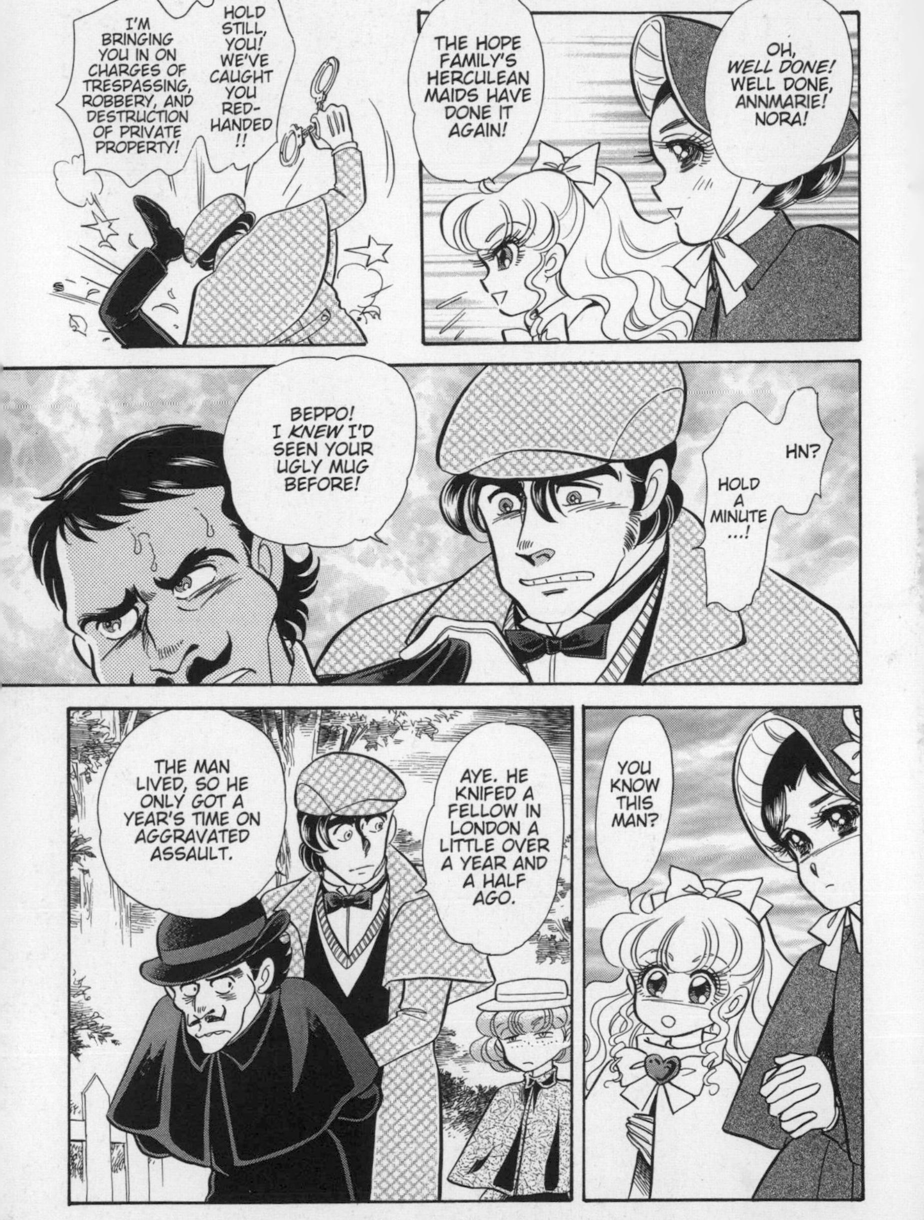
OH, *WELL DONE!* WELL DONE, ANNMARIE! NORA!
THE HOPE FAMILY'S HERCULEAN MAIDS HAVE DONE IT AGAIN!
HOLD STILL, YOU! WE'VE CAUGHT YOU RED-HANDED!!
I'M BRINGING YOU IN ON CHARGES OF TRESPASSING, ROBBERY, AND DESTRUCTION OF PRIVATE PROPERTY!
HN?
HOLD A MINUTE...!
BEPPO! I *KNEW* I'D SEEN YOUR UGLY MUG BEFORE!
YOU KNOW THIS MAN?
AYE. HE KNIFED A FELLOW IN LONDON A LITTLE OVER A YEAR AND A HALF AGO.
THE MAN LIVED, SO HE ONLY GOT A YEAR'S TIME ON AGGRAVATED ASSAULT.

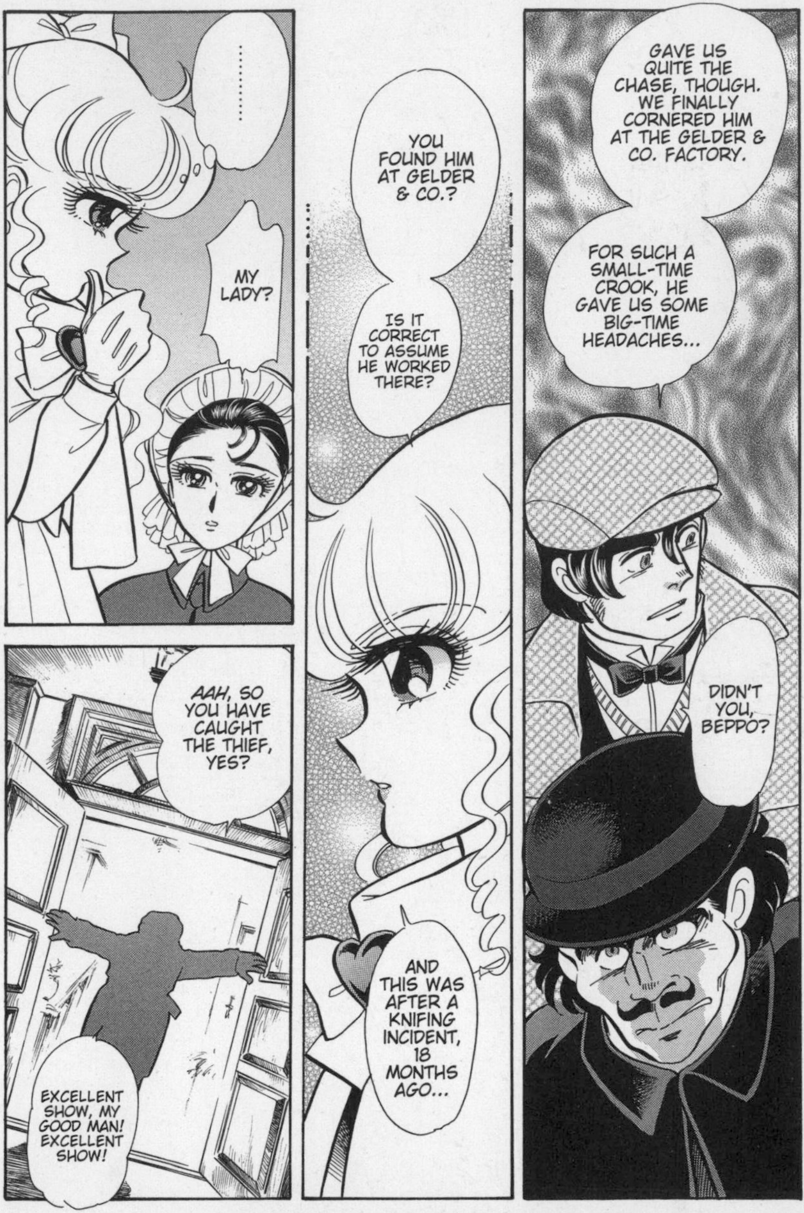
GAVE US QUITE THE CHASE, THOUGH. WE FINALLY CORNERED HIM AT THE GELDER & CO. FACTORY.
FOR SUCH A SMALL-TIME CROOK, HE GAVE US SOME BIG-TIME HEADACHES...
DIDN'T YOU, BEPPO?
YOU FOUND HIM AT GELDER & CO.?
IS IT CORRECT TO ASSUME HE WORKED THERE?
AND THIS WAS AFTER A KNIFING INCIDENT, 18 MONTHS AGO...
......
MY LADY?
AAH, SO YOU HAVE CAUGHT THE THIEF, YES?
EXCELLENT SHOW, MY GOOD MAN! EXCELLENT SHOW!

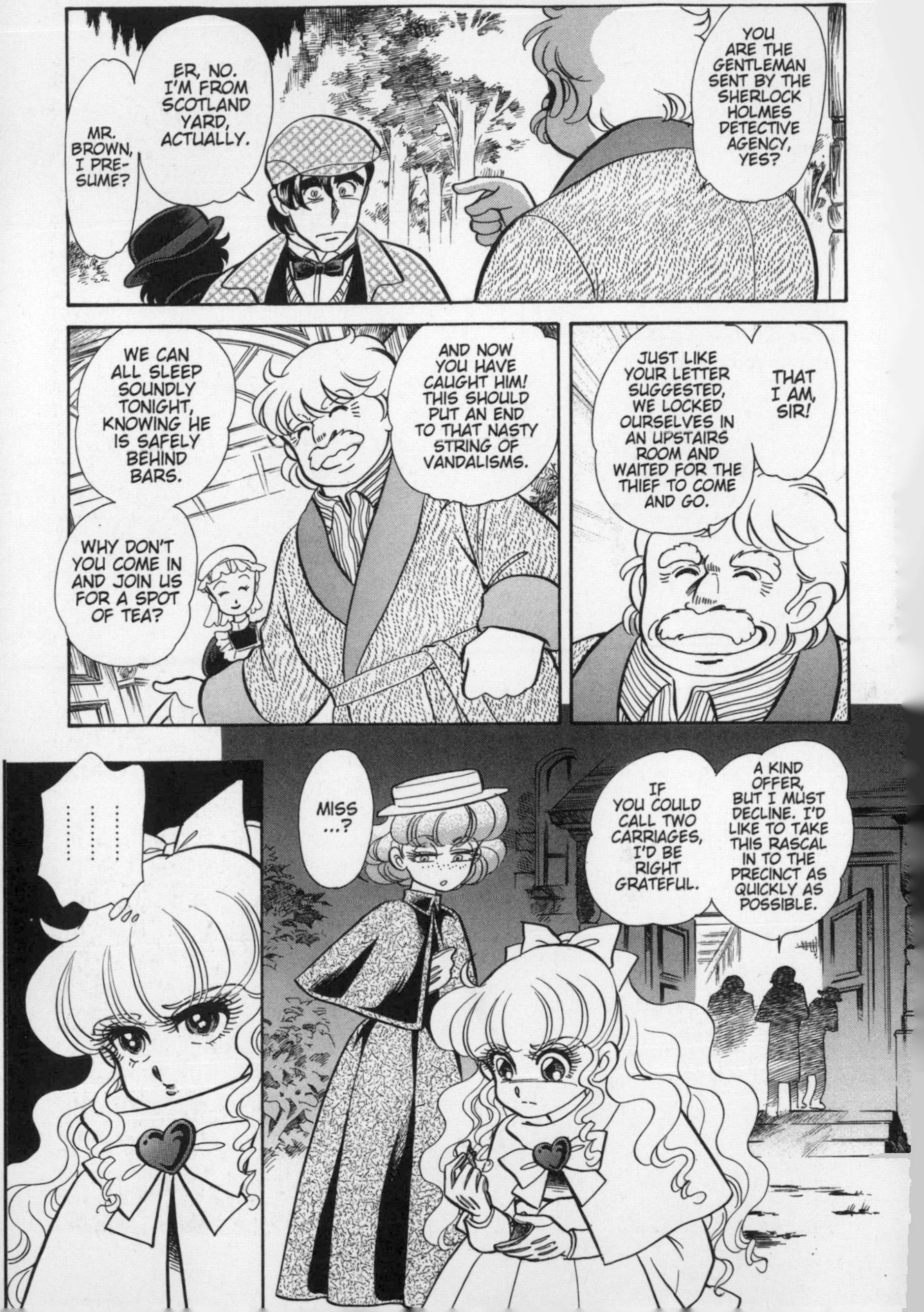
YOU ARE THE GENTLEMAN SENT BY THE SHERLOCK HOLMES DETECTIVE AGENCY, YES?
ER, NO. I'M FROM SCOTLAND YARD, ACTUALLY.
MR. BROWN, I PRESUME?
THAT I AM, SIR!
JUST LIKE YOUR LETTER SUGGESTED, WE LOCKED OURSELVES IN AN UPSTAIRS ROOM AND WAITED FOR THE THIEF TO COME AND GO.
AND NOW YOU HAVE CAUGHT HIM! THIS SHOULD PUT AN END TO THAT NASTY STRING OF VANDALISMS.
WE CAN ALL SLEEP SOUNDLY TONIGHT, KNOWING HE IS SAFELY BEHIND BARS.
WHY DON'T YOU COME IN AND JOIN US FOR A SPOT OF TEA?
A KIND OFFER, BUT I MUST DECLINE. I'D LIKE TO TAKE THIS RASCAL IN TO THE PRECINCT AS QUICKLY AS POSSIBLE.
IF YOU COULD CALL TWO CARRIAGES, I'D BE RIGHT GRATEFUL.
MISS ...?
......

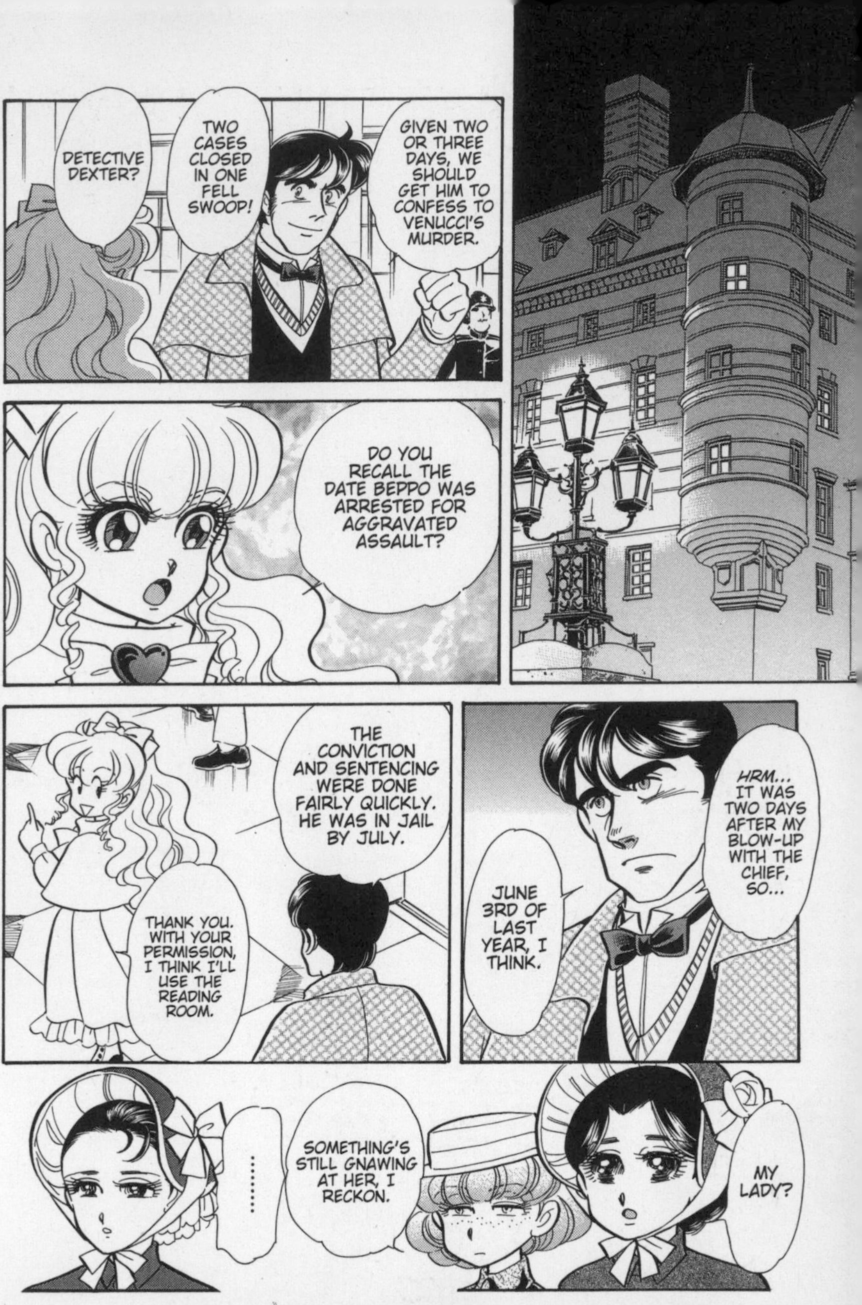
GIVEN TWO OR THREE DAYS, WE SHOULD GET HIM TO CONFESS TO VENUCCI'S MURDER.
TWO CASES CLOSED IN ONE FELL SWOOP!
DETECTIVE DEXTER?
DO YOU RECALL THE DATE BEPPO WAS ARRESTED FOR AGGRAVATED ASSAULT?
HRM... IT WAS TWO DAYS AFTER MY BLOW-UP WITH THE CHIEF, SO...
JUNE 3RD OF LAST YEAR, I THINK.
THE CONVICTION AND SENTENCING WERE DONE FAIRLY QUICKLY. HE WAS IN JAIL BY JULY.
THANK YOU. WITH YOUR PERMISSION, I THINK I'LL USE THE READING ROOM.
MY LADY?
SOMETHING'S STILL GNAWING AT HER, I RECKON.
......

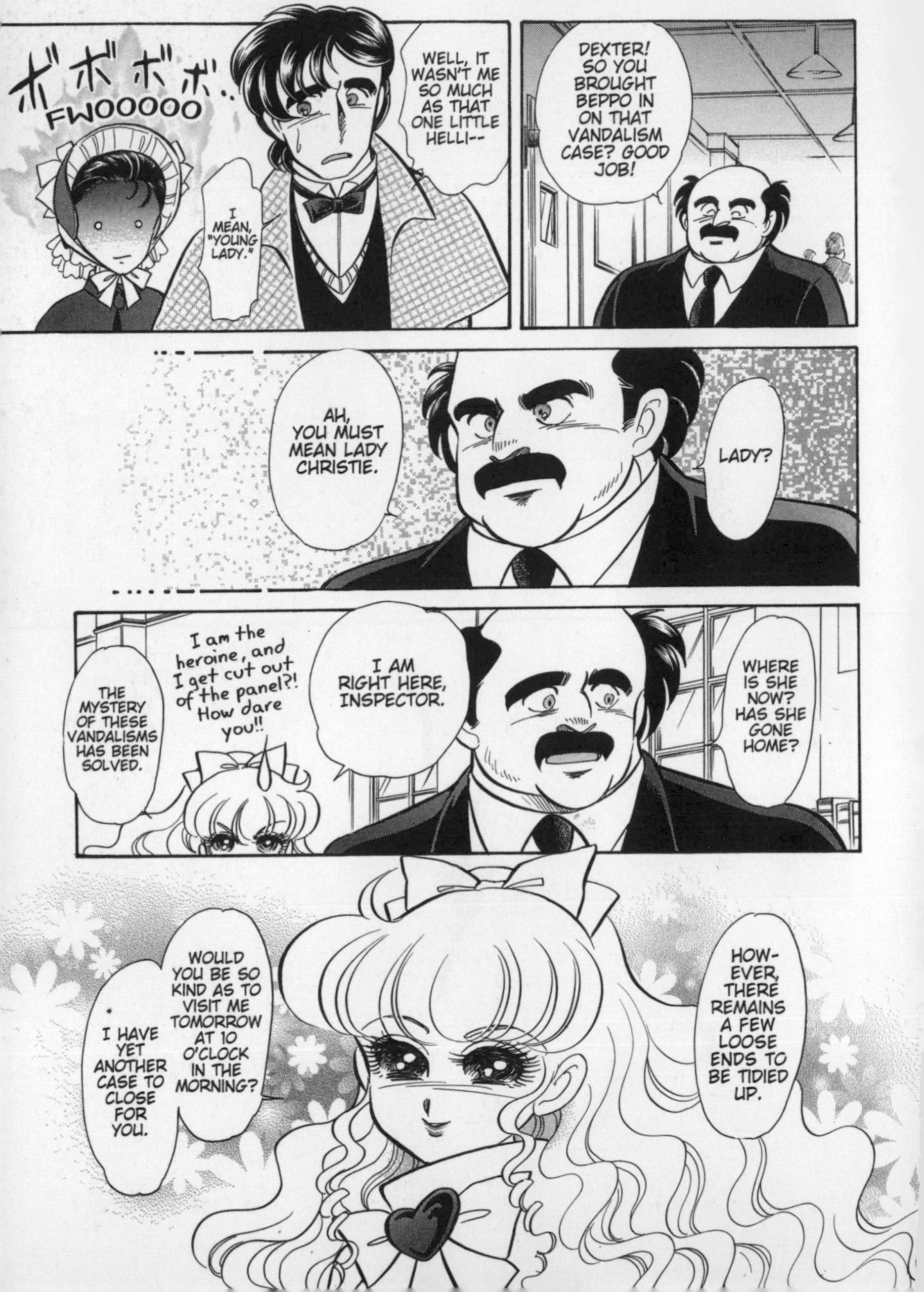
DEXTER! SO YOU BROUGHT BEPPO IN ON THAT VANDALISM CASE? GOOD JOB!
WELL, IT WASN'T ME SO MUCH AS THAT ONE LITTLE HELLI--
I MEAN, "YOUNG LADY."
ボボボボ..
FWOOOOO
LADY?
AH, YOU MUST MEAN LADY CHRISTIE.
WHERE IS SHE NOW? HAS SHE GONE HOME?
I AM RIGHT HERE, INSPECTOR.
I am the heroine, and I get cut out of the panel?! How dare you!!
THE MYSTERY OF THESE VANDALISMS HAS BEEN SOLVED.
HOW-EVER, THERE REMAINS A FEW LOOSE ENDS TO BE TIDIED UP.
WOULD YOU BE SO KIND AS TO VISIT ME TOMORROW AT 10 O'CLOCK IN THE MORNING?
I HAVE YET ANOTHER CASE TO CLOSE FOR YOU.

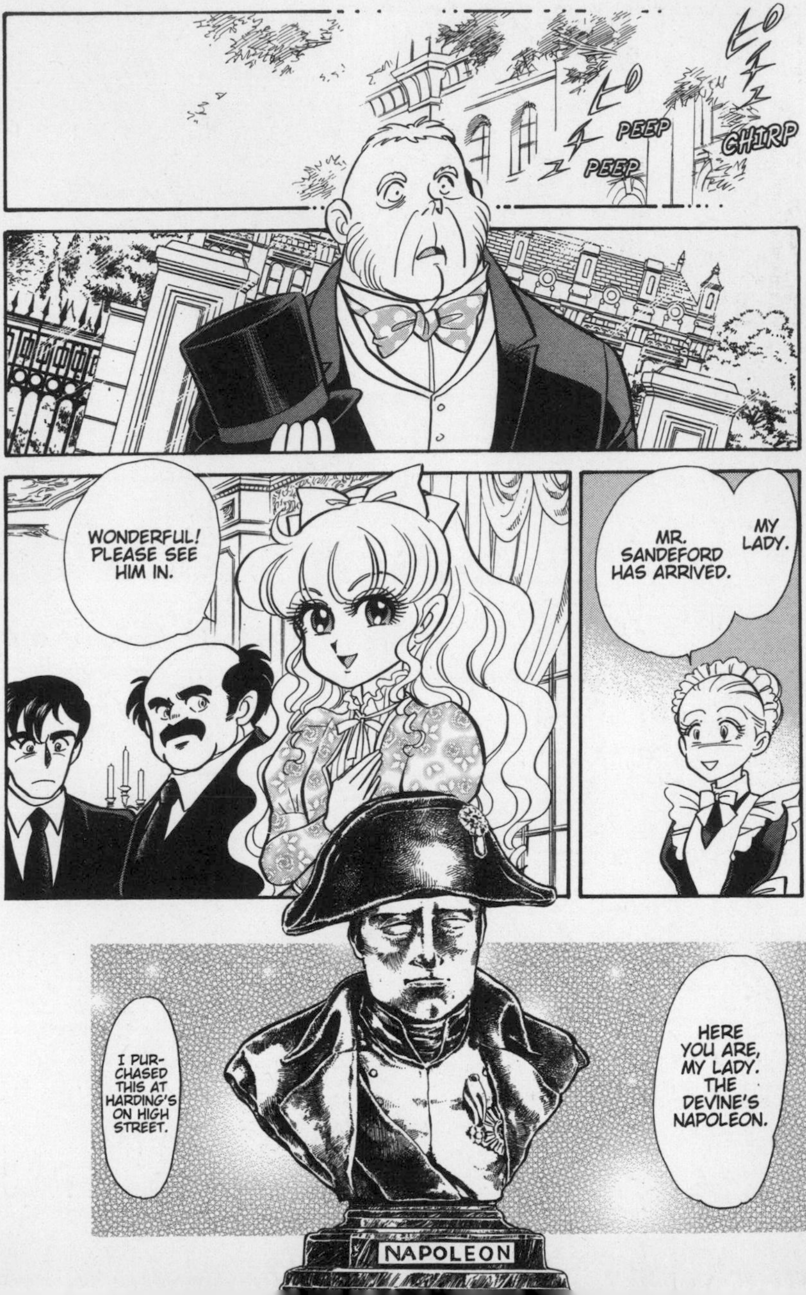
CHIRP
PEEP
PEEP
MY LADY.
MR. SANDEFORD HAS ARRIVED.
WONDERFUL! PLEASE SEE HIM IN.
HERE YOU ARE, MY LADY. THE DEVINE'S NAPOLEON.
I PUR-CHASED THIS AT HARDING'S ON HIGH STREET.
NAPOLEON

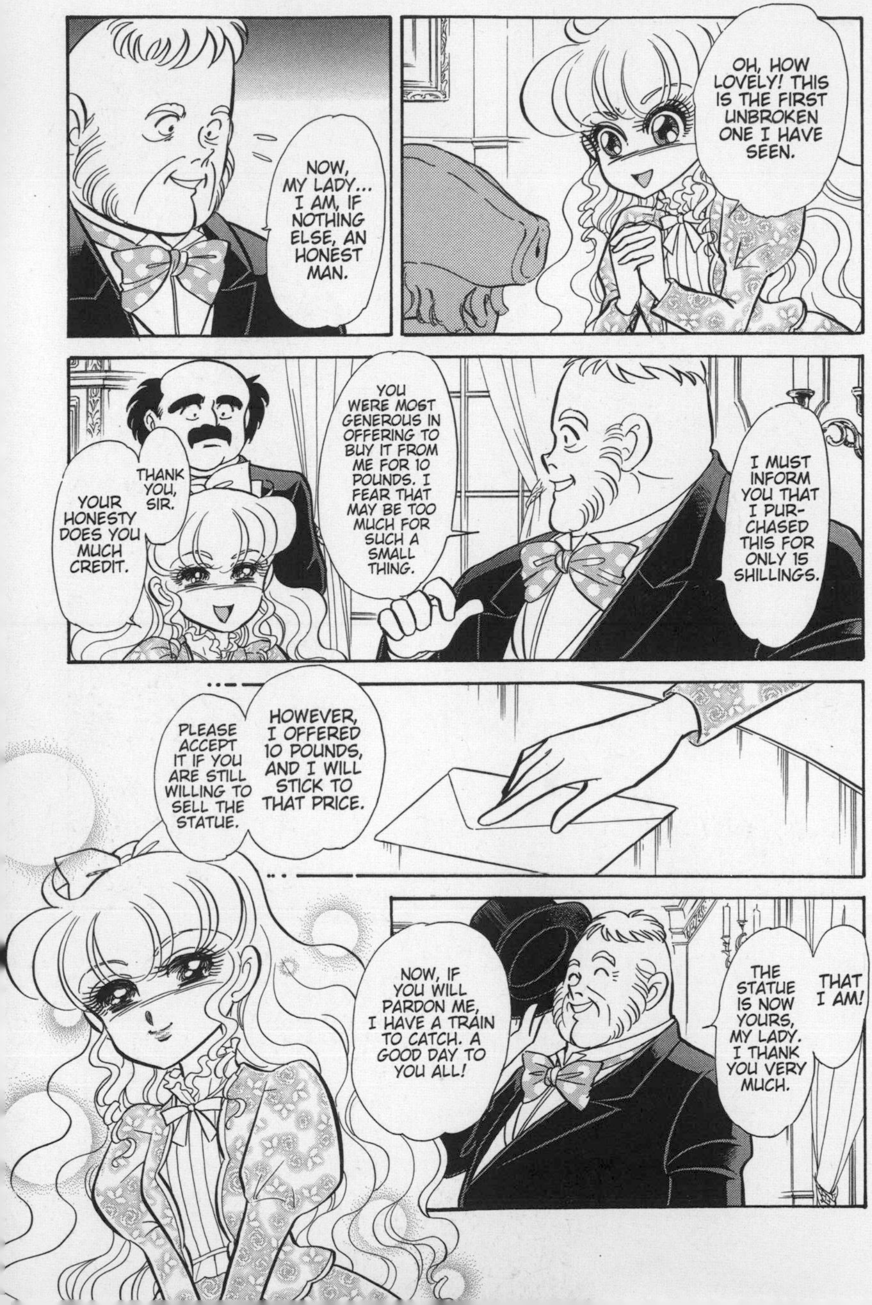
OH, HOW LOVELY! THIS IS THE FIRST UNBROKEN ONE I HAVE SEEN.
NOW, MY LADY... I AM, IF NOTHING ELSE, AN HONEST MAN.
I MUST INFORM YOU THAT I PUR-CHASED THIS FOR ONLY 15 SHILLINGS.
YOU WERE MOST GENEROUS IN OFFERING TO BUY IT FROM ME FOR 10 POUNDS. I FEAR THAT MAY BE TOO MUCH FOR SUCH A SMALL THING.
THANK YOU, SIR.
YOUR HONESTY DOES YOU MUCH CREDIT.
HOWEVER, I OFFERED 10 POUNDS, AND I WILL STICK TO THAT PRICE.
PLEASE ACCEPT IT IF YOU ARE STILL WILLING TO SELL THE STATUE.
THAT I AM!
THE STATUE IS NOW YOURS, MY LADY. I THANK YOU VERY MUCH.
NOW, IF YOU WILL PARDON ME, I HAVE A TRAIN TO CATCH. A GOOD DAY TO YOU ALL!

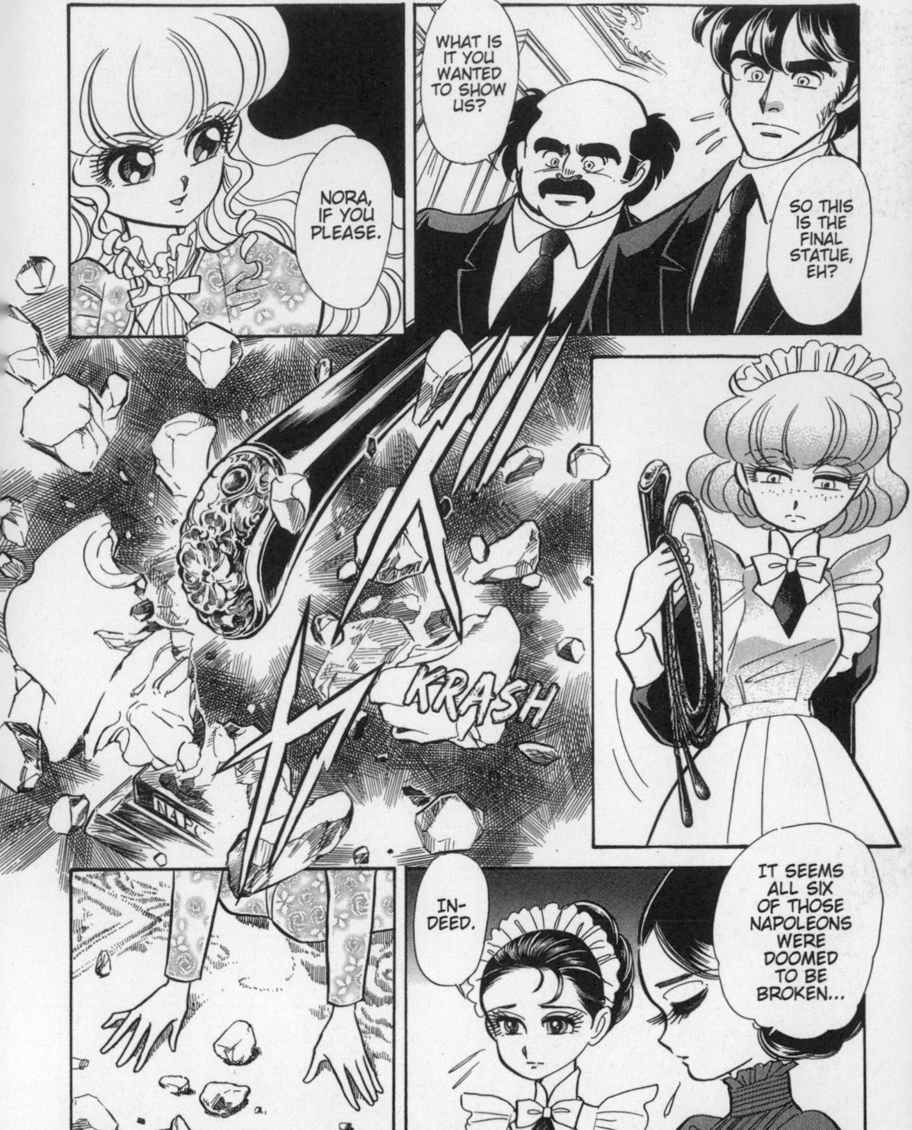
WHAT IS IT YOU WANTED TO SHOW US?
SO THIS IS THE FINAL STATUE, EH?
NORA, IF YOU PLEASE.
KRASH
IT SEEMS ALL SIX OF THOSE NAPOLEONS WERE DOOMED TO BE BROKEN...
IN-DEED.

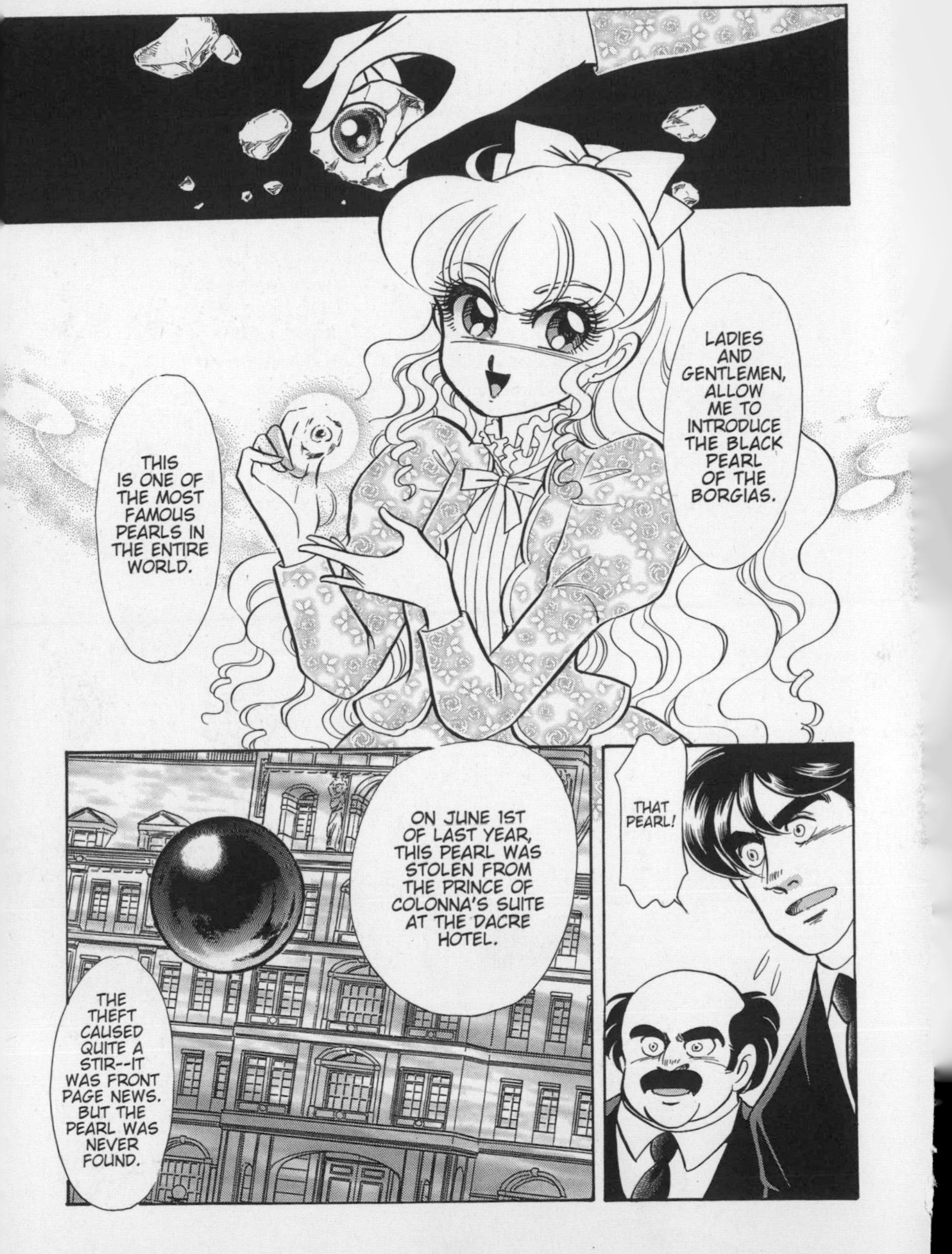
LADIES AND GENTLEMEN, ALLOW ME TO INTRODUCE THE BLACK PEARL OF THE BORGIAS.
THIS IS ONE OF THE MOST FAMOUS PEARLS IN THE ENTIRE WORLD.
THAT PEARL!
ON JUNE 1ST OF LAST YEAR, THIS PEARL WAS STOLEN FROM THE PRINCE OF COLONNA'S SUITE AT THE DACRE HOTEL.
THE THEFT CAUSED QUITE A STIR--IT WAS FRONT PAGE NEWS. BUT THE PEARL WAS NEVER FOUND.

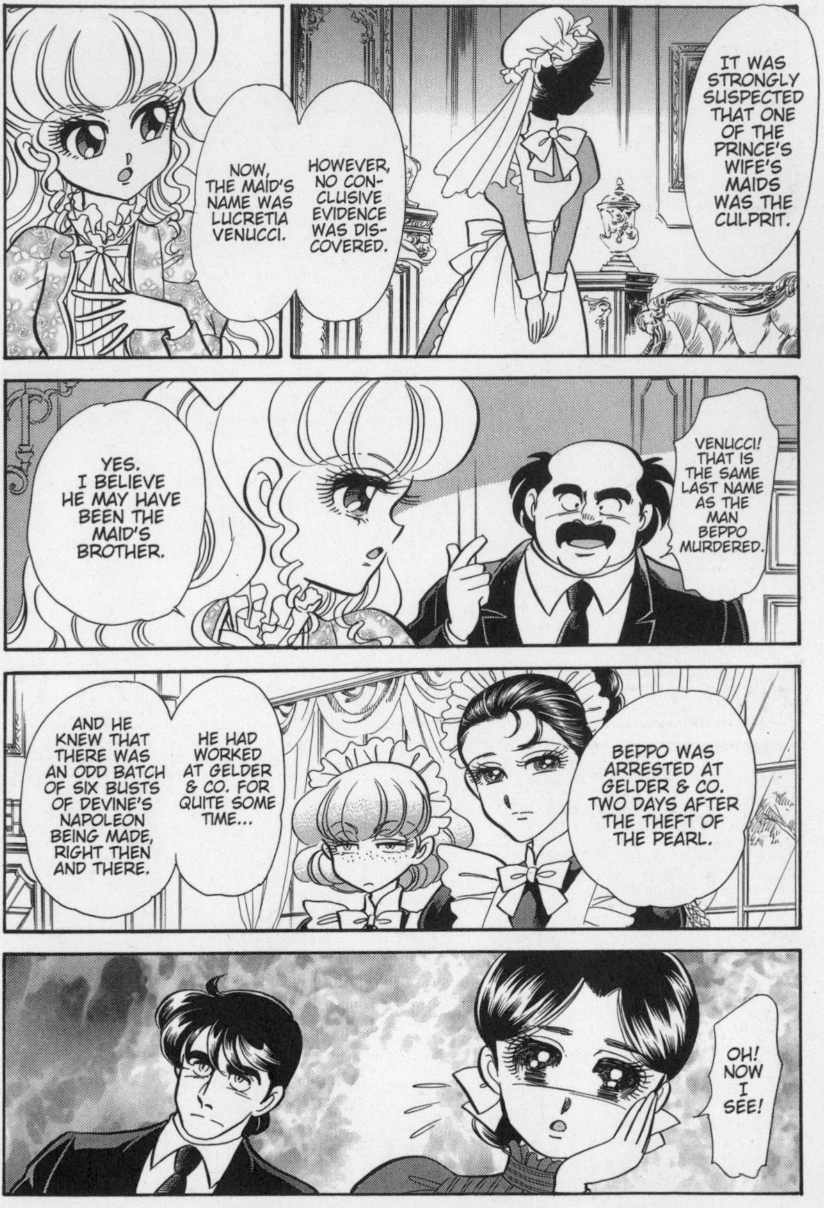
IT WAS STRONGLY SUSPECTED THAT ONE OF THE PRINCE'S WIFE'S MAIDS WAS THE CULPRIT.
HOWEVER, NO CON-CLUSIVE EVIDENCE WAS DIS-COVERED.
NOW, THE MAID'S NAME WAS LUCRETIA VENUCCI.
VENUCCI! THAT IS THE SAME LAST NAME AS THE MAN BEPPO MURDERED.
YES. I BELIEVE HE MAY HAVE BEEN THE MAID'S BROTHER.
BEPPO WAS ARRESTED AT GELDER & CO. TWO DAYS AFTER THE THEFT OF THE PEARL.
HE HAD WORKED AT GELDER & CO. FOR QUITE SOME TIME...
AND HE KNEW THAT THERE WAS AN ODD BATCH OF SIX BUSTS OF DEVINE'S NAPOLEON BEING MADE, RIGHT THEN AND THERE.
OH! NOW I SEE!

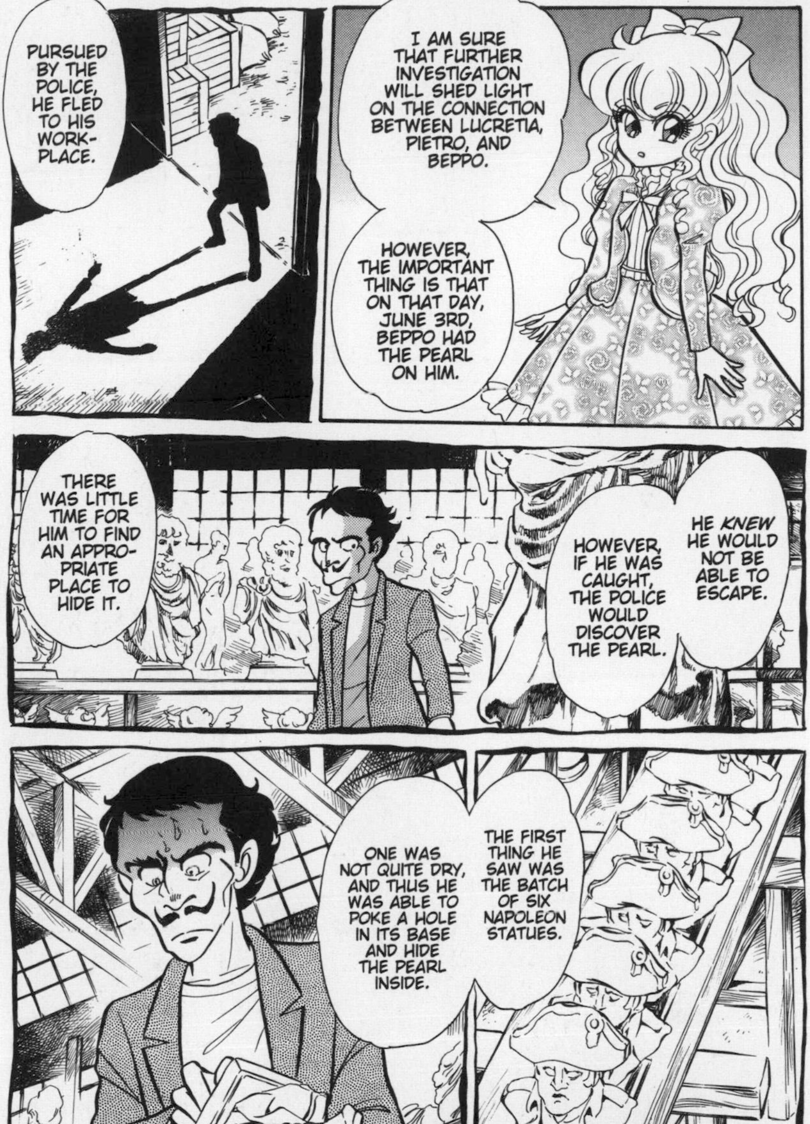
I AM SURE THAT FURTHER INVESTIGATION WILL SHED LIGHT ON THE CONNECTION BETWEEN LUCRETIA, PIETRO, AND BEPPO.
HOWEVER, THE IMPORTANT THING IS THAT ON THAT DAY, JUNE 3RD, BEPPO HAD THE PEARL ON HIM.
PURSUED BY THE POLICE, HE FLED TO HIS WORK-PLACE.
HE *KNEW* HE WOULD NOT BE ABLE TO ESCAPE.
HOWEVER, IF HE WAS CAUGHT, THE POLICE WOULD DISCOVER THE PEARL.
THERE WAS LITTLE TIME FOR HIM TO FIND AN APPRO-PRIATE PLACE TO HIDE IT.
THE FIRST THING HE SAW WAS THE BATCH OF SIX NAPOLEON STATUES.
ONE WAS NOT QUITE DRY, AND THUS HE WAS ABLE TO POKE A HOLE IN ITS BASE AND HIDE THE PEARL INSIDE.

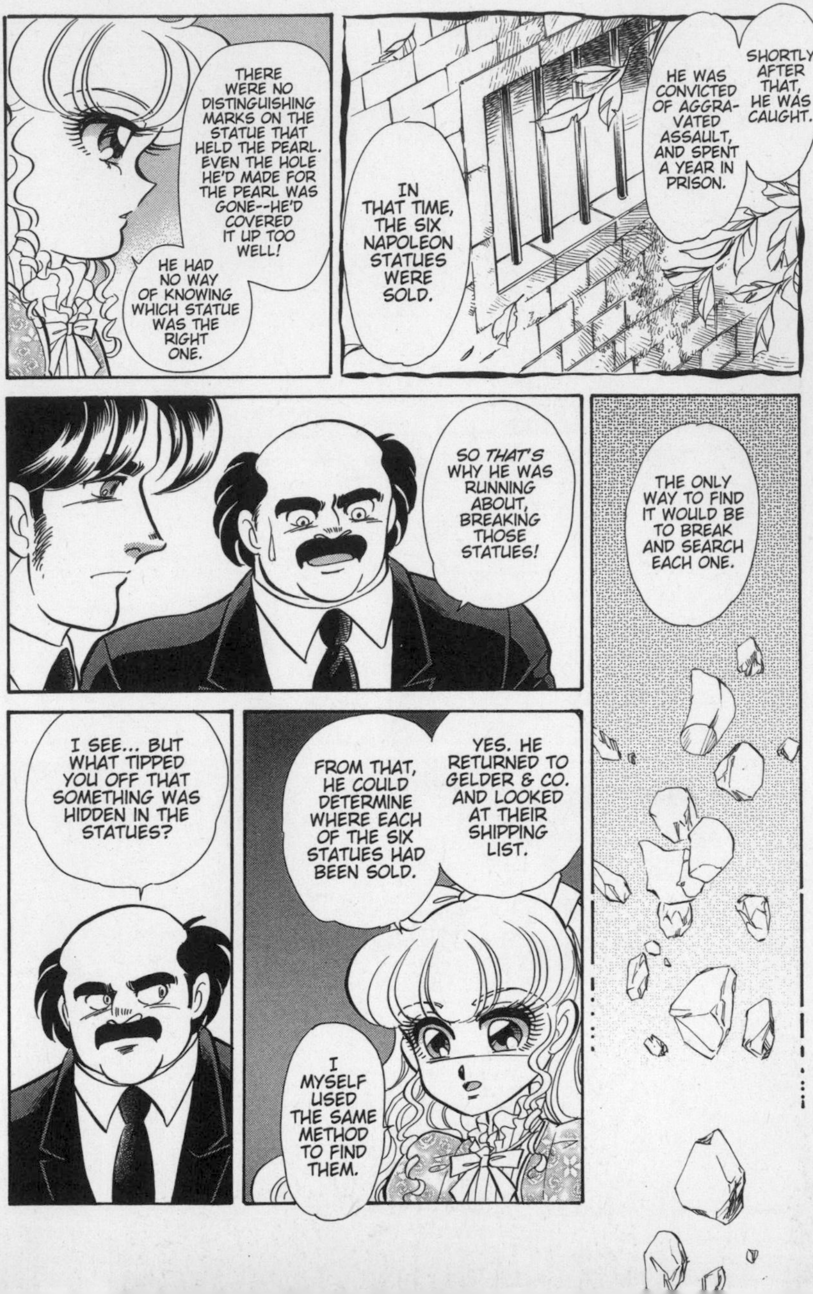
SHORTLY AFTER THAT, HE WAS CAUGHT.
HE WAS CONVICTED OF AGGRA-VATED ASSAULT, AND SPENT A YEAR IN PRISON.
IN THAT TIME, THE SIX NAPOLEON STATUES WERE SOLD.
THERE WERE NO DISTINGUISHING MARKS ON THE STATUE THAT HELD THE PEARL. EVEN THE HOLE HE'D MADE FOR THE PEARL WAS GONE--HE'D COVERED IT UP TOO WELL!
HE HAD NO WAY OF KNOWING WHICH STATUE WAS THE RIGHT ONE.
THE ONLY WAY TO FIND IT WOULD BE TO BREAK AND SEARCH EACH ONE.
SO *THAT'S* WHY HE WAS RUNNING ABOUT, BREAKING THOSE STATUES!
YES. HE RETURNED TO GELDER & CO. AND LOOKED AT THEIR SHIPPING LIST.
FROM THAT, HE COULD DETERMINE WHERE EACH OF THE SIX STATUES HAD BEEN SOLD.
I MYSELF USED THE SAME METHOD TO FIND THEM.
I SEE... BUT WHAT TIPPED YOU OFF THAT SOMETHING WAS HIDDEN IN THE STATUES?

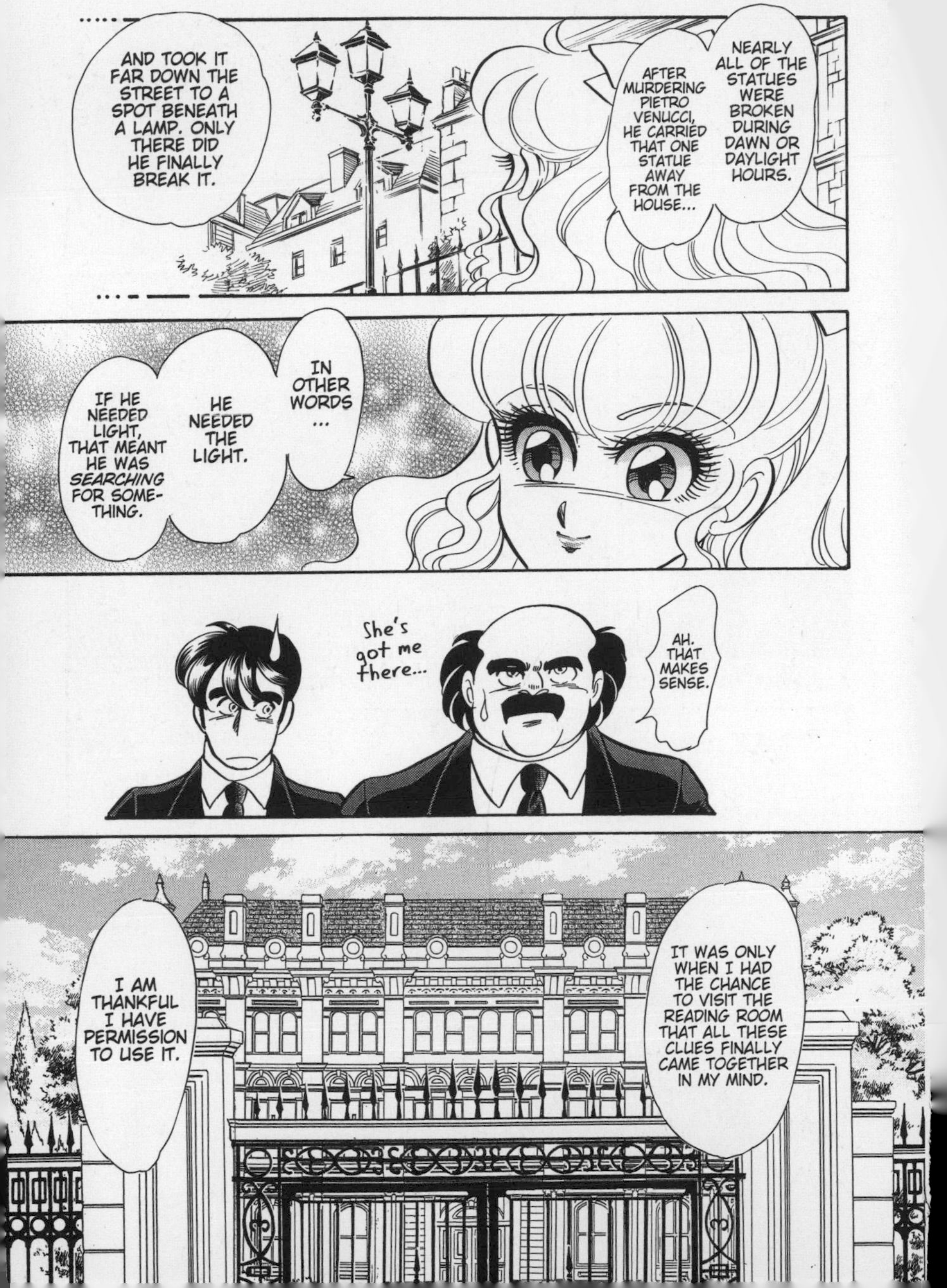
NEARLY ALL OF THE STATUES WERE BROKEN DURING DAWN OR DAYLIGHT HOURS.
AFTER MURDERING PIETRO VENUCCI, HE CARRIED THAT ONE STATUE AWAY FROM THE HOUSE...
AND TOOK IT FAR DOWN THE STREET TO A SPOT BENEATH A LAMP. ONLY THERE DID HE FINALLY BREAK IT.
IN OTHER WORDS ...
HE NEEDED THE LIGHT.
IF HE NEEDED LIGHT, THAT MEANT HE WAS *SEARCHING* FOR SOMETHING.
AH. THAT MAKES SENSE.
She's got me there...
IT WAS ONLY WHEN I HAD THE CHANCE TO VISIT THE READING ROOM THAT ALL THESE CLUES FINALLY CAME TOGETHER IN MY MIND.
I AM THANKFUL I HAVE PERMISSION TO USE IT.

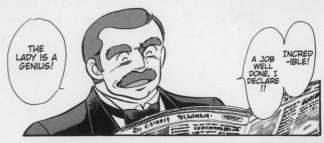

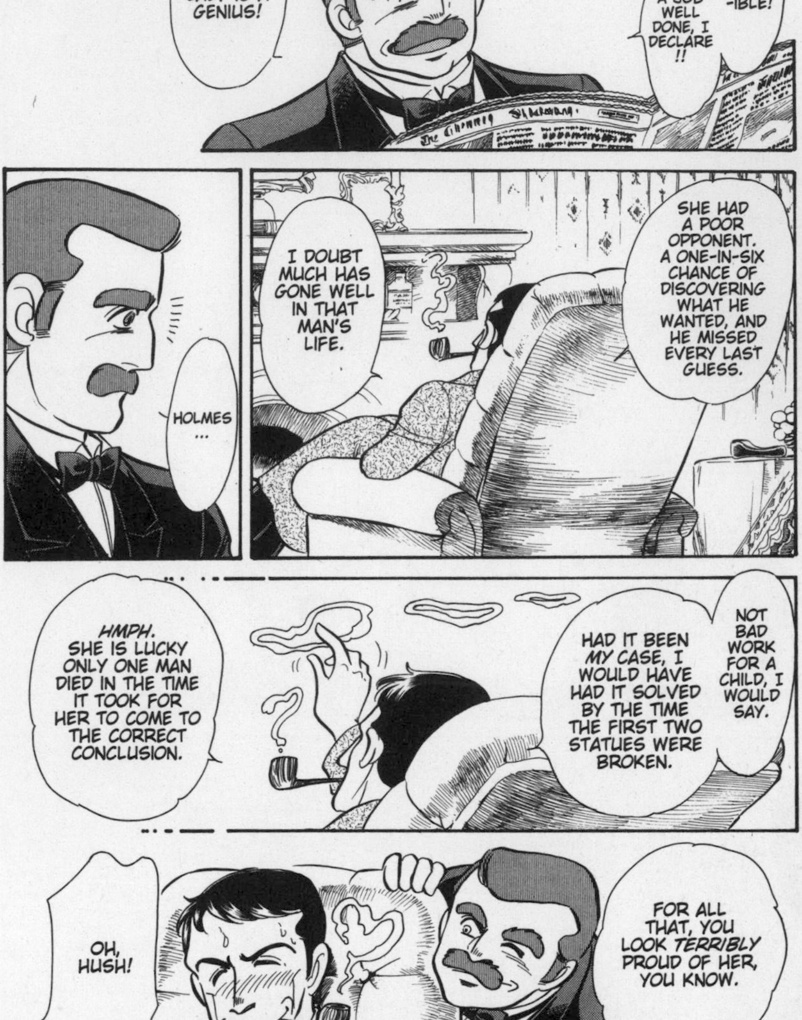
INCRED-IBLE!
A JOB WELL DONE, I DECLARE!!
THE LADY IS A GENIUS!
SHE HAD A POOR OPPONENT. A ONE-IN-SIX CHANCE OF DISCOVERING WHAT HE WANTED, AND HE MISSED EVERY LAST GUESS.
I DOUBT MUCH HAS GONE WELL IN THAT MAN'S LIFE.
HOLMES...
NOT BAD WORK FOR A CHILD, I WOULD SAY.
HAD IT BEEN *MY* CASE, I WOULD HAVE HAD IT SOLVED BY THE TIME THE FIRST TWO STATUES WERE BROKEN.
HMPH. SHE IS LUCKY ONLY ONE MAN DIED IN THE TIME IT TOOK FOR HER TO COME TO THE CORRECT CONCLUSION.
FOR ALL THAT, YOU LOOK *TERRIBLY* PROUD OF HER, YOU KNOW.
OH, HUSH!

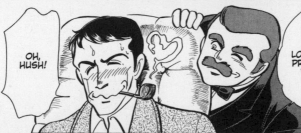

The Memories of Nora

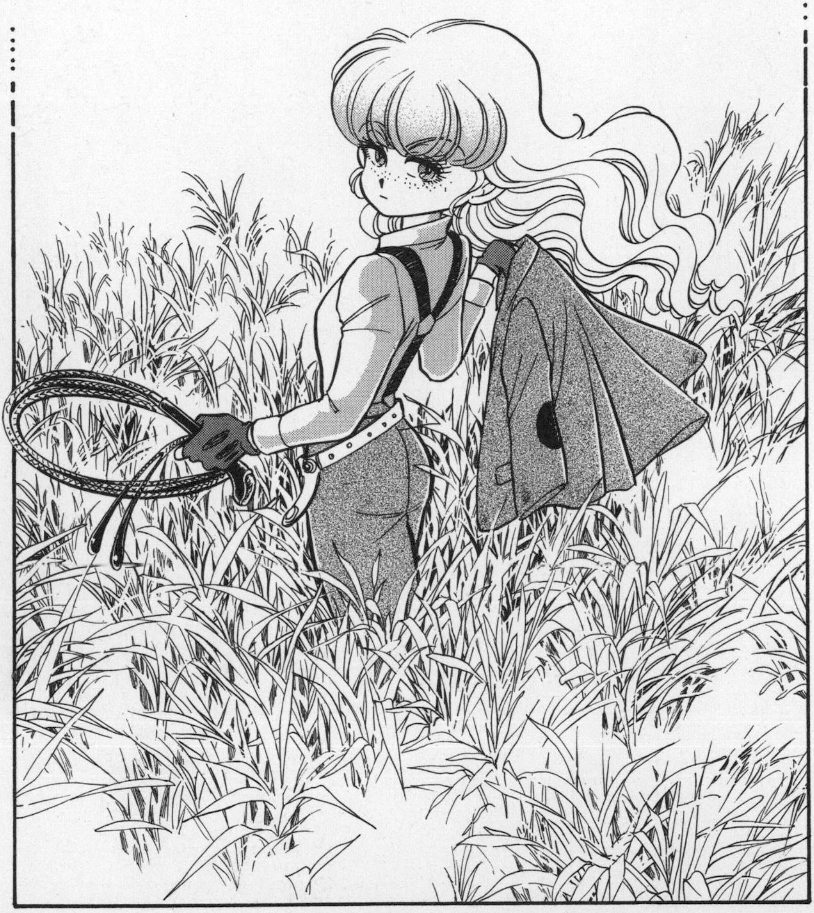

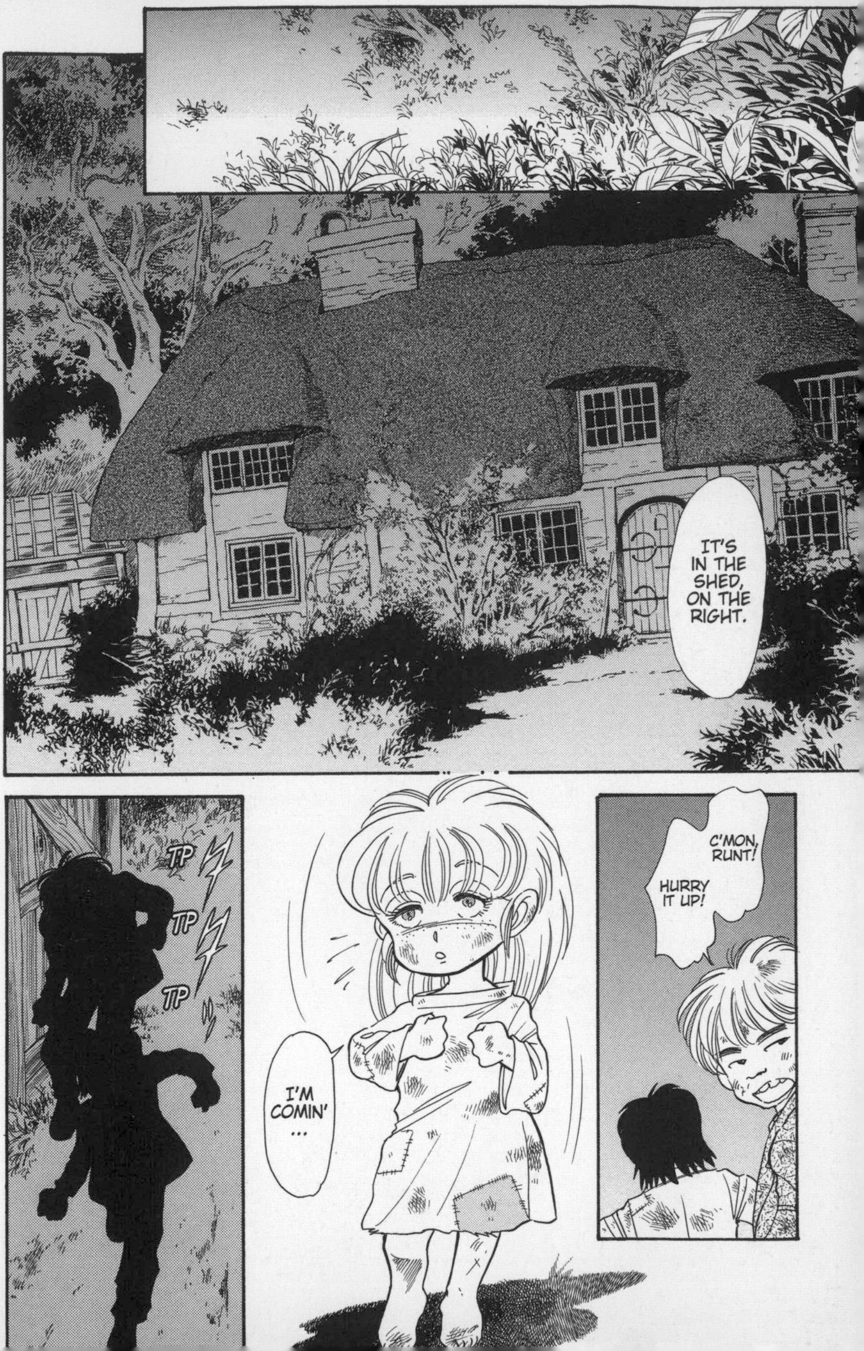

IT'S IN THE SHED, ON THE RIGHT.
C'MON, RUNT!
HURRY IT UP!
I'M COMIN' ...
TP
TP
TP

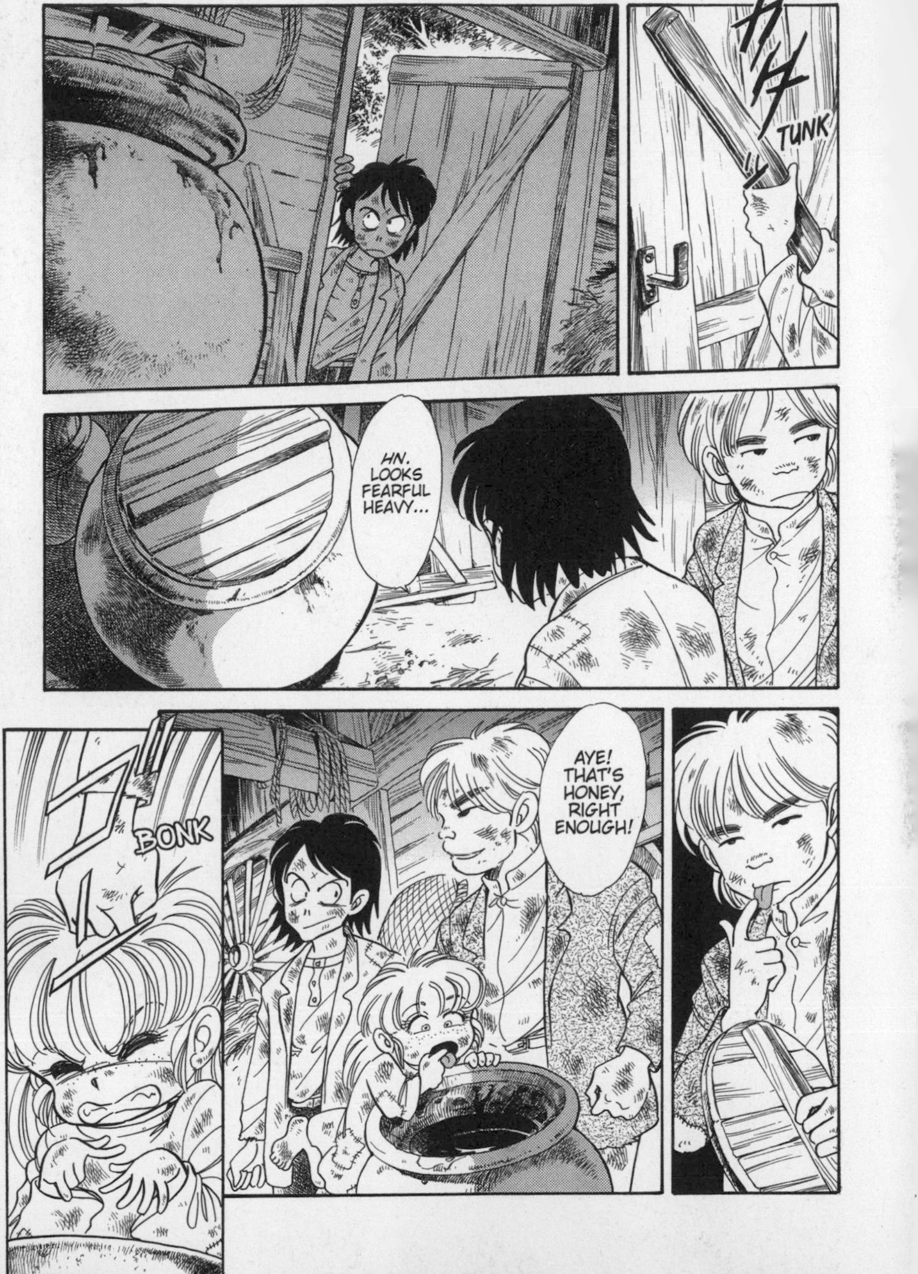
TUNK
HN. LOOKS FEARFUL HEAVY...
AYE! THAT'S HONEY, RIGHT ENOUGH!
BONK

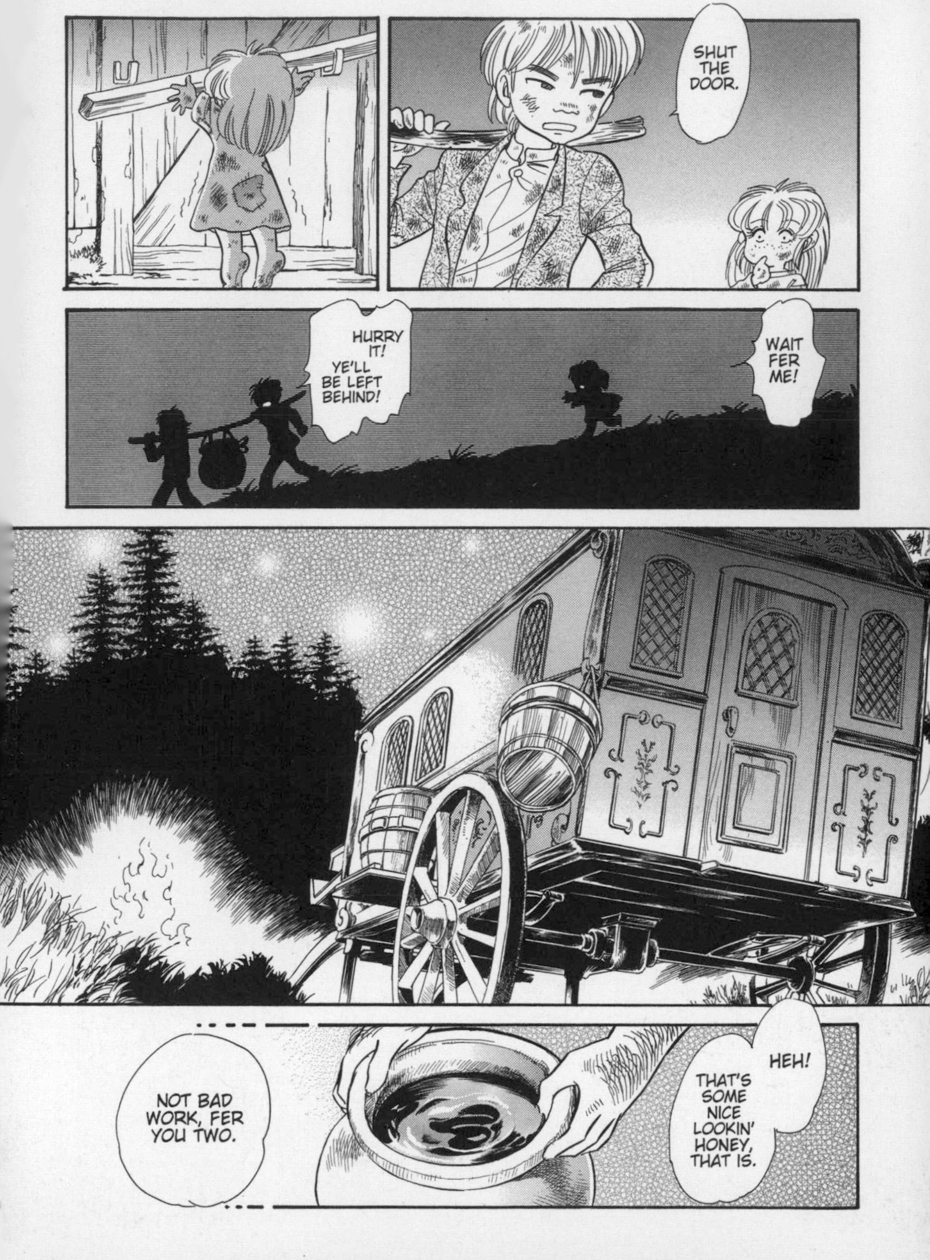
SHUT THE DOOR.
WAIT FER ME!
HURRY IT! YE'LL BE LEFT BEHIND!
HEH!
THAT'S SOME NICE LOOKIN' HONEY, THAT IS.
NOT BAD WORK, FER YOU TWO.

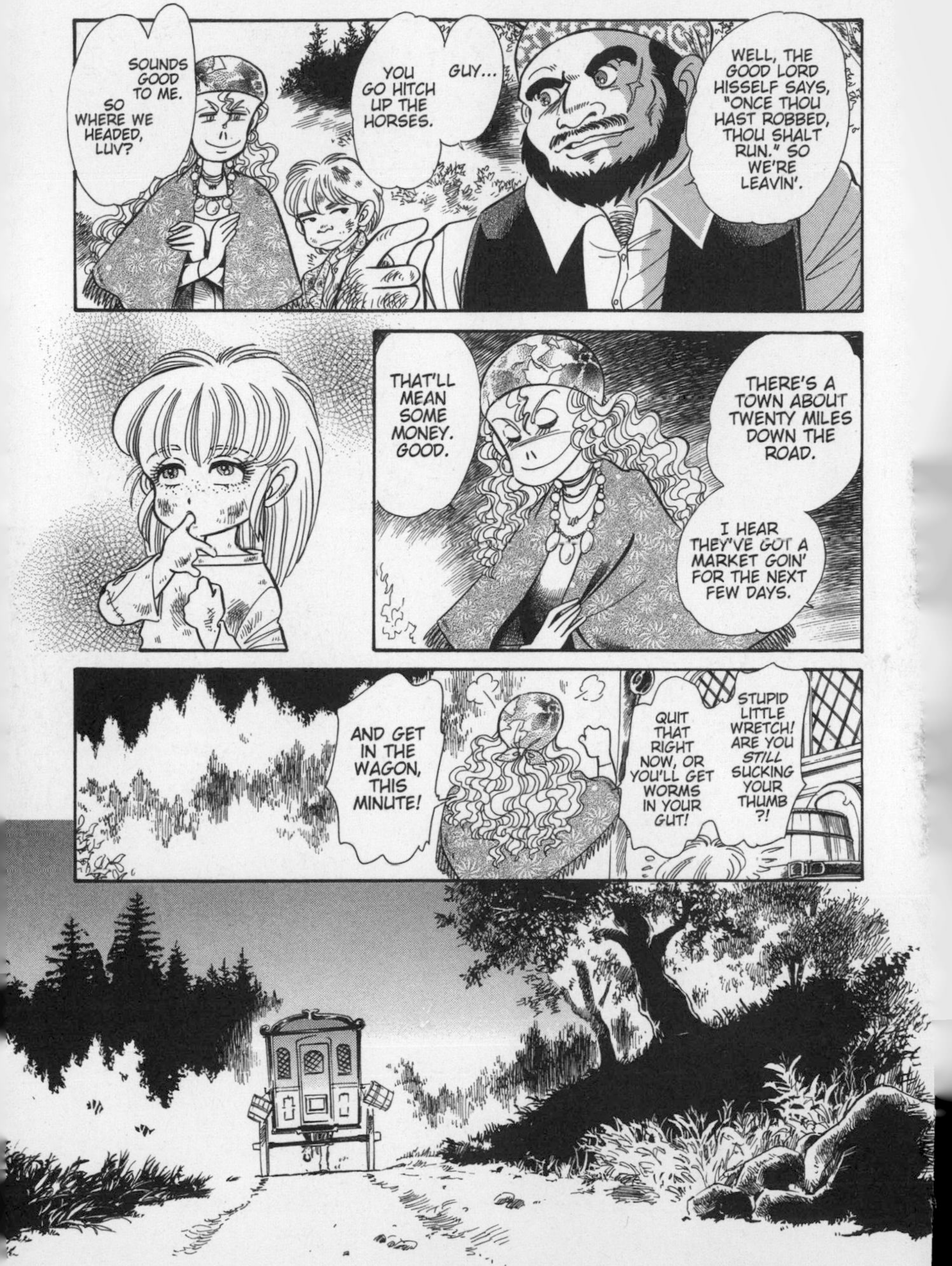
WELL, THE GOOD LORD HISSELF SAYS, "ONCE THOU HAST ROBBED, THOU SHALT RUN." SO WE'RE LEAVIN'.
GUY... YOU GO HITCH UP THE HORSES.
SOUNDS GOOD TO ME. SO WHERE WE HEADED, LUV?
THERE'S A TOWN ABOUT TWENTY MILES DOWN THE ROAD.
I HEAR THEY'VE GOT A MARKET GOIN' FOR THE NEXT FEW DAYS.
THAT'LL MEAN SOME MONEY. GOOD.
STUPID LITTLE WRETCH! ARE YOU *STILL* SUCKING YOUR THUMB?!
QUIT THAT RIGHT NOW, OR YOU'LL GET WORMS IN YOUR GUT!
AND GET IN THE WAGON, THIS MINUTE!

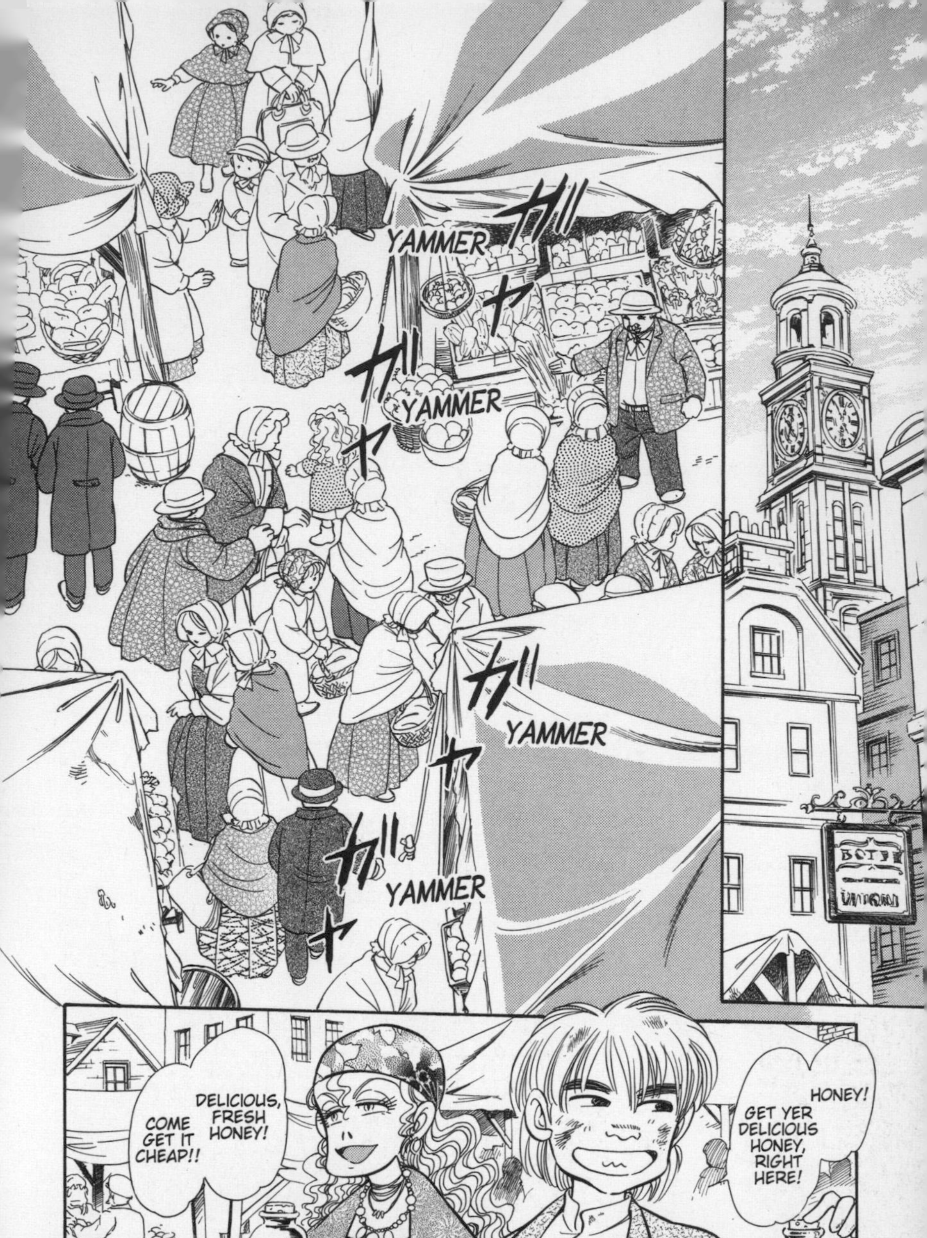

ガヤ
YAMMER
ガヤ
YAMMER
ガヤ
YAMMER
ガヤ
YAMMER
HONEY!
GET YER DELICIOUS HONEY, RIGHT HERE!
DELICIOUS, FRESH HONEY!
COME GET IT CHEAP!!

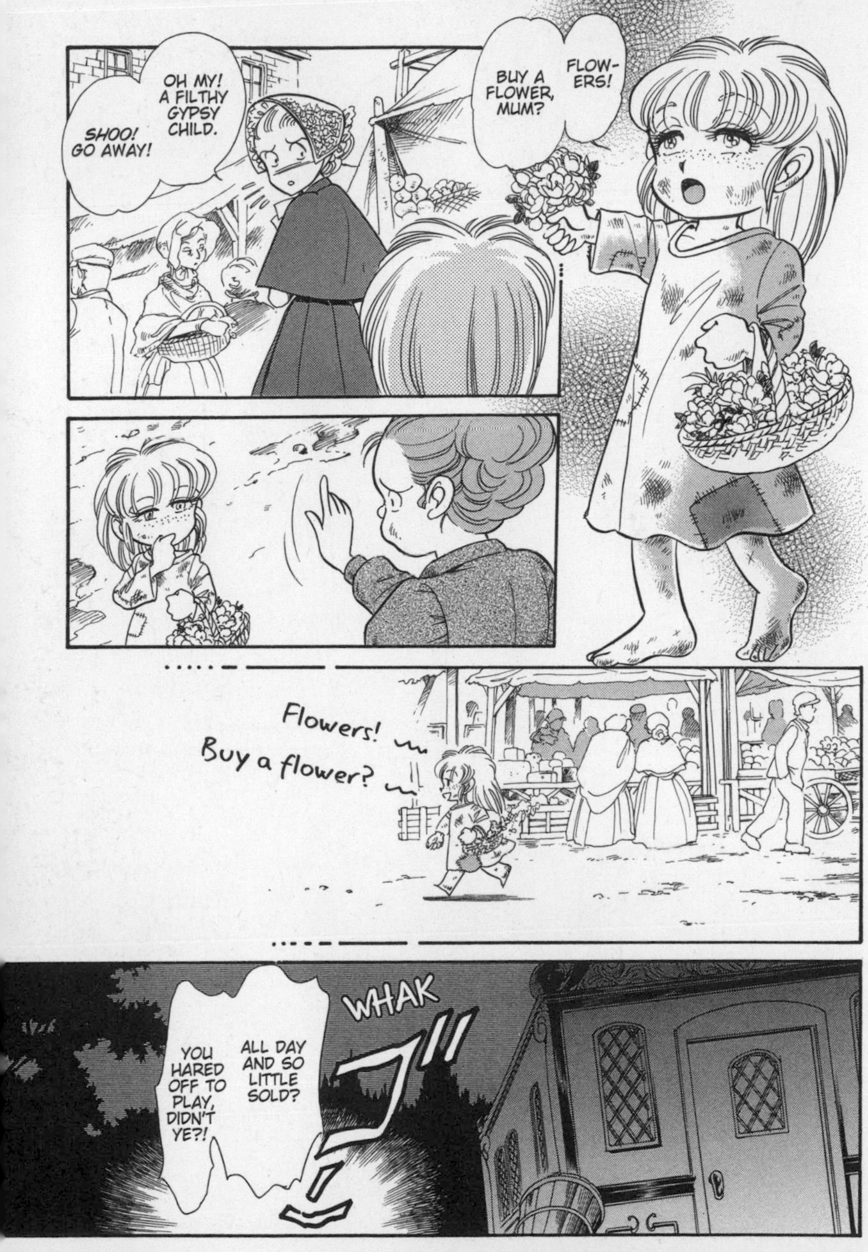
FLOW-ERS!
BUY A FLOWER, MUM?
OH MY! A FILTHY GYPSY CHILD.
SHOO! GO AWAY!
Flowers!
Buy a flower?
WHAK
ALL DAY AND SO LITTLE SOLD?
YOU HARED OFF TO PLAY, DIDN'T YE?!

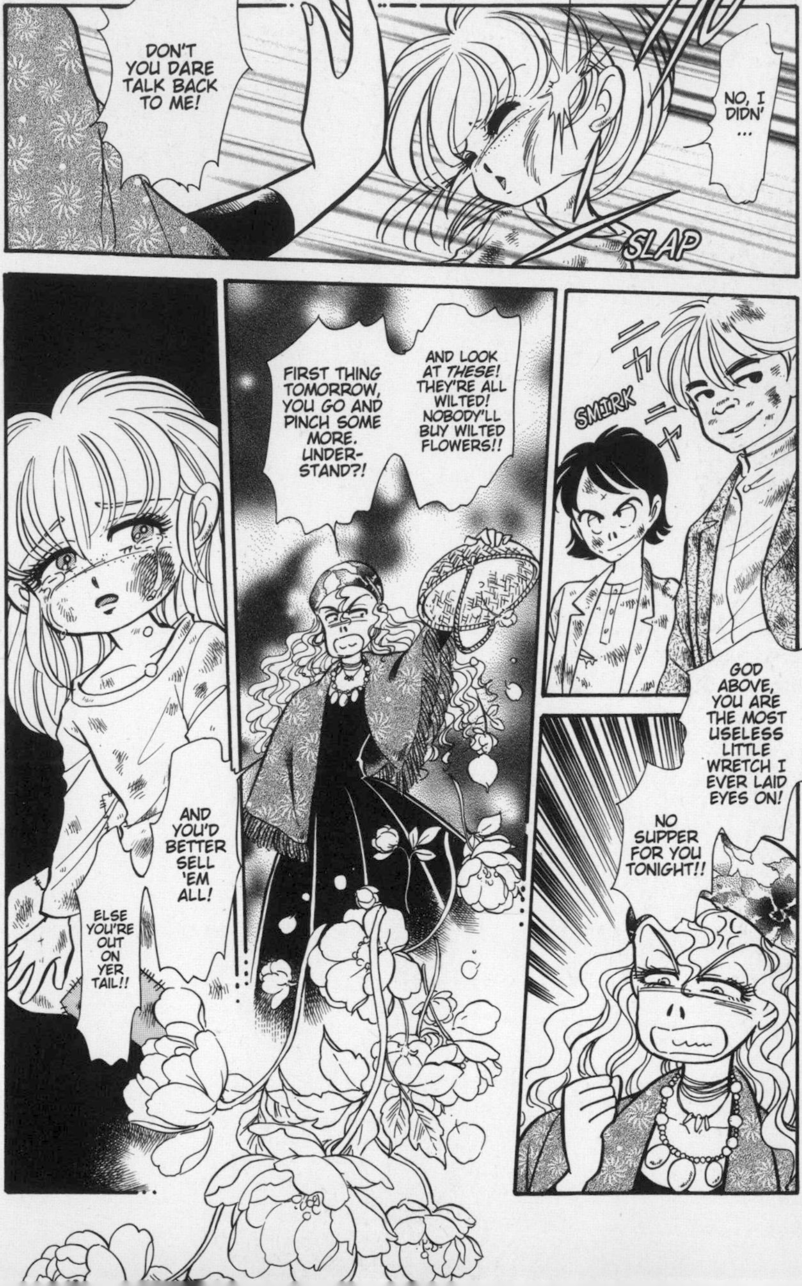
NO, I DIDN' ...
SLAP
DON'T YOU DARE TALK BACK TO ME!
ニヤ
SMIRK
ニヤ
GOD ABOVE, YOU ARE THE MOST USELESS LITTLE WRETCH I EVER LAID EYES ON!
NO SUPPER FOR YOU TONIGHT!!
AND LOOK AT *THESE*! THEY'RE ALL WILTED! NOBODY'LL BUY WILTED FLOWERS!!
FIRST THING TOMORROW, YOU GO AND PINCH SOME MORE. UNDER-STAND?!
AND YOU'D BETTER SELL 'EM ALL!
ELSE YOU'RE OUT ON YER TAIL!!

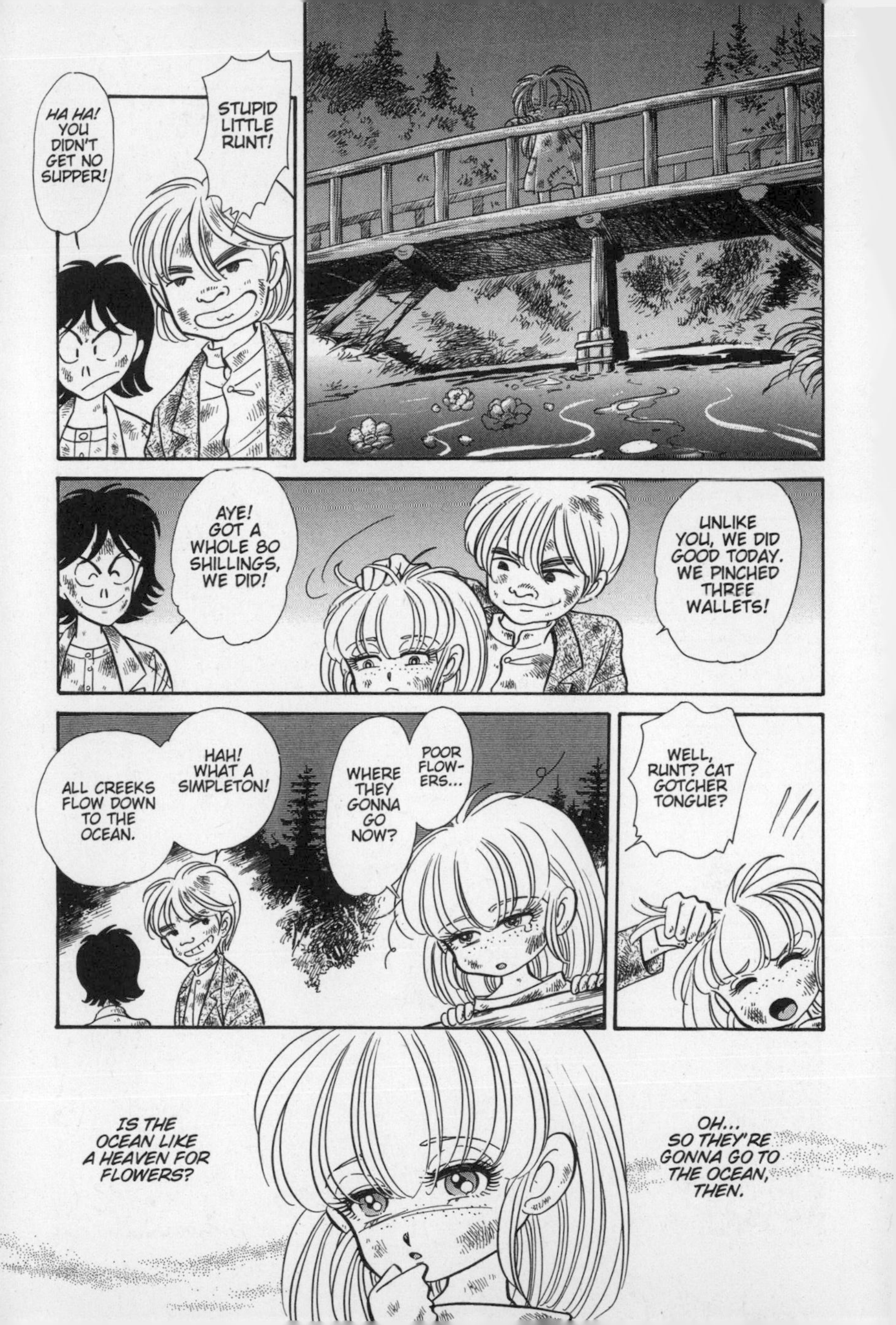
STUPID LITTLE RUNT!
HA HA! YOU DIDN'T GET NO SUPPER!
UNLIKE YOU, WE DID GOOD TODAY. WE PINCHED THREE WALLETS!
AYE! GOT A WHOLE 80 SHILLINGS, WE DID!
WELL, RUNT? CAT GOTCHER TONGUE?
POOR FLOWERS...
WHERE THEY GONNA GO NOW?
HAH! WHAT A SIMPLETON!
ALL CREEKS FLOW DOWN TO THE OCEAN.
OH... SO THEY'RE GONNA GO TO THE OCEAN, THEN.
IS THE OCEAN LIKE A HEAVEN FOR FLOWERS?

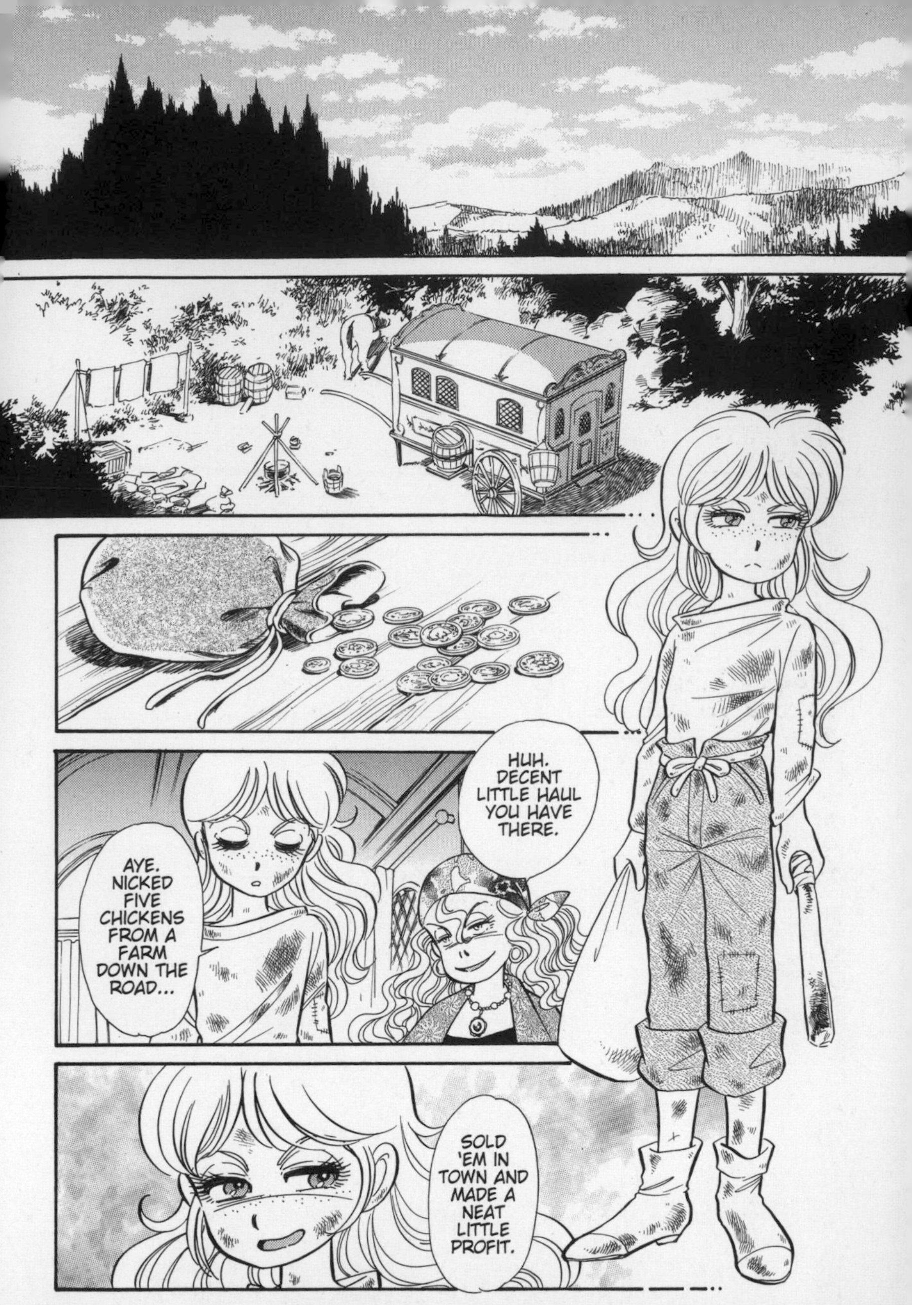
HUH. DECENT LITTLE HAUL YOU HAVE THERE.
AYE. NICKED FIVE CHICKENS FROM A FARM DOWN THE ROAD...
SOLD 'EM IN TOWN AND MADE A NEAT LITTLE PROFIT.

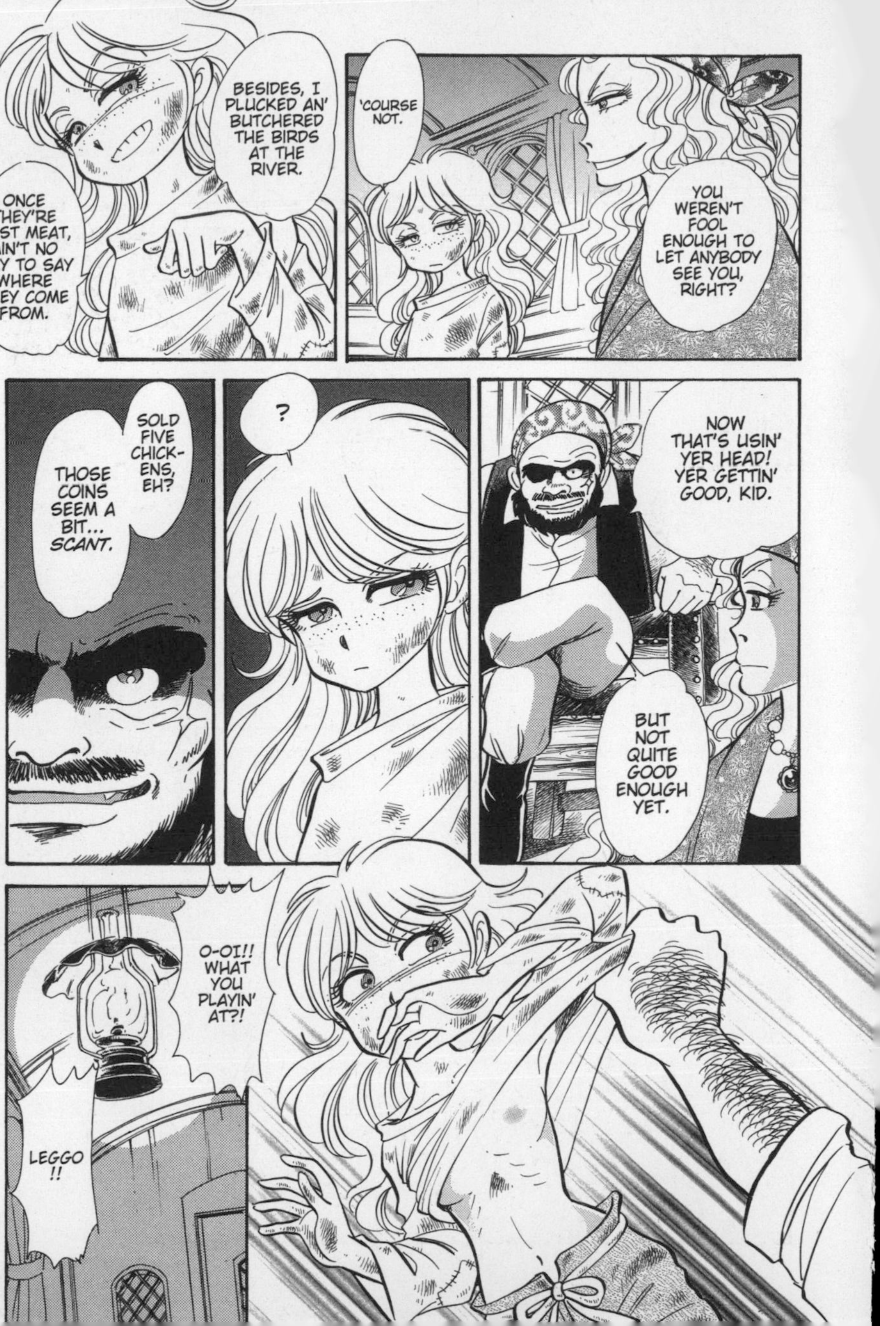
YOU WEREN'T FOOL ENOUGH TO LET ANYBODY SEE YOU, RIGHT?
'COURSE NOT.
BESIDES, I PLUCKED AN' BUTCHERED THE BIRDS AT THE RIVER.
ONCE THEY'RE JUST MEAT, AIN'T NO WAY TO SAY WHERE THEY COME FROM.
NOW THAT'S USIN' YER HEAD! YER GETTIN' GOOD, KID.
BUT NOT QUITE GOOD ENOUGH YET.
?
SOLD FIVE CHICK-ENS, EH?
THOSE COINS SEEM A BIT... *SCANT.*
O-OI!! WHAT YOU PLAYIN' AT?!
LEGGO !!

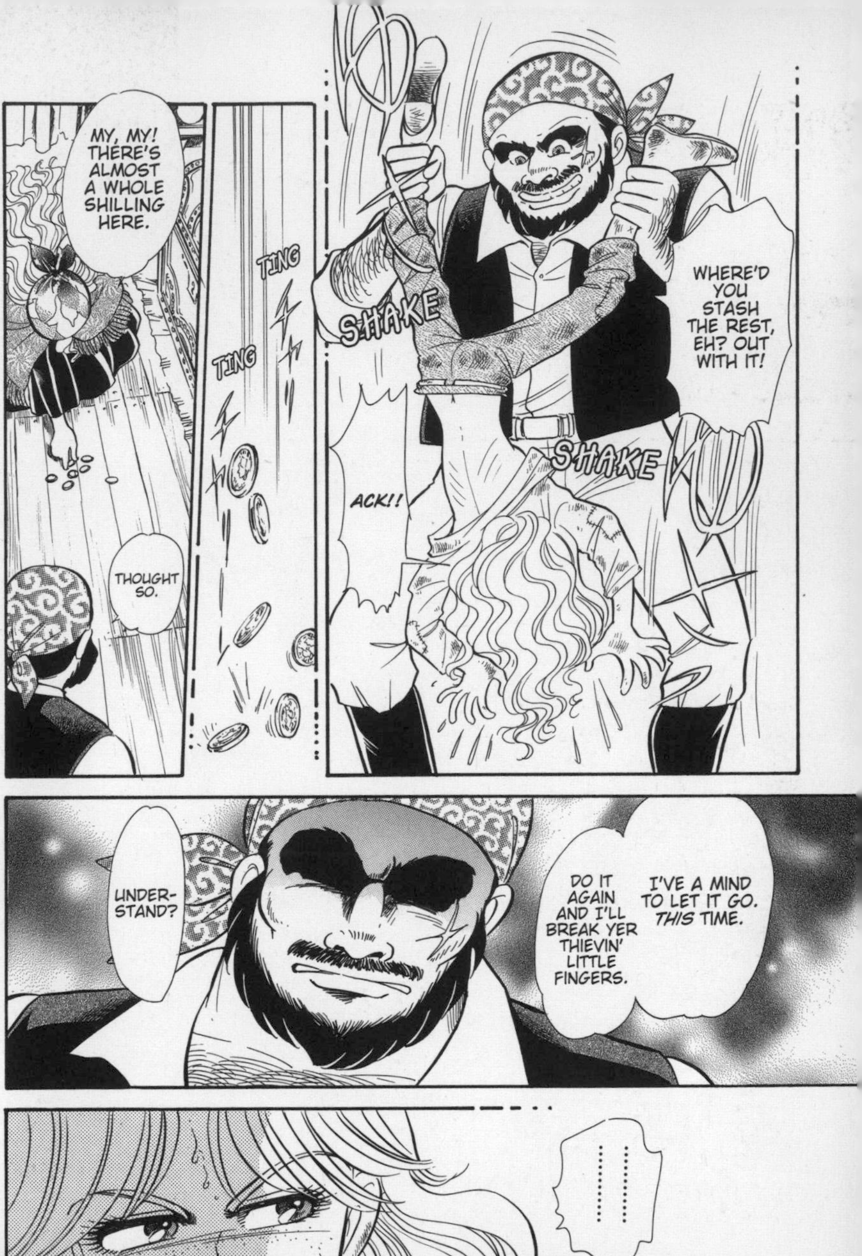
WHERE'D YOU STASH THE REST, EH? OUT WITH IT!
SHAKE
SHAKE
ACK!!
TING
TING
MY, MY! THERE'S ALMOST A WHOLE SHILLING HERE.
THOUGHT SO.
I'VE A MIND TO LET IT GO. *THIS* TIME.
DO IT AGAIN AND I'LL BREAK YER THIEVIN' LITTLE FINGERS.
UNDER-STAND?
……

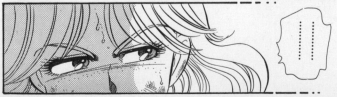

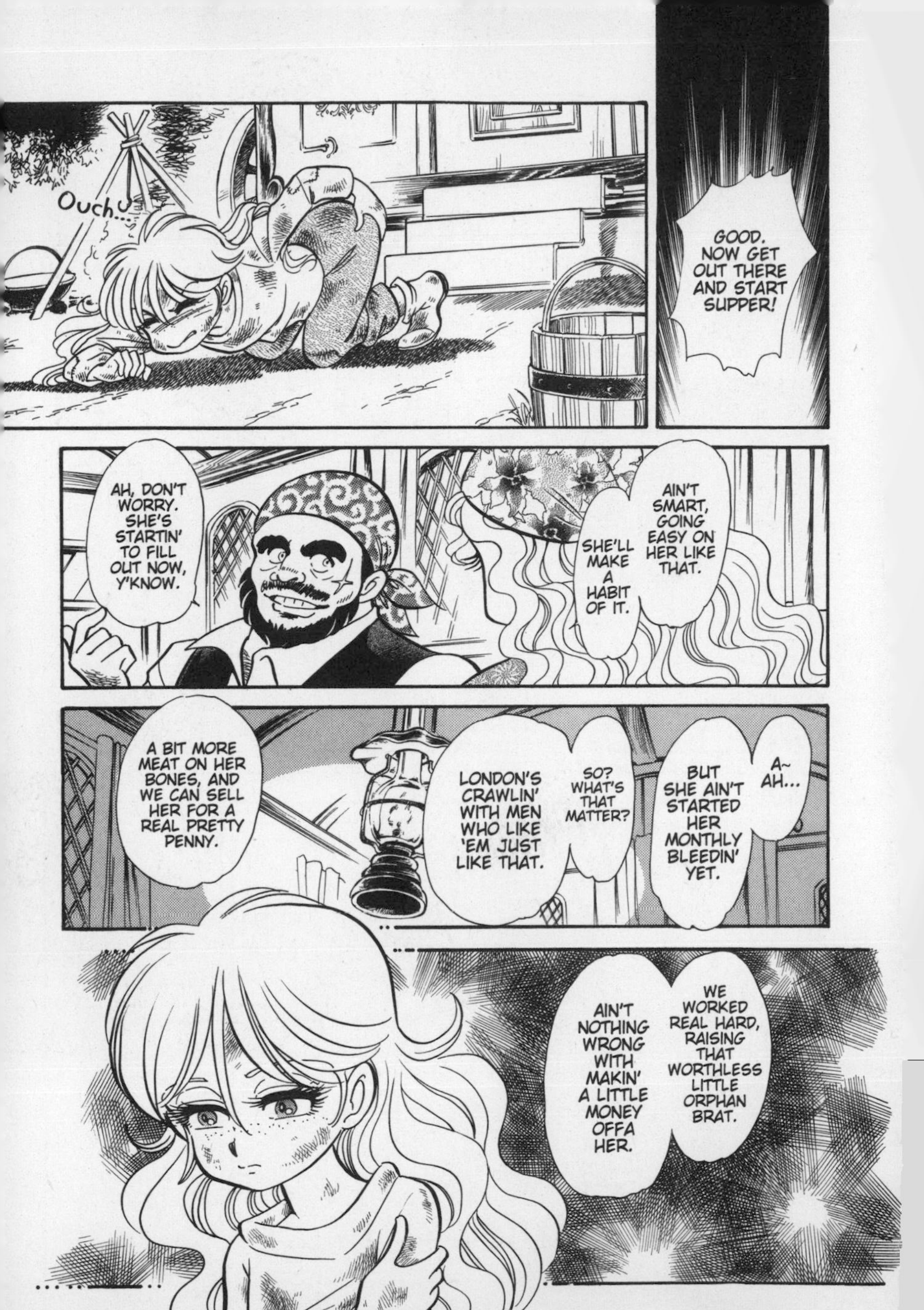
GOOD. NOW GET OUT THERE AND START SUPPER!
Ouch...
AIN'T SMART, GOING EASY ON HER LIKE THAT.
SHE'LL MAKE A HABIT OF IT.
AH, DON'T WORRY. SHE'S STARTIN' TO FILL OUT NOW, Y'KNOW.
A~ AH...
BUT SHE AIN'T STARTED HER MONTHLY BLEEDIN' YET.
SO? WHAT'S THAT MATTER?
LONDON'S CRAWLIN' WITH MEN WHO LIKE 'EM JUST LIKE THAT.
A BIT MORE MEAT ON HER BONES, AND WE CAN SELL HER FOR A REAL PRETTY PENNY.
WE WORKED REAL HARD, RAISING THAT WORTHLESS LITTLE ORPHAN BRAT.
AIN'T NOTHING WRONG WITH MAKIN' A LITTLE MONEY OFFA HER.

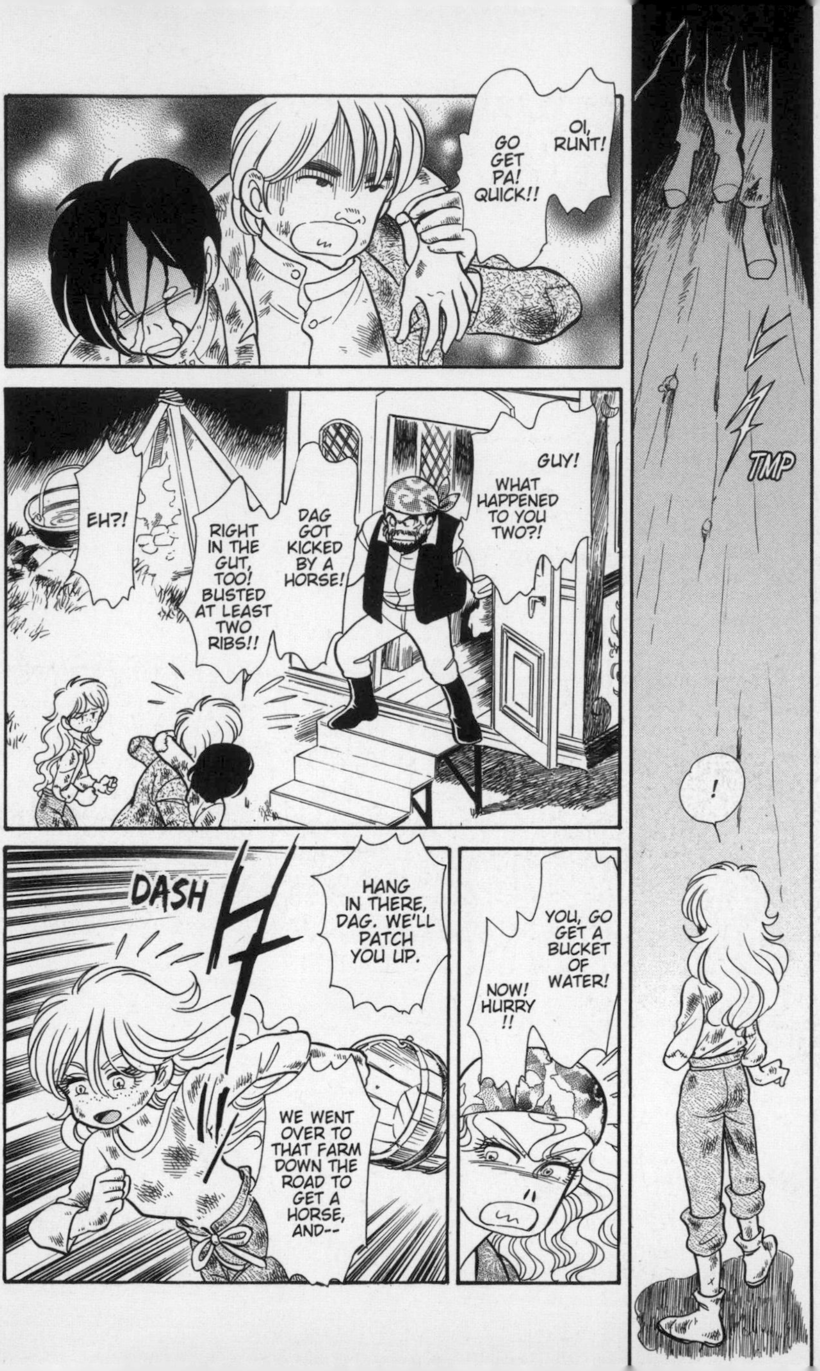
TMP
!
OI, RUNT!
GO GET PA! QUICK!!
GUY! WHAT HAPPENED TO YOU TWO?!
DAG GOT KICKED BY A HORSE!
RIGHT IN THE GUT, TOO! BUSTED AT LEAST TWO RIBS!!
EH?!
YOU, GO GET A BUCKET OF WATER!
NOW! HURRY!!
HANG IN THERE, DAG. WE'LL PATCH YOU UP.
DASH
WE WENT OVER TO THAT FARM DOWN THE ROAD TO GET A HORSE, AND--

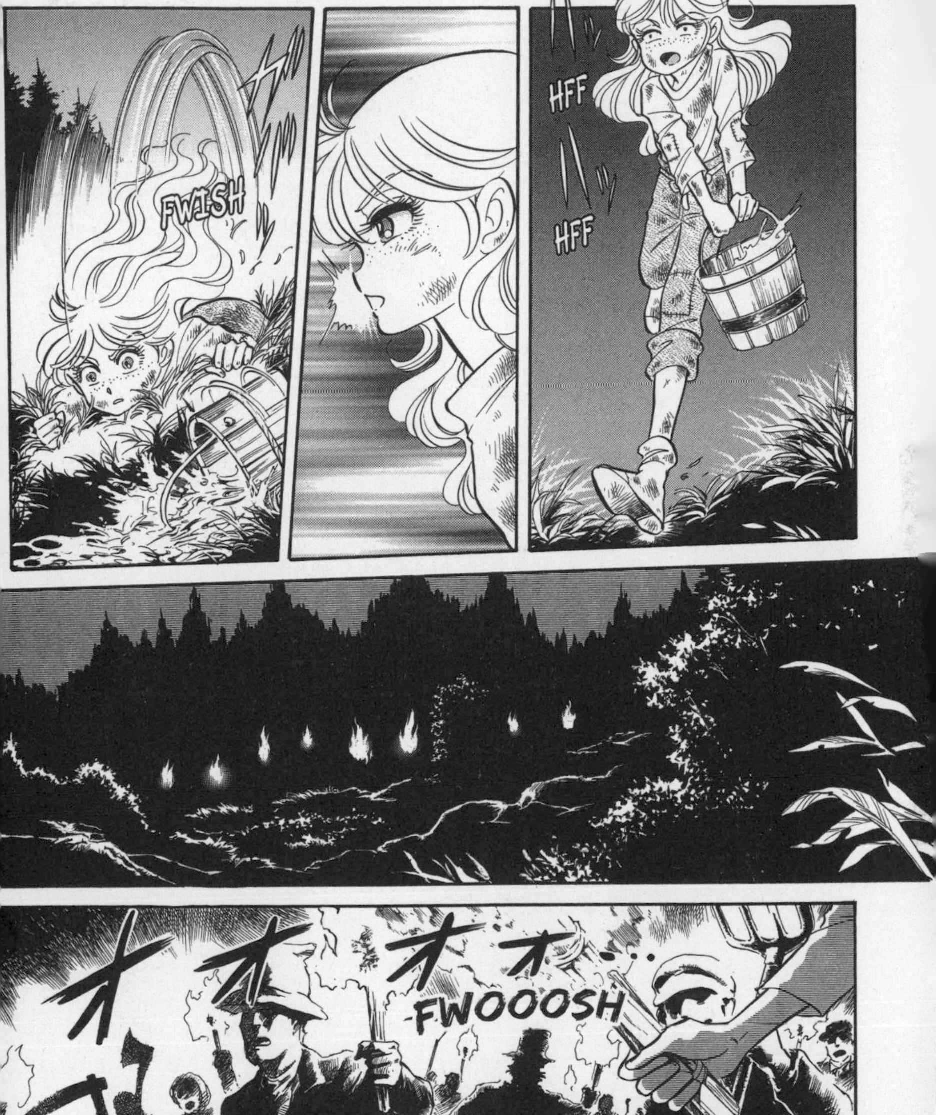
HFF
HFF
FWISH
オオオオ…
FWOOOSH

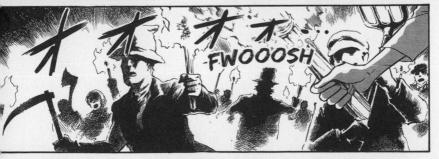

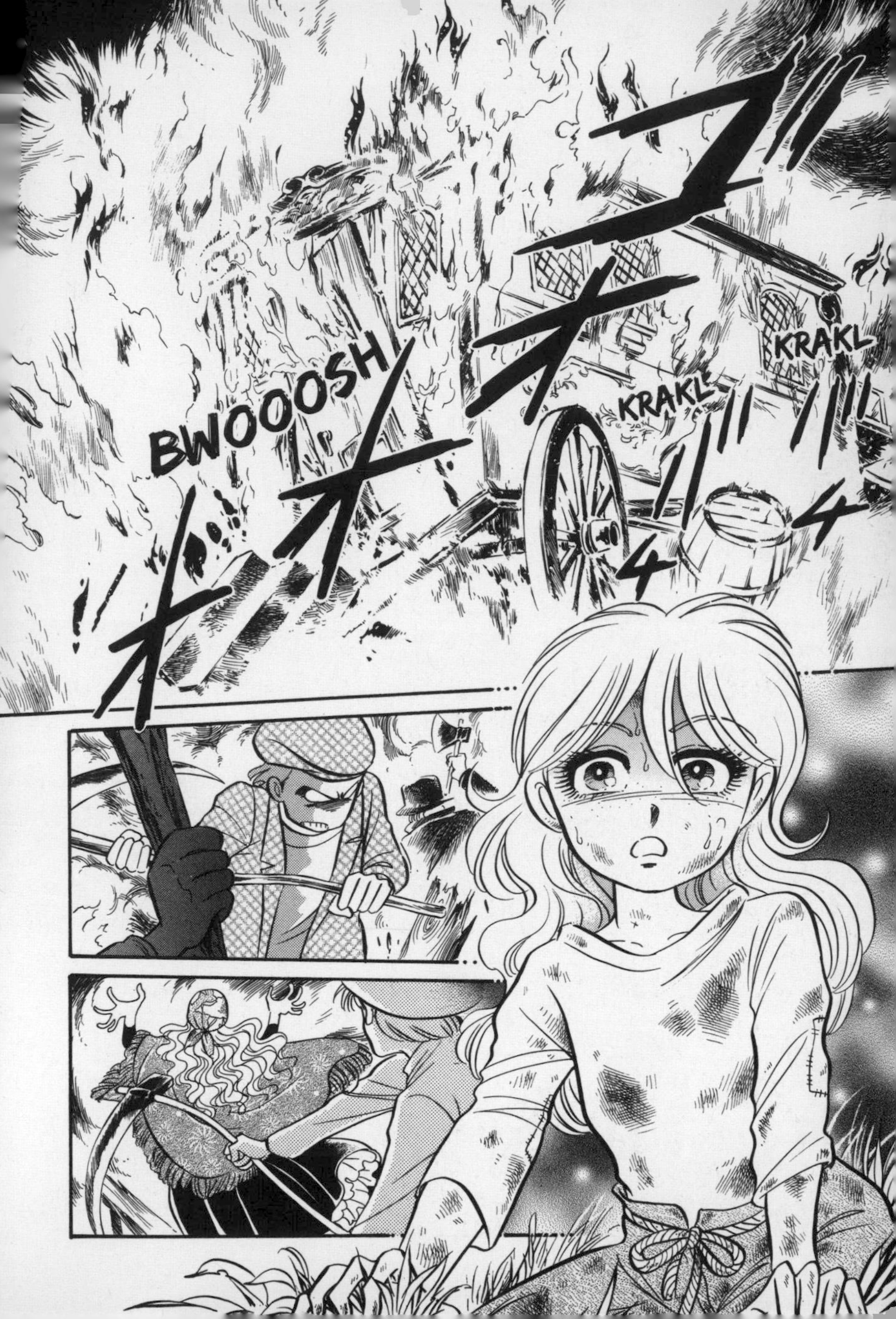
BWOOOSH
KRAKL
KRAKL

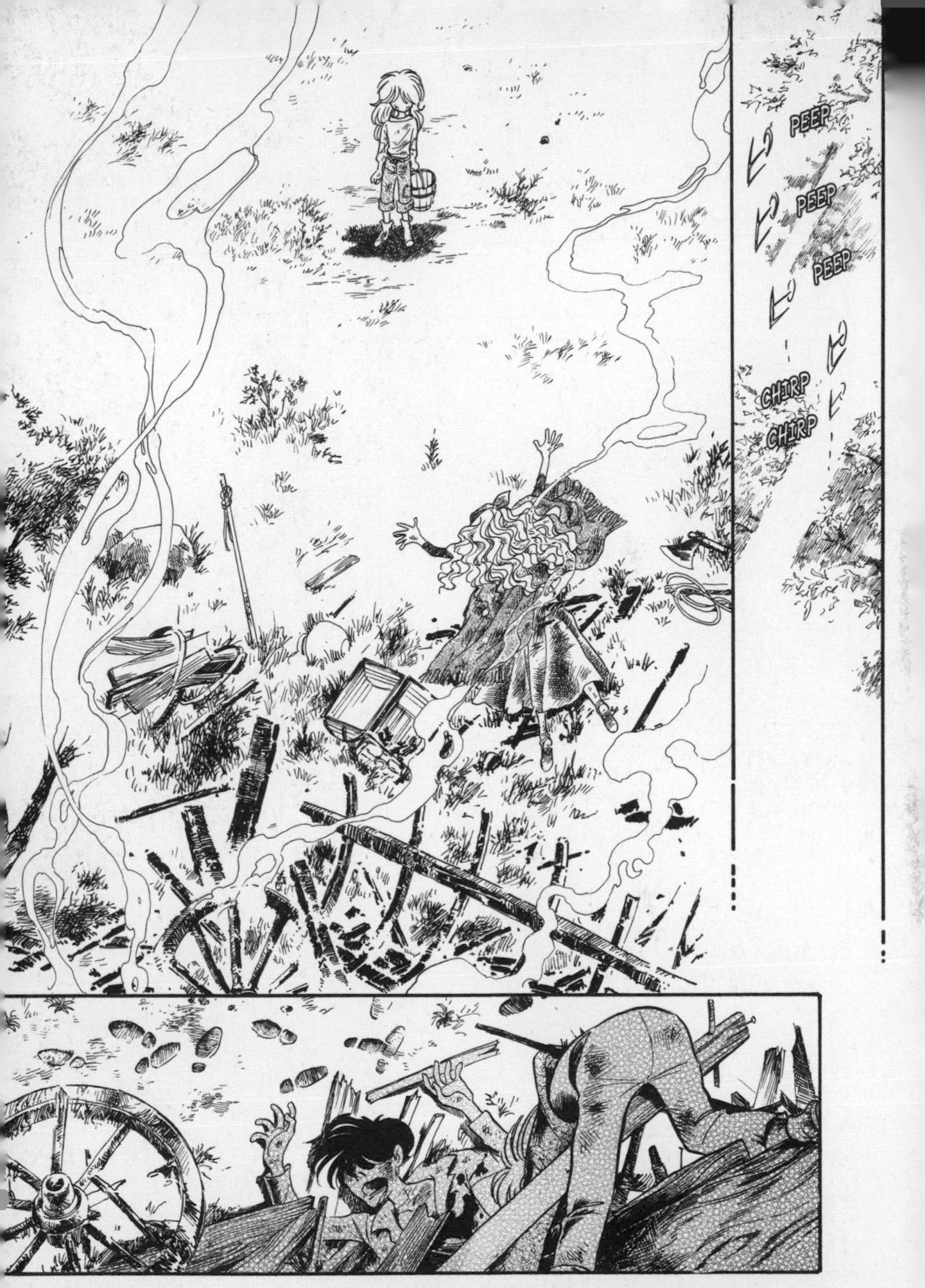
PEEP
PEEP
PEEP
CHIRP
CHIRP

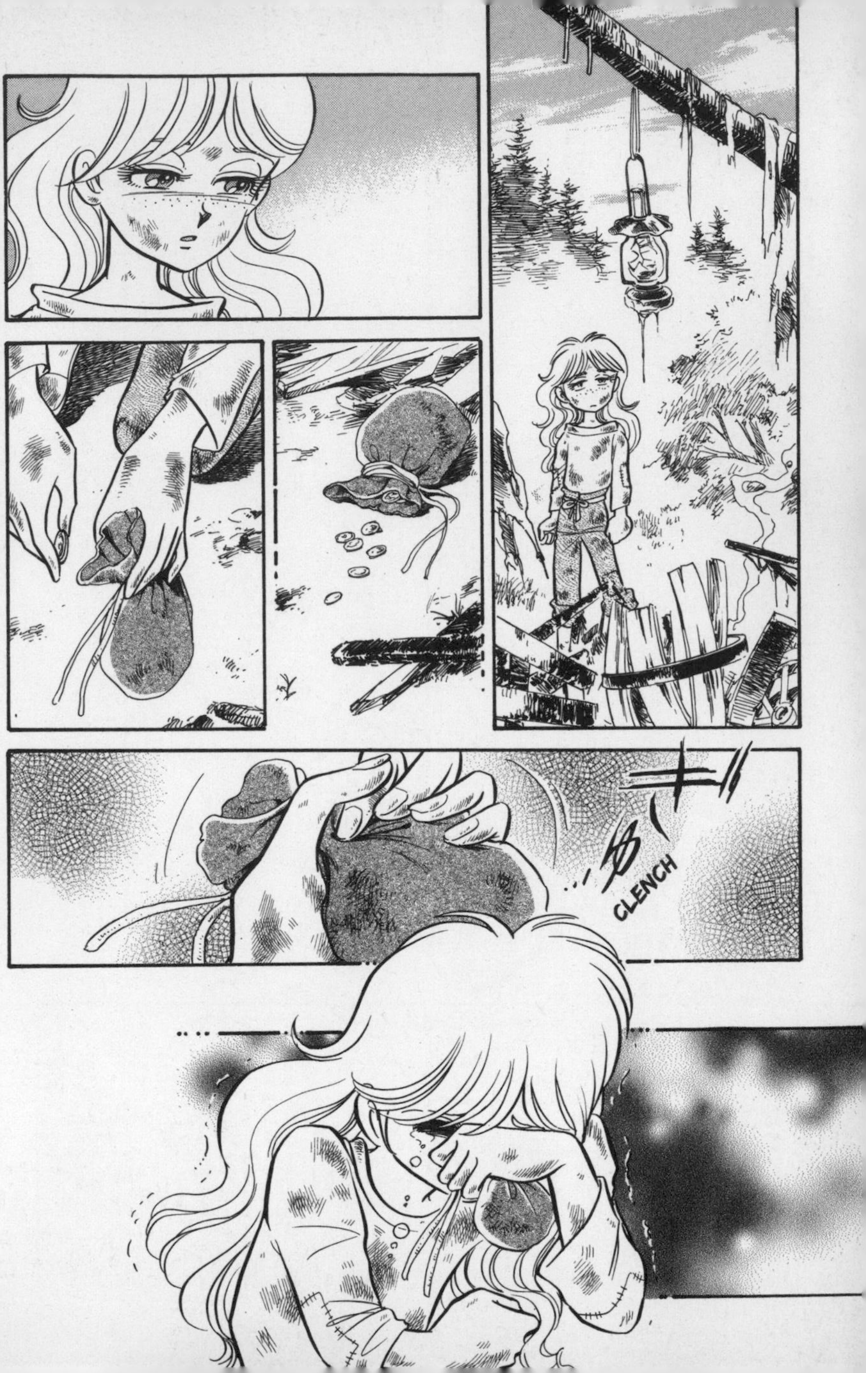
CLENCH

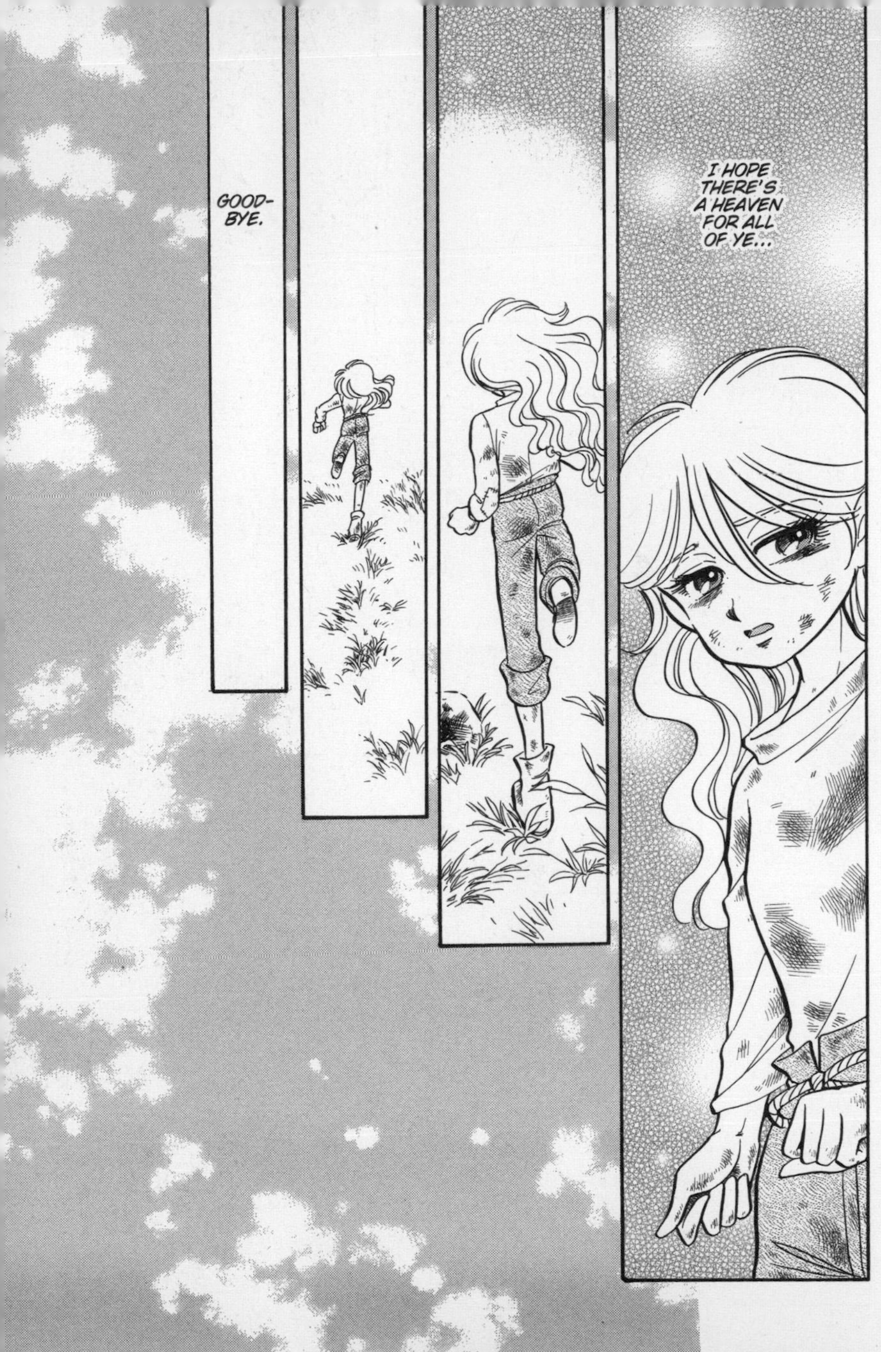
I HOPE THERE'S A HEAVEN FOR ALL OF YE...
GOOD-BYE.

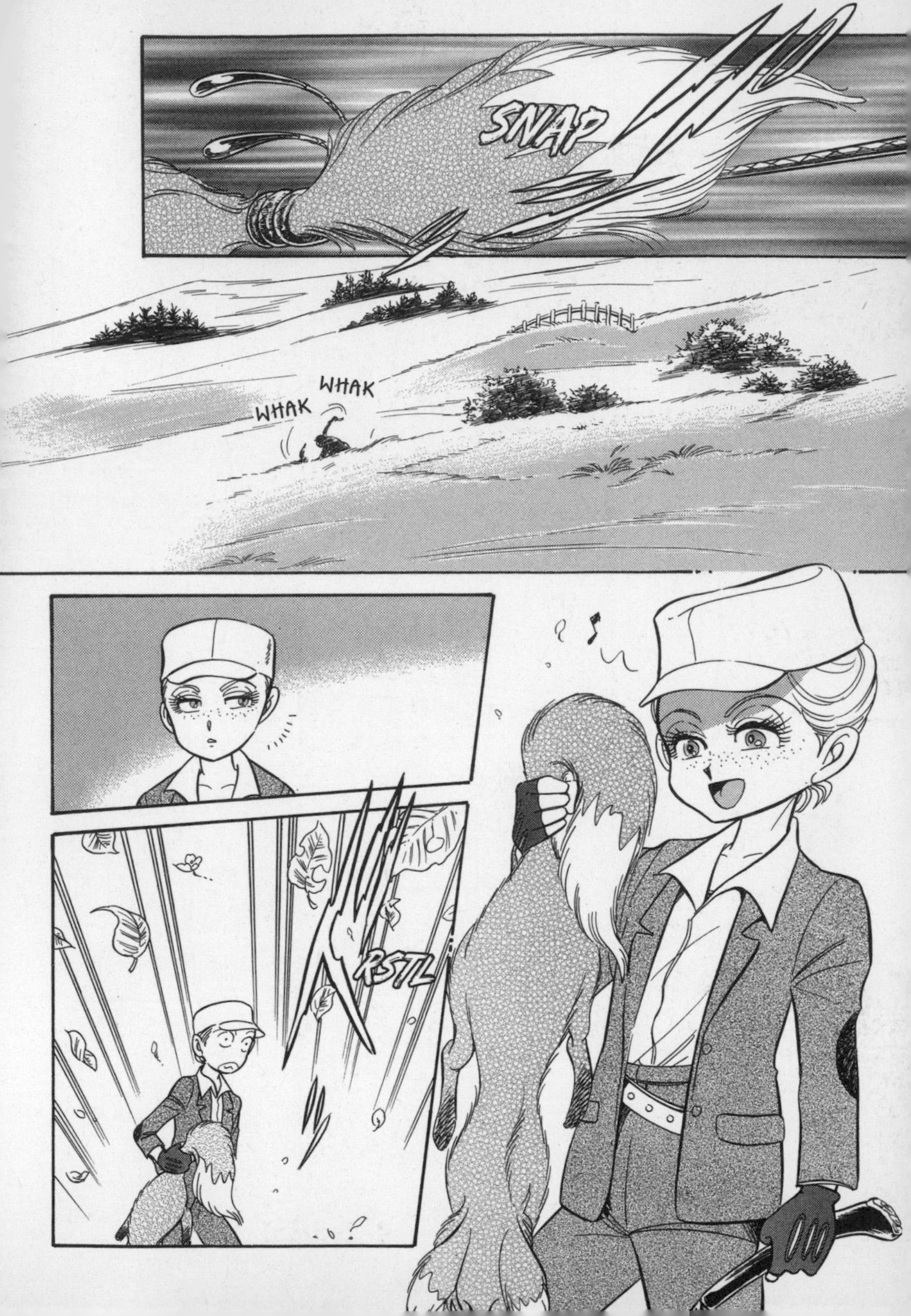
SNAP
WHAK
WHAK
RSTL

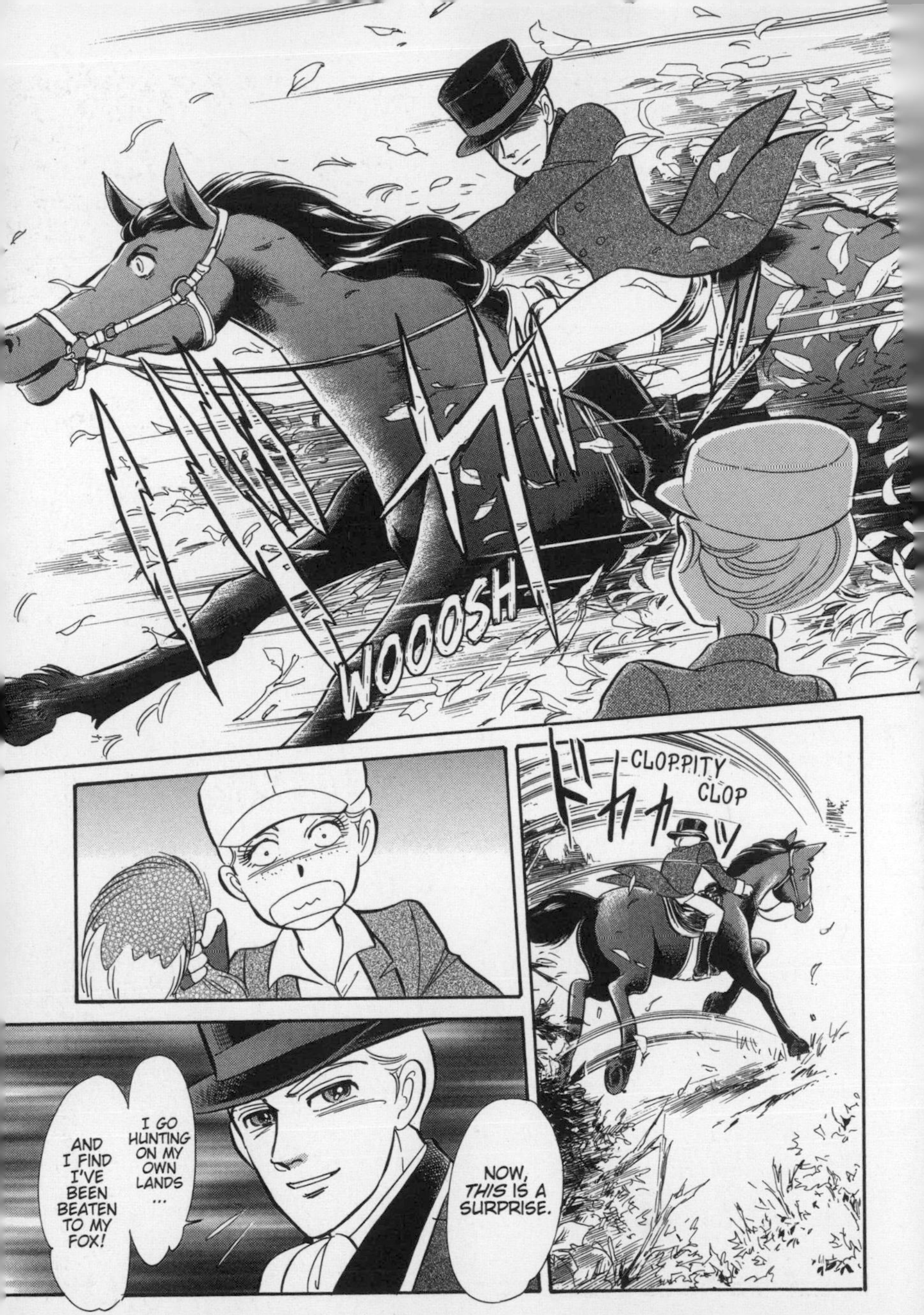
WOOOSH
ドカカッ
CLOPPITY CLOP
NOW, *THIS* IS A SURPRISE.
I GO HUNTING ON MY OWN LANDS ...
AND I FIND I'VE BEEN BEATEN TO MY FOX!

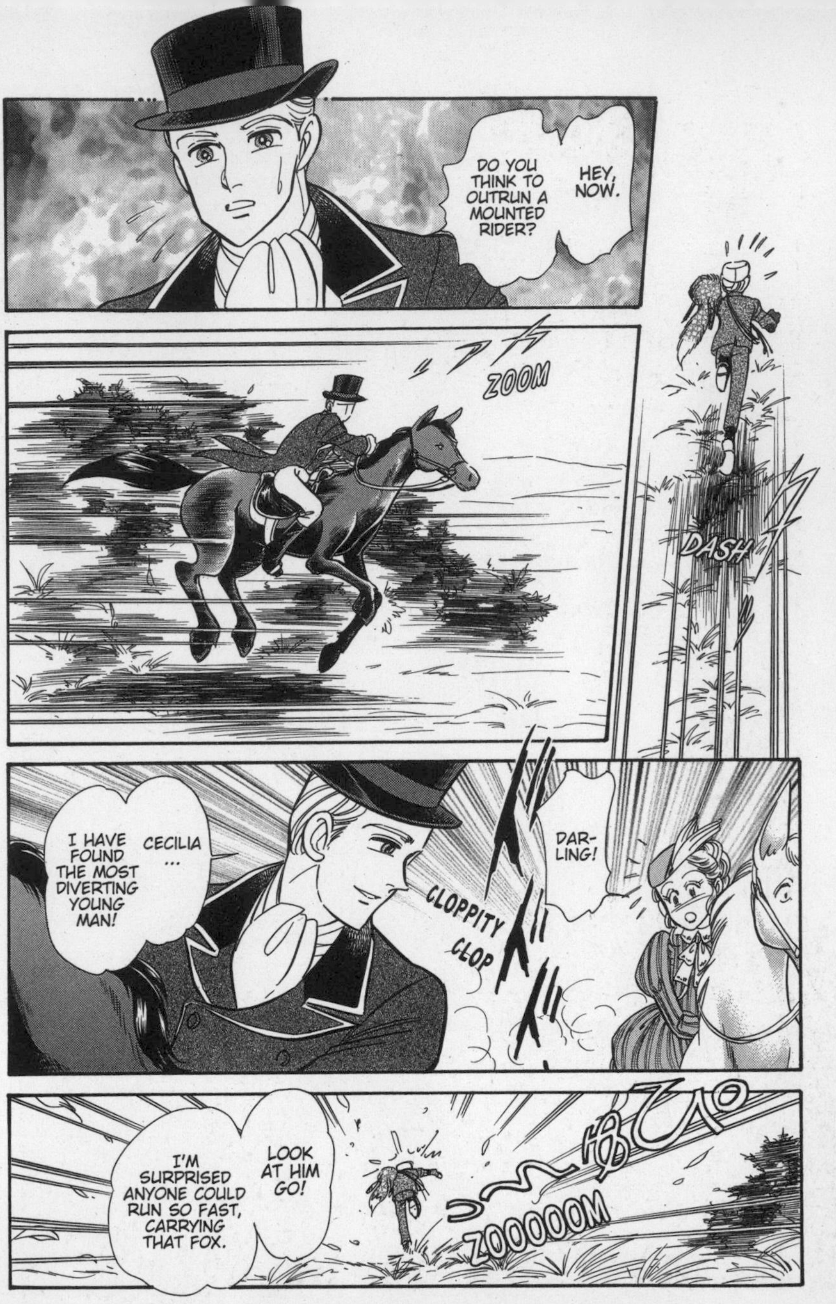
HEY, NOW.
DO YOU THINK TO OUTRUN A MOUNTED RIDER?
DASH
ZOOM
DAR-LING!
CLOPPITY CLOP
CECILIA...
I HAVE FOUND THE MOST DIVERTING YOUNG MAN!
ZOOOOOM
LOOK AT HIM GO!
I'M SURPRISED ANYONE COULD RUN SO FAST, CARRYING THAT FOX.

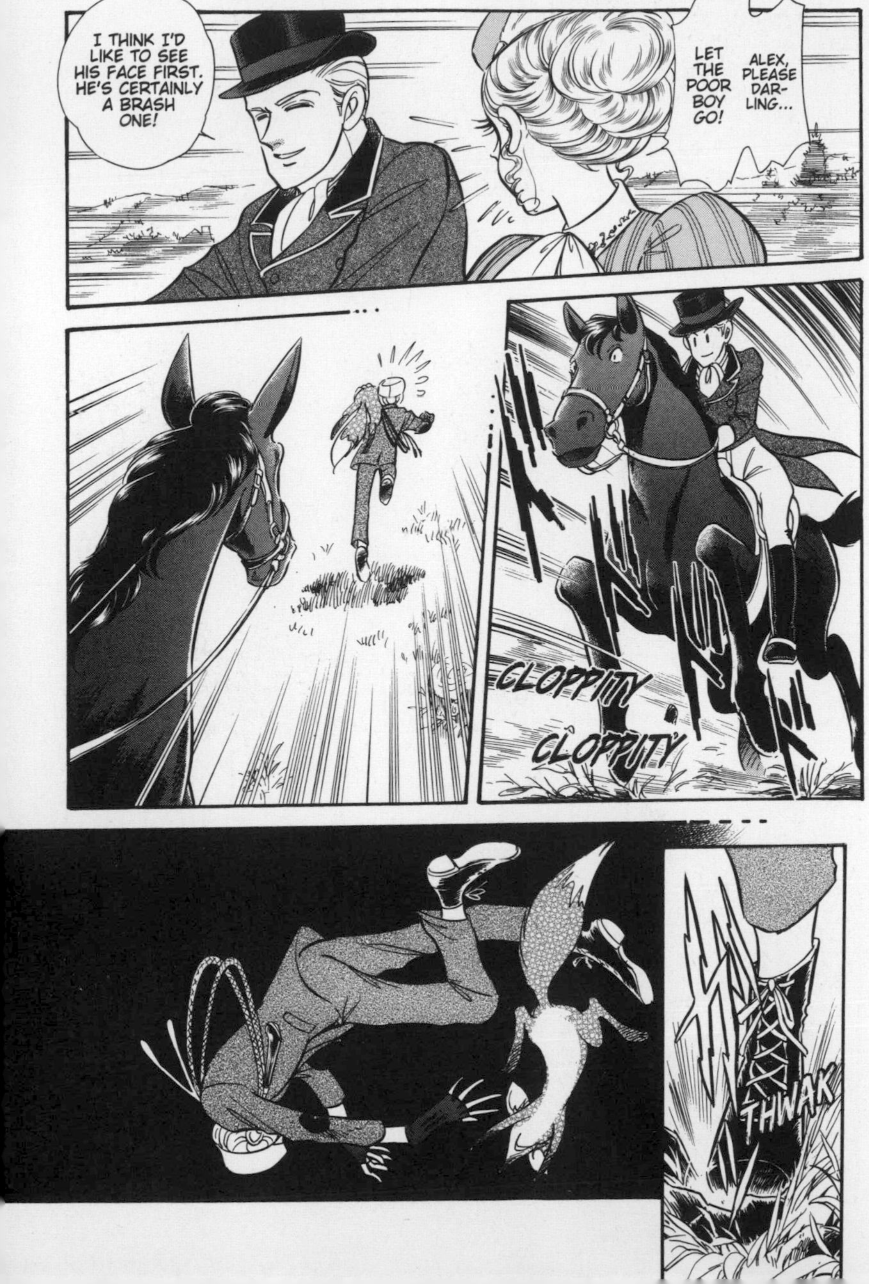
ALEX, PLEASE DARLING...
LET THE POOR BOY GO!
I THINK I'D LIKE TO SEE HIS FACE FIRST. HE'S CERTAINLY A BRASH ONE!
CLOPPITY CLOPPITY
THWAK

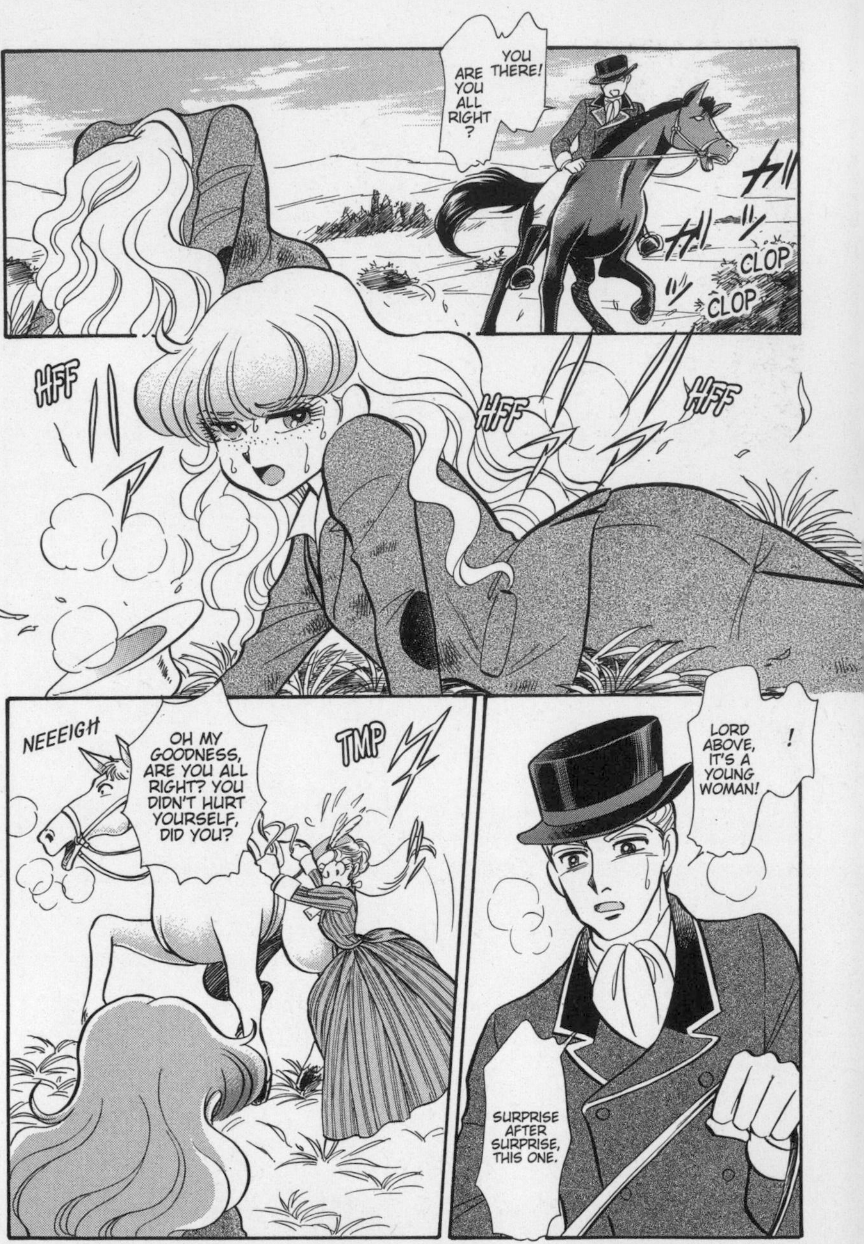
YOU THERE! ARE YOU ALL RIGHT?
CLOP
CLOP
HFF
HFF
HFF
!
LORD ABOVE, IT'S A YOUNG WOMAN!
SURPRISE AFTER SURPRISE, THIS ONE.
TMP
OH MY GOODNESS, ARE YOU ALL RIGHT? YOU DIDN'T HURT YOURSELF, DID YOU?
NEEEIGH

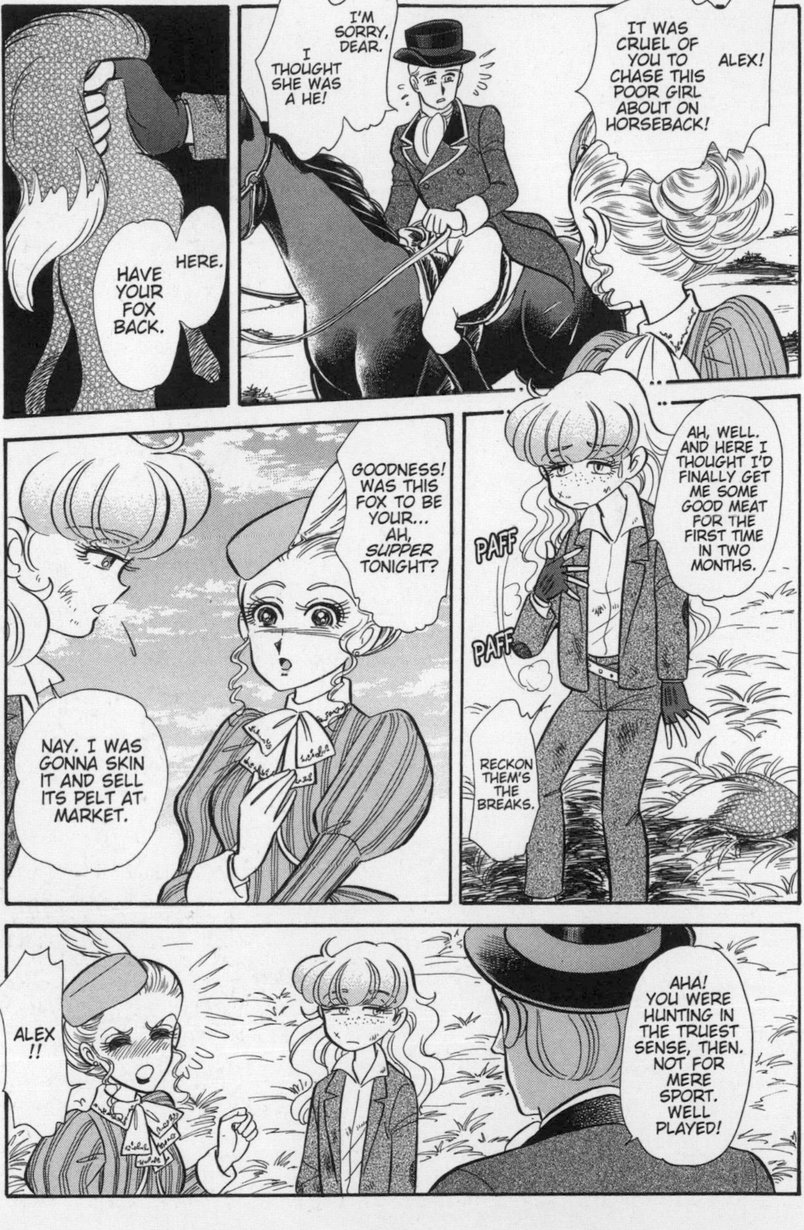
ALEX!
IT WAS CRUEL OF YOU TO CHASE THIS POOR GIRL ABOUT ON HORSEBACK!
I'M SORRY, DEAR.
I THOUGHT SHE WAS A HE!
HERE.
HAVE YOUR FOX BACK.
AH, WELL. AND HERE I THOUGHT I'D FINALLY GET ME SOME GOOD MEAT FOR THE FIRST TIME IN TWO MONTHS.
PAFF
PAFF
RECKON THEM'S THE BREAKS.
GOODNESS! WAS THIS FOX TO BE YOUR... AH, *SUPPER* TONIGHT?
NAY. I WAS GONNA SKIN IT AND SELL ITS PELT AT MARKET.
AHA! YOU WERE HUNTING IN THE TRUEST SENSE, THEN. NOT FOR MERE SPORT. WELL PLAYED!
ALEX !!

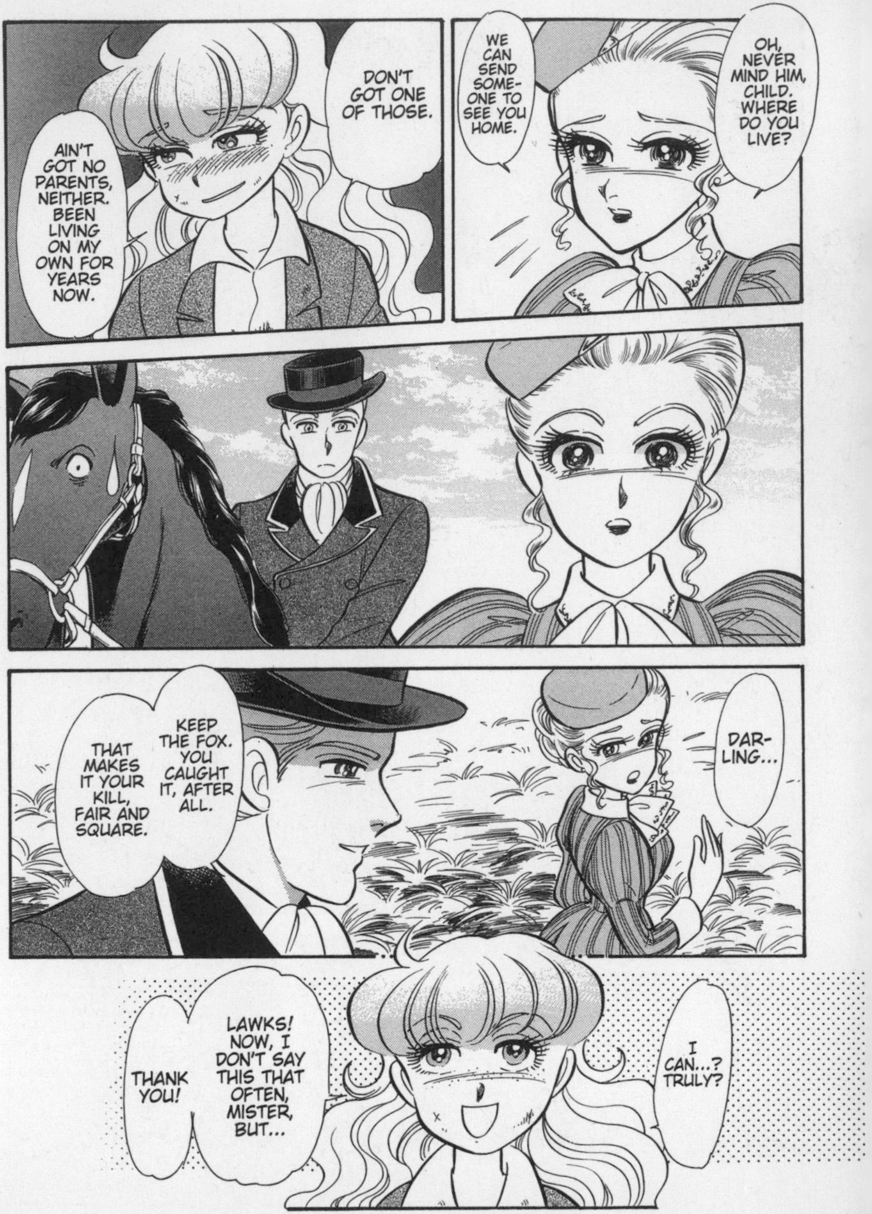
OH, NEVER MIND HIM, CHILD. WHERE DO YOU LIVE?
WE CAN SEND SOME-ONE TO SEE YOU HOME.
DON'T GOT ONE OF THOSE.
AIN'T GOT NO PARENTS, NEITHER. BEEN LIVING ON MY OWN FOR YEARS NOW.
DAR-LING...
KEEP THE FOX. YOU CAUGHT IT, AFTER ALL.
THAT MAKES IT YOUR KILL, FAIR AND SQUARE.
I CAN...? TRULY?
LAWKS! NOW, I DON'T SAY THIS THAT OFTEN, MISTER, BUT...
THANK YOU!

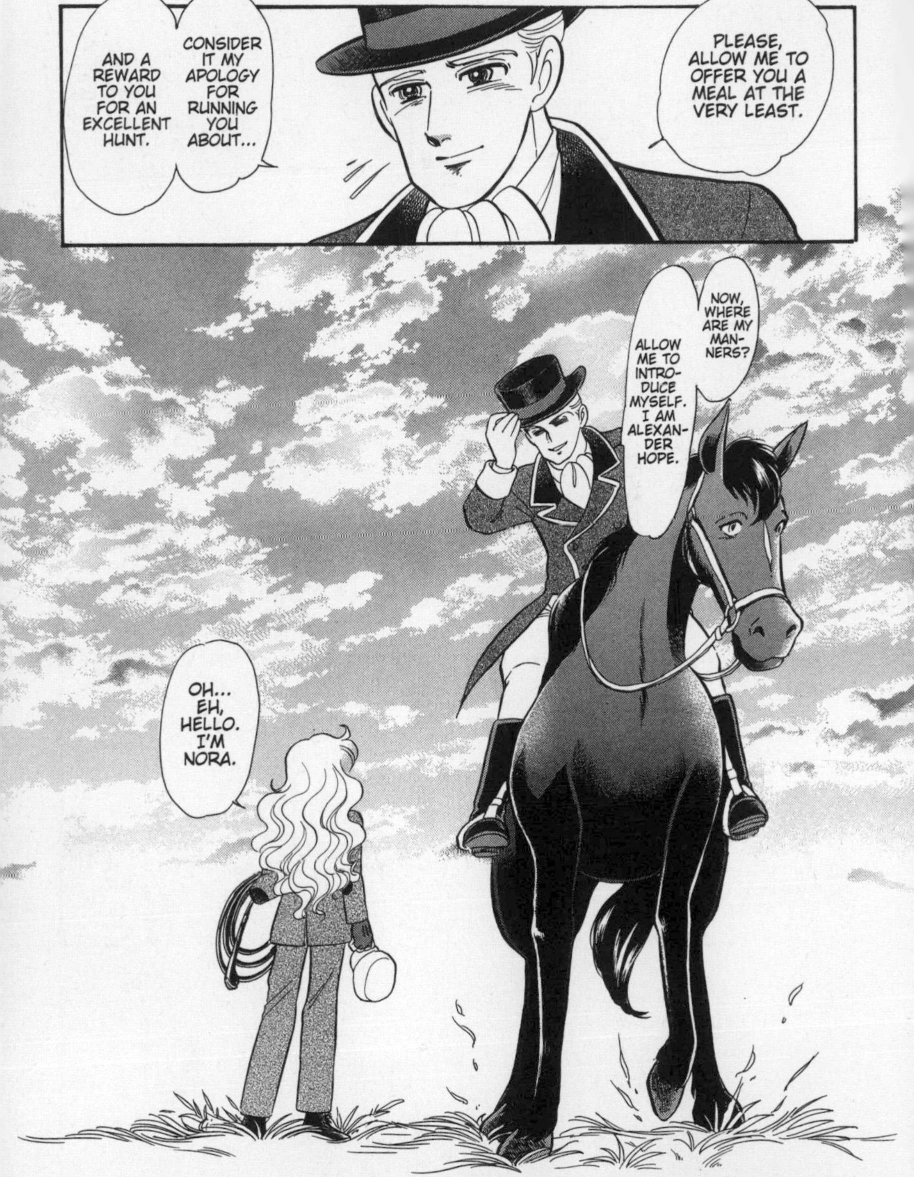
PLEASE, ALLOW ME TO OFFER YOU A MEAL AT THE VERY LEAST.
CONSIDER IT MY APOLOGY FOR RUNNING YOU ABOUT...
AND A REWARD TO YOU FOR AN EXCELLENT HUNT.
NOW, WHERE ARE MY MAN-NERS?
ALLOW ME TO INTRO-DUCE MYSELF. I AM ALEXAN-DER HOPE.
OH... EH, HELLO. I'M NORA.

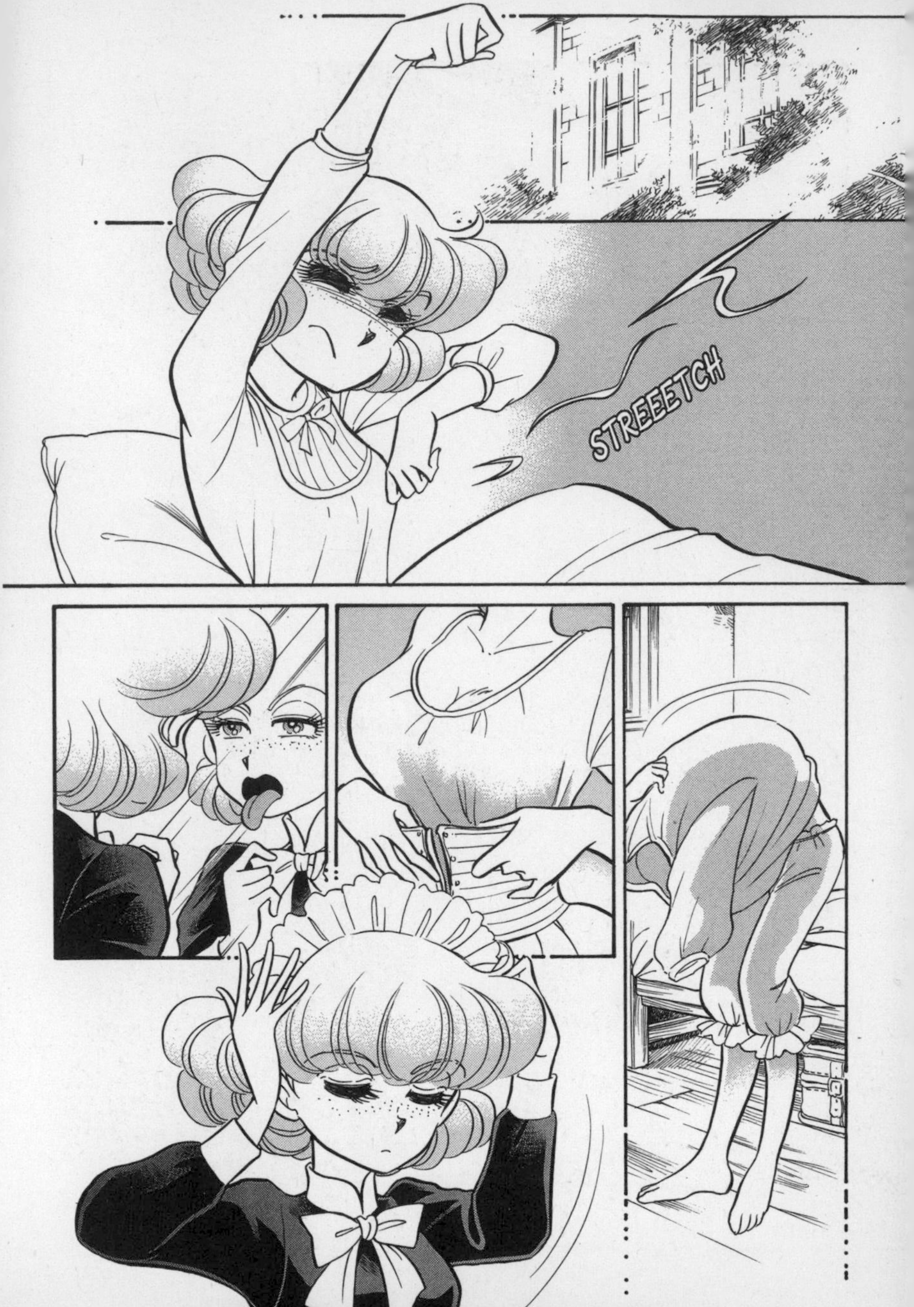
STREEETCH

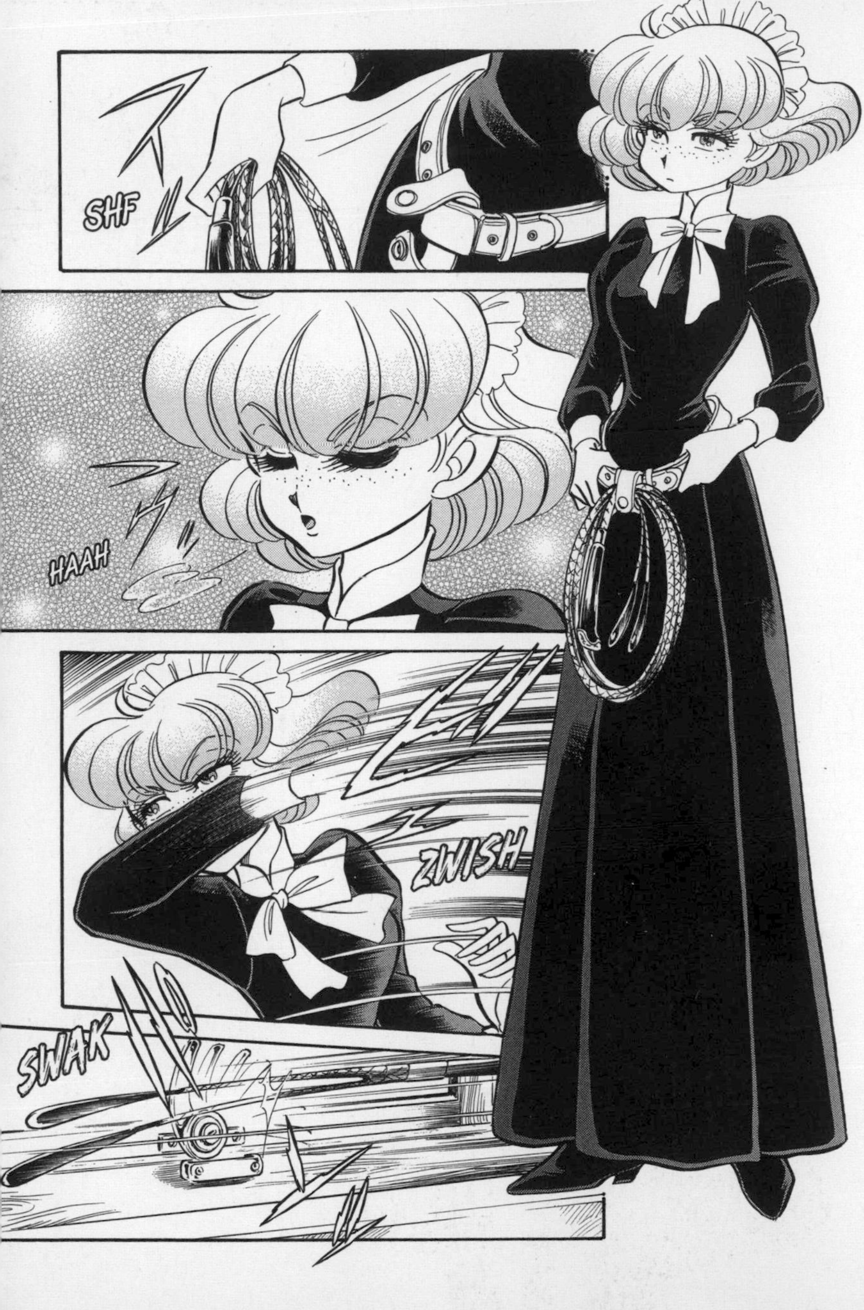
SHF
HAAH
ZWISH
SWAK

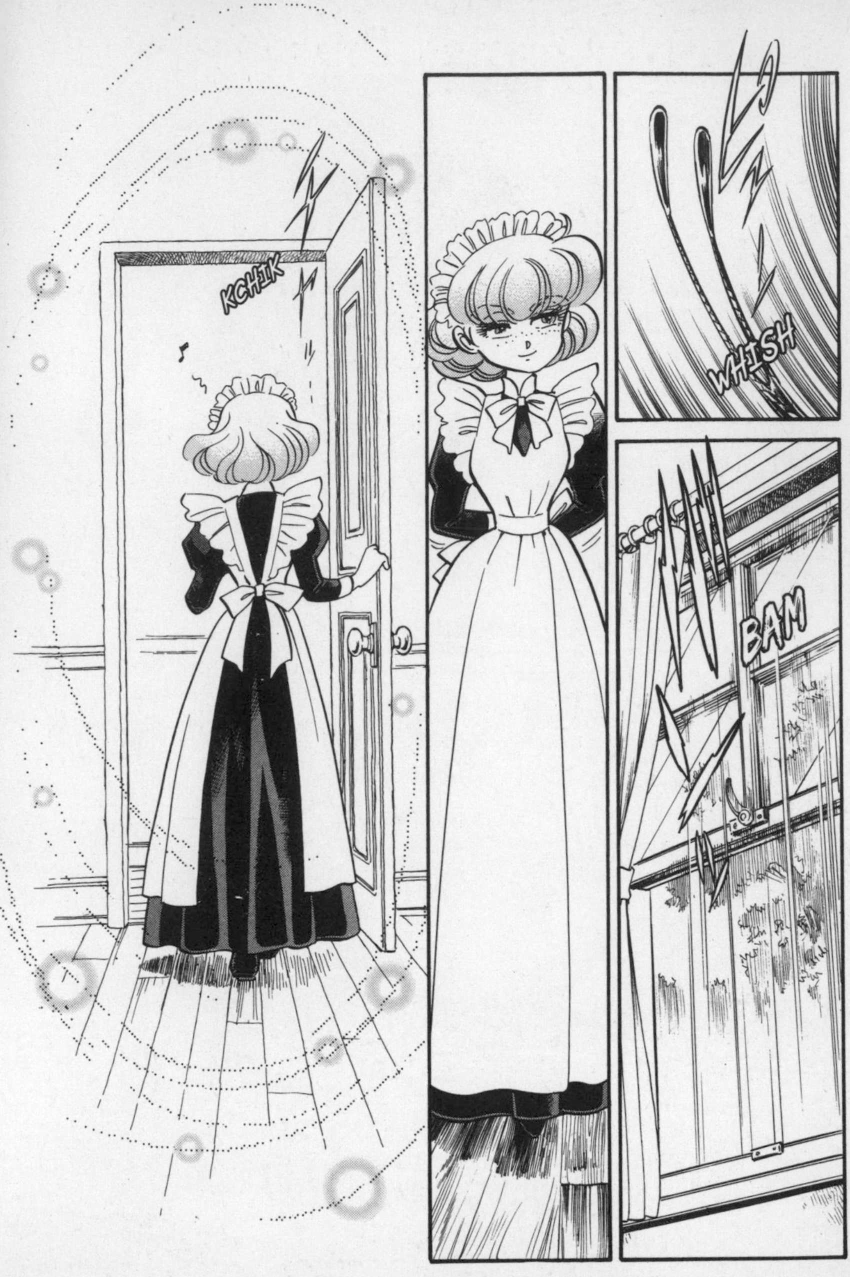
WHISH
BAM
KCHIK

The Five Orange Pips (1)

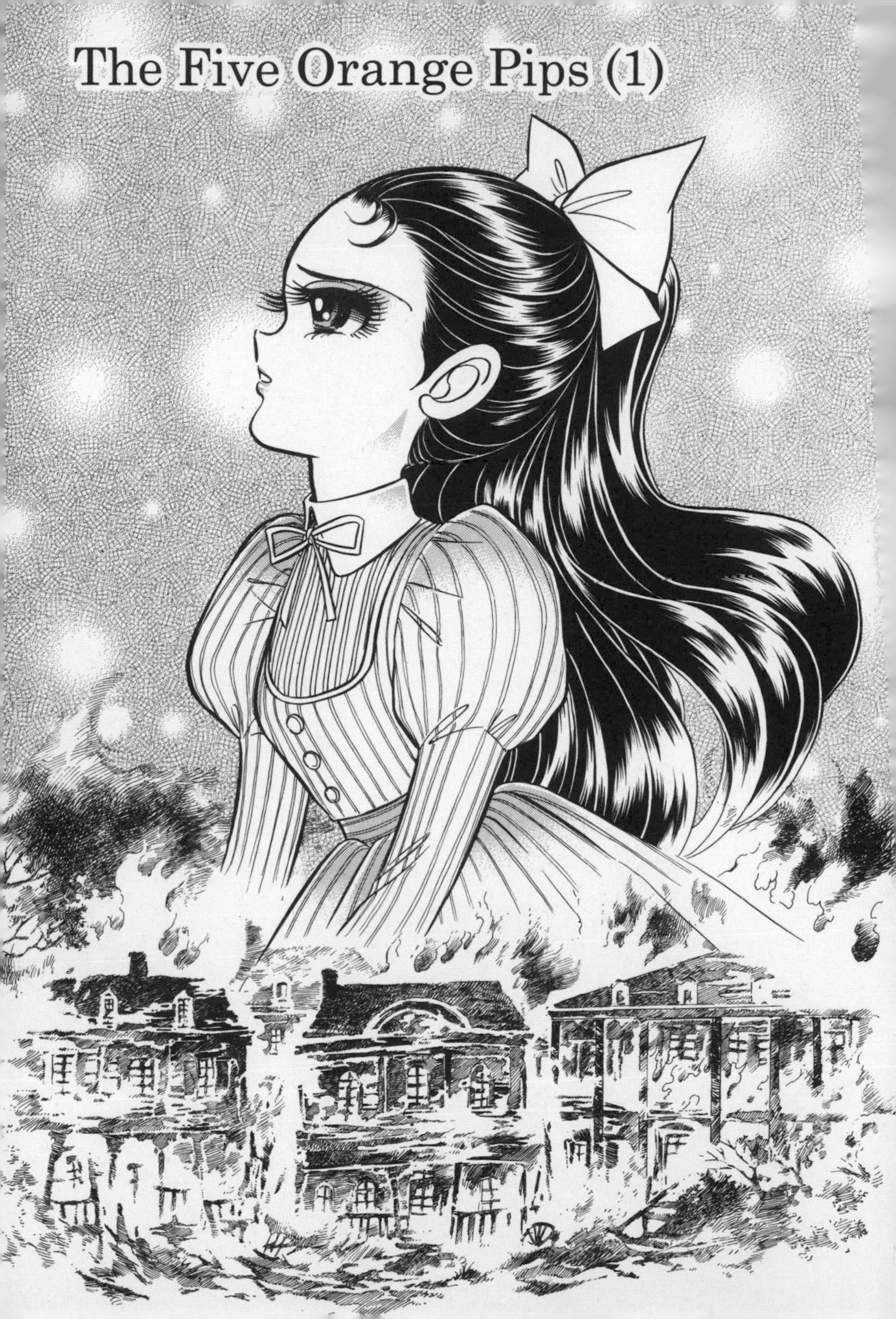

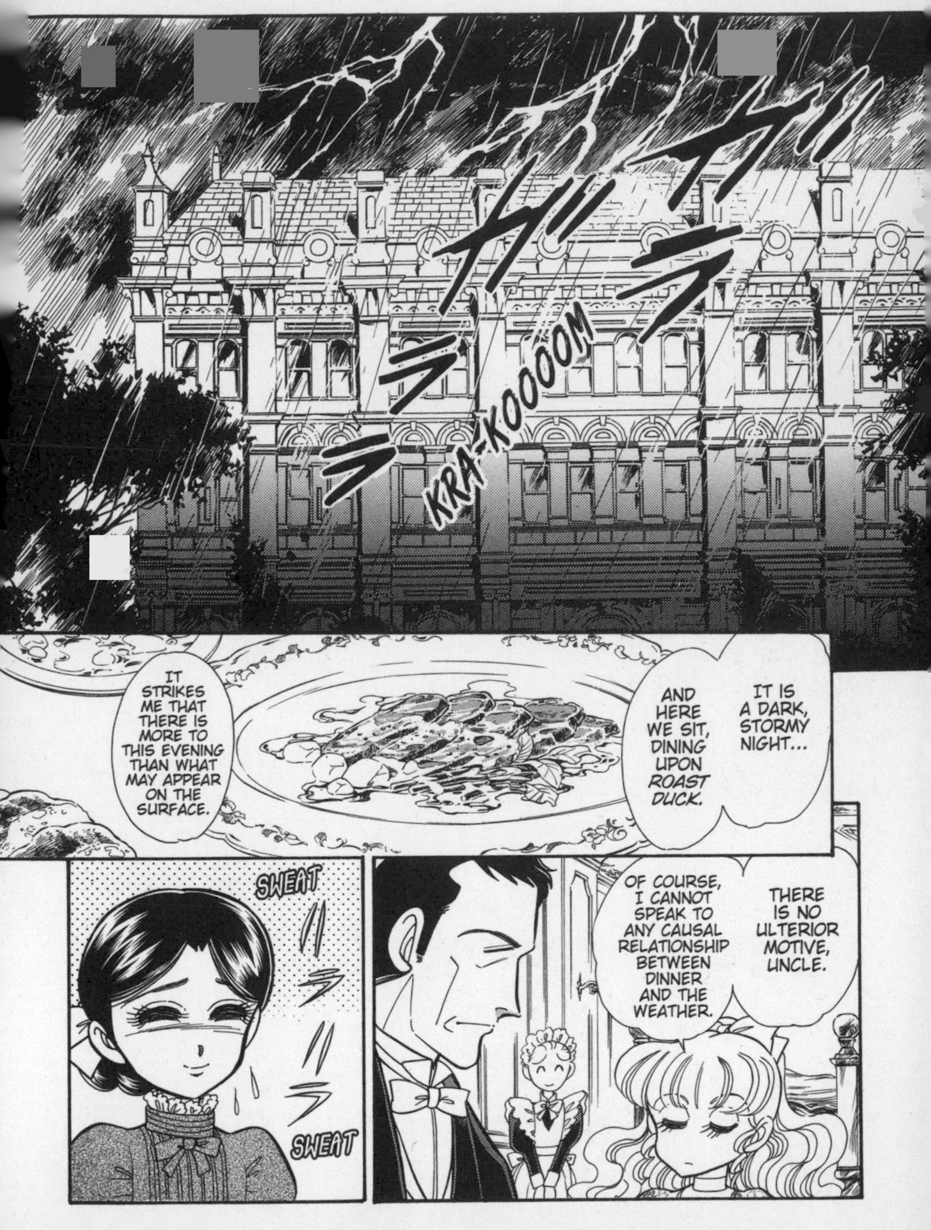
KRA-KOOOOM
IT IS A DARK, STORMY NIGHT...
AND HERE WE SIT, DINING UPON *ROAST DUCK.*
IT STRIKES ME THAT THERE IS MORE TO THIS EVENING THAN WHAT MAY APPEAR ON THE SURFACE.
THERE IS NO ULTERIOR MOTIVE, UNCLE.
OF COURSE, I CANNOT SPEAK TO ANY CAUSAL RELATIONSHIP BETWEEN DINNER AND THE WEATHER.
SWEAT
SWEAT

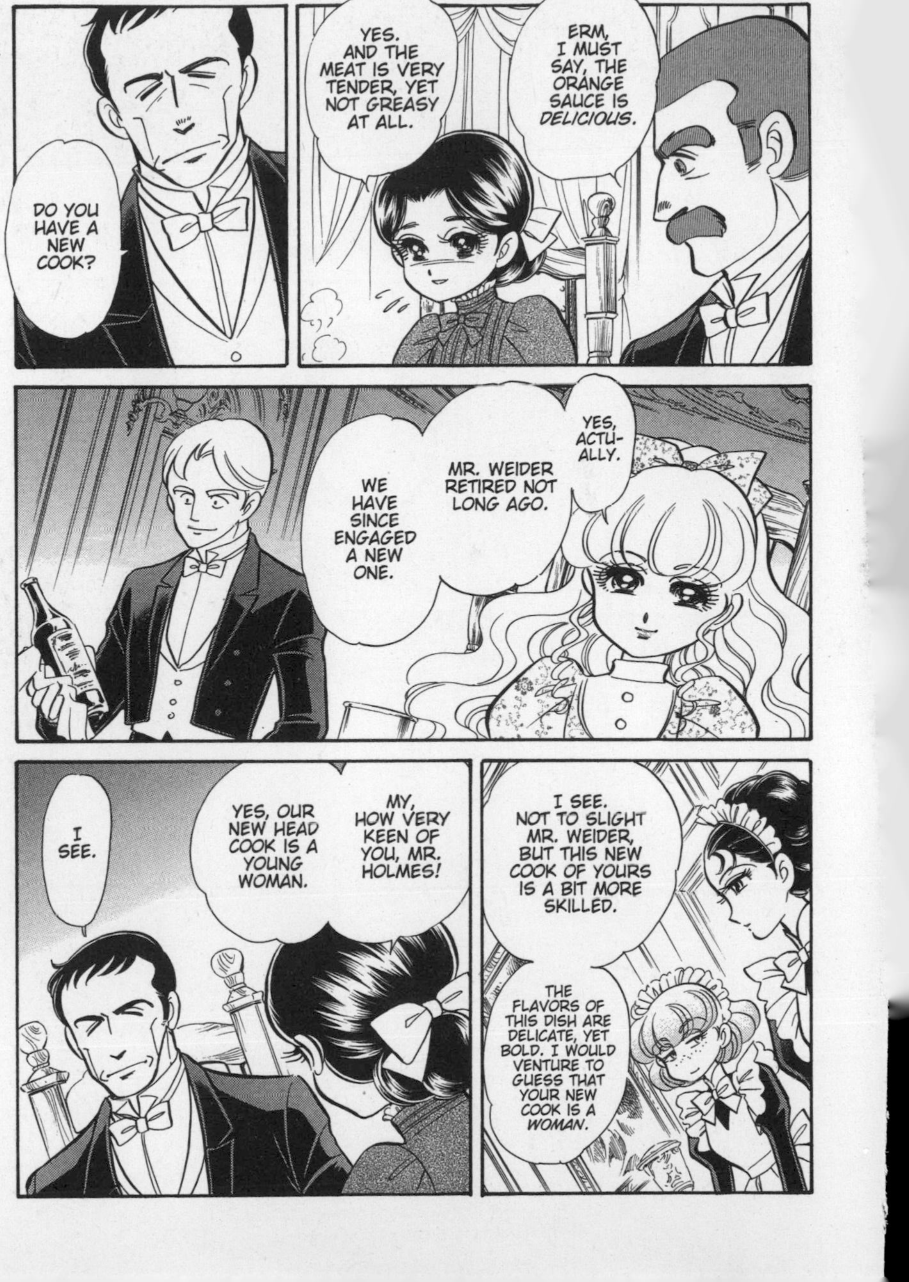
ERM, I MUST SAY, THE ORANGE SAUCE IS *DELICIOUS.*
YES. AND THE MEAT IS VERY TENDER, YET NOT GREASY AT ALL.
DO YOU HAVE A NEW COOK?
YES, ACTUALLY.
MR. WEIDER RETIRED NOT LONG AGO.
WE HAVE SINCE ENGAGED A NEW ONE.
I SEE. NOT TO SLIGHT MR. WEIDER, BUT THIS NEW COOK OF YOURS IS A BIT MORE SKILLED.
THE FLAVORS OF THIS DISH ARE DELICATE, YET BOLD. I WOULD VENTURE TO GUESS THAT YOUR NEW COOK IS A *WOMAN.*
MY, HOW VERY KEEN OF YOU, MR. HOLMES!
YES, OUR NEW HEAD COOK IS A YOUNG WOMAN.
I SEE.

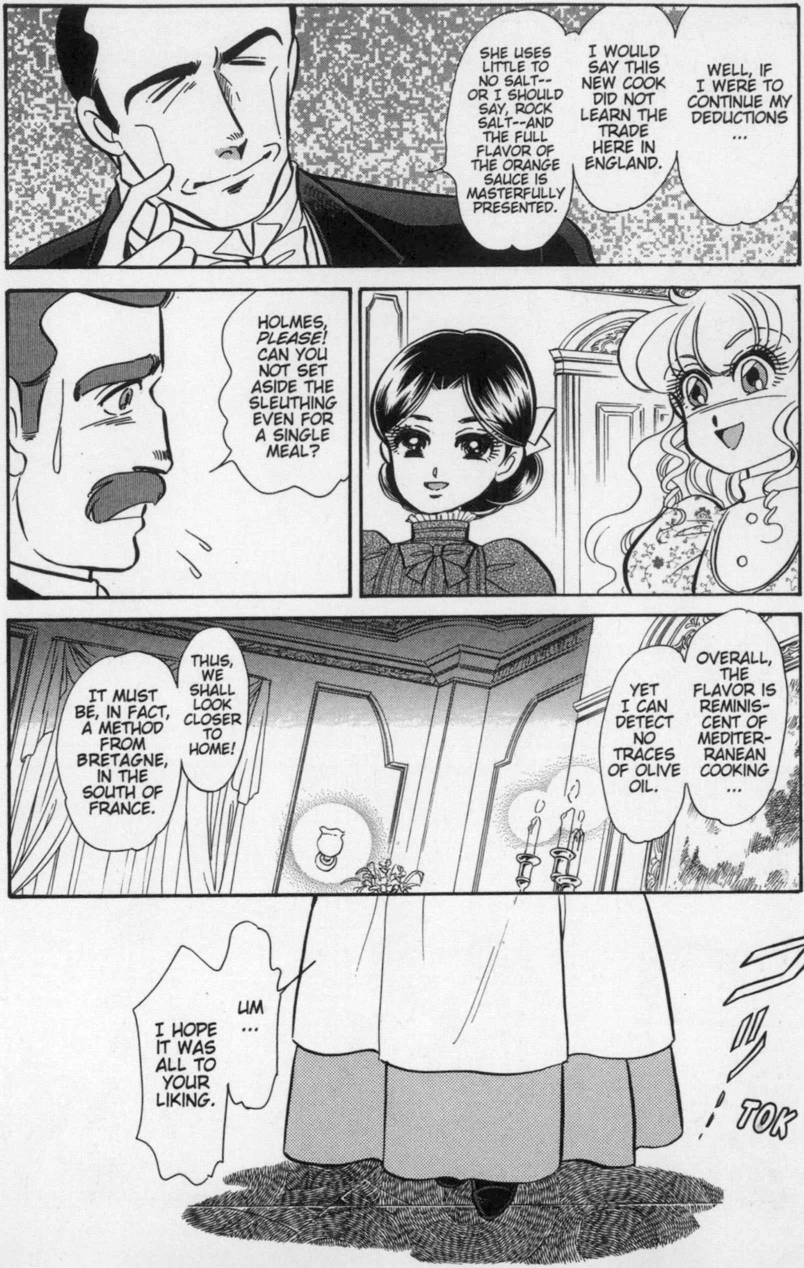

WELL, IF I WERE TO CONTINUE MY DEDUCTIONS ...
I WOULD SAY THIS NEW COOK DID NOT LEARN THE TRADE HERE IN ENGLAND.
SHE USES LITTLE TO NO SALT--OR I SHOULD SAY, ROCK SALT--AND THE FULL FLAVOR OF THE ORANGE SAUCE IS MASTERFULLY PRESENTED.
HOLMES, *PLEASE!* CAN YOU NOT SET ASIDE THE SLEUTHING EVEN FOR A SINGLE MEAL?
OVERALL, THE FLAVOR IS REMINISCENT OF MEDITERRANEAN COOKING ...
YET I CAN DETECT NO TRACES OF OLIVE OIL.
THUS, WE SHALL LOOK CLOSER TO HOME!
IT MUST BE, IN FACT, A METHOD FROM BRETAGNE, IN THE SOUTH OF FRANCE.
TOK
UM ...
I HOPE IT WAS ALL TO YOUR LIKING.

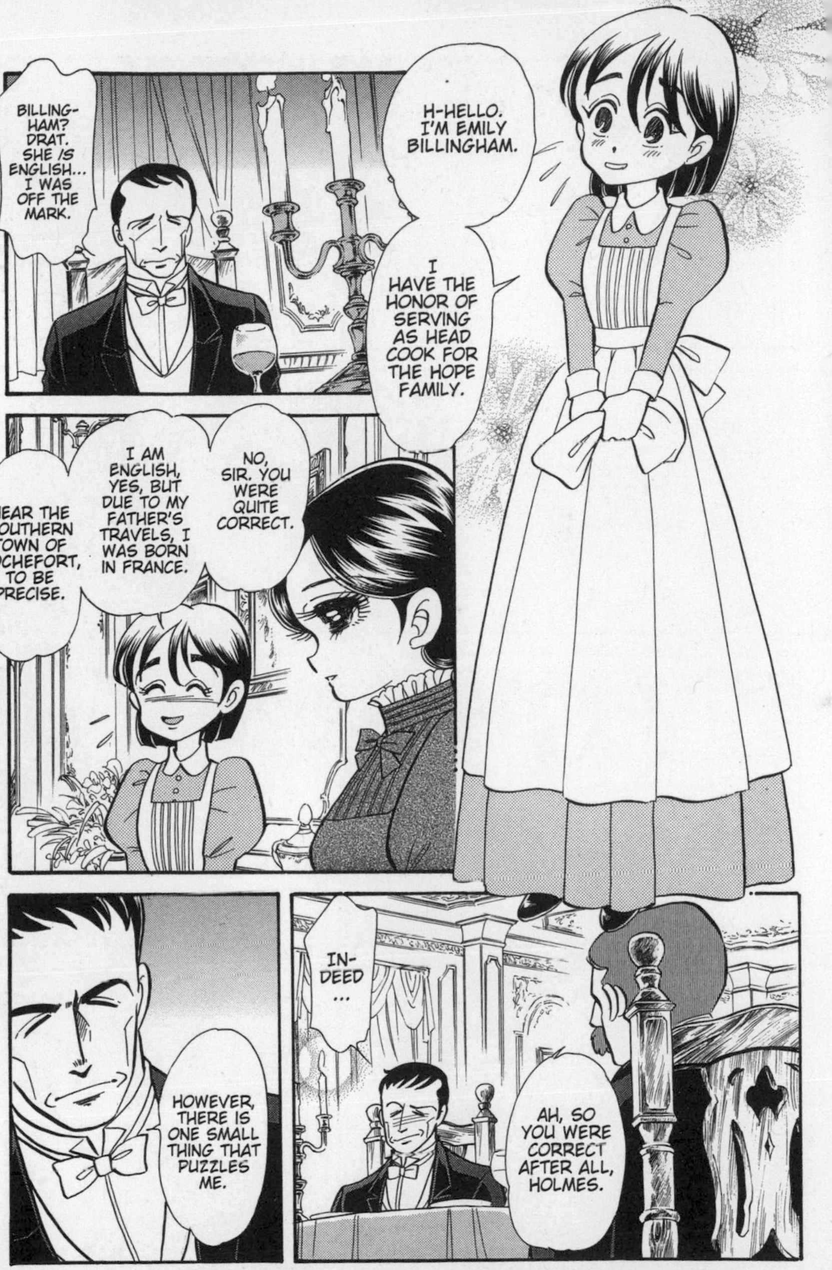
H-HELLO. I'M EMILY BILLINGHAM.
I HAVE THE HONOR OF SERVING AS HEAD COOK FOR THE HOPE FAMILY.
BILLING-HAM? DRAT. SHE *IS* ENGLISH... I WAS OFF THE MARK.
NO, SIR. YOU WERE QUITE CORRECT.
I AM ENGLISH, YES, BUT DUE TO MY FATHER'S TRAVELS, I WAS BORN IN FRANCE.
NEAR THE SOUTHERN TOWN OF ROCHEFORT, TO BE PRECISE.
AH, SO YOU WERE CORRECT AFTER ALL, HOLMES.
IN-DEED...
HOWEVER, THERE IS ONE SMALL THING THAT PUZZLES ME.

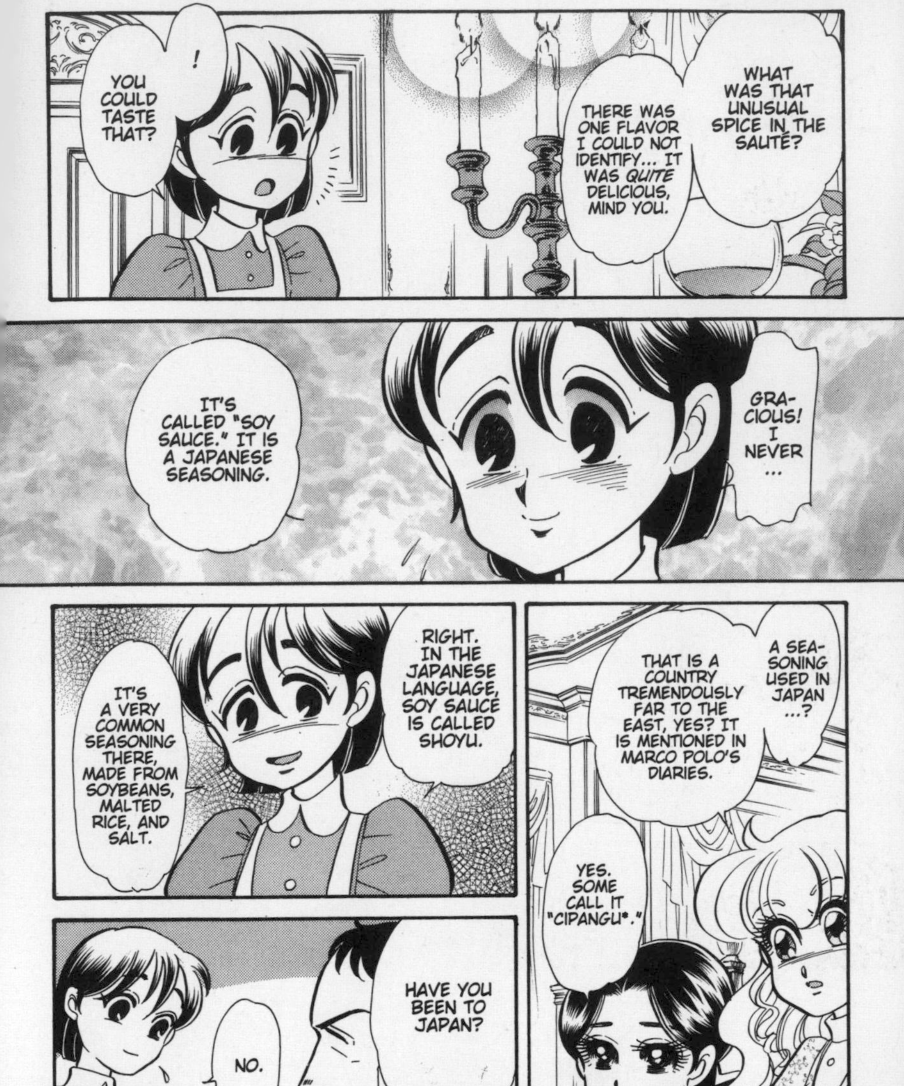
WHAT WAS THAT UNUSUAL SPICE IN THE SAUTÉ?
THERE WAS ONE FLAVOR I COULD NOT IDENTIFY... IT WAS *QUITE* DELICIOUS, MIND YOU.
!
YOU COULD TASTE THAT?
GRA-CIOUS! I NEVER ...
IT'S CALLED "SOY SAUCE." IT IS A JAPANESE SEASONING.
A SEA-SONING USED IN JAPAN ...?
THAT IS A COUNTRY TREMENDOUSLY FAR TO THE EAST, YES? IT IS MENTIONED IN MARCO POLO'S DIARIES.
YES. SOME CALL IT "CIPANGU*."
RIGHT. IN THE JAPANESE LANGUAGE, SOY SAUCE IS CALLED SHOYU.
IT'S A VERY COMMON SEASONING THERE, MADE FROM SOYBEANS, MALTED RICE, AND SALT.
HAVE YOU BEEN TO JAPAN?
NO.

*Cipangu is the name of Japan in Marco Polo's diaries. It originates from the Portuguese recording of the early Mandarin or Wu Chinese name for Japan, "Cipan," and the word for "realm" or "kingdom."

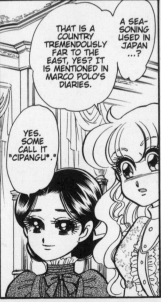

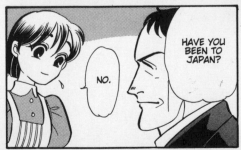

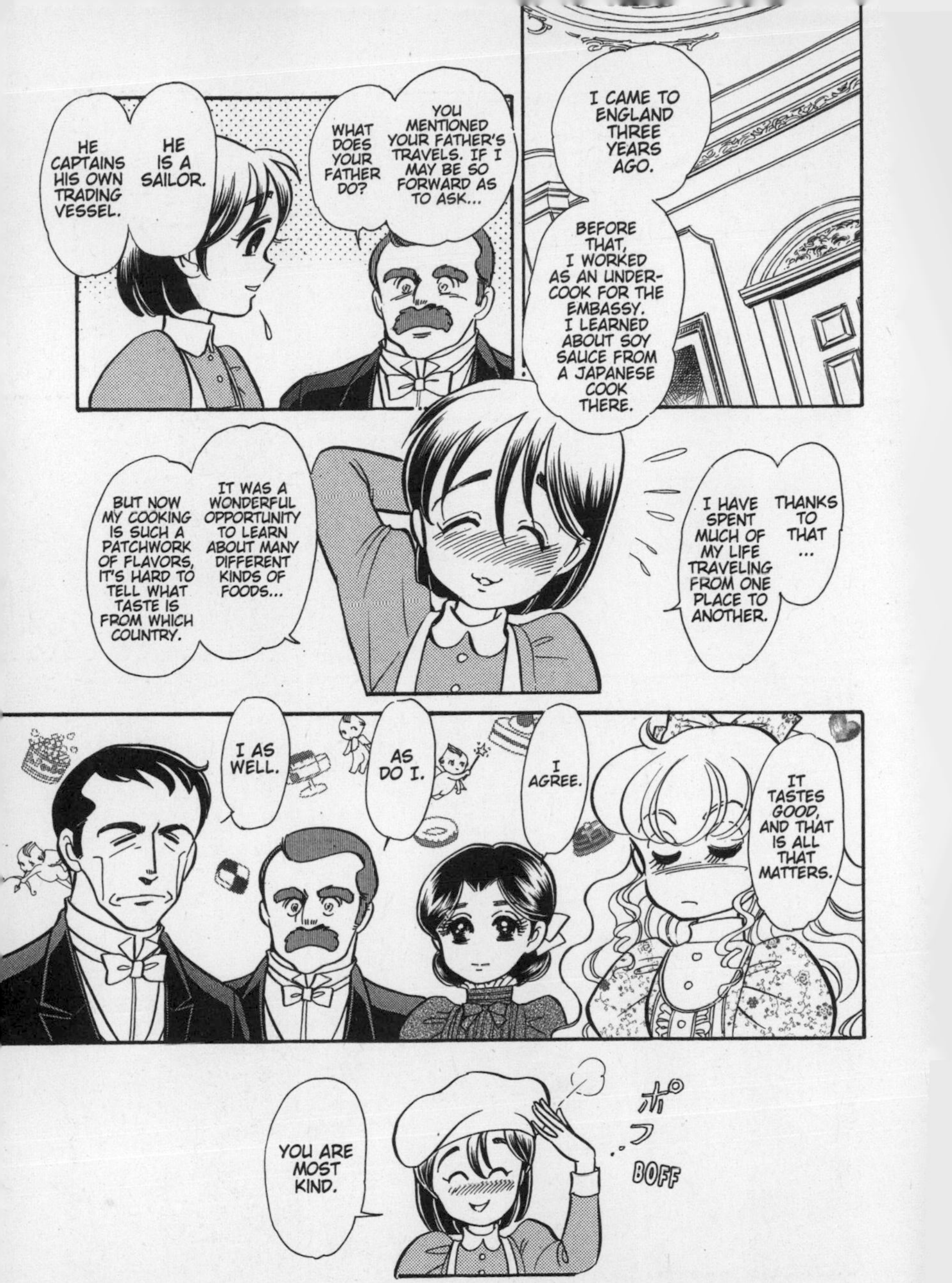
I CAME TO ENGLAND THREE YEARS AGO.
BEFORE THAT, I WORKED AS AN UNDER-COOK FOR THE EMBASSY. I LEARNED ABOUT SOY SAUCE FROM A JAPANESE COOK THERE.
YOU MENTIONED YOUR FATHER'S TRAVELS. IF I MAY BE SO FORWARD AS TO ASK...
WHAT DOES YOUR FATHER DO?
HE IS A SAILOR.
HE CAPTAINS HIS OWN TRADING VESSEL.
THANKS TO THAT...
I HAVE SPENT MUCH OF MY LIFE TRAVELING FROM ONE PLACE TO ANOTHER.
IT WAS A WONDERFUL OPPORTUNITY TO LEARN ABOUT MANY DIFFERENT KINDS OF FOODS...
BUT NOW MY COOKING IS SUCH A PATCHWORK OF FLAVORS, IT'S HARD TO TELL WHAT TASTE IS FROM WHICH COUNTRY.
IT TASTES GOOD, AND THAT IS ALL THAT MATTERS.
I AGREE.
AS DO I.
I AS WELL.
ポフ
BOFF
YOU ARE MOST KIND.

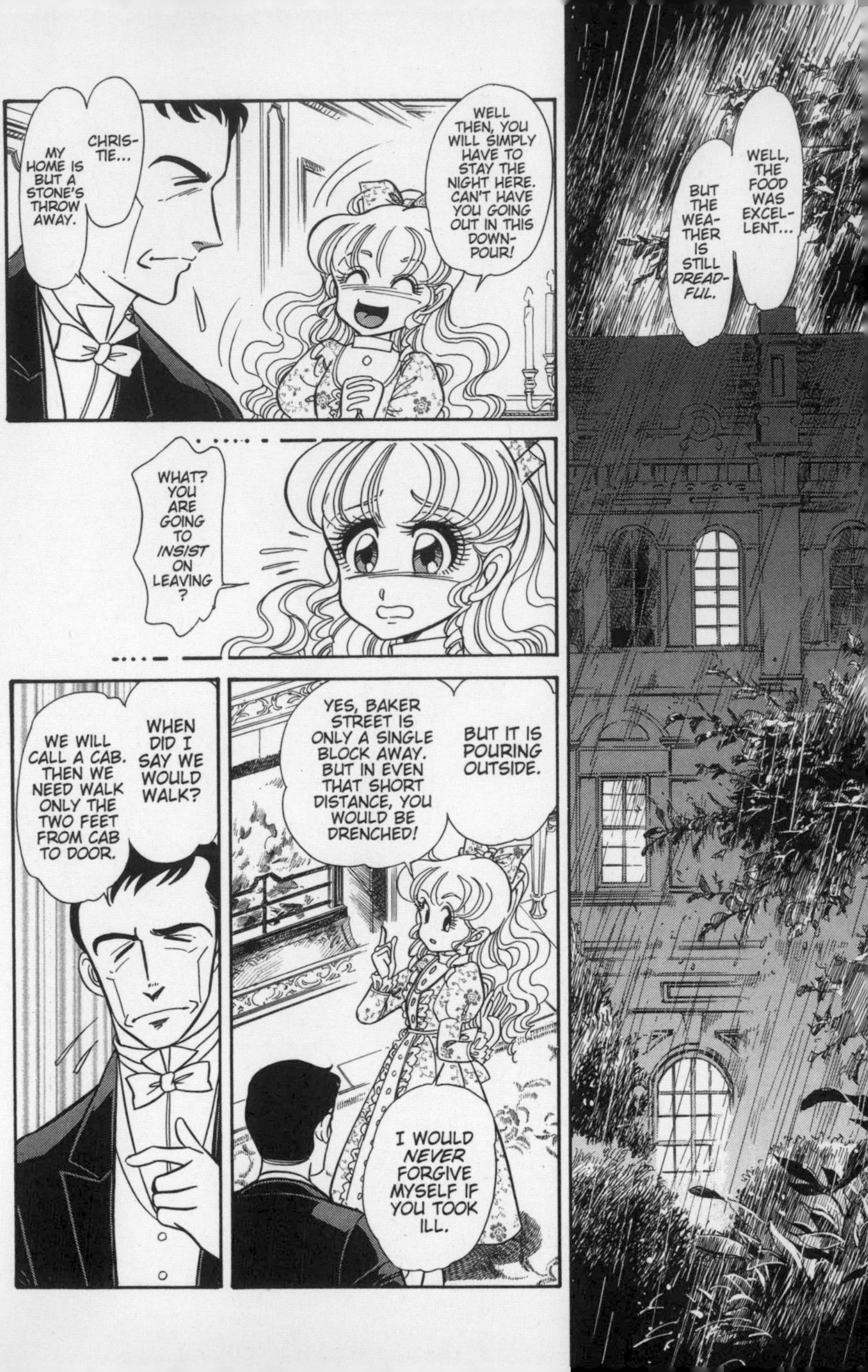
WELL, THE FOOD WAS EXCEL-LENT...
BUT THE WEA-THER IS STILL *DREAD-FUL.*
WELL THEN, YOU WILL SIMPLY HAVE TO STAY THE NIGHT HERE. CAN'T HAVE YOU GOING OUT IN THIS DOWN-POUR!
CHRIS-TIE...
MY HOME IS BUT A STONE'S THROW AWAY.
WHAT? YOU ARE GOING TO *INSIST* ON LEAVING?
BUT IT IS POURING OUTSIDE.
YES, BAKER STREET IS ONLY A SINGLE BLOCK AWAY. BUT IN EVEN THAT SHORT DISTANCE, YOU WOULD BE DRENCHED!
I WOULD *NEVER* FORGIVE MYSELF IF YOU TOOK ILL.
WHEN DID I SAY WE WOULD WALK?
WE WILL CALL A CAB. THEN WE NEED WALK ONLY THE TWO FEET FROM CAB TO DOOR.

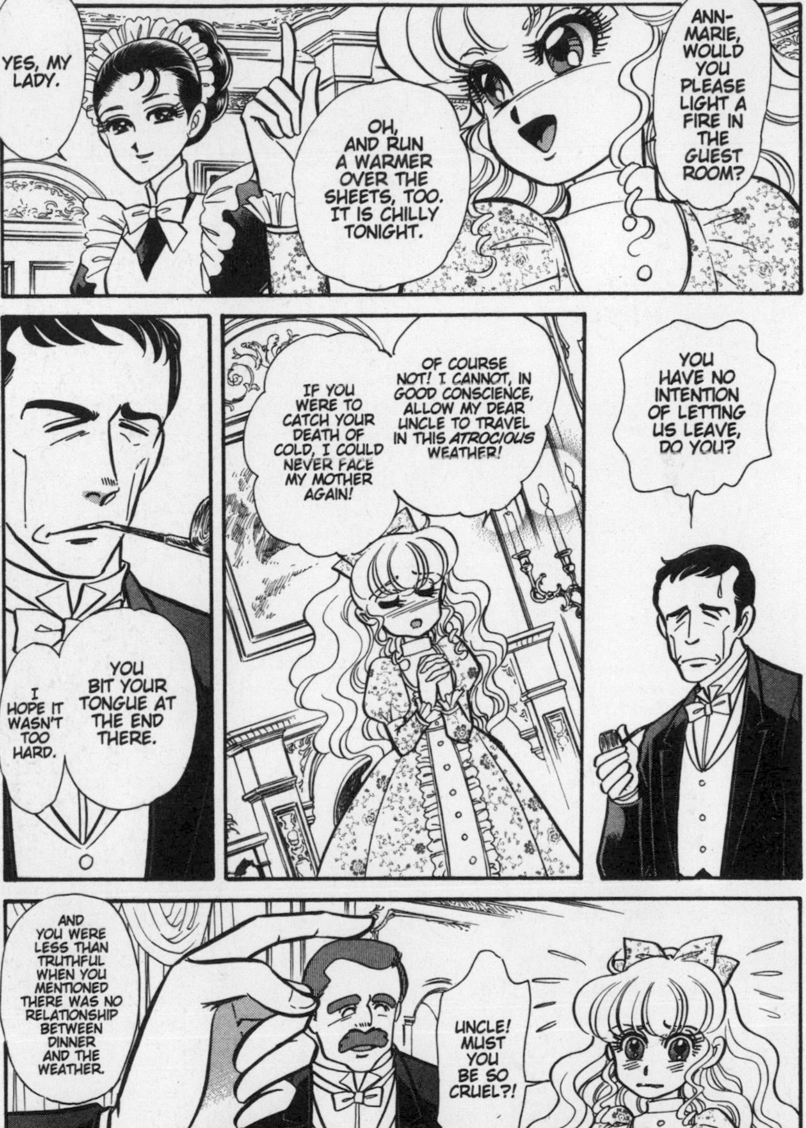
ANN-MARIE, WOULD YOU PLEASE LIGHT A FIRE IN THE GUEST ROOM?
OH, AND RUN A WARMER OVER THE SHEETS, TOO. IT IS CHILLY TONIGHT.
YES, MY LADY.
YOU HAVE NO INTENTION OF LETTING US LEAVE, DO YOU?
OF COURSE NOT! I CANNOT, IN GOOD CONSCIENCE, ALLOW MY DEAR UNCLE TO TRAVEL IN THIS *ATROCIOUS* WEATHER!
IF YOU WERE TO CATCH YOUR DEATH OF COLD, I COULD NEVER FACE MY MOTHER AGAIN!
YOU BIT YOUR TONGUE AT THE END THERE.
I HOPE IT WASN'T TOO HARD.
AND YOU WERE LESS THAN TRUTHFUL WHEN YOU MENTIONED THERE WAS NO RELATIONSHIP BETWEEN DINNER AND THE WEATHER.
UNCLE! MUST YOU BE SO CRUEL?!

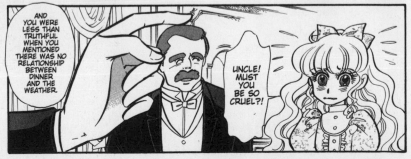

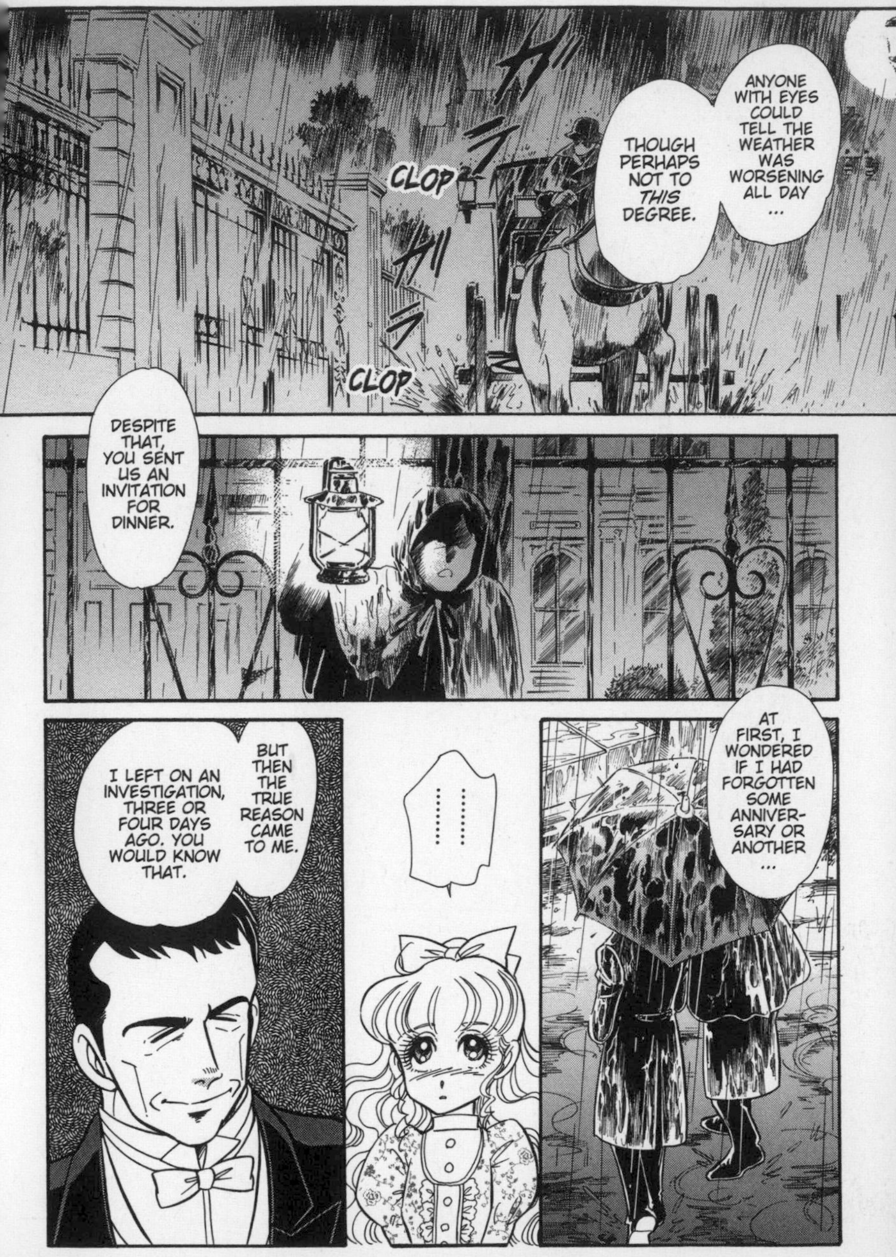
ANYONE WITH EYES COULD TELL THE WEATHER WAS WORSENING ALL DAY ...
THOUGH PERHAPS NOT TO *THIS* DEGREE.
CLOP
CLOP
DESPITE THAT, YOU SENT US AN INVITATION FOR DINNER.
AT FIRST, I WONDERED IF I HAD FORGOTTEN SOME ANNIVERSARY OR ANOTHER ...
......
BUT THEN THE TRUE REASON CAME TO ME.
I LEFT ON AN INVESTIGATION, THREE OR FOUR DAYS AGO. YOU WOULD KNOW THAT.

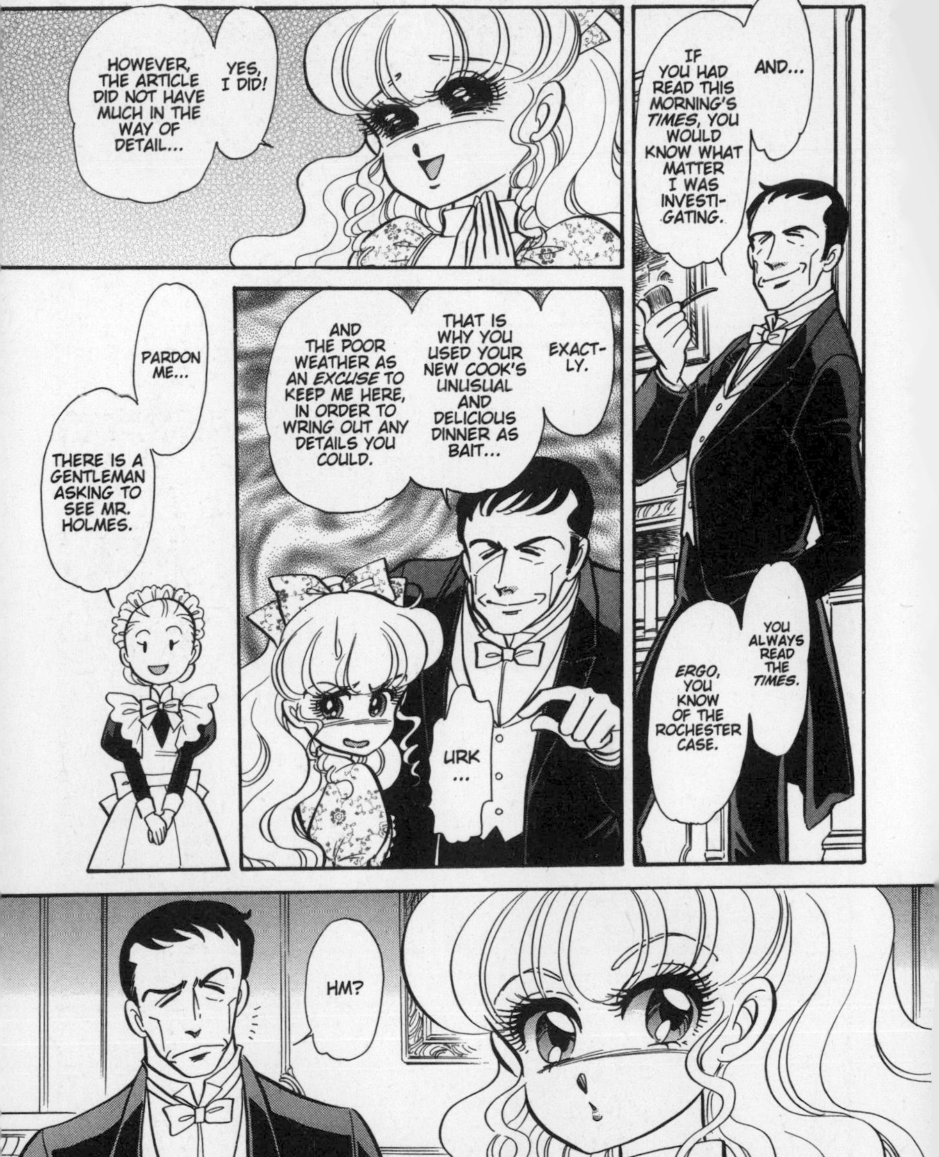
AND...
IF YOU HAD READ THIS MORNING'S *TIMES*, YOU WOULD KNOW WHAT MATTER I WAS INVESTIGATING.
YOU ALWAYS READ THE *TIMES*.
ERGO, YOU KNOW OF THE ROCHESTER CASE.
YES, I DID!
HOWEVER, THE ARTICLE DID NOT HAVE MUCH IN THE WAY OF DETAIL...
EXACTLY.
THAT IS WHY YOU USED YOUR NEW COOK'S UNUSUAL AND DELICIOUS DINNER AS BAIT...
AND THE POOR WEATHER AS AN *EXCUSE* TO KEEP ME HERE, IN ORDER TO WRING OUT ANY DETAILS YOU COULD.
URK...
PARDON ME...
THERE IS A GENTLEMAN ASKING TO SEE MR. HOLMES.
HM?

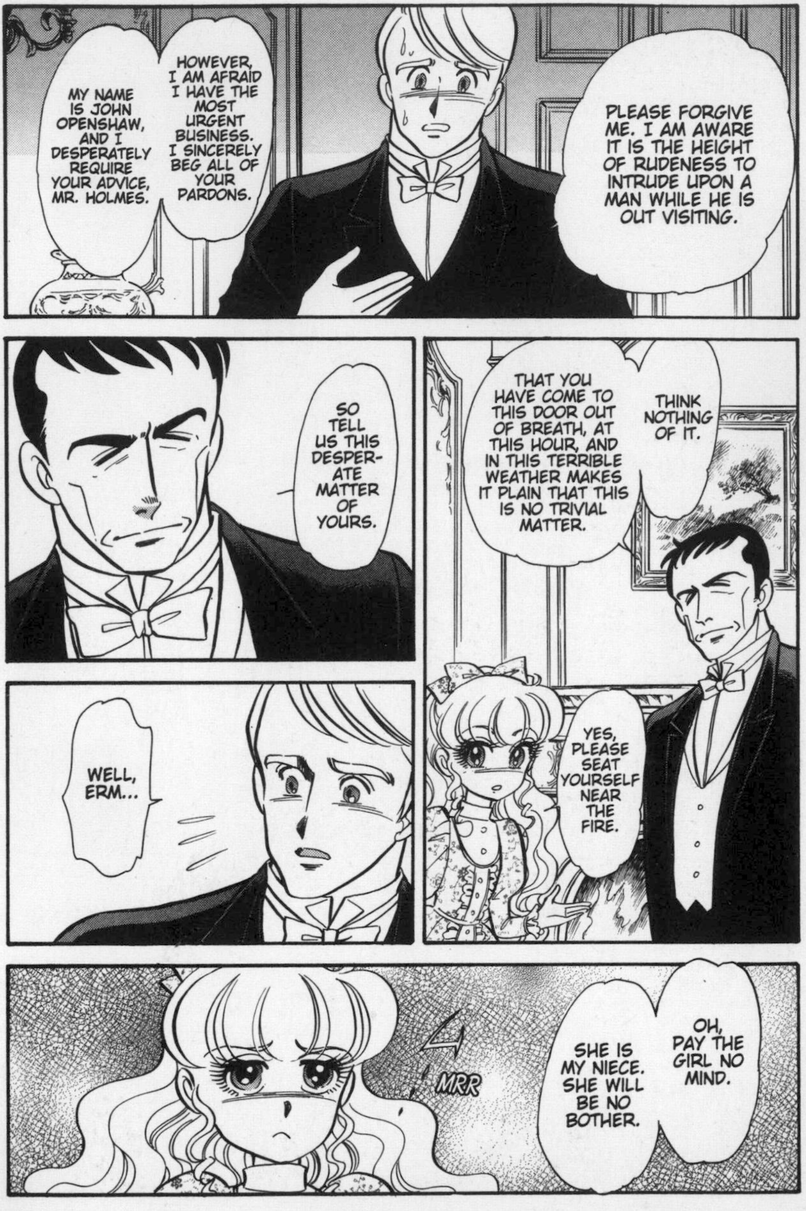
PLEASE FORGIVE ME. I AM AWARE IT IS THE HEIGHT OF RUDENESS TO INTRUDE UPON A MAN WHILE HE IS OUT VISITING.
HOWEVER, I AM AFRAID I HAVE THE MOST URGENT BUSINESS. I SINCERELY BEG ALL OF YOUR PARDONS.
MY NAME IS JOHN OPENSHAW, AND I DESPERATELY REQUIRE YOUR ADVICE, MR. HOLMES.
THINK NOTHING OF IT.
THAT YOU HAVE COME TO THIS DOOR OUT OF BREATH, AT THIS HOUR, AND IN THIS TERRIBLE WEATHER MAKES IT PLAIN THAT THIS IS NO TRIVIAL MATTER.
YES, PLEASE SEAT YOURSELF NEAR THE FIRE.
SO TELL US THIS DESPERATE MATTER OF YOURS.
WELL, ERM...
OH, PAY THE GIRL NO MIND.
SHE IS MY NIECE. SHE WILL BE NO BOTHER.
MRR

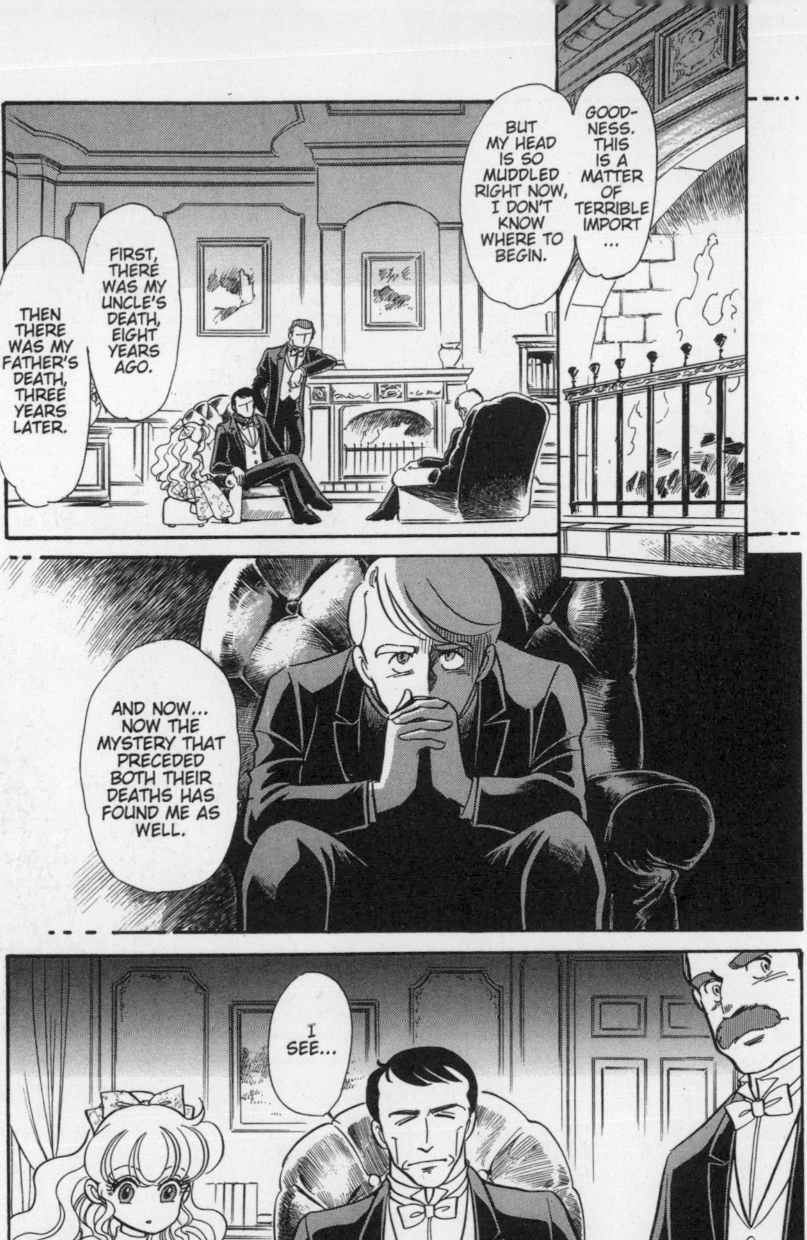
GOOD-NESS. THIS IS A MATTER OF TERRIBLE IMPORT ...
BUT MY HEAD IS SO MUDDLED RIGHT NOW, I DON'T KNOW WHERE TO BEGIN.
FIRST, THERE WAS MY UNCLE'S DEATH, EIGHT YEARS AGO.
THEN THERE WAS MY FATHER'S DEATH, THREE YEARS LATER.
AND NOW... NOW THE MYSTERY THAT PRECEDED BOTH THEIR DEATHS HAS FOUND ME AS WELL.
I SEE...

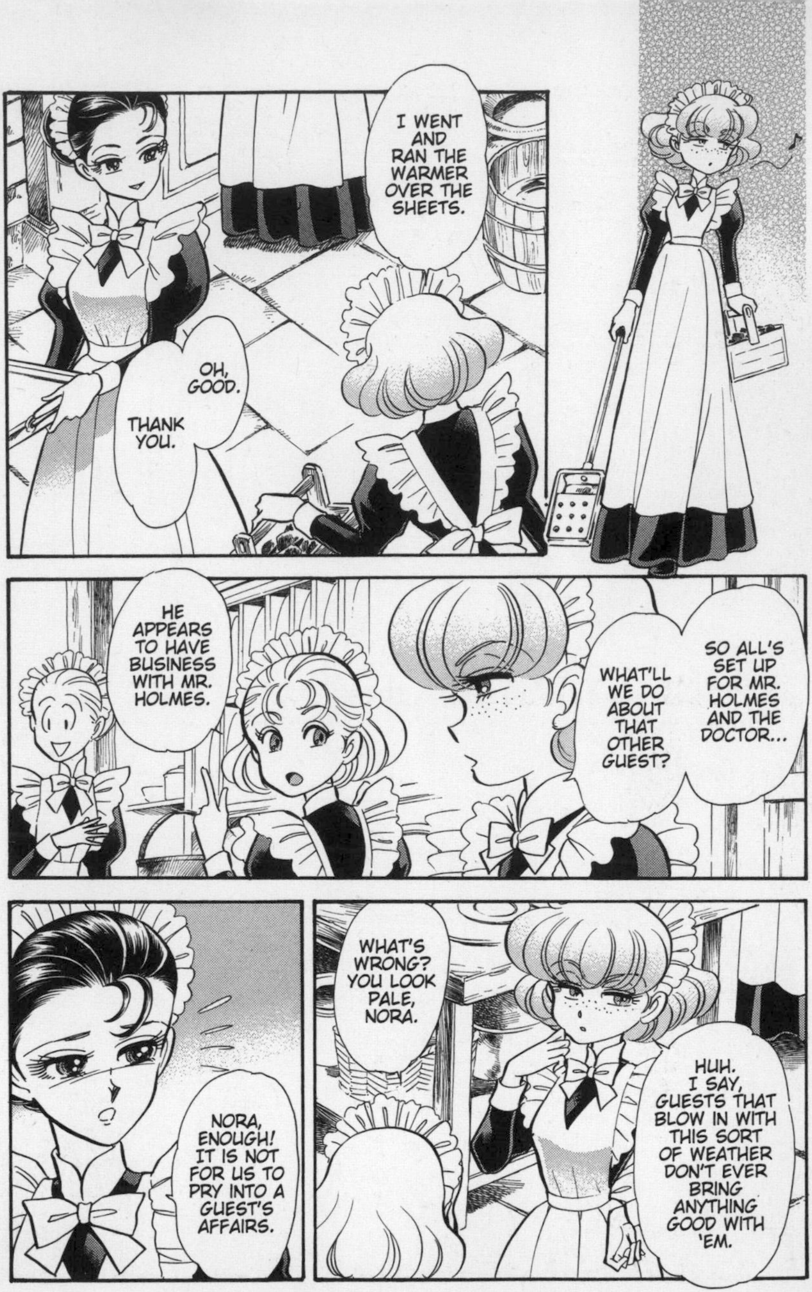
I WENT AND RAN THE WARMER OVER THE SHEETS.
OH, GOOD.
THANK YOU.
SO ALL'S SET UP FOR MR. HOLMES AND THE DOCTOR...
WHAT'LL WE DO ABOUT THAT OTHER GUEST?
HE APPEARS TO HAVE BUSINESS WITH MR. HOLMES.
HUH. I SAY, GUESTS THAT BLOW IN WITH THIS SORT OF WEATHER DON'T EVER BRING ANYTHING GOOD WITH 'EM.
WHAT'S WRONG? YOU LOOK PALE, NORA.
NORA, ENOUGH! IT IS NOT FOR US TO PRY INTO A GUEST'S AFFAIRS.

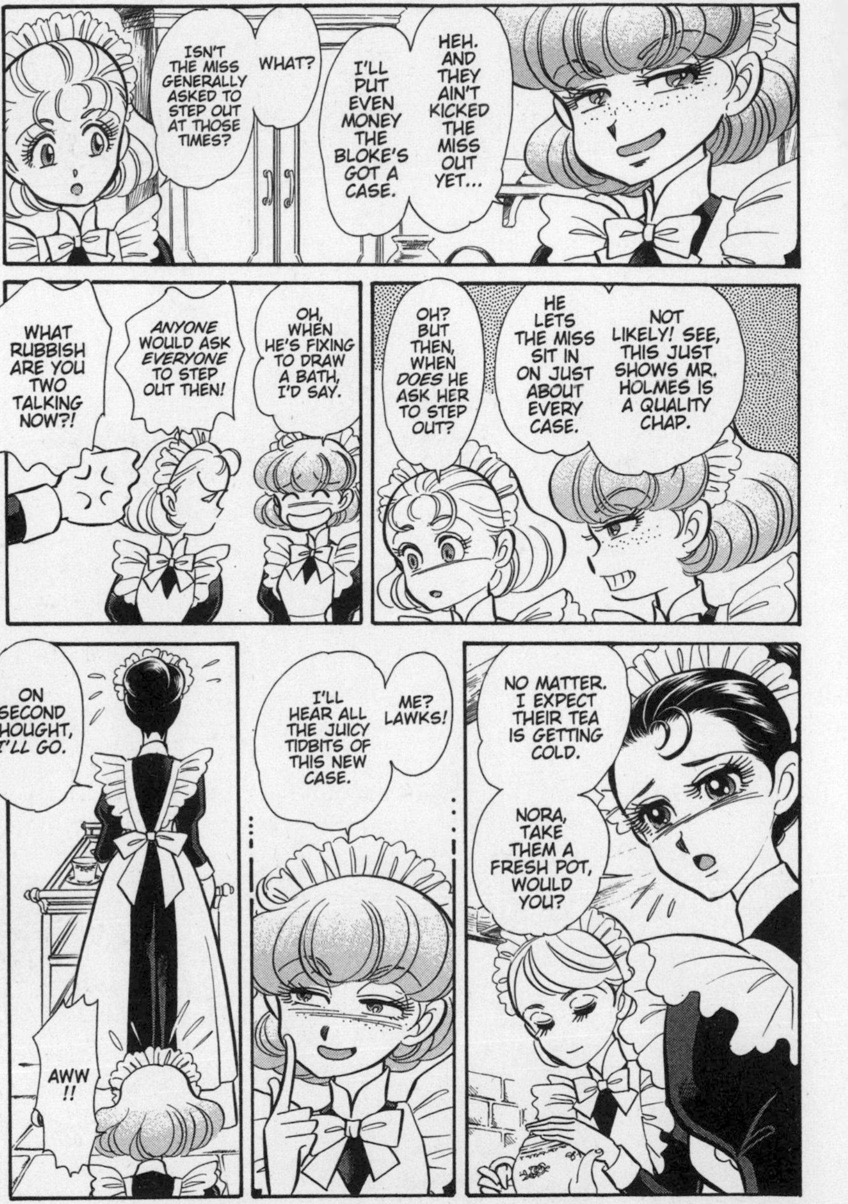
HEH. AND THEY AIN'T KICKED THE MISS OUT YET...
I'LL PUT EVEN MONEY THE BLOKE'S GOT A CASE.
WHAT?
ISN'T THE MISS GENERALLY ASKED TO STEP OUT AT THOSE TIMES?
NOT LIKELY! SEE, THIS JUST SHOWS MR. HOLMES IS A QUALITY CHAP.
HE LETS THE MISS SIT IN ON JUST ABOUT EVERY CASE.
OH? BUT THEN, WHEN *DOES* HE ASK HER TO STEP OUT?
OH, WHEN HE'S FIXING TO DRAW A BATH, I'D SAY.
ANYONE WOULD ASK *EVERYONE* TO STEP OUT THEN!
WHAT RUBBISH ARE YOU TWO TALKING NOW?!
NO MATTER. I EXPECT THEIR TEA IS GETTING COLD.
NORA, TAKE THEM A FRESH POT, WOULD YOU?
ME? LAWKS!
I'LL HEAR ALL THE JUICY TIDBITS OF THIS NEW CASE.
ON SECOND THOUGHT, *I'LL GO.*
AWW !!

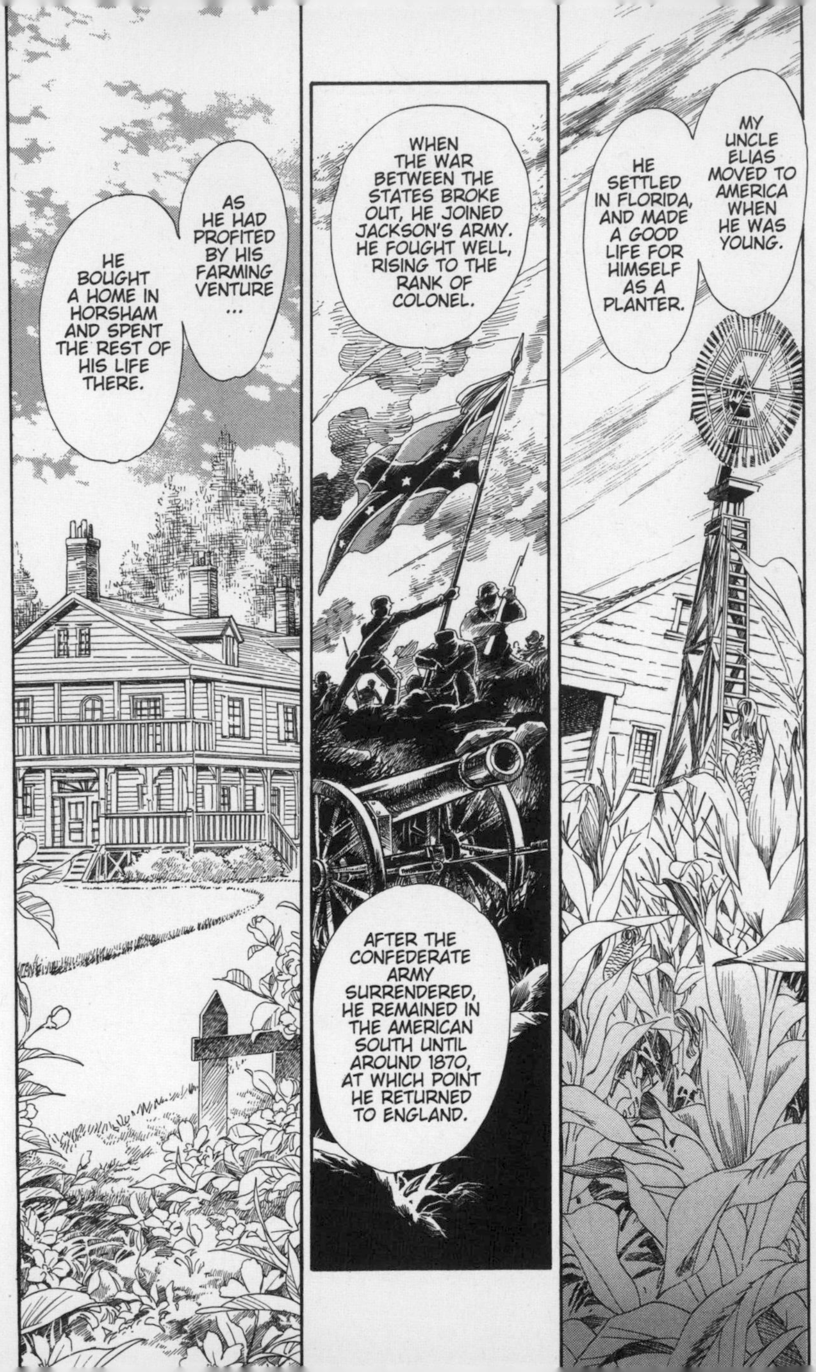
MY UNCLE ELIAS MOVED TO AMERICA WHEN HE WAS YOUNG.
HE SETTLED IN FLORIDA, AND MADE A GOOD LIFE FOR HIMSELF AS A PLANTER.
WHEN THE WAR BETWEEN THE STATES BROKE OUT, HE JOINED JACKSON'S ARMY. HE FOUGHT WELL, RISING TO THE RANK OF COLONEL.
AFTER THE CONFEDERATE ARMY SURRENDERED, HE REMAINED IN THE AMERICAN SOUTH UNTIL AROUND 1870, AT WHICH POINT HE RETURNED TO ENGLAND.
AS HE HAD PROFITED BY HIS FARMING VENTURE ...
HE BOUGHT A HOME IN HORSHAM AND SPENT THE REST OF HIS LIFE THERE.

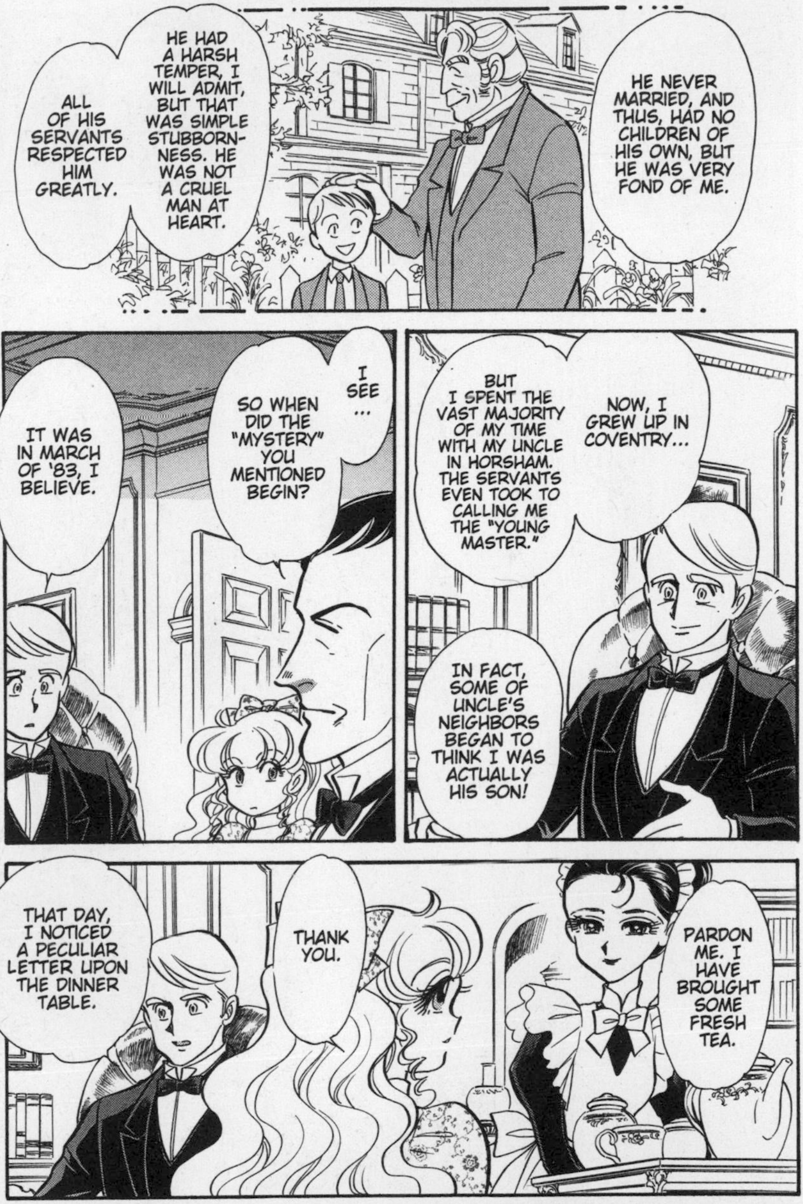
HE NEVER MARRIED, AND THUS, HAD NO CHILDREN OF HIS OWN, BUT HE WAS VERY FOND OF ME.
HE HAD A HARSH TEMPER, I WILL ADMIT, BUT THAT WAS SIMPLE STUBBORNNESS. HE WAS NOT A CRUEL MAN AT HEART.
ALL OF HIS SERVANTS RESPECTED HIM GREATLY.
NOW, I GREW UP IN COVENTRY...
BUT I SPENT THE VAST MAJORITY OF MY TIME WITH MY UNCLE IN HORSHAM. THE SERVANTS EVEN TOOK TO CALLING ME THE "YOUNG MASTER."
IN FACT, SOME OF UNCLE'S NEIGHBORS BEGAN TO THINK I WAS ACTUALLY HIS SON!
I SEE...
SO WHEN DID THE "MYSTERY" YOU MENTIONED BEGIN?
IT WAS IN MARCH OF '83, I BELIEVE.
PARDON ME. I HAVE BROUGHT SOME FRESH TEA.
THANK YOU.
THAT DAY, I NOTICED A PECULIAR LETTER UPON THE DINNER TABLE.

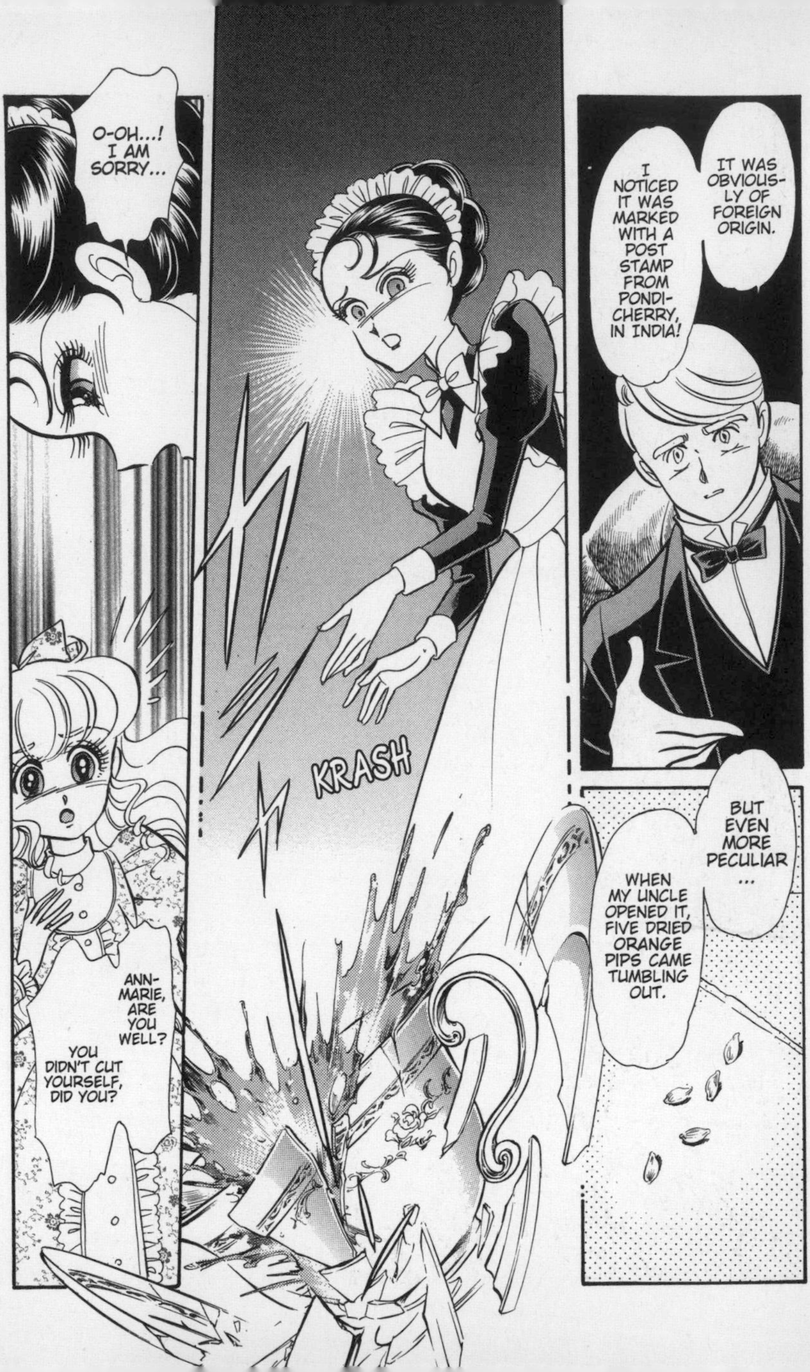
IT WAS OBVIOUSLY OF FOREIGN ORIGIN.
I NOTICED IT WAS MARKED WITH A POST STAMP FROM PONDICHERRY, IN INDIA!
BUT EVEN MORE PECULIAR ...
WHEN MY UNCLE OPENED IT, FIVE DRIED ORANGE PIPS CAME TUMBLING OUT.
KRASH
O-OH...! I AM SORRY...
ANN-MARIE, ARE YOU WELL?
YOU DIDN'T CUT YOURSELF, DID YOU?

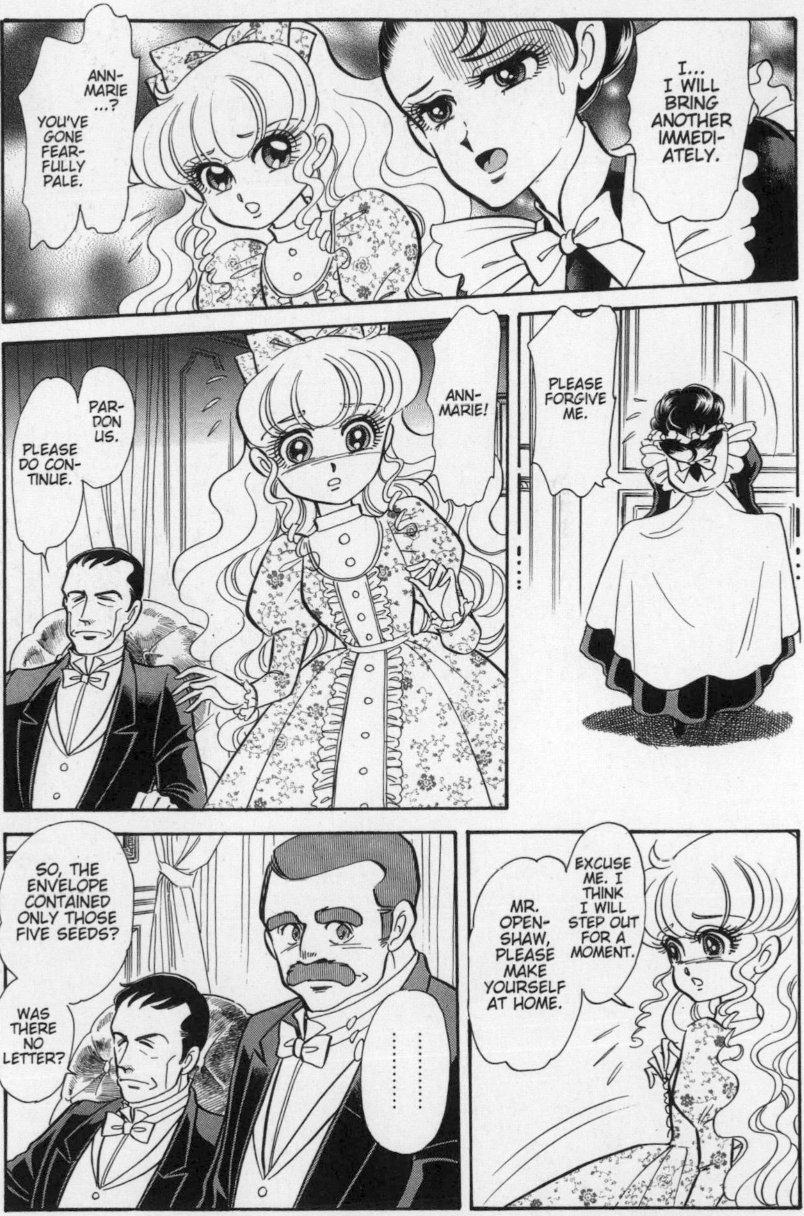
I... I WILL BRING ANOTHER IMMEDIATELY.
ANNMARIE ...? YOU'VE GONE FEARFULLY PALE.
PLEASE FORGIVE ME.
......
ANN-MARIE!
PARDON US. PLEASE DO CONTINUE.
EXCUSE ME. I THINK I WILL STEP OUT FOR A MOMENT.
MR. OPENSHAW, PLEASE MAKE YOURSELF AT HOME.
......
SO, THE ENVELOPE CONTAINED ONLY THOSE FIVE SEEDS?
WAS THERE NO LETTER?

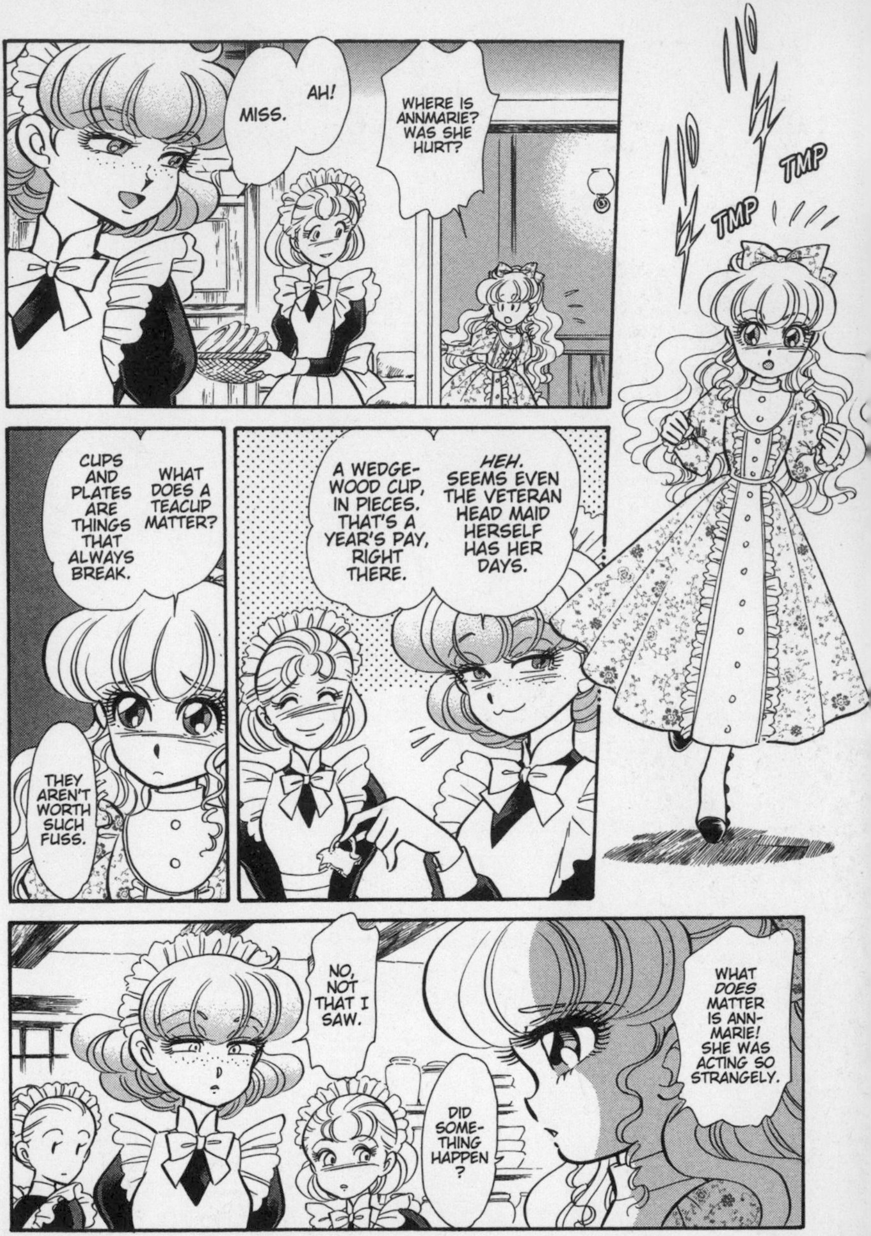
TMP
TMP
AH! MISS.
WHERE IS ANNMARIE? WAS SHE HURT?
HEH. SEEMS EVEN THE VETERAN HEAD MAID HERSELF HAS HER DAYS.
A WEDGE-WOOD CUP, IN PIECES. THAT'S A YEAR'S PAY, RIGHT THERE.
WHAT DOES A TEACUP MATTER?
CUPS AND PLATES ARE THINGS THAT ALWAYS BREAK.
THEY AREN'T WORTH SUCH FUSS.
WHAT *DOES* MATTER IS ANN-MARIE! SHE WAS ACTING SO STRANGELY.
DID SOME-THING HAPPEN?
NO, NOT THAT I SAW.

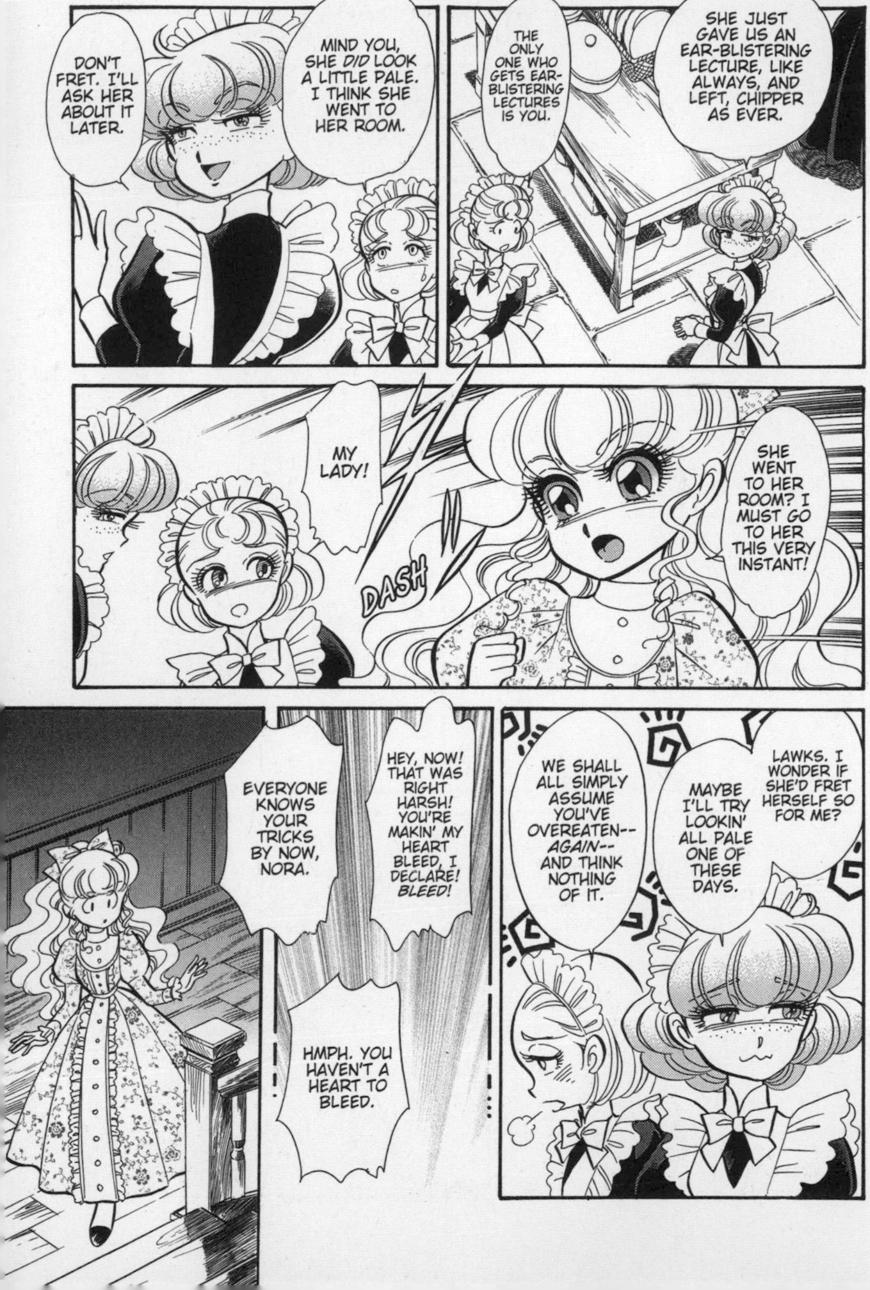
SHE JUST GAVE US AN EAR-BLISTERING LECTURE, LIKE ALWAYS, AND LEFT, CHIPPER AS EVER.
THE ONLY ONE WHO GETS EAR-BLISTERING LECTURES IS YOU.
MIND YOU, SHE *DID* LOOK A LITTLE PALE. I THINK SHE WENT TO HER ROOM.
DON'T FRET. I'LL ASK HER ABOUT IT LATER.
SHE WENT TO HER ROOM? I MUST GO TO HER THIS VERY INSTANT!
DASH
MY LADY!
LAWKS. I WONDER IF SHE'D FRET HERSELF SO FOR ME?
MAYBE I'LL TRY LOOKIN' ALL PALE ONE OF THESE DAYS.
WE SHALL ALL SIMPLY ASSUME YOU'VE OVEREATEN--*AGAIN*--AND THINK NOTHING OF IT.
HEY, NOW! THAT WAS RIGHT HARSH! YOU'RE MAKIN' MY HEART BLEED, I DECLARE! *BLEED!*
EVERYONE KNOWS YOUR TRICKS BY NOW, NORA.
HMPH. YOU HAVEN'T A HEART TO BLEED.

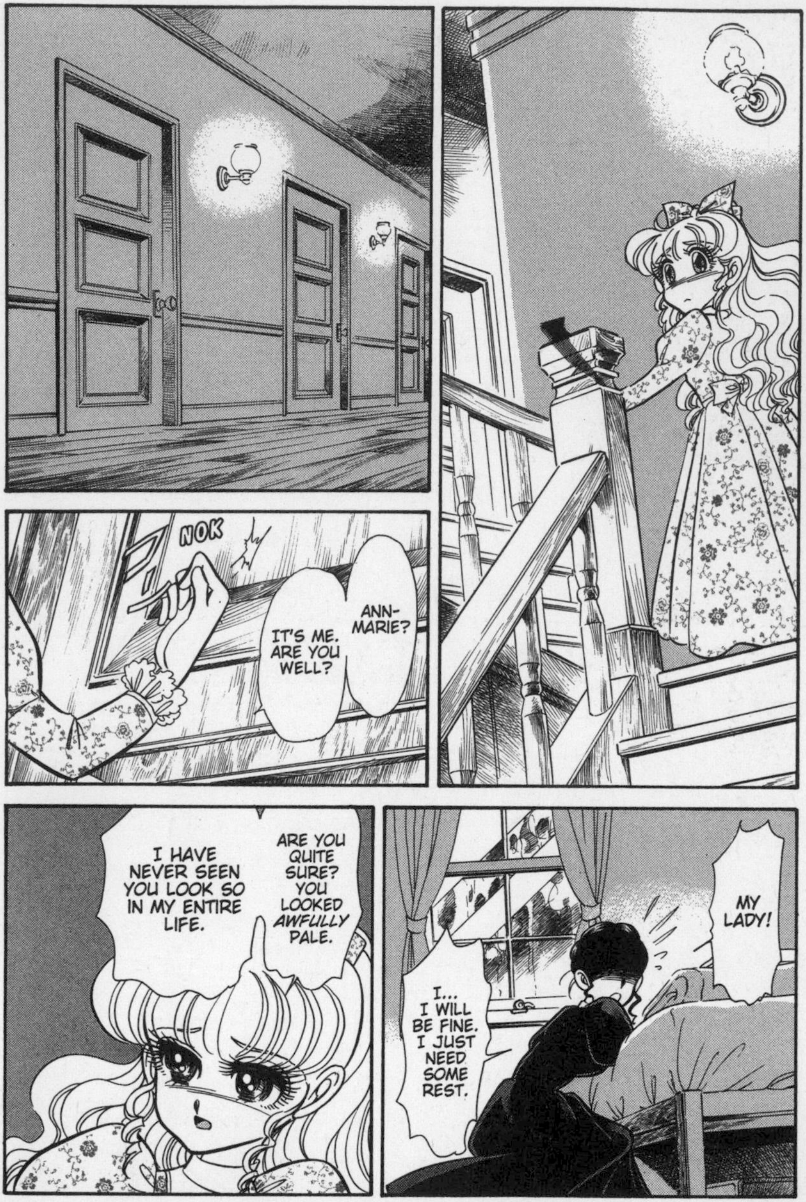
NOK
ANN-MARIE?
IT'S ME. ARE YOU WELL?
MY LADY!
I... I WILL BE FINE. I JUST NEED SOME REST.
ARE YOU QUITE SURE? YOU LOOKED AWFULLY PALE.
I HAVE NEVER SEEN YOU LOOK SO IN MY ENTIRE LIFE.

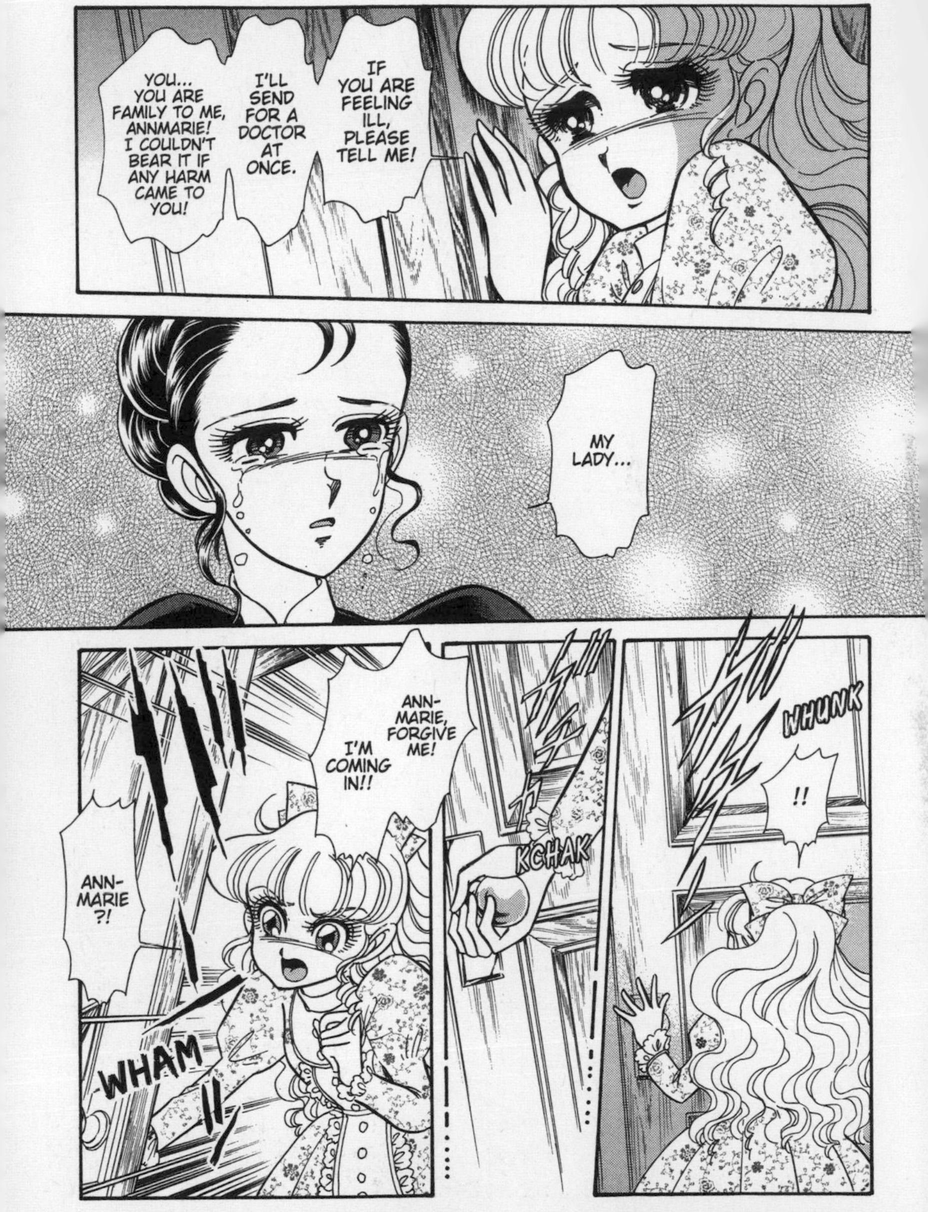
IF YOU ARE FEELING ILL, PLEASE TELL ME!
I'LL SEND FOR A DOCTOR AT ONCE.
YOU... YOU ARE FAMILY TO ME, ANNMARIE! I COULDN'T BEAR IT IF ANY HARM CAME TO YOU!
MY LADY...
WHUNK
!!
ANN-MARIE, FORGIVE ME!
KCHAK
I'M COMING IN!!
ANN-MARIE?!
WHAM

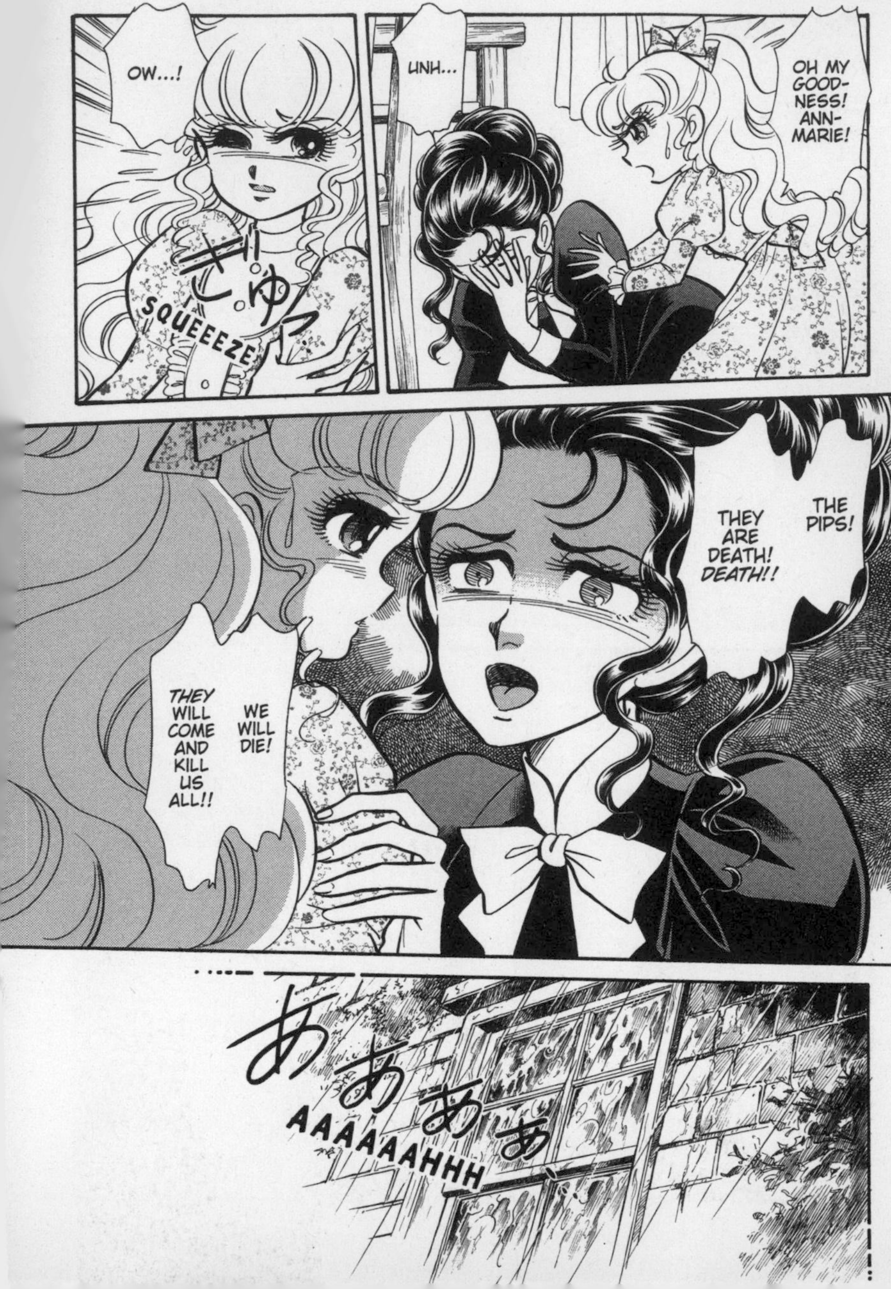
OH MY GOODNESS! ANN-MARIE!
UNH...
OW...!
SQUEEEEZE
THE PIPS!
THEY ARE DEATH! DEATH!!
WE WILL DIE!
THEY WILL COME AND KILL US ALL!!
AAAAAAAHHH

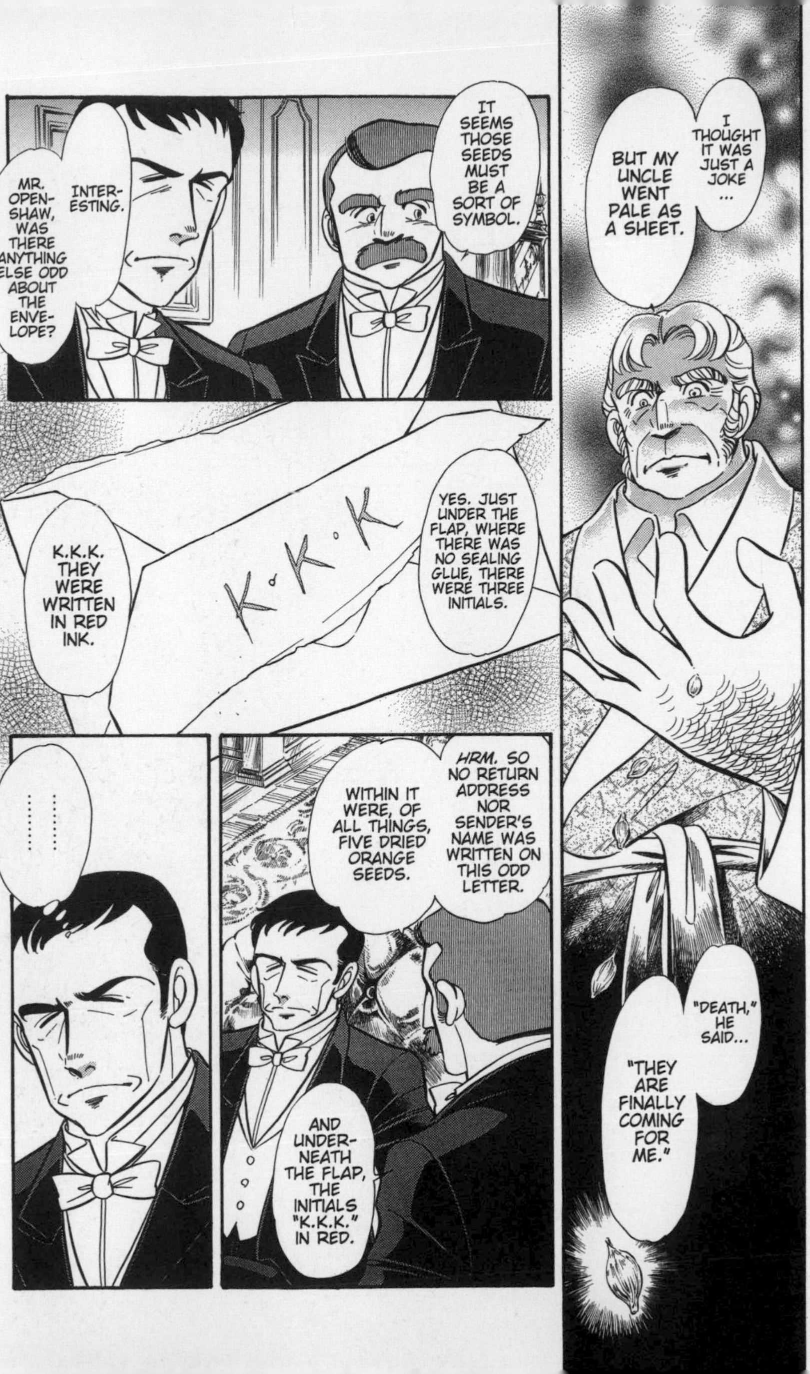
I THOUGHT IT WAS JUST A JOKE ...
BUT MY UNCLE WENT PALE AS A SHEET.
"DEATH," HE SAID...
"THEY ARE FINALLY COMING FOR ME."
IT SEEMS THOSE SEEDS MUST BE A SORT OF SYMBOL.
INTERESTING.
MR. OPENSHAW, WAS THERE ANYTHING ELSE ODD ABOUT THE ENVELOPE?
YES. JUST UNDER THE FLAP, WHERE THERE WAS NO SEALING GLUE, THERE WERE THREE INITIALS.
K.K.K
K.K.K. THEY WERE WRITTEN IN RED INK.
HRM. SO NO RETURN ADDRESS NOR SENDER'S NAME WAS WRITTEN ON THIS ODD LETTER.
WITHIN IT WERE, OF ALL THINGS, FIVE DRIED ORANGE SEEDS.
AND UNDERNEATH THE FLAP, THE INITIALS "K.K.K." IN RED.
......

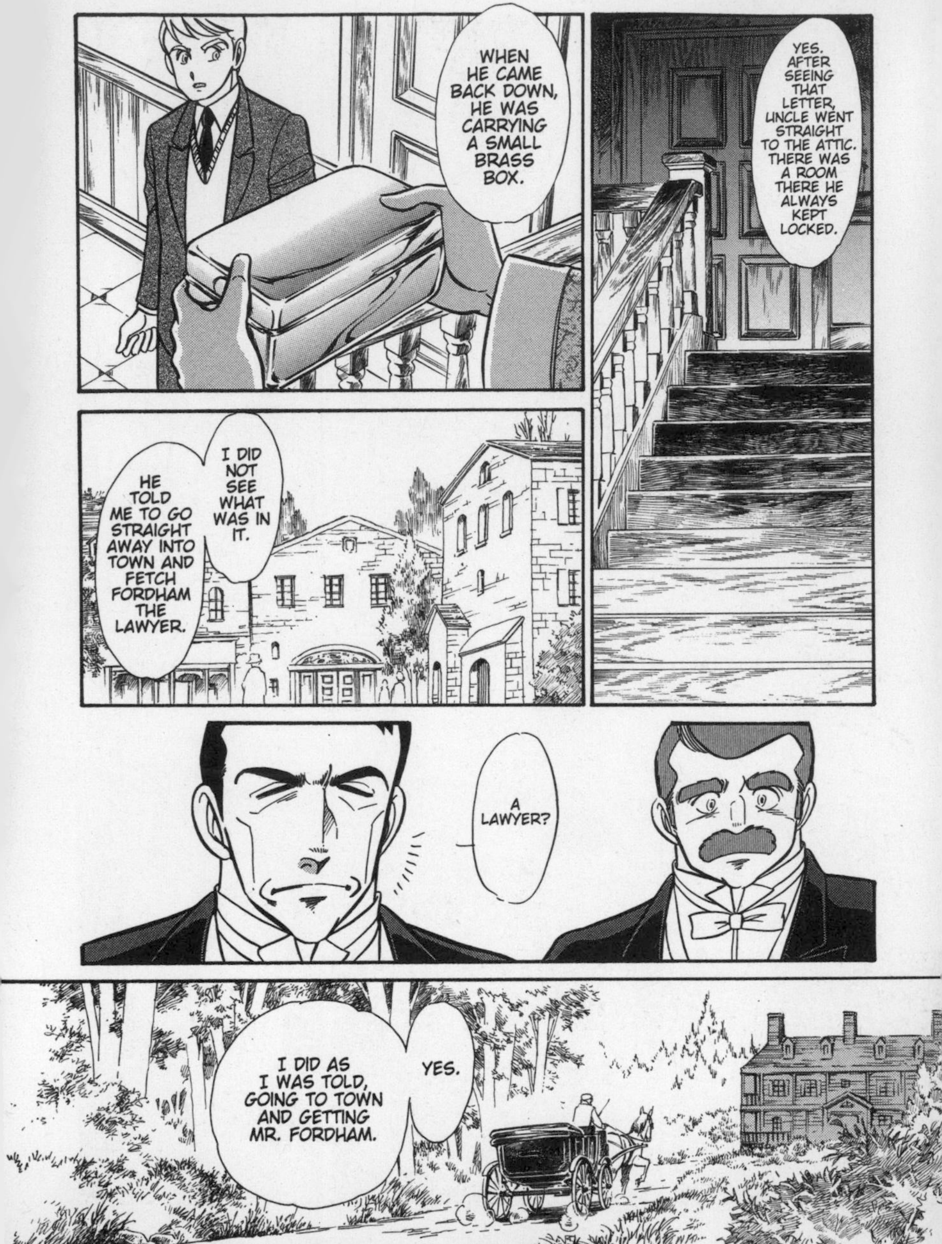
YES. AFTER SEEING THAT LETTER, UNCLE WENT STRAIGHT TO THE ATTIC. THERE WAS A ROOM THERE HE ALWAYS KEPT LOCKED.
WHEN HE CAME BACK DOWN, HE WAS CARRYING A SMALL BRASS BOX.
I DID NOT SEE WHAT WAS IN IT.
HE TOLD ME TO GO STRAIGHT AWAY INTO TOWN AND FETCH FORDHAM THE LAWYER.
A LAWYER?
YES.
I DID AS I WAS TOLD, GOING TO TOWN AND GETTING MR. FORDHAM.

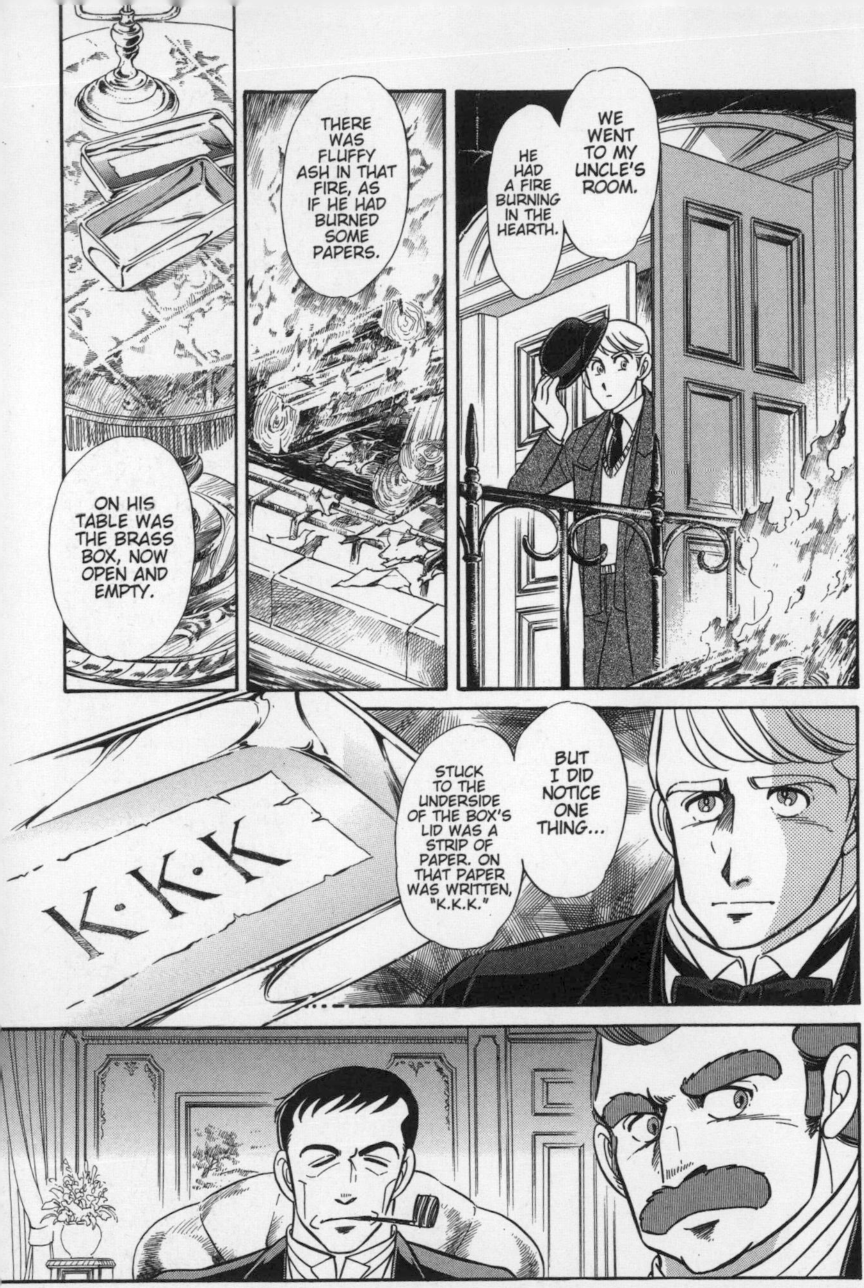
WE WENT TO MY UNCLE'S ROOM.
HE HAD A FIRE BURNING IN THE HEARTH.
THERE WAS FLUFFY ASH IN THAT FIRE, AS IF HE HAD BURNED SOME PAPERS.
ON HIS TABLE WAS THE BRASS BOX, NOW OPEN AND EMPTY.
BUT I DID NOTICE ONE THING...
STUCK TO THE UNDERSIDE OF THE BOX'S LID WAS A STRIP OF PAPER. ON THAT PAPER WAS WRITTEN, "K.K.K."
K·K·K

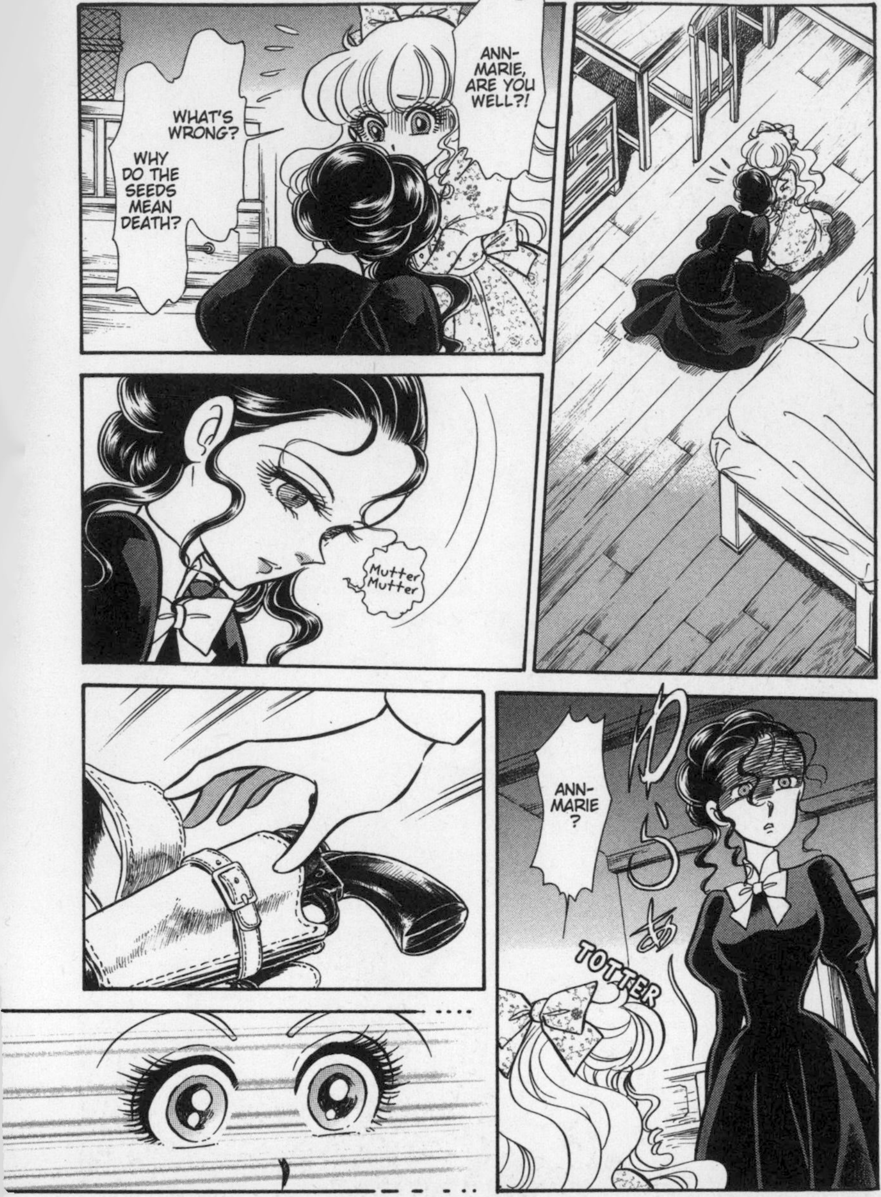
ANN-MARIE, ARE YOU WELL?!
WHAT'S WRONG?
WHY DO THE SEEDS MEAN DEATH?
Mutter Mutter
ANN-MARIE?
TOTTER

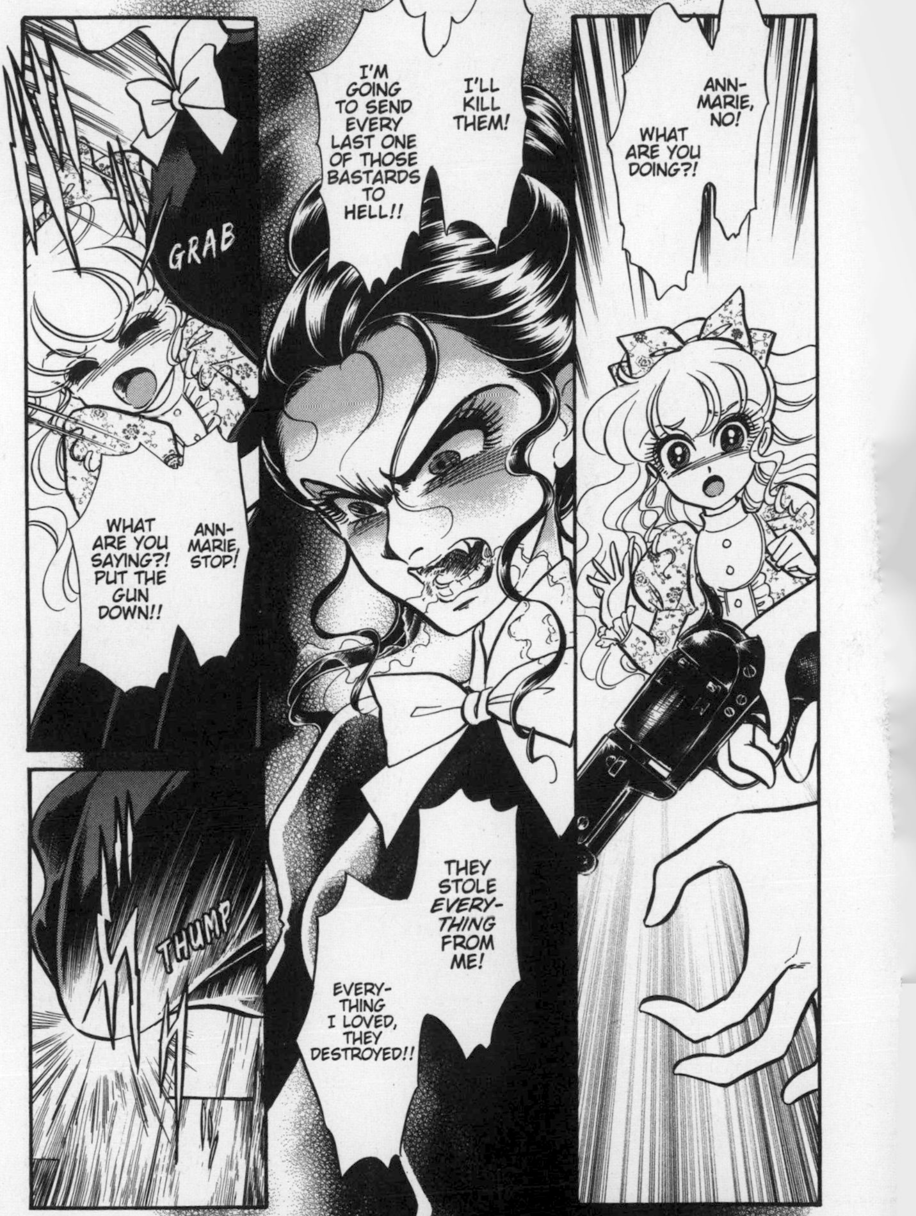
ANN-MARIE, NO!
WHAT ARE YOU DOING?!
I'LL KILL THEM!
I'M GOING TO SEND EVERY LAST ONE OF THOSE BASTARDS TO HELL!!
THEY STOLE EVERYTHING FROM ME!
EVERYTHING I LOVED, THEY DESTROYED!!
GRAB
ANN-MARIE, STOP!
WHAT ARE YOU SAYING?! PUT THE GUN DOWN!!
THUMP

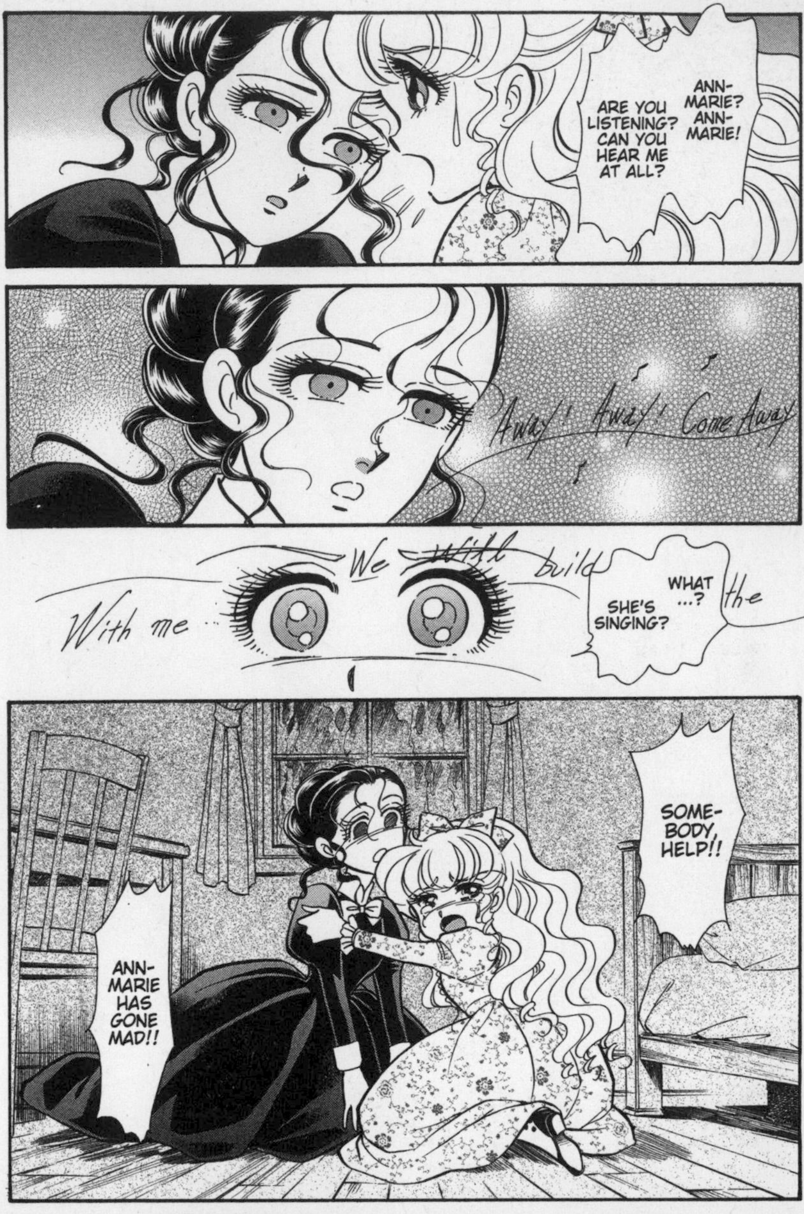
ANN-MARIE? ANN-MARIE!
ARE YOU LISTENING? CAN YOU HEAR ME AT ALL?
Away! Away! Come Away
WHAT ...?
SHE'S SINGING?
With me ... We will build the
SOME-BODY, HELP!!
ANN-MARIE HAS GONE MAD!!

The Five Orange Pips (2)

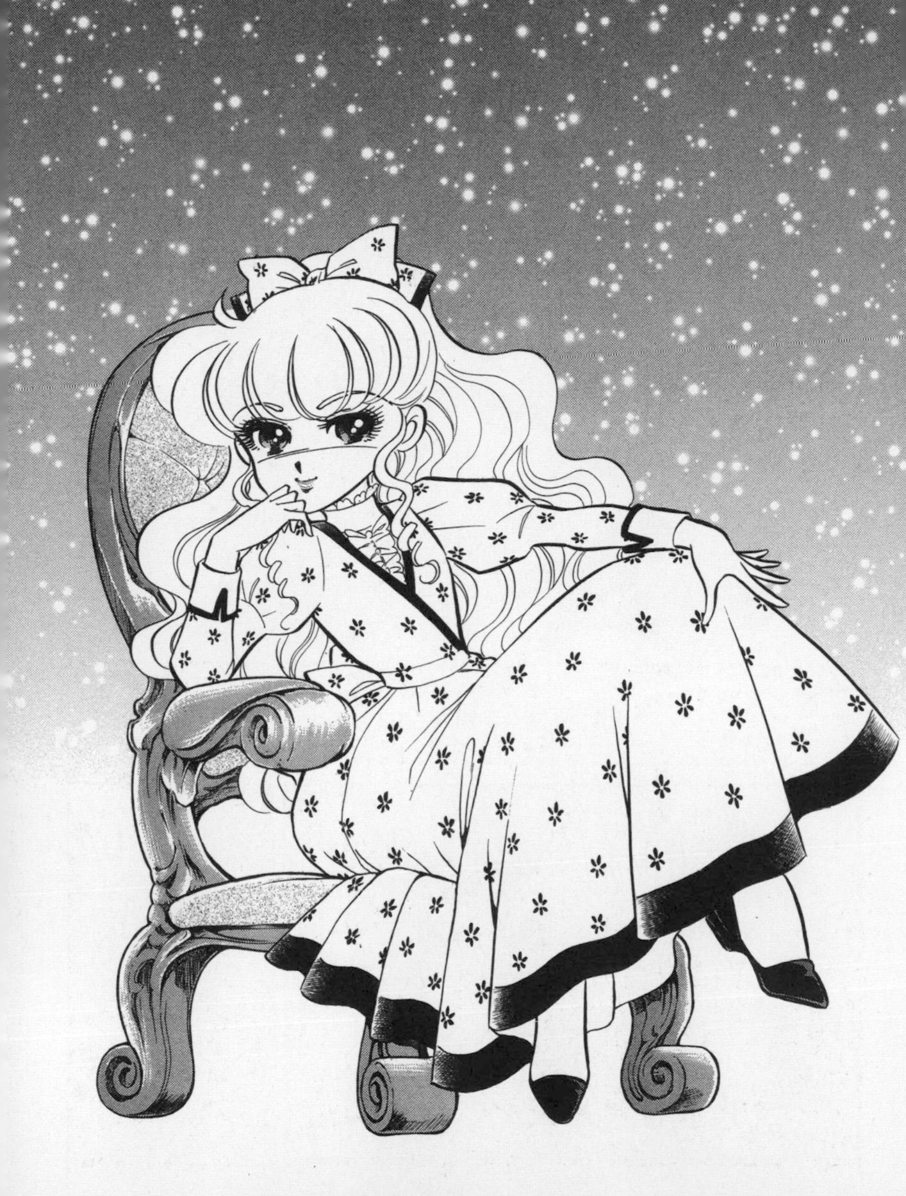

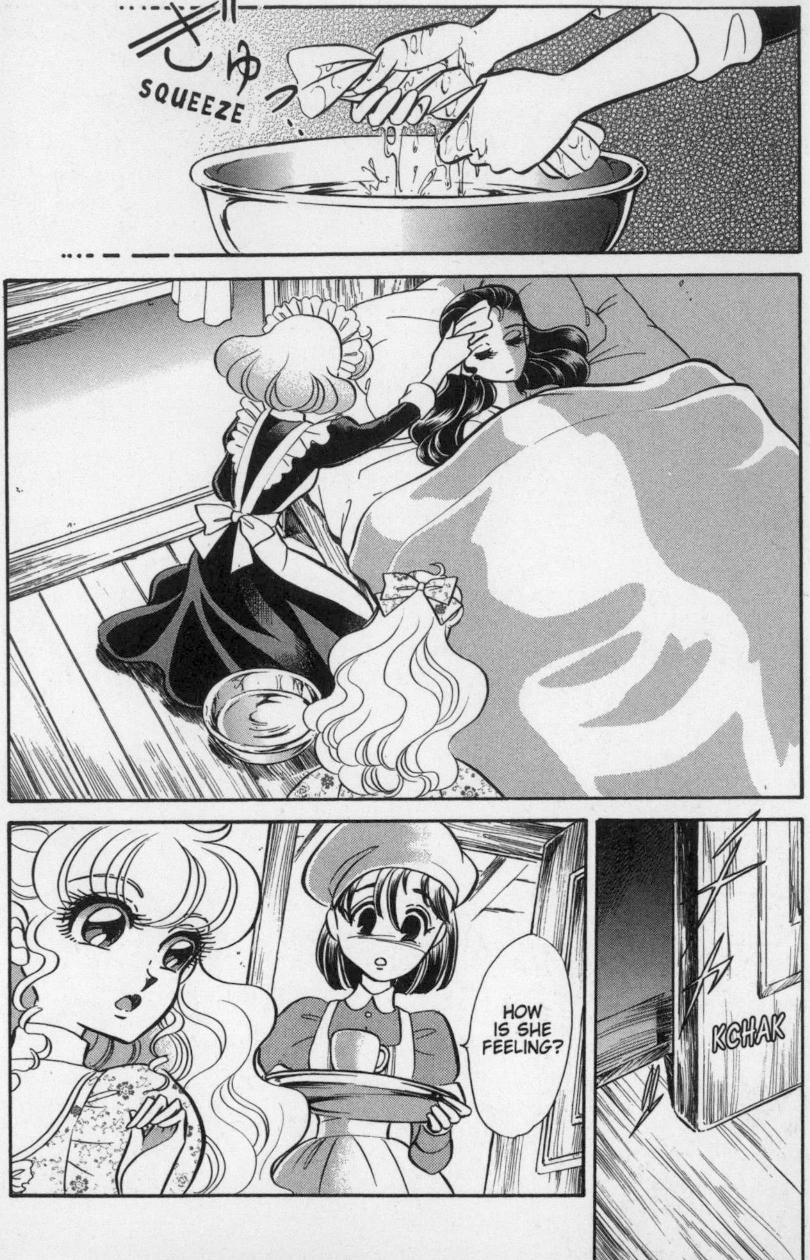
ぎゅっ
SQUEEZE
KCHAK
HOW IS SHE FEELING?

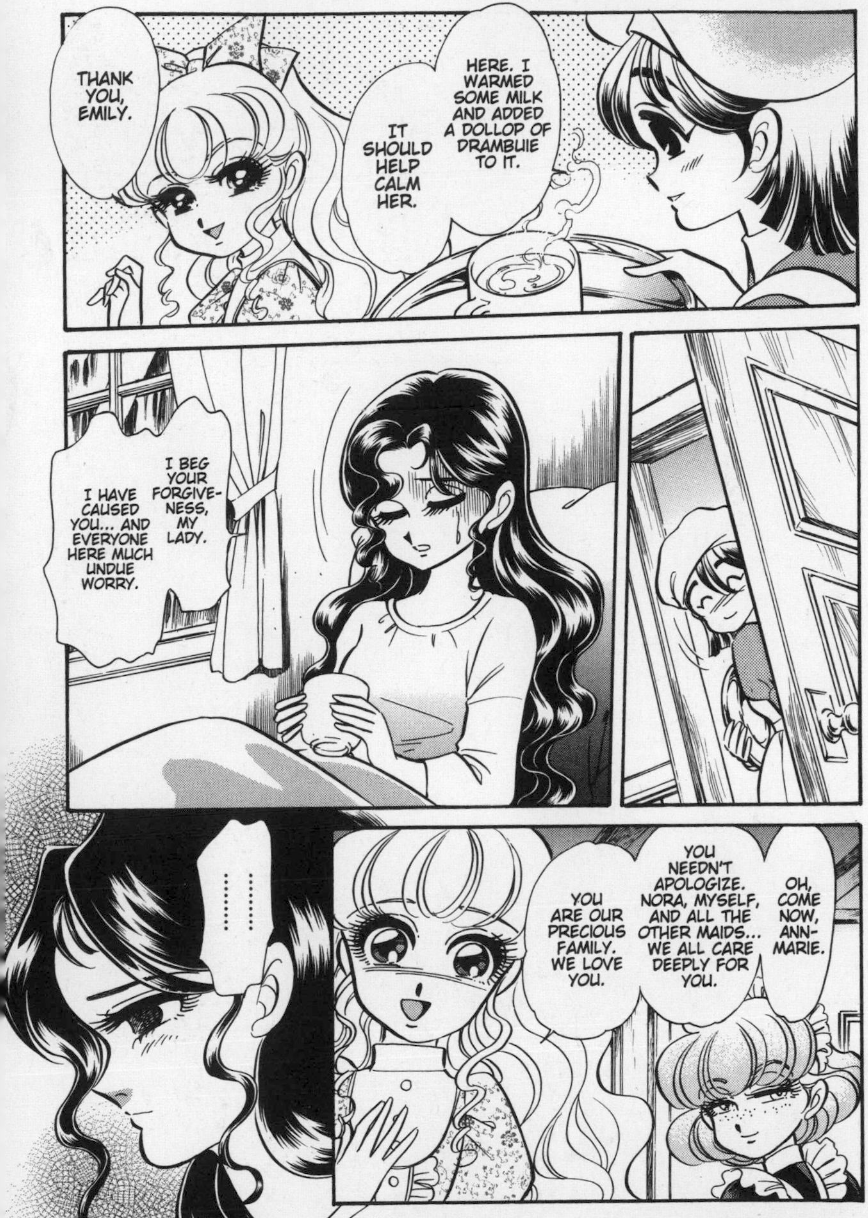
HERE. I WARMED SOME MILK AND ADDED A DOLLOP OF DRAMBUIE TO IT.
IT SHOULD HELP CALM HER.
THANK YOU, EMILY.
I BEG YOUR FORGIVENESS, MY LADY.
I HAVE CAUSED YOU... AND EVERYONE HERE MUCH UNDUE WORRY.
OH, COME NOW, ANN-MARIE.
YOU NEEDN'T APOLOGIZE. NORA, MYSELF, AND ALL THE OTHER MAIDS... WE ALL CARE DEEPLY FOR YOU.
YOU ARE OUR PRECIOUS FAMILY. WE LOVE YOU.
......

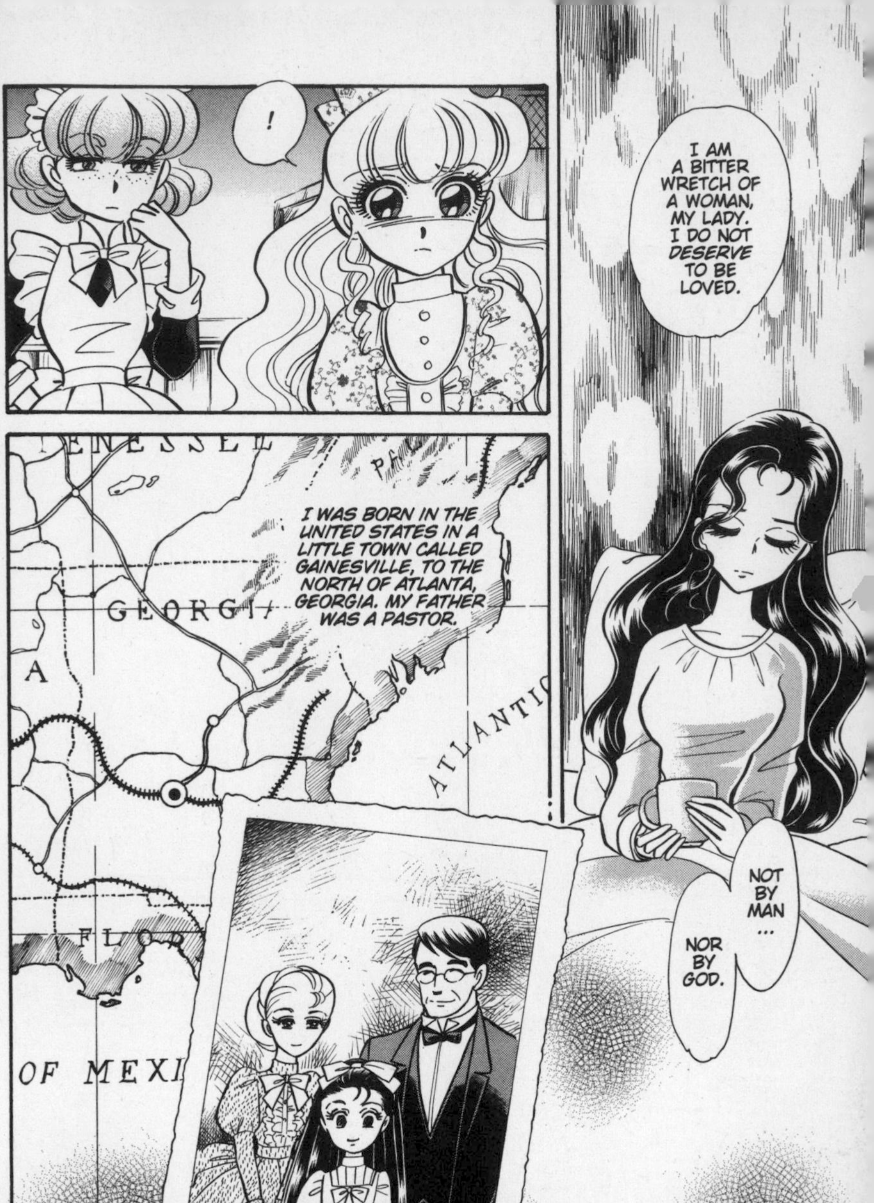
I AM A BITTER WRETCH OF A WOMAN, MY LADY. I DO NOT *DESERVE* TO BE LOVED.
NOT BY MAN ...
NOR BY GOD.
!
I WAS BORN IN THE UNITED STATES IN A LITTLE TOWN CALLED GAINESVILLE, TO THE NORTH OF ATLANTA, GEORGIA. MY FATHER WAS A PASTOR.

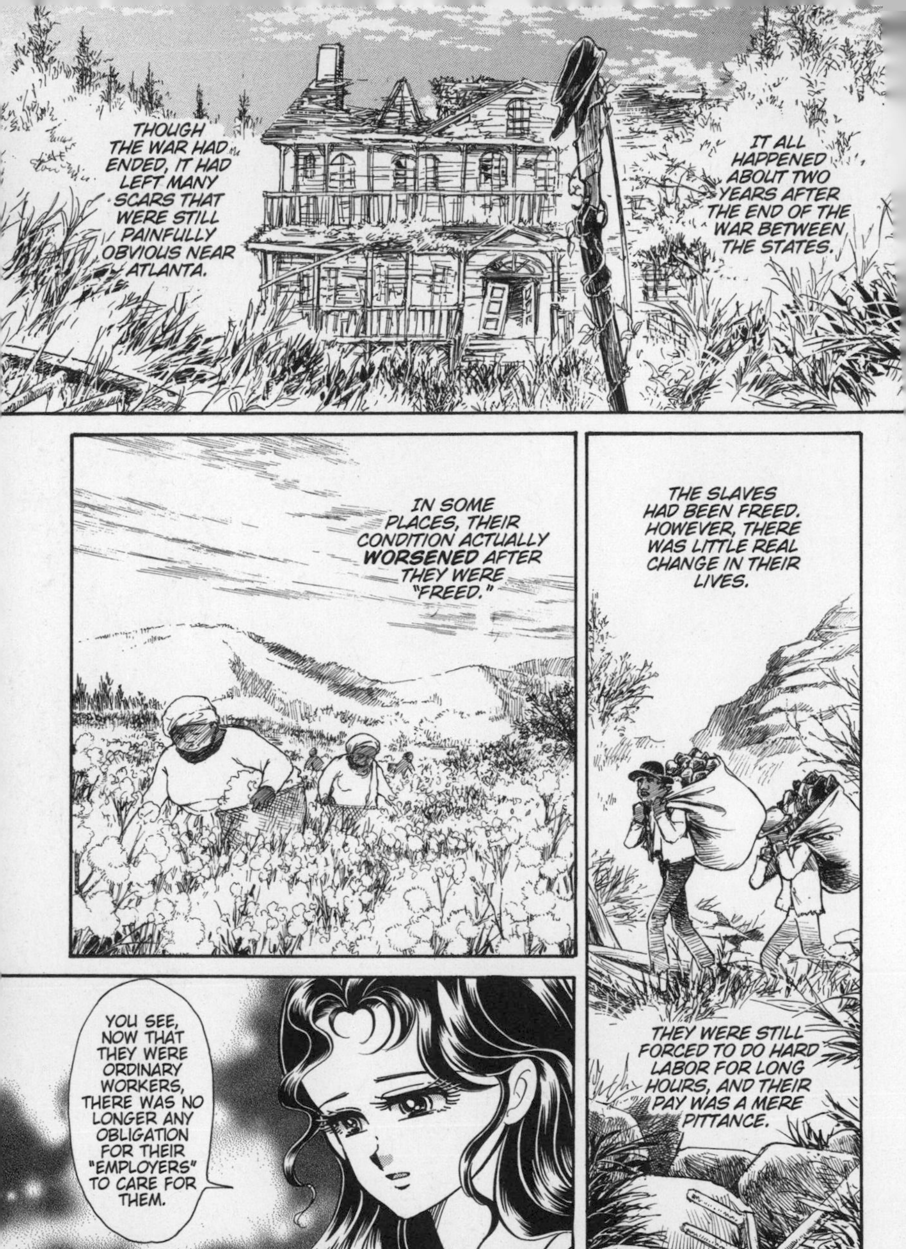
IT ALL HAPPENED ABOUT TWO YEARS AFTER THE END OF THE WAR BETWEEN THE STATES.
THOUGH THE WAR HAD ENDED, IT HAD LEFT MANY SCARS THAT WERE STILL PAINFULLY OBVIOUS NEAR ATLANTA.
THE SLAVES HAD BEEN FREED. HOWEVER, THERE WAS LITTLE REAL CHANGE IN THEIR LIVES.
THEY WERE STILL FORCED TO DO HARD LABOR FOR LONG HOURS, AND THEIR PAY WAS A MERE PITTANCE.
IN SOME PLACES, THEIR CONDITION ACTUALLY **WORSENED** AFTER THEY WERE "FREED."
YOU SEE, NOW THAT THEY WERE ORDINARY WORKERS, THERE WAS NO LONGER ANY OBLIGATION FOR THEIR "EMPLOYERS" TO CARE FOR THEM.

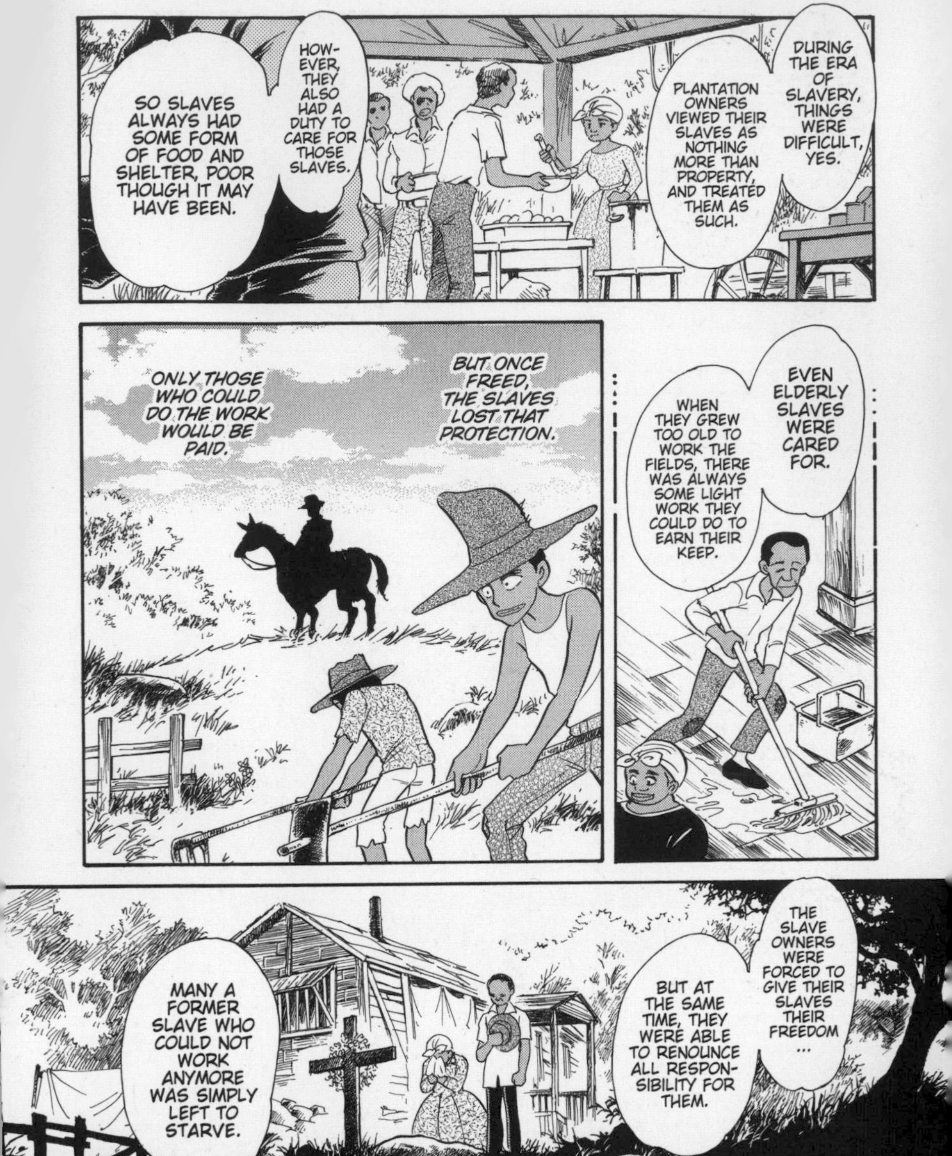
DURING THE ERA OF SLAVERY, THINGS WERE DIFFICULT, YES.
PLANTATION OWNERS VIEWED THEIR SLAVES AS NOTHING MORE THAN PROPERTY, AND TREATED THEM AS SUCH.
HOW-EVER, THEY ALSO HAD A DUTY TO CARE FOR THOSE SLAVES.
SO SLAVES ALWAYS HAD SOME FORM OF FOOD AND SHELTER, POOR THOUGH IT MAY HAVE BEEN.
EVEN ELDERLY SLAVES WERE CARED FOR.
WHEN THEY GREW TOO OLD TO WORK THE FIELDS, THERE WAS ALWAYS SOME LIGHT WORK THEY COULD DO TO EARN THEIR KEEP.
BUT ONCE FREED, THE SLAVES LOST THAT PROTECTION.
ONLY THOSE WHO COULD DO THE WORK WOULD BE PAID.
THE SLAVE OWNERS WERE FORCED TO GIVE THEIR SLAVES THEIR FREEDOM ...
BUT AT THE SAME TIME, THEY WERE ABLE TO RENOUNCE ALL RESPON-SIBILITY FOR THEM.
MANY A FORMER SLAVE WHO COULD NOT WORK ANYMORE WAS SIMPLY LEFT TO STARVE.

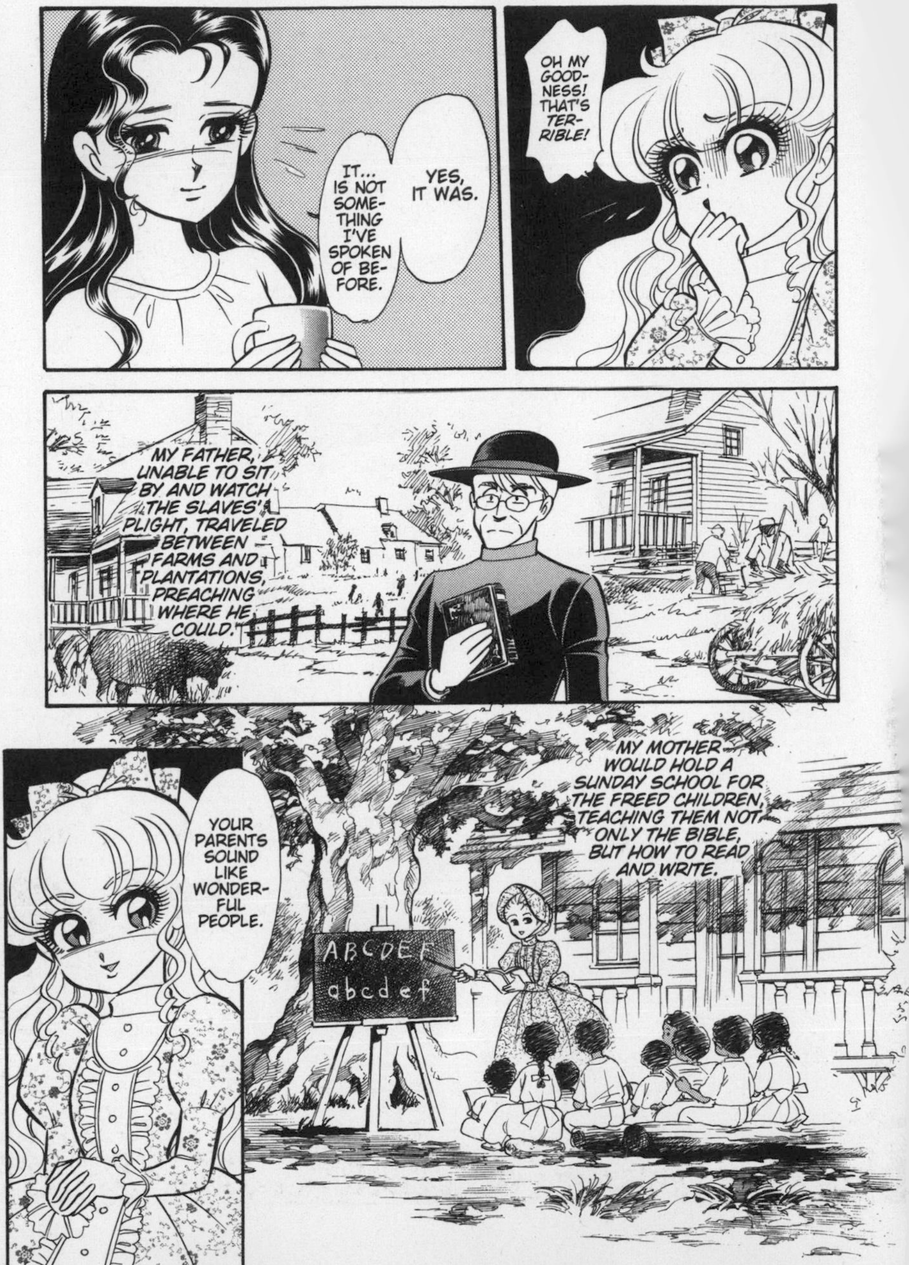
OH MY GOODNESS! THAT'S TERRIBLE!
YES, IT WAS.
IT... IS NOT SOMETHING I'VE SPOKEN OF BEFORE.
MY FATHER, UNABLE TO SIT BY AND WATCH THE SLAVES' PLIGHT, TRAVELED BETWEEN FARMS AND PLANTATIONS, PREACHING WHERE HE COULD.
MY MOTHER WOULD HOLD A SUNDAY SCHOOL FOR THE FREED CHILDREN, TEACHING THEM NOT ONLY THE BIBLE, BUT HOW TO READ AND WRITE.
ABCDEF
abcdef
YOUR PARENTS SOUND LIKE WONDERFUL PEOPLE.

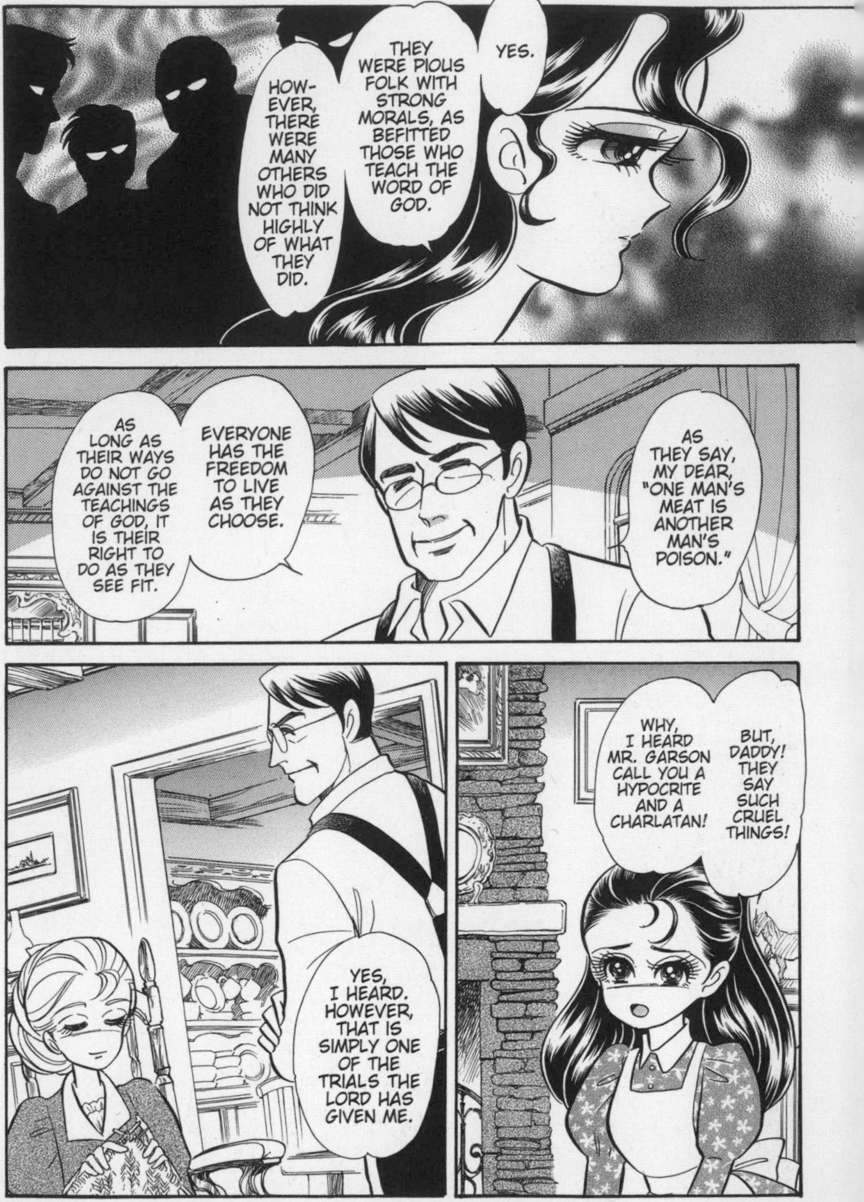
YES.
THEY WERE PIOUS FOLK WITH STRONG MORALS, AS BEFITTED THOSE WHO TEACH THE WORD OF GOD.
HOW-EVER, THERE WERE MANY OTHERS WHO DID NOT THINK HIGHLY OF WHAT THEY DID.
AS THEY SAY, MY DEAR, "ONE MAN'S MEAT IS ANOTHER MAN'S POISON."
EVERYONE HAS THE FREEDOM TO LIVE AS THEY CHOOSE.
AS LONG AS THEIR WAYS DO NOT GO AGAINST THE TEACHINGS OF GOD, IT IS THEIR RIGHT TO DO AS THEY SEE FIT.
BUT, DADDY! THEY SAY SUCH CRUEL THINGS!
WHY, I HEARD MR. GARSON CALL YOU A HYPOCRITE AND A CHARLATAN!
YES, I HEARD. HOWEVER, THAT IS SIMPLY ONE OF THE TRIALS THE LORD HAS GIVEN ME.

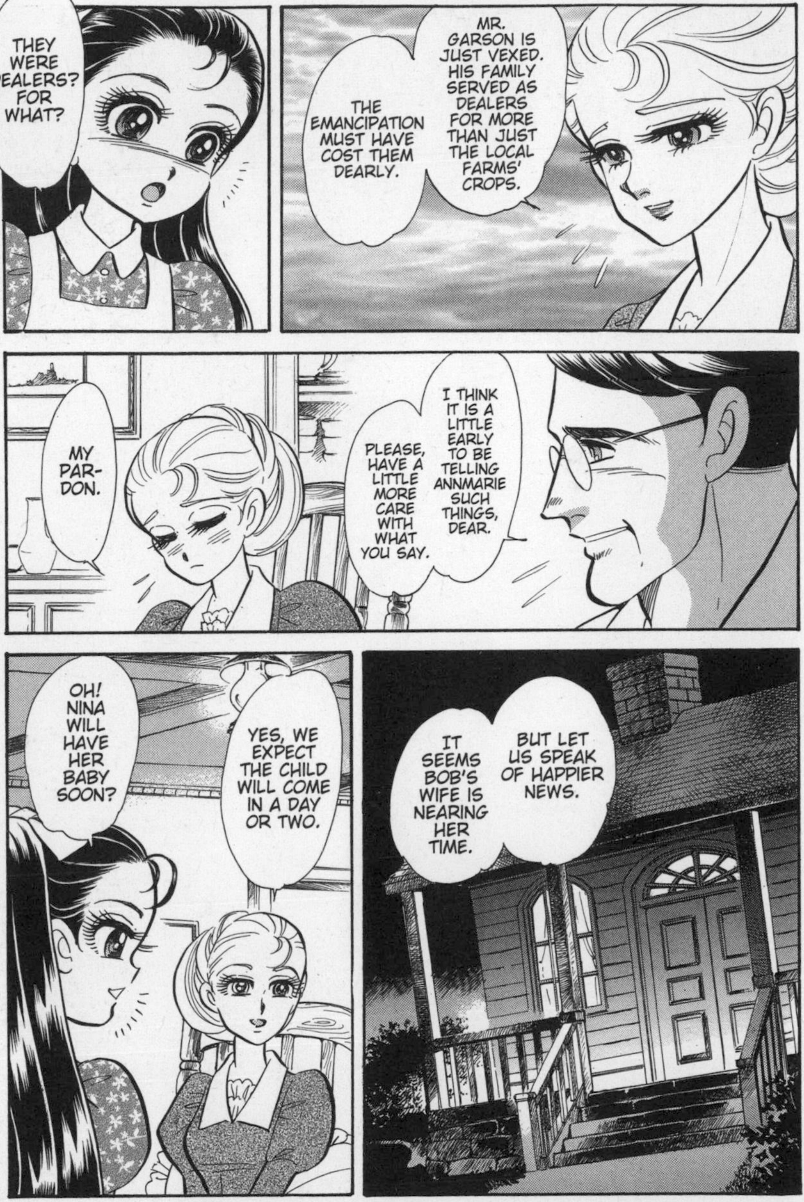
MR. GARSON IS JUST VEXED. HIS FAMILY SERVED AS DEALERS FOR MORE THAN JUST THE LOCAL FARMS' CROPS.
THE EMANCIPATION MUST HAVE COST THEM DEARLY.
THEY WERE DEALERS? FOR WHAT?
I THINK IT IS A LITTLE EARLY TO BE TELLING ANNMARIE SUCH THINGS, DEAR.
PLEASE, HAVE A LITTLE MORE CARE WITH WHAT YOU SAY.
MY PAR-DON.
BUT LET US SPEAK OF HAPPIER NEWS.
IT SEEMS BOB'S WIFE IS NEARING HER TIME.
OH! NINA WILL HAVE HER BABY SOON?
YES, WE EXPECT THE CHILD WILL COME IN A DAY OR TWO.

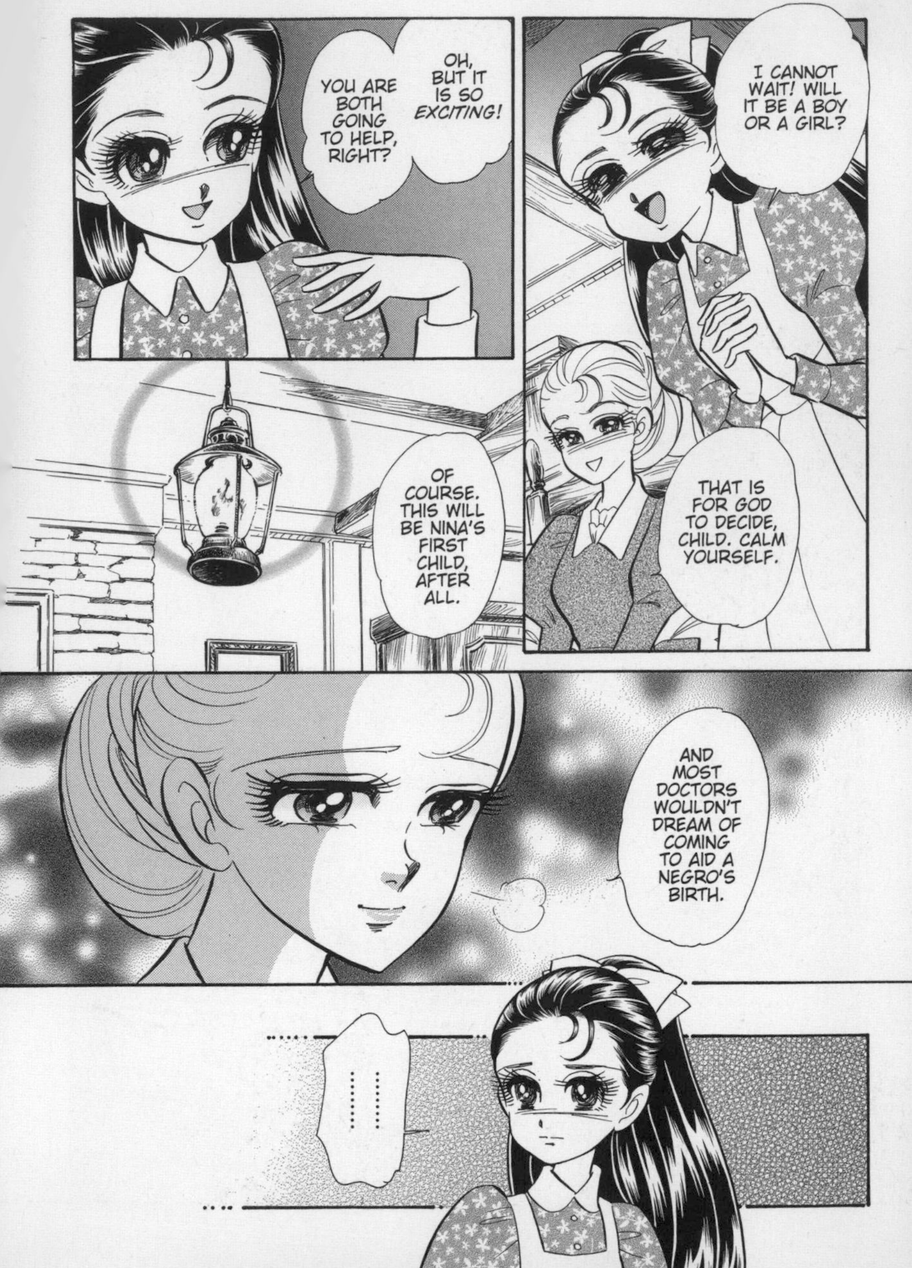
I CANNOT WAIT! WILL IT BE A BOY OR A GIRL?
THAT IS FOR GOD TO DECIDE, CHILD. CALM YOURSELF.
OH, BUT IT IS SO *EXCITING!*
YOU ARE BOTH GOING TO HELP, RIGHT?
OF COURSE. THIS WILL BE NINA'S FIRST CHILD, AFTER ALL.
AND MOST DOCTORS WOULDN'T DREAM OF COMING TO AID A NEGRO'S BIRTH.
......

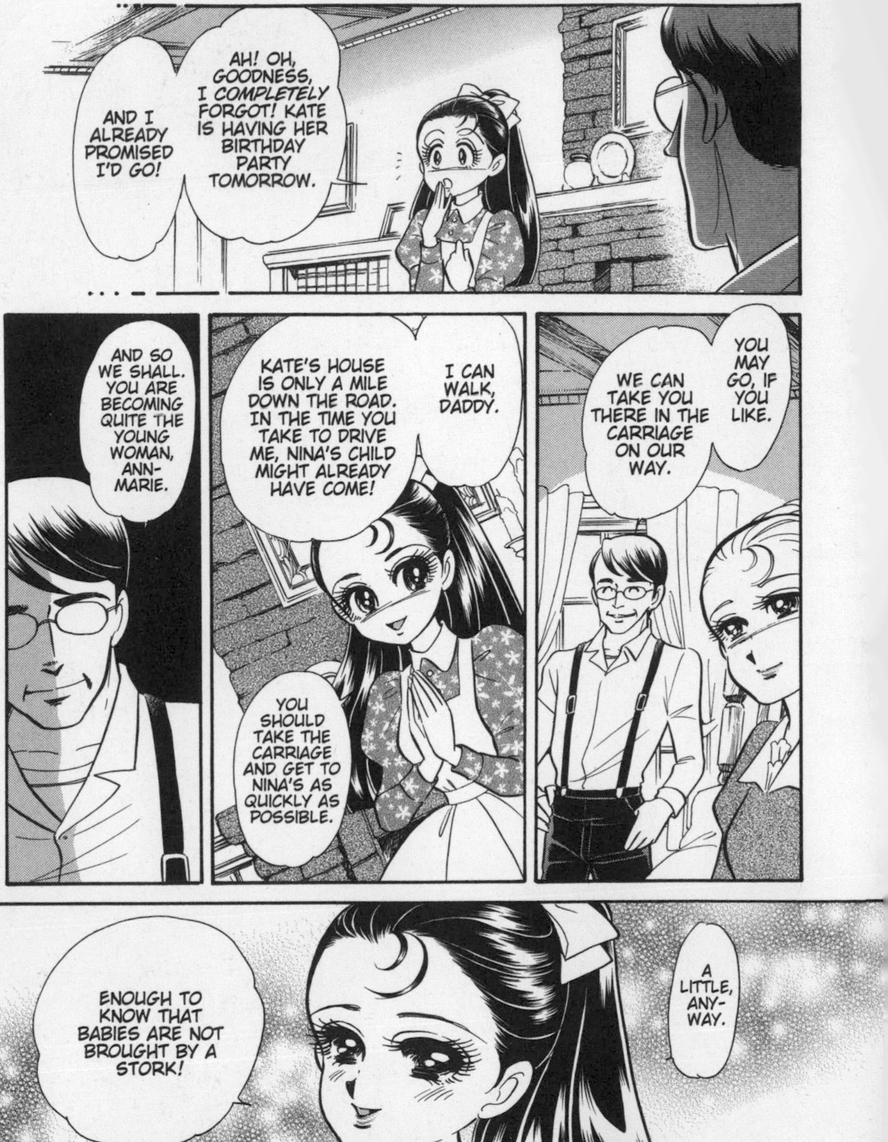
AH! OH, GOODNESS, I *COMPLETELY* FORGOT! KATE IS HAVING HER BIRTHDAY PARTY TOMORROW.
AND I ALREADY PROMISED I'D GO!
YOU MAY GO, IF YOU LIKE.
WE CAN TAKE YOU THERE IN THE CARRIAGE ON OUR WAY.
I CAN WALK, DADDY.
KATE'S HOUSE IS ONLY A MILE DOWN THE ROAD. IN THE TIME YOU TAKE TO DRIVE ME, NINA'S CHILD MIGHT ALREADY HAVE COME!
YOU SHOULD TAKE THE CARRIAGE AND GET TO NINA'S AS QUICKLY AS POSSIBLE.
AND SO WE SHALL. YOU ARE BECOMING QUITE THE YOUNG WOMAN, ANN-MARIE.
A LITTLE, ANY-WAY.
ENOUGH TO KNOW THAT BABIES ARE NOT BROUGHT BY A STORK!

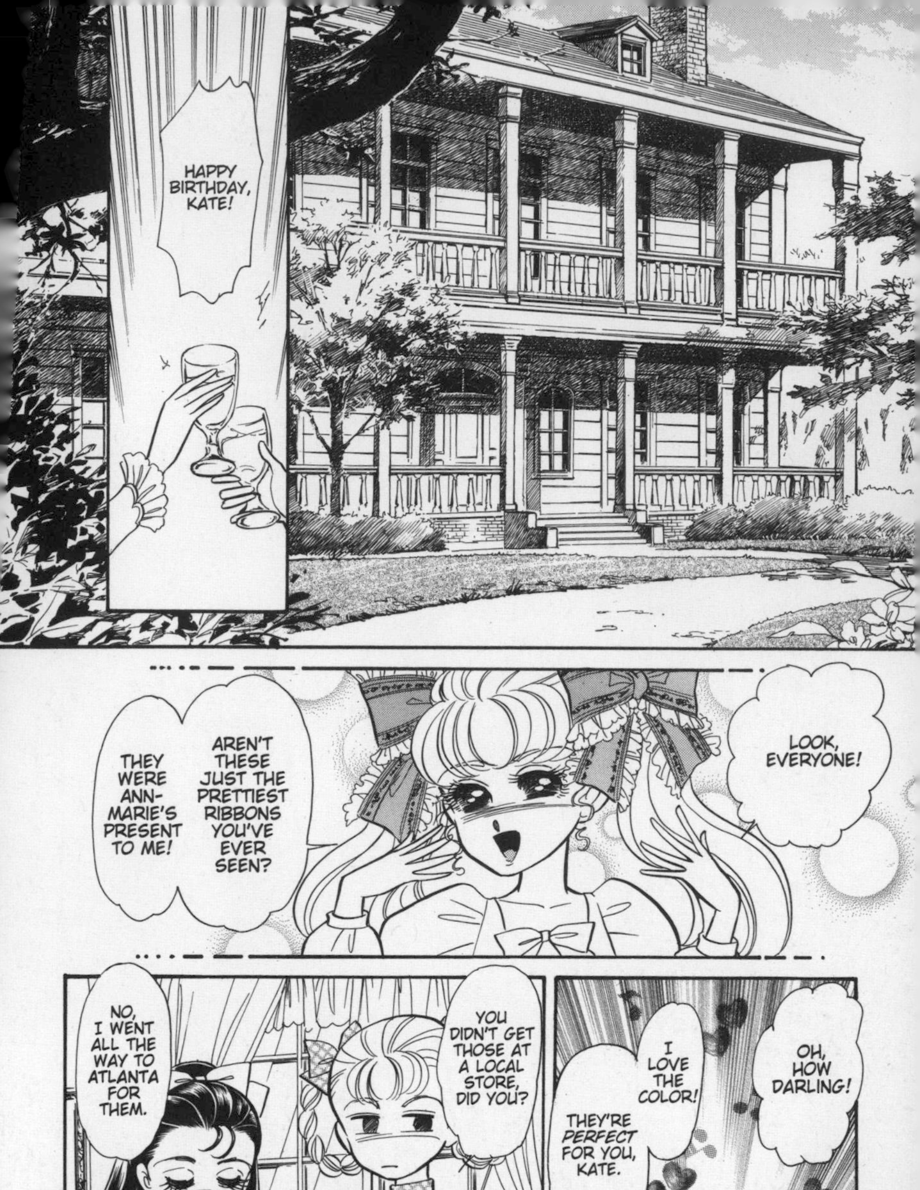
HAPPY BIRTHDAY, KATE!
LOOK, EVERYONE!
AREN'T THESE JUST THE PRETTIEST RIBBONS YOU'VE EVER SEEN?
THEY WERE ANN-MARIE'S PRESENT TO ME!
OH, HOW DARLING!
I LOVE THE COLOR!
THEY'RE *PERFECT* FOR YOU, KATE.
YOU DIDN'T GET THOSE AT A LOCAL STORE, DID YOU?
NO, I WENT ALL THE WAY TO ATLANTA FOR THEM.

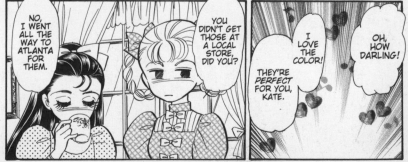

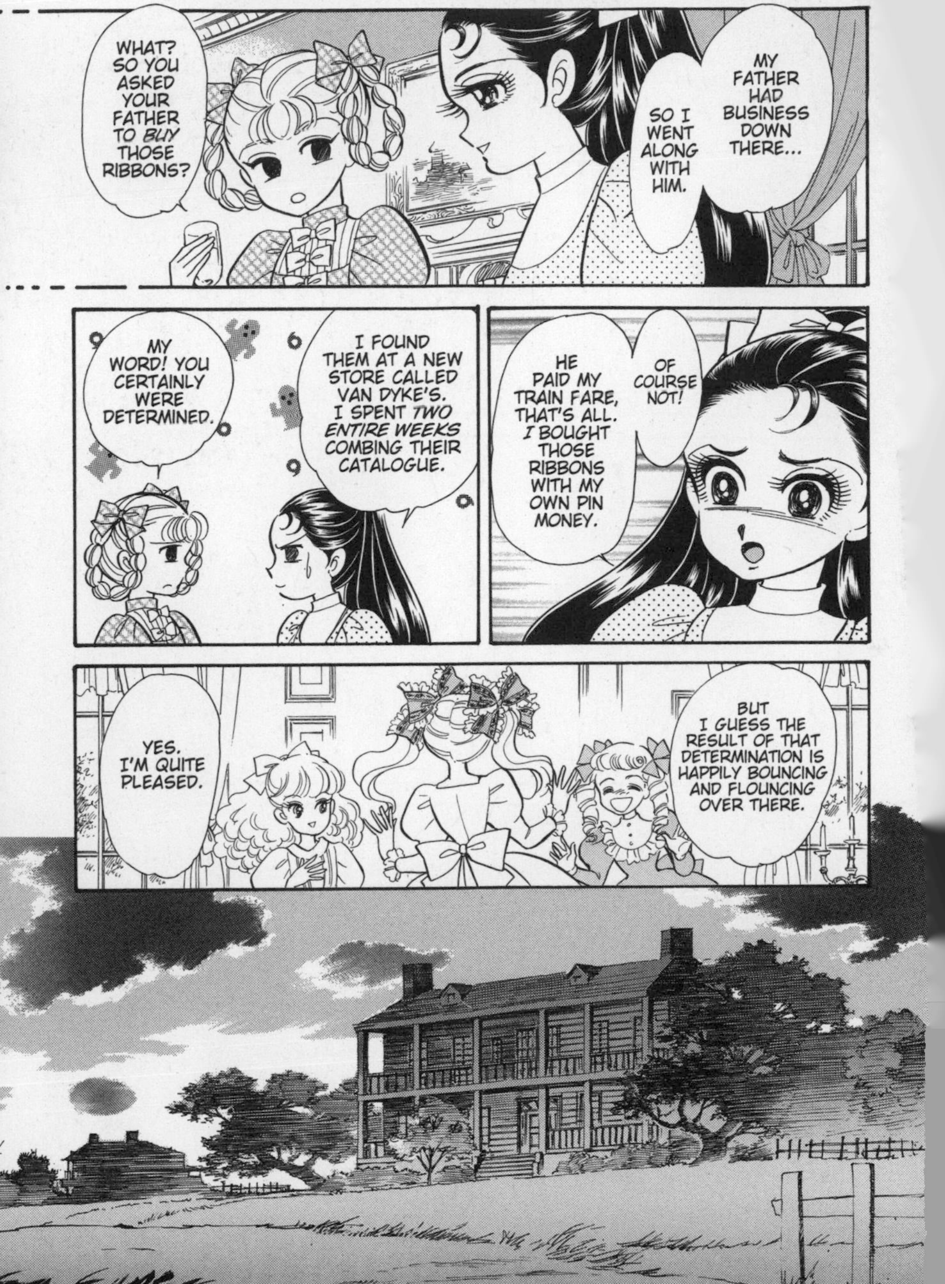
MY FATHER HAD BUSINESS DOWN THERE...
SO I WENT ALONG WITH HIM.
WHAT? SO YOU ASKED YOUR FATHER TO *BUY* THOSE RIBBONS?
OF COURSE NOT!
HE PAID MY TRAIN FARE, THAT'S ALL. *I* BOUGHT THOSE RIBBONS WITH MY OWN PIN MONEY.
I FOUND THEM AT A NEW STORE CALLED VAN DYKE'S. I SPENT *TWO ENTIRE WEEKS* COMBING THEIR CATALOGUE.
MY WORD! YOU CERTAINLY WERE DETERMINED.
BUT I GUESS THE RESULT OF THAT DETERMINATION IS HAPPILY BOUNCING AND FLOUNCING OVER THERE.
YES. I'M QUITE PLEASED.

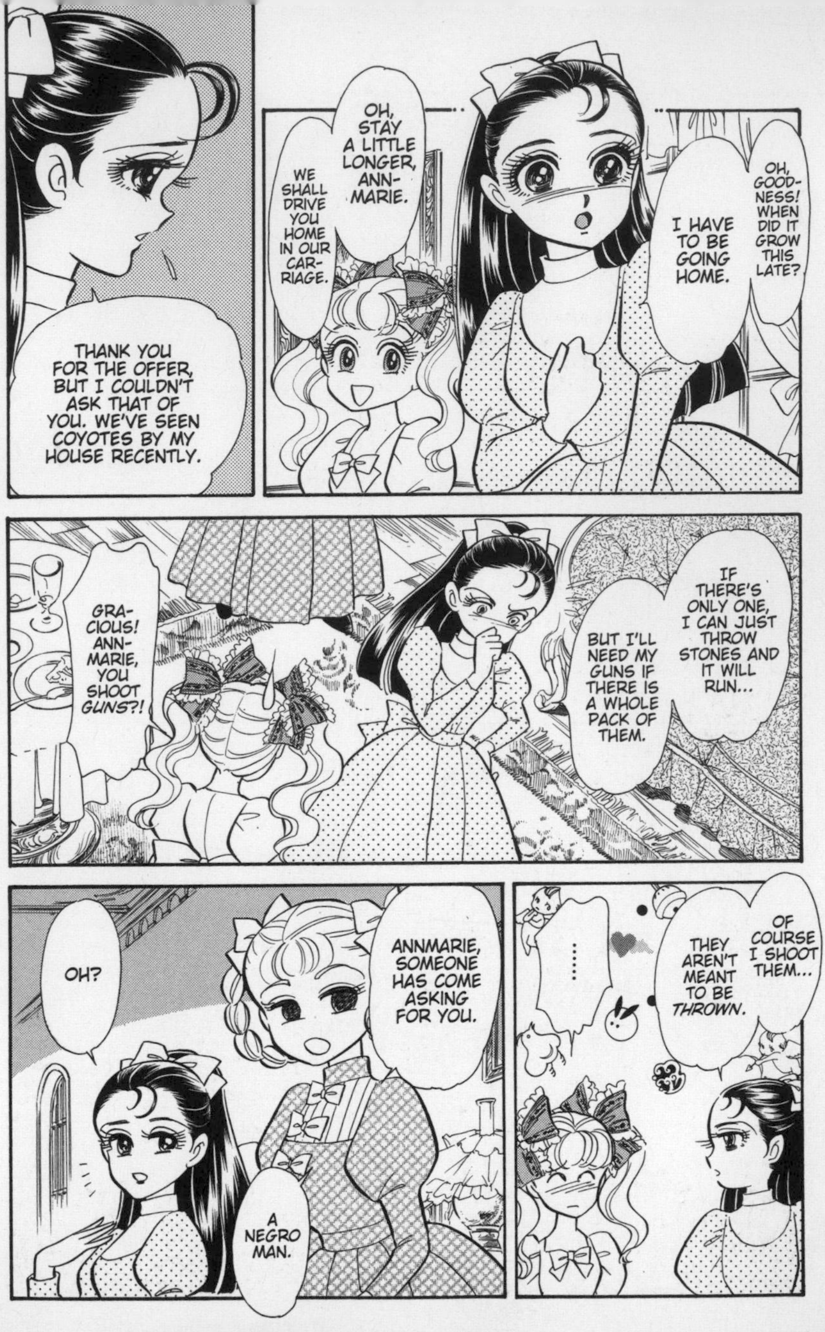
OH, GOODNESS! WHEN DID IT GROW THIS LATE?
I HAVE TO BE GOING HOME.
OH, STAY A LITTLE LONGER, ANN-MARIE.
WE SHALL DRIVE YOU HOME IN OUR CAR-RIAGE.
THANK YOU FOR THE OFFER, BUT I COULDN'T ASK THAT OF YOU. WE'VE SEEN COYOTES BY MY HOUSE RECENTLY.
IF THERE'S ONLY ONE, I CAN JUST THROW STONES AND IT WILL RUN...
BUT I'LL NEED MY GUNS IF THERE IS A WHOLE PACK OF THEM.
GRA-CIOUS! ANN-MARIE, YOU SHOOT GUNS?!
OF COURSE I SHOOT THEM...
THEY AREN'T MEANT TO BE *THROWN*.
......
ANNMARIE, SOMEONE HAS COME ASKING FOR YOU.
OH?
A NEGRO MAN.

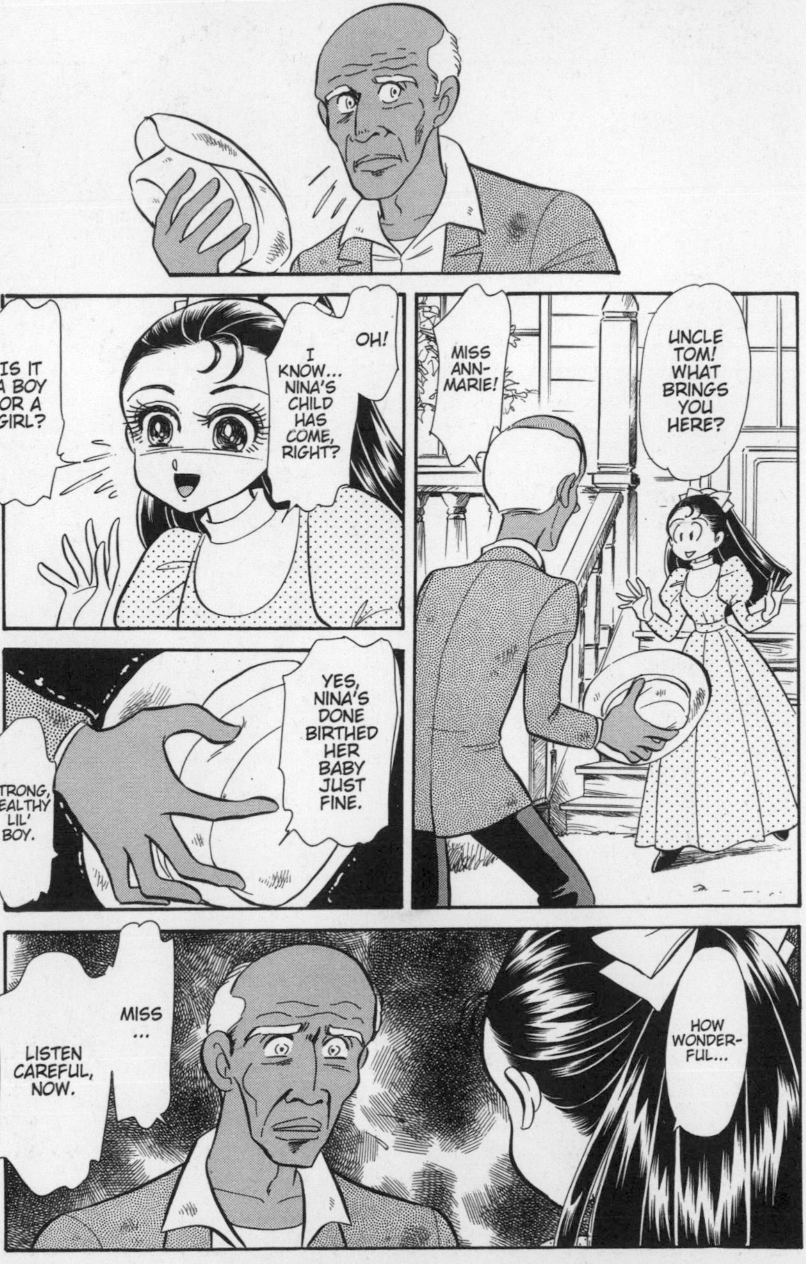
UNCLE TOM! WHAT BRINGS YOU HERE?
MISS ANN-MARIE!
OH!
I KNOW... NINA'S CHILD HAS COME, RIGHT?
IS IT A BOY OR A GIRL?
YES, NINA'S DONE BIRTHED HER BABY JUST FINE.
STRONG, HEALTHY LIL' BOY.
HOW WONDERFUL...
MISS ...
LISTEN CAREFUL, NOW.

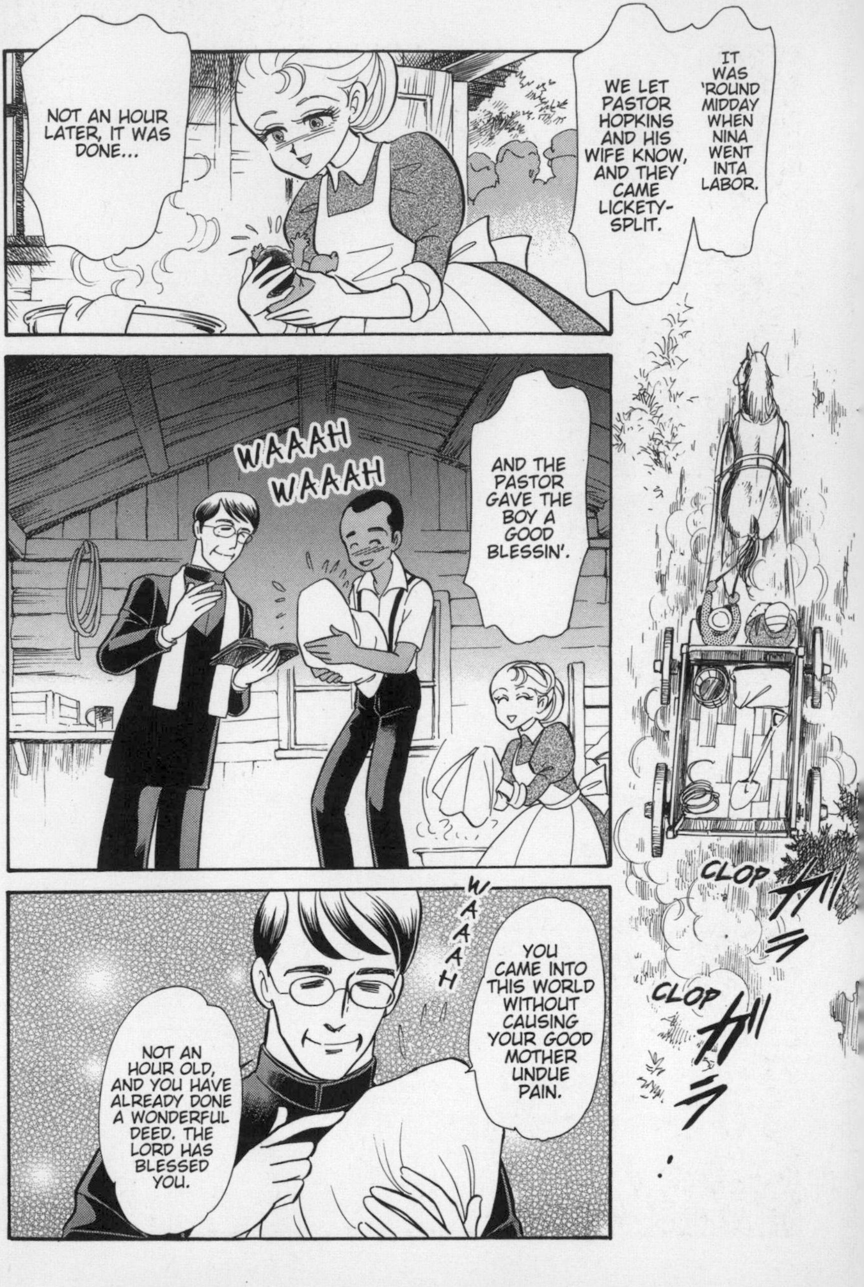
IT WAS 'ROUND MIDDAY WHEN NINA WENT INTA LABOR.
WE LET PASTOR HOPKINS AND HIS WIFE KNOW, AND THEY CAME LICKETY-SPLIT.
CLOP
CLOP
NOT AN HOUR LATER, IT WAS DONE...
AND THE PASTOR GAVE THE BOY A GOOD BLESSIN'.
WAAAH WAAAH
WAAAAH
YOU CAME INTO THIS WORLD WITHOUT CAUSING YOUR GOOD MOTHER UNDUE PAIN.
NOT AN HOUR OLD, AND YOU HAVE ALREADY DONE A WONDERFUL DEED. THE LORD HAS BLESSED YOU.

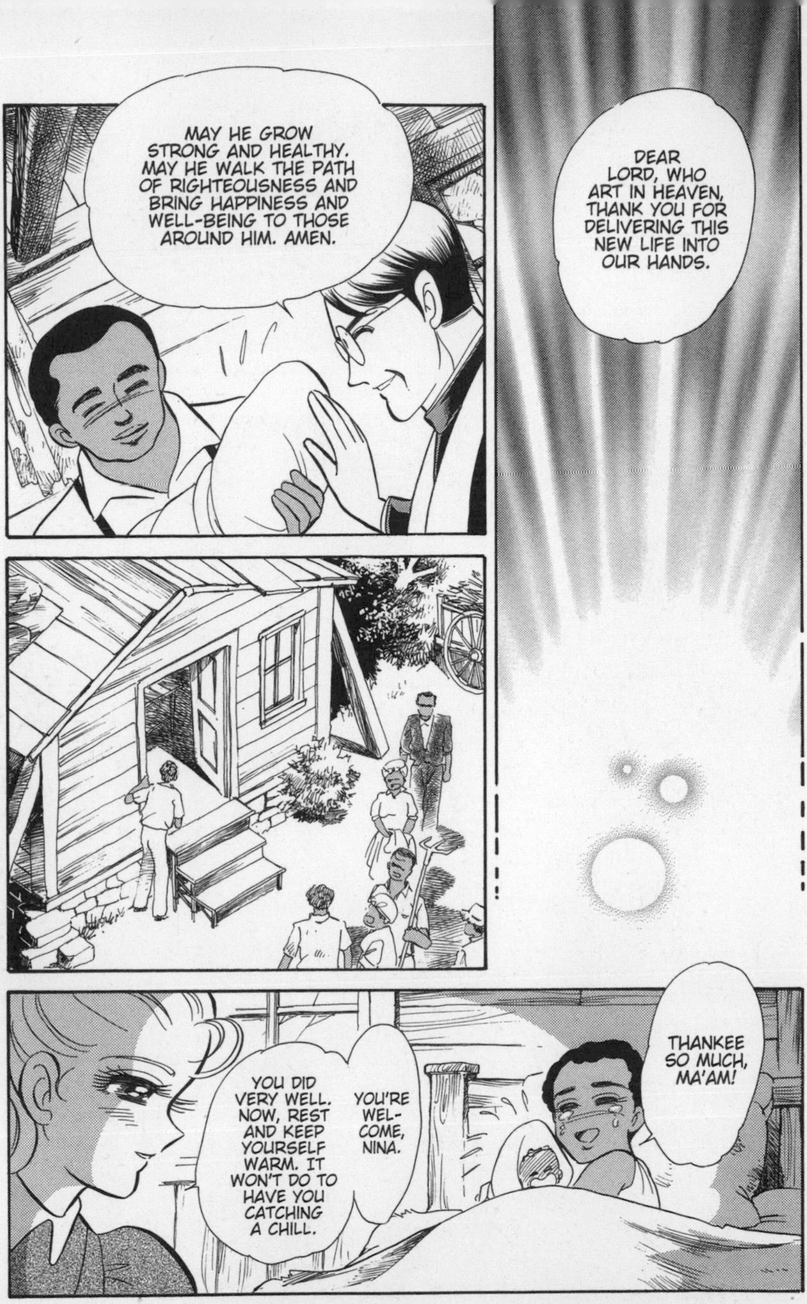
DEAR LORD, WHO ART IN HEAVEN, THANK YOU FOR DELIVERING THIS NEW LIFE INTO OUR HANDS.
MAY HE GROW STRONG AND HEALTHY. MAY HE WALK THE PATH OF RIGHTEOUSNESS AND BRING HAPPINESS AND WELL-BEING TO THOSE AROUND HIM. AMEN.
THANKEE SO MUCH, MA'AM!
YOU'RE WEL-COME, NINA.
YOU DID VERY WELL. NOW, REST AND KEEP YOURSELF WARM. IT WON'T DO TO HAVE YOU CATCHING A CHILL.

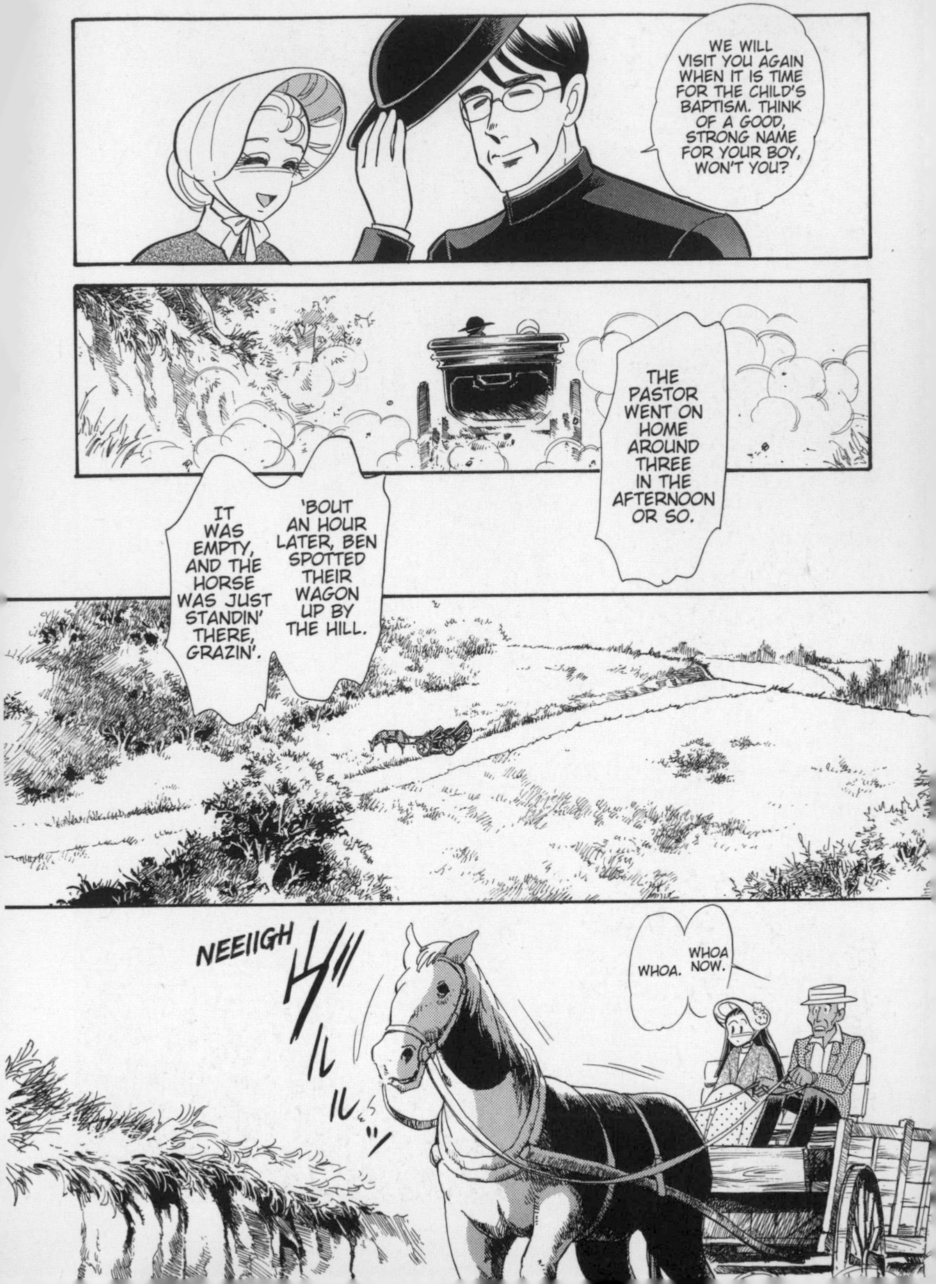
WE WILL VISIT YOU AGAIN WHEN IT IS TIME FOR THE CHILD'S BAPTISM. THINK OF A GOOD, STRONG NAME FOR YOUR BOY, WON'T YOU?
THE PASTOR WENT ON HOME AROUND THREE IN THE AFTERNOON OR SO.
'BOUT AN HOUR LATER, BEN SPOTTED THEIR WAGON UP BY THE HILL.
IT WAS EMPTY, AND THE HORSE WAS JUST STANDIN' THERE, GRAZIN'.
WHOA NOW.
WHOA.
NEEIIGH

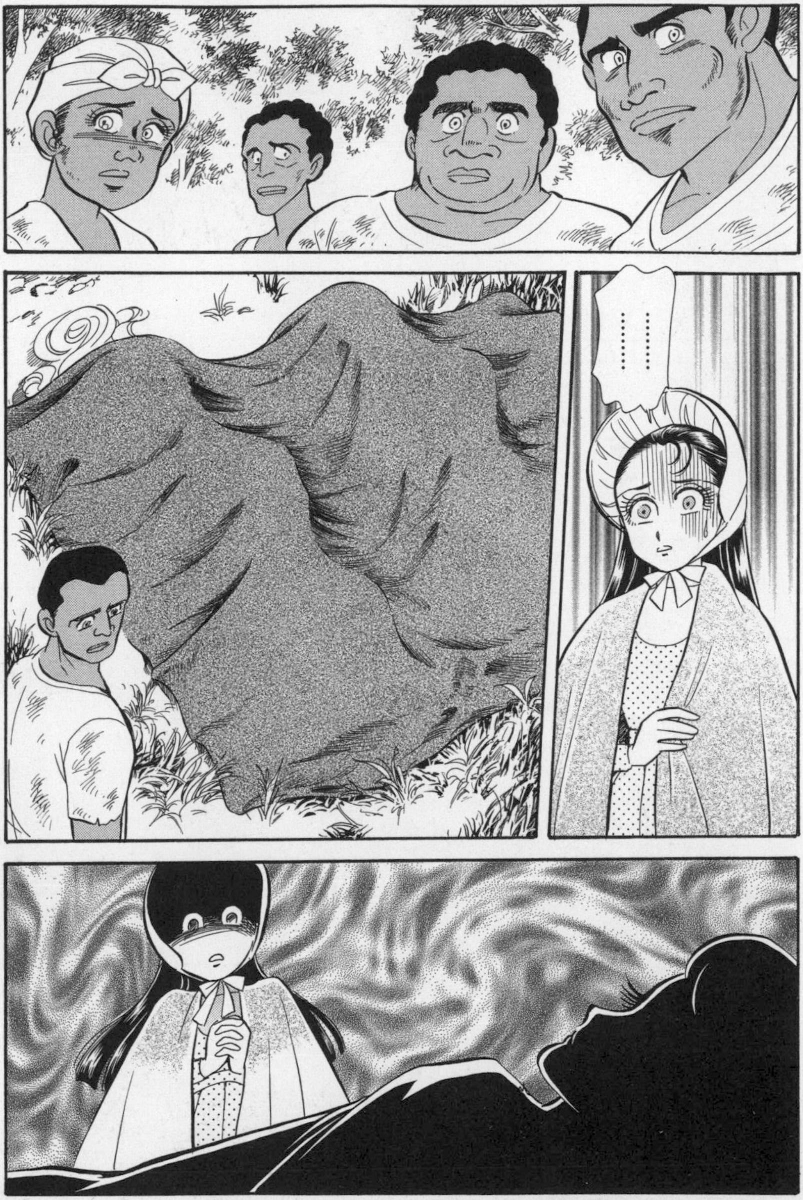
……

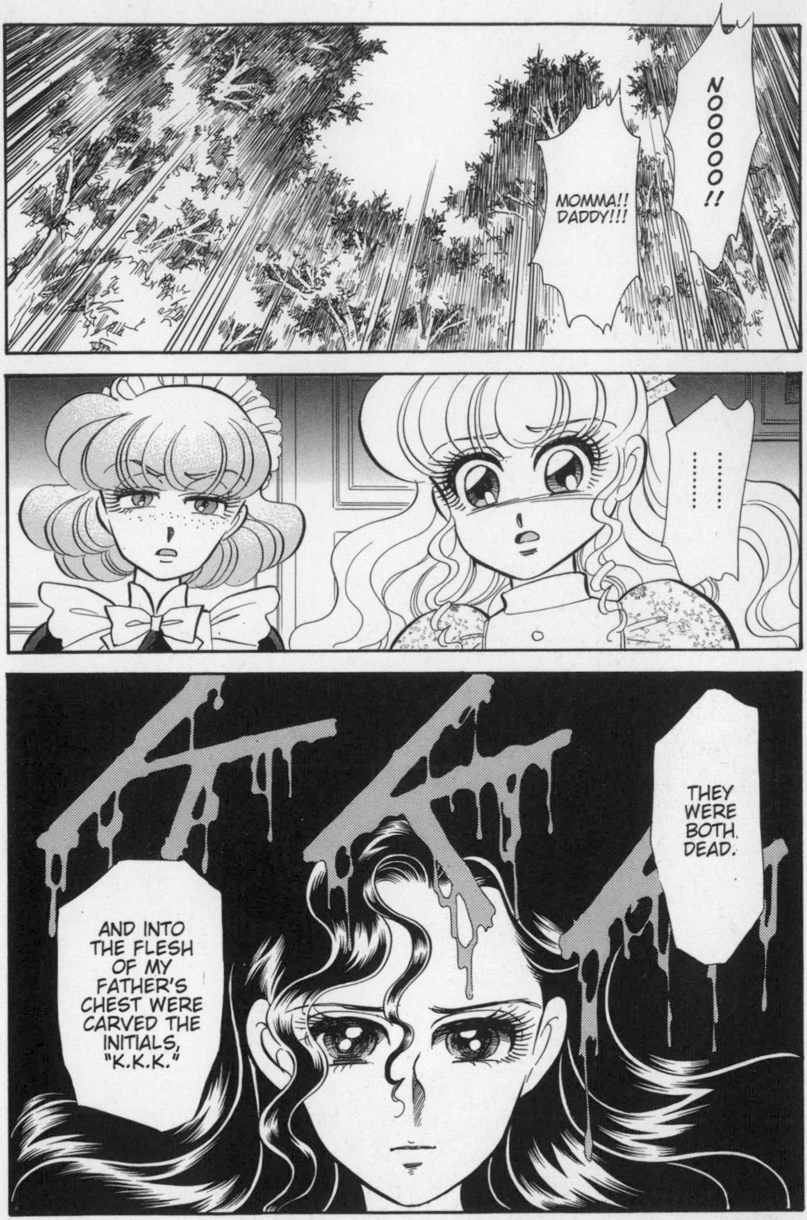
NOOOOOO!!
MOMMA!! DADDY!!!
......
THEY WERE BOTH DEAD.
AND INTO THE FLESH OF MY FATHER'S CHEST WERE CARVED THE INITIALS, "K.K.K."

The Five Orange Pips (3)

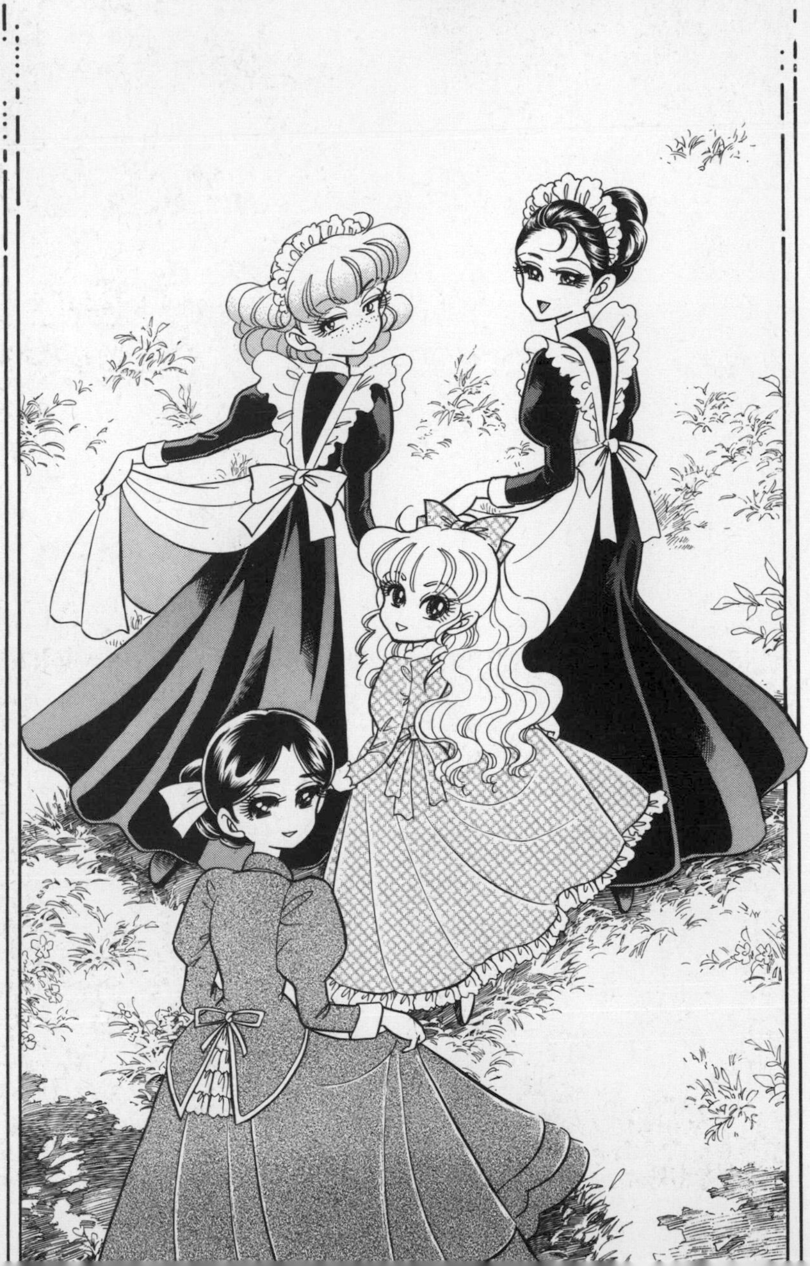

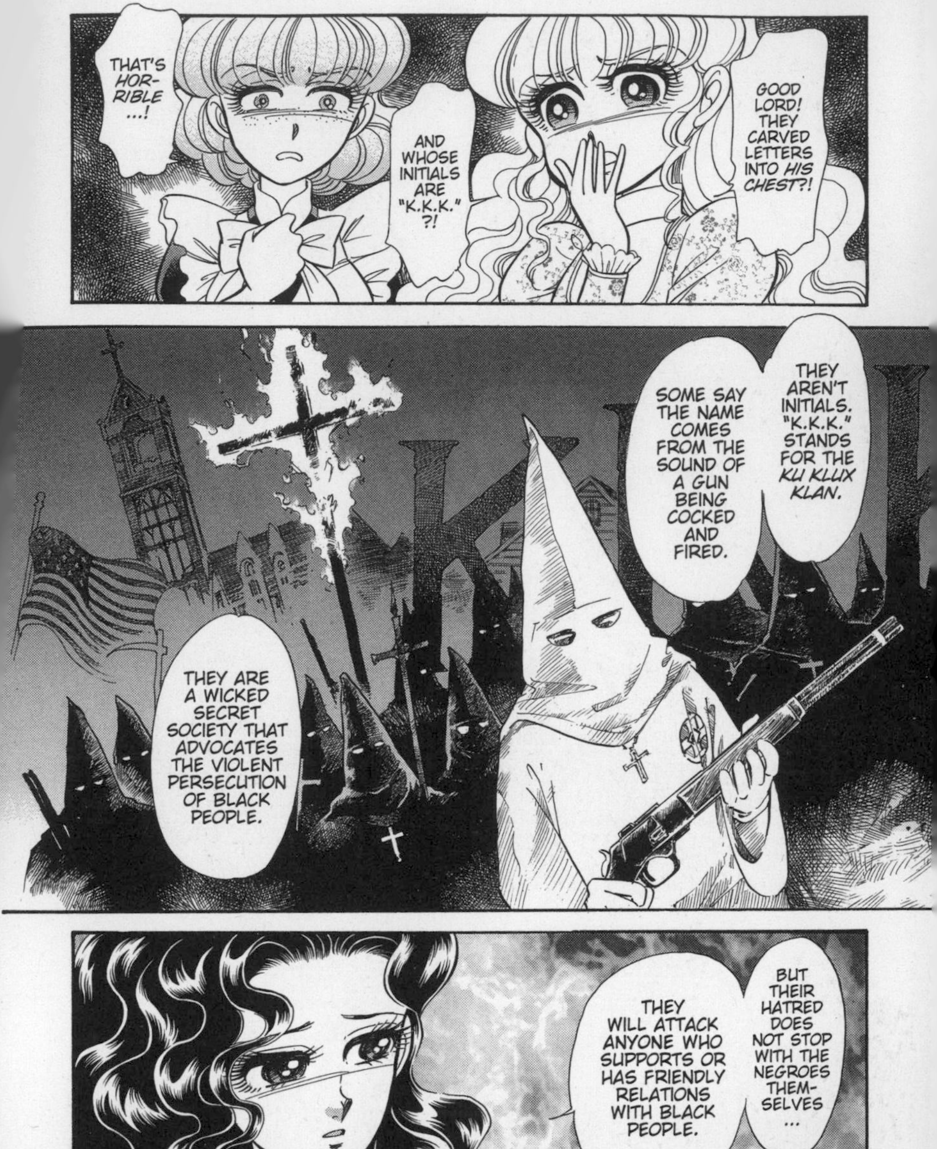
GOOD LORD! THEY CARVED LETTERS INTO HIS CHEST?!
AND WHOSE INITIALS ARE "K.K.K."?!
THAT'S HOR-RIBLE...!
THEY AREN'T INITIALS. "K.K.K." STANDS FOR THE KU KLUX KLAN.
SOME SAY THE NAME COMES FROM THE SOUND OF A GUN BEING COCKED AND FIRED.
THEY ARE A WICKED SECRET SOCIETY THAT ADVOCATES THE VIOLENT PERSECUTION OF BLACK PEOPLE.
BUT THEIR HATRED DOES NOT STOP WITH THE NEGROES THEM-SELVES...
THEY WILL ATTACK ANYONE WHO SUPPORTS OR HAS FRIENDLY RELATIONS WITH BLACK PEOPLE.

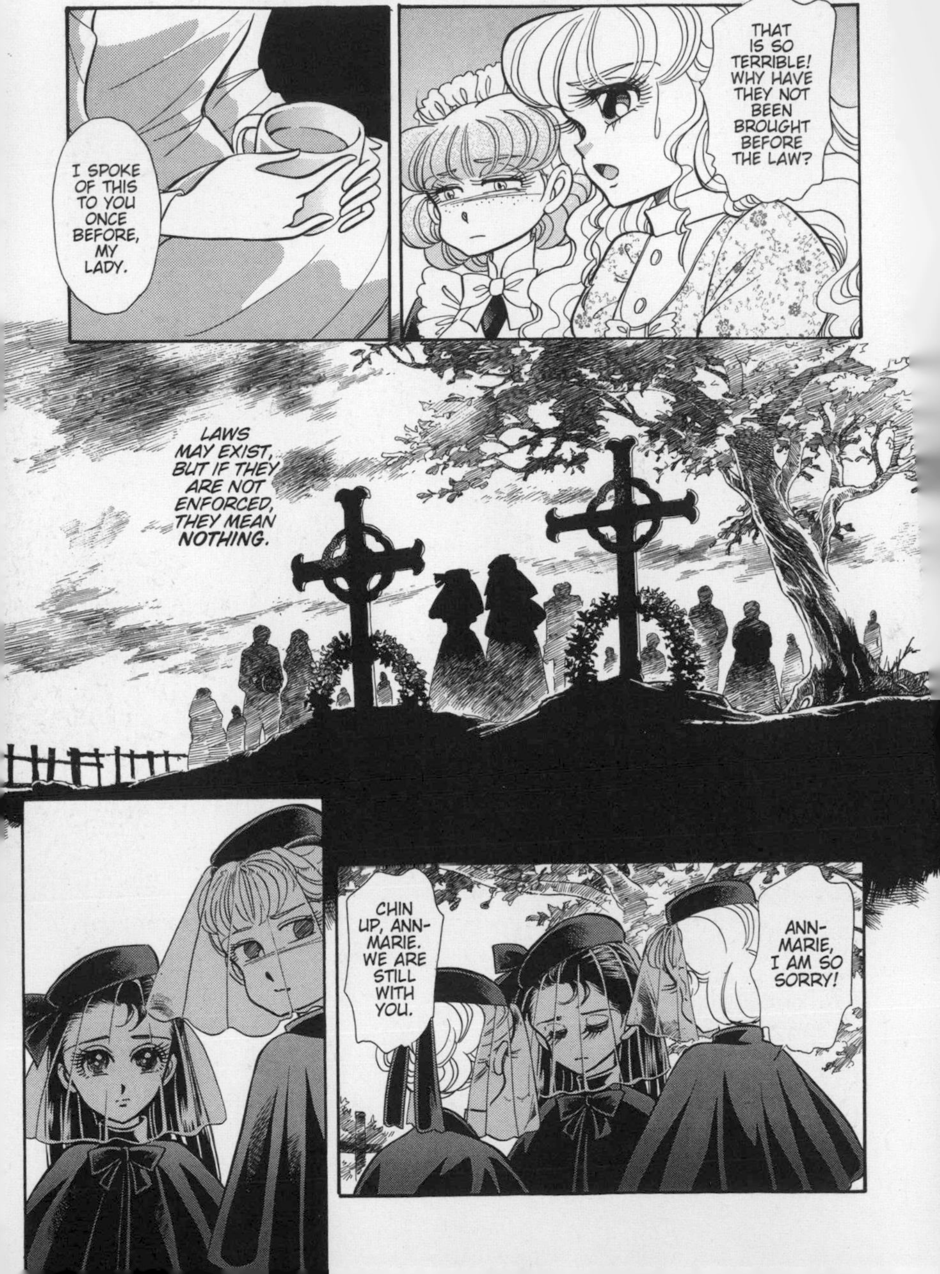
THAT IS SO TERRIBLE! WHY HAVE THEY NOT BEEN BROUGHT BEFORE THE LAW?
I SPOKE OF THIS TO YOU ONCE BEFORE, MY LADY.
LAWS MAY EXIST, BUT IF THEY ARE NOT ENFORCED, THEY MEAN NOTHING.
ANN-MARIE, I AM SO SORRY!
CHIN UP, ANN-MARIE. WE ARE STILL WITH YOU.

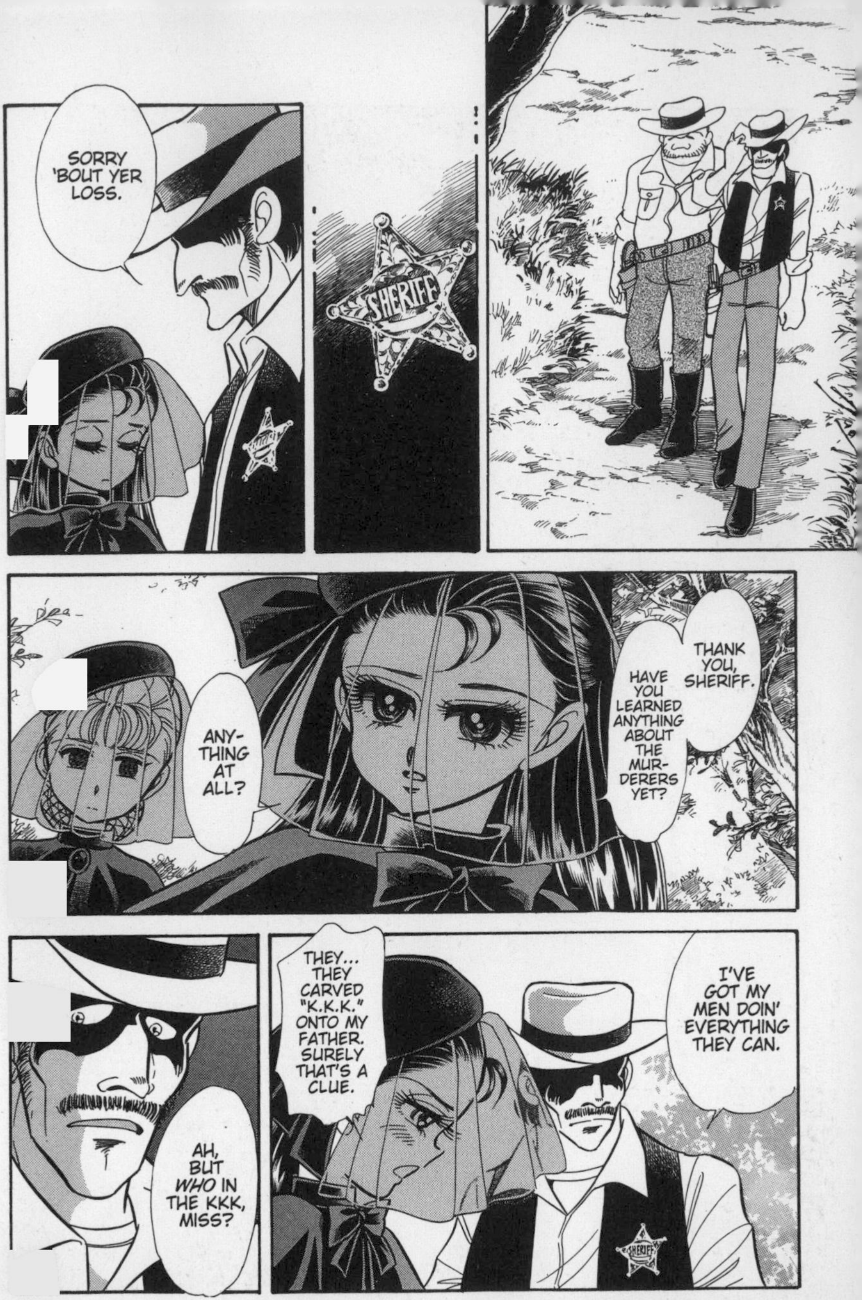
SHERIFF
SORRY 'BOUT YER LOSS.
THANK YOU, SHERIFF.
HAVE YOU LEARNED ANYTHING ABOUT THE MURDERERS YET?
ANYTHING AT ALL?
I'VE GOT MY MEN DOIN' EVERYTHING THEY CAN.
THEY... THEY CARVED "K.K.K." ONTO MY FATHER. SURELY THAT'S A CLUE.
AH, BUT *WHO* IN THE KKK, MISS?
SHERIFF

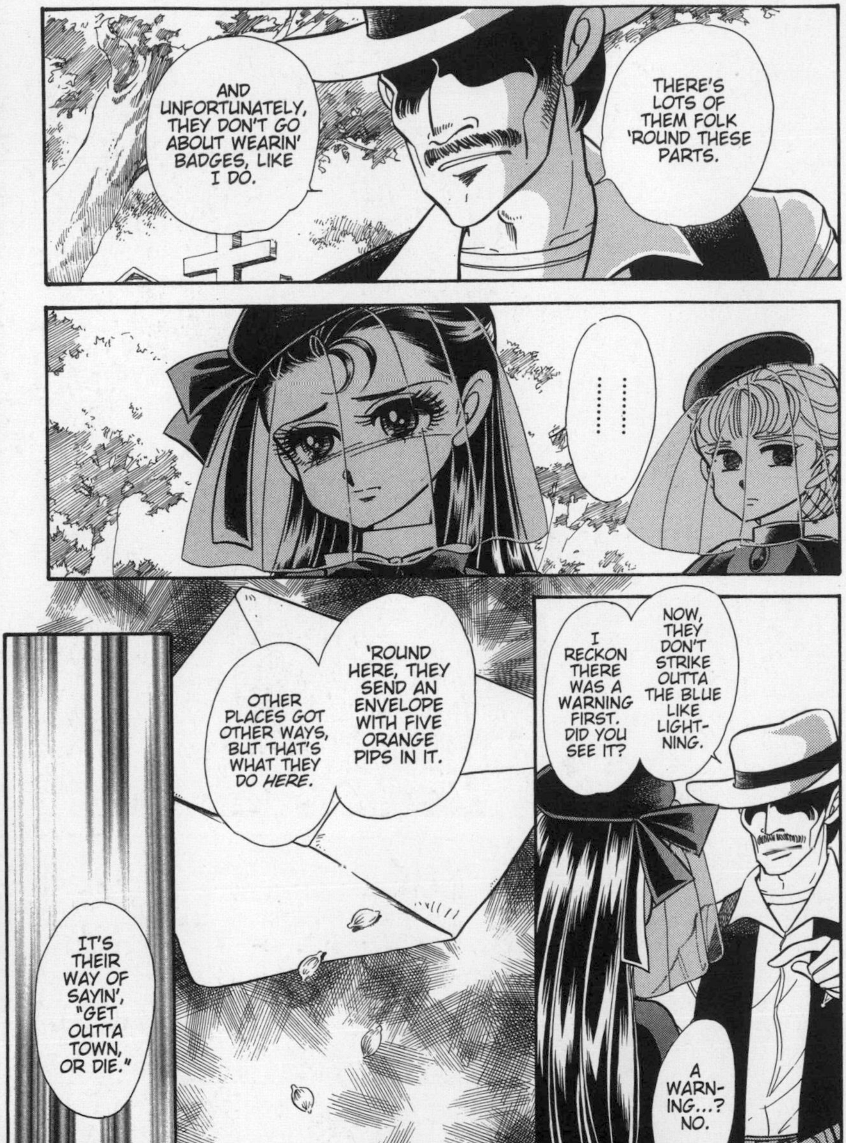
THERE'S LOTS OF THEM FOLK 'ROUND THESE PARTS.
AND UNFORTUNATELY, THEY DON'T GO ABOUT WEARIN' BADGES, LIKE I DO.
......
NOW, THEY DON'T STRIKE OUTTA THE BLUE LIKE LIGHT-NING.
I RECKON THERE WAS A WARNING FIRST. DID YOU SEE IT?
A WARN-ING...? NO.
'ROUND HERE, THEY SEND AN ENVELOPE WITH FIVE ORANGE PIPS IN IT.
OTHER PLACES GOT OTHER WAYS, BUT THAT'S WHAT THEY DO *HERE*.
IT'S THEIR WAY OF SAYIN', "GET OUTTA TOWN, OR DIE."

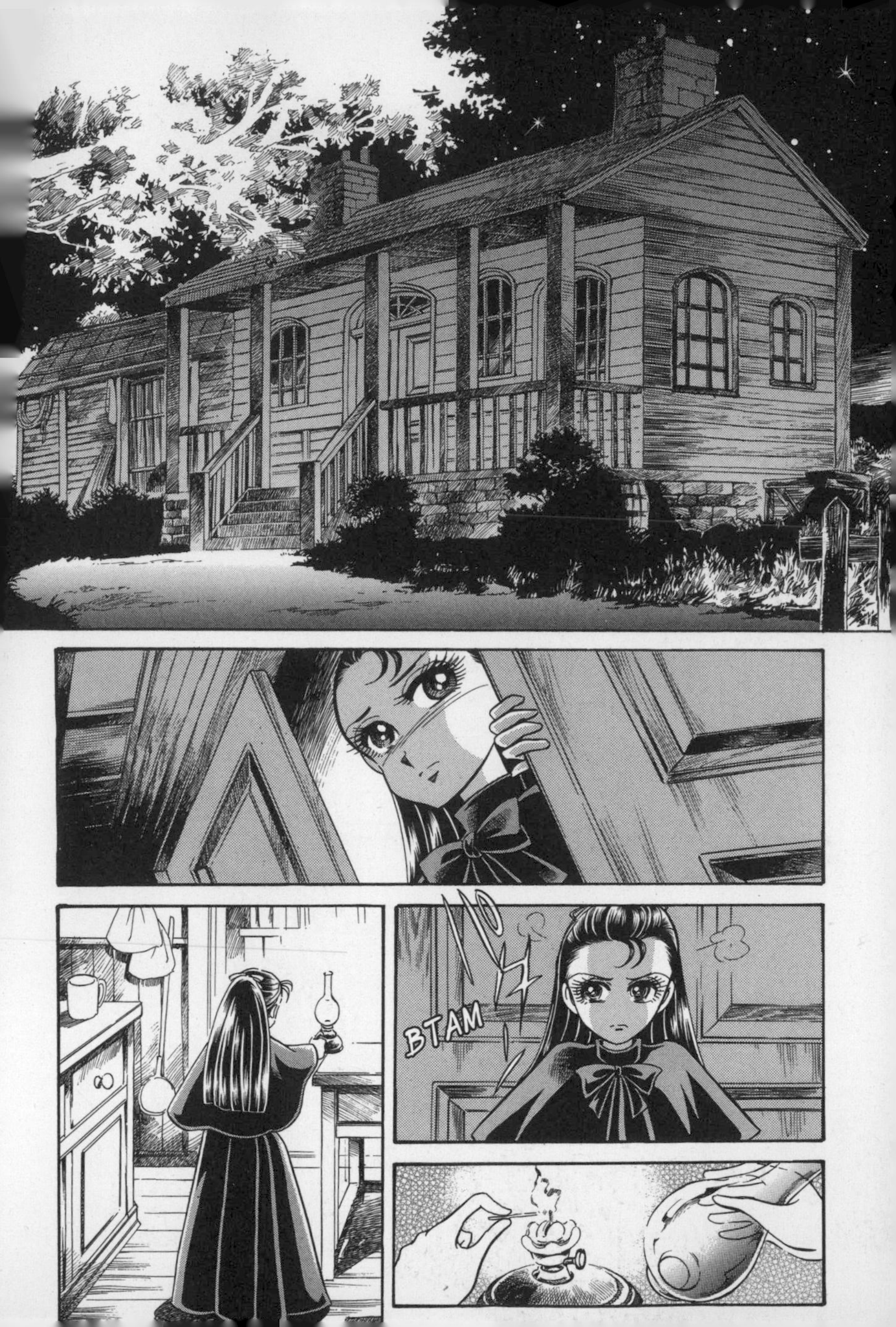
BTAM

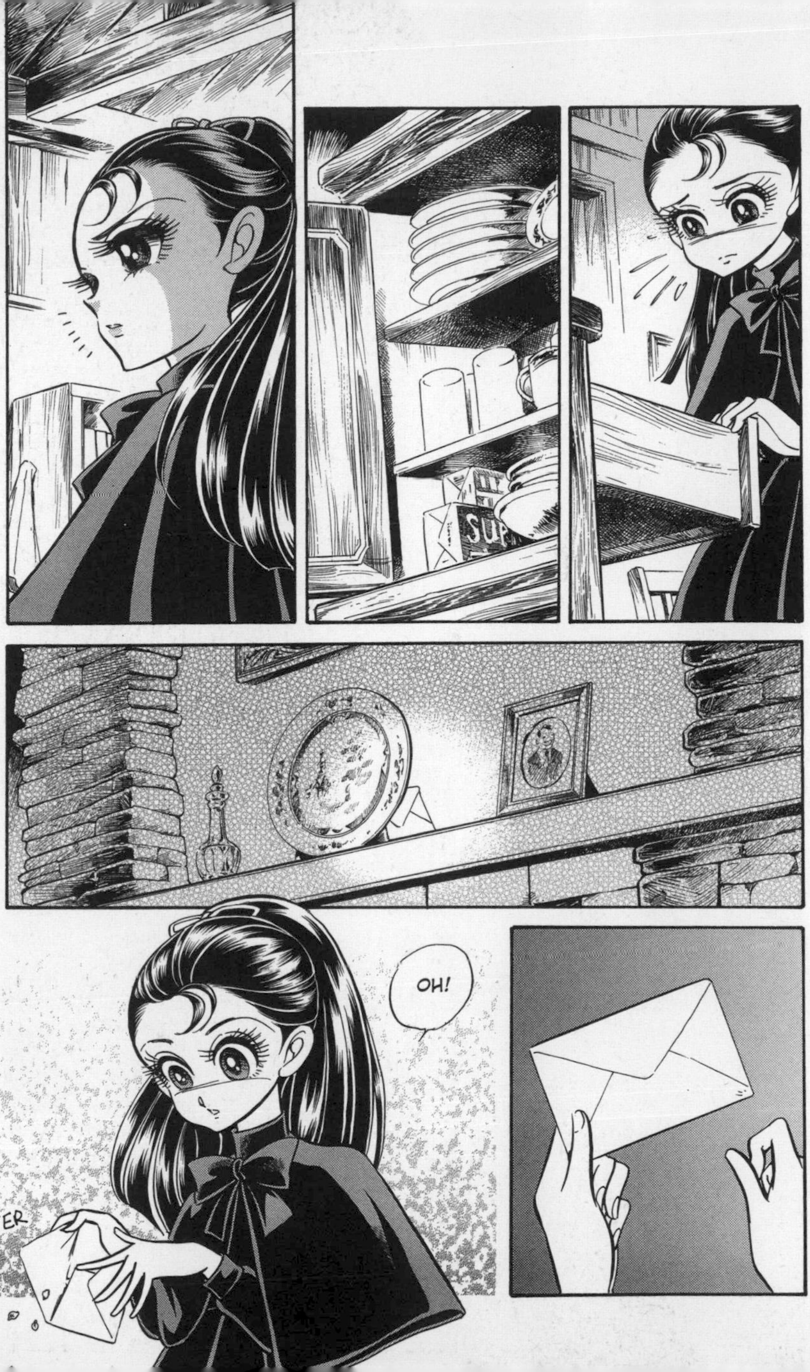
OH!
PATTER

ORANGE
SEEDS...
FIVE OF
THEM.

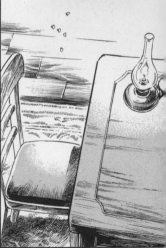

SLUMP

LORD
SAVE
ME...

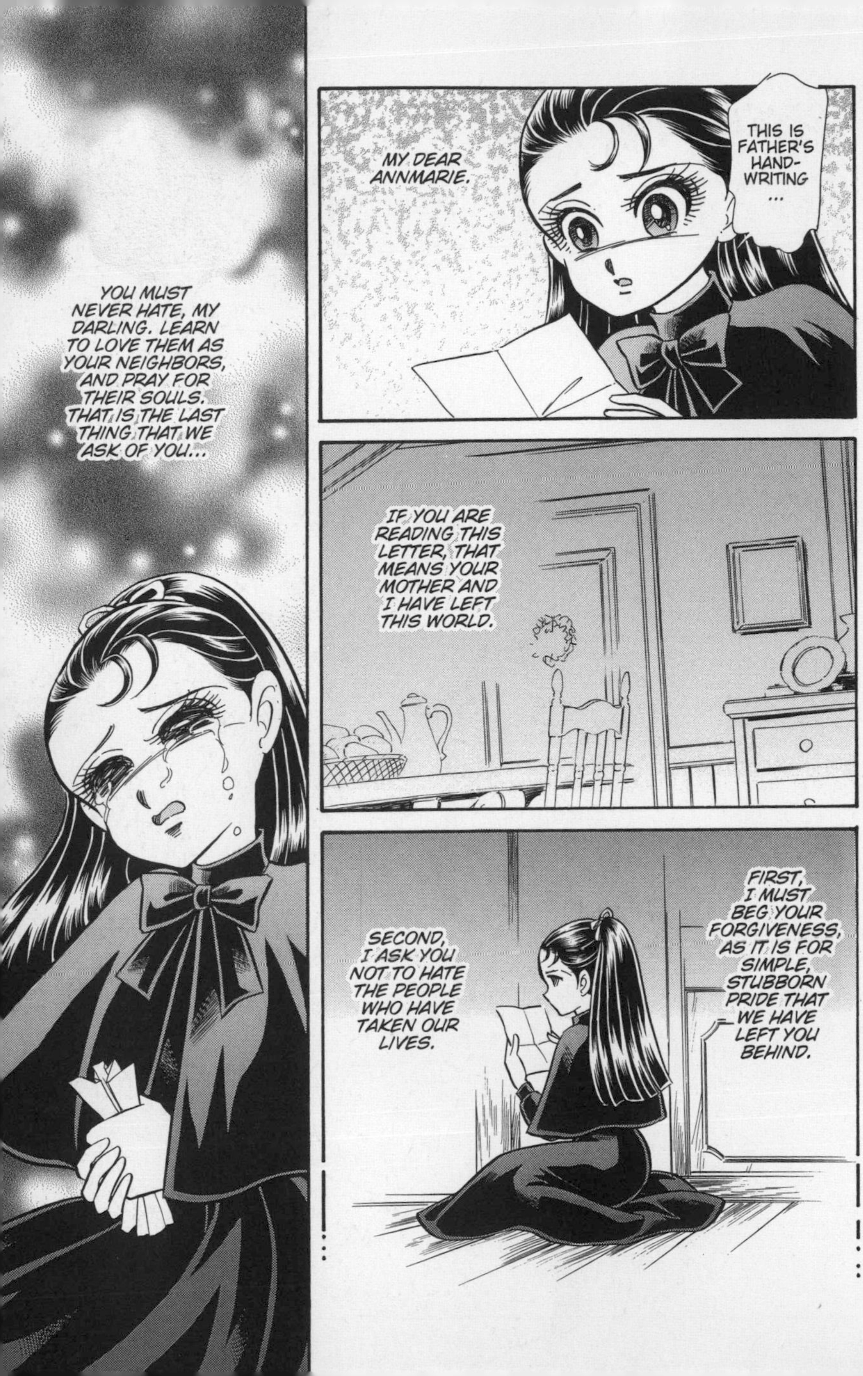
THIS IS FATHER'S HAND-WRITING ...
MY DEAR ANNMARIE.
IF YOU ARE READING THIS LETTER, THAT MEANS YOUR MOTHER AND I HAVE LEFT THIS WORLD.
FIRST, I MUST BEG YOUR FORGIVENESS, AS IT IS FOR SIMPLE, STUBBORN PRIDE THAT WE HAVE LEFT YOU BEHIND.
SECOND, I ASK YOU NOT TO HATE THE PEOPLE WHO HAVE TAKEN OUR LIVES.
YOU MUST NEVER HATE, MY DARLING. LEARN TO LOVE THEM AS YOUR NEIGHBORS, AND PRAY FOR THEIR SOULS. THAT IS THE LAST THING THAT WE ASK OF YOU...

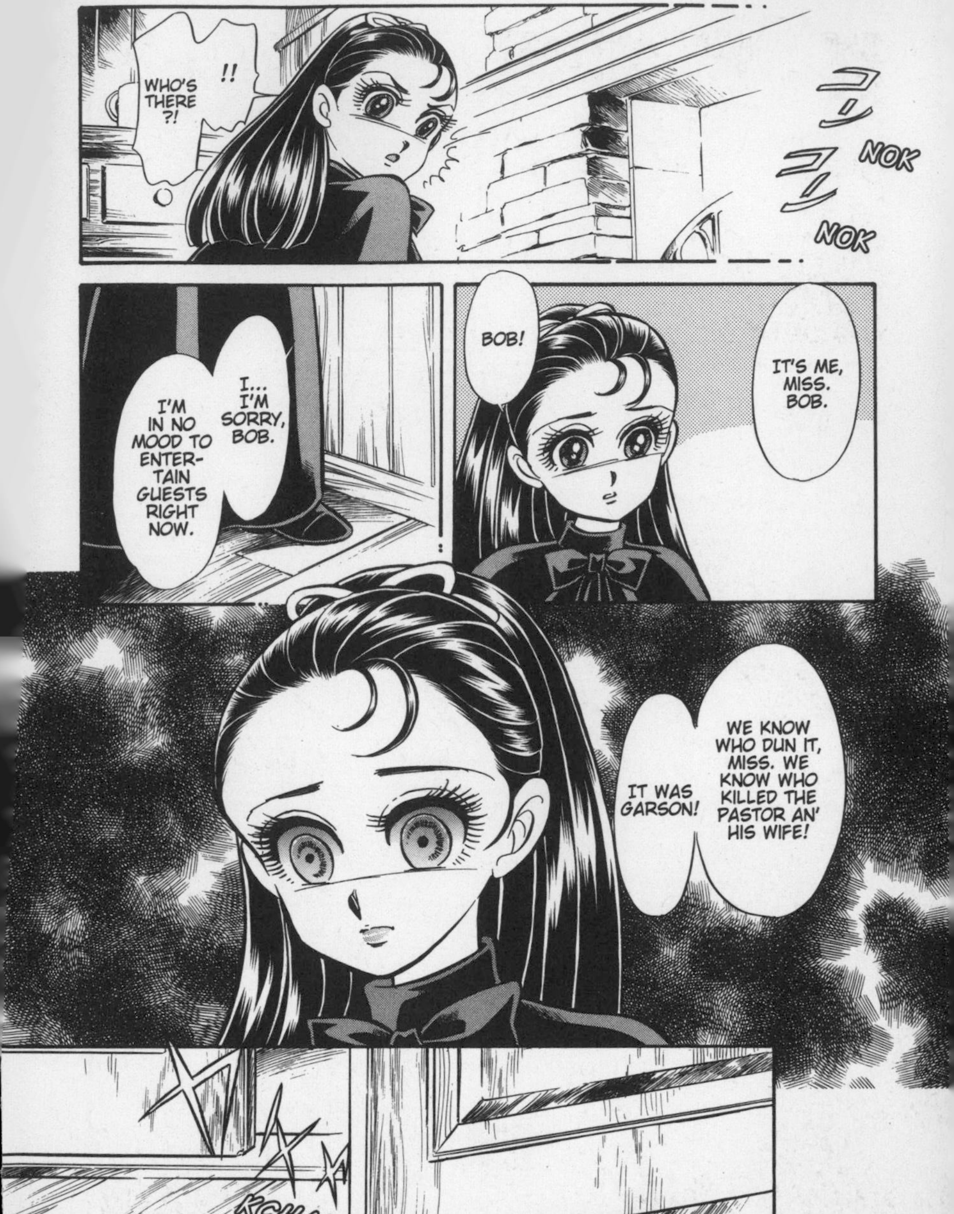
NOK
NOK
!!
WHO'S THERE ?!
IT'S ME, MISS. BOB.
BOB!
I... I'M SORRY, BOB.
I'M IN NO MOOD TO ENTER- TAIN GUESTS RIGHT NOW.
WE KNOW WHO DUN IT, MISS. WE KNOW WHO KILLED THE PASTOR AN' HIS WIFE!
IT WAS GARSON!
KCHAK

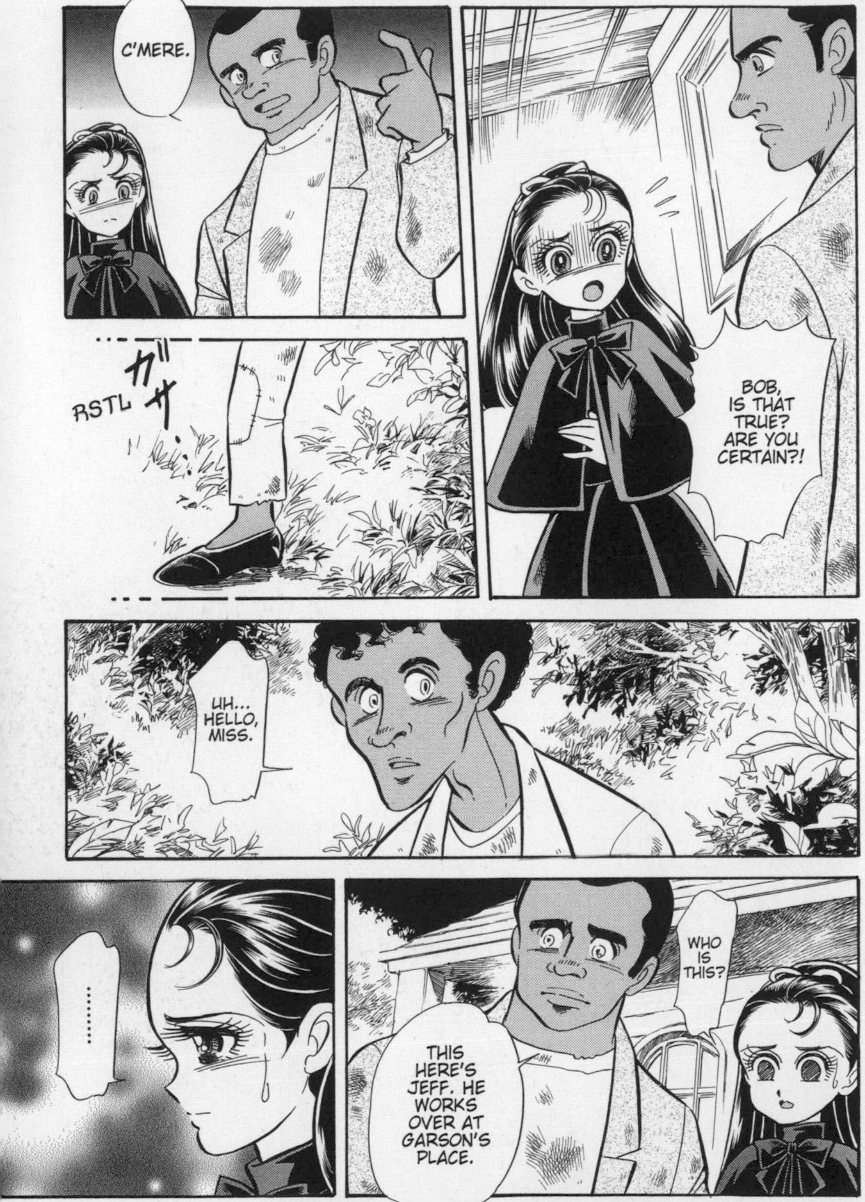
BOB, IS THAT TRUE? ARE YOU CERTAIN?!
C'MERE.
ガサ
RSTL
UH... HELLO, MISS.
WHO IS THIS?
THIS HERE'S JEFF. HE WORKS OVER AT GARSON'S PLACE.
....

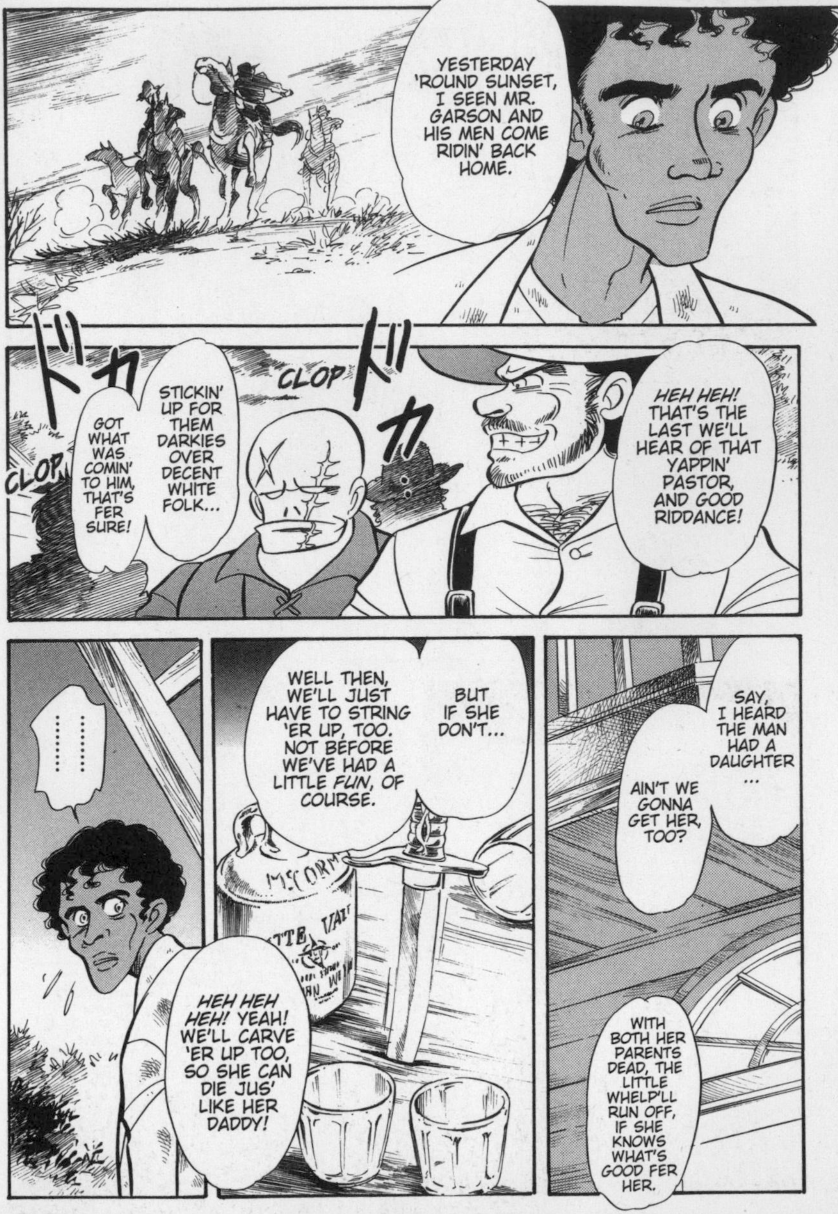
YESTERDAY 'ROUND SUNSET, I SEEN MR. GARSON AND HIS MEN COME RIDIN' BACK HOME.
HEH HEH! THAT'S THE LAST WE'LL HEAR OF THAT YAPPIN' PASTOR, AND GOOD RIDDANCE!
ドカ
CLOP
STICKIN' UP FOR THEM DARKIES OVER DECENT WHITE FOLK...
GOT WHAT WAS COMIN' TO HIM, THAT'S FER SURE!
ドカ
CLOP
SAY, I HEARD THE MAN HAD A DAUGHTER...
AIN'T WE GONNA GET HER, TOO?
WITH BOTH HER PARENTS DEAD, THE LITTLE WHELP'LL RUN OFF, IF SHE KNOWS WHAT'S GOOD FER HER.
BUT IF SHE DON'T...
WELL THEN, WE'LL JUST HAVE TO STRING 'ER UP, TOO. NOT BEFORE WE'VE HAD A LITTLE *FUN*, OF COURSE.
HEH HEH HEH! YEAH! WE'LL CARVE 'ER UP TOO, SO SHE CAN DIE JUS' LIKE HER DADDY!
......

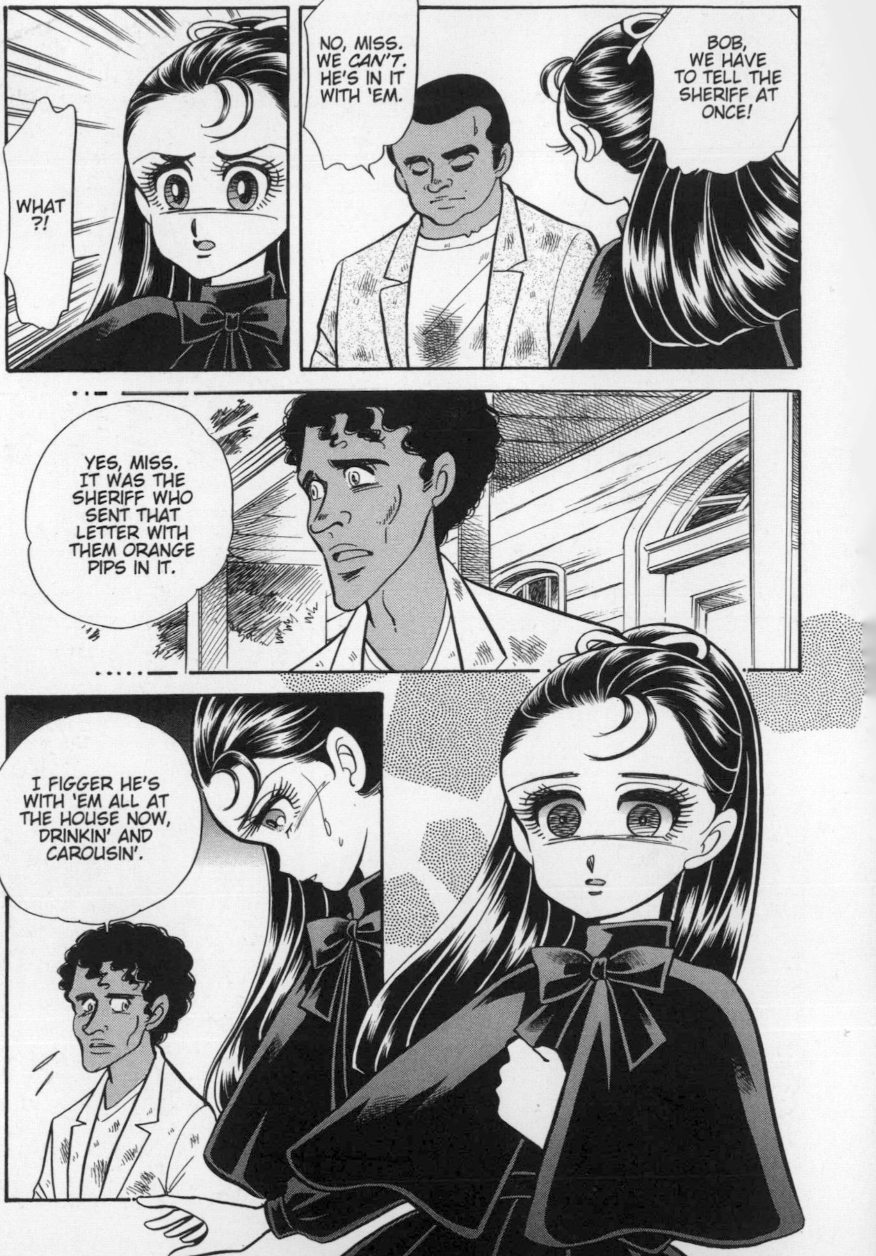
BOB, WE HAVE TO TELL THE SHERIFF AT ONCE!
NO, MISS. WE *CAN'T*. HE'S IN IT WITH 'EM.
WHAT ?!
YES, MISS. IT WAS THE SHERIFF WHO SENT THAT LETTER WITH THEM ORANGE PIPS IN IT.
I FIGGER HE'S WITH 'EM ALL AT THE HOUSE NOW, DRINKIN' AND CAROUSIN'.

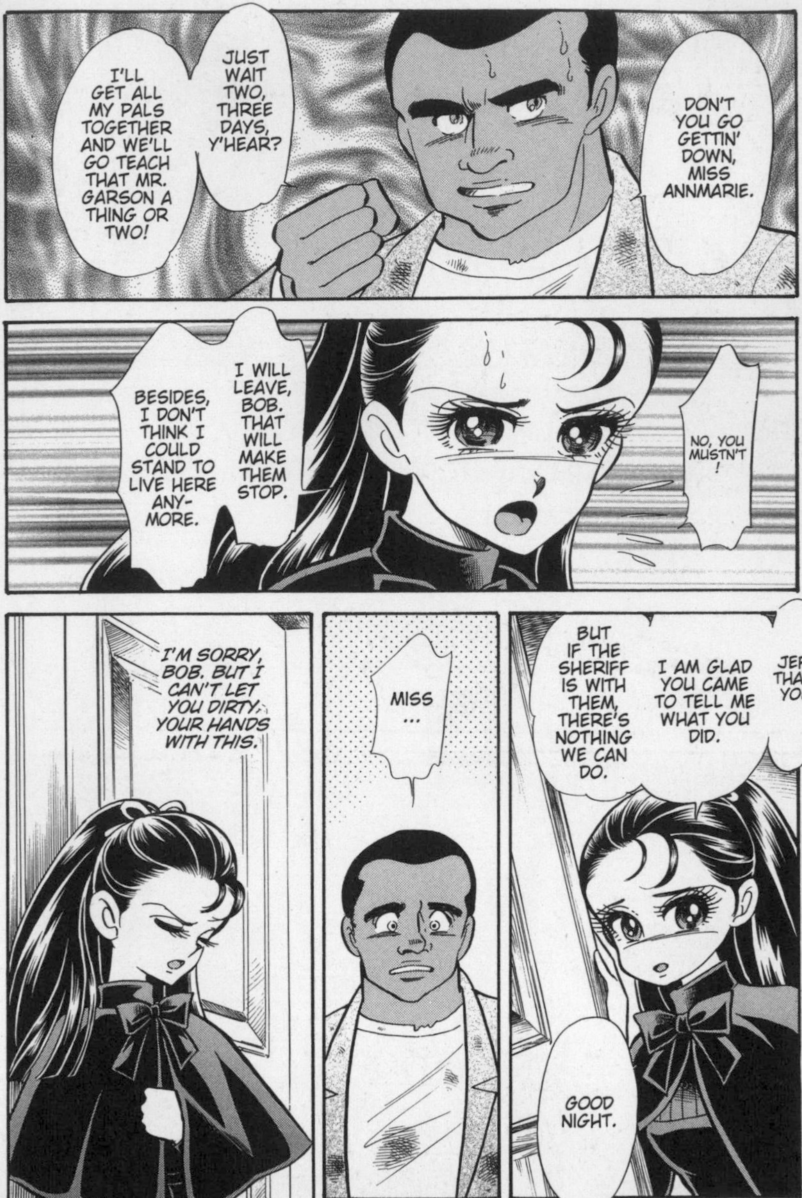

DON'T YOU GO GETTIN' DOWN, MISS ANNMARIE.
JUST WAIT TWO, THREE DAYS, Y'HEAR?
I'LL GET ALL MY PALS TOGETHER AND WE'LL GO TEACH THAT MR. GARSON A THING OR TWO!
NO, YOU MUSTN'T!
I WILL LEAVE, BOB. THAT WILL MAKE THEM STOP.
BESIDES, I DON'T THINK I COULD STAND TO LIVE HERE ANY-MORE.
JEFF, THANK YOU.
I AM GLAD YOU CAME TO TELL ME WHAT YOU DID.
BUT IF THE SHERIFF IS WITH THEM, THERE'S NOTHING WE CAN DO.
GOOD NIGHT.
MISS ...
I'M SORRY, BOB. BUT I CAN'T LET YOU DIRTY YOUR HANDS WITH THIS.

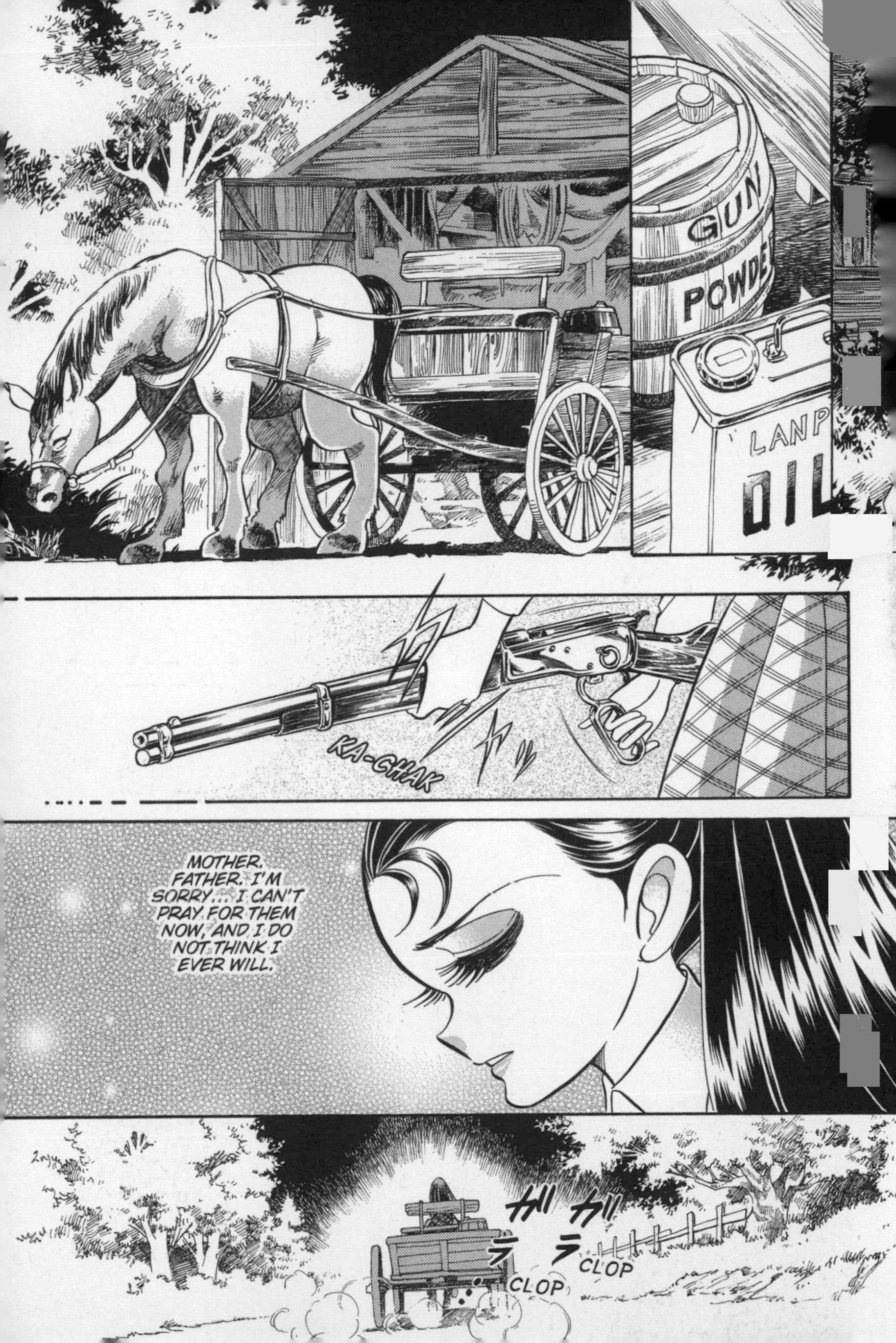
GUN POWDER
LAMP OIL
KA-CHAK
MOTHER. FATHER. I'M SORRY... I CAN'T PRAY FOR THEM NOW, AND I DO NOT THINK I EVER WILL.
ガラ
ガラ
CLOP
CLOP

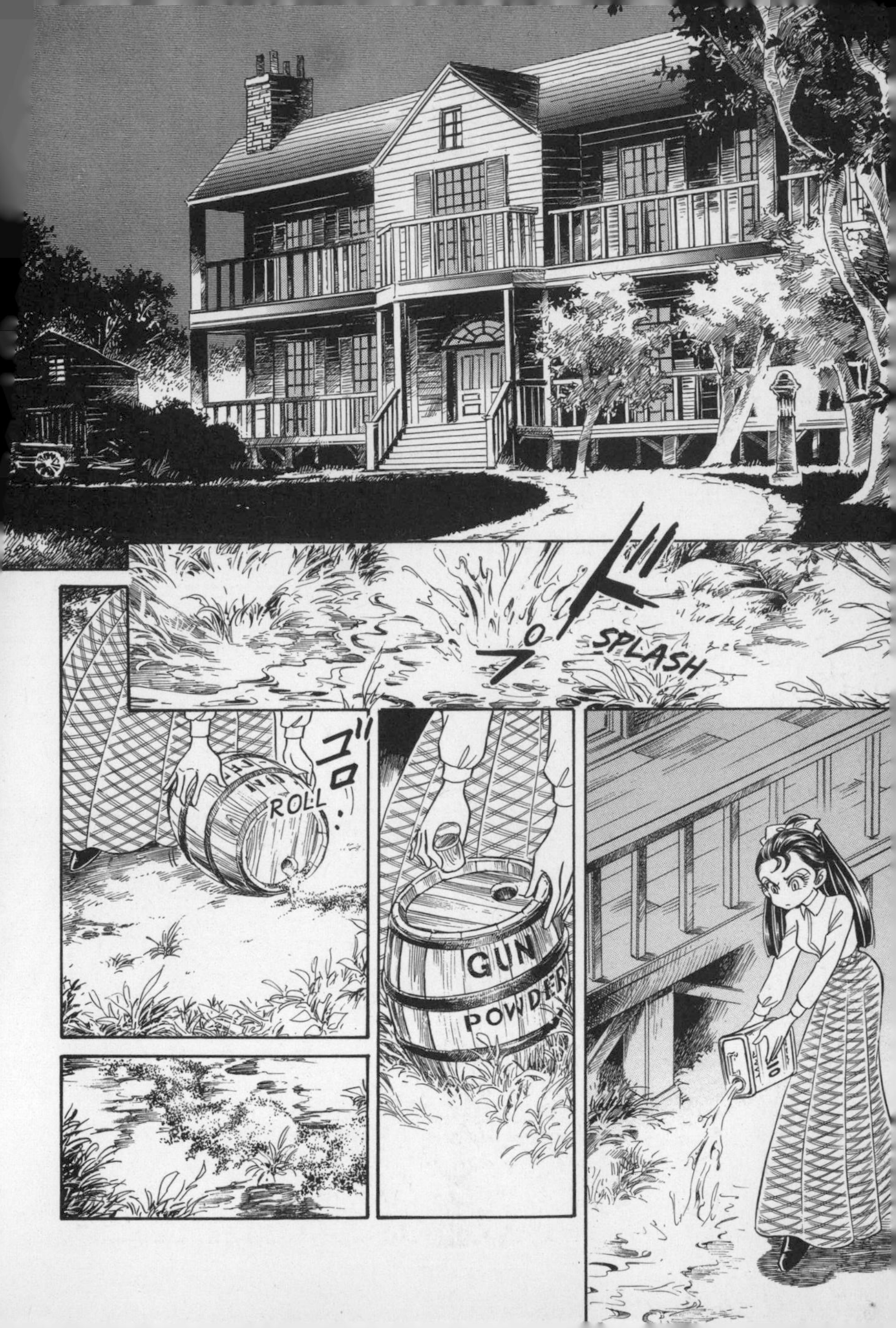
ドプ
SPLASH
GUN
POWDER
ゴロ
ROLL

BLAM

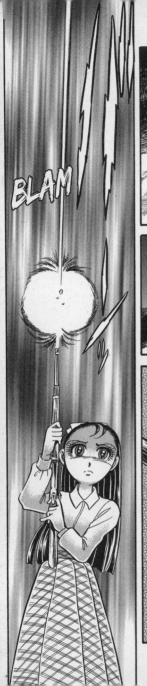

HFF

HFF

KLIK

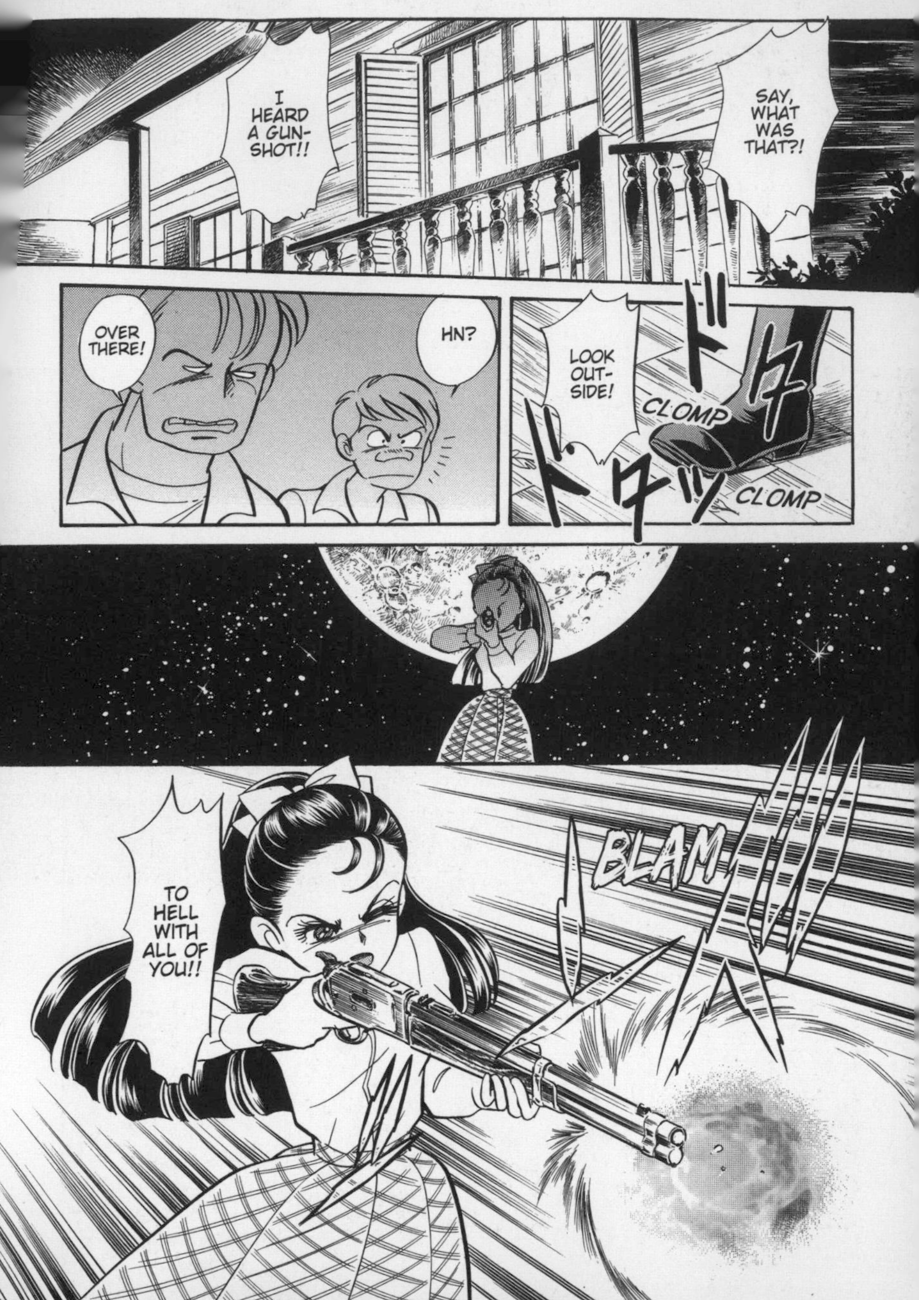
SAY, WHAT WAS THAT?!
I HEARD A GUN-SHOT!!
LOOK OUT-SIDE!
CLOMP
CLOMP
HN?
OVER THERE!
BLAM
TO HELL WITH ALL OF YOU!!

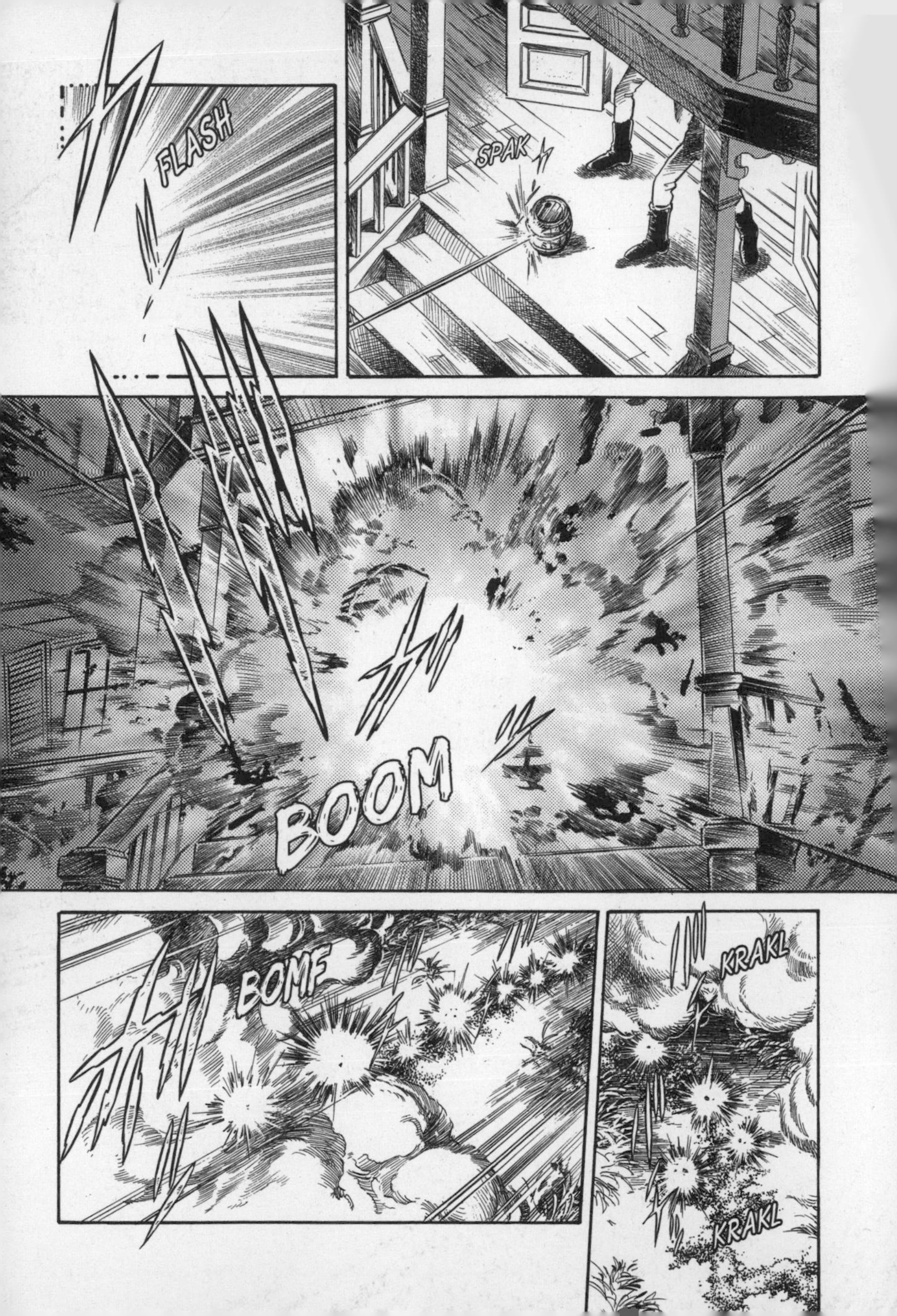
SPAK
FLASH
BOOM
KRAKL
KRAKL
BOMF

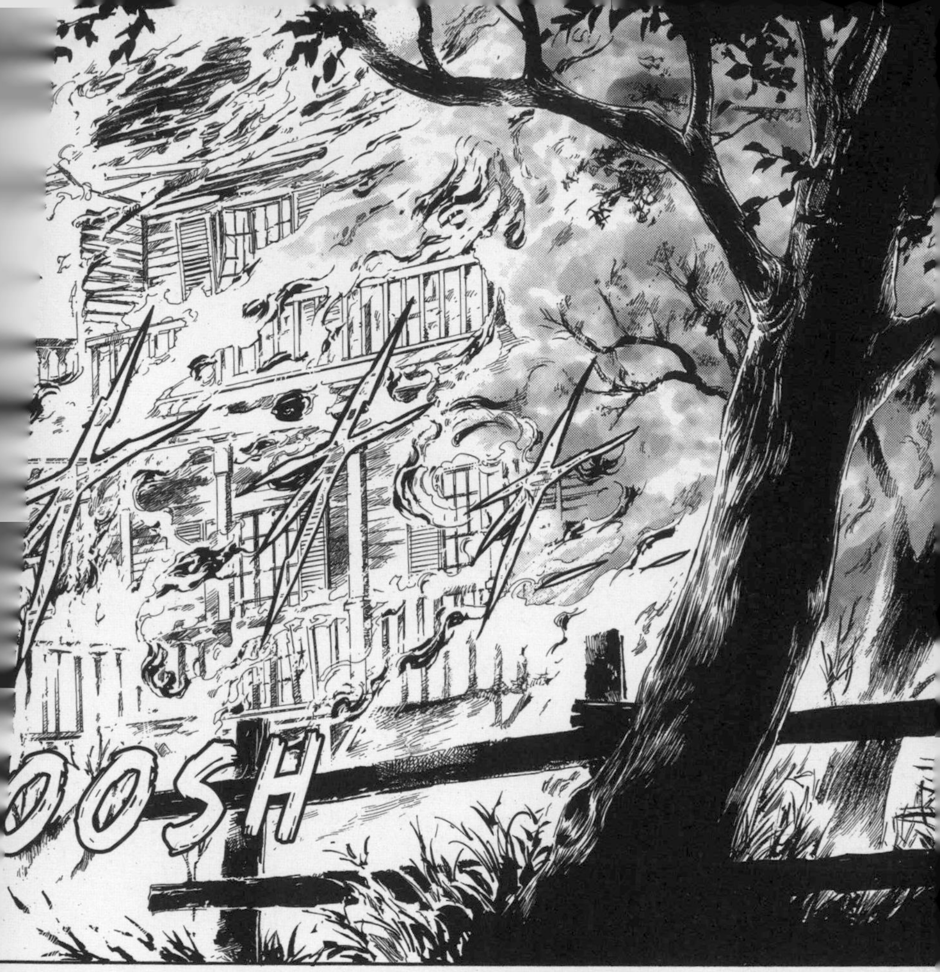
OOSH

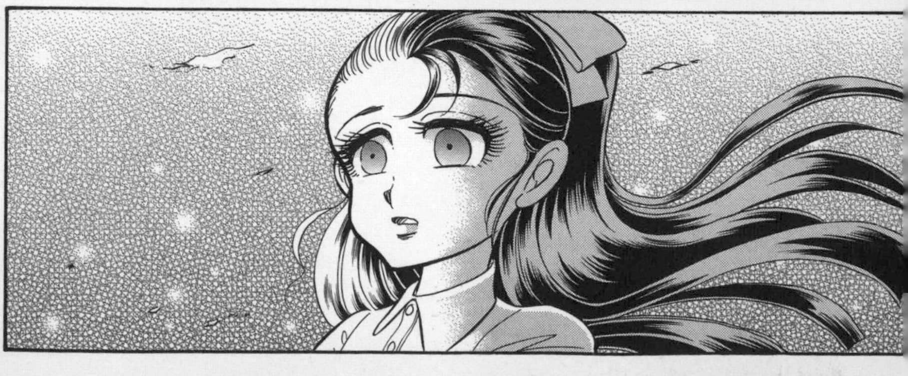

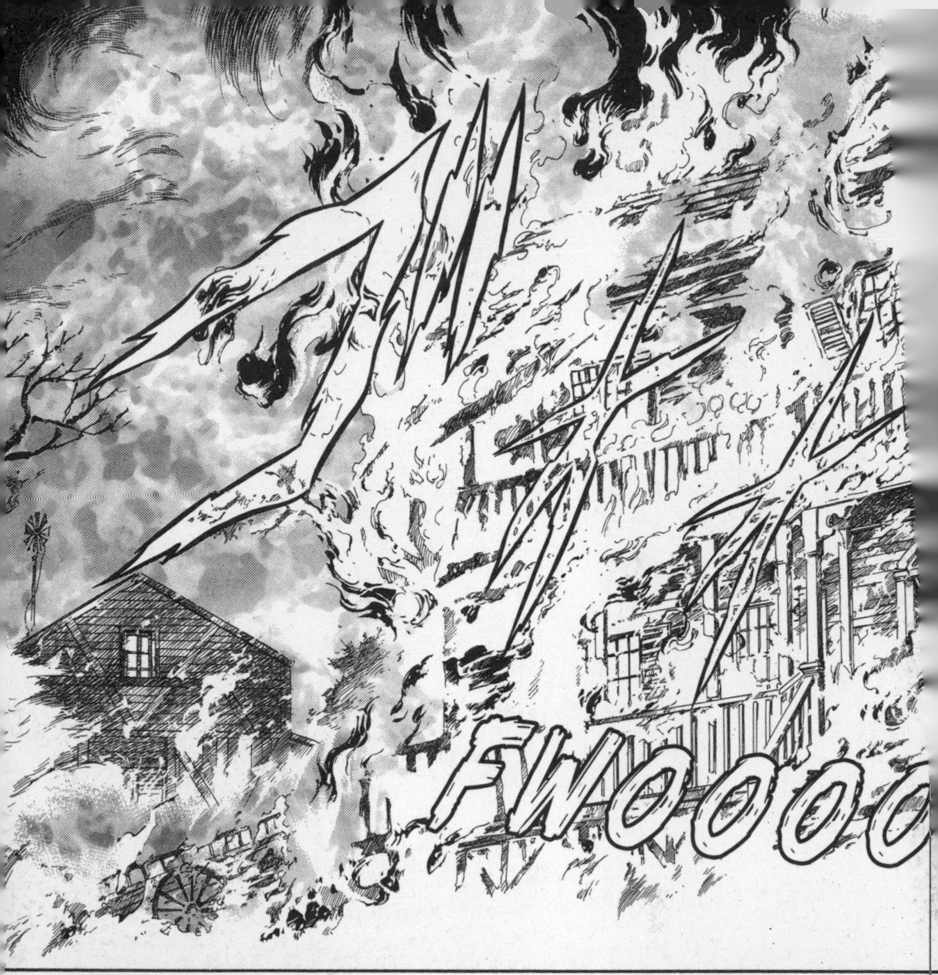
FWOOOO
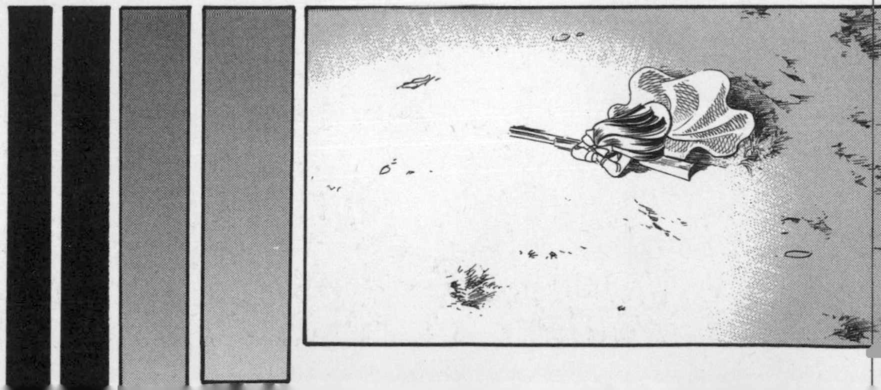

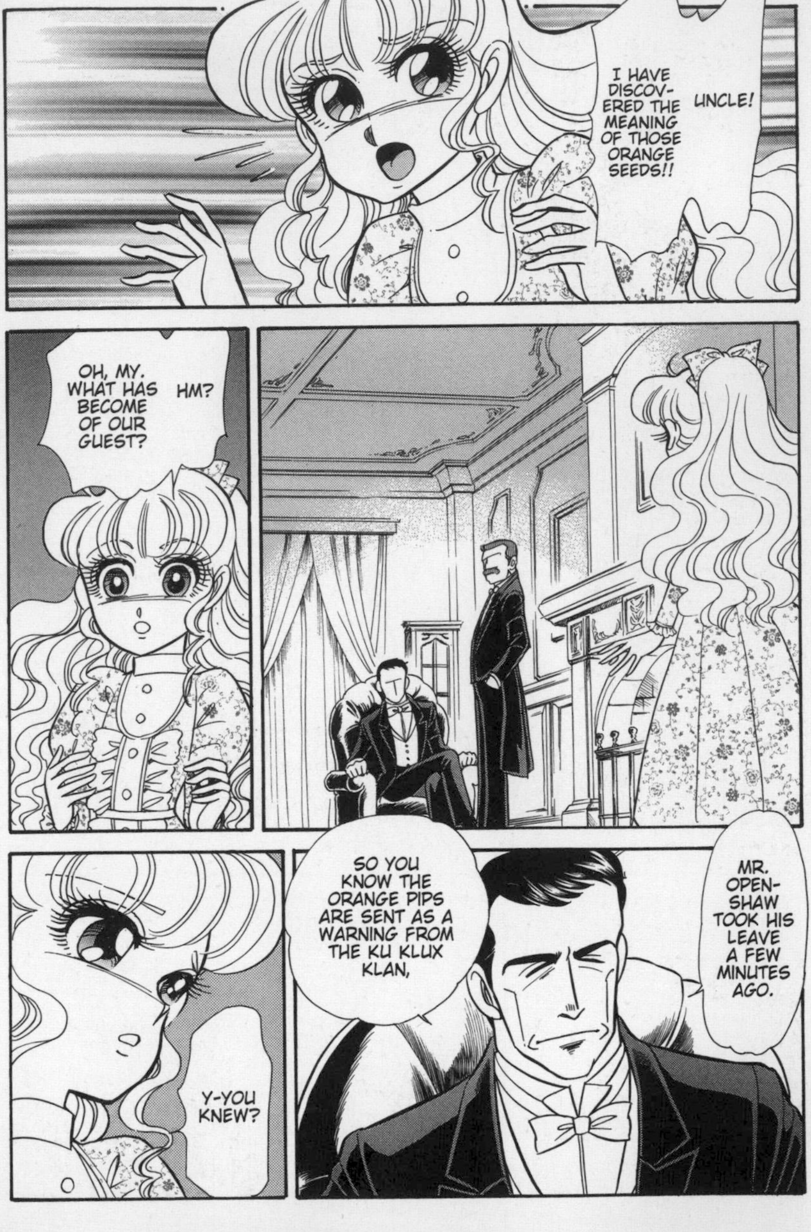
UNCLE!
I HAVE DISCOVERED THE MEANING OF THOSE ORANGE SEEDS!!
HM?
OH, MY. WHAT HAS BECOME OF OUR GUEST?
MR. OPENSHAW TOOK HIS LEAVE A FEW MINUTES AGO.
SO YOU KNOW THE ORANGE PIPS ARE SENT AS A WARNING FROM THE KU KLUX KLAN,
Y-YOU KNEW?

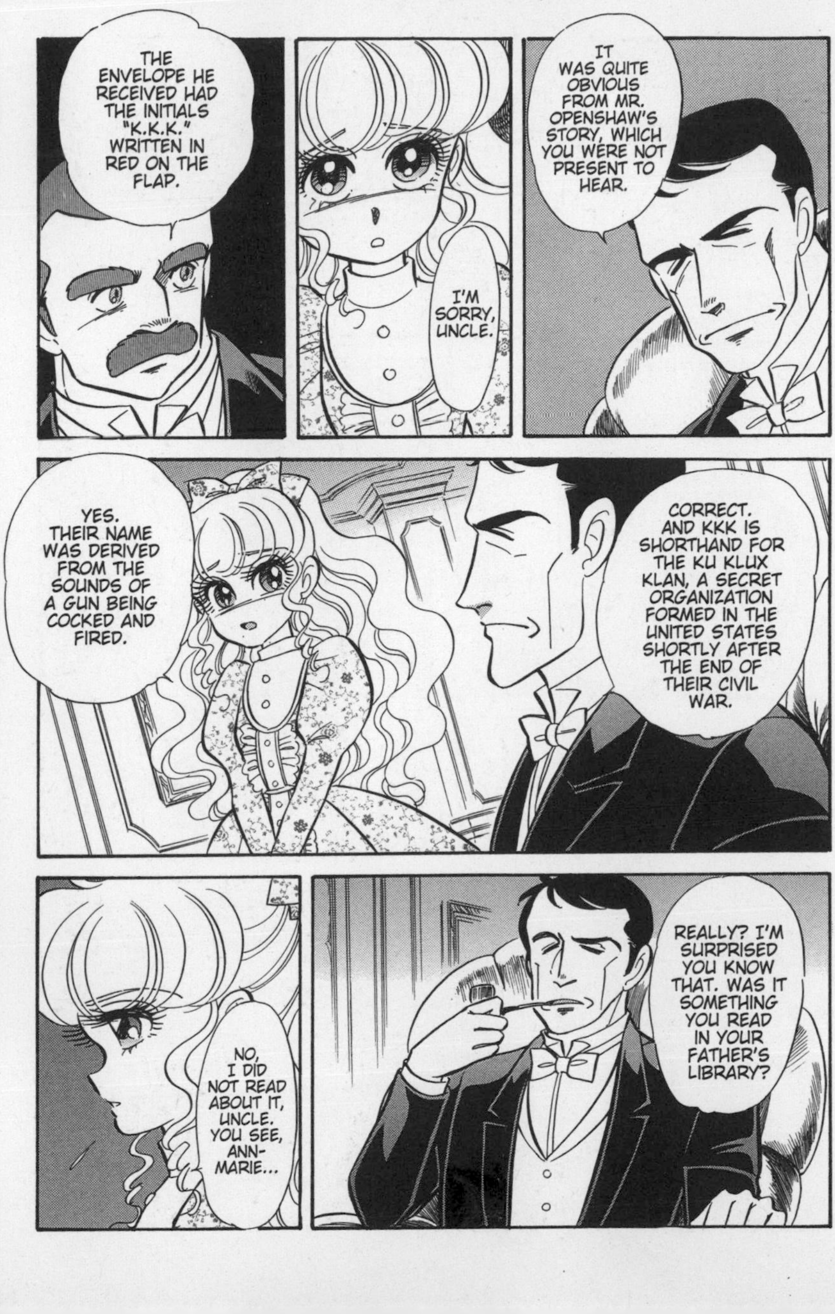
IT WAS QUITE OBVIOUS FROM MR. OPENSHAW'S STORY, WHICH YOU WERE NOT PRESENT TO HEAR.
I'M SORRY, UNCLE.
THE ENVELOPE HE RECEIVED HAD THE INITIALS "K.K.K." WRITTEN IN RED ON THE FLAP.
CORRECT. AND KKK IS SHORTHAND FOR THE KU KLUX KLAN, A SECRET ORGANIZATION FORMED IN THE UNITED STATES SHORTLY AFTER THE END OF THEIR CIVIL WAR.
YES. THEIR NAME WAS DERIVED FROM THE SOUNDS OF A GUN BEING COCKED AND FIRED.
REALLY? I'M SURPRISED YOU KNOW THAT. WAS IT SOMETHING YOU READ IN YOUR FATHER'S LIBRARY?
NO, I DID NOT READ ABOUT IT, UNCLE. YOU SEE, ANN-MARIE...

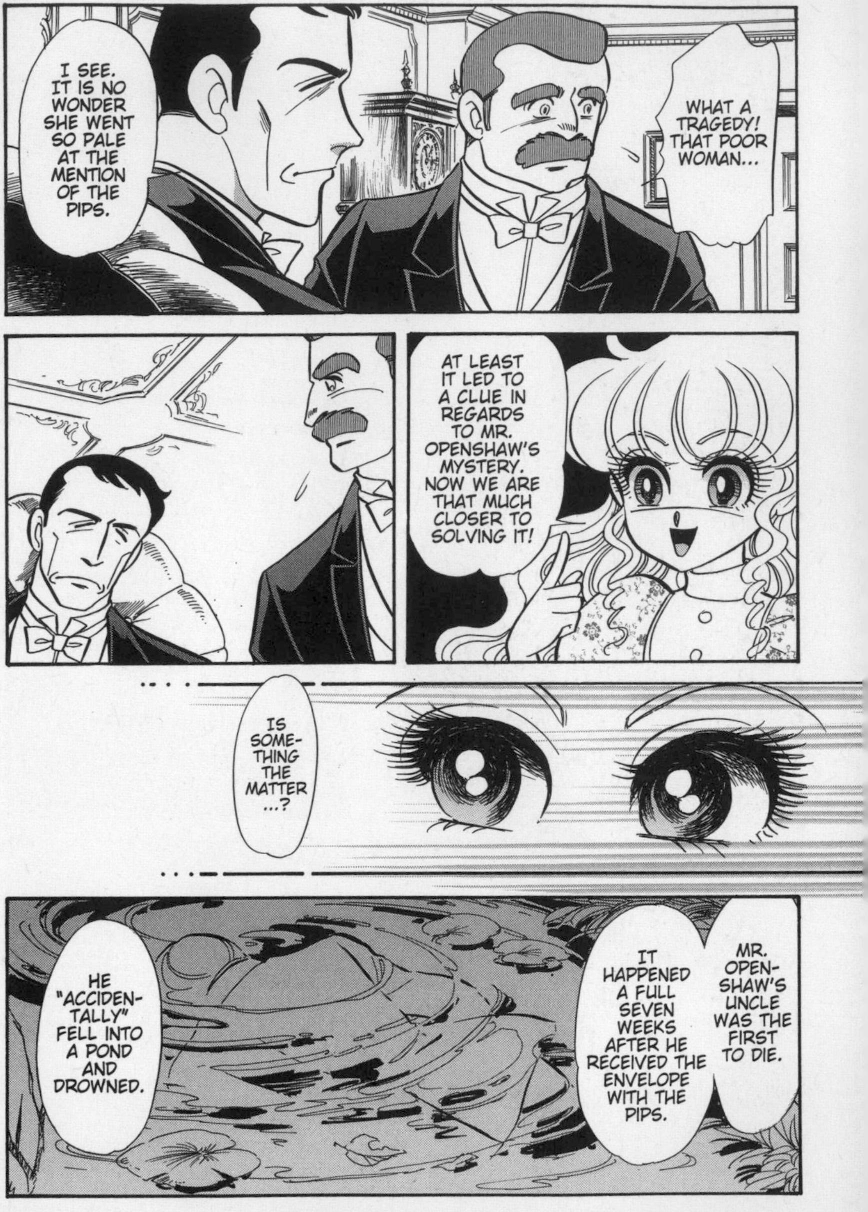
WHAT A TRAGEDY! THAT POOR WOMAN...
I SEE. IT IS NO WONDER SHE WENT SO PALE AT THE MENTION OF THE PIPS.
AT LEAST IT LED TO A CLUE IN REGARDS TO MR. OPENSHAW'S MYSTERY. NOW WE ARE THAT MUCH CLOSER TO SOLVING IT!
IS SOME-THING THE MATTER ...?
MR. OPEN-SHAW'S UNCLE WAS THE FIRST TO DIE.
IT HAPPENED A FULL SEVEN WEEKS AFTER HE RECEIVED THE ENVELOPE WITH THE PIPS.
HE "ACCIDEN-TALLY" FELL INTO A POND AND DROWNED.

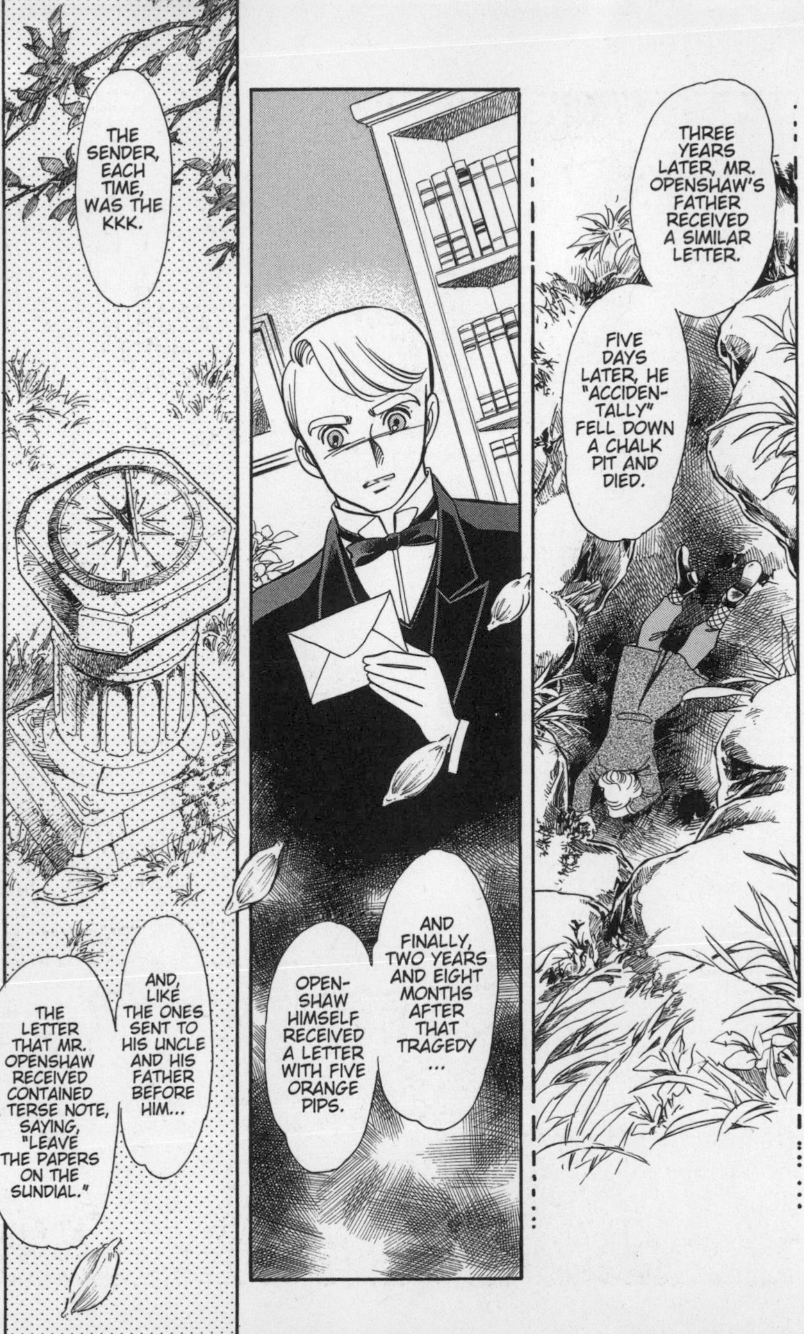
THREE YEARS LATER, MR. OPENSHAW'S FATHER RECEIVED A SIMILAR LETTER.
FIVE DAYS LATER, HE "ACCIDENTALLY" FELL DOWN A CHALK PIT AND DIED.
AND FINALLY, TWO YEARS AND EIGHT MONTHS AFTER THAT TRAGEDY...
OPENSHAW HIMSELF RECEIVED A LETTER WITH FIVE ORANGE PIPS.
THE SENDER, EACH TIME, WAS THE KKK.
AND, LIKE THE ONES SENT TO HIS UNCLE AND HIS FATHER BEFORE HIM...
THE LETTER THAT MR. OPENSHAW RECEIVED CONTAINED A TERSE NOTE, SAYING, "LEAVE THE PAPERS ON THE SUNDIAL."

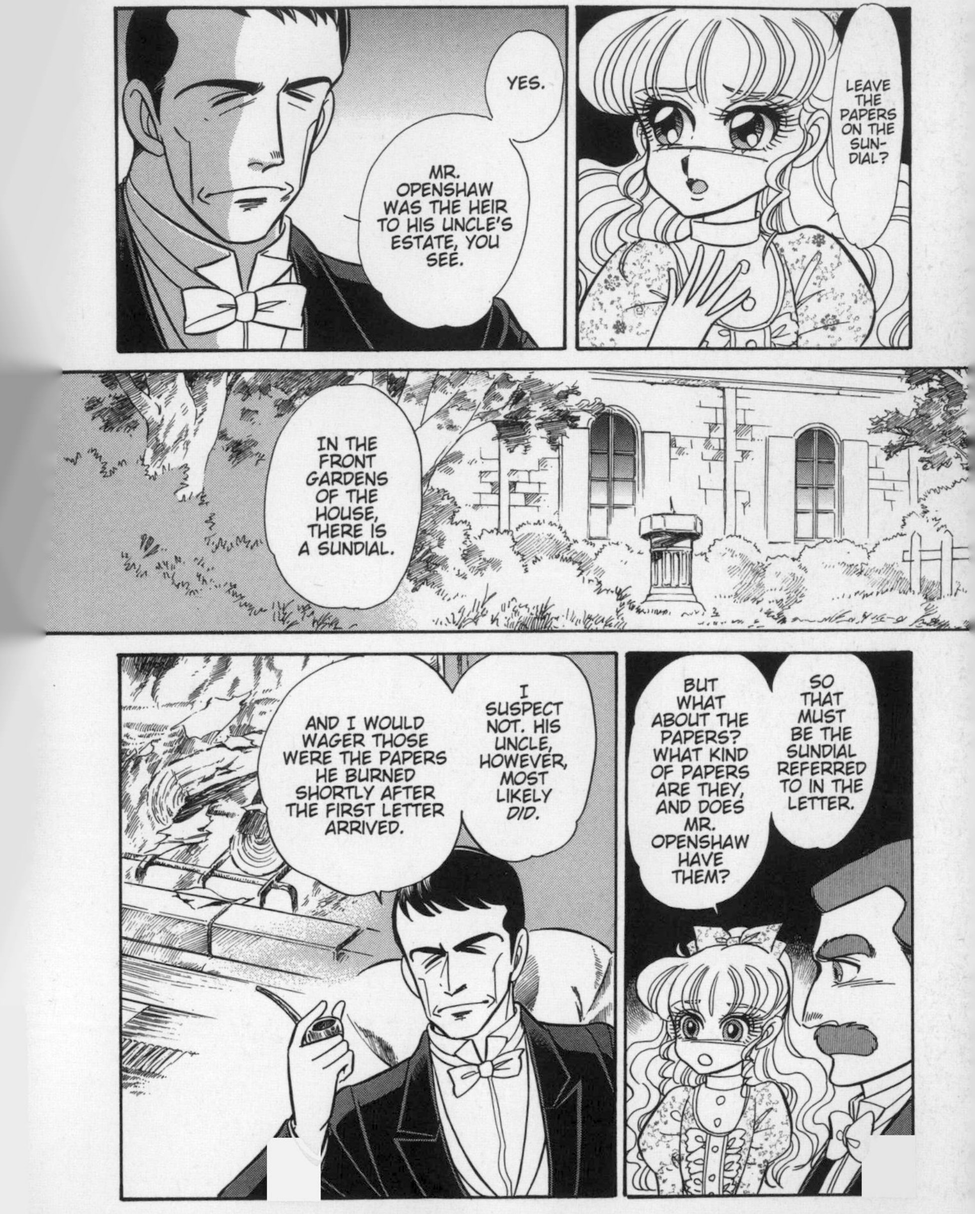
LEAVE THE PAPERS ON THE SUN-DIAL?
YES.
MR. OPENSHAW WAS THE HEIR TO HIS UNCLE'S ESTATE, YOU SEE.
IN THE FRONT GARDENS OF THE HOUSE, THERE IS A SUNDIAL.
SO THAT MUST BE THE SUNDIAL REFERRED TO IN THE LETTER.
BUT WHAT ABOUT THE PAPERS? WHAT KIND OF PAPERS ARE THEY, AND DOES MR. OPENSHAW HAVE THEM?
I SUSPECT NOT. HIS UNCLE, HOWEVER, MOST LIKELY *DID*.
AND I WOULD WAGER THOSE WERE THE PAPERS HE BURNED SHORTLY AFTER THE FIRST LETTER ARRIVED.

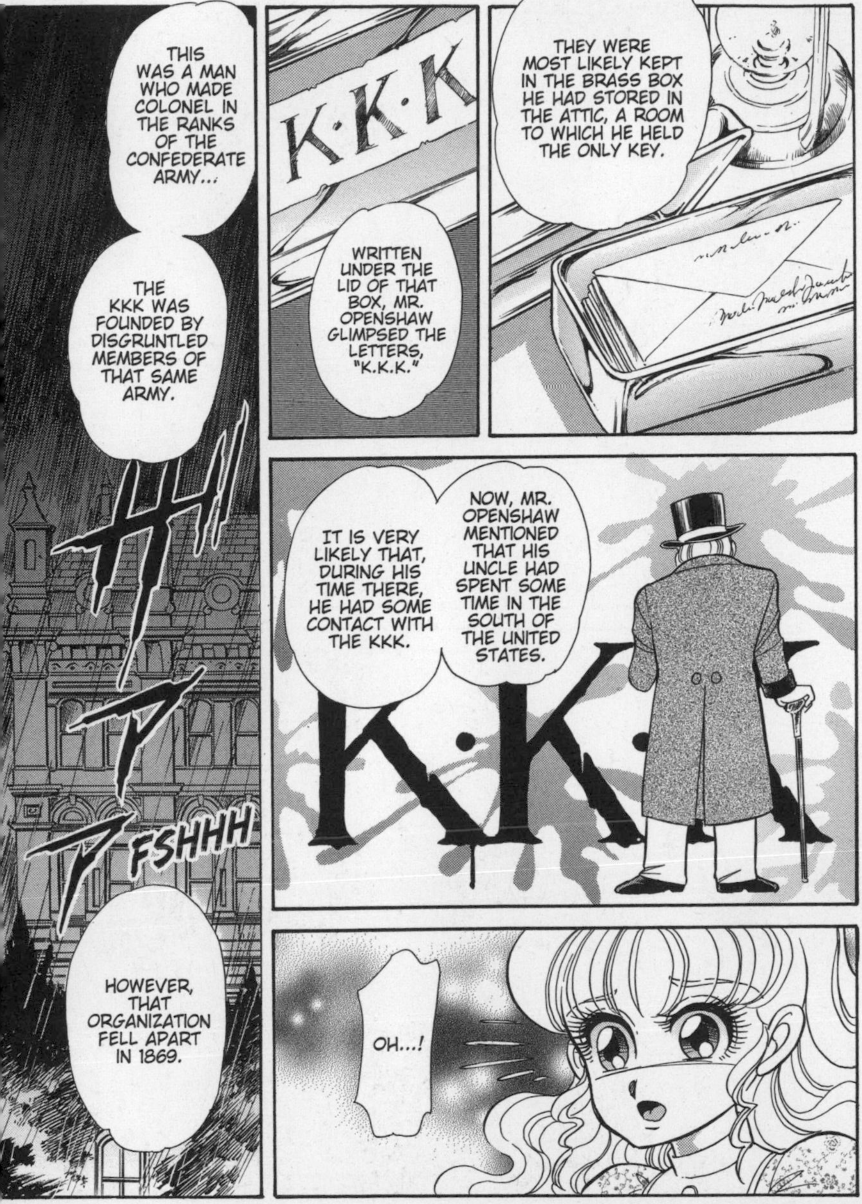
THEY WERE MOST LIKELY KEPT IN THE BRASS BOX HE HAD STORED IN THE ATTIC, A ROOM TO WHICH HE HELD THE ONLY KEY.
K·K·K
WRITTEN UNDER THE LID OF THAT BOX, MR. OPENSHAW GLIMPSED THE LETTERS, "K.K.K."
NOW, MR. OPENSHAW MENTIONED THAT HIS UNCLE HAD SPENT SOME TIME IN THE SOUTH OF THE UNITED STATES.
IT IS VERY LIKELY THAT, DURING HIS TIME THERE, HE HAD SOME CONTACT WITH THE KKK.
OH...!
THIS WAS A MAN WHO MADE COLONEL IN THE RANKS OF THE CONFEDERATE ARMY...
THE KKK WAS FOUNDED BY DISGRUNTLED MEMBERS OF THAT SAME ARMY.
FSHHH
HOWEVER, THAT ORGANIZATION FELL APART IN 1869.

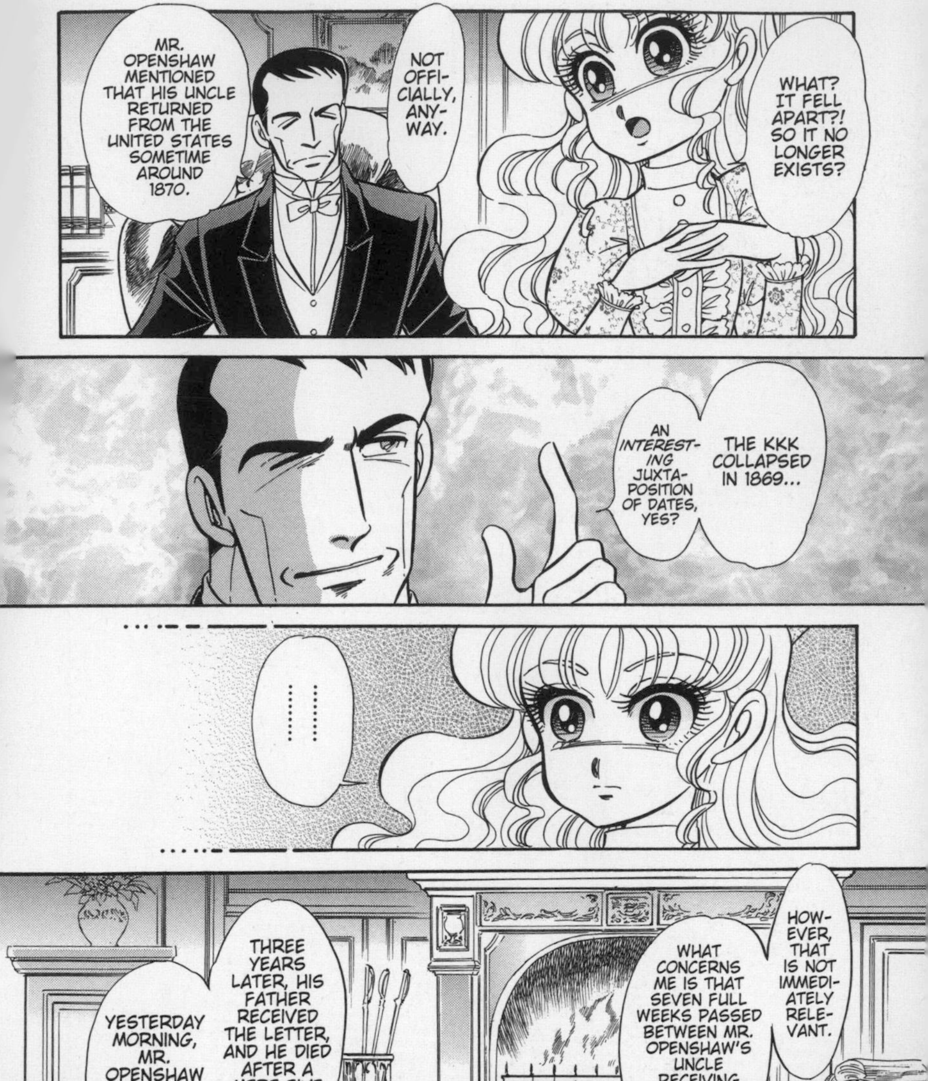
WHAT? IT FELL APART?! SO IT NO LONGER EXISTS?
NOT OFFICIALLY, ANYWAY.
MR. OPENSHAW MENTIONED THAT HIS UNCLE RETURNED FROM THE UNITED STATES SOMETIME AROUND 1870.
THE KKK COLLAPSED IN 1869...
AN *INTERESTING* JUXTAPOSITION OF DATES, YES?
......
HOWEVER, THAT IS NOT IMMEDIATELY RELEVANT.
WHAT CONCERNS ME IS THAT SEVEN FULL WEEKS PASSED BETWEEN MR. OPENSHAW'S UNCLE RECEIVING THE LETTER AND HIS DEATH.
THREE YEARS LATER, HIS FATHER RECEIVED THE LETTER, AND HE DIED AFTER A MERE FIVE DAYS.
YESTERDAY MORNING, MR. OPENSHAW HIMSELF RECEIVED THE LETTER.

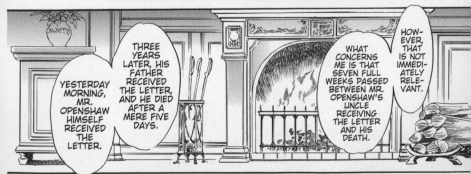

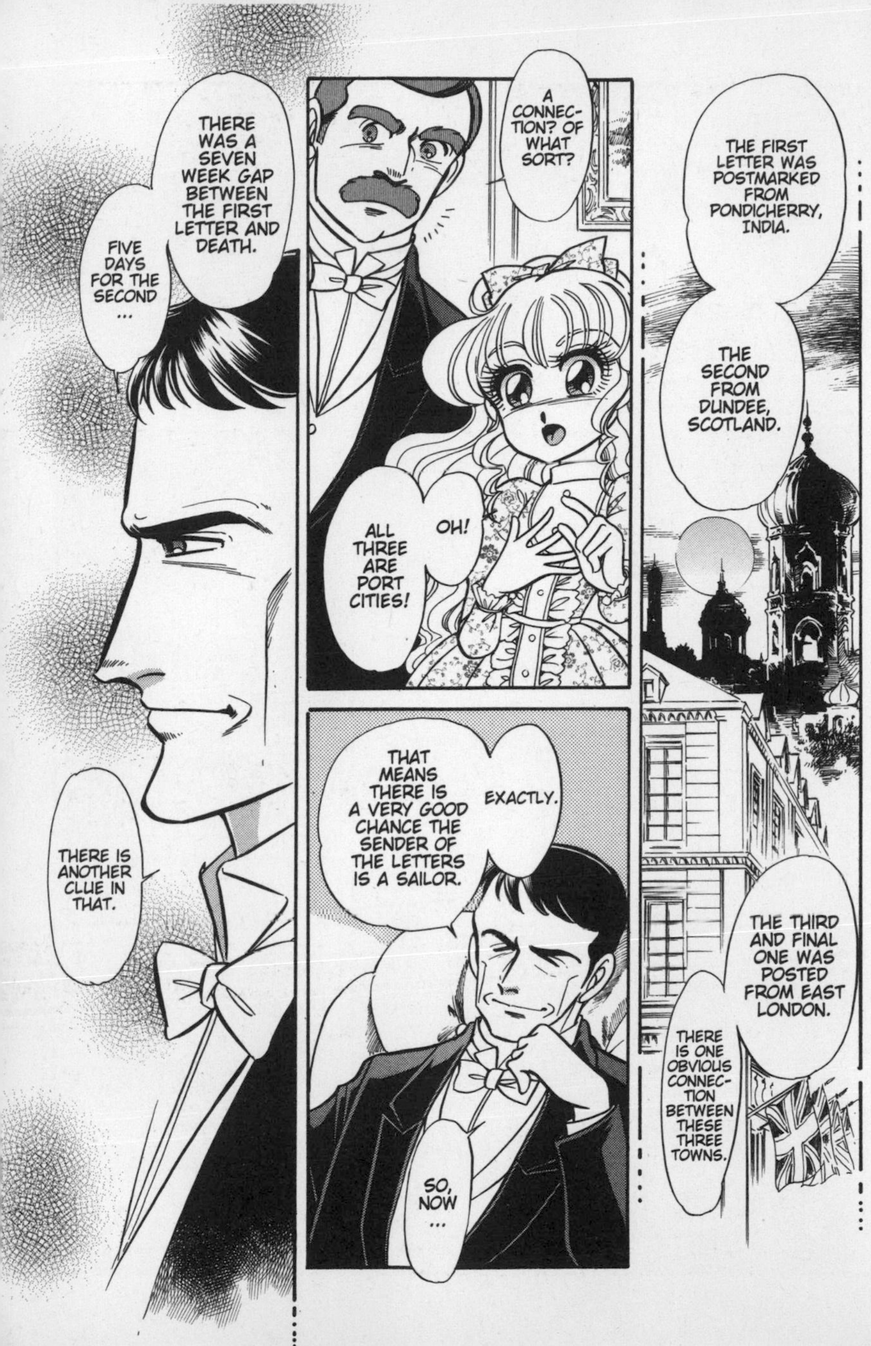
THE FIRST LETTER WAS POSTMARKED FROM PONDICHERRY, INDIA.
THE SECOND FROM DUNDEE, SCOTLAND.
THE THIRD AND FINAL ONE WAS POSTED FROM EAST LONDON.
THERE IS ONE OBVIOUS CONNEC-TION BETWEEN THESE THREE TOWNS.
A CONNEC-TION? OF WHAT SORT?
OH!
ALL THREE ARE PORT CITIES!
EXACTLY.
THAT MEANS THERE IS A VERY GOOD CHANCE THE SENDER OF THE LETTERS IS A SAILOR.
SO, NOW ...
THERE WAS A SEVEN WEEK GAP BETWEEN THE FIRST LETTER AND DEATH.
FIVE DAYS FOR THE SECOND ...
THERE IS ANOTHER CLUE IN THAT.

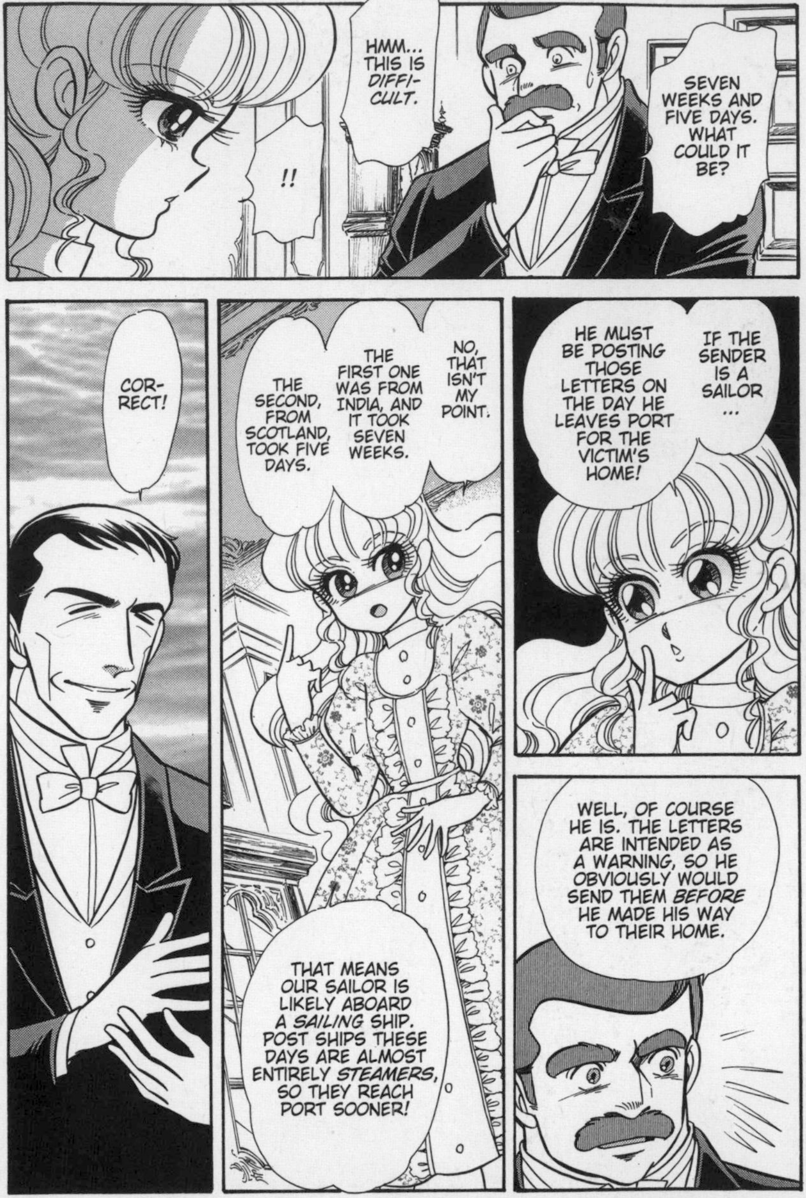
SEVEN WEEKS AND FIVE DAYS. WHAT COULD IT BE?
HMM... THIS IS DIFFI-CULT.
!!
IF THE SENDER IS A SAILOR ...
HE MUST BE POSTING THOSE LETTERS ON THE DAY HE LEAVES PORT FOR THE VICTIM'S HOME!
WELL, OF COURSE HE IS. THE LETTERS ARE INTENDED AS A WARNING, SO HE OBVIOUSLY WOULD SEND THEM *BEFORE* HE MADE HIS WAY TO THEIR HOME.
NO, THAT ISN'T MY POINT.
THE FIRST ONE WAS FROM INDIA, AND IT TOOK SEVEN WEEKS.
THE SECOND, FROM SCOTLAND, TOOK FIVE DAYS.
THAT MEANS OUR SAILOR IS LIKELY ABOARD A *SAILING* SHIP. POST SHIPS THESE DAYS ARE ALMOST ENTIRELY *STEAMERS*, SO THEY REACH PORT SOONER!
COR-RECT!

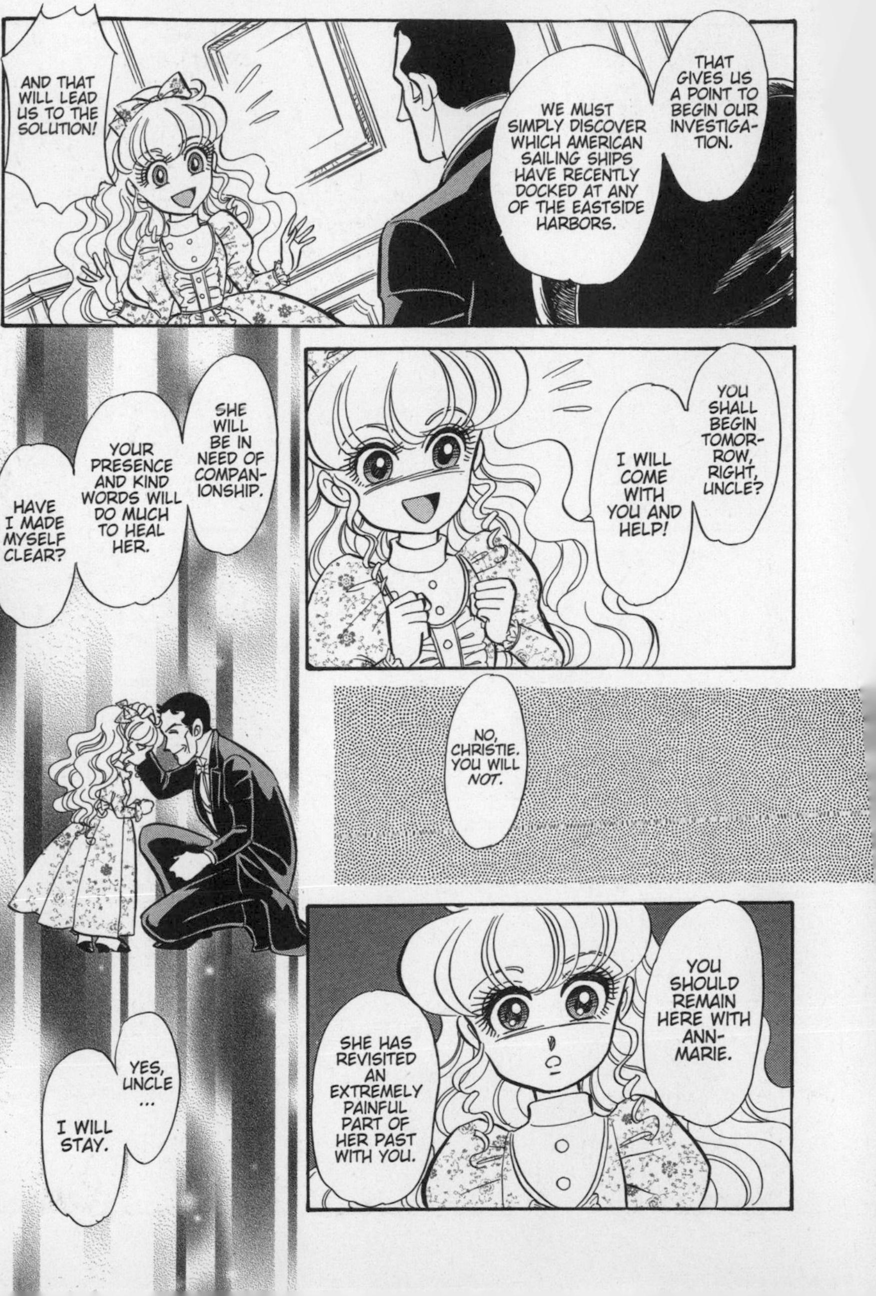
THAT GIVES US A POINT TO BEGIN OUR INVESTIGATION.
WE MUST SIMPLY DISCOVER WHICH AMERICAN SAILING SHIPS HAVE RECENTLY DOCKED AT ANY OF THE EASTSIDE HARBORS.
AND THAT WILL LEAD US TO THE SOLUTION!
YOU SHALL BEGIN TOMORROW, RIGHT, UNCLE?
I WILL COME WITH YOU AND HELP!
NO, CHRISTIE. YOU WILL *NOT*.
YOU SHOULD REMAIN HERE WITH ANN-MARIE.
SHE HAS REVISITED AN EXTREMELY PAINFUL PART OF HER PAST WITH YOU.
SHE WILL BE IN NEED OF COMPANIONSHIP.
YOUR PRESENCE AND KIND WORDS WILL DO MUCH TO HEAL HER.
HAVE I MADE MYSELF CLEAR?
YES, UNCLE ...
I WILL STAY.

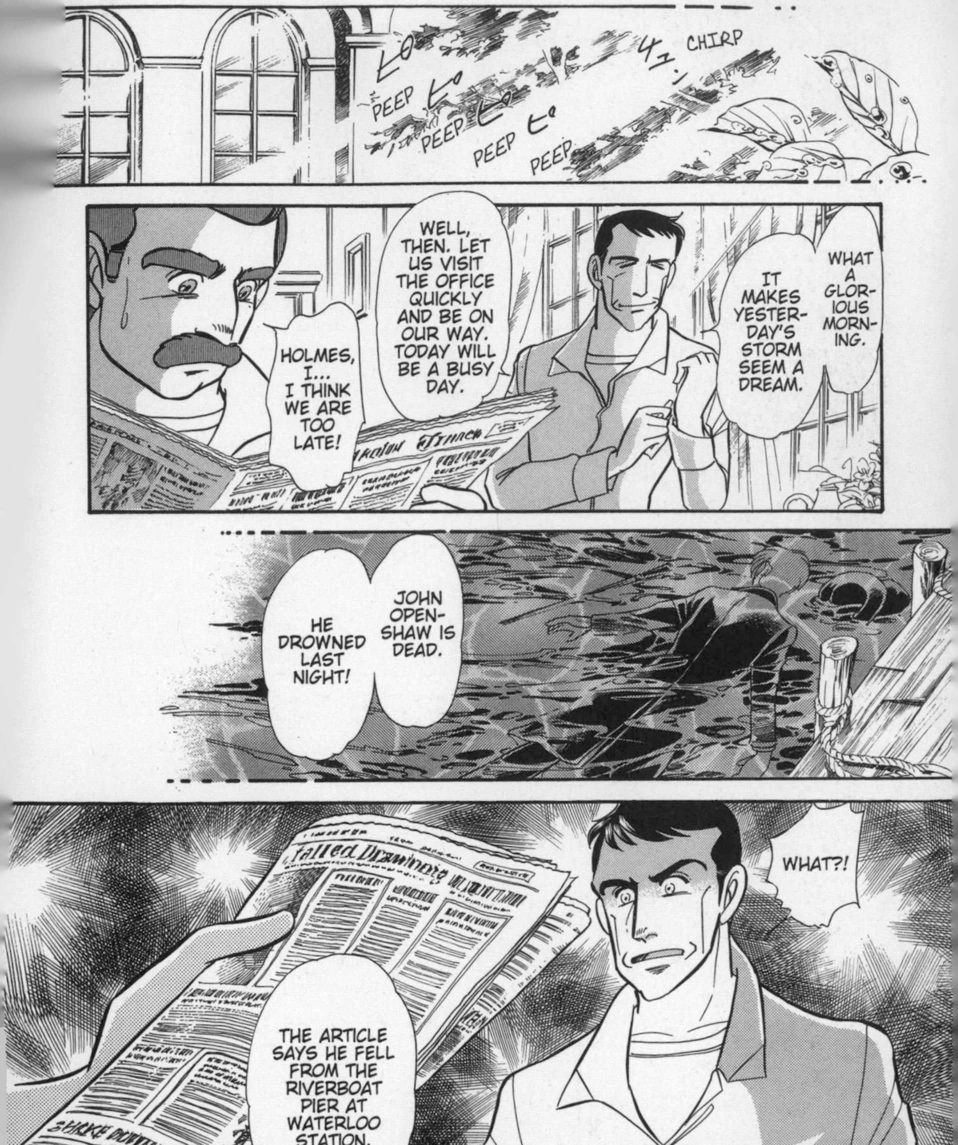
CHIRP
PEEP
PEEP
PEEP
PEEP
WHAT A GLOR-IOUS MORN-ING.
IT MAKES YESTER-DAY'S STORM SEEM A DREAM.
WELL, THEN. LET US VISIT THE OFFICE QUICKLY AND BE ON OUR WAY. TODAY WILL BE A BUSY DAY.
HOLMES, I... I THINK WE ARE TOO LATE!
JOHN OPEN-SHAW IS DEAD.
HE DROWNED LAST NIGHT!
WHAT?!
THE ARTICLE SAYS HE FELL FROM THE RIVERBOAT PIER AT WATERLOO STATION.

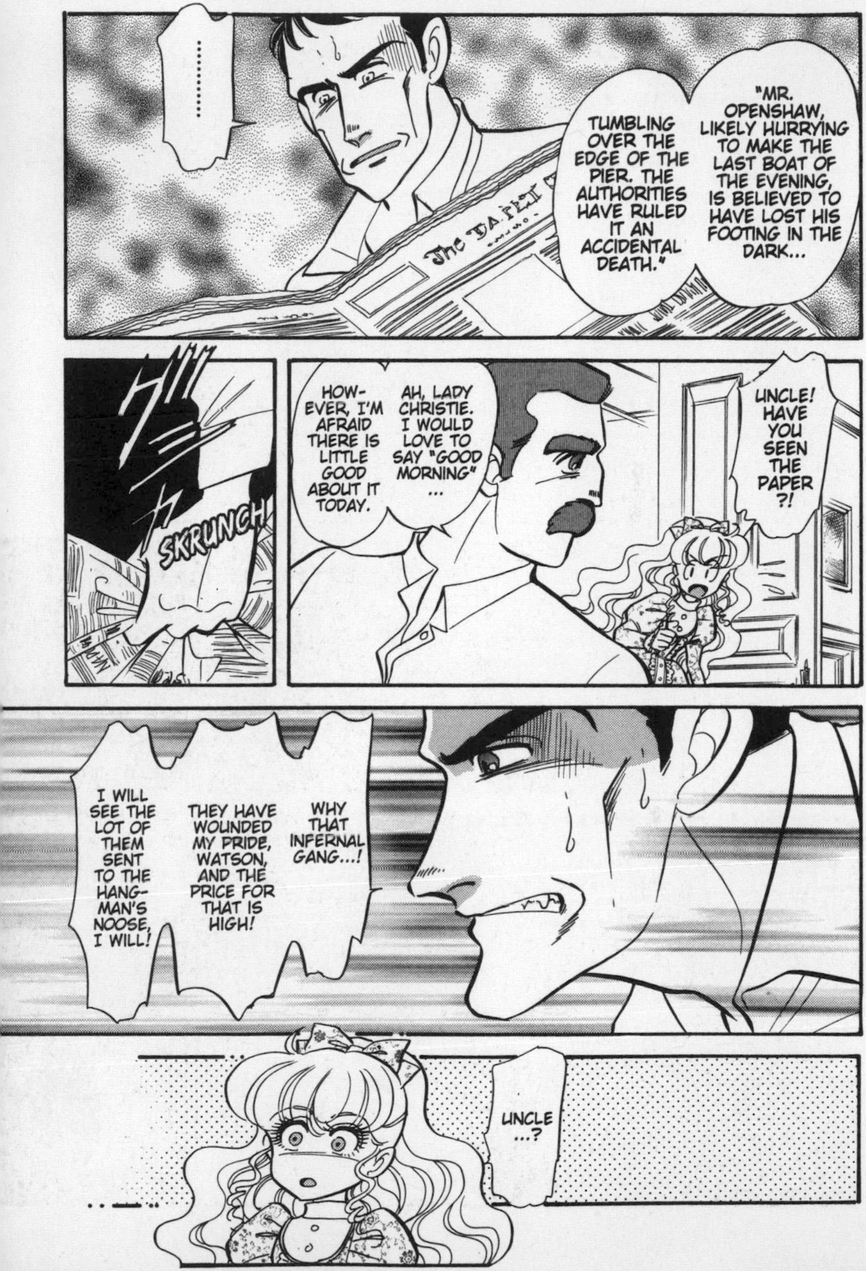
"MR. OPENSHAW, LIKELY HURRYING TO MAKE THE LAST BOAT OF THE EVENING, IS BELIEVED TO HAVE LOST HIS FOOTING IN THE DARK...
TUMBLING OVER THE EDGE OF THE PIER. THE AUTHORITIES HAVE RULED IT AN ACCIDENTAL DEATH."
......
UNCLE! HAVE YOU SEEN THE PAPER?!
AH, LADY CHRISTIE. I WOULD LOVE TO SAY "GOOD MORNING"...
HOW-EVER, I'M AFRAID THERE IS LITTLE GOOD ABOUT IT TODAY.
SKRUNCH
WHY THAT INFERNAL GANG...!
THEY HAVE WOUNDED MY PRIDE, WATSON, AND THE PRICE FOR THAT IS HIGH!
I WILL SEE THE LOT OF THEM SENT TO THE HANG-MAN'S NOOSE, I WILL!
UNCLE ...?

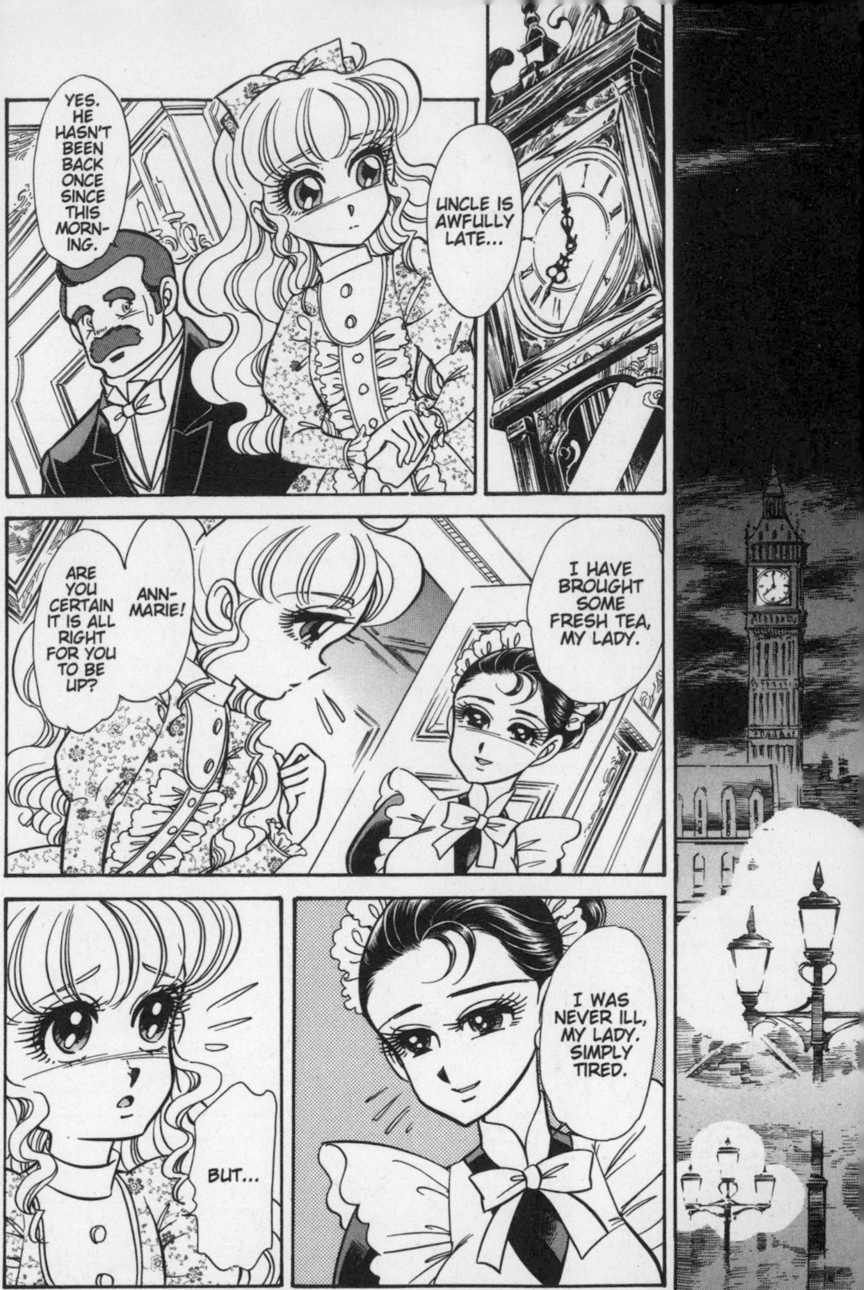
UNCLE IS AWFULLY LATE...
YES. HE HASN'T BEEN BACK ONCE SINCE THIS MORNING.
I HAVE BROUGHT SOME FRESH TEA, MY LADY.
ANN-MARIE!
ARE YOU CERTAIN IT IS ALL RIGHT FOR YOU TO BE UP?
I WAS NEVER ILL, MY LADY. SIMPLY TIRED.
BUT...

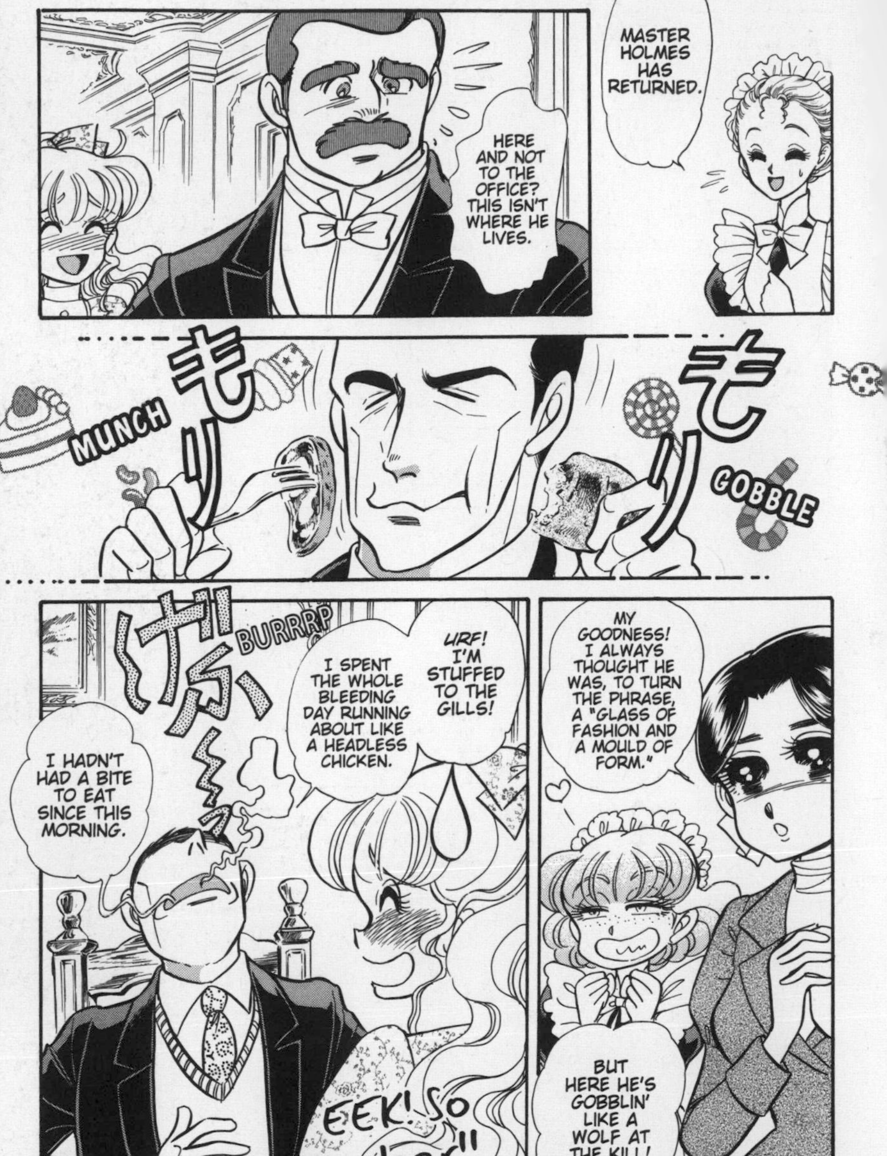
MASTER HOLMES HAS RETURNED.
HERE AND NOT TO THE OFFICE? THIS ISN'T WHERE HE LIVES.
もり
GOBBLE
もり
MUNCH
MY GOODNESS! I ALWAYS THOUGHT HE WAS, TO TURN THE PHRASE, A "GLASS OF FASHION AND A MOULD OF FORM."
BUT HERE HE'S GOBBLIN' LIKE A WOLF AT THE KILL!
URF! I'M STUFFED TO THE GILLS!
I SPENT THE WHOLE BLEEDING DAY RUNNING ABOUT LIKE A HEADLESS CHICKEN.
BURRRP
げふ
I HADN'T HAD A BITE TO EAT SINCE THIS MORNING.
EEK! So vulgar!!

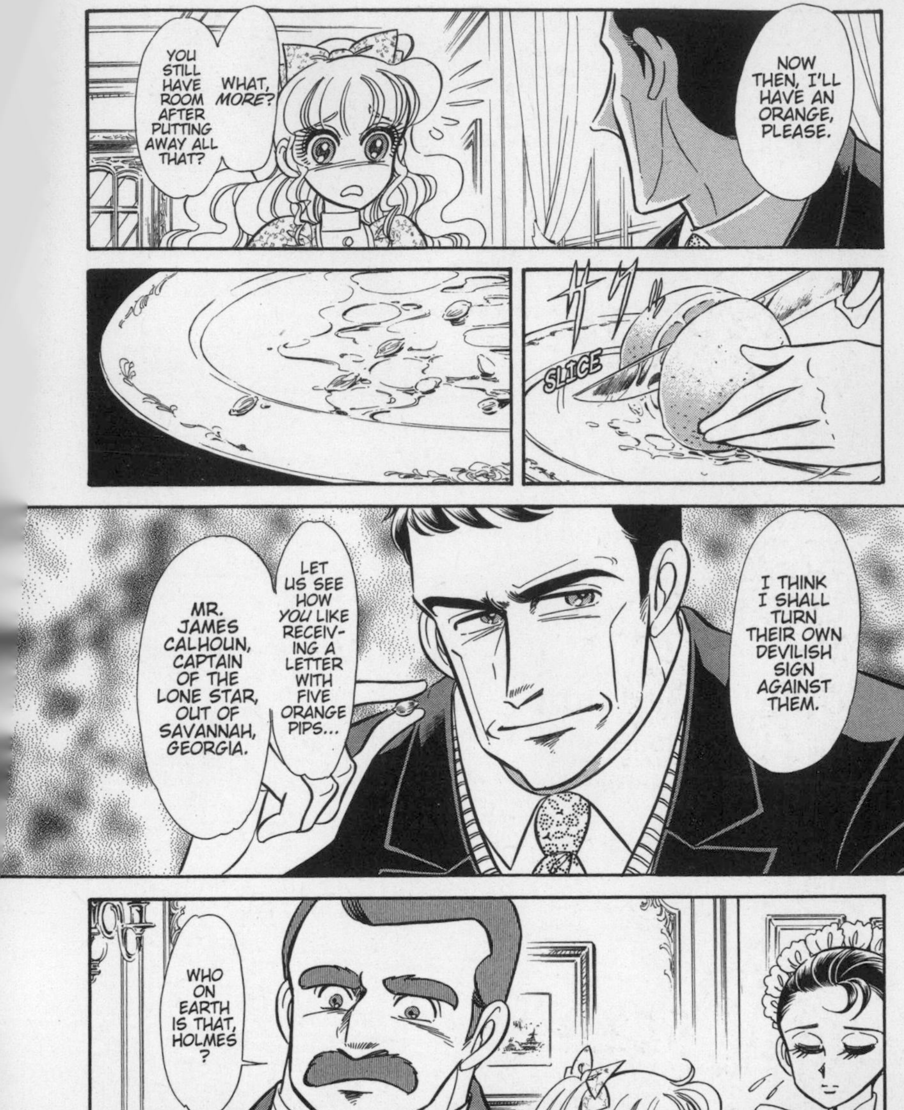
NOW THEN, I'LL HAVE AN ORANGE, PLEASE.
WHAT, *MORE?*
YOU STILL HAVE ROOM AFTER PUTTING AWAY ALL THAT?
SLICE
I THINK I SHALL TURN THEIR OWN DEVILISH SIGN AGAINST THEM.
LET US SEE HOW *YOU* LIKE RECEIVING A LETTER WITH FIVE ORANGE PIPS...
MR. JAMES CALHOUN, CAPTAIN OF THE LONE STAR, OUT OF SAVANNAH, GEORGIA.
WHO ON EARTH IS THAT, HOLMES?

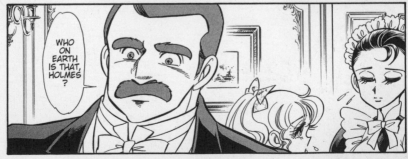

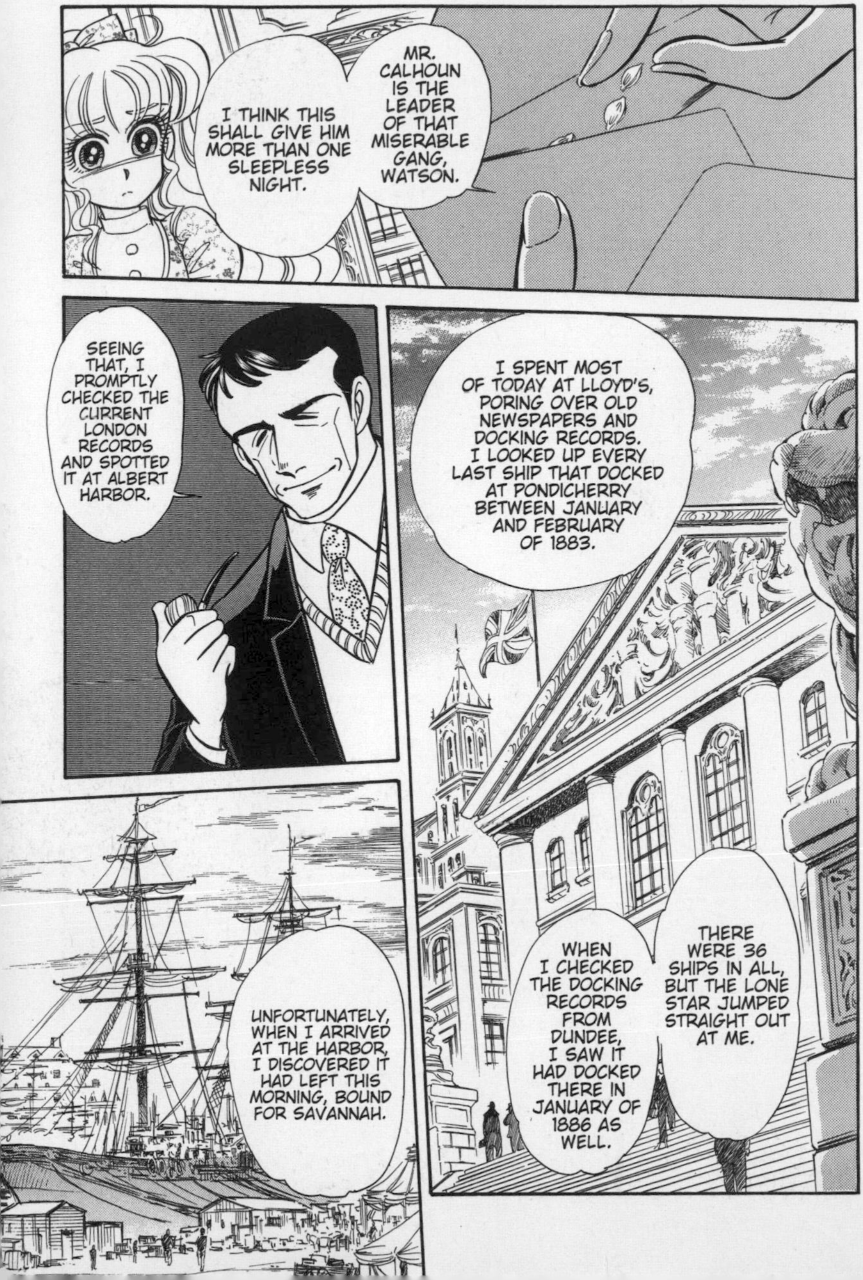
MR. CALHOUN IS THE LEADER OF THAT MISERABLE GANG, WATSON.
I THINK THIS SHALL GIVE HIM MORE THAN ONE SLEEPLESS NIGHT.
I SPENT MOST OF TODAY AT LLOYD'S, PORING OVER OLD NEWSPAPERS AND DOCKING RECORDS. I LOOKED UP EVERY LAST SHIP THAT DOCKED AT PONDICHERRY BETWEEN JANUARY AND FEBRUARY OF 1883.
THERE WERE 36 SHIPS IN ALL, BUT THE LONE STAR JUMPED STRAIGHT OUT AT ME.
WHEN I CHECKED THE DOCKING RECORDS FROM DUNDEE, I SAW IT HAD DOCKED THERE IN JANUARY OF 1886 AS WELL.
SEEING THAT, I PROMPTLY CHECKED THE CURRENT LONDON RECORDS AND SPOTTED IT AT ALBERT HARBOR.
UNFORTUNATELY, WHEN I ARRIVED AT THE HARBOR, I DISCOVERED IT HAD LEFT THIS MORNING, BOUND FOR SAVANNAH.

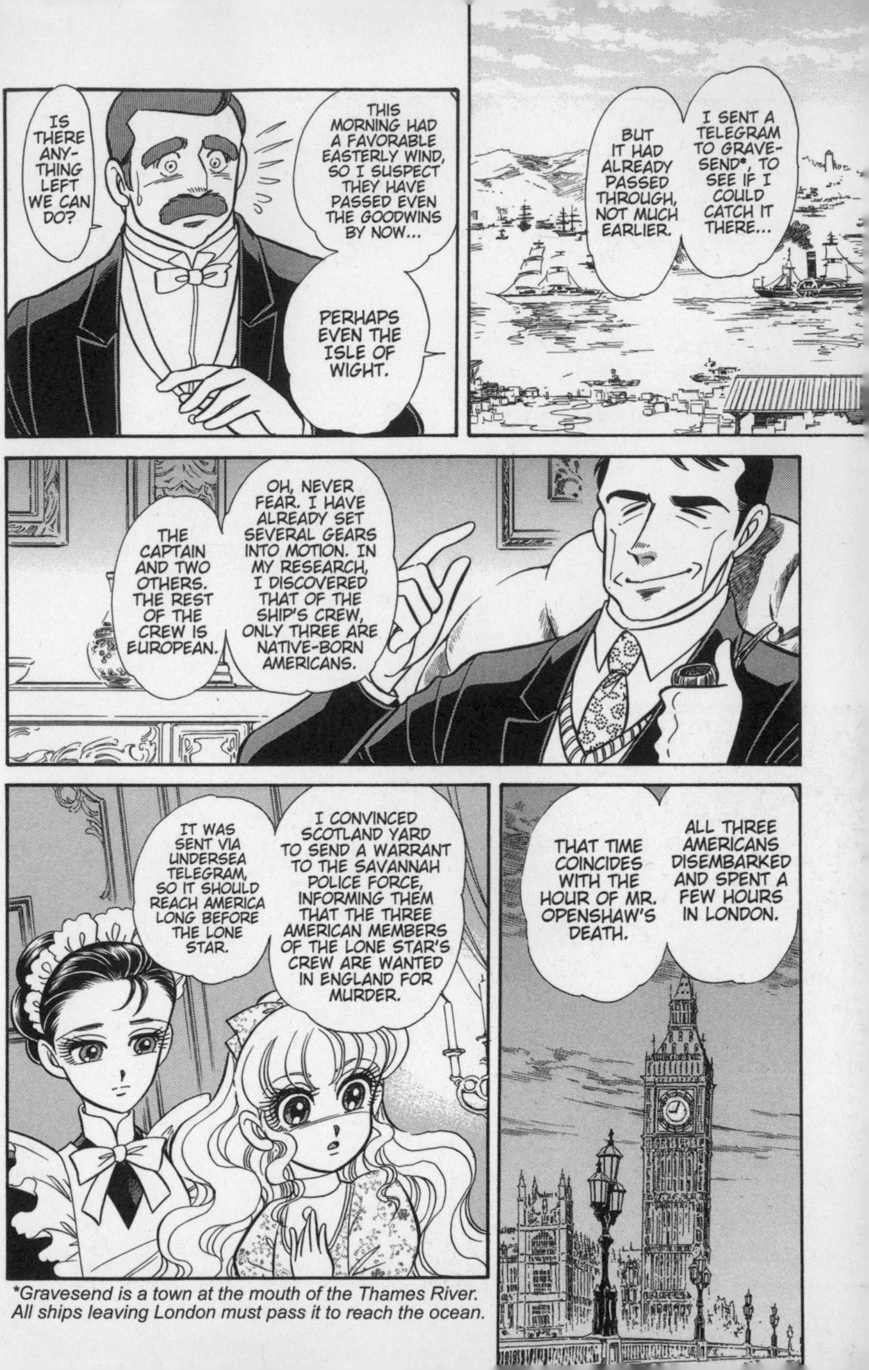
I SENT A TELEGRAM TO GRAVESEND*, TO SEE IF I COULD CATCH IT THERE...
BUT IT HAD ALREADY PASSED THROUGH, NOT MUCH EARLIER.
THIS MORNING HAD A FAVORABLE EASTERLY WIND, SO I SUSPECT THEY HAVE PASSED EVEN THE GOODWINS BY NOW...
PERHAPS EVEN THE ISLE OF WIGHT.
IS THERE ANYTHING LEFT WE CAN DO?
OH, NEVER FEAR. I HAVE ALREADY SET SEVERAL GEARS INTO MOTION. IN MY RESEARCH, I DISCOVERED THAT OF THE SHIP'S CREW, ONLY THREE ARE NATIVE-BORN AMERICANS.
THE CAPTAIN AND TWO OTHERS. THE REST OF THE CREW IS EUROPEAN.
ALL THREE AMERICANS DISEMBARKED AND SPENT A FEW HOURS IN LONDON.
THAT TIME COINCIDES WITH THE HOUR OF MR. OPENSHAW'S DEATH.
I CONVINCED SCOTLAND YARD TO SEND A WARRANT TO THE SAVANNAH POLICE FORCE, INFORMING THEM THAT THE THREE AMERICAN MEMBERS OF THE LONE STAR'S CREW ARE WANTED IN ENGLAND FOR MURDER.
IT WAS SENT VIA UNDERSEA TELEGRAM, SO IT SHOULD REACH AMERICA LONG BEFORE THE LONE STAR.

Gravesend is a town at the mouth of the Thames River. All ships leaving London must pass it to reach the ocean.

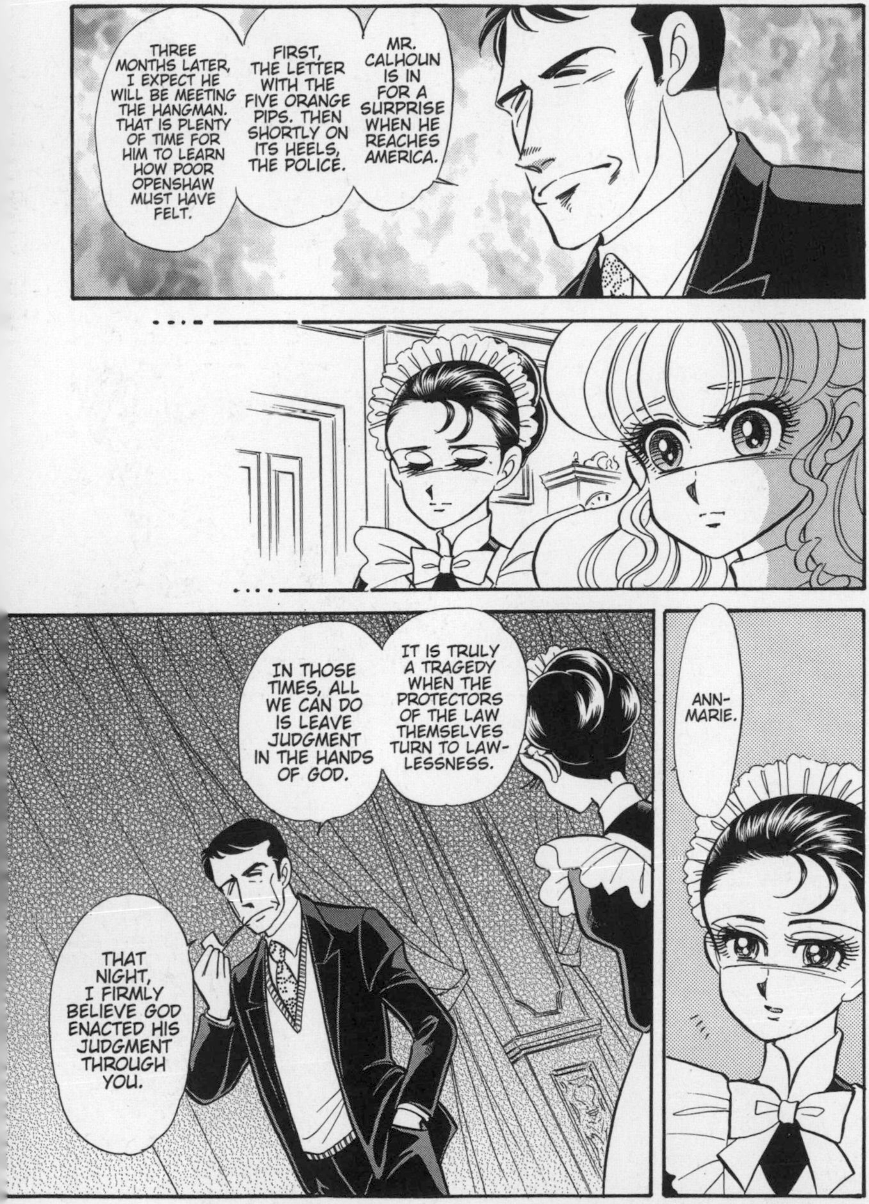
MR. CALHOUN IS IN FOR A SURPRISE WHEN HE REACHES AMERICA.
FIRST, THE LETTER WITH THE FIVE ORANGE PIPS. THEN SHORTLY ON ITS HEELS, THE POLICE.
THREE MONTHS LATER, I EXPECT HE WILL BE MEETING THE HANGMAN. THAT IS PLENTY OF TIME FOR HIM TO LEARN HOW POOR OPENSHAW MUST HAVE FELT.
ANN-MARIE.
IT IS TRULY A TRAGEDY WHEN THE PROTECTORS OF THE LAW THEMSELVES TURN TO LAW-LESSNESS.
IN THOSE TIMES, ALL WE CAN DO IS LEAVE JUDGMENT IN THE HANDS OF GOD.
THAT NIGHT, I FIRMLY BELIEVE GOD ENACTED HIS JUDGMENT THROUGH YOU.

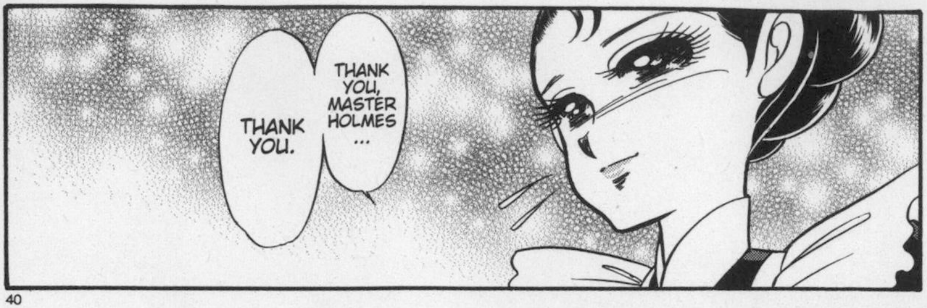
THANK YOU, MASTER HOLMES ...
THANK YOU.

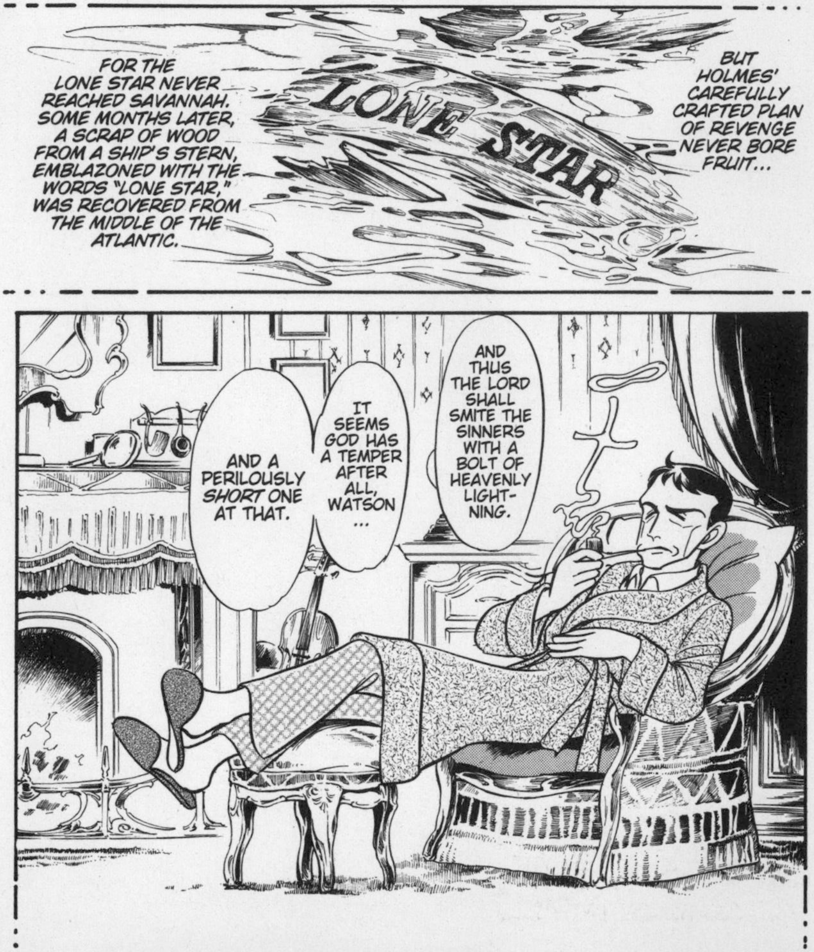
BUT HOLMES' CAREFULLY CRAFTED PLAN OF REVENGE NEVER BORE FRUIT...
LONE STAR
FOR THE LONE STAR NEVER REACHED SAVANNAH. SOME MONTHS LATER, A SCRAP OF WOOD FROM A SHIP'S STERN, EMBLAZONED WITH THE WORDS "LONE STAR," WAS RECOVERED FROM THE MIDDLE OF THE ATLANTIC.
AND THUS THE LORD SHALL SMITE THE SINNERS WITH A BOLT OF HEAVENLY LIGHT-NING.
IT SEEMS GOD HAS A TEMPER AFTER ALL, WATSON ...
AND A PERILOUSLY *SHORT* ONE AT THAT.

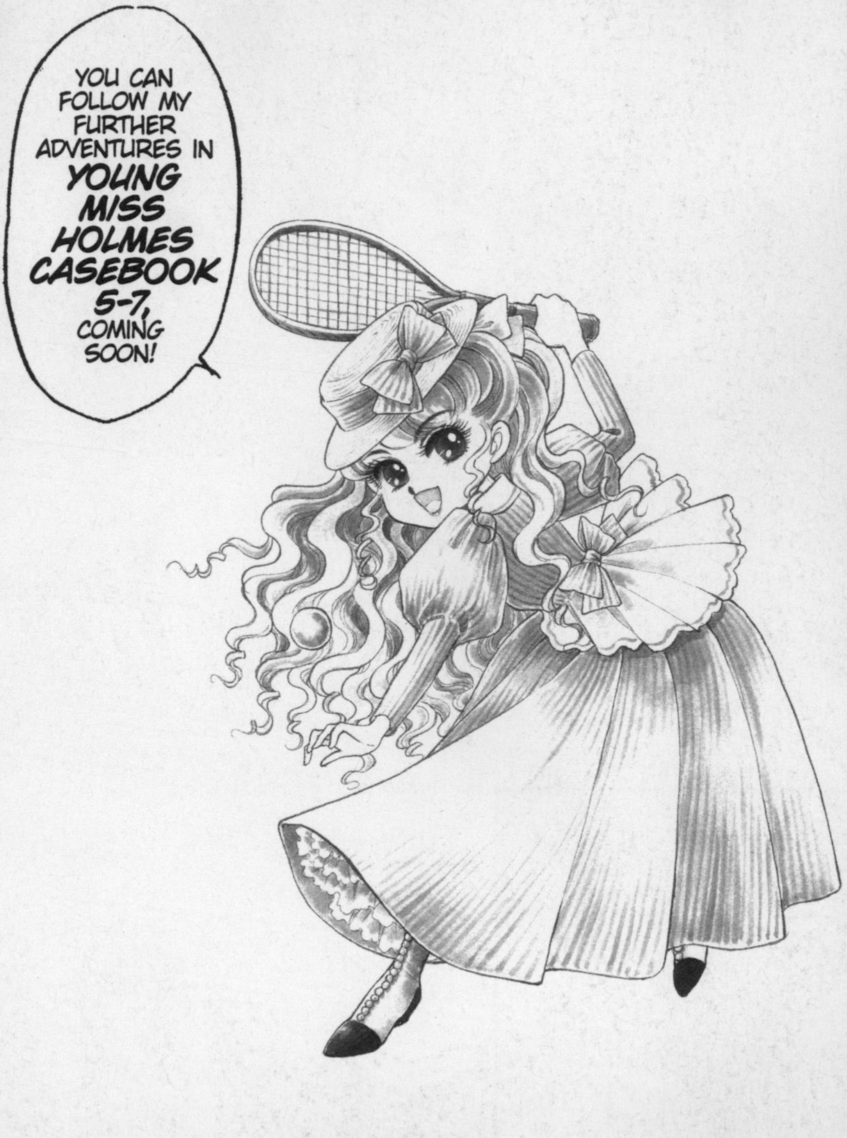
YOU CAN FOLLOW MY FURTHER ADVENTURES IN YOUNG MISS HOLMES CASEBOOK 5-7, COMING SOON!

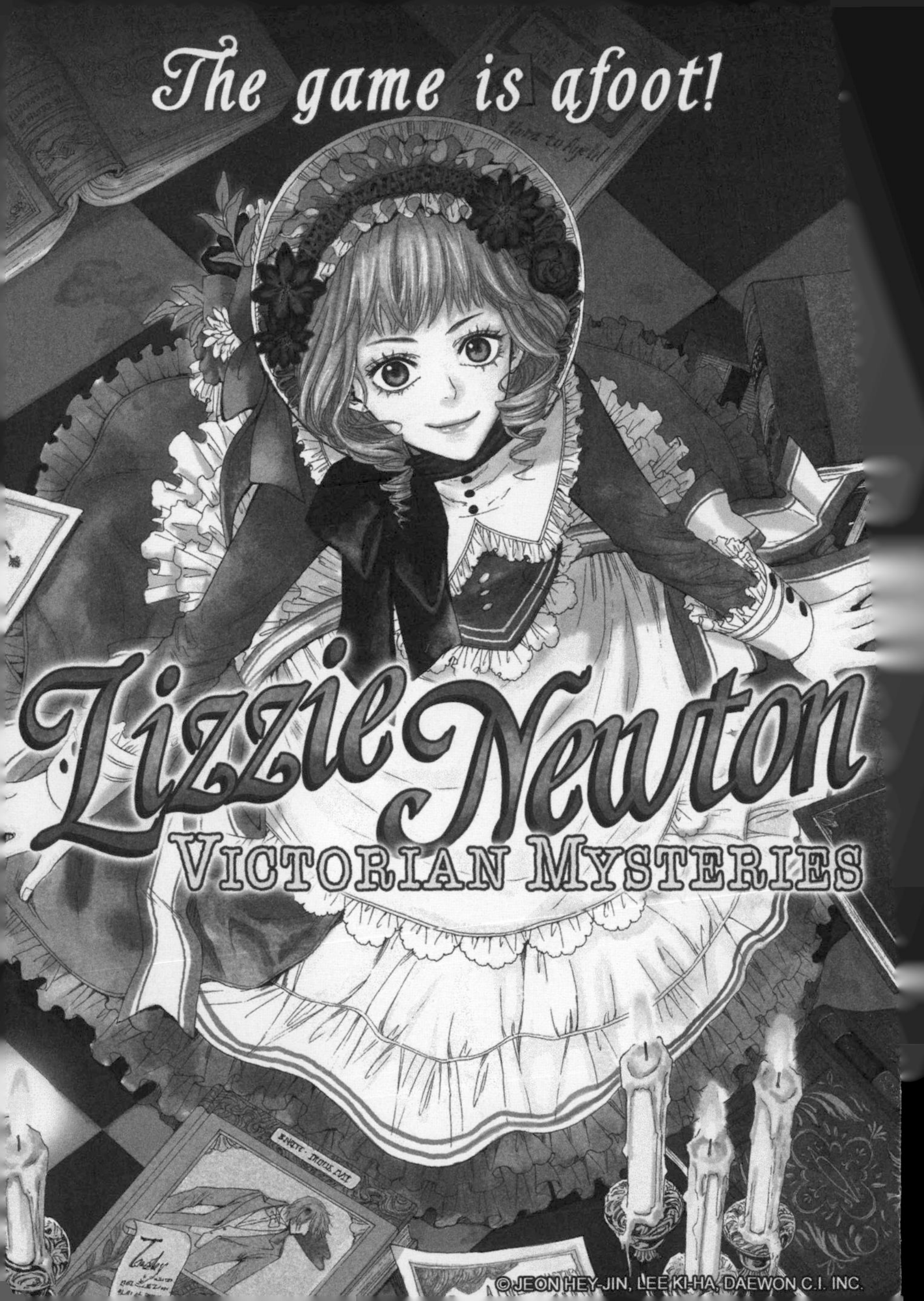
The game is afoot!
Lizzie Newton
VICTORIAN MYSTERIES
© JEON HEY-JIN, LEE KI-HA, DAEWON C.I. INC.

WITCH HUNTER

Witches, beware! Tasha Godspell and Halloween have come to town!

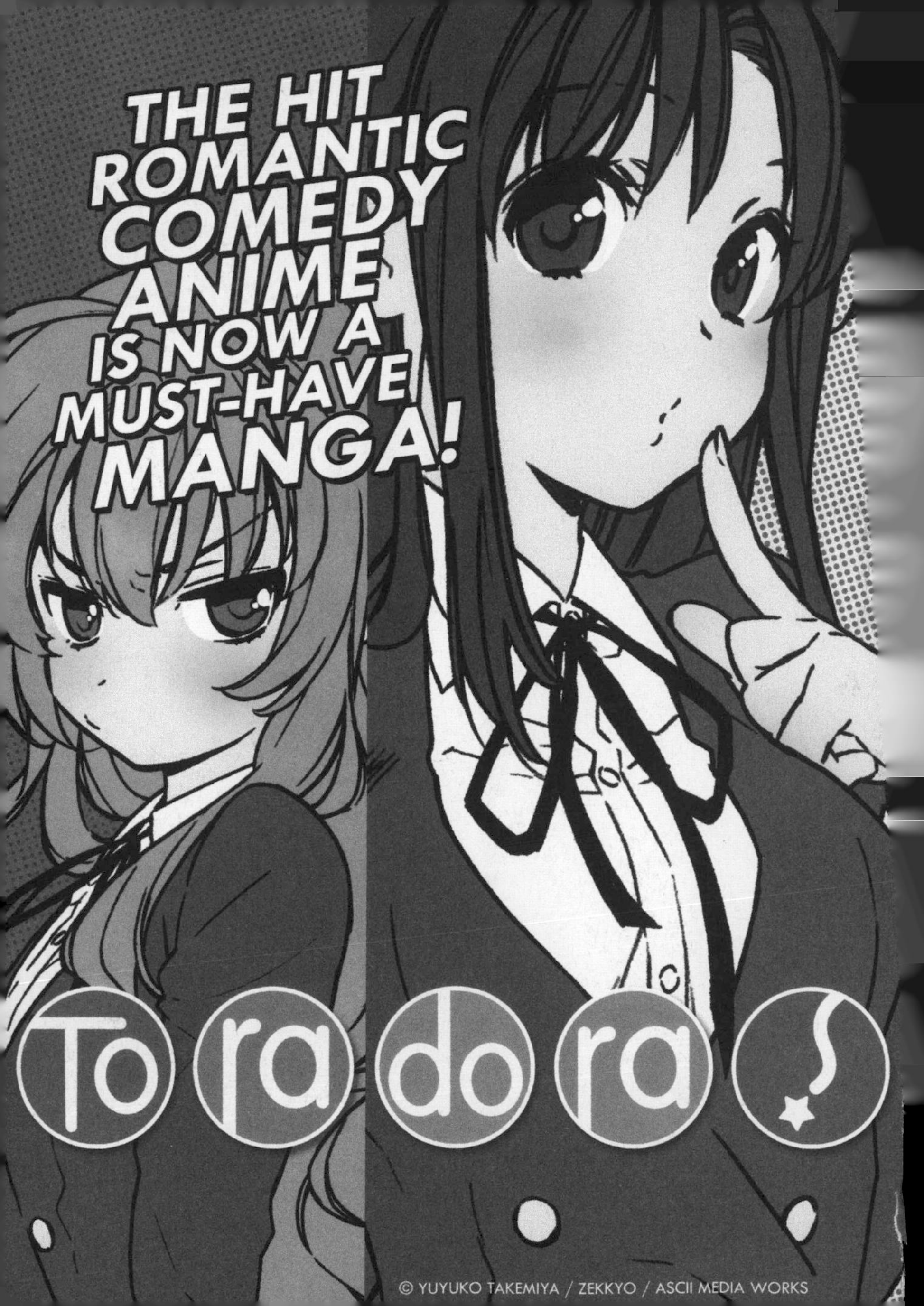
THE HIT ROMANTIC COMEDY ANIME IS NOW A MUST-HAVE MANGA!
To ra do ra !
© YUYUKO TAKEMIYA / ZEKKYO / ASCII MEDIA WORKS

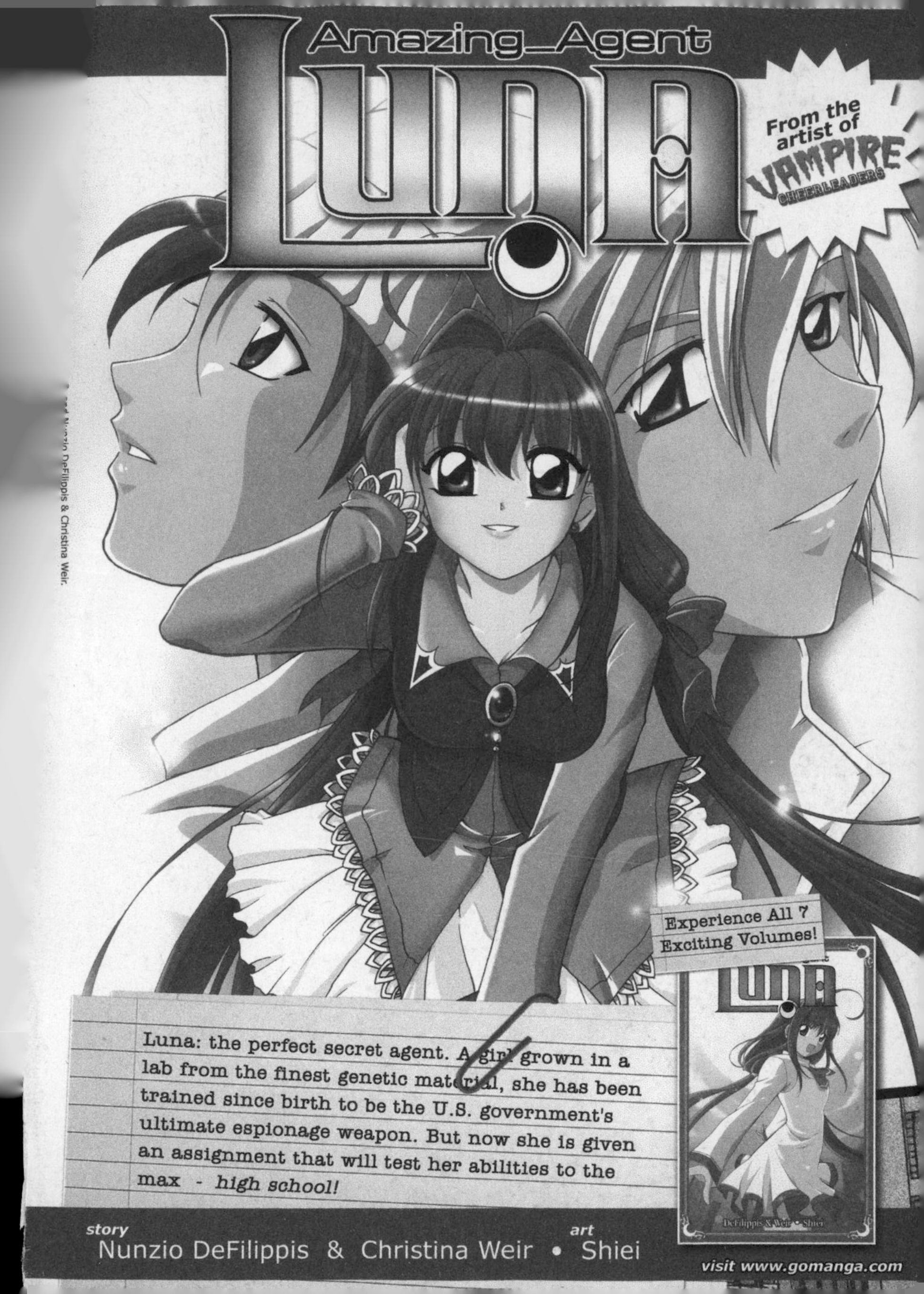
Amazing Agent
LUNA
From the artist of VAMPIRE CHEERLEADERS
Nunzio DeFilippis & Christina Weir.
Experience All 7 Exciting Volumes!
LUNA
DeFilippis & Weir • Shiei
Luna: the perfect secret agent. A girl grown in a lab from the finest genetic material, she has been trained since birth to be the U.S. government's ultimate espionage weapon. But now she is given an assignment that will test her abilities to the max - *high school!*
story
Nunzio DeFilippis & Christina Weir • Shiei
art
visit www.gomanga.com

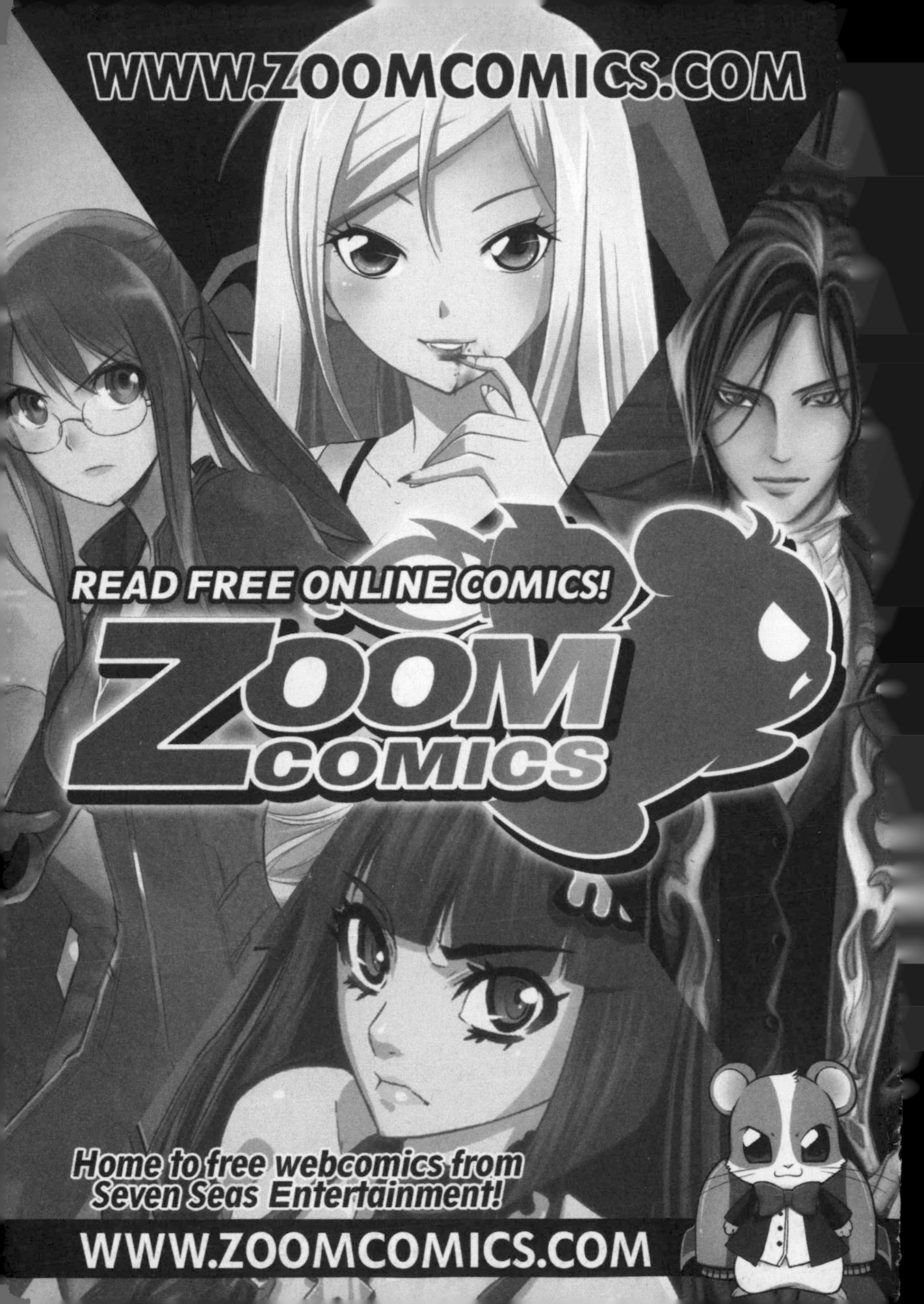
WWW.ZOOMCOMICS.COM
READ FREE ONLINE COMICS!
ZOOM COMICS
Home to free webcomics from
Seven Seas Entertainment!
WWW.ZOOMCOMICS.COM